The Metamorphoses of Kinship

The Metamorphoses of Kinship

Maurice Godelier

TRANSLATED BY NORA SCOTT

VERSO

London • New York

Many thanks to the corporate foundation EISAI

First published in English by Verso 2011
© Verso 2011
Translation © Nora Scott 2011
First published as *Métamorphoses de la parenté*
© Librairie Arthème Fayard 2004

1 3 5 7 9 10 8 6 4 2

Verso
UK: 6 Meard Street, London W1F 0EG
US: 20 Jay Street, Suite 1010, Brooklyn, NY 11201
www.versobooks.com

Verso is the imprint of New Left Books

ISBN-13: 978-1-84467-746-7

British Library Cataloguing in Publication Data
A catalogue record for this book is available from the British Library

Library of Congress Cataloging-in-Publication Data
A catalog record for this book is available from the Library of Congress

Typeset in Minion by Hewer UK Ltd, Edinburgh
Printed in the US by Maple Vail

To Lina.

To Alexandre.

Contents

Introduction

The last thirty years of the twentieth century witnessed an upheaval in family relations and in ideas about the family. We also saw profound mutations in people's lives – I am thinking first of all of the lives of the millions of individuals of both sexes, of all ages and conditions, who make up the traditionally Christian, capitalist and democratic societies of the Western world, and who will be our principal reference here. These mutations have reshaped the practices, mental outlooks and institutions that define what are known as kinship relations between both individuals and the groups engendered by these relations: nuclear families, what are mistakenly called 'extended' families, kindred, and so forth.

Several facts testify to this transformation, including the sharp decline in marriages and the even sharper rise in the number of separations and divorces, resulting in the appearance and multiplication of single-parent families, 'recomposed' families, etc. But if the conjugal tie is proving increasingly fragile, the parents' desire to continue to shoulder their child-raising responsibilities, even after separation and divorce, is nevertheless a social fact that is constantly and strongly asserted. It is an aspect and one of the effects of the tendency to value childhood and children that emerged in Western Europe in the nineteenth century and became fully fledged by the mid twentieth. In short, among the metamorphoses of the conjugal family, if the marriage axis has weakened, the axis of filiation is still solidly in place.[1]

But filiation itself is likely tomorrow to be no longer what it was yesterday, and defining it has already been made more complex by recent discoveries in biology and the development of new reproductive technologies. Whereas it used to seem a matter of common sense to say that, while paternity may always be open to doubt, there can be no doubt about who the mother is – she is the woman who carried the child in her womb and brought it into the world – nowadays this may no longer be the case. Today, it is possible to transfer an egg fertilized in the body of one woman into the uterus of another woman, where it will continue to develop until the child is born. Whereas formerly, in our societies, the woman who gave birth to a child was perceived as being both the child's genetrix and its mother, as it becomes possible artificially to separate these three *naturally* indivisible stages – fertilization, gestation and parturition – the question arises of what, for the child born under these conditions, are the various

---

1 Cf. I. Théry (ed.), *Couple, filiation et parenté aujourd'hui. Le droit face aux mutations de la famille et de la vie privée* (Paris, Odile Jacob, 1998). Commissioned by the Ministère de l'Emploi et de la Solidarité et au garde des Sceaux, ministre de la Justice, this report, which is careful with the facts and nuanced in their interpretation, was most useful.

women who, one after another, contributed to its birth? Generally speaking, because of the importance our culture places on the biological aspect of kinship relations and the genealogical representation of these ties, the question usually comes down to asking: which of these women is the 'real' mother?[2]

For if all these transformations – which sometimes lead in opposite directions – have deeply altered the world of kinship, they have not yet shaken an axiom that, in Europe, has for centuries been the basis of its definition and representation, namely: that kinship is fundamentally a world of both biological and genealogical ties between same-sex or opposite-sex individuals of the same generation or of different generations following in time.

Nevertheless, for some twenty years now, formerly prohibited and repressed unions have emerged into broad daylight and been more or less tacitly accepted by public opinion. Furthermore, these unions are contesting, head-on and for the first time, the genealogical principle that was traditionally seen as the core of kinship: I am talking about homosexual couples. The affirmation and multiplication of such unions has had an impact on family relations as a whole. There are two reasons for this. First, because homosexual couples are demanding legal recognition of their union and that this recognition should allow for a form of marriage. Second, because a minority of these couples wants to go further, demanding the right to raise a family by adopting children engendered outside the couple or by artificial insemination with the help of a more-or-less anonymous sperm donor.

We are thus caught in a paradox. Marriage is increasingly shunned by heterosexuals, while being demanded by homosexuals. Children who, until the appearance of new procreation technologies, owed their birth to sexual relations between men and women who may not have desired children, are now wanted by homosexual couples who, on principle, exclude heterosexual intercourse from their desire. Another paradox for some would be the fact that in homosexual families parenthood may be fully realized simply by becoming a more or less social and affective reality: If a woman can choose to be the 'father' and act accordingly, or a man choose to be the 'mother' and act accordingly, if both choose to be parents apart from any reference to their biological sex, would this not be undeniable proof that parenthood is basically not biological but social, thus confirming a thesis dear to many kinship specialists?

These contemporary developments would once again seem to confirm the pre-eminent role of anthropology when it comes to thinking about kinship, as might be substantiated by the number of jurists, politicians and psychologists who seek out anthropologists to help them better understand the mysteries of

---

2   Cf. R. Fox, *Reproduction and Succession: Studies in Anthropology, Law and Society* (New Brunswick NJ, Transactions Publisher, 1993), p. 120. See also M. Strathern, *Reproducing the Future: Essays on Anthropology, Kinship and the New Reproduction Technologies* (Manchester, Manchester University Press, 1992), pp. 39–53.

modern kinship before intervening in its evolution. But do anthropologists still want, or are they even able, to answer the questions put to them, when the majority ceased to be interested in kinship as far back as the 1980s?

Before examining what has become of their work on kinship, long considered to be a specialist field and the very flower of anthropology, let us step back and look at the principles of our own kinship system.

The Western European system has three components, which combine with each other to constitute the deep structure of kinship relations in our societies, the framework within which the Westerner is born and lives. The first component is the family, which is nuclear and monogamous. The second is the network of families related by consanguinity or affinity.[3] These networks associate individuals of different generations linked mainly by direct or collateral ties of descent on both the father's and the mother's side. For, in Western societies, one side counts nearly as much as the other, which is why this kinship system is called 'cognatic'. Nevertheless, in so far as it is the father who hands his name on to the children, and other elements of social life pass principally or exclusively through him, we say that our cognatic system has a 'patrilineal bias'. These networks of related families, who associate with each other and whose members feel bound together by ties of solidarity, who help one another and exchange goods and services, are sometimes misnamed 'extended families'. This expression should actually be reserved for groups of kin – usually a father and his married sons living under one roof and comprising a single domestic unit, or household, and who also often function as a production unit. These 'extended' families properly speaking existed in various parts of rural France and Europe under the Ancien Régime, and for a portion of the nineteenth century, but today they have practically disappeared.

The third component is Ego's kindred. This, too, is a network of people related by ties of kinship, but it is centered on the individual. It covers, on the one hand, all those relatives the individual 'inherited' at birth – on both the father's and the mother's side – as well as the affines of his or her consanguines and the consanguines of his or her affines. This birth kindred is shared by all the children of a particular father and mother, that is, by all siblings. But, when the individual in question marries (or as is often the case today, lives with someone) and has children, then he or she becomes the starting point for a new kindred, which differs from that of his siblings. The two networks, the one formed by the families and the one formed by the related individuals, are open, with boundaries that depend on a number of factors which have nothing to do with kinship:

---

3 The alliance can be official if there was a marriage or declaration of cohabitation between the two individuals, or it can be unofficial if they simply live together in what the French call 'free union'.

spatial proximity of the families and the individuals; changes in the social status of certain families or individuals, who may no longer see each other; families or individuals who die or disappear due to epidemics, wars, and so on.

These three ingredients, which comprise the field of kinship, existed under the Ancien Régime, but they were associated with other components as well, which either disappeared after the French Revolution and the promulgation in 1804 of the Napoleonic Code or underwent a change of status in the new society and the new moral and sexual order that ensued. Under the Ancien Régime, marriage was a religious act, a sacrament that made the bond between a man and a woman indissoluble. Divorce was forbidden by the Church, unless the marriage could be proven not to have been consummated. Children had to be baptized, and the baptism (like the birth) was recorded on the rolls of the parish that had administered the sacrament. The child's father was theoretically supposed to be the husband of its mother, and he had authority over his wife and his children.

This configuration of rights, practices and values characteristic of the Ancien Régime began to change with the institution of 'civil' marriage in 1804. In principle, the civil marriage was not mandatory, but it rapidly became a de facto obligation in the eyes of the majority of the population, which was quick to understand that the new institution would become the only legal means of legitimizing the children that would be born to a couple. Their birth was henceforth recorded by the state registry office.

In the nineteenth century cohabitation was still stigmatized as a practice of the lower classes or of individuals who had chosen to break with social conventions – artists, for example.[4] Children born out of wedlock had no rights. They were bastards and were treated less well than those of the Ancien Régime nobility. There was strong social pressure on young people to marry within their own social class. The only member of the family to exercise authority was the father. He was vested with paternal authority, a right and a concept that go back to Roman Antiquity. It was the husband's duty to ensure the family's material conditions of existence. The married woman was under her husband's authority and was legally incapable. Marriage – whether civil or religious – was still the act that founded the couple. Initially recognized, divorce would be abolished in 1816. Exploration of sexuality and love before marriage was stifled. Of course, homosexuality was forbidden and regarded as an unnatural desire, as a sin by believers, as a pathology in medical circles; and homosexual couples were forced to conceal their relationship.

This quick glance back over the nineteenth century is meant merely to

---

4   Reform of 4 June 1970, laws of 22 July 1987 and 8 January 1993. See Théry, *Couple, filiation, parenté*, pp. 189–207.

suggest the changes that have been multiplying since the 1960s, when a new society took shape and began to thrive in the wake of the upheaval wrought in Western Europe by the Second World War and the subsequent division of the world into two blocs.

In France in 1970, the notion of paternal authority was abolished and replaced by that of parental authority,[5] shared equally between the father and the mother, to whom were enjoined responsibilities toward their children in matters of health, education, safety and morality,[6] even in the event of separation or divorce. Parental authority is thus considered to be a function of public order, guaranteed by the state.

In 1975 divorce by 'mutual consent' was made possible in France. In 2009, thirty-nine per cent of all marriages ended in divorce. To this figure must be added the large number of separations that do not go through divorce. This is obviously the case for the separation of cohabiting couples. Hence the growing number of single-parent households, and 'recomposed' families, which are not an alternative model but simply social configurations that occur at different stages in people's lives, as the spectacular increase in longevity compared to the nineteenth century now allows individuals to contract several kinds of alliance in their lifetime.

Generally speaking, then, in our society, marriage is no longer the act that founds the couple.[7] The couple forms *before* the marriage, which, if they eventually decide to marry, often takes place only after the couple becomes convinced of the necessity to stabilize their union. But marriage alone no longer makes a family. The family truly comes into being only when a child or two are born. It would therefore be false to claim that we are seeing a wholesale rejection of marriage when the institution has merely lost some of its social importance. At the same time, negative attitudes toward cohabitation have largely disappeared, as has the opprobrium cast on children born out of wedlock.

Networks of related families exist and continue to lend support to their members, beyond the boundaries of their birth or conjugal families, especially in times of economic recession or youth unemployment. But these networks are beginning to shrink, contracting around the axes of direct descent, and increasingly excluding close or distant collaterals. The same is true of the kindred to which an individual feels attached, which also tends to dwindle to a small number of relatives by blood or by marriage with whom he or she has chosen to keep up ties.

What are the forces that have modified the forms and practices of kinship

---

5 J. Rubellin-Devichi (ed.), *Des concubinages dans le monde* (Paris, Centre National de la Recherche Scientifique, 1990).

6 Article 371–2 of the French Civil Code.

7 F. Battagliola, *La Fin du mariage?* (Paris, Syros/Alternatives, 1988).

in Western societies since the mid twentieth century? The first is the emphasis on the right to freely choose the other with whom to found a couple. This choice has been freed of social constraints and conventions such as the moral duty to marry within one's class, to transmit a family name or perpetuate a social group, etc. Desire, love and sentiment now prevail over other, less subjective, more social criteria. In addition, teenage lovemaking is no longer taboo, and everything points to a new attitude toward sexuality. In this context, the loss of desire and/or love for the other have become sufficient reason for splitting up and making oneself available for new ties and a new life.

The second force helping to reshape kinship relations arose out of changes in gender relations and the increasing social pressure for greater equality between the sexes in all areas of social and personal life. The establishment of parental authority and divorce by mutual consent attest to this change.[8] The pressure for greater sexual equality can also be explained by the fact that increasing numbers of women are entering the economy and making an essential contribution to the material life of their couple or family. In doing so, they (also) acquire greater material autonomy with respect to their spouse or partner.

The third force that gradually affected the field of kinship and the family was the progressive valorization of the child and childhood, whereby the child was no longer seen as a being more or less 'incapable of reasoning' but as already a person, one whose arrival in the family was no longer endured but rather desired and even, thanks to medical progress, programmed. The child thus came to occupy a much greater place in the family's affective and economic life. But, at the same time, and as an effect of the action of the two previous forces, many couples made an effort to create a space for themselves alongside and beyond their parental tasks and duties. Obviously, women have the most to gain from family life not being reduced entirely to their mothering role. Finally, having a 'big' family is no longer an ideal – if it ever was – and for many groups the new model is instead that of a family comprised of working parents and two children, a boy and a girl.

All of these changes are borne along by a deeper current that did not arise in the field of kinship but which flows through it and continuously acts within it, just as it courses through all areas of social life and acts on them. It is the current that propels promotion of the individual as such, independently of his or her initial attachments to family or social group, that lends value to autonomous behaviour and the capacity to take the initiative, to accept responsibilities, and that enables the individual to rise within the public and private institutions that constitute the economic and political structure of our societies. This

---

8   1975 reform, which also created a new non-judicial type of divorce: 'divorce by common declaration'.

upward propulsion of the individual occurs in a historical context where acts of authority on the part of power holders in the state or private companies, regarding persons in their control, spark criticism, resistance and opposition when forcibly imposed without room for dialogue. In short, Western society increasingly prefers deserved or negotiated authority over the kind that is inherited or imposed. The positive side of this trend can be seen in the abolition of paternal authority and the promotion of shared 'parental' authority 'guaranteed' by the state. To this must be added the fact that children, recognized as beings who must be treated as persons from birth, remain 'children' for a shorter period, since they become 'adult' at the age of eighteen. Parents have thus been forced to invent forms of authority that did not exist when they themselves were children, forms designed to convince rather than to coerce, based on dialogue rather than violence.[9]

It has become harder to be a parent, and we are now seeing many families undergoing a profound crisis of parental authority, one that affects the father more than the mother in so far as he was traditionally the one who embodied the law and authority. We thus sometimes find, when the parents separate or divorce, a veritable dissolution of the father figure: eighty per cent of children of separated or divorced parents live with their mother, as compared to eight per cent with their father and six per cent with someone else. Furthermore only twenty per cent of children who live with their mother see their father at least once a week.

If the father and/or the mother remarry, the children find themselves in families composed of fragments of former families. The child then lives with a stepfather or a stepmother, has half-brothers and/or half-sisters if the couple have children together, and stepbrothers or stepsisters if the person with whom the father or mother has chosen to live brings children from a previous marriage. Children in recomposed families therefore have a hard time finding their bearings and their place in these new configurations of persons and ties, and first of all deciding what to call their new 'parents'. Finally, as separation and divorce become more widespread, many children fear that their parents are going to split up and that they will only see their father or mother once a week, on Sundays, or for part of a vacation.

In short, pulled hither and thither by these opposing and even contradictory currents, the family at the dawn of the twenty-first century certainly no longer looks like the stable basis or keystone of society, if it ever was. And the increasing numbers of homosexual couples demanding the right to raise children they themselves did not engender add new uncertainties about the future of parenthood, the family and marriage.

---

9   The same development occurred in schools, where children spend as much time as they do at home, and forced teachers to change their methods.

Globally, and with hindsight, all of the changes that have recently occurred in the family appear to be in keeping with the overall evolution of Western democratic societies, which favour individual initiatives and interests, and which therefore in principle reject despotic forms of public – but also private – authority. To these features must be added other, more specific traits, which can be explained only by the influence of the Christian tradition, either because it continues to affect the lives of individuals and institutions or because it has prompted reactions and breakaways specific to the Western world, particularly in the areas of sexuality or the family. One such example is the institution of civil marriage, which has become the only legal form of marriage in a number of European countries (making religious marriage a matter of personal and private choice).

No one foresaw this evolution when it began to emerge some ten years after the Second World War, and no one today knows exactly where it will lead. Especially since the facts that condition it are both complex and insufficiently known, and the problems, even the most visible ones (like the difficulty parents have in retaining authority over their children, or school teachers over their pupils), have to be shouldered by each person, individually, alone and with no real help from public debate or a sharing of experience.

To say that the evolution of the family is linked to the global evolution of society as a whole amounts to viewing many pronouncements on marriage, the family, love and desire as so many ideological manifestos. For those who condemn the evolution of Western societies in the name of an idealized past, the world has become a jungle in which everyone is condemned to fight with everyone else to impose his particular interests and appetites, even to the detriment of his parents, family and friends. For those who hold this view, the family, once the sanctuary of eminently social values – respect, solidarity, mutual aid – is doomed, and is already nearly dead. For others, on the contrary, we are the first in the history of the world to allow individuals to live as they desire and feel. Ours is a world in which each person freely chooses those with whom he or she will live, ignoring prejudice and convention, and discounting relations of class, caste or any other system of social ranking.

It seems obvious that, between the demonization of today's society and its 'angelization', there is room for another attitude that consists in conducting a detailed inventory of actual situations and practices before making a judgement. This attitude implies setting aside theoretical assumptions and listening to what people have to say about themselves and others, about their past and their present, and trying to confront discourse with actual practice. To be sure, these discourses and practices must be placed in a much longer time frame than that of an individual's personal memories and references: this time frame is that of the modern history of European societies.

Such an attitude entails combining various approaches and methods from the social sciences, first among which are those used by historians, who try to bring to life a past more often unknown than forgotten or invented, and those used by anthropologists, whose profession demands long immersion in a contemporary society and its observation, at a remove, as it were, but also from within. What does the anthropologist have to say about this evolution?

Let us imagine someone who knows little of the latest developments in anthropology but who is knowledgeable about the social sciences and is now seeking quickly to discover what has become of kinship studies. This reader would likely start her investigation with the formerly widely accepted opinion that the study of kinship 'is to anthropology what logic is to philosophy or the nude is to art; it is the basic discipline of the subject'. Despite the somewhat dubious comparisons, this formulation by Robin Fox, author of a still-useful book on kinship,[10] seemed at the time of its publication (1961) to state a long-established given.

Without necessarily returning to the founding fathers of anthropology (in particular L. H. Morgan, who in 1871 published his huge *Systems of Consanguinity and Affinity of the Human Family*[11]), the mere mention of a few of the great names in the discipline – Pitt-Rivers, Kroeber, Radcliffe-Brown, Evans-Pritchard, Fortes, Murdock, Lévi-Strauss, Lounsbury, Dumont, Needham – all of whom owe something of their renown to their contribution to kinship studies, should be enough to reassure the non-specialist that kinship is indeed an area in which anthropology excels and an object whose study is more or less its specialty.

Our reader would therefore probably be astonished, as she scrolls through the various available sources on the computer screen, to discover that the study of kinship has practically disappeared from the course lists of numerous American university anthropology departments as well as a certain number in Europe who have followed suit.

In the space of forty years, kinship – which seemed to have come out rather well in the many tough battles through which competing generations of anthropologists sought to define or redefine the object, its principles and (biological and/or social) foundations – had finally dissolved of its own accord. It had become a non-object for many anthropologists themselves, even before today's self-styled 'postmodernists' appeared on the scene and set about 'deconstructing' their discipline. This is indicated by the fact that the leading figures of this movement – Marcus, Fisher, Clifford, et al. – made practically no mention of

10   R. Fox, *Kinship and Marriage* (London, Penguin Books, 1967), p. 10.
11   L. H. Morgan, *Systems of Consanguinity and Affinity of the Human Family* (Washington DC, Smithsonian Institution, 1871).

kinship in the many books in which they draw up a critical inventory of anthropology and propose new objects of study for its reconstruction.[12]

In reality, as the rest of the present work intends to show, this apparent absence stems from the fact that, far from having vanished, the object 'kinship' has emigrated to other areas of anthropology where it is being refashioned and linked to new questions. In other words, the analysis of kinship has simply deserted those places where anthropology had been running in circles for decades, bogged down in insoluble problems by false principles. The blanks left by this desertion are not necessarily a sign that the announced death has occurred.

But let us begin at the beginning.

MORGAN, THE FOUNDER

Why begin with the American Lewis Henry Morgan? Because he epitomizes the contradictions facing anthropology from the start. At the same time, he also shows the conditions under which fieldwork and the interpretations anthropologists propose of what they have observed can slowly acquire a scientific character and constitute a new type of knowledge of the other and oneself, one that no longer merely projects onto this other the prejudices of the anthropologist and his or her culture, garbed in discourse borrowed from the exact sciences.

By way of a reminder, let us recall that, in Morgan's time (1818–81), the paradigm of scientific explanation was Darwin's theory of the evolution of species. It was in this context that Morgan – a jurist by profession, a railroad company lawyer in Rochester, New York, and friend and defender of the Indians in their struggle against expropriation and other exactions inflicted by European settlers – became fascinated by Indian customs and decided to devote his life to their study.[13]

While doing fieldwork among the Seneca, a tribe of the Iroquois confederation, Morgan discovered that their kinship relations displayed a logic of their own that was very different from that of the European and American-European systems. He noted that, where Europeans use two terms to designate the father and the father's brothers ('uncles'), the Seneca do not make this distinction and

---

12   G. E. Marcus and M. J. Fisher, *Anthropology as Cultural Critique: An Experimental Moment in the Human Sciences* (Chicago, University of Chicago Press, 1986); G. E. Marcus, *Ethnography through Thick and Thin* (Princeton, Princeton University Press, 1998); J. Clifford and G. E. Marcus, *Writing Culture: The Poetics and the Politics of Ethnography* (Berkeley, University of California Press, 1986).

13   T. Trautmann, *Lewis Henry Morgan and the Invention of Kinship* (Berkeley, University of California Press, 1987); R. Care, *Lewis Henry Morgan: American Scholar* (Chicago, University of Chicago Press, 1960).

use the same term for these men as well as for all those they classify in the same category with respect to an individual of reference (Ego). He also discovered that, vice versa, where Europeans have a single term 'cousin' to designate the children of both father's and mother's brothers and sisters, the Seneca have two: one for the children of the father's brothers and the mother's sisters, and another for the children of the father's sisters and the mother's brothers. In other words, they use different terms to designate the children of their parents' same-sex and opposite-sex collaterals, distinguishing between what anthropologists have called parallel cousins and cross cousins. And since the terms for parallel cousins of both sexes are the same as those used for brothers and sisters, and since brothers and sisters cannot marry each other, parallel cousins cannot marry each other either, on pain of committing incest. On the other hand, it will often be possible, and even recommended, to marry one's cross cousin. Finally, owing to the fact that, in contrast to kinship terminologies that classify several individuals under a single term – for instance, the father and all his brothers – European terminologies proceed by describing step by step the relations linking one individual to another, as in the expression 'my grandfather's grandfather is my great-great-grandfather', Morgan concluded that there is a fundamental difference in the principles governing these terminologies. He would call the first 'classificatory terminologies' and the second 'descriptive terminologies'. This opposition would subsequently draw strong criticism, and was later emended.

Morgan also discovered that the composition of the Iroquois exogamous groups could be explained using a descent rule that traced descendants exclusively through the women's line, whereas in Europe descent is traced through both men and women. He used a Latin word, *gens*, to designate those groups of individuals who regarded themselves as descending through women from a common female ancestor. This was not a matter of chance. And he called the principle governing these kinship groups the 'matrilineal descent' rule. He also noted that, once men married, they left their clan and took up residence with their wife's people. Lastly, he concluded from these observations that all these elements formed a coherent whole with its own logic, in other words, a 'system'.

When he extended his study to other North American Indian tribes with different languages and cultures, he discovered that, beyond these differences, a number of them used kinship terminologies that had the same structure as that of the Seneca. This type of structure would come to be called 'Iroquois'. Other groups, however, such as the Crow and the Omaha, had very different terminologies and marriage rules. Confronted with this diversity but also these convergences, Morgan decided to launch a worldwide survey of kinship terminologies and marriage rules. He drew up a questionnaire describing nearly a hundred possible kin ties with respect to a male or a female Ego, which constituted a sort of family tree ending or starting with Ego, and he sent out nearly one thousand copies to missionaries, civil servants and colonial administrators all over the world.[14]

Thanks to their replies, Morgan was the first person in history to dispose of such a quantity and diversity of information on kinship practices in societies dispersed widely over the face of the earth. Analysis and comparison of this data showed that the dozens of terminologies collected in totally unrelated languages turned out to be varieties or variants of a few types, which he dubbed Punaluan, Turanian, etc., and which we now, following Murdock, call 'Hawaiian', 'Dravidian', etc. As a consequence, European kinship systems, too, would appear as varieties of one of these structure types, the one that would come to be known as 'Eskimo'. In 1871 Morgan gathered part of the data together with his theoretical conclusions into his famous *Systems of Consanguinity and Affinity of the Human Family*, published under the auspices of the Smithsonian Institution, in the conclusion to which he stressed the importance of kinship relations in human history and particularly in 'non-civilized' societies.

We thus see how Morgan endowed anthropology with one of its objects of study (kinship), with a method for studying it (the genealogical questionnaire), and with a first batch of findings including the discovery of some of the rules non-European societies had chosen to organize ties of descent and alliance between the individuals and the groups that make up these societies.

But all this was possible only because of Morgan's remarkable and persistent effort to decentre his thinking with respect to the categories of his own (Euro-American) society and culture. This decentring itself was made possible only by suspending judgement, by temporarily placing in brackets those things that were taken for granted and shared by the members of his society and culture. To be sure, suspension of judgement alone would not have given Morgan's research a scientific character. He also had to learn to turn factual observations into problems to be solved, questions to be asked, in sum into a new way of considering the facts, breaking them down and putting them back together. But he also had to invent a method for observing facts in the field, concepts for describing them and hypotheses for attempting to explain them. Last of all, he had to pose the principle that, in order to understand the data collected in any society, one must compare it with data gathered in other societies, similar or not, close by or not.

Morgan's approach thus marked a profound rupture with the spontaneous ethnography practised by missionaries, military officers, colonial administrators, traders and other representatives of the Western world, all of whom had been striving since the sixteenth century to improve their knowledge of the

---

14   See Trautmann, *Lewis Henry Morgan*.

customs of the populations they were trying to convert, control or administer, and who had, in certain cases, set down their observations in letters, reports or accounts of their travels.

THE INCOMPLETE DECENTRING

But there is another side to Morgan's work. As soon as his *Systems* was published, he turned to the task of marshalling all his data and analyses with a view to reconstructing, as so many were attempting at the time, the evolution of humankind. In 1877, he published *Ancient Society*,[15] in which he described how humanity had gone from a primitive 'savage' state (scarcely differing from that of the animal world, and where promiscuity reigned between the sexes) through to the 'civilized' state. On this account, the greatest inventions of this last state had appeared in Western Europe and were continued in the United States of America in a new society, created by Europeans to be sure, but without the after effects of feudalism, which in the mid nineteenth century continued to hobble the march of progress and democracy in most nations of the Old World. In a speculative schema purported to explain the evolution of humankind via three successive stages of social development (the primitive savage state, the barbarian state and the civilized state), Morgan went on to assign to one or another of these stages each of the various exotic societies whose kinship terminologies he had collected and analyzed. Polynesian societies with their chiefs and complex social structures thus became witnesses to and vestiges of the age when, having just emerged from the primitive state of animal-like promiscuity, groups of brothers 'married' groups of sisters – a 'fact' that 'explained', according to Morgan, the characteristically small number of terms in 'Hawaiian' kin terminologies and their extensions, wherein all of the men and all of the women in the generation above an individual are his 'fathers' and 'mothers' and those of his own generation are his 'brothers' and 'sisters'.

In short, the same man who had managed to decentre his own thinking with regard to Western categories and had engendered a new discipline, this time around harnessed his findings to a speculative ideological version of history that – once again, though now with new arguments – made Europe and America the mirror in which humankind could at once contemplate its origins and measure its evolution, in a process that had left a great number of peoples far behind.

This explains why, twenty years earlier, Morgan had designated the Iroquois descent groups with the Latin term *gens*. As a jurist schooled in Roman law, he

---

15   L. H. Morgan, *Ancient Society or Research in the Lines of Human Progress from Savagery through Barbarism to Civilization* (Tucson, University of Arizona Press, 1985) (first edition 1887).

considered that the Iroquois clans held the key to understanding the Roman *gens* or the *genos* of the ancient Greeks. The kinship system of the nineteenth-century Iroquois was thus projected onto ancient Roman society. But, as the Iroquois *gens* (it would later be called 'clan') was matrilineal and the Roman *gens* patrilineal, the Iroquois were taken as providing evidence of an even more archaic state of the *gens*. This vision would rapidly (in 1884) be adopted by Friedrich Engels in his *Origin of the Family, Private Property and the State*, in which he attempted to bring Morgan's evolutionist speculations into line with Karl Marx's historical materialism.

In the end, by presenting the Western nuclear – and monogamous – family as the most rational form of family, as that form in which the 'blood' ties connecting a child to his or her (real) father and to his or her (real) mother were finally visible, Morgan, despite his efforts to decentre his thinking with regard to the values and representations of his own society, was never able to treat the Western way of organizing kinship, the family and marriage as merely one cultural model among others, a model that was just as ethnocentric and therefore equally as 'rational' or 'irrational' as the others.

We now understand why Morgan's work immediately drew so much criticism, targeted at his evolutionism, which, as it quickly became clear, had to be jettisoned if progress was to be made in exploring the domain he himself had helped to found as an object of scientific knowledge and upon which his work on the *Systems of Consanguinity and Affinity* had conferred its first letters of nobility.

For decades following Morgan, hundreds of field surveys, conducted in so-called 'tribal' societies of Africa, Asia, America and Oceania, or in 'peasant' societies in Europe, Asia and Latin America, confirmed the importance of kinship relations in the functioning of these societies.

LÉVI-STRAUSS AND HIS CRITICS

Once kinship ties began to appear as the very basis of these societies, their study was regarded as providing the key to understanding the way societies worked. This in turn resulted in a proliferation of studies on the subject, including works by some of the biggest names in anthropology, making kinship studies the lynchpin of the new social science. Indeed, because this theoretical context endowed kinship systems with a twofold primacy – ontological in relation to the life of societies and epistemological in terms of their scientific study – George Peter Murdock was able to entitle a book almost entirely devoted to the inventory and analysis of kin terminologies and systems throughout the world, *Social Structure* (1949).[16] The publication, in the same year, of Claude Lévi-Strauss' *The*

---

16   G. P. Murdock, *Social Structure* (New York, Macmillan, 1949).

Elementary Structures of Kinship[17] was to confirm the importance of kinship in the appearance, development and destiny of humankind.

Lévi-Strauss changed the scope of kinship studies by postulating that the incest taboo had been the primary condition both for the emergence of kinship relations and for the appearance of 'genuine' human society, henceforth separate from the animal-like state and pursuing its development in another world, a man-made one, the world of culture. The goal was no longer simply to understand tribal or peasant societies but to circumscribe and apprehend that which was truly human in man – in short, and as the philosophers say, to grasp his essence.

The goal thus singularly outstripped the standard theoretical ambitions and limits of anthropology, and of the other social sciences taken separately. Lévi-Strauss' thesis set out a global vision of humankind that resembled Morgan's minus the evolutionism, since Morgan had made the exclusion of incest (which he believed to have been gradual), in other words of primitive, animal-like promiscuity between the sexes, the driving force behind the changes in the family and in kinship relations, and one of the conditions of human progress. It is perhaps for this reason that Lévi-Strauss dedicated his book to Morgan. Furthermore, he was implicitly in agreement with Freud, who half a century earlier, in *Totem and Taboo*,[18] had explained the emergence of kinship relations by the sons' murder of a despotic and incestuous father. (The sons, so the theory goes, after having killed their father in order to gain access to their sisters and their mother, decided to renounce incestuous relations with them so as to avoid being obliged eventually to kill each other. Kinship relations would theoretically have appeared once the brothers began to exchange their sisters and their mothers, whom they had renounced, with other groups of men, who theoretically had done likewise.)

Yet, in *The Elementary Structures of Kinship*, Lévi-Strauss paid scant attention to the fact that Freud had based kinship relations on the exchange of women and had made this exchange the consequence of the incest taboo – an attitude that can probably be ascribed to Freud's claim that, in order to emerge from animal-like sexual promiscuity, it was necessary first to kill the father who tyrannized the primal horde. This was a thesis smelling of brimstone, which foregrounded sexuality and its repression, and claimed to explain by a unique

---

17   C. Lévi-Strauss, *Les Structures élémentaires de la parenté* (Paris, Presses Universitaires de France, 1949); English translation: *The Elementary Structures of Kinship*, translated by James Harle Bell, John Richard von Sturmer and Rodney Needham (Boston, Beacon Press, 1969).

18   S. Freud, *Totem and Taboo*, translated by James Strachey (London, Routledge and Kegan Paul, 1961), Chapter 4. Freud quotes J. G. Frazer, *Totemism and Exogamy* (London, Macmillan, 1910), p. 97: 'It is not easy to see why any deep human instinct should need to be reinforced by law. There is no law commanding men to eat and drink or forbidding them to put their hands in the fire.'

act – one that was unverifiable but whose consequences were irreversible – and furthermore by a murder, what Lévi-Strauss claimed to explain by the shock resulting from the emergence of language and symbolic thought in the human species.

With Lévi-Strauss, it was possible to believe that the study of kinship, thus elevated, had a considerable future and that its importance would no longer be contested. After the publication of his book, having turned his attention to American Indians' mythology, Lévi-Strauss would progressively leave the task of continuing the pursuit to his students, but not without having laid out the course of research for others.[19] Naturally he believed that this task could be carried out only by disciples or colleagues who shared his thesis that the explanation of the differences in the various kinship systems lay in the forms of sister-exchange, and that these had to be analyzed using a method he called 'structural analysis'. Many took up the challenge, and some made important findings.[20]

But the edifice was already cracking under the strain of criticism from various parts. I will give only a few examples. Feminist anthropologists, in particular, rapidly rejected the idea that kinship was *necessarily* based on the exchange of women by men, objecting that this amounted to making male domination the primary, insurmountable and therefore 'natural', as it were, condition of the existence of kinship relations and society.[21] If this was true, an insuperable limit was set on the progress women could hope to make toward greater gender equality.

Leach, for his part, having greeted Lévi-Strauss' ideas with interest and introduced them in Great Britain, later undertook a critique. Already in his book, *Pul Elya, a Village in Ceylon: A Study of Land Tenure and Kinship*,[22] he had written that the (Dravidian) kin ties between the people of this village were no more than an idiom, a language in which social realities were expressed and dissimulated and which carried more weight than kinship. These realities were: relations with the land, land ownership, ties apart from which 'kinship systems had no reality'. This was a provocation of the kind Leach was fond of launching, but the formula produced its effect. His criticism prefigured by several years that which certain self-styled Marxist anthropologists – Claude Meillassoux and Emmanuel Terray in France, Joel Khan in England, among others – would

---

19   C. Lévi-Strauss, 'The future of kinship studies', *Proceedings of the Royal Anthropological Institute*, vol. 1 (1965), pp. 13–22.

20   F. Héritier, *L'Exercice de la parenté* (Paris, Gallimard/Seuil, 1981).

21   R. Reiter (ed.), *Toward an Anthropology of Women* (New York, Monthly Review Press, 1975), see particularly G. Rubin's text: 'The Traffic of Women: Notes on the "Political Economy" of Sex', pp. 157–210.

22   E. Leach, *Pul Elya, a Village in Ceylon: A Study of Land Tenure and Kinship* (Cambridge, Cambridge University Press, 1961).

direct against the thesis that kinship relations (rather than relations of production) were at the root of human society.[23]

Leach's iconoclastic blow was to be followed by many others, and they came from the two British temples of anthropology of kinship: Cambridge and Oxford. One after another, the concepts of kinship, marriage, incest and descent, together with Meyer Fortes' notion of complementary filiation, prescription or preference in the choice of a spouse in elementary systems, were dissected and confronted with various facts that contradicted the accepted definitions. Once again Leach had paved the way, in another book published the same year as *Pul Elya* (1961) but whose title, *Rethinking Anthropology*,[24] clearly suggested that the time of comforting self-evident notions was already over: in it he declared that marriage was not an institution that could be given a universal definition. Finally, in 1969, the Association of Social Anthropologists, presided over by Leach himself, declared that the time had come to put anthropology on a sound footing and decided that the first question up for discussion should obviously be: kinship. Rodney Needham was given the task of organizing a major symposium on 'Kinship and Marriage'. Some of the papers presented on this occasion appeared in 1971 in the volume *Rethinking Kinship and Marriage*,[25] a title clearly indicating that the authors were approaching these questions from the same critical angle as Leach.

This important book deserves a mention here, for through it runs a major contradiction that illuminates the nature of this first big wave of criticism directed against kinship studies by top anthropologists who were experts in the field. Needham's two introductory texts provide a spectacular illustration. First of all, certain chapters, such as Thomas Beidelman's on the representation of kinship among the Kaguru of Tanzania, or J. Fox's 'Sister's child as plant', on metaphors of consanguinity in Roti, an Indonesian island, as well as long passages in which Needham restates and develops his earlier analysis of the Purum, on the Wikmunkan or on the notion of prescriptive marriage, are by no means criticisms of kinship studies but, on the contrary, direct and enriching extensions.

On the other hand, in some passages Needham and Leach hoist the rebel flag. Needham, for instance, claimed to be a structuralist, while at the same time criticizing Lévi-Strauss for having yielded to the 'passion for generalities', an

---

23   M. Godelier, *Rationalité et irrationalité en économie* (Paris, Maspero, 1966); and *Horizons, trajets marxistes en anthropologie* (Paris, Maspero, 1973), English translation: *Perspectives in Marxist Anthropology*, translated by Robert Brain (Cambridge, Cambridge University Press, 1977); C. Meillassoux, *Femmes, greniers et capitaux* (Paris, Maspero, 1969); M. Bloch (ed.), *Marxist Analyses and Social Anthropology* (London, Malaby Press, 1975).

24   E. Leach, *Rethinking Anthropology* (London, University of London/The Athlone Press, 1963).

25   R. Needham, *Rethinking Kinship and Marriage* (London, Tavistock Publications, 1971).

expression borrowed from Wittgenstein[26] (of whom Needham was a fervent admirer). The criticism was aimed not solely at Lévi-Strauss and this theory of incest, but also at Meyer Fortes, for having posited the existence of a complementary filiation present in unilineal kinship systems. This thesis correctly claimed that, in a patrilineal society, for example, the child's ties with its mother's lineage or clan, without constituting actual 'descent' ties, had a strong existence that was recognized and which in many circumstances completed the descent ties. For Needham, considering the extreme diversity of the facts, all general definitions of incest, marriage, etc., looked very much like 'all-purpose words', abusive generalizations. But at the same time, he rightly criticized his colleagues who had not yet grasped that: 'it is not only that we cannot make sociological inferences, about institutions, groups, and persons, from the structure of a terminology, but we cannot even infer that the statuses denoted by any one term will have anything significant in common'.[27]

It is from this viewpoint that we must read the following declarations, which created quite a stir at the time:

> By this account, 'kinship' is certainly a thoroughly misleading term and a false criterion in the comparison of social facts. It does not denote a discriminable class of phenomena or a distinct type of theory, and it does not admit of special canons of competence and authority. Accordingly, it cannot be said that a social anthropologist is 'good at kinship'; what he is good at is analysis. What that means depends on whatever he happens to be analysing.[28]

Or elsewhere: 'To put it very bluntly, then, there is no such thing as kinship, and it follows that there can be no such thing as kinship theory.'[29]

In the same volume, Leach would go even further than Needham, putting the latter in the same bag as the anthropologists he had criticized: 'All of which adds up to saying that, in my view, the utility of the study of kin-term systems as sets – which runs from Morgan to Rivers to Radcliffe-Brown to Goodenough to Lounsbury and, by a different route, to Lévi-Strauss and Rodney Needham – is pretty well worked out.'[30] Provocations and paradoxes, as we can see, were Leach's daily bread.

Needham evinces the same attitude when, having buried the concept of kinship together with any attempt to work out a general theory of kinship, he stresses in terms taken from strictly classical anthropology that, 'the deeper the

---

26   L. Wittgenstein, *The Blue and Brown Books* (Oxford, Blackwell, 1958), pp. 43–4.
27   Needham, *Rethinking Kinship and Marriage*, p. cvii.
28   Ibid., p. cviii.
29   Ibid., p. 5.
30   Ibid., pp. 76–7, cviii.

analyst goes, the more he is obliged to concentrate on singularities of *cultural signification*: this involves trying to put a coherent construction both on an unpredictable variety of meanings and functions that any individual term may have and on the set of terms in combination'.[31]

Wise words, which show that Needham's and Leach's rejection of the notion of kinship and their criticism of all general theories did not at the time mean a death sentence for kinship studies but the declaration, in deliberately excessive and gratifying terms, not that the study of kinship should be halted but that it should be *conducted on different bases, not stopping at terminologies but going on to the links between kinship and economy, power, religion, etc.*

This was no longer the case fifteen years later with the publication of David Schneider's book *Critique of the Study of Kinship* (1984).[32] For many, this appeared to be the final blow to the majestic edifice of kinship writings. After having described how, twenty years earlier, he had analyzed the kin system of the Yap Islanders (in Micronesia), where he had begun his fieldwork, Schneider launched into a radical self-critique of his early writings and proposed another interpretation of the same data, and particularly of the basic unit of Yap society, the *tabineau*. Previously he had defined it as an extended patrilocal family combined with a matrilineal kinship system. In his second version, Schneider stressed that it seemed to him that, for the Yap Islanders, what bound together the members of a *tabineau* was not kinship but actual cooperation in working the same piece of land, and that it was this alone which founded an individual's right to the land. In sum, he no longer regarded the *tabineau* as a kin group or Yap society as kin based, but as being based on other relations (economic) and other values (religious and economic). Schneider's auto-critique concurred with Leach's position on kinship in Pul Elya. In spite of this convergence, though, Schneider merely mentioned it in passing, without dwelling on it, and aimed a first criticism at 'almost all anthropologists' who had gone before (and against himself in his former life): that of having abusively posed the principle that kinship was a *universally recognized basic* value in all societies. This was the very opposite of Lévi-Strauss' view.

Schneider nevertheless decided to go on and sift through the principal definitions of kinship from Morgan to Scheffler and Lounsbury. When he had finished, he felt entitled to say that all studies on kinship, from Morgan on, had been explicitly or implicitly based on the same ethnocentric definition. For Europeans and Euro-Americans,[33] kinship concerns essentially procreation, the

---

31   Ibid., p. cviii; emphasis added.
32   D. M. Schneider, *A Critique of the Study of Kinship* (Ann Arbor, University of Michigan Press, 1984).
33   Schneider himself launched a large-scale survey of the cultural values associated with kin relations in the United States, which resulted in the publication of *American Kinship: A Cultural*

reproduction of human beings. This reproduction is primarily a biological process, and therefore the genealogical ties between individuals are biological ties, 'blood' ties. For Westerners, the nuclear family is the place where the parents' blood mingles in and is shared by the children. Finally he deemed that anthropological theories reflect the Western idea – found equally in Malinowski, Meyer Fortes or Scheffler – that, whatever cultural values and social attributes may be associated with these genealogical ties in a given society, there lies at the heart of all kinship systems a universal genealogical structure that is inescapable and indissoluble, which proceeds from the nuclear family. It is from this structure, regarded as the core of 'primary' kinship relations, that, by the twofold process of direct extension and unilateral reinterpretation, all of the other kin relations are derived.[34] Schneider's general conclusion that 'the study of kinship derives directly and practically unaltered from the ethnoepistemology of European culture . . . [that] Blood is presumably Thicker than Water'[35] became a pseudo-scientific postulate which he called 'the Doctrine of the Genealogical Unity of Mankind'.[36] This postulate, he conjectured, was the basis of the genealogical method, perfected by Morgan, Rivers and others, that all field anthropologists used to explore the kinship system in the society they had chosen to study. This being the case, all were doomed to failure, since, because they were using a method that incorporated Western cultural prejudices assumed to be universal sociological truths, their work could only produce results that confirmed these universal truths.

For Schneider there was only one conclusion, and it was simple and clear: from Morgan onward, kinship studies had simply gone in circles, and the objective analysis of kinship had not yet truly begun.

In the course of the present work, I will examine and reply to these criticisms one by one. Some are simply inadmissible. But I cannot pass over in silence the fact that numerous anthropologists had shown, well before Schneider, that in one or another society the kin terms people use to refer to those they regard as relatives do not correspond to 'real' genealogical ties but to relations between categories of individuals considered to be in the same social relationship to each

Account (Englewood Cliffs NJ, Prentice Hall, 1968) and of another volume in collaboration with R. T. Smith, *Class Differences and Sex Roles in American Kinship and Family Structure* (Englewood Cliffs NJ, Prentice Hall, 1973). We are also indebted to Schneider for such remarkable articles as 'The Meaning of Incest', *The Journal of the Polynesian Society*, vol. 85, no. 3 (1976), pp. 149–69, and his introduction to the book *Matrilineal Kinship*, co-edited with Kathleen Gough (Berkeley, University of California Press, 1961), which Leach regarded as a small 'masterpiece'. My criticism of Schneider is not addressed to his work as a whole but to his 1984 volume, which had the greatest impact.

34   B. Malinowski, 'Parenthood. The basis of social structure', in V. F. Calverton and D. Schmalhausen (eds.), *The New Generation: The Intimate Problems of Modern Parents and Children* (New York, Macaulay, 1930), p. 196, quoted in Schneider, *A Critique of the Study of Kinship*, p. 171.

35   Schneider, *A Critique of the Study of Kinship*, p. 174.

36   Ibid.

other. Durkheim had already noted as much concerning Australian Aboriginal peoples – for which Schneider praised him while reproaching him for not having sought to show how this social relationship was precisely a kinship relation rather than something else. Many others had followed in Durkheim's steps, such as Hocart, Leach and Dumont, whom Schneider does not cite.

Moreover, even in societies where informants emphasize genealogical ties between individuals, it is hard, if one takes cultural representations of procreation seriously, to reduce these genealogical ties to biological ones as they are understood in European culture, in other words, as relations that entail the sharing and mingling of the parents' blood. Furthermore it is widely accepted that cultural representations of the role of blood in making babies are a matter not of biology (as an experimental science) but of ideology.

There is nothing mechanical about culture. It suffices to cite societies where the 'descent rule', as anthropologists say, is patrilineal and yet no mention is made of the possible role of sperm or blood in making a child. Furthermore, while it is true that the presence of an Iroquois-type terminology in certain societies in Africa, Oceania and America says nothing about how each of them sees the process of conceiving a child and therefore how they represent what we call motherhood, fatherhood, etc., it remains to be explained why so many societies having different cultures use kinship terminologies whose formal structure is similar. This point, too, Schneider passed over in silence, seeking as he was to imprison his colleagues in a false syllogism. Starting, on the one hand, from the real fact that one never knows in advance what kinship is in a non-European society and, on the other hand, from the fact that we know that Europeans use kinship as a set of biological *and* social relations which link individuals of the two sexes in the process of reproducing life and the succession of generations, Schneider contended that trying to discover how other societies thought of this process always came down to finding in others that which one already had in oneself and had transported to the other society. Anthropologists would thus merely be 'discovering' in other cultures pretexts for erecting mirrors in which their own image would be reflected infinitely, but garbed in the features of the other.

In sum, if for Leach and Needham the term 'kinship' finally did not designate a distinct class of facts or any distinct type of theory, they had nevertheless continued to study the facts of kinship and attempted to theorize them. Schneider, on the other hand, considered that there was indeed such a thing as kinship, but only in Western societies. Or more precisely, that it might exist in other societies, but that one could not postulate this existence and that any attempt to discover it was bound to fail if one counted on the genealogical-survey method. After Schneider, was it still worth spending even one hour on kinship?

In reality things did not turn out as Schneider had predicted. Kinship had, in the meantime, become entangled with other issues and had emigrated to other sites, where its object had begun to be reshaped and enriched. Anthropologists had, for example, become increasingly interested in gender relations and in the questions of the form and foundations of male or female powers in the private and public spheres. Kinship was also increasingly being seen no longer as a separate area but as an aspect of the global process of social reproduction. Or again, at the other pole from this global approach but in complement to it, kin ties were being considered as a part of the process of constructing the person, the self.

By shifting sites in this way, the study of kinship had finally deserted those places where it had been running in circles for decades, exhausting itself in an attempt to answer false questions to which Leach, Needham and also Schneider had the merit of drawing attention. Since the 1980s, almost no one has proposed to deduce the structure of a society from the formal analysis of its kin terminology. And vice versa, no one now explains the presence of a given kinship terminology by the existence of a particular mode of production or political system.

So the predicted death has not occurred! And, taking a closer look, we see that today's preferred topics of study (construction of the person, gender relations, kinship in the global functioning of a society, etc.) are not really new. What is new is first of all that these topics have moved to the forefront of research concerns. The explanation does not lie in scientific reasons alone, but also in what is going on in our societies, for example, the social struggles and pressures for greater gender equality. New, too, is the fact that in our search for answers we can no longer rely on notions that were only recently still taken for granted, such as the idea that so-called 'primitive' societies are 'kin based' or that the family is the basis of society. To these reasons we must add the fact that, in the present context of the fast-growing globalization of the capitalist economy and the inclusion of all societies in this world system, the process of the overall reproduction of each local society rests less and less on that society's own bases, so that the kinship relations that may once have played an important role in this process now contribute increasingly less to the social reproduction of its groups and individuals.

The conclusion to be drawn from this brief overview of the transformations in kinship studies on the ground and in theory seems clear. Anthropology cannot exist as a scientific discipline unless it constantly submits its concepts, its methods and its findings to criticism and criticizes them itself, always placing this self-examination in historical context, taking in not only the history of anthropology and the social sciences, but also the history of the societies in which anthropologists learned their trade as well as that of the societies in which they later exercised it.

It is in this perspective that I am now going to revisit my own work, in order to show how I studied kinship in the field, among the Baruya, a society in New Guinea where I lived and worked for a total of more than seven years between 1967 and 1988.

CHAPTER ONE

Kinship in the Field
The Baruya of New Guinea

Analyzing and interpreting the realm and the exercise of kinship in contemporary societies is obviously not simply a matter of theories and choosing among the different hypotheses and doctrines advanced by one or another anthropologist. One must also have tried one's hand at conducting a systematic study of the relations and representations of kinship and the family in a real society. This holds not only for anthropologists, but for sociologists and other social scientists engaged in the study of contemporary societies.

THE TOOLBOX

It is also obvious that, before undertaking such a study, anthropologists cannot clear their head of everything they have previously read, heard, learned or understood about kinship. Deliberate amnesia of this sort is impossible. What is possible, however, and even to be recommended, is to adopt a stance of critical vigilance or awareness so as to be ready, if necessary, to revise or abandon concepts one previously considered to be analytically founded or field methods one had held to 'pay off', etc. In the meantime, one must begin to work with the theories and methods at hand and which seem useful for doing what one has set out to do.

This was, of course, true in my own case when in 1967 I decided to study kinship relations in the Baruya society, a New Guinea Highlands population with whom I had chosen to live and 'do fieldwork', as we said then. How did I proceed? What results did I obtain and what shifts did my observations prompt in my theories? This is what I will now attempt to describe.

In 1967, as mentioned above, Lévi-Strauss' theoretical work in kinship held sway in France and had already won a large following in Great Britain and the United States. To be sure, Leach had already formulated his first criticisms in *Rethinking Anthropology*, but the stage was still largely occupied by the debates and disputes between those for whom descent was the primordial axis of kinship relations and those for whom this role fell to alliance, in short: between Meyer Fortes, Evans-Pritchard, Jack Goody, etc., on one side, and Lévi-Strauss, Rodney Needham, Louis Dumont, Leach, etc., on the other. Of course, some in each camp had already begun to point out that there was no commonly agreed definition of family, marriage, incest, etc., and, above all, none that applied to all societies. But no one at the time seriously doubted that such institutions as descent, filiation, marriage, the family, transmission of names and ranks, relations with the ancestors, dowry, and exchange of women belonged to the field of kinship and its exercise.

Everyone was also familiar with Murdock's categories of kinship terminologies: 'Hawaiian', 'Sudanese', 'Eskimo' and so on, whose construction rules and formal structures had been isolated and therefore could be identified in the field. And finally, although it was already well known (since Hocart at least)[1] that in many societies in Australia, Oceania, Asia and America kin terms designated not only (or not at all) a person's genealogical position with respect to another taken as a reference (an abstract male or female Ego), but (often) relations between 'categories' of individuals who were related to each other in the same way without necessarily having a genealogical tie, no one in France, by 1959, had yet formulated a radical criticism of the use of the genealogical method for the study of kinship. Novice anthropologists were merely advised not to force their informants to invent genealogies simply to please the ethnographer and to be aware that informants may have all sorts of reasons for manipulating the genealogies they recite – reasons that may be motivated by self-interest and therefore are interesting for anthropologists, as long as they realize this and can discover why.

In short, it was with this theoretical baggage and critical advice – shared by the other young anthropologists of the time – that I set out in October 1966 for New Guinea. I arrived in 1967, having stopped off in Australia to learn Melanesia Pidgin in the University of Canberra's language laboratory, run by A. Wurm. Robert Glasse, Andrew Strathern and others had alerted me to the importance of Pidgin for anyone travelling in New Guinea. But why New Guinea? And why the Baruya, with whom, a few months later, I would decide to live and work?

WHY NEW GUINEA?

It was on the advice of Claude Lévi-Strauss that I finally chose this country for some 'real' fieldwork. After having studied philosophy and then economics, I had decided to become an anthropologist and to look into an as yet little-developed domain: the economic systems of tribal and peasant societies; in sum, I wanted to go into economic anthropology. I had made this choice in a Marxist perspective, for at the time I believed that studying the modes of production and circulation of subsistence goods and wealth (a topic generally neglected by anthropologists in favour of kinship or religion, with some illustrious exceptions like R. Firth, A. Richard, Herskovitz, Bohannan and a few others), was a better approach to explaining the origin and functioning of kinship and political

---

1   A. Hocart, 'Kinship systems', *Anthropos*, vol. 32 (1937), pp. 545–51.

systems. I went to Lévi-Strauss, who accepted me in his group and took me on as his assistant, giving me the task of studying the 'infrastructures' of the societies he was working on, while he analyzed their 'superstructures', kinship and religion. At the time Lévi-Strauss still readily used such Marxist vocabulary.[2]

An opportunity soon arose for me to involve myself clearly in the domain of economic anthropology when Unesco offered me the chance to study the effects of the implementation of a planned socialist economy on the development of village communities and ethnic groups in Mali. This move had been decided by President Modibo Keita and his Rassemblement Démocratique Africain (RDA) after Mali had broken with France and become independent. Having spent some weeks in the country, I concluded that there was indeed a ministry and a minister of the Plan, but no plan to speak of, and that what there was did not have a very positive impact on Mali's development. And so I spent my time travelling around and reading the literature on economic anthropology I had brought with me. A year later when I returned to Paris, disappointed, I was ready for some real fieldwork.[3]

I first went for advice to my friend Alfred Métraux (1902–63). He suggested that, rather than returning to Africa, I go to Bolivia and work among some of the Indian groups he had visited thirty years earlier. I was tempted by the idea and discussed it with him on several occasions so as to shape the project. But on the evening of 12 April 1963, a few hours after we had talked at length, Métraux took his life. Never in the course of our conversation had he let slip a hint of his decision, if he had already made it. When, a few days later at his funeral, I told Lévi-Strauss about our idea of a site for fieldwork, he advised against it, explaining that a large number of French anthropologists were already working in Africa or America and that there was something better: go to New Guinea, the last country where one could find societies less devastated by colonialism and Western culture than elsewhere, and where a few major figures of the discipline had distinguished themselves – Malinowski, Thurnwald, Mead, Fortune, etc. I capitulated and spent the next two years preparing myself to go to New Guinea.

In January 1967, I arrived armed with a list of names of tribes or local groups that my colleagues – R. Rappaport, P. Vayda, R. Glasse, A. Strathern, R. Crocombe, etc., who had already worked in New Guinea – had suggested I visit before making my choice. These tribes were generally neighbours of those among whom my colleagues had worked, so they knew they had not yet been studied and thought it was worthwhile and would enrich the material in view of future comparisons. The Baruya were not on the list.

---

2   C. Lévi-Strauss, *La Pensée sauvage* (Paris, Plon, 1962); English translation: *The Savage Mind* (Chicago, University of Chicago Press, 1969) (no translator mentioned).

3   In the meantime, I wrote up a synthesis of my readings on Mali, which appeared in the journal *L'Homme*, under the title 'Objet et méthodes de l'anthropologie économique', vol. 5, no. 2 (1965), pp. 32–91.

WHY THE BARUYA?

My encounter with the Baruya came about by chance, even if my decision to choose them for my fieldwork did not. In fact, the first name on my list of groups to visit was the Waffa, a tribe that lived several days' walk south of the Markham River and which in 1967 no one had visited for some ten years. After various adventures (such as crossing the Markham without benefit of a ford or a bridge, being abandoned in the bush by my guides before crossing the Waffa River, the sudden emergence from the forest of three men who would, so they said, take me to the Waffa), I found myself several days later at the foot of a high cliff atop which one could make out a village whose inhabitants were observing our arrival. Among them were two Europeans. I then learned from my three guides that I had not reached the Waffa at all but the Watchakes, and that the Europeans were two sisters from the Summer Institute of Linguistics (SIL) who had been living there for years so as to learn the language, translate the Bible and convert the people to Christianity. I was furious to have been tricked, but they explained that in fact the Waffa lived too far away and they had thought it would be useful for me to meet the Best sisters since they knew the area and spoke English. Forty years later, I still thank them for their initiative.

I spent some time with the Watchakes listening to and questioning the Best sisters who were at that time collecting and translating stories about the origin of the Pleiades star cluster, cultivated plants, etc. One day when I was talking about my plans, one of the sisters pointed to the highest peak in the chain of mountains that barred the horizon and said: 'Why not go see the Baruya? It was only in 1960 that the Administration set up a patrol post to control their region and only since 1965 that one can circulate freely there. We have a missionary couple, the Lloyds, who live in a village a few hours walk from the Wonenara patrol post. You'll see, the Baruya still dress like the Watchakes used to. Only recently they were still at war with their neighbours.'

I let myself be tempted and, a few days later, found myself at Wonenara, on the edge of a small landing strip where Dick Lloyd met me and took me to Yanyi, 'his' village. I learned from him that the Baruya had been 'discovered' in 1951 by Jim Sinclair,[4] a young patrol officer who had mounted an expedition to find out about the 'Batia', whose reputation as the makers of bars of salt used as a sort of exchange currency had reached the region he patrolled.[5] I also learned

---

4   J. P. Sinclair, *Behind the Ranges: Patrolling in New Guinea* (Melbourne, Melbourne University Press, 1966).

5   M. Godelier, 'La Monnaie de sel des Baruya de Nouvelle-Guinée', *L'Homme*, vol. 11, no. 2 (1969), pp. 5–37, and 'Outils de pierre, outils d'acier chez les Baruya de Nouvelle-Guinée', *L'Homme*,

that the Baruya belonged to a large group of tribes disparagingly called the 'Kukakuka', or 'thieves', by their enemies (a term carelessly adopted by the Australian administration to refer to them), and that the 'Kukakuka' had resisted the penetration of Australian patrols and European gold prospectors by killing or wounding a few, among whom was a young officer by the name of J. McCarthy,[6] who, having fallen into an ambush, managed to escape and walk for several days with an arrow in his abdomen. Later McCarthy would become a district Commissioner for Papua New Guinea and relate his adventures among the 'Kukakuka' in his memoirs, published in 1963, four years before my arrival in New Guinea.

I left the Lloyds and the village of Yanyi for Baruya country. The Baruya live at an altitude of 2,000 meters in two valleys of a mountain chain culminating in the volcano, Mount Yelia. The mountainsides are a patchwork of grass fields deforested by fire and broad stretches of primary or secondary rainforest. I was struck by the beauty of the landscape, but I would quickly discover that New Guinea abounds in impressive landscapes. I left the Wonenara Valley, crossed the mountains and found myself in the Marawaka Valley, the part of the Baruya territory not yet directly under Australian control.

I went from village to village, sleeping in the men's house where the young initiates lived. At that time all the men and adolescent boys carried their bows and arrows wherever they went. The women and young girls walking on the footpaths would stop and hide their faces in their bark capes whenever they met or were overtaken by married men or young initiates. In certain places there was a system of parallel paths, one for men and a lower one for women and children. Close to the waterways were fields of salt canes, with scattered constructions: these were ovens for producing the bars of crystallized salt. The population lived in villages of between 200 and 300 inhabitants, perched high on the mountainside to protect them from enemy attacks and dominated by one or several 'men's houses'.

Two weeks later I left the Baruya, taking with me my observations and impressions, and set out finally to visit the groups on my list. After some weeks, I found myself in the region of Mount Ialibu, blocked by a flooding river and forced to wait until the water fell sufficiently for us to cross to the Huli, a group living in the direction of Mendi, where Robert Glasse had worked. It was there that I decided to end this reconnaissance once it had become clear that nothing I had seen appealed to me as much as the Baruya.

vol. 13, no. 3 (1973), pp. 187–220.
6   J. K. McCarthy, *Patrol into Yesterday: My New Guinea Years* (Melbourne, F. W. Cheshire, 1963).

Several rational criteria entered into this choice. One, of course, was the fact that no anthropologist had ever worked among the Baruya, and I was going to be the first.[7] But at the time in New Guinea it was still easy and common for an anthropologist to be the first somewhere. Other reasons carried even more weight. The first was the Baruya's reputation for producing a sort of salt 'currency'. My head was full of Malinowski, Kula exchanges and so on; and I was delighted at the idea of studying another regional exchange network. The second was the fact that the Baruya initiated their boys (at the time I did not know that girls too were initiated) and that, until their marriage, these boys lived apart from the women's world in the famous men's houses built high on a mountainside or in the village. The third was the fact that the Baruya had the reputation of being warlike and that other tribes in the same 'ethnic' group (known as Kukakuka) had mounted an armed resistance to European penetration. Fourth was the fact that the Baruya lived in fairly big villages, and I would not have to spend my days hiking to little groups of ten or fifteen people dispersed in the forest, which would have been the case had I chosen to live with the highly nomadic groups to the south of Mount Hagen or Mount Bosavi, which were on my list. As my family was scheduled to join me, the fact of being able to live in a fairly well-populated village and only a few hours walking time from an airstrip also counted significantly in my choice.

In all, between 1967 and 1988, I spent, as I said, over seven years with the Baruya, usually in the same village, Wiaveu, which I left periodically to visit other Baruya villages or those of neighbouring – friendly or hostile – tribes. During my various stays, I conducted, simultaneously or successively, several major studies, among which was one on kinship (which I completed at least three times over the course of the twenty years). I should add that, in 1975, Australia granted Papua New Guinea its independence, and the Baruya, one of the last tribes to come under the control of a colonial power, found themselves willy-nilly citizens of an emerging state, which would almost immediately become a member of the United Nations. The society in which I lived and worked was thus not frozen in the past or even clinging to it. It was a society about to undergo rapid and profound changes, which were the work not only of the colonial power but of the Baruya themselves coming to grips with these new situations.

---

7   But this was not the only reason. In the years that followed, I invited young anthropologists to work with me and to develop their own research: Jean-Luc Lory, who wanted to work on Baruya shamanism and horticulture; Pierre Lemonnier, interested in salt-making and the Baruya's techniques; and Annick Coudart, a young archeologist who wanted to study the marks left in the ground by a village of horticulturalists and to compare them with those left by populations of slash-and-burn agriculturalists in the Neolithic.

During the first months of my stay, I applied myself to collecting the genealogies of the people around me. At that time, my main informants were not-yet-initiated boys and young unmarried girls, in short, youngsters for whom my presence was an unusual and continual source of entertainment and who accompanied me in packs from morning to night.

After several months, I submitted my first genealogies to some adult informants – married men and women with children. All conveyed to me that almost everything I had noted was inexact. In the sense that the young people did not know or confused the birth order of their uncles and aunts (on both sides), their grandparents' names and places of birth, and so on.

But I had also begun to collect the Baruya terms for kin ties – father of, son of, etc. – which I had compared with a much fuller list that had been drawn up before my arrival by Richard and Joy Lloyd, the missionaries from the Summer Institute of Linguistics.[8] In spite of that, and for different reasons, my survey had gotten off to a bad start, and I decided to take time out and turn to something else I had in mind: a study of how the Baruya produced their salt money and made their gardens. This entailed measuring the areas of their sweet potato, taro and yam patches; identifying the composition of the groups of men and/or women who worked together on a given step of the production process; calculating the number and areas of the patches in each garden; getting the names of the women who worked them; and with their help, learning their kin ties with the owners of the land they tended, the names of those who had first cleared each garden, the names of those who had the right to cultivate the gardens in 1967, and so forth. All of this was necessary in order to understand the principles underpinning the ownership and use rights in the areas of tribal territory, forests, grasslands and rivers used for hunting, gardening or fishing.

Every day for over six months I visited the gardens, where, respecting the customary rules for entering, I spent hours with the people working there. With their help, I made a topographical map of each garden, a study of the soil using Baruya categories, and noted the number and areas of the plots. Finally, for each of the gardens cultivated by the inhabitants of Wiaveu that year (over 180 gardens divided into at least 600 plots), I made a fairly complete file.

8   R. G. Lloyd, 'The Angan Language Family', in K. Franklin (ed.), *The Linguistic Situation in the Gulf District and Adjacent Areas, Papua New Guinea.* (Canberra, The Australian University, 1973), pp. 31–110; and 'Baruya Kith and Kin', in D. Shaw (ed.), *Kinship Studies in Papua New Guinea* (Ukarumpa, Summer Institute of Linguistics, 1974), pp. 97–114; J. A. Lloyd, *A Baruya–Tok Pisin–English Dictionary* (Canberra, The Australian University, 1992; Pacific Linguistic series).

ANOTHER WAY IN AND THE RIGHT WAY AROUND

At that point my relations with the Baruya changed altogether, and they would subsequently include me in all their activities, including the most secret aspects of their initiation rites. For, like many Melanesians, the Baruya are enthusiastic gardeners, keen to discuss the pros and cons of different pieces of land, the origin or the flavour of a given variety of taro or sweet potato, etc. And of course, it is no time before they give you the name of their ancestor, the first one, who cleared one or another piece of the forest with a stone adze. Then they will volunteer that this was when the Baruya were at war with such and such a tribe – the Yuwarrounatche, for example – and that during this war, one of their great warriors, an *aoulatta*, was killed at a particular spot but that they had avenged him by killing three enemies, one of whom was a woman, and so on. It was also explained to me that, next to a certain garden, it was forbidden to cut trees or clear land, and above all not to stop there to make love because the spot was inhabited by spirits who could attack you or make off with the semen and vaginal fluids that might have seeped into the earth and who could then kill you by multiplying these substances and using them against you. In sum, the garden study constantly spilled over into kinship, war, religion and, always, the Baruya's collective or individual history. It was at that point that I decided – while waiting for the chance to attend the large-scale initiation ceremonies planned for the end of 1968[9] – to resume my study of the Baruya kinship system.[10]

I therefore started over from scratch, but this time taking an altogether different approach. While studying the gardens, I had noticed that a fairly elderly woman, Djirinac, from the Baruya clan (the clan that gave the tribe its name and which is the 'centre post'), had such an immense knowledge of genealogies and an ability to reconstruct series of exchanges of women between lineages that people from other clans would consult her to fill in the gaps in their memories. I therefore asked her if she would help me conduct the survey, and she agreed, at least in so far as the inhabitants of the Wonenara Valley were concerned, because she wanted to be able to go home every evening to feed her family and her pigs. Two men older than she, Warineu and Kandavatche – one

---

9   The male initiation ceremonies are held every three years or so. Over the next twenty years, I would attend several of these as well as two initiations for young girls having reached menarche and finally in 1988 a ceremony initiating new shamans, held every ten or twelve years. Cf. M. Godelier, *La Production des Grands Hommes. Pouvoir et domination masculine chez les Baruya de Nouvelle Guinée* (Paris, Fayard, 1982); English translation: *The Making of Great Men: Male Domination and Power among the New Guinea Baruya*, translated by Rupert Swyer (Cambridge, Cambridge University Press, 1986).

10   In the following years, with the help of Jean-Luc Lory, I would make a second complete survey of the gardens cultivated by the Wiaveu villagers.

the former bodyguard of a great warrior and the other a salt-maker who no longer did much gardening – joined us. For a month our little band went from village to village reconstructing the genealogies of the valley's inhabitants.

When we had to cross the mountains to continue our work in the neighbouring Marawaka Valley, Djirinac left us, as we had agreed. As luck would have it, an elderly man from the Valley offered to take her place – Nougrouvandjereye, from the Nounguye clan, whom Djirinac would consult when he came to Wonenara if she wanted specific details on the genealogies or marriages of Baruya living in the Marawaka villages, whom she knew less well. Nougrouvandjereye's memory was as vast and as clear as Djirinac's, and, like her, he knew the kin ties between hundreds of people, which I would then go with him to verify. In addition to all the kin ties, Nougrouvandjereye's memory also covered all of the wars waged on or by the Baruya, and he was able to detail the circumstances of each war, the battle sites, the names of those killed, the reprisals and compensations, etc. Djirinac had nothing particular to say on these topics, quite simply because war stories did not interest her.

I had also developed a sort of standard note card for this survey, which I obliged myself to fill in for each individual whose name I had collected and whose genealogy I tried to reconstruct – with the person concerned if he or she was living and agreeable, or with others if the person was deceased or a child. Since in the meantime I had learned many things about the Baruya's marriage rules, descent principles and forms of hierarchy, my cards recorded the answers to such questions as: What is your mother's lineage? What woman from your father's lineage was exchanged (*ginamare*) for your mother? Since your father (father's group) did not give a woman in exchange for your mother, which of your 'sisters' is going to take your mother's place and marry your mother's brother's son (marriage with the matrilateral cross cousin)? Was your father an *aoulatta* (great warrior)? A *koulaka* (shaman)? Who were your father's co-initiates? Are any still living? And so on. A number of these questions could be put to either a man or a woman. But others could not, and I had to respect this taboo strictly.

Finally, at the end of this first systematic survey (which took over six months), with one or two exceptions, I had covered practically all of the living Baruya, including the men who had left to work on the coastal plantations, the women who had married into neighbouring friendly or enemy tribes, the boys the Lutheran missionaries had sent away to continue their studies begun at the Wonenara Bible School, etc.

Having watched me go from village to village, all of the Baruya in the Wonenara and Marawaka valleys knew me, and soon I knew somewhat more than their youngsters did about their ancestors and their lineage history. Over the following twenty years, I continued to record deaths, births, marriages, moves, changes in social circumstances, etc. I even made a second complete survey of the whole population, village by village. I inquired about why, in the interval, someone had married so and so or had moved house. What did this woman die from? In childbirth? By sorcery? Killed by her husband? In short, by 1988, the date of my last prolonged stay with the Baruya,[11] I had information accumulated over twenty years of observation on what, during this whole time, the Baruya had decided to do when it came to marrying, transmitting ranks to their children, etc. To make sense of this data concerning the exercise of kinship relations, it is necessary to bear in mind certain indispensable information about the Baruya's history and the type of society in which they live, act and reproduce themselves.

WHAT ARE THE BARUYA?

What does the word 'Baruya' mean? It is the name of an insect with red wings speckled with black spots (*baragaye*), which was formerly chosen by one of the tribe's clans to designate itself and which members of this clan are forbidden to kill. Its red wings remind them of the fiery sky-path followed by their Dream-time ancestor, Djivaamakwe, whom the Sun had sent to Bravegareubaramandeuc to found a village and a tribe by gathering to himself everyone living there, to whom he is said to have given their clan name and their roles in the perform-ance of the initiation rites. Today Bravegareubaramandeuc is the site of a long-deserted village perched on a hilltop near Menyamya, a few days' walk from the Baruya's valleys, a village that used to be inhabited by clans of the now-extinct Yoyue tribe.

This mythic account justifies the primary position the 'Baruya' clan holds in the male initiations and explains why this clan was destined to give its name to the territorial group that was to emerge when the Yoyue split. It is followed by a 'historical' account, which refers to facts on which all tribes in the area concur.

The facts are the following: toward the end of the eighteenth century (according to my calculations), certain Yoyue clans seem to have secretly arranged for the inhabitants of Bravegareubaramandeuc to be massacred by the Yoyue's traditional enemies, the Tapatche. But, on the day, the Baruya and members of some other clans were away in the forest, and their wives and young children were with them, as happens on the large-scale hunts that precede initi-ations. When they learned that all of their young initiates had been massacred in the men's house, together with a few others who had stayed behind, those who had gone hunting scattered in different directions to seek refuge with

---

11   I was there to take part in a big initiation ceremony for new shamans – both men and women, an event held every ten or fifteen years and which I had never been able to attend.

friendly tribes. A large group of refugees, including the members of the Baruya clan, reached the Andje, a tribe living in the Marawaka Valley, at the foot of Mount Yelia, where they asked for temporary refuge and protection. Their request was granted, and they moved in with their hosts – particularly with the Ndelie, a local clan that allowed them to use some of their growing and hunting lands.

After a number of years, the refugees decided, with the Ndelie's complicity, to take over their hosts' territory. In the meantime they had adopted their hosts' language (very similar to their own) and had their children initiated by the Andje. One day they lured the Andje into a trap, massacred some and put the rest to flight. History was repeating itself. After a series of battles, the Andje abandoned their territory and moved to the other side of Mount Yelia. At the conclusion of these events, a new local group, new 'tribe', was formed which took the name of the Baruya clan – probably because the Baruya already played an important role in the Yoyue male initiations through their possession of sacred objects and powerful ritual knowledge.

Now a 'tribe', the Baruya pursued their expansion throughout the nineteenth century and into the first decades of the twentieth, to the detriment of the neighbouring groups. At the beginning of the nineteenth century, they penetrated into the Wonenara Valley – where I was to encounter them in 1967 – drove out two groups already living there and settled on their lands. When peace was restored, certain Baruya lineages gave women to enemy lineages, thus making them affines. When wars broke out anew between the tribes, the Baruya, if victorious, would leave those of their enemies who were affines the choice of either fleeing with the rest of their tribe or coming to live with the Baruya and thus preserving their lives and their lands. Thus it was, when I arrived in 1967, that the Baruya society was composed of fifteen 'clans', eight of which descended from the Bravegareubaramandeuc refugees and seven from local lineages that had intermarried or joined with the Baruya. As a reward for having betrayed the Andje and helped the Baruya seize their territory, the Ndelie had been given a certain number of sacred objects and been allowed to take part in Baruya initiations. By contrast, although the six other local lineages had kept their lands and provided warriors, they played no role in these rites on the pretext (which turned out to be unfounded) that they had never owned *kwaimatnie*[12] and were therefore not sons of the Sun like the Baruya from Bravegareubaramandeuc, but were born there from droppings left by the cassowary, a wild woman who lives deep in the forest.

---

12   Sacred objects used in the boys' initiation ceremonies; the Baruya believe they were gifts from the gods to their ancestors. This affirmation was hotly contested in my presence by the representative of one of the lineages that had joined the Baruya.

WHAT IS A 'TRIBE'?

Let us leave the Baruya for a moment, now they are a 'tribe', and try to define what we mean in this context by 'tribe', 'ethnic group' and, of course, 'clan'.[13]

A 'tribe', as we just saw with the story of the Baruya, *is a local group which forms when a certain number of kin groups band together to defend and share the resources of a territory they exploit individually and/or in common.* This territory has either been inherited from ancestors or conquered by force. In the Baruya's case, a tribe is also a largely endogamous territorial group, since the kin groups that comprise it prefer to marry among themselves rather than with members of neighbouring friendly or hostile tribes. We will see why, finally, everyone cooperates directly (*kwaimatnie*-owning clans) or indirectly (associated local clans) to initiate their boys together and make them into warriors, shamans and so forth.

It is important to note that, in the Baruya language, the word *tsimiyaya* ('what *tsimia* do you belong to?') is used to ask someone what local group (what I here call a 'tribe') they belong to. *Yaya* means 'name'. *Tsimia* designates the big ceremonial house erected by the Baruya and neighbouring tribes, who speak the same language and share the same culture, in which they perform the rites that introduce a new generation of boys into the men's world and promote the other generations to the next initiation stage. This temporary structure is built by all of the adult men and women in the Baruya villages, whatever their clan and village. The word *tsimie* designates the 'big centre post' that holds up the roof of the ceremonial house. This post is called 'grandfather' during the initiations, and from its top a dangerous wild animal is thrown to its death, the meat from which is then presented to the oldest man in the valley. This gift signifies that his generation will have vanished before the next initiations are held three or four years hence, when a new generation of boys will be initiated and thus testify that the Baruya, as a tribe, continue to exist.

In short, by banding together to defend a territory, exchange women and initiate their children, the kin groups that make up the tribe act in such a way that each depends on all the others to reproduce itself, and in so doing reproduces the others. All of these kin groups share the same language and the same culture. By *culture*, I mean *the whole set of representations of the universe, rules for organizing society, positive and negative values and behavioural standards to which the individuals and groups that make up the Baruya society refer*[14] *when*

---

13   M. Godelier, 'Ethnie, tribu, nation chez les Baruya de Nouvelle-Guinea', *Journal de la Société des océanistes*, vol. 41, no. 81 (1985), pp. 159–68, and 'Le Concept de tribu. Crise d'un concept ou crise des fondements empiriques de l'anthropologie?', *Diogène*, no. 81 (1973), pp. 3–28.

14   To refer to does not necessarily mean to apply. But even not to apply shared rules is still to refer to them. Cf. M. Godelier, *L'Idéel et le matériel. Pensée, économie, sociétés* (Paris, Fayard,

acting on other groups, themselves or the world around them. This world that surrounds the Baruya is made up of trees, rivers and streams, animals and spirits of the dead, neighbouring friendly or enemy tribes, evil underground-dwelling spirits, the Python (god of rain and menstruation) and the two shining heavenly bodies, the Sun and the Moon – two powers that govern the seasons and human destiny well beyond tribal frontiers. Of course, nowadays, the Baruya's world also includes Europeans, the police, the army and the Administration – instruments of a new institution that is the state. Not forgetting the presence of a new god as well, Jesus Christ, and his adversary, Satan.

One very important fact will now allow us to distinguish between the realities we designate by the terms 'tribe' and 'ethnic group', and to show that *a shared culture is not enough* – as Schneider and his disciples had advanced – *to make a set of local groups, kin groups or others, into a society; that is to say, into a whole capable of representing itself to itself as such, and which must reproduce itself as a whole in order to go on existing as such.*

FROM TRIBE TO ETHNIC GROUP

Let us therefore come back to the fact that, with the exception of a single group,[15] all of the Baruya's neighbours – Wantekia, Usarumpia, Bulakia, Yuwarrounatche, Andje, etc. – speak the same language and have nearly the same customs as the Baruya. All wear the same kinds of clothing, the same insignia; all say that their remote ancestors lived in the Menyamya area.

In fact, the Baruya and their neighbours form the northwestern edge of a set of local groups that speak related languages and occupy a vast territory stretching from the high valleys in the north to a few kilometres from the shores of the Gulf of Papua in the south. Neighbouring tribes understand each other's speech, but individuals from tribes located on opposite sides of this immense territory do not. According to linguists using glottochronology, all of these languages split off from a common trunk spoken in the vicinity of Menyamya, and their differentiation probably occurred over the span of a millennium. But it was not only the languages that diverged; the social structures also display striking differences.

The northern groups, to which the Baruya belong, worship the Sun, emphasize the role of sperm in making babies, and initiate their boys by isolating them

---

1984); English translation: *The Mental and the Material: Thought, Economy and Society*, translated by Martin Thom (London/New York, Verso, 1986) and the chapter 'Quelles cultures pour quels primates: définition faible ou définition forte de la culture?' in A. Ducros, J. Ducros and P. Joulain (eds.), *La Culture est-elle naturelle?* (Paris, Errance, 1998), pp. 217–23.

15   The Kenazé, who belong to the broad Awa-Tairora language group and with whom the Baruya regularly trade but never fight.

in men's houses, where they engage in ritualized homosexual practices.[16] The southern groups, on the other hand, emphasize menstrual blood, their initiations do not include homosexual practices, and they separate their young male initiates from their mothers and the world of women for only a short time.[17] Yet in spite of these cultural and social differences, all of these tribes recognize a shared origin, which goes back to the Dreamtime of their mythic ancestors (*wandjinia*), a common origin attested by the clothing and the insignia worn by the men and the women, which are nearly identical in all groups.[18]

But recognizing their common origins and their shared cultural identity does not stop these tribes from fighting each other, massacring their neighbours or seizing all or part of their territory – as the history of the Baruya themselves shows. This shared identity is also recognized by bordering tribes that belong to other linguistic and cultural groups. Moreover, some use derogatory terms, like *kukakuka*, to designate all of the groups living between Menyamya and the Gulf of Papua. Since *Kuka* means 'to steal' in Baruya, one imagines that the Baruya and their neighbours who share the same culture do not use a term for themselves or each other that evokes a society of thieves whose lethal raids once devastated enemy villages.[19]

By ethnic group, I mean *the whole set of these local groups – Baruya, Andje, Bulakia, etc. – that recognize each other as having a common origin, speak closely related languages, and share ways of thinking and living, that is to say, representations of the universe and rules of organization which show by their very differences that they belong to one tradition within which these differences appear as possible transformations.*[20]

---

16   Cf. J. Mimica, 'The incest passions: An outline of the logic of Ye social organization, Part I–II', *Oceania*, vol. 62, no. 2 (1991), pp. 34–58, and *Intimations of Infinity* (Oxford, Berg, 1988).

17   P. Bonnemère, *Le Pandanus rouge. Corps, différence des sexes et parenté chez les Ankave* (Paris, Editions du CNRS/Editions de la Maison des Sciences de l'Homme, 1996), pp. 293–94, and 'Maternal nurturing substance and paternal spirit: The making of a Southern Anga society', *Oceania*, vol. 64, no. 2 (1993), pp. 159–86.

18   See the article by P. Lemonnier, 'Mipela wan bilas. Identité et variabilité socioculturelle chez les Anga de Nouvelle-Guinée', in S. T. Tcherkézoff and F. Marsaudon (eds.), *Le Pacific sud aujourd'hui: identités et transformations culturelles* (Paris, Editions du CNRS, 1998), pp. 196–227; English translation: S. T. Tcherkézoff and F. Maursaudon (eds.), *The Changing South Pacific: Identities and Transformations* (Canberra: Pandanus Books, Rspas, the Australian National University, 2005).

19   The term 'Kukakuka' was unfortunately adopted by the Australian administration to designate the Baruya and other tribes of the same culture. After independence, it was replaced by a neutral term suggested by Dick Lloyd, 'Anga', which is common to all of these languages and designates 'the house'. The term was adopted by the Baruya and their neighbours as a way of underscoring their shared identity within the Menyamya District to which they now belong.

20   This definition concords with Fredrik Barth's pioneering work in the area; Barth accorded a variable degree of importance to ethnic belonging in understanding the identity of individuals and local groups. Barth had worked among the Pathans of Afghanistan and Pakistan, a culturally and sociologically very complex region where different groups met and intersected:

It is important to stress that the fact that a Baruya or an Andje belongs to the same ethnic group and knows this does not entitle him (or her) to either *land or a spouse*, and does not give him any power or *authority* outside the boundaries of his own local group; neither does it keep the tribes belonging to this ethnic group from making war on each other. In short, the ethnic group is a social and cultural reality, *but an ethnic group is not a 'society'*. Conversely, a territorial group such as the Baruya or the Andje does constitute a society. What makes the Baruya a society is first of all the fact that this group has an identity that is expressed by a 'big name', a single overarching name that subsumes the names of the particular groups (clans and lineages) and those of the individuals that compose them, and endows everyone with a specific all-encompassing identity they recognize and which is also recognized by the other territorial groups around them (who also have a big name, e.g. Bulakia, Andje, Wantekia, etc.).

This big name always goes with a territory whose boundaries are known, if not respected or accepted, by the neighbouring groups and over which the group exercises a sort of sovereignty, in the two senses of the term. Sovereignty in the sense that the clans and lineages that make up the Baruya society thereby have the exclusive right to appropriate and exploit parts of this territory in order to extract the bulk of their means of existence. Sovereignty, too, in the sense that the Baruya do not give groups other than themselves the right to resolve the sometimes bloody conflicts that arise between their members. No outside intervention is accepted or requested, save in exceptional circumstances.

So we see what makes the difference between an ethnic group, which is a social reality without being a society, and a 'tribe', which, on the other hand, is a society. The Baruya, the Wantekia, the Usarumpia, etc., speak the same language or closely related dialects, share the same culture and follow the same rules of social organization (sister exchange, male and female initiations, etc.). These facts attest that they belong to a single group of linguistically and culturally related populations, and it is this set of populations that we call an ethnic group, a social reality whose existence was recognized by these populations, who referred to it by a periphrasis: 'those who wear the same ornaments as we'.

---

language groups – Persophones, Arabophones, Turcophones etc.; agriculturalists and pastoral nomads; invading and conquered groups; as well as town and country. Barth showed the alternatives extended to these groups, owing to their history, for defining or choosing their identity. The Baruya's situation, by contrast, was simple to understand, but also showed that the awareness of belonging to a single ethnic group had not stopped them from developing very differently. Cf. F. Barth, *Political Leadership among Swath Pathans* (New York/London, Athlone Press, 1959). See Also F. Barth (ed.), *Ethnic Groups and Boundaries: The Social Organization of Culture Difference* (Boston, Little, Brown and Company, 1969; London School of Economics Monographs on Social Anthropology, no. 19).

What thus makes the Baruya, the Wantekia, etc., different societies within the same ethnic set is that each of these groups controls a distinct *territory*. Because they exploit the resources and extract the bulk of their material means of existence from it, this territory is therefore the first condition for the reproduction of the social groups that make up these societies, and therefore for the reproduction of the social relations that bind them together through marriage, initiations, ritual practices, solidarity in times of war, etc. For a society to exist (as a whole able to reproduce itself), there must be in addition to the 'mental' components of social life (representations of the universe, rules for organizing society, values, standards of conduct), a relation of social and material appropriation to the territory from which the group's members draw a significant fraction of their material means of existence.[21]

THE BARUYA ARE A SOCIETY, THE ANGA ETHNIC GROUP IS A COMMUNITY

This whole that must reproduce itself as such and which constitutes a society consists concretely of a certain number of persons of both sexes and different generations, born into distinct kin groups, often having different social, ritual or other functions, but who exercise in common what could be called a sort of 'sovereignty' over their natural environment which ends as soon as they step outside their territorial boundaries. Because of this, all these individuals and groups have a common identity and carry a common name that is added to their personal names (these indicate the person's lineage, sex, etc.). In addition, all these individuals and groups entertain a certain number of connected but distinct relations – of kinship, material or ritual dependence, subordination of one gender to the other, etc. – such that, for a society to continue to exist, not only must those who die be *replaced* by others, but the *relationships* between individuals and groups which characterize this type of society (relations shaped by the kinship system or by the existence of an initiation system) must also be *reproduced*. And, of course, just as individuals cannot – save in exceptional circumstances – stop producing and reproducing their social relations, neither can they avoid producing their material conditions of existence, which not only ensure their subsistence but also consist in producing or assembling the material conditions necessary for exercising kinship relations, performing initiations, making war, etc.

Yet the story of the Yoyue and the Baruya shows us just as clearly that these territorial groups operate as societies, as overarching local units, only for a time. Before the arrival of Europeans, which froze the habitually unstable state of relations between neighbouring tribes, numerous conflicts of interest (over

---

21   For the notion of 'mental' (*idéel*) realities, see Godelier, *The Mental and the Material*.

women, land, game, trading partners) opposed lineages and individuals (even close relatives) from the same tribe. Ultimately, in certain circumstances, the tacit agreement between lineages and individuals to live together breaks down, the unity of the tribe is shattered, and the tribe splits into fragments that join with neighbouring tribes or come together to create a new tribe, as in the case of the Baruya. However, it must be noted that, if, before the Europeans arrived, local groups came together, split up and joined with others, *the tribal form of these groups*, by contrast, *did not disappear and was promptly reproduced by each of the new groups.*

The fact of having shown that the Baruya existed as a society from the moment they exercised a sort of sovereignty over a territory (a sovereignty that was, if not recognized, at least known by their neighbours), and of having then applied the concept of tribe to this society because the social units sharing the territory are kin groups, still tells us nothing about the internal structure of the society, a structure that engenders distinct functions and social positions hierarchically distributed among individuals as well as among the kin groups into which they are born.

SOME INSTITUTIONS ARE BROADER THAN KINSHIP RELATIONS AND KIN GROUPS

There are other divisions running through Baruya society than those between clans or lineages. Two of these are of particular importance because they cut across the whole society: one is between the sexes and the other between clans.

Baruya gender relations were, in 1967, and indeed still are, relations of complementarity and cooperation at the same time as relations of domination and subordination. The complementarity is visible in the division of labour and in the domains of activity assigned to each sex (hunting, warfare, child-raising, weaving, etc.), ensuring that each gender makes its distinct contribution to the ongoing production of the Baruya's material and social conditions of existence. But this cooperation works on the basis of a characteristic overarching relationship of domination, which one could describe as that of the generalized subordination of women to men.[22]

This gender inequality is affirmed at the child's birth, but does not reach its fully fledged and definitive form until the moment when, around the age of nine or ten, all the boys in that age group are taken away from their mothers and sisters and, after having their noses pierced, are secluded in the 'men's house' that dominates every Baruya village. Women are strictly forbidden to approach

---

22   Since my first encounter with the Baruya, gender relations have evolved toward a lesser degree of subordination (or submission) of women to men.

this house. The separation and the marking of the boys' bodies are the first in a long series of initiatory ordeals that, after ten or more years and four stages of initiation, ultimately rid them of everything that tied them to the maternal world. They will now be masculine enough to cope with the world of women, and to leave the men's house and marry a girl who has been chosen for them and for whom their lineage has given a 'sister'.

Over the course of these years, the boys will be led deep into the forest or into the dimly lit men's house and placed in contact with the sacred objects held by the clans in charge of the various initiation rites. They will hear the sound of the bull-roarers and will discover that this noise – which terrifies the women and the uninitiated, who have been led to believe they are hearing the voices of the forest spirits come to visit the men and the new initiates in the midst of their ceremonies – is actually man-made. It will be revealed to them – but they must not speak of it to women or children on pain of death – that it was really the women who invented the flutes, bows and many other things, and that these were subsequently stolen by the first men, and now the women can neither own them nor even look on them. It will also be explained to them that the men were compelled to take the bows from the women because they used them ill-advisedly, killing too much game and compromising the cosmic and social orders by defiling everything with the menstrual blood running down their thighs. They will learn that the women's sexual organ and sexual relations with women are a constant threat to men, who risk being deprived of their strength, their good looks and their superiority.

During this all-male period, which lasts for years,[23] the boys will be secretly 're-engendered' by the men, but his time without the help of women. The older boys in the last two stages of initiation – young men between the ages of fifteen and twenty or twenty-two, who have not yet had intercourse with a women – often give the young boys their semen to drink, through homosexual relations that grow up between the older initiates and the newcomers. Later, these boys will in turn give their semen, equally free of all female defilement, to those boys who follow them into the men's house.

Little by little, these young boys and adolescents come to see it as right and proper that Baruya women are not allowed to inherit their ancestors' land, bear arms, make salt money, have contact with the sacred objects, and so on. Little by little, too, the physical, psychological and social violence the men do to

---

23   It should be stressed that Baruya boys leave their family at the age of nine or ten. They see their mothers from afar but cannot approach them. Every evening one of their sisters brings a netbag containing food prepared by their mother and hangs it on the fence of the men's house after having called their brother's name. Inside the men's house, these same boys rarely see their fathers except when the married men gather there to sing with the boys or carry out rituals. It is the older boys who look after them on a daily basis.

women, or at least to their wives – never to their mothers or their sisters – appears as being justified. For during the long lessons they are subjected to, the masters of the initiations also teach them that women, too, have rights, and that it is their duty to know and respect them. That is why the men's domination is not based only on the violence they inflict on women and which the latter often resist in a variety of ways. It also rests on the fact that, up to a certain point, women consent to this domination in so far as they share with the men the same mythical-religious representations which blame women for the disorder that threatens the reproduction of the social and cosmic orders and which they do not want to inflict on their kinsmen or their children.

It is from the setting in motion of this formidable machinery for differentiating the social nature of the sexes, for growing men in the Baruya imaginary but also for (really) elevating them socially above women, that the second cross-cutting division takes its origin and its meaning. This time the line runs not between individuals according to their gender but between the kin groups into which these individuals were born and according to their genealogical position in these groups.

For only the representatives of the clans that descend from the Bravegareu-baramandeuc refugees as well as from the Ndelie clan, which helped them seize their hosts' territory, have the right to initiate the tribe's boys, on the pretext that only their ancestors received from the Sun the sacred objects and secret formulae enabling them to sever the boys from the female world and make them into men, warriors, shamans, etc. For this reason, the native clans that joined with the Baruya are excluded from leading the political-religious activities which cement the unity of all the kin groups and all the generations, and affirm their common identity in front of neighbouring tribes. Moreover, whenever initiations are held, these neighbours are invited to come and admire the number and strength of the young Baruya warriors as they leave the *tsimia*, which the Baruya call the 'body' of their tribe. The initiates will then dance around the *tsimia* and sing for hours, adorned in their feathers, wearing their new bark capes, and armed with their weapons, under the admiring gaze of their mothers, sisters and fiancées massed together in the front row. The reason invoked for excluding these autochthonous tribes from leading the ceremonies is the claim that their ancestors came from forest creatures and never possessed *kwaimatnie* or secret knowledge (something these representatives vehemently deny when questioned).

It is thus the Baruya's history that explains the hierarchy among those clans that have the right to initiate the boys and those that do not. On the top rung of this social ladder stands the Baruya clan, which gave the tribe its name, and in particular one of the clan's two lineages, the Baruya Kwarrandariar, who are in charge of passing the initiates from the second to the third stage, when they will be considered warriors and will be prepared for marriage as soon as their fiancée reaches menarche and is in turn initiated by the women. This political-religious ranking of the clans also creates a hierarchy among individuals in so far as the clan representatives who exercise the various functions in the male initiations are considered 'Great Men', a status they acquire at the same time as their function and the sacred objects and formulae that allow them to carry it out.

The male and female initiations are not the Baruya's only cycle, however. There is another, which concerns only shamans and gives rise to ceremonies performed every ten or twelve years, during which the training of the men and women who have shown exceptional personal powers is completed. At the close of these ceremonies, their ability to attend to victims of evil-spirit attacks and to visit death or sickness on their enemies is publicly validated or invalidated. Shamanism is also the only area of social life in which men and women can test their capacities directly, without mediation. But the functions of the 'master' of the shaman initiations belong exclusively to a clan that stems from the Brave-gareubaramandeuc refugees, the Andavakia, and are always transmitted through the men of one of this clan's lineages.

Alongside these very few inherited functions and ranks, there are others that can be acquired by showing exceptional talent and merit. Being at war with some neighbouring tribes and at peace with others, then making an alliance with the first to fight the second, means that the Baruya live in a constant state of war. This explains the fact that all men are trained from childhood in the arts of warfare and hunting, and never go anywhere without their weapons. Yet only certain men are considered to be 'great' warriors, *aoulatta*, because they have killed several enemy warriors in single combat, with their axe after having issued a public challenge. The rest are considered (ironically) by the Baruya themselves as merely *wopai*, 'sweet potatoes', ordinary warriors who make a lot of noise but are content to shoot their arrows from a distance and then duck behind their shield when the volley is returned.

In a society where warfare is given so much importance, the representatives of the clans that own the sacred objects indispensable for initiating boys or shamans do not go to war, in order to avoid being killed before having passed on their powers to their eldest son. For their untimely death would deprive the tribe of some of the spiritual forces that ensure its existence and reproduction. (The names of the *kwaimatnie* owners are also concealed from neighbouring tribes.) This is also the case of the *tanaka*, men considered by one and all to be 'great' horticulturalists, because they clear big gardens and place their harvests at the disposal of those who go to war and therefore cannot look after their own plots.

Some distinguish themselves in other domains and they, too, can become Great Men: certain shamans and a few expert trappers of cassowary, the wild woman who lives deep in the forest and whose flesh – forbidden to the hunters and to women – is eaten by the initiates in the men's house. Last of all, far behind the rest, a few expert makers of the salt-bars used by the Baruya as a currency before the Europeans arrived can also acquire certain renown.

Furthermore, in each generation, some women are promoted to the rank of 'Great Women', without this calling into question the official ideology that men are in principle superior to women. 'Great' women are those who have a large number of living children whom they succeed in raising, those who are inured to the tasks of making fine gardens and raising many pigs, those who as shamans have worked spectacular cures, etc. These women are allowed to express themselves when the members of their village meet to discuss problems of general import – the consequences of an act of adultery, the threat of armed conflict with a neighbouring tribe, and so forth.

In the case of women, however, everything must be won by merit; nothing or almost nothing is inherited.[24] Men alone inherit functions and ranks that automatically set them apart. This is just one more proof of male dominance, and of the control men exercise over the way this society works. We should remember that the inherited functions and ranks are divided among the eight clans of refugees from Bravegareubaramandeuc, to which must be added the Ndelie, one of the seven native clans that joined the Baruya and who were granted a *kwaimatnie* and a role in the initiations.[25] Apart from these reserved ranks, all of the positions an individual could acquire through his own qualities were open to men and women from any of the clans.

We see, then, that despite a political-religious division between refugees and natives, which lasted until 1967 and was carefully nurtured, the structure of Baruya society made it impossible for any one clan, and even less for a person of renown, to have the monopoly of armed violence – which would have enabled them to impose their desires on the rest of society and to work for their own interests. Thus, for example, decisions having an impact on everyone – clearing a large garden, collecting the materials needed to build the ceremonial house, preparing to make war on a neighbouring group and securing the help of allies, or, today, planting large tracts of forest in coffee – were taken in the course of public debates in which male voices predominated, to be

---

24 Nevertheless women inherit shamanistic powers from their mother or their father.

25 If all political-ritual functions were concentrated in one or two clans and transmitted within the clan from one generation to the next, the society would be divided into a sort of hereditary aristocracy and a majority of 'commoners' – in short, it would operate as a sort of chiefdom, something that is rare in Papua New Guinea. Nevertheless see the example of the Mekeo, studied by Marc Mosco, and of course the Trobriand Islanders studied by Malinowski: M. Mosko, *Quadripartite Structures: Categories, Relations and Homologies in Bush Mekeo Culture* (Cambridge, Cambridge University Press, 1985) and 'Rethinking Trobriand chieftainship', *Journal of the Royal Anthropological Institute*, vol. 1, no. 4 (1995), pp. 763–85.

sure, in which young people and ordinary women did not intervene publicly, but in which the Great Women voiced their opinions and were listened to.

Against this backdrop of unequally shared sovereignty, the other more visible forms of authority and power stand out: those of the ritual masters, great warriors, shamans, etc.

One of the first theoretical conclusions that can be drawn from this analysis is that the existence of kin groups is not enough to make a society or to make this society a 'tribe'. These groups, or most of them, must also – and above all – exercise a sort of political and ritual sovereignty over the population as a whole and over a territory defended by everyone, whose boundaries are known (if not recognized) by their neighbours. And if this is true, we can already see how erroneous it is to affirm – as the majority of anthropologists continue to do – that societies without classes or castes, 'primitive' societies, etc., are *kin based*.

A PLURAL BARUYA IDENTITY

The second theoretical conclusion that can be drawn from these analyses is that a person's identity – Baruya, Wantekia, etc. – never comes down to the common, overarching identity he or she has by virtue of being a member of his or her tribe or society. Identity is always multiple. A person has as many identities as the social groups he or she belongs to simultaneously through his or her different aspects. He is a man and not a woman. He is the co-initiate of . . . She is a woman, she is the co-initiate of . . . He or she is a shaman. He is a master of the initiations who inherited his role and status from his father. He is the son of, the brother of . . . She is the sister of, the mother of . . . All of these identities are crystallizations within the individual of different relationships with others, with roles and ranks, which either end with this person and stamp themselves in him or her or start with this person and stamp themselves in others. An individual draws the content and shape of all of his or her identities from the specific social relationships that characterize his or her society, from the particularities of its structure to the way it functions. All of these make up the concrete multiplicity of social identity, which is never a simple addition of distinct identities or particular relationships. An individual's personal, private identity is always the product of a singular life history, which is reproduced nowhere else and is constructed amid life circumstances that are never the same for any two individuals, however closely related they may be.

Even before Europeans set foot in Wonenara in 1951, a Baruya's identity was made up of aspects of him- or herself that were broader than his or her society. He or she was aware of belonging to a group of tribes related by language and customs, what we have called an ethnic group, and which constituted a community[26] that encompassed the Baruya society and was linked to it through a shared distant past. But the ethnic group did not function for the Baruya individual as 'his' or 'her' society. This feature – engendered by an individual's belonging to groups that were broader than and that encompassed the birth society – would grow in importance after 1951.

THE WEST ARRIVES, AND THE BARUYA LOSE SOVEREIGNTY OVER THEIR TERRITORY AND THEMSELVES

It was in that year, without having either requested or foreseen it, that the Baruya received a new common identity by becoming 'subjects' of His Majesty, the King of England, and were placed under the authority of a colonial state created and governed by Europeans of Australian origin, assisted by other Continental or North American Europeans. In 1975, again without having desired it, the same Baruya were informed that they had become 'citizens', this time of a post-colonial state whose independence and constitutional regime had not been their own work but had been granted them by Australia, their former colonial guardian. And so they found themselves embarked on an accelerated process of multicultural nation-building which had to succeed at all costs in order to flesh out a state that had been created wholesale by foreigners and forced on all inhabitants of Papua New Guinea, whatever their tribal or ethnic origin, as the obligatory framework for their future life.

In this new historical context, Baruya children (at first only the boys) went to the Lutheran mission school to go on to become policemen, or aid-post orderlies, or church pastors or professors at the Lutheran university in Lae. More recently, beginning in 1981, many of the adults – especially the women – began turning to Christianity and joined one of the various Protestant churches, which have vied for decades to teach the Baruya the message of Christ and root out their old beliefs, which were held to come from Satan. The number of shamans declined, as did their prestige. The Great Warriors have all died. Now when war sporadically erupts with a neighbouring tribe, it is no longer waged by the same rules or with the same weapons. Only men are killed. The women and children are often spared because there is more risk of police intervention if news gets out that women and children have been killed in the clashes.

---

26   By 'community', I mean a social group resulting from the sharing among individuals and/or groups of common realities – a language, a religion, a function, a history, a myth, etc. – transmitted to them by birth or chosen by them in the course of their life. But the sharing of one or several common components by its members is not enough to make a community into a society. Concerning the concepts 'society', 'community', 'culture', see M. Godelier, 'Introspection, rétrospections, projections: un entretien avec Hosham Dawood', *Gradhiva*, no. 25 (1999), pp. 1–25; English translation: 'Insights into an Itinerary. An Interview with Maurice Godelier', by Hosham Dawod (translated by N. Scott), *Folk*, vol. 41 (1999), pp. 5–44.

Of course, the articulation of these old and new identities does not occur without conflict, especially in so far as some claim to exclude others. For a Baruya, becoming a citizen of Papua New Guinea meant losing the right to bear arms and to use one's own laws to settle the offences and crimes committed by individuals or groups from the tribe. It meant trusting unknown policemen and judges who cited other laws for securing compensation and justice. In another vein, being baptized and becoming a Christian meant joining a universal community that affirmed the equality of all – white, black, yellow – before a god who had come to save humankind; but it also meant abandoning polygamy and initiations, and giving up the rites for driving away evil spirits or ensuring a good harvest.

In short, all those Baruya who became aid-post orderlies or health officers or converted to Christianity ceased, one after the other, individually or as a group, to produce *certain* social relations that had characterized their society before the Europeans arrived – or, if they continue to reproduce these relations, they only do so partially while deeply altering their meaning. Pre-colonial relations did not thus vanish of their own accord, but as a consequence of certain individuals and groups refusing to reproduce them in their dealings with other members of their society. This was not only a question of private, personal choice. It was often also an act of submission to external constraints, such as the ban on war, on exposing the dead on platforms, etc. In short, it was the effect of a power struggle between the former society that had once had sovereignty over its territory and the new society that had deprived it of this sovereignty in one fell swoop, which was then appropriated by a hitherto unknown institution, the state.

Little by little, through these deliberate or forced choices, a new society emerged which extended over and into the local societies. For to become a policeman or an aid-post orderly, to produce coffee for the market or work as a bank clerk, is not only to become part of these new 'communities'; it is also to enable these institutions to live and develop. The latter now play an active role throughout the territory of the state of Papua New Guinea and impose themselves on all groups – local, tribal, urban, etc. Furthermore, all of these institutions – the police, hospitals, the university, the market – did not come about by accident and are not unconnected with each other. They are the components of a new world society, imported and imposed from outside, and they combine two familiar formulae: the development of a market economy and the creation of a multi-party parliamentary democracy. To which must be added the effects of the spread of a militant religion also imported from the West: Christianity, which emphasizes individual and personal salvation, and casts discredit on ancestral religions. Ultimately these new global societies will probably supplant the different local societies that existed in New Guinea at the time of the European arrival. For this to happen, however, the former societies would have to lose or refuse their capacity to go on affording their members non-commercial access to the land and other forms of mutual aid rooted in kinship or other social relations implying solidarity and sharing among those bound by these relationships. Such an outcome is perfectly plausible, but in the meantime, at the time of this writing (2004), these two types of 'societies' – local and national – rely on each other to function and to keep on reproducing themselves for a certain time to come – albeit in a context of a process of globalization ever more closely tied to the capitalist economy and to institutions that arose in the West.[27]

Finally, at the dawn of the twenty-first century, the Baruya live or are being born into a hybrid society that has been deeply altered by the direct or indirect interventions of powerful outside forces – the colonial and then post-colonial state, the market, Christianity – which, though they will no doubt be even stronger tomorrow, will not completely obliterate whole swathes of the old social organization and ancestral ways of thinking, even if in preserving them the Baruya have had to adapt and reshape them.

We have seen that the Baruya's history, their sovereignty over their territory, the political-ritual hierarchy among kin groups and, finally, the distinction between Great Men and Women, on the one hand, and the rest of the people, on the other, did not originate in the world of kinship relations, although they encompass this world and fashion it from within. Yet it would be completely erroneous to conclude that, in Baruya society, kinship is a minor – or even marginal – aspect of social life. For, while the Baruya exist as a 'society' because they exercise shared sovereignty over their territory, this territory is distributed among the kin groups; therefore what actually gives individuals access to the material conditions of their social existence – land for gardens and a territory for hunting – is the fact of being born into and thus belonging to one of these groups.

But land is not the only resource that falls to an individual by virtue of belonging to a lineage or a clan. Such belonging also means that the individual can count on the solidarity and support of the members of the group and of his or her affines in the event of a serious conflict with members of another lineage. It also implies that, in the event of conflict with a member of his (or her) own lineage, he submits to internal arbitration by the lineage elders. In addition, everyone is entitled to the help and participation of his or her lineage in finding a spouse. Lastly, for those kin groups having a hereditary role in the

---

27   See M. Godelier, 'Les Baruya de Nouvelle-Guinée, un exemple récent de subordination économique, politique et culturelle d'une société 'primitive' à l'Occident', in M. Godelier (ed.), *Transitions et subordinations au capitalisme* (Paris, Editions de la Maison des Sciences de l'Homme, 1999), pp. 379–99.

performance of the male initiations, the eldest sons of the representatives of these lineages know that, if they are not handicapped in some way, they will inherit these functions together with the sacred objects and ritual formulas that give the right to exercise them. Functions, objects and inherited statuses circulate through certain kin ties binding persons of the same sex and different generations.

KINSHIP AND SOCIETY AMONG THE BARUYA

The universe of kinship, that world which receives and surrounds each individual at birth, is comprised of intimacy, affection, protection, authority and respect. It is from this world that the little Baruya boys will suddenly be torn when they are around ten, and placed not under their father's authority but under that of older boys who are not yet married but soon will be. And it is from their ingested sperm that these boys will be reborn to full manhood, rid of any remaining vestiges of having come from a woman's womb and having until then been raised in a primarily female world. A girl's destiny, on the other hand, is not to be reborn outside the world of kinship. Until puberty, and beyond, she will live at home and will leave her family only to marry and found a new one. At this time, nothing will prevent her from becoming a Great Woman, a shaman or the mother of many children. When she marries she does not cease to belong to her birth lineage, however, even if she is now under her husband's authority and her children belong to their father's lineage.

In Baruya society, kin groups are formed according to a rule of descent that passes exclusively through the male side and creates patrilineal lineages and clans. This does not mean that a child's maternal kin do not matter or have no rights in relation to the child. It means that the names, lands, ranks or statuses a child will receive over his lifetime come from his ancestors through his father and his father's brothers (who are also fathers for him and are designated by the same term, in accordance with the Iroquois-type kinship terminology used by the Baruya). Genealogical memory does not go back more than three, sometimes four, generations above Ego. Beyond that only a few names escape oblivion. These are the names of Great Men, legendary heroes – Bakitchatche, for example, the ancestor of the Tchatche, who while still young killed a great many Andje with the help of supernatural powers and enabled the Baruya to seize the territory of the Andje, who had taken them in and protected them. In addition, the patrilineal principle skews the lists of the most remote ancestors an individual remembers.

All of these lists begin with a man, sometimes several, listed by order of birth. Rarely is the name of a woman – a sister of one of these men – given at this level (G^{+5}, G^{+4}), and this woman is never the eldest. The memory of kin ties is therefore doubly marked by the patrilineal principle, which results in the almost general forgetting of the names of the women of the lineage in the great-grandparents' generation and, furthermore, the systematic attribution of the position of eldest to a man.

I would add that people's names (and perhaps their spirits) are passed on in alternate generations – from grandfathers to grandsons, from paternal great-aunts to their grand-nieces. These names go in twos, a first name is given when the child is born; it will be replaced by a second name when the child's septum has been pierced and he or she has been initiated. From then on it is forbidden to call this person by the former name, which would be a grave insult and require compensation.

HOW DO THE BARUYA TALK ABOUT KINSHIP?

Sometimes we have called the Baruya's kin groups clans and sometimes lineages. What do the Baruya call them? They use two terms, which underscore different but related aspects of these groups. The first term, *navaalyara*, comes from *avaala*, which means 'the same' and foregrounds the fact that all members of these groups share the same identity. The second term, *yisavaa*, refers to a tree, *yita*, and emphasizes the descent rule, the ramification of the tree's branches from its trunk and the growth of the trunk from the roots. Both terms can be used to designate either a particular lineage or several lineages with the same name. The term *yisavaa* is favoured in the second case to designate a set of lineages sharing the same overarching name, a group we have, with numerous precautions, called 'clan'. To give an example, the name 'Bakia' turns up in several lineage names: Kuopbakia, Boulimmanbakia, etc. But what is the impact of these realities in practice?

Let us take the kin group that calls itself the Baruya. It is made up of two lineages, which bear the names of two toponyms in the Marawaka Valley (where their ancestors, having fled Bravegareubaramandeuc, settled upon reaching the Andje). One of the lineages now calls itself the Baruya Kwarrandariar, and the other, the Baruya Wombouye. Both know they are Baruya, but they are unable to trace the ties connecting them to a common ancestor. This ancestor is said to have been a certain Djivaamakwe, a Dreamtime hero. It is he who is said to have received the first *kwaimatnie* from the Sun, established the initiations and assigned each of the other clans a specific role in their performance.

But the Kwarrandariar claim Djivaamakwe as their own ancestor, and if they give the Wombouye a role in their ritual tasks, it is a minor one. Therefore, if we use the word 'clan' to designate these two lineages that bear the same big name, Baruya, we see that it has no true existence outside the political-religious sphere, since the two lineages also sometimes exchange women and otherwise behave like exogamous units. If we compare these practices with the way certain anthropologists have defined the clan (as an 'exogamous' group), we see that, if the fact that the Kwarrandariar and the Wombouye both carry the name Baruya gives the impression that the two form one clan, either this clan is not 'exogamous' or what is covered by this shared name is not a 'clan'. I lean toward the first interpretation. They are a 'clan' in the sense of a set of lineages that have retained the memory of a shared origin and name, but this clan is not exogamous. Lineages which are physically separated or which have only a very remote genealogical tie with each other contract marriages that they do not repeat before at least three generations, as we will see when we analyze Baruya marriage practices.

In principle, when sons marry, they are supposed to build their house next to their father's, if he is living, or next to the site of his old house if he is deceased. But if this rule were systematically applied, we should find whole villages inhabited by all of the male descendants of a group of brothers who lived in the same place three or four generations before. This is not the case, however, because one or several of a man's sons frequently choose to live near one of their brothers-in-law and so move to another village. Similarly, a brother-in-law may decide to come and live near one of the sons, the one to whom he 'gave' a sister as a wife. The result of these comings and goings is that villages and hamlets[28] are comprised of several lineage segments gathered around the lineage of the village founders. These settlements were regrouped and fortified in times of war, but in peacetime the families would disperse and often lived next to their gardens.

The Baruya find it advantageous to invite one or several of their affines to live nearby or to allow one of their own to move next to their affines. The presence of these affines lessens the conflicts that frequently crop up between two brothers or two brothers' sons (parallel cousins). There is no lack of reasons to quarrel or clash: a man tries to bed his brother's wife; the wife of one brother is embroiled in a quarrel with the wife of another brother or mistreats one of this wife's children. More seriously: a man clears a garden in an area originally cleared by his father's brother, but without telling him, and so on. Some quarrels end in murder, and in this case the murderer and his family are forced to seek refuge with affines who will protect them and perhaps even allow them to stay with them indefinitely and use their growing lands and hunting grounds. After a number of years, the murderer can even be taken into his hosts' lineage, following a ceremony in which the host gives a considerable number of salt-bars and lengths of cowry shells to the murderer's lineage. The lineage elder then declares that this man is no longer one of them and has lost

28   In 1979 the Baruya had 17 for a population of 2,159, or an average of 127 persons per hamlet or village.

all rights in the lands and the groves of pandanus trees (whose fruit is prized) planted by his ancestors. Henceforth his descendants will carry a double name composed of the lineage that absorbed them and the name of their original lineage. They will become, for example, Ndelouwaye – i.e. Yowaye who have become Ndelie.

A KINSHIP TERMINOLOGY OF THE IROQUOIS TYPE

The Baruya use what is called an Iroquois-type kinship terminology. What does this mean? We call 'kinship terminology' a fraction of the vocabulary of a language, a limited set of terms, that designates the ties a person, characterized exclusively by his or her sex, has, on the one hand, with a certain number of individuals of both sexes from whom he or she descends or who descend from him or her, and, on the other hand, with other individuals to whom he or she is related by marriage (affines) or who are related by marriage to his or her paternal or maternal kin – or sometimes are even affines of affines.

In the West we are accustomed to designate all paternal and maternal kin, together with their descendants, as 'consanguines', and all relatives by marriage as 'affines'. But these terms do not have a universal definition and have the disadvantage of projecting onto kinship systems different from our own distinctions that give rise to confusion and deform or mask the actual facts. In the Baruya's case, it would be absurd to call the 'maternals' 'consanguines', which would suggest that they share their blood with the child, whereas, as we will see, a child's blood and bones are believed to come from its father's sperm, while its spirit comes from a male or female ancestor (depending on the child's sex) who also belongs to the father's lineage. Moreover – but this will be discussed later – we know that in many kinship terminologies, Dravidian and Australian in particular, there are no specific terms for affines and that the mother's brother is called by the same term as the wife's father, a term that subsumes two relations which in the West are divided between the vocabulary of consanguinity (maternal uncle) and that of affinity (father-in-law). We thus understand why an observer must decentre his thinking with respect to the categories and representations of kinship used in the West.

What aspects of Baruya kinship terminology cause us to classify it as being of the Iroquois type? (Of course, the Baruya themselves are not aware that their terminology is of the same type as that collected at the end of the nineteenth century by Morgan among the Iroquois.) First, the fact that father's brothers' children and mother's sisters' children are called by the same terms used to designate Ego's brothers and sisters. All are brothers and sisters, which is expressed in anthropological jargon by the statement: parallel cousins are (equivalent or identical to) siblings. Alternatively, father's sisters' children and mother's brothers' children – Ego's cross cousins – are called by a distinct term. Since male and female parallel cousins are brothers and sisters, in theory they cannot marry each other. But the Baruya can sometimes marry their matrilateral parallel cousin. Cross cousins, on the contrary, are potential spouses. But, in reality, the Baruya do not marry their mother's brother's daughter – their matrilateral cross cousin – because it is forbidden to repeat the father's marriage and take a wife from the mother's lineage. The distinction between parallel and cross cousins does not carry over several generations, as in Dravidian systems. It is the outcome, in Ego's generation, of an exchange of women in the preceding generation (G^{+1}), but it is not the consequence of a rule obliging Ego to marry one of his cross cousins or a rule that in a less constraining manner would have him *prefer* her to other possible choices.

The absence of a prescriptive or preferential marriage rule explains the existence in the Baruya language of specific terms for affines, which is a second feature typical of Iroquois-type kinship terminologies that distinguishes them from Dravidian terminologies. The existence of this specific terminology means that the rule is not to marry someone who is closely related on the father's or mother's side, but to marry into a lineage into which your line has not yet married (or at least not for three generations). In short, a potential spouse is an unrelated or distantly related Baruya, but not an outsider, for the Baruya tribe is overwhelmingly endogamous. When someone marries an outsider, it is usually in order to seal a trading or a political alliance. In this case, depending on the context, one exchanges either a woman (in the case of a political alliance) or a certain quantity of goods (in view of trading): salt-bars, cowries, bark capes, feathers and so on, in short, wealth for a woman, or bridewealth.

Let us come back to the fact that Ego's father's brothers' children and Ego's mother's sisters' children are Ego's brothers and sisters. This implies that Ego's father's brothers are also fathers for Ego and that Ego's mother's sisters are also mothers for Ego. We are dealing here with a 'classificatory' terminology, where the term for 'father' designates a category of individuals who stand in the same relation to Ego as the man who is married to Ego's mother. The notion of paternal 'uncle' therefore does not exist in this language and 'fatherhood' does not mean the same thing as it does in French or English, since the Baruya word *noumwe* places in the same category people and relationships that we would distinguish. Likewise for the mother's side, where the notion of 'maternal' aunt does not exist because all of Ego's mother's sisters are Ego's mothers. But since not all of these 'mothers' are either Ego's father's co-wives or potential or real wives of Ego's father's brothers – Ego's other fathers – we immediately see that the word *noua*, which I translate as 'mother', takes in people and relationships that are distinguished from each other in the European kinship system.

Furthermore, Ego's mother's brothers are indeed Ego's uncles, but owing to the fact that Baruya marriage is based on the exchange of 'sisters' between two men, one of my father's sisters is likely the wife of one of Ego's mother's brothers (MB=FZH). Alternatively, Ego's mother's other brothers will be married to women from other lineages, in accordance with the rule that two brothers are not supposed to take wives in the same lineage. The notions 'father', 'brother', 'sister' and so on thus refer to an indefinite number of individuals who stand in the same category of relation to Ego and Ego's siblings.

Given the existence of such classificatory terminologies designating categories of individuals standing in equivalent relationships, kinship specialists wondered whether these categories were constructed by extension, as for example when the word 'father' is the extension (and projection) of the father–children relationship created within the nuclear family to all of the father's brothers, who are not part of this nuclear family and are not married to Ego's mother. Kinship, however, as we will see, is never simply a matter of the nuclear family – or any other kind – and kin groups are never constructed by simply extending and multiplying the relationships found within the nuclear family, which some, following Murdock, insist on calling 'primary' kinship relations. We must therefore look for the explanation in an equivalence posited between the relations linking Ego and the class of his or her substitutes ('brothers' and 'sisters') with another class of individuals. Furthermore this equivalence can subsume genealogically very different relationships, and even link individuals who have no direct or indirect genealogical tie with each other.

English and French kinship terminologies, which are of the Eskimo type, also use classificatory terms that subsume under the same word individuals who stand at equivalent distances and in equivalent relations to Ego, whereas their relationship with Ego is distinct. The term 'aunt', for instance, designates both father's and mother's sister; the term 'nephew', a brother's and a sister's son; each time one has to clarify the relationship by adding 'on my father's side', 'on my mother's side', and so on. Likewise for the Baruya. To distinguish mother's brothers from all of the men who belong to the same lineage and who are their 'brothers' and therefore Ego's classificatory uncles, the Baruya say that they are *api aounie* – 'mother's brothers' (*api*) 'of the breast' (*aounie*) – and their children are called *migwe aounie* – 'cross cousins' (*migwe*) 'of the breast' – to distinguish them from all other cross cousins. In the same manner, father's sisters' children are called *migwe kale* – 'cross cousins of the liver' (*kale*) – to distinguish them from the children of all of the father's classificatory sisters. Likewise, father's brothers are called 'little' fathers, to distinguish them from the father who is the mother's husband; and mother's sisters, 'little' mothers, to distinguish them from the mother who is the father's wife.

When it comes to attitudes, rights and duties, all of Ego's fathers (father and father's brothers) have authority over Ego. And if Ego does not have a sister to exchange for a wife, he is entitled to expect his other fathers to give him one of their daughters (who are his classificatory 'sisters') for the exchange. In addition, as we will see, all of these fathers and all of their children were made from the same sperm as that of Ego's father and as that of Ego (in the case of a male Ego). Which explains why, even though he also calls the daughters of his mother's sisters, 'sisters', he cannot use them to exchange for a wife: they were not made from the same sperm that made the women of his lineage whom he calls 'sisters'. Likewise, even though Ego's mother's sisters are mothers too, when he addresses his mother, he says *Nouaou* and when he addresses her sisters, he says *Amawo*. Finally, grandparents and grandchildren use reciprocal terms, *ate* (grandfather, grandson) and *ata* (grandmother, granddaughter). And if your great-grandfather is living and you are a boy, he will call you *Gwagwe* ('little brother') and you will call him *Dakwe* ('big brother'). This means that beyond three generations, individuals who carry the same name 'merge', and that this merging begins with the third generation, when the grandson carries the same name as his paternal grandfather, the grandmother the same name as her paternal great-aunt, etc. This is direct evidence that for the Baruya an ancestor's spirit does not die, and to give his or her name to a newborn child is the same as giving this spirit a body in which to reincarnate.

Baruya kinship terminology is thus characterized by three principal features: first, it is a 'classificatory' terminology that makes a distinction between cross and parallel kin, the latter being assimilated to siblings; this distinction is present only in Ego's generation (Go) and not in the ascending and descending generations, as in Dravidian systems. Second, this terminology also possesses specific forms for designating affines, which is also a feature of Iroquois-type systems and distinguishes them from Dravidian systems. Third, the terminology does not carry any indication of the kind of descent rule at work in this society, which is patrilineal. It should be recalled that the Iroquois Indians described by Morgan were matrilineal and that some Iroquois-type terminologies are also associated with undifferentiated, non-lineal descent rules, which we term cognatic. We can already conclude from the above that there is therefore no necessary connection between the existence of a particular terminology and the presence of a particular descent rule.

Finally one last remark: children learn to use these kin terms at a very early age. They are usually taught by their mothers, in concrete situations, and they are quick to grasp that they are supposed to call a given man, distinct from their father, by the same term as they use for their father, *noumwe*, and that they are supposed to call this man's children 'brothers' and 'sisters', and so on.

MARRIAGE RULES

What are the principles governing Baruya marriage alliances? The first rule is a negative one: one does not marry in one's own lineage. This is regarded as behaving like a dog, which mates with his siblings, and is regarded as incest, and incest is usually punished by death. It is also forbidden for a man to marry his matrilateral cross cousins, in other words his mother's brothers' daughters, even though he is allowed to make blatantly sexual jokes with them in public. He enjoys the same joking relationship with his patrilateral cross cousins, his father's sisters' daughters, but these he can marry. And this is precisely what the Baruya do each time a wife-taking lineage has not given a woman in exchange. In this event, one of the woman's daughters will come and marry one of her mother's brothers' sons (a patrilateral cross-cousin marriage).

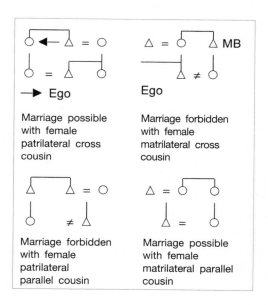

Why don't the Baruya marry their matrilateral cross cousins, since they treat them like potential spouses? In order not to take a wife from the same lineage in two successive generations, in other words so as not to repeat their father's marriage and not to immediately reproduce the same alliance. At least three generations must pass before repeating an alliance with the same group. It is also forbidden for two brothers to take wives in the same lineage. Over generations and depending on the number of male and female members, each lineage thus finds itself allied with five or six different lineages. This multiplication of marriages and the refusal to reproduce them before several generations have elapsed means that Baruya kinship practices resemble what are called 'semi-complex' systems. What differentiates the Baruya system is that their form of marriage is based fundamentally on the direct exchange of (close or distant) 'sisters' between two men and two lineages, which is typical of what are called 'elementary' systems.

But, if a man cannot marry his matrilateral cross cousins even though they are potential wives, he nevertheless sometimes marries a matrilateral parallel cousin, a 'sister', since her mother is also his mother. Why can he marry these 'sisters' whereas his own sister is forbidden? Because, unlike his sisters on his father's side (siblings and female parallel cousins), his sisters on his mother's side are not made from the same sperm as that which made him and his (real) sisters. This is clearly not the case with the mother's sisters' daughters – in virtue of the rule that dictates the dispersal of alliances in each generation, they cannot marry a man from their father's lineage and thus repeat their sister's marriage. They therefore marry into other lineages and bear children made from a different sperm and who are therefore potential spouses.

THE FIVE MARRIAGE TYPES

The Baruya distinguish five types of marriage. The basic rule is direct exchange of women between two lineages or segments. This rule has a name: *ginamare*. The exchange can be organized by the families either at the time of the children's birth or at the time of puberty if the girl has not yet been promised. The boy's family always makes the first move, and the mother of the small or adolescent girl has a great deal of say in deciding whether or not to promise her daughter to the lineage seeking her for one of its sons.

The second type of marriage derives from the first. It is practised when a boy's father has given one of his sisters in marriage without receiving – for himself or someone in his lineage – a woman in exchange. In this case he has rights over one of his sister's daughters – usually the eldest – who will marry his son as a counter-gift for her mother. This is patrilateral cross-cousin marriage; it is therefore not a general rule but complementary to the rule of direct 'sister' exchange. This rule, too, has a name: *kouremandjinaveu*. The term evokes the shoot that grows at the base of the banana tree (*koure*), which will replace the old tree when it stops bearing fruit.

The third type takes the form of a staged abduction. Two young people who want to marry against the will of their families, who have already chosen other spouses for them, simulate an abduction with the help of the young man's co-initiates. This is a serious matter, for many interests are compromised and many promises of alliance are left in tatters. The men of the girl's family pursue the young man, who allows himself to be struck until blood flows. If he can then mark the girl, whom his accomplices have brought along, with his blood, marriage becomes necessary as a compensation for the blood spilled. In this case, either the young man's lineage gives one of their daughters to the lineage to whom the reluctant girl had been promised or, when the couple is married, they promise one of their daughters to the wife's lineage. This brings us back to the second type of marriage. Marriage by abduction or capture also has a name: *tsika*, a term that evokes the fact that the young man makes a show of twisting one of the girl's fingers and then drags her along behind him, pretending to tighten his grip if she struggles.

The fourth type of marriage is very rare. A young orphan with no sister to exchange, no father to help him, and no father's brother who will come to his aid by allowing him to exchange one of his daughters, marries the daughter of a couple who has no son to help them in their old age. Last of all, sometimes the Baruya marry women from tribes with whom they trade but never fight. In this case, they make a compensation payment of a large quantity of goods – salt-bars, cowries, weapons, etc. This type of marriage, which implies a bridewealth, is never practised between Baruya themselves.

Of the more than 1,000 marriages I recorded, covering four generations, only eleven took place between a Baruya man and a woman from a neighbouring tribe. All of the other marriages were between Baruya and, with the exception of fewer than ten cases, all had involved an immediate exchange of women (*ginamare*) or an exchange deferred to the following generation (*kouremandjinaveu*). A prime example of an endogamous society.

The Baruya thus follow two rules when it comes to marriage: exchange of a woman for a woman, and exchange of wealth for a woman; in other words, one rule which, according to Lévi-Strauss, is typical of elementary kinship structures, and another which is typical of complex structures. The principle of exchanging wealth for women is forbidden in Baruya society but is occasionally practised with outsiders (their trading partners). In other parts of New Guinea, where we find a form of society characterized by Big Men instead of Great Men, who amass women and wealth and win their renown and their authority through the ceremonial competitive giving of gifts and counter-gifts, the practice of 'direct' sister exchange is, on the contrary, known but forbidden. The reason alleged is that direct exchange of women would encourage lineages to be content with equivalent exchanges, without rivalry, without competition, and therefore to forsake the network of ceremonial exchanges that reaches beyond the village and the local group to encompass an entire region, bringing face to face in a giving-war the representatives of clans from a great number of tribes that, in other circumstances, might fight over land or for other reasons.

Thus we see that, in Big Man societies, the principle of direct sister exchange has become purely abstract, known but forbidden, and that the practice of giving wealth for a woman – bridewealth – is the very rule that the Baruya apply only exceptionally in their relations with more or less remote tribes with whom they entertain friendly trade relations. Alternatively, the Baruya occasionally exchange women with neighbouring tribes, and we have seen why. In making brothers-in-law among their former enemies, they hope that, the next time war breaks out, these affines will forsake their own tribe and join with the Baruya in exchange for protection of their lands, their goods and, of course, their lives. The Baruya rule is that a Baruya will not kill enemies who are at the same time affines. But he can kill his sister if she has run away to an enemy group and married there without the consent of her lineage and without compensation for the marriage – in the form of a woman or wealth. Cleverly managed alliances thus serve not only to divide groups but also to unite and bring them closer together.

GIFTS AND COUNTER-GIFTS: DEBTS THAT CANNOT BE CANCELLED

We need to come back here to a very important point, one that is not always easy for a Westerner to understand. When a Baruya (lineage) gives a woman and receives another in return, the two parties are not even, their debts are not cancelled.[29] The debts balance out and are the raison d'être for many exchanges of goods and services between the two men and their lineages. And these exchanges will continue throughout their lives. By giving, one makes the other one's debtor and by receiving, one becomes the debtor of the one who has given. At the close of these reciprocal exchanges, each lineage is at the same time 'superior' and 'inferior' to the other: superior because it has given a woman and inferior because it has received one. Their debts are now equal, but on the basis of a double inequality that will fuel a flow of reciprocal prestations over a lifetime.

Several features must be clarified here concerning marriage and alliance between two lineages. First of all, a girl who wants to break a marriage that has been forcibly arranged for her (and that will enable her brother to marry) can use other means than getting herself abducted by the man she wants to marry. She can also wait for the onset of her first menstrual period and then refuse the gifts and the game her fiancé, with the help of his brothers and other men from his and her lineages, has gathered for her and has had delivered to the menstrual hut where she is fasting while waiting to undergo the puberty rites. This supposes a great deal of courage on the girl's part, but it does happen (and

---

29   M. Godelier, *L'Enigme du don* (Paris, Fayard, 1996), in particular pp. 153–201, 'Objets sacrés, objets précieux et objets monnaie chez les Baruya de Nouvelle-Guinée'; English translation: *The Enigma of the Gift*, translated by N. Scott (Chicago/Cambridge, University of Chicago Press/Polity Press, 1998).

increasingly often today). A great deal of courage because, in refusing to marry the man to whom she was promised, she prevents her brother from marrying this man's sister, who was promised to him. She breaks the ties that were contracted between the two lineages when she was promised as a child, ties that translated over the years into exchanges of services, pork and so on.

A girl is not absorbed into her husband's lineage when she marries. She keeps her identity and remains a life-long member of her own lineage. But this lineage has ceded its authority over her. It is not unusual to see a man beating his wife in the presence of her brother, who remains silent. For her brother is the husband of the man's sister. In the course of a secret ritual that takes place at the base of a giant tree in the forest, the future husband, at the time of his fiancée's menarche when she undergoes the initiation performed for girls, calls upon the Sun and declares that this woman is no longer under her father's authority but under his own. At the same moment, in another part of the forest, hundreds of women surround the girl, shouting and pounding her head with their digging sticks, telling her that the time for playing is over, that from now on she will have to obey her husband, not try to seduce his co-initiates – otherwise he will beat her and kill her.

This is proof that the exchange of women concerns not only the two men involved but their lineages as well, which have a collective right over the women they give, in that when a man dies his wife is inherited by one of his brothers or uncles, who may be scarcely older than the deceased. Furthermore, the Baruya forbid divorce. A man can repudiate a wife and give her to one of his brothers, but he cannot send her back to her family or agree to let her leave and make a new start elsewhere.

THE FAMILY

Up to now I have not said much about families. Yet families are what I see every-day in the field. It is rare that the men and women of a lineage get together; the sisters live in their husband's house, since residence is virilocal. It is rarer still that the village meets to discuss matters concerning everyone – initiations, building an airstrip for the mission planes, etc. The family is a living unit, and also a production and consumption unit. In Baruya, the word for family is *kuminidaka*, which designates the group formed by the man, his wife and his children. *Kumi* means 'everyone/all'. The family is thus all of these people together. Married men sleep in the men's house when their wives are menstruating or have just given birth. Their wives must purify themselves before resuming life with their husband and cooking for him once more. Theoretically, a married man should not cook his own food and, in the event of conflict with his wife, if she takes the risk of refusing to cook for him or if she takes his children and goes to stay with her mother for several weeks, the man – somewhat embarrassed – gets his sisters to invite him by turns. Polygamous families are not unusual, but a young man who wants to marry two women will marry them on the same day so that neither can claim to be the first wife and mistreat the other. This is not the case with widows inherited together with their children by a man. They are usually subjected to harassments and humiliations by the first wife or wives.

Let us now come back to the moment of the marriage and look at the role played by several types of social relations and groups – the future spouse's lineages, their age groups, the inhabitants of the village where the couple is going to live, and who will build their house. A week or two before the ceremony, the groom's father comes to the men's house where the young man has been living since he had his nose pierced and tells him to get together the different kinds of wood needed to build the floor and the walls of his future house. He will have to gather the materials discreetly and hide them in the forest on the village outskirts. I never obtained an explanation of the reasons for this discretion, which in no way prevents the whole village from being in the know.

The day the house is to be built, all of the young men in the groom's age group arrive to frame the house and lay the floor. The mood is festive. Meanwhile the village girls, especially those of the same age as the bride, file to the site with bundles of grasses for the roof. The future couple watch the others work but do not participate. In general the house is raised in a day. The next day, the men of the husband's lineage arrive to construct the hearth, using flat stones and clay they have carried to the site. The groom is not present. His father and his uncles light the first fire and chew betel around the brand new hearth while telling stories about their ancestors and talking about current events. The day after, a member of the Bakia clan comes to affix the four sharpened sticks, called 'the Sun's flowers', on the peak of the roof. They will henceforth connect the house and those who live in it with the Sun, the father of all Baruya.

The wedding takes place the following day, in the presence of the members of the allied lineages and their kinfolk and guests. The two young people are seated side by side and listen in silence to the speeches addressed to them, usually by men reputed for their rhetorical skills. They address the bride and the groom successively, exhorting them to remember that they must not commit adultery, must work hard in the gardens, and must raise and protect their children. They are also publicly reminded of their shortcomings, or of certain childhood incidents – thefts, quarrels, etc.

At the end of the day, the young groom spends the night in his new house surrounded by the not-yet-initiated village boys, who come to sleep beside him. Next evening, it's the bride's turn to spend the night with the village girls. From then on, the couple sleeps in the house, but they are theoretically forbidden to make love before soot from the fire in their new fireplace has blackened the walls of their house. This can take several weeks. During this time, though the couple abstains from actual intercourse, the young man has the young woman drink his sperm so that her breasts will fill out and she will later have plenty of milk to nourish the children she will bear. From this time on, the young man can no longer have homosexual relations with the young initiates living in the men's house.

We can thus see how a number of factors come into marriage: kinship relations (for example the husband's lineage, which constructs the fireplace); the age groups linked to initiation, which build the house; ritual relations; the intervention of a clan, the Bakia, which owns the sacred objects and ritual formulas that will allow this new house and family to be connected to the Sun, father of all Baruya.

Inside the family home, the man sleeps with his sons at the back of the house, on the other side of the central fireplace, while his wife or wives sleep next to the door with their daughters and babies. A woman will never enter the male space without permission and will never step over the hearth set in the middle of the floor. For her vulva might open over the fire where she cooks the food that goes into her husband's mouth, and that would pollute it. It would be sorcery on her part, and, if her husband were to catch her in the act, he would beat her or even kill her on the spot. A woman may resist her husband physically, but she must never strike him in the face – and even less on the nose, which is pierced and adorned with his initiation insignia. Husband and wife do not address each other by name but by using the words 'man' and 'woman'. And they never touch each other or make intimate gestures in public.

The fact that the man and the woman have usually not chosen each other, the existence of all these bodily constraints, and the affirmation of male domination and the fear of sexual relations, do not prevent numerous couples from feeling deep affection for each other, and it is not uncommon for a man or a woman to hang him- or herself when the spouse dies. It is also not unusual for a widower or a widow to wear on a necklace for the rest of their life their spouse's hair or certain bones removed at the time of the second funeral for the deceased, when the bones are collected and placed in a tree in the ancestral forest.

WHAT IS A CHILD FOR THE BARUYA?

The Baruya's view of child conception testifies to the dominant status of men in the kinship system and more broadly in the society as a whole. For the Baruya, it is the man's sperm that makes the better part of the child in its mother's womb – its bones, blood and skin. The woman's uterus is simply a 'bag' in which the foetus develops, nourished for the first months by the sperm of the husband, who increases his sexual relations with his wife once she discovers she is pregnant. The woman's vaginal fluids (and not her blood) play their role in the child's identity. If they are 'stronger' than the sperm, it will be a girl, if the sperm prevails, it will be a boy.

Nevertheless, the sperm, which makes the foetal body and nourishes it, does not suffice to bring it to its final form. It still does not have fingers and toes, and especially a nose, which will be pierced when the future boy or girl is initiated. The Baruya believe that the Sun 'completes' the embryo in the woman's womb. Each Baruya man and woman thus has two fathers: the first engenders three quarters of the child with his sperm and gives it a social identity as a male or female member of a lineage; the second is a heavenly power which completes the foetus with a nose, the seat of intelligence and understanding, as well as hands and feet to move about and act with. Later, when the child has survived for at least a year, the father's lineage presents the mother's with a series of goods during a ceremony at the close of which the child will receive its first name, the name it will carry until it is initiated and which is the first name of a male or female lineage ancestor.

But it seems that the child receives more than just the ancestor's name. Something like part of this ancestor's spirit (in the sense of soul, *anima*, which is associated with the Sun) is transmitted along with the name. Sperm is therefore the life force. It is what justifies male domination in society. Even the milk that swells the new mother's breasts is, according to Baruya men, their sperm changed into milk. And it is to work this transformation that, during the first weeks of marriage, the young man has his young wife drink his sperm every day so that she will later have plenty of milk to nourish their children. On several occasions, however, I observed that not all of the women entirely shared this representation of the male origin of their milk, and in particular almost none of the younger generation, who have gone to school and been Christianized, any longer believe this.

The sperm concealed in the woman's womb becomes life, but at the expense of a mortal threat to the men's strength and even to the reproduction of the cosmos. To make love is to take risks, and to put society and the universe at risk as well. When a married couple makes love, they cannot work in the gardens that day, and the man cannot make salt or go hunting. In short, sexuality (heterosexuality) must be tightly controlled because it is a threat to the social and cosmic orders. This is, in the final analysis, because heterosexuality entails a man uniting with a woman whose menstrual blood periodically runs down her thighs and threatens to deplete not only the force and strength of the men, but also that of the plants or the game that feed them. Alternatively, the sperm that the initiates give the younger boys in the men's house, in so far as it is free of any contact with a woman's vagina, contributes to their rebirth as stronger and more handsome men.

It is therefore understandable that the Baruya forbid a married man to give his sperm to a boy. Once a penis has entered a woman's vagina, it can no longer enter a boy's mouth. It is similarly understandable that a woman is forbidden to straddle the man during coitus, for her vaginal fluids would run out onto his abdomen and pollute it, and so on.

In sum, in this society as in many others (and not only in Oceania), 'sexuality-as-desire' is subordinated to 'sexuality-for-reproduction', and the heterosexual nature of the latter is seen as a threat to the reproduction of society and the cosmos. Women in particular are the bearers of this threat, and because they are responsible they are therefore guilty. Their menstrual blood is seen as the opposite of sperm, an anti-sperm, as it were. The ambivalence of all these representations is glaring. For the first flow of menstrual blood, the arrival of a girl's first period, is also the sign that one day she will bear children, will enable a lineage to reproduce itself by providing descendants, sons who will inherit their ancestors' lands and powers, and daughters who will procure wives for their brothers. Furthermore, it was the Moon, the Sun's wife (in the exoteric, popular version) or his younger brother (in the esoteric version of the shamans) who one day opened the path in the girl's body that enables the menstrual blood to flow. At the heart of these myths and practices lies the men's fear of women, a sort of constantly denied envy of women's life-giving power, and the desire, too, to appropriate a share of this power for themselves.

For a Baruya woman has the right to kill her newborn child – at least during the time she is isolated in the birthing hut she has built. This hut stands down-hill from the village in a space strictly off-limits to men. When a man sees his wife coming home without a baby in her arms, he immediately accuses her of having killed their child and suspects that it surely must have been a boy, a son his wife deprived him of. To be sure, a certain number of children die at birth. But it also happens that a woman gets rid of the child, either because she already has too many or because of births too close together; she thinks she will not be able to feed this child and raise it. But some women also told me they had killed their baby because they did not want to give any more children to a loathsome husband who beat them, or to a man who wanted to take a second wife. By killing their child, the women offer men one more proof that, if they can give life, they can also take it back. And it was precisely this power that the first men had been trying to appropriate when they stole the women's flutes (whose secret name designates both the foetus and the new initiate).

This explains why the sacred objects (*kwaimatnie*) come in pairs and why the more powerful, or 'hotter', of the two is a 'female object', which the masters of the initiations grasp and use to strike the chest of the initiates after having held the object up to the Sun. The word *kwaimatnie* is a compound of *kwala* ('man') and *nyimatnie* ('to cause to grow'). It is with the women's power to give life that the men are confronted even as they claim to have appropriated it for themselves in the imaginary workings of the myths they mime in the symbol-laden enactment of the secret male initiation rites, in the course of which they cause the boys to be reborn independently of a woman's womb. To engender themselves – such seems to be the men's secret desire, present at the heart of these myths and rites. But could such a wish come true other than in the imaginary? – and by means of purely symbolic practices.[30]

In conclusion, I would like to stress that it is not enough to show that the sphere of kinship, in Baruya society, is a domain of social practice that enacts the domination of one gender over the other, of men over women. The entire social division of labour illustrates this reality. It is equally important to show that, above and beyond women's individual and collective subordination to men, there is the impersonal, structural subordination of a whole set of social relations – kinship relations – to the reproduction of the political-ritual relations that enable the Baruya tribe to exist as a whole, as a local society with sovereignty over its territory and governed by the men, who have taken upon themselves the right to represent this whole, of which they are only a part.

THE PRE-EMINENCE OF POLITICAL-RELIGIOUS RELATIONS

I will recall here a few facts that I have already stated, to which I will add others that also testify to the subordination of kinship relations to the political-ritual relations that enable the Baruya society to exist as such.

First is the fact that the Sun is supposed to complete the foetus in the woman's womb. But it is the men who monopolize access to the Sun, since they are the ones who possess that which the Sun gave their ancestors in the Dream-time, namely: the sacred objects and the formulae that allow them to grow boys into men, into warriors capable of confronting their enemies and husbands capable of dealing with their wives.

Second is the fact that, when the *tsimia* is constructed, each post stands for a new initiate and is prepared and brought to the site by a boy's father. The fathers of the initiates then form a circle that marks the periphery of the future ceremonial house. They stand side by side, arranged not by lineage but *by village*, and all together, at a signal from the masters of the initiations, sink the poles – the new generation of initiates – into the ground. Politics is thus more important than kinship. At the same time, metaphorically speaking, kinship symbolizes politics, for the Baruya say that the *tsimia* is the image of the tribe's

---

30   The new twenty-first-century techniques of reproduction, like cloning, could now make it possible to satisfy such a desire in reality and no longer just symbolically.

'body', and the posts are its 'bones', planted in the ground by the men, and the thatch the 'skin', brought by the women.

A third fact points in the same direction. As soon as he is initiated, a young boy immediately becomes the *elder* of all his sisters, including his older sisters, who will from then on address him as 'elder brother' (*gwagwe*) destined to replace their father. This mental transformation performed on genealogical ties by virtue of the men's political-ritual promotion clearly shows the subordination of kinship relations to the relations that organize power within the society.

This evokes a fourth fact, which this time revises linguistic usages. In the Baruya language, once a game animal is *dead* it becomes *feminine*.

Fifth, in the course of the first-stage initiation ceremony, a long, wide plank is brought and laid across the threshold of the men's house, where the new initiates have just been secluded. Later they will learn that this board is the image of *all* the married women, a symbol the married men step on when they enter the house to join their sons. Nor must we forget that *kwaimatnie* come in pairs, and that the hotter one, the more powerful and dangerous of the two, is always the 'female' one.

And finally, when I first arrived among the Baruya, in 1967, the mountain-sides were covered with paired paths, one a few metres above the other: the higher one was for men, the lower one for women, girls and children.

MODERN TIMES

As the Baruya enter the twenty-first century, their gender relations have changed profoundly. There is no longer any sign of the paired, gendered paths. These disappeared quite suddenly, in the 1970s, in other words twenty years after the first contacts with Europeans, ten years after the first patrol post and the first Lutheran mission. Another thing that was quick to disappear was the habit of women and girls stopping when a group of men approached and turning their backs while hiding their faces behind a flap of their bark capes. Next the men began to shorten the duration of the taboo on eating in front of their mother before they had fathered at least two children and had gone through a ceremony to lift this prohibition. This taboo was doubled by a ban on addressing their mother or speaking to someone in her presence. By 1980 the men had decided they could lift this ban and once again eat in their mother's presence and speak to her a few months after the birth of their first child. Men who, before the Europeans arrived, had never touched a baby, regarding it as a dirty being that soiled the netbag in which the mother carried it everywhere she went – slung on her back or across her chest – would one by one begin to hold their small children in their arms, first the boys and a year or two later, the girls as well. Meanwhile most of the women had stopped going bare-breasted and now covered their

chest and shoulders with cheap cotton blouses bought at the Lutheran mission –
which were soon reduced to tatters by sweat, rain and the heavy loads they
carried on their back.[31]

A few girls were sent to primary school, where they excelled, but their
parents were unwilling to let them go away to high school, as the boys did.
Nevertheless they had learned to speak Pidgin and read the Bible. The custom
of newly wed girls practising fellatio to 'swell their breasts' with their husband's
sperm also disappeared fairly soon, and the old women still blame this disappearance for the diseases that sometimes carry off young women for no apparent
reason.

In 1981 the girls of Wiaveu, the village where the Baruya had allowed me to
live in 1967, would play basketball on a court made in the centre of the village by
the non-initiated boys who attended school and with the help of other boys of
their age who had been initiated and lived in the men's house. Everyone attended
the games between the girls' teams and did not hesitate to comment on the size
of their breasts, their skill or their clumsiness, a scene reminiscent of village life
in Europe and far removed from the sexual segregation I had found in 1967.

Today more and more young Baruya men who have left for two or three
years to work on the plantations come home with a foreign wife, taken from a
group living on the coast or in one of the high interior valleys in the vicinity of
the towns of Goroka or Hagen. They have sometimes had to give several thousand *kina* (a *kina* is worth slightly less than one US dollar) to their wife's clan in
order to conclude the marriage. And once these women, who are not from the
area and who know nothing of the Baruya language and traditions, get to
Wonenara or Marawaka, they lead a very hard life, which sometimes drives
them to run away, with or without their children. The young men who brought
them back from their stay in town or on the plantations are very proud to have
obtained a wife without incurring a debt to their lineage, thus keeping the
possibility of exchanging their 'sisters' for a Baruya wife.

Last of all, men and women have begun planting and harvesting coffee as a
cash crop; and the children who used to spend their days playing, especially the
little boys, are now recruited for one or two hours a day to sort the coffee beans
drying in the sun on bamboo mats. In short, all levels of the population now
often work in order to 'do business', but the money earned from the sale of their
harvests serves only to buy rice and tinned fish from Japan, which replace the
game formerly used in ceremonies; or to purchase shoes, sunglasses, umbrellas,
machetes and soap. A few Baruya have started putting their money on savings

31   M. Godelier, 'L'Occident est-il le modèle universel de l'humanité? Les Baruya de
Nouvelle-Guinée entre transformation et décomposition', *Revue internationale des sciences sociales*,
no. 128 (1991), pp. 411–23.

passbooks distributed by the Administration, so that they no longer see their 'real' money, which is collected regularly and taken away in sacks for deposit in the bank vault in Goroka. A last fact, which is important: numbers of Baruya women – more than the men – have joined one of a number of Christian denominations that send missionaries to the area – today nearly all natives of Papua New Guinea – even as far as Wonenara and Marawaka. Once the adults have been converted and baptized, they renounce their personal name – for example Gwataie, Maye, which immediately tell a Baruya that the first is an Andavakia and the second a Baruya Kwarrandariar. Henceforth they are called John, David, or Mary, followed by their clan name: John Andavakia, David Bakia. Their children are baptized, go to the mission school and are no longer initiated. For the rest of their life they will carry Old or New Testament first names. They have stopped living as the reincarnation of one of their lineage or clan ancestors.

Before concluding, I would like to say something about my approach to Baruya kinship in the field. As we saw, it was a mistake to try to start fieldwork with a study of the kinship system without sufficient knowledge of the language and using informants who were too young. The error was due to lack of experience. It was a good decision to drop this study and start another on an aspect of Baruya life that occupies the men several months of the year and the women on a daily basis, namely: clearing large gardens in the forest, planting sweet potatoes or taros, tending them and then progressively harvesting while starting new gardens well before the old ones are exhausted. These are relentless tasks that mobilize every able man and woman to produce this essential portion of their material means of existence, their means of subsistence. No one is exempted from these tasks without an exceptional reason.

It was only when I spent months with the Baruya in their gardens, taking down the names of the ancestors who had first cleared the land and those of their descendants who had inherited the right to use it today, listing the names of the men who had worked together to cut the trees and build the fences around each garden to keep out the wild pigs, the names of the women – the wives, sisters, sisters-in-law, eldest daughters, etc. – among whom the plots had been divided, that a path opened up enabling me to gradually approach what the domain of kinship and ties to the land meant for the Baruya, the women's ties to the plants they grew, the presence of the spirits, the history of their wars and so on. Little by little I learned the kin ties that allowed given groups of men and women to cultivate such and such a plot, which of them held the right to make the garden, and which affines or maternal kin were invited to join them on this occasion, which would be reciprocated.

Over these months, day after day, I got to know dozens (and even hundreds) of Baruya personally. And they in turn formed their judgement of me and almost always accepted my presence with them in their gardens or on their hunting grounds. Some were reluctant, though, and I did not press them.

It became increasingly easy to question them on their genealogy. It was they who volunteered their ties of consanguinity or affinity with those who shared the use of the land. All adults had direct knowledge of these ties, but many were incapable of going back very far, no more than two generations. When someone was in doubt or admitted ignorance, they readily appealed to someone else, generally an elderly man or woman, known for remembering old alliances or the names of ascendants who had died young or gone to live in neighbouring friendly – or even hostile – tribes. These knowledgeable persons were not necessarily members of the questioner's lineage. But the size of the Baruya tribe and the fact that, in virtue of the ban on repeating marriages from the preceding generations, each lineage was ultimately allied with six or seven others, together with the need to keep all these marriages straight so as to know when they could be repeated, meant that people like old Djirinac or Nougrouvandjereye had to remember the genealogies of almost all of the tribe's members over several generations.

But the memory of even the most knowledgeable and reliable informants is always skewed by the (unconscious) interference of the patrilineal descent rule – in the Baruya's case – which meant that in the generations farthest from Ego (G^{+3} or G^{+4}), the first names cited were always those of men, as though all of the firstborn of these generations had been male. The women's names were generally forgotten or mentioned only in second or third position in their generation. Reciting genealogies was not only an exercise in 'kinship'; the sound of certain names spontaneously elicited copious comments on such and such a personality, famous for his deeds or misdeeds, the memory of bloody clashes between brothers over such and such a woman or garden.

I remember one time when Nougrouvandjereye, who had spent the day with other Baruya constructing for me the genealogies of certain lineages in the Marawaka Valley, went home to his village, where he was attacked and wounded on the arm by a man wielding a machete. The aggressor had heard – probably from one of the (many) Baruya usually at my house – that sometime that day Nougrouvandjereye had voiced doubts in my presence about the aggressor's lineage's rights in a certain number of pandanus trees (which produce highly appreciated berries), whereas Nougrouvandjereye had told me that it was not one of his own ancestors who had planted the trees.

GENEALOGIES: MADE-UP STORIES FOR THE WHITE MAN?

In short, genealogies did indeed exist for the Baruya, and they involved many stakes and interests. Asking the Baruya to reconstruct their genealogies, therefore, did not amount to imposing a Eurocentric vision of kinship. Nor was it a matter of projecting our vision of consanguinity, our notions of fatherhood and motherhood. The Baruya taught me two things in this regard, which kept me from projecting my own representations of paternity, consanguinity, etc., onto theirs. The first was that the Baruya have only one word for father and father's brothers, and another for mother and mother's sisters; as a consequence, their children are brothers and sisters. The notions of father, mother and siblings therefore cannot mean the same thing for a Baruya as for a Western European born into a kinship system centred on the nuclear family and which places in the same category (that of uncle) father's brother and mother's brother, following the terminology known as Eskimo, which characterizes the Western European and American kinship systems.

Second, and above all, for the Baruya a child is made from its father's sperm, which makes its blood, its bones, its skin and even the milk with which its mother nourishes it. But the child is also the work of the Sun, which as I have said makes the foetus in the woman's womb into a human child. In short, when one understands how the Baruya envision the process of making a baby, and the respective roles played by the man, the woman and the Sun, it is impossible to project one's own concept of consanguinity onto their way of thinking and living, and to affirm that for them, too, 'blood is thicker than water'. For the Baruya – to parody Schneider – sperm is thicker and stronger than blood, milk and so forth, which come from what the Baruya call 'penis water' (*lakala alieu*).

Lastly, and this is the weightiest argument against Schneider's criticisms, just as questioning people about their genealogies in no way prompts the anthropologist to project onto them the Western notion of consanguinity and thus to put both maternal and paternal kin in the same category, so too discovering the importance of kinship relations and the associated norms and values for the Baruya in no way compels the anthropologist to conclude that theirs is a 'kin-based society'.

We have seen that, in the Baruya's case, the existence of kin groups and kin ties between individuals and between the groups they form is not enough to make a society, in the sense of a territorial group that exists and must reproduce itself as a whole, that represents itself to itself as a whole and acts as such at the political-religious level. In sum, no one is obliged to conclude, after having reconstructed genealogies, that kinship is the universal basis of societies that have no classes or castes. No one is compelled to overrate the importance of kinship and its real functions in the production and reproduction of a given society. On this point I agree with Schneider. But I go further, for I maintain that there is no such thing as kin-based societies, on the one hand, and, on the other, societies based on other kinds of social relations – classes, for instance. To my mind, *no society* as a social group that presents itself to its members as a whole and is reproduced as such by them can be kin based. That kinship is the basis of societies is an axiom of social anthropology that does not seem to me to have been demonstrated and which I now reject after having accepted it for years.

To conclude this chapter, I would like to step back from the Baruya and place their case in a broader context. We have seen how a young anthropologist had no difficulty discovering that the Baruya's kinship terminology belongs to what is called the Iroquois type. Of course, the Baruya were unaware of this, and their ignorance had no effect on the way they led their lives. They lived their relationships as they found them, striving to reproduce them if it suited them; but to compare their relationships with those existing in other societies, about which they ignored everything down to their very existence, would have been meaningless to them.

And yet the fact that a number of societies with very different languages, cultures and structures never having had any historical contact with each other possess kinship terminologies with the same structure raises a whole series of questions. What is an Iroquois-type terminology? How many variants of this type are there? Where in the world are other examples found? Is there a connection between this type of terminology and the Baruya marriage rule of direct 'sister' exchange? Is there a connection between this type of terminology and the existence, in Baruya society, of a patrilateral descent principle? The Iroquois that Morgan studied followed a different rule, in which descent was calculated through the female line, thus a matrilineal principle. Furthermore, if the Baruya recognize themselves as being the son or daughter of a father and a mother, and thus represent themselves as being in a bilateral relationship of filiation with their paternal and maternal kin, what is the significance of favouring the ties that go through the men, starting from a common ancestor, to constitute the kin groups we have called lineages and, with more reserve, clans? Finally, is it because this descent rule is patrilineal and the children belong to their father's lineage that the Baruya give so much importance to sperm in their representations of child conception? And yet we know that there are societies where the kinship terminology is of the Iroquois type and descent reckoning is patrilineal and which nevertheless do not hold sperm to be of much importance, for instance the Paici of New Caledonia. Nor should we forget that, for the Baruya, the husband's sperm is not enough to make a child, since the Sun must intervene to complete its formation in the mother's womb. But the Sun is a male power, which acts as a father to all Baruya, whatever their lineage.

In short, these questions take us to another level, that of the theoretical analysis of the field data, an analysis that can be carried out only by comparing the Baruya's ways of living and thinking with those found in other human groups that are close or distant over space or in time. It is not that the Baruya do not compare their own ways of doing and thinking with those of their close or more remote neighbours – and, since 1951, with those of Europeans – but they do this by enumerating the differences, without being able actually to explain the reasons, except to say: this is how it's been for a very long time and the ancestors (and the gods) of the various groups are the ones who made it so.

What makes the difference between the spontaneous empirical comparisons everyone can make with nearby societies and the comparisons that anthropologists construct are, on the one hand, the terms of comparison and, on the other, the breadth and diversity of the selection of cases to be compared. For when we compare Baruya kinship terminology with the neighbouring systems, we are comparing not only vocabularies but also sets of relationships engendered by a certain number of principles (descent, marriage, etc.), which structure a set of kin terms. This structure defines the system as belonging to a type, usually already identified (Iroquois, Dravidian, Sudanese, etc.). One can also compare the Baruya with other examples of the same Iroquois-type terminology found in New Guinea, America or Oceania, in societies the Baruya have never heard of. But a kinship terminology is a logical-linguistic set of some thirty words, on average, whose content is of a different order of abstraction than the Baruya representations of, say, the process of making a baby and the role played by the father, mother and Sun. This set of representations can in turn be compared with those that have been worked out in other societies, nearby or far away, with various kinship systems.

Although the comparison of representations of how a baby is made is every bit as 'constructed' as the comparison of terminologies, the results do not put the Baruya in as vast a category as that of Iroquois-type terminologies, but into a smaller set; that of patrilineal societies stressing the primary role of sperm. But, if we add the role of the Sun, the Baruya's cultural singularity shifts to the fore and gives them a specific identity, though not one that is unique, since six or seven of their neighbours – who speak the same language and initiate their boys in the same way – also see the roles of sperm and the Sun in a like manner. But other groups – to the west and the south of the Baruya and their neighbours and who belong to the same big linguistic group, such as the Ankave – lay the stress not on sperm but on menstrual blood, do not go in for ritual homosexuality, and do not give the same importance to the Sun.[32] Why?

In short, the global comparison of societies is clearly not a good way to start. The analysis needs to deconstruct the social relations in a society before

---

32 See P. Lemonnier, 'Maladies, cannibalisme et sorcellerie chez les Anga de Papouasie-Nouvelle-Guinée', in M. Godelier and M. Panoff (eds.), *Le Corps humain supplicié, possédé, cannibalisé* (Amsterdam, Archives Contemporaines, 1998), pp. 7–28; P. Bonnemère, 'Considérations relatives aux représentations des substances corporelles en Nouvelle-Guinée', *L'Homme*, vol. 114 (April–June 1990), pp. 101–20, and 'L'Anthropologie du genre en Nouvelle-Guinée. Entre analyse sociologique, psychanalyse et psychologie du développement', *L'Homme*, vol. 161 (January– March 2002), pp. 205–24.

attempting to place them in the overall dynamic configuration from which they were detached in an abstract fashion. This global configuration exists in all societies, since it is by reproducing it that societies reproduce themselves and ensure their historical existence. To be capable of creating an analytical reconstruction of these various global configurations that make each society singular is the most ambitious aim of the social sciences, of which anthropology is but one particular discipline. Successes along this path are few and far between, and a high degree of methodological rigour and prudence are called for if one wants the comparison between societies taken as a whole, defined by a few structures and values judged to be characteristic of their functioning and identity, to have any true meaning for science.

I will therefore not be comparing societies 'globally' in the following chapters. These caveats having been stated, I will try briefly to describe the components of the domain of social life that anthropology designates by the term 'kinship'. But first I will recapitulate what I have learned in terms of theory and methods from my fieldwork about the nature of kinship relations and their role in the Baruya society of New Guinea.

The first lesson is that there is no assurance of carrying out a successful study of kinship if one starts by trying to resolve the questions this poses, because kinship is closely bound up with all sorts of practices and areas of life that may be much more important to the anthropologist than to the actors themselves.

The second lesson is that systematically recording genealogies does not mean that one has yielded to a genealogical vision of kinship. The Baruya themselves make a distinction between classificatory kinship and kin ties based on genealogical links. It must therefore be concluded that kinship categories are broader than genealogies without being completely separate.

The third lesson is that making a systematic survey of genealogies does not mean that one has in mind the Western concepts of consanguinity. As soon as one works from the local ideas about procreation, the conception of a child and its development in its mother's body, and so on, one is no longer reproducing the Western concept of consanguinity as shared blood. In one society, the blood will come from the father, as will the bones; in another, the bones will come from the father and the blood from the mother. All one can say is that, in all societies, individuals have paternal and maternal kin. But that in no way dictates the content of the concepts of fatherhood, motherhood, marriage and alliance in a given society.

The fourth lesson is that an anthropologist has no difficulty rapidly identifying Baruya kinship terminology as a variety of the Iroquois type. This shows that the conceptual findings of scientific inquiry into the forms of organization of human societies and their attendant cultural representations do not coincide with the actors' own experience; that is to say, with their own awareness of themselves and their institutions. From the moment one discovers that Baruya kinship terminology is a variety of the Iroquois type, a problem arises that is not part of the Baruya's experience, namely: where, on the face of the earth, do we find societies using the same terminology, despite the fact that there is no historical record of contact between the groups in question? Which in turn raises other questions: can we understand, for example, the reasons why, in places so far apart and at such different times in history, terminologies having the same formal structure appear?

Fifth lesson: Baruya kinship terminology tells us nothing about the descent rule they have adopted to manage their kin ties. The Baruya principle is patrilineal, whereas descent reckoning among the Iroquois, who gave their name to the terminology, is matrilineal. There is, therefore, no necessary tie between kinship terminology and descent rule. This needs explaining.

Sixth lesson: Do the Baruya have clans? No, if we regard exogamy as a constituent principle of the existence of a clan; yes, if a clan is merely a group that sees itself as having a political-ritual identity based on a unilineal descent principle without this necessarily making it exogamous. Finally, we have seen that in the same society two types of exchange can be used to establish a marriage alliance. The Baruya exchange either a woman for a woman or wealth for a woman. According to the first rule, they conform to the category of elementary kinship structures; according to the second, they have already entered the realm of complex structures. We must 'think' this duality and identify in a more global manner how it appears in other contexts.

Seventh lesson: Taking several paths through some complex realities, we have come to the conclusion that kinship is not the basis of Baruya society. But we went further and affirmed more generally that, to exist as such, a society must exist as a whole that *unites* all of the groups that form it and at the same time encompasses them, because this whole lies at another level, the level of political-religious relations, which cement its unity in a largely (for us) imaginary and symbolic manner and ensure, by means that are not all imaginary or symbolic (e.g. warfare, access to hunting grounds, etc.), its overall reproduction. Which raises the question of the axiom reiterated throughout the past by most anthropologists, namely, that 'primitive societies', in other words, societies without class or caste structures, are 'kin based'. This axiom becomes meaningless if kinship is never enough to make a set of kin groups into a society.

Eighth and last lesson, which is also important: Throughout our analysis of Baruya kinship relations, we have seen that these relationships are subject to the dynamics of the power relations in this society. And we have also seen that gender relations are a privileged site of the articulation between kinship and power. This appeared in the representations of male and female bodily substances – as well as in numerous other social and cultural facts that implement and illustrate the forms and mechanics of the domination of one sex over the other, in the present case of men over women. It is therefore not possible to understand kinship relations without analyzing the place occupied by men and women, and in a broader perspective the social attributes attaching to each, and which make them different genders.

CHAPTER TWO

The Components of Kinship

The following pages are intended to provide the non-specialist with a few basic indications of the diversity of the forms and content of kinship. It will also give me the occasion to clarify my position on certain basic problems, such as whether 'the exchange of women by men' (and for men) is indeed the universal basis of all kinship systems, as Lévi-Strauss asserted in 1945. I will also discuss recent progress made in the analysis of certain kinship systems – Dravidian and Iroquois – which once again raises the question of the reversibility or non-reversibility of transformations of kinship systems over the course of their historical evolution. Finally, I will take the opportunity to outline the large blank areas that it would be useful to explore, for example: how the Sudanese and Hawaiian systems work. I will temporarily leave to one side other questions, such as the relationship between the body, kinship and power or the foundations of the incest taboo, which will be dealt with in later chapters.

Let us therefore attempt an overview of the domains of kinship by means of a rapid inventory of its components, letting the Baruya guide us. What was at issue, for the Baruya and for ourselves, when together we analyzed what kin ties were for them? The existence of social groups made up of men and women claiming to descend – through the male line exclusively – from one or several common ancestors. The members of these 'patrilineal descent' groups were dispersed among the different Baruya villages, with the married men usually continuing to live with their father and their brothers while, the women left their family to go with their husband. These groups had different names, which gave their members a particular identity: Andavakia, Bakia and so on. The fact that a person belonged to one group or to another was due to birth or to adoption by the family of one of the married men in the group. Families – whether monogamous or polygamous – thus presented themselves as social groups, distinct from descent groups, from lineages and from clans but directly tied to lineages, since the families in question were those of married male members of these lineages and clans.

Within these families, however, the children are sons and daughters of both their father and their mother, and these bilateral ties of filiation link them to both their paternal and their maternal kin. It is the family that initially socializes the children and ensures the production of the bulk of the individuals' means of subsistence, and it is in the family setting that the consumption takes place. Moreover, the Baruya use separate terms for family (*kuminidaka*) and descent group (*navaalyara* or *yisavaa*) (see Chapter 1). It is the descent groups and not the families that hold in common growing lands and hunting territories, names and functions. At birth men and women alike receive names that were already carried by their ancestors. Only men inherit land, however. And some of them, the eldest sons of the masters of the initiations, inherit the formulae and sacred objects, which are lineage property; if the sons prove capable, they succeed their fathers in taking responsibility for part of the male initiation rites.

In the family as in the lineage, authority is exercised primarily by the men, and, within the same generation, by the older brother over his younger brothers and over all his sisters, including those older than he. The members of a descent group generally feel a duty of solidarity toward each other when it comes to finding a spouse for the young men and avenging a murder or a grave offence affecting one of their group. But in reality, in a good number of cases, owing to marriage with women from different lineages, men of a same lineage may take sides, each going to the aid of his own affines and therefore sometimes finding themselves fighting with other group members.

The first basic components of the kinship domain thus encompass modes of descent and descent groups, filiation, the family, residence, and material and immaterial realities that are inherited or transmitted from one generation to the next. They also include marriage rules and authorized alliances between individuals and between the descent groups to which they belong. The Baruya had two types of such rules: positive and even prescriptive, which made the exchange of women between lineages the obligatory form of marriage within the tribe; and negative, which forbid men of the same generation taking a wife in their mother's lineage and thus repeating their father's marriage, or two brothers taking a wife in the same lineage. And, of course, they were forbidden to marry their real or their classificatory sisters, or at least not the closest classificatory sisters, since Baruya marry women from their clan who may be geographically or genealogically distant. But as I have pointed out, a Baruya can marry his mother's sister's daughter, who is a 'sister' for him. This is a second fundamental component of kinship: it includes marriage rules, alliance strategies, prohibition of incest (and once again residence after marriage, the family and the lineage).

All of the relationships a Baruya man or woman entertains with the members of his or her birth or adoptive family, with the members of his or her lineage, with direct affines as well as with the affines of his or her consanguines (e.g. a brother's wife's brother) and with the consanguines of affines (e.g. the brother-in-law's brother) are designated by terms that often subsume several of these ties (e.g. 'father' is used for father's brothers as well, etc.). The set of terms allowing a Baruya speaker to address other persons (address terms) while taking into account their kin ties, or to express the relations that link them with others, or that link other Baruya with each other (reference terms), are a local variety of a type of terminology identified a long time ago and known as the Iroquois type.

Another basic ingredient of the kinship domain is thus the existence of a particular vocabulary which allows an individual (Ego), defined by his or her sex, to address other individuals who are related in various ways, or to describe the kin ties that bind individuals, who may or may not be personally related to the speaker (e.g. X is the *migwe*, cross cousin, of Y because his father A married . . . and so on).

But I ran into kinship once again when I asked the Baruya to explain what a child is, how they represented the process of its conception, the man's role (the father), the woman's role (the mother) and the Sun's role in forming the child that the woman was going to bring into the world. Such representations exist in every society. And they bear the mark of their kinship systems (patrilineal, matrilineal, etc.) as well as that of the political and economic systems that determine relations (usually unequal) between individuals according to gender, clan, caste, religion, etc. Finally, investigating kinship also meant identifying the rights and duties of those who regard themselves as kin of a child born to or adopted into their group, and their respective responsibilities in its education and transformation from a child into a responsible adult. And of course this includes the child's reciprocal duties and rights with regard to the various categories of people related to it.

It is by bringing together all of these factors that we can finally understand what it means to be a parent, a relative or a child in a given society, to be a given kind of relative and a given kind of child, and thus what is covered in other societies by what we designate by the terms 'father', 'mother', 'siblings', 'affines', etc.

In sum, analyzing the domain of kinship in a society amounts to exploring and reconstructing the ties between the following aspects of the society's organization:

(1) The modes of descent reckoning and the groups they engender; filiation; material and immaterial realities that are inherited and transmitted from one generation to the next; and family and residence.

(2) Marriage rules and alliance strategies; the incest taboo (and once again residence after marriage, family, lineage, etc.) (But we must be careful here: there are societies in which there is no marriage [the Na of Yunnan] or where it is only simulated [the Nyar in India].)

(3) Representations of what a child is, of the process of the child's conception, of its development and of what is meant in different cultures by

what we designate by the words 'fatherhood', 'motherhood', 'consanguinity', 'affinity', as well as the rights and duties that bind various kinds
of kin.

Like all other social relations, kinship relations do not exist purely *between*
individuals (and between the groups to which they belong – family, lineage,
household, caste, etc.), they also and at the same time exist *within* the individuals. One is defined as the son or daughter of . . . as the (real or classificatory)
father or mother of . . . These ties are stamped into people's very being, into
their consciousness and their sexed body. For to be born a Baruya man or
woman is to know that one's body has been made and nourished in one's mother's womb by one's father's sperm and that it was then completed by the Sun
before the spirit of an ancestor from the father's lineage entered the body and
took possession.

It is for this reason that it is impossible fully to understand the nature and
workings of kinship relations by analyzing them once they have been detached,
disjoined from the ways they are thought and experienced by those who were
born to these relations and (more or less) compelled in the course of their existence to take them on and reproduce them. It is for this reason, too, that the field
of kinship in any society is marked out by two series of representations. On the
one hand, there is a vocabulary of some thirty words on average, learned and
known by all members of the society, which enable each person, according to
his or her sex and generation, to situate all others with respect to him- or herself
or with respect to others within the types of kinship relations existing in the
society and which have their own logic. X is my *migwe aounie* – my cross cousin
(*migwe*) on the breast (*aounie*) side, that is to say, my mother's side. Y is so-and-
so's younger brother, and so on. At the other pole are those representations that
a society has of what a child is, of how it is conceived, of what it receives from
the father, from the mother or from the ancestors (and from which side), of
what it will grow up to be if it is a boy or a girl, etc.

All of these representations work their way into the individual's consciousness from infancy and delineate the cultural form of the intimate relationship
the individual will have with him- or herself and with others. At the heart of the
representations that delineate each person's private relationship with him- or
herself according to gender lie not only complementary gender relations, but
also relations of authority and domination that work in favour of one of the two
sexes, not only in the sphere of kinship but beyond, within the economic, political or religious relations between the groups and individuals that make up the
society.

To sum up, let us say that, in the overwhelming majority of known societies, kinship relations arise from the implementation by individuals and by the

groups to which they belong of principles commonly accepted in their society. These rules define whom it is possible or forbidden to marry and specify who the children born of the couple will belong to. In many but not all societies it is also possible to adopt children and even adults, and to treat them as full members of the adoptive family or clan. Polynesian societies and the Inuit engage intensely in the giving of children as gifts between families. Here, too, there are rules that determine the circumstances in which a kin group (family, lineage, household) can adopt someone and whom it can adopt.[1]

All of these rules prescribing what individuals can and cannot do and often what they should or should not do are the source of positive or negative 'values' attached to the actions of individuals and groups and to the social relations to which their actions give rise. Rules and values are mental (*idéel*)[2] realities that are by no means an epiphenomenon of kinship relations but one of the conditions of their production. For in a society one cannot get married without knowing what marriage is and whom, in this society, one is allowed or forbidden to marry. And once a marriage has taken place, what was formerly a mental condition now becomes an internal component.

Of course, every society has individuals who ignore in practice the (positive or negative) norms in use. Some even oppose them openly, often at their own peril. Contradictions between norms and practices obviously do not stem purely from individual decision, though they tend to multiply when a society undergoes rapid and deep changes that make it increasingly hard to reproduce the old structures. So it is today in certain Australian Aboriginal groups, where up to 25 per cent of marriages are 'irregular', in other words correspond to unions traditionally forbidden by their system. One of the reasons for this situation is the demographic collapse of these groups, which means that there are no longer enough permissible spouses in certain of the 'sections' into which Aboriginal society is divided. A number of men have therefore married women from their own section or from their own 'moiety', and who are therefore their 'sisters', thus breaking the incest taboo and the rule of exogamy on which their kinship system was based.

---

1 I. Brady (ed.), *Transactions in Kinship, Adoption and Fosterage* (Honolulu, The University Press of Hawaii, 1976) (ASAO monograph. no. 4); V. Caroll (ed.), *Adoption in Eastern Oceania* (Honolulu, The University Press of Hawaii, 1970) (ASAO monograph no. 1); M. Corbier (ed.), *Adoption et fosterage* (Paris, De Boccard, 1997); A. Fine (ed.), *Adoptions: ethnologie des parentés choisies* (Paris, Editions de la Maison des Sciences de l'Homme, 1998); S. Lallemand, *La Circulation des enfants en société traditionnelle: prêt, don, échange* (Paris, L'Harmattan, 1993).

2 Translator's note: We have translated the French *idéel* as 'mental', fully aware that this does not cover the full range of the French term, which 'takes into account thought in all its forms and processes, conscious and unconscious, cognitive and non-cognitive', in the words of the publisher's note to the English translation of M. Godelier's *L'Idéel et le matériel, pensée, économie, sociétés* (Paris, Fayard, 1984); English translation: *The Mental and the Material: Thought, Economy and Society*, translated by Martin Thom (London/New York, Verso, 1986).

Such facts give us an opportunity to clarify an important point. All of the transformations that occur in a kinship system always (if the society continues to exist) lead to the establishment of another type of kinship relations, to the appearance of another kinship system. *Changes in kinship never produce anything but more kinship*; and kinship relations can never turn into, for example, caste or class relations. If this is true, we must therefore turn elsewhere to explain the emergence, around 4000 BCE in the Near East and around 2000 BCE in the New World, of the first societies differentiated into castes or classes, in which new institutions were to appear – such as various forms of centralized power, chiefdoms, states and empires.

Before the appearance of these new forms of power, all human societies were probably organized according to combinations of different types of kinship relations with different kinds of political-religious relations, different from kinship relations but directly articulated with and encompassing them. It is this direct articulation that disappears, more or less rapidly and more or less completely, with the development of caste- and class-based societies. India is an example of a single political-religious system in which the system of castes is articulated and coexists with three types of kinship systems: Indo-European in northern India, Munda[3] in central India, and Dravidian in the South.[4]

KINSHIP, POWER AND WEALTH

I will end this overview with a few words about the relationship between kin ties, power(s) and wealth. In many societies, concluding a marriage alliance between two groups gives rise to transfers of wealth and services, sometimes even political and/or religious titles, between wife-givers and wife-takers. The young couple may receive a dowry from their respective families, or the groom's family may pay bridewealth to the family of the bride, or, in the event that two women exchange brothers (as among the Rhades of Vietnam[5] or the Tetum of Timor[6]), the woman's family may pay the sisters of the future husband a 'groom-price'. In short, the establishment of a matrimonial alliance is the occasion for transfers of wealth – in the form of cattle, jewellery, and sometimes land or titles – which give rights in persons and are often followed by counter-gifts in various proportions. Generally speaking, however, the greatest flow of wealth,

3   R. Parkin, *The Munda of Central Asia: An Account of their Social Organization* (Delhi, Oxford University Press, 1992).

4   T. Trautmann, 'India and the Study of Kinship Terminologies', *L'Homme*, no. 154–55 (2000), pp. 559–72.

5   A. de Hautecloque-Howe, *Les Rhades: une société de droit maternel* (Paris, Editions du CNRS, 1985).

6   G. Francillon, 'Un profitable échange de frères chez les Tetum du Sud. Timor central', *L'Homme*, vol. 29, no. 1 (1989), pp. 26–43.

functions, titles and crests, and knowledge, circulates between ascending and descending generations along certain kin ties and following rules that regulate the procedures of inheritance and succession.

Several remarks are called for here. All of these titles, these functions, this knowledge, this wealth, circulate in the form of *gifts* that always have a personal character because establishing new kinship relations or reproducing old ones always means entering into relationships that subsequently bind the individuals or the groups of individuals involved, even if the personal character of these bonds varies with the distance that separates the parties. These gifts are not simply a demonstration of generosity on the part of the givers, they are part of the obligations incumbent on them (and on the groups to which they belong) because they are or wish to become kin.

In short, once they have entered the universe of kinship, this wealth, this knowledge, these functions or titles, however they may have been acquired, circulate along relations of descent or alliance as gifts, unilateral gifts with no possible or expected reciprocation, or as gifts followed by counter-gifts, as reciprocal gifts. Which leads us to another important point. Generally speaking, the exchanges that occur within the domain of kinship and in the name of kinship do not come under the heading of commercial exchanges and do not obey market logic. This can give rise to idealization of kin ties in societies where the bulk of exchanges have become impersonal and are carried out through commercial relations. In contemporary Western societies, the relationship between money and kinship is ambiguous if not a subject of conflict. There are some relatives from whom you do not dare buy anything because they will never accept payment, and this creates a debt that is hard to live with. There are those who give you a good deal 'because you're a relative'. There are some who never give you a 'break' and whom you secretly reproach for treating you like a stranger, in other words like non-kin. These are relatives who do not feel 'obligated' to do something for you, even though you are a relative. For in all societies, kin ties, or at least the closest ties, are a source of obligations and debt – and are lived as such.

A few concluding remarks on the relationship between kin ties and political-religious powers, and with the production of the material conditions of existence and wealth. Because political and/or religious functions come into the possession of certain kin groups (family, lineage, household) and are transmitted to persons occupying a certain position within the kinship relations that structure these groups (from father to eldest or youngest son, from maternal uncle to nephew, etc.), the perpetuation of these groups – in other words the reproduction of the kinship relations that allow them to exist – is one of the major conditions for the reproduction of the political-religious system, which in turn enables the society to exist as a whole. It is important to remember here that, *even though these functions reside within kin groups, this does not mean they are kinship relations.* If we look at all of the functions and titles, which are always unequally distributed among kin groups – as is the case in Polynesian chiefdoms such as Tonga – we see that taken together they constitute a global system of political-religious relations obtaining between all local kin groups but which are not the same thing as the kinship relations that actually exist between these groups; on the contrary, the political-religious relations co-opt kinship relations and use them for their own reproduction.

It is the existence of this global system and the hierarchy between the various titles and functions that oblige or forbid various kin groups (household, clan, lineage) to contract a given type of alliance and that oblige men and women to marry within their status or to develop complex strategies to marry above their rank (in the hope of procuring a more elevated title). In such societies, certain kin groups (clans, houses) can disappear, others may lose their title, while yet others rise to a higher status; but these events merely change the place of the person within the system, they do not compromise its existence, quite the opposite.

Alongside ownership of titles and functions which are often not redistributed among all of the kin groups that make up a society but concern only a fraction of them (for example the eight Baruya clans that own the Kwaimatnie and cooperate in the initiation of the boys of all of the clans, including those that do not have sacred objects), there are other forms of property: horticultural lands, hunting or fishing grounds, tools and weapons. Owning these forms of property in combination with the labour and know-how of the members of the kin groups (and/or their dependents, clients, servants, slaves, etc.) enables these groups to produce the bulk (or a significant portion) of their material means of existence, in other words both their means of subsistence and the share of material wealth they need to exchange or redistribute on the occasion of weddings or funerals, or which will be offered to the gods, or paid as tribute to the chief or as taxes to the state.

In short, in many societies, kin groups are at the same time units of production, of redistribution, of consumption and of exchange of means of subsistence and wealth. Depending on the society – and I will give some examples below – land can be owned in common by a lineage while being redistributed for use by the families of the lineage, who work it separately. Sometimes each of these families keeps their harvest in their own silo, sometimes they gather their harvests into a common silo placed under the authority of the lineage elders, who set aside the portion to be used as seed the next year and then, each day, mete out to each family the amount it needs.[7] In short, on the basis of the social

---

7   For instance, among the Guro of Ivory Coast. Cf. C. Meillassoux, *Anthropologie*

division of labour between the sexes and generations, which is not itself part of kinship, the production and the redistribution of the means of subsistence and wealth are carried out by persons occupying different positions in the relations that structure their kin group.

The authority wielded over those involved in the work process or in the redistribution of subsistence goods or wealth is identical to that found in the kinship relations, *which thus take on directly the functions of social relations organizing production.* The redistribution and the consumption of the material conditions of existence in these contexts, and the material tasks necessary to the existence and the reproduction of the kin group, thus *appear as obligations* imposed on its members by their kin ties, as *attributes of kinship relations.* It is also an obligation connected with kinship that compels the elder men of a lineage to collect the bridewealth (pigs, bird-of-paradise feathers, money) that will enable one of their young men to marry when he comes of age. Once again, kinship appears as a universe of personal ties – ties of solidarity and sharing, but also of dependence and authority – between the individuals that comprise the group, not only those born to the group but also those who have entered it through adoption or marriage.

A remark is necessary concerning economic relations and functions as compared to political-religious functions and relations. The role of the economy and its connections with kinship relations are not the same in societies without castes or classes and in societies where these exist. In the first case, there is no, or only a limited, social division of labour. In the second case, in caste-based societies for example, everything that serves material reproduction (means of subsistence, wealth, services) is produced in these societies by different social groups, each of which is specialized in the production of certain products (blacksmiths, farmers, fishers) or certain services (barbers, gravediggers, etc.).

Alongside these castes whose labour contributes directly to the production of goods and services are others that do not participate in these various work processes but control them socially and receive a share of the product, either because they own the land that the others cultivate or because they exercise religious or political-military functions, and a share of what is produced is allotted them so that they may devote all their time to the exercise of their function. In these societies, of which India is the classic example, each kin group produces whatever its caste is supposed to produce and receives from others the goods and services owed it in exchange. In this case, the economy is a *global* system that binds together all castes and thereby the kin groups that compose them. No kin group can therefore be materially self-sufficient, if one understands by

---

économique des Gouro de Côte-d'Ivoire (Paris/La Haye, Mouton, 1964) and *Femmes, greniers et capitaux* (Paris, Maspero, 1969).

material conditions of existence much more than the mere means of subsistence. Such a global system, without excluding the use of money and the development of commercial exchanges, operates basically according to other rules than those of the market.[8]

In contemporary Western societies, where the capitalist economy rests on the mass production of goods and services bought and sold as commodities, where there is a much more complex social division of labour than in caste-based societies (which rested more on agriculture than on industry), and where a person's status and activity are not definitively settled at birth since there are social classes of owners and non-owners of the means of production and exchange whose access is theoretically open, the economy also constitutes a global system that links all the groups in the society, all the families and all the individuals, through the market (or rather markets – of labour, of industrial products, of money, etc.). Each person must derive the bulk of his means of social existence from whatever he sells or buys in the marketplace. In this context, with the exception of certain sectors such as agriculture, crafts and (small) businesses, families no longer function as production units but rather as consumption units. For those who own the principal means of production and exchange, by virtue of which they intervene in various sectors of the capitalist system, the family is a unit of wealth accumulation, of asset management and sometimes, more rarely, of the direct management of a firm producing goods or services.

In contrast, in societies where there is no social division of labour, or if there is then it concerns only the production of certain goods or certain services, *the economy does not function as a global system* linking together in their production and distribution all of the kin groups that compose a society whose sovereignty over a territory, its resources and the men and women living there is known (if not recognized) by the neighbouring groups. In such societies, of which the Baruya are an example, the economic activities of production, redistribution and consumption of goods and services remain local and separate, and do not cause kin groups to depend directly and daily on each other in order to reproduce themselves. Nevertheless their material cooperation is necessary and expected in times of war, when most of the men are away fighting and the women cannot venture unaccompanied to their gardens to gather what they need to feed their family and their pigs. This is also the case when it comes time for the initiations, which run for weeks and require big gardens to be planted in advance with a view to liberally feeding the hundreds of guests. But these are

8   L. Dumont, *Homo hierarchicus. Le système des castes et ses implications* (Paris, Gallimard, 1966); English translation: *Homo Hierarchichus: The Caste System and Its Implications*. Complete revised English edition, translation by Mark Sansbury, Louis Dumont and Basia Gulati (Chicago, University of Chicago Press, 1970).

exceptional circumstances, in which the economy is placed in the service of the reproduction of the society as a whole, in the service of the social relations that, precisely, encompass all kin groups and cause them to exist within this whole.

In conclusion, let me say that it is clear that kinship is not only about establishing ties of alliance and descent between individuals and between the groups to which they belong. Other realities – material, political, religious – reside within kinship relations and are reproduced along with them. These realities are so many stakes which, depending on circumstances, bring together or divide those who recognize each other as being closely or less closely related. It is not enough to have tender memories of sharing the maternal breast to keep brother from turning against brother or daughter against mother. The passion for power and wealth break ties, sweep away the feelings and obligations that 'should' exist between family members.[9]

And it is because all kinds of social relations that do not come down to kinship relations also reside in them and are reproduced in part along with them that it is *impossible to know in advance the importance of kinship* in the workings of any given society at any given period. Any general claim concerning the real nature and importance of kinship in society is meaningless.[10] And going even further, for a peasant without anything to transmit and a lord who has titles, lands and a glorious genealogy to hand on, kinship can have neither the same meaning nor the same importance, even if both use identical kin terms.

We will now look at each of the four blocks of facts and concepts that make up the field of kinship, both on the ground and in theory – filiation and descent, alliance, residence, and kinship terminologies. These will be the subjects of the next four chapters.

---

9   This dark side of kinship is often masked or marginalized. As in Hiatt or Meyer Fortes, the face of kinship usually displayed is what Hiatt calls 'an ethics of generosity', and Meyer Fortes, 'amity', which is more than friendship and the opposite of enmity. Amity is a mutual understanding whereby members of a family agree to lend each other the support that enables them to maintain a 'code of good conduct' in view of fulfilling the 'legitimate interests of each'. See Meyer Fortes, *Kinship and the Social Order* (London, Routledge and Kegan Paul, 1969), p. 110; see also L. Hiatt, *Kinship and Conflict: A Study of an Aboriginal Community in Northern Arnhem Land* (Canberra, Australian National University, 1965), p. 146.

10   I come to the same conclusion as David Schneider here, but by a different path and without stigmatizing kinship studies as the product of a Western ethnocentric illusion leading to a theoretical impasse.

CHAPTER THREE

Filiation and Descent
(First Component)

Filiation and descent: While both words are translated by the French *filiation*, Anglo-Saxon anthropologists make a distinction between the two terms. The majority of French anthropologists do not, and range themselves behind Lévi-Strauss,[1] who, in a debate with Leach[2] claimed that the distinction was not useful. This is not my opinion; I think that it is not only pertinent but important. For Meyer Fortes, Leach and Needham, who agree on this point at least, the term 'filiation' should be kept to designate the fact that every individual is at birth (or becomes by adoption) the son or daughter of a father or fathers and a mother or mothers who are themselves sons and daughters of a father or fathers and a mother or mothers, and so on. In a word, filiation is the set of ties that link children to their paternal and maternal kin. Filiation is bilateral and cognatic; it links the individual to both agnates and uterines.

DESCENT MODES

Descent is governed by other principles. The calculation of descent can be unilineal, duolineal, bilineal or non-lineal. In the case of unilineal systems, descent is traced through only one of the sexes. When descent is reckoned through men, it is patrilineal. When it is traced through women only, it is matrilineal. In the first case, a man's sons and daughters belong to his descent group, but only sons

---

1 Cf. C. Lévi-Strauss, 'Réponse à Edmund Leach', *L'Homme*, vol. 18, no. 2–3 (1977), pp. 131–3. Lévi-Strauss' reply was particularly scathing: 'To Leach, these locutions are nonsense perhaps. But allow us to prefer Durkheim's brand of caution in deciding how one should go about expressing oneself in French.' Lévi-Strauss goes on to quote Trévoux's *Dictionnary*, Diderot and d'Alembert's *Encyclopédie*, the *Larousse du XXe siècle* and the *Petit Robert* dictionary, without ever addressing the crux of the problem.
2 Cf. E. Leach, 'The atom of kinship, filiation and descent: error of translation or confusion of ideas?', *L'Homme*, vol. 17, no. 2–3 (1977), pp. 127–9. Leach criticizes the confusions that appear in the English translation of Lévi-Strauss' article, 'Réflexions sur l'atome de parenté', *L'Homme*, vol. 13, no. 3 (1973), pp. 5–30, stemming from the fact that the French word *filiation* has two meanings: 'filiation' – the tie that links an individual to his/her father and his/her mother – and 'descent', i.e. the individual's tie to a kin group, which can be traced through the father, through the mother or through both of them. Leach wrote that: 'both in the original French text of Lévi-Strauss (1945) and in its successor (*id.*, 1958) there is a radical confusion which stems from the fact that the single French term *filiation* is made to cover two quite separate concepts which in English language anthropological writing are now distinguished as *filiation* and *descent*. The issue is not just a matter of mistranslation or Anglo-Saxon obtuseness' ('The atom of kinship . . .', p. 128).

DESCENT PRINCIPLES AND FILIATION	
Unilineal principles	
	Patrilineal descent: Children of A and B belong to A (patrilineage, clan, etc.) and are under the authority of A. / **Matrilineal descent:** Children of A and B belong to B (matrilineage, matriclan, etc.) and are under the authority of B.
Ambilineal principle	**Ambilineal descent:** Principle of double descent reckoning: Children of A and B belong simultaneously to the patrilineal clan of A and to the matrilineal clan of B, and receive distinct things from each clan: for example land from A and titles from B.
Parallel/cross bilineal principles	**Parallel bilineal descent:** boys belong to A, girls to B, their mother's lineage. / **Cross bilineal descent:** girls belong to A, boys to B.
Undifferentiated principle	**Undifferentiated principle** Undifferentiated, cognatic descent: children's descent is traced equally through A and B. Filiation and descent are fused here, unless some other principle is introduced (co-residence, for example).

transmit this belonging. In the second case the opposite holds true: a woman's sons and daughters belong to her descent group, but only daughters transmit the belonging. The systems termed ambilineal or duolineal combine the preceding unilineal systems, such that each child belongs to its father's group by virtue of a patrilineal principle and to its mother's group by virtue of a matrilineal principle. Alternatively, bilineal systems are rare. They come in two kinds. Either descent is parallel, and the sons of a couple belong to the father's lineage and the daughters to the mother's. Or descent is crossed, and a couple's daughters belong to their father's lineage, and the sons to their mother's.

Lastly, in non-lineal systems, the individual's sex makes no difference, and descent is traced indifferently through the men and through the women. All descendants, in the male or the female line, of an ancestral couple can refer to this ascendance in order to claim rights to titles or land use, for instance. The sons, daughters, grandsons and granddaughters of this ancestral couple have of course married into other groups, and their descendants belong to these groups. Undifferentiated kinship systems therefore require other rules than ascendance to constitute coherent, bounded descent groups.

PATRILINEAL DESCENT

Among the societies that reckon descent grosso modo by a patrilineal principle, we find ancient Greece and Rome, ancient and contemporary China, the Nuer in Sudan, the Tallensi in Ghana, the Cyrenian Bedouins, the Iraqi Kurds, the Juang[3] in central India, the Kachin in Burma, the Purum[4] in India, the Melpa or the Baruya in New Guinea, the Tupinamba in Amazonia, and so on. These societies differ profoundly from one another. The Melpa prohibit the direct exchange of women and instead exchange wealth for wives. For the Baruya, direct sister exchange is the principal marriage rule, but they practise payment of bridewealth in the case of marriage with other groups. The Katchin forbid wife-takers to be wife-givers as well. When the givers are superior to the takers, the women circulate in the opposite direction of the wealth (which 'rises' from the takers toward the givers).

Let us spend a moment with the Juang, studied by McDougal (1964) and by Parkin in his monographic work on the Munda (1992).[5] The Munda descent system is divided into three levels of segmentation. The first consists of eighteen patriclans (*bok*), which are exogamous, do not hold property in common, are dispersed in

3   C. McDougal, *The Social Structure of the Hill Juang* (Ann Arbor, University Microfilms, 1963).
4   R. Needham, 'A Structural Analysis of Purum Society', *American Anthropology*, vol. 60, no. 1 (1958), pp. 75–101.
5   R. Parkin, *The Munda of Central India: An Account of Their Social Organization* (Delhi, Oxford University Press, 1992).

various villages but have different individual 'totems'. These clans are in turn divided into thirty-eight local descent groups, each of which usually resides in its own village. The local groups are exogamous, and it is between these groups that marriages take place. The third level is formed by the lineages, which are of shallow genealogical depth, three or four generations on average, with two or three lineages living in the same village. They cooperate to gather the payment needed for their young men to marry, and redistribute the brideprice received when their daughters marry. Marriage must take place between persons with different totems, and therefore from different clans. Residence after marriage is virilocal. Lands and goods are inherited within the lineage, which also functions as a ritual unit.

MATRILINEAL DESCENT

Among the societies whose mode of descent reckoning is matrilineal, we can mention the Ashanti of Ghana, the Pende of Kasai, the Khasi of northeast India, the Nayar of South India, the Trobriand Islanders, the Maenge of New Britain, the Mnong-Gar and the Rhades of Vietnam, the Tetum of Timor, the Na of China, the Nagovisi of Bougainville, the Iroquois and the Hopi of North America. The Khasi are divided into matriclans (*kur*).[6] The couple's residence after marriage is uxorilocal, but in the daytime the family is composed of brothers and sisters living together with the sisters' children. At night, the brothers join their own wives and children while the sisters' husbands take their place. Na families, too, are composed of brothers and sisters and the sisters' children. At night the men circulate among the houses and become the temporary lover of one or another of the women living in these houses. Marriage as a ceremony officializing a union exists only for village headmen's families, and the kinship vocabulary, according to the Chinese ethnologist, Cai Hua, has no word for 'husband' or 'father'.[7]

DUOLINEAL DESCENT

Duolineal systems are a rarity. We can cite the Yako of Nigeria, the Herrero of South Africa, and the Kondaiyankottai Maravar, a South Indian subcaste. The Kondaiyankottai Maravar have two kinds of clan: patrilineal (*kottu*) and matrilineal (*kilai*).[8] Children belong to both clans. The patrilineal clans correspond to

6   C. Nakane, *Garos and Khasis: A Comparative Study in Matrilineal Systems* (Paris, Ecole Pratique des Hautes Etudes, Cahiers de L'Homme, Nouvelle Serie V; The Hague, Mouton & Co., 1967).
7   C. Hua, *Une société sans père ni mari. Les Na de Chine* (Paris, Presses Universitaires de France, 1997).
8   A. Good, *The Female Bridegroom: A Comparative Study of the Life Crisis Rituals in India and Sri Lanka* (Oxford, Clarendon Press, 1991) and 'Prescription, Preference and Practice: Marriage Patterns among the Kondaiyankottai Maravar of South India', *Man*, vol. 16, no. 1 (1981), pp. 108–29.

local, exogamous descent groups. They control inheritance of land and other forms of property, and settle successions. They are religious and ritual units that ensure the worship of family gods. The matrilineal clans are not localized but they too are exogamous. Every marriage must take into account each group member's double clan affiliation. In duolineal systems, children belong to both clans, regardless of sex; but the continuation of the clan and the transmission of rights and statuses rest on unilineal principles: from the father to his sons for the patrilineal clan and from the mother to her daughters for the matrilineal clan.

BILINEAL DESCENT

Bilineal systems, whether parallel or cross, are even more rare. Examples of the first case are the Orokolo[9] and the Omie;[10] and of the second, the Mundugumor,[11] three New Guinea societies, the first two of which live in the South in the Gulf of Papua, and the third in the North, in the Sepik. In the first case, an individual's belonging to a lineage is transmitted from same sex to same sex (from father to sons and from mother to daughters), unlike unilineal or duolineal systems, in which children of both sexes belong either to their father's or to their mother's clan or to both at once. In cross systems, the clan to which boys and girls belong switches with each generation. Among the Mundugumor, a son belongs to his mother's kin group, a daughter to the father's. The son carries the name of his maternal grandfather, the daughter that of her paternal grandmother. This has been called a 'rope' system. Land is transmitted from father to son, but the father's weapons and his group's sacred flute are transmitted from father to one of his daughters, who will pass them on to her sons.

UNDIFFERENTIATED DESCENT

Examples of societies with an undifferentiated mode of descent are the Maori of New Zealand and a great many Polynesian societies – Samoa, Tonga, etc. At one end of the great axis of the Malayo-Polynesian migrations, we find the Imerina and several other societies of Madagascar. And between the two, the Penan of Borneo and other groups in Indonesia. Among the Maori,[12] the descent group (*hapu*) stems, as its name indicates, from a group of ancestors to which the group members are connected by ties that run indifferently through the male or the female line. These ties can go back as many as ten generations or more. A

9   P. E. Williams, *Drama of Orokolo* (Oxford, Clarendon Press, 1940).
10   M. Rohatynskyj, *The Larger Context of Omie Sex Affiliation* (New York, Morrow, 1990).
11   M. Mead, *Sex and Temperament in Three New-Guinea Societies* (New York, Morrow, 1935).
12   R. Firth, 'A Note on Descent Groups in Polynesia', *Man*, no. 57 (1957), pp. 4–8.

person can belong to several *hapu*, but the fact of residing in one of them consolidates the rights to which he is entitled. Marriages very often take place within the same *hapu*, which is therefore strongly endogamous. Each *hapu* is under the political and religious authority of a chief, who descends in the male line from the eldest son of the founding ancestor. Each of the family lines that descend from the founding ancestor has a different status, determined by its distance from the family line of the eldest son. This line is a sort of aristocracy within the *hapu*, whereas younger sons of younger sons were treated as people of inferior status, as commoners. This example shows that in cognatic systems it is also possible to resort to unilineal principles for the purpose of transmitting certain functions and establishing various forms of hierarchy. In addition, real or potential belonging to several *hapu* offers individuals choices and strategies that are more open and broader than in strictly 'lineal' societies. In this case residence plays an important role in consolidating rights and reducing these choices.

HOUSE SYSTEMS

To the various modes of descent reckoning, long known to anthropologists, we will add a mode of constituting groups that calls upon both descent principles and marriage rules. This mode creates kinship groups that we in the West call 'houses'; however such groups are also found in the aristocratic families of Japan and in the societies on the northwest coast of the United States and Canada characterized by 'ranks and houses', such as the Kwakiutl and their neighbours, or in certain politically ranked cognatic societies of Indonesia. In Europe, alongside the 'royal' houses and the various minor or great houses that made up the family lines of the feudal aristocracy (vestiges of which still exist) we find various peasant 'houses', such as the *casa* in Catalonia or the *ostau* of the Lavedan region.

When Lévi-Strauss made a close analysis of the workings of the *numayn* – the Kwakiutl 'houses' whose underlying structure (patrilineal and/or matrilineal principles)[13] Boas, who had been the first to describe them, admitted having great difficulties in discovering – he drew anthropologists' and histori-

---

13 Boas had largely opened the way for his successors, writing in 'The social organization of the Kwakiutl': 'The fundamental principle seems to be that primogeniture, regardless of sex, entitles the first-born child to the highest rank held by one of its parents. Rank is, on the whole, determined by the order of birth, and the noblest line is the line of the firstborn. The lowest in rank that of the youngest born' (p. 116). 'We may say that the *numayms* are based on descent with a preference for the paternal line' (p. 118). 'The peculiar transfer of name, position and privileges from the woman's father to his son-in-law has been described by me before' (p. 118). See F. Boas, 'The Social Organization of the Kwakiutl', *American Anthropologist*, vol. 22 (1920), pp. 111–26, and Francis Zimmerman's comments in *Enquête sur la parenté* (Paris, Presses Universitaires de France, 1993), pp. 145–9.

ans' attention to this type of institution. A *numayn* is one of a hierarchy of 'houses' each of which has a rank and a seat defined by a name and a crest. According to Lévi-Strauss:

> The house is first of all a legal entity, in possession of a domain composed of material and immaterial goods . . . by material [I mean] the possession of a real domain, fishing sites and hunting grounds . . . The immaterial domain includes names, which are owned by houses, legends, the exclusive right to perform certain dances of rituals . . . [A house] perpetuates itself by handing down its name, its wealth and its titles in a direct or fictitious line regarded as legitimate on condition that this continuity can be expressed in the language of kinship or marriage, and most often both at once . . . There is so much freedom in this area that one can say that alliance and descent are interchangeable.[14]

It is thus not the house that belongs to the people but the people who belong to the house, together with material and immaterial assets which are indivisible and kept to be transmitted to their firstborn male or female descendants in the direct line. Alternatively, other parts of the domain can be temporarily detached and given to the husbands of the daughters of the house, sons-in-law, who then have the duty to transmit them in turn to their firstborn. The first rule in this system, the rule of primogeniture, implies gender equivalence for succession to certain titles and ranks. At this level, the system is cognatic, but skewed to the paternal line. The second principle – by virtue of which certain of the house's titles are provisionally alienated by giving them to the men who marry the daughters of the house with the obligation to transmit them to their own children, who are therefore the giver's grandchildren – posits a partial equivalence between alliance and descent. In short, instead of opposing descent through the male line and descent through the female line (or radically opposing descent and alliance), this system plays on all kinship relations in order to maintain a 'house' and conserve its name and its seat, in other words a rank, a crest and privileges in the political-religious system that encompasses all houses and ranks them with respect to all others within a territorial group which Boas calls a 'tribe'. Furthermore, this system defines not only the rank and place of each house but the rank and place of each individual in the house according to birth order and sex.

Far from being merely a 'language', as Lévi-Strauss suggests,[15] reiterating a

---

14   C. Lévi-Strauss, 'La notion de maison: entretien avec Claude Lévi-Strauss', *Terrain*, no. 9 (Oct. 1989), pp. 34–9.

15   Ibid.

thesis stated well before by Beattie[16] and then by Leach,[17] Tambiah[18] and others, kinship relations actually function as relations of appropriation and transmission of the material and social conditions of the houses' existence (fishing and hunting territories), and determine their capacity to amass the wealth that will be entered in the potlatches, the competition by means of gift-giving between *numayn* for titles or to legitimize their transmission. But these titles, ranks, crests and myths, the immaterial property of the 'houses', are not attributes of kinship. They do not exist physically as do the hunting and fishing territories that each house has appropriated. They exist socially as part of a political-religious system of titles and privileges distributed hierarchically, and therefore unequally, between the 'houses'; and in virtue of this distribution they come to reside in the workings of the kinship relations that structure them. But, as I said, titles, ranks, crests and privileges are not attributes of kinship; they belong to a component of society that encompasses all kin groups and places them permanently at its service for its own reproduction: this part of society is the political-ritual system which enables the society to exist as a whole, and represents it as such. This political-religious system is therefore not to be confused with the worship each 'house' may pay its ancestors or the tutelary gods that afford support and protection. These acts of veneration of course apply to a universe of representations, myths and rites shared by all members of the society, but in themselves they are part of the specific identity of each 'house'.

Lastly, there is one point that Claude Lévi-Strauss, Pierre Lamaison and the others who participated in the discussion on the notion of house neglected, and that is the fact that there are two major differences between the tribal aristocracy of the Kwakiutl 'houses' and the 'houses' of the feudal aristocracy of Europe and Japan. Kwakiutl society was self-governing, there was no state. In Europe and in Japan, there were various forms of state, of central power embodied in a royal or imperial house (in Japan it was the families of the emperor and the shogun). Among the Kwakiutl, commoners were kinsmen of the aristocrats, they were the younger siblings of descendants of family lines who had no seat or crest; they were freemen. In Europe and in Japan, commoners had no kin ties with the aristocratic families, and marriage was forbidden between these social classes – on pain, for the aristocrats, of forfeiting their title and their condition. Furthermore, commoners were not freemen. They were serfs or dependants, living on lands owned by the noble families, which they were allowed to use in

16   J. H. M. Beattie, 'Kinship and Social Anthropology', *Man*, no. 130 (1964), pp. 1–23.

17   E. Leach, *Pul Elya, a Village in Ceylon: A Study of Land Tenure and Kinship* (Cambridge, Cambridge University Press, 1961).

18   S. J. Tambiah, 'The Structure of Kinship and Its Relationships to Land Possession and Residence in Pata Dumbara, Central Ceylon', *Journal of the Royal Anthropological Institute*, vol. 88, no. 1 (1958), pp. 21–44.

exchange for payment of rents in labour, produce or money, thus enabling the nobles to live in keeping with their condition, surrounded by the signs of their distinction.

A certain similarity is created between the tribal and the feudal 'houses' (and in their successoral practices) by the fact that a large portion of the functions, and therefore of the state's power, was shared between the families and family lines of the feudal hierarchy, who exercised these functions over their lands and their people – the right to sit in judgement, the right to raise troops and make war, the right to preside the village meeting, the right to collect taxes on the goods circulating or sold on their lands, and so forth. But, in Europe, there was yet another type of 'house', found more specifically in mountainous regions, where the economy was based on a combination of farming of privately owned lands and stock-raising on communal pastures, jointly owned by all members of the community. In these regions, one found village communities also organized into 'houses'. Each had a name attached to it, whatever its owners' patronym. Owing to the importance of their 'house' (i.e. the wealth composed of farming lands and livestock), these owners held a distinct rank in the organization of village power, and their voice carried more or less weight in managing community lands and business. Each 'house' also had its own pew in the parish church. In order to reproduce itself, the system required that each 'house' be transmitted as a block to a single descendant, usually the eldest son, but sometimes, if there were no sons, to the eldest daughter, whose husband would move into the 'house' and take its name. The system thus implied the creation of a strongly marked hierarchy between the descendants and, in general, the exclusion of all of the younger children from the inheritance; they in turn were obliged to leave the house and become priests, or soldiers, or stay at home but remain bachelors and become virtual servants to the brother or sister who had inherited the name and the property. In short, what is perpetuated in these systems is not a family line but a name and a domain that is conserved through the families which become the successive owners.

Having come this far, since we live in Europe where the feudal aristocracies have been replaced by 'bourgeois' dynasties – rarely very old and always turning over – and the system of peasant 'houses' has become residual (livestock raising no longer having the same importance in the mountain economy or being done indoors, and the French government having outlawed primogeniture), I will say a few words about another system, which was much more prevalent in Europe than 'houses' and continues to exist in almost all strata of our societies: this is the system of 'kindreds'. Which brings us back to kinship.

Today's world is populated with millions of monogamous nuclear families, often reconstituted, following a divorce, on the part of one member of the couple if not both, and including the children of this previous marriage. These individuals' memories of their ascendants rarely go back beyond their grand-parents. And the vast majority of them have forgotten the existence and the names of their grandparents' collaterals, if they ever knew them. They may remember a few great uncles and great aunts and some of their descendants, distant cousins. Generally speaking these are descendants of their father's and mother's brothers and sisters, close cousins, whom one sees most often, as well as these cousins' married or unmarried children. This is on average the extent of the genealogical memory and knowledge of most members of Western Euro-pean societies and of those in the Americas who have European roots.

THE KINDRED

In this sea of nuclear families, where there is no general affiliation principle that might group them more or less mechanically into lineages and clans, there are nevertheless fuzzy collections of kin, whose existence is never guaranteed and whose longevity is always temporary. These groups are of two kinds and overlap in part.

The first is exclusively centred on an individual. This is what is called his or her 'kindred'.[19] The other kind is not centred on an individual but contains him or her. These are groups of families whose members are related to each other, and who see each other regularly and help each other; up to a certain point, they feel a bond of mutual solidarity. In so far as the family into which an individual is born (or adopted) is part of such a group, it can be said that this individual's belonging is initially automatic. He (or she) will be socialized in childhood, at the same time as his siblings, within a group of families and kin that will over-spill to a greater or lesser degree the bounds of the nuclear birth or adoptive family. In so far as these groups continue to exist, even if one or another of the individuals in them decides to break with his family or disappears, it can be said that they are decentred with respect to Ego and partially independent from Ego. They existed before Ego was born, but he determines whether they continue to exist through him. For an individual can decide to stop seeing certain relatives and their families, or vice versa certain relatives and their families can decide not to see Ego. In a word, the individual finds himself at the centre of a network of kin whom, depending on circumstances, he sees or ignores and who, for, the same reasons or others, see or ignore him.

A person's kindred is first of all a network of individuals who are either directly attached to him, and he is at the centre; or are related by ties that start or end with him. To the ascendants and descendants we must add Ego's brothers

---

19   See D. Freeman, 'On the Concept of Kindred', *Journal of the Royal Anthropological Institute*, vol. 91 (1961), pp. 192–220.

and sisters, who share the same ascendants, Ego's half-brothers and half-sisters, who share some of them, their spouses, brothers-in-law and Ego's nieces, etc. A person's kindred includes not only paternal and maternal kin in the direct and collateral lines, but also their close affines – and of course those of Ego if he or she is married.

A kindred is thus not a descent group, in the sense of a lineage or a clan; it is a collection of people related by various close or distant ties with whom Ego maintains relations and whom, for example, Ego will invite to his wedding or whose funeral he will attend; whereas he will ask only certain ones – a brother-in-law rather than a brother, a maternal uncle rather than his father – for help or advice in certain circumstances. Quite often, the ties with certain kinsmen fade even before these relatives die because they have moved away or their position or social class has changed thereby creating too much distance with respect to Ego, not because of their kin ties, which do not change, but because of their social success or comedown – or even decline (in the eyes of society and/or Ego).

But we must not forget that, in addition to Ego's kindred, there is another network, formed by his friends, some of whom are neighbours, others, more numerous, having become friends in other contexts – school, workplace, sports, etc. With his friends, the network of Ego's personal relations with a portion of society's members – people he will listen to or who will listen to him, people he will help or who will help him – expands.

Nevertheless, in Europe, as in America and Australia, with their myriads of families with short memories, there are a few who conserve (and even cultivate) the memory of ancestors going back several generations, of kin in the direct line but also collaterals. Without belonging to the European aristocracy, now of marginal social importance, these families carry a name that raises them above other families at the local, regional, national or even international level. This can be the name of an industrial dynasty, like the Schneiders in France, or a political dynasty, like the Kennedys or the Bushes in the United States. Because certain members of these families have made a name for themselves through various deeds whereby the family has gained exceptional prestige, their descendants are invited to preserve the memory of their ties with these famous ancestors.

The name becomes an immaterial shared asset that is usually unaccompanied by any other form of shared property – material or other – but which may be used by those who carry it as social capital. Moreover, it is in their interest to do so. Some even feel obliged to show themselves worthy of their name, either by doing as well as their illustrious ancestor in the same area or by excelling in others.

We thus see the spontaneous creation of cognatic pseudo-descent groups strongly skewed to the male line, which bring together all those who have inherited a name and pass it on to their children (men) or who carried the name in childhood but do not transmit it to their children (women) although they teach them that they have a stake in this name through their mother, and so on. Much less visible, and as though dotted, female lines thus grow up alongside the immediately visible male lines. Sometimes these groups, who keep their family tree up to date – including direct descendants and affines – hold family reunions, which everyone or almost everyone attends to get to know each other personally and count their members (like the Monods, whose reunions can number up to 700 persons from several countries in Europe). All that would need to happen is for these groups of families to own in common material wealth – land, factories, banks – or inherit political (or other) functions in order for genuine descent groups to come into being that would adopt rules for distributing the use of these resources among the families and for transmitting the task and honour of carrying out these functions to one or another of their number. It is clear, in this case, that the generalization of private, individual and family-held property, of the means of production and of money, make it difficult for descent groups to come into being, for they would tend to close ranks through the systematic application of a criterion of kinship (perhaps completed by other criteria allowing the inclusion or exclusion of certain types of kin).

Proof that this possibility once existed in Europe can be found by observing the customs of the inhabitants of Karpathos Island in the Aegean Sea. Until sometime in the 1920s, in order to avoid dividing the family assets, the rare farming lands and the houses, only first-born children married: the eldest son of one family with the eldest daughter of another.[20] The eldest children bore a name, Kanacares, which distinguished them from their younger siblings. The latter were obliged to emigrate or, if they stayed on, to serve their elder sibling after he or she married. The assets that formed the dowry of each of the spouses were again passed on to the next generation, to the eldest sons and daughters. These marriage rules ultimately ensured the circulation of land, houses and statuses in two parallel lines of descent and inheritance, one male and the other female. The system disappeared sometime between the two World Wars, when the value of land fell and money became the principal form of wealth: the younger siblings who had emigrated to the United States or Australia and had made money came home and were able to marry an eldest daughter. The old logic was broken and did not survive.[21] Today Karpathos has roughly the same matrimonial regime as the rest of Greece.

It must be stressed that kindred systems are not restricted to Europe. They are found in Borneo, among the Iban, where the kindred underpins the

---

20   See B. Vernier, *Frère et sœur. La genèse sociale des sentiments* (Paris, Editions de l'Ecole des Hautes Etudes en Sciences Sociales, 1991).

21   See our review of Bernard Vernier's book in *L'Homme*, no. 130 (1993), pp. 191–5.

organization of the 'long houses', the *Bilek*, described by Derek Freeman,[22] and in New Guinea among the Garia,[23] and so on.

And if we extend a person's kindred to all those individuals linked to him by cognatic ties, we will find ourselves in the Polynesian or Malagasy systems, where the kindred is a principle that works in tandem with the existence of cognatic descent groups. Taking yet another step, we will point out that the extended kindred, as the collection of Ego's cognates and affines, exists in all descent systems – unilineal, bilineal and non-lineal. But it is usually pushed into the background, placed in sleep mode, or completely masked by the interplay of rules that assigns an individual to a descent group that is not Ego-centered. The Nuer,[24] a society whose patrilineal system stresses agnatic kinship and lineages descending from a common ancestor, a relationship they designate by the term *buth*, use another word, *jimarida*, for Ego's kindred, that is to say not only paternal and maternal kin but also the affines of Ego's lineage.

The elegant table below, borrowed from Needham,[25] shows the various descent modes that have been discussed. The letters m and f stand for 'male' and 'female'.

$m \rightarrow m$	patrilineal	Nuer, Tallensi,[26] Turk,[27] Baruya, Juang, etc.
$f \rightarrow f$	matrilineal	Trobriand, Khasi, Iroquois, Ashanti, Nagovisi, Hopi, etc.
$[m \rightarrow m] + [f \rightarrow f]$	duolineal	Yako, Herrero, Kondaiyankottai Maravar
$[m \rightarrow f] + [f \rightarrow m]$	cross bilineal	Mundugumor
$[m \rightarrow m] + [f \rightarrow f]$	parallel bilineal	Orokolo, Omie, Apinaye
$mf \rightarrow mf$	non-lineal	Maori, Imerina,[28] Penan

The formula $mf \rightarrow mf$, when it does not function as a rule for constructing cognatic descent groups, as in Polynesia, also represents (European, Euro-American) kindred-based systems, which are cognatic as well but do not give rise to genuine long-lasting descent groups.

---

22   Freeman, 'On the Concept of Kindred'; see also J. Rousseau, *The Social Organization of the Baluy Rayan* (Cambridge, Cambridge University Press, 1973) and V. T. Ring (ed.), *Essays on Borneo Societies* (Oxford, Hull, 1978).

23   P. Lawrence, *The Garia* (Melbourne, Melbourne University Press, 1984).

24   E. E. Evans-Pritchard, *Kinship and Marriage among the Nuer* (Oxford, Clarendon Press, 1951), pp. 5–7.

25   R. Needham, *Rethinking Kinship and Marriage* (London, Tavistock Publications, 1971), p. 10. Cf. A. Barnard and A. Good, *Research Practices in the Study of Kinship* (London, Academic Press, 1984), pp. 70–1.

26   M. Fortes, *The Dynamics of Clanship among the Tallensi* (Oxford, Oxford University Press, 1945) and *The Web of Kinship among the Tallensi* (Oxford, Oxford University Press, 1949).

27   C. Delaney, *The Seed and the Soil: Gender and Cosmogony in a Turkish Village Society* (Berkeley, University of California Press, 1991).

28   On the Imerina, cf. A. Razafintsalama, *Les Tsimahafotsy d'Ambohimanga* (Paris, Selaf, 1984) and C. Vogel, *Les 'Quatres Mères' d'Ambohibaho* (Paris, Selaf, 1982).

DISTRIBUTION OF DESCENT MODES

Although we are far from having even a relatively complete inventory of the descent modes characteristic of the some 10,000 societies or local groups that currently exist on the face of the earth, taking our cue from the figures advanced by Roger Keesing,[29] we can suggest the following distribution:

Patrilineal	Matrilineal	Duo-bilineal	Cognatic
45%	12%	4%	39%

1. Patrilineal systems predominate in the Chinese zone, in India, in the expansion zone of Islam, in a portion of sub-Saharan Africa, in New Guinea and in numerous North and South American Indian groups.

2. Matrilineal systems are numerous in Central Africa (the 'matrilineal' belt of Africa), in part of North America, in eastern New Guinea and in the Solomon Islands, and in a few minorities of Southeast Asia or China.[30]

3. Duo- and bilineal systems are few and far between; we find them here and there in Africa, Asia and Oceania.[31]

4. Cognatic descent systems are plentiful in the expansion zone of Malayo-Polynesian-speaking societies, which stretches from Madagascar to Easter Island, by way of Taiwan, which is close to this expansion zone. Large numbers are also found in Amazonia.

5. Cognatic systems based on kindred prevail in Europe, in populations of European origin in North and South America, in Japan and in certain areas of Malaysia and Indonesia.

In the absence of a map of the world-distribution of these systems, it is evident that we cannot go very far toward finding correlations between the nature of these systems and other aspects of the culture and structures of their associated societies.

---

29   R. Keesing, *Kin Groups and Social Structure* (New York, Holt, Rinehart and Winston, 1975), pp. 134–5.
30   D. Schneider and K. Gough (eds.), *Matrilineal Kinship* (Berkeley, University of California Press, 1961). See E. Leach's review in, *American Journal of Sociology*, vol. 67, no. 6 (1962), pp. 705–7.
31   D. Forde, 'Double Descent among the Yako', in A. R. Radcliffe-Brown and D. Forde (eds.), *African Systems of Kinship and Marriage* (London, Oxford University Press, 1950), chap. 7.

I will complete this inventory by examining several theoretical problems raised by the analysis of these systems over the last decades.

Application of a descent rule, whether lineal or non-lineal, gives rise to groups of individuals of both sexes, in several successive generations, that have been dubbed 'lineages' and 'clans, in the case of uni-, duo- and bilineal systems, and 'branches' or 'demes' – terms unfamiliar to the public – sometimes used to designate cognatic descent groups. Whereas applying the descent rule in lineal and bilineal groups suffices to define and close the boundaries of the groups, in the case of undifferentiated, non-lineal groups, other principles are needed to define a descent group and give it boundaries (individuals having resided on an ancestral site for a long time, for instance).

CONCERNING THE IMAGINARY CHARACTER OF DESCENT PRINCIPLES

An initial remark is needed here to underscore the abstract, social, and in part imaginary character of these rules and therefore of the kinship relations they engender. To favour the relations that pass exclusively through the male or exclusively through the female line is to attribute a different social status to the two sexes by *overdetermining* one to the detriment of the other in the production of social ties between the generations and, in each generation, between the sexes. Even in cognatic systems, where the rule of gender equivalence ensures the transmission of descent and the continuity of the group, in certain contexts only the men or only the women, the eldest or the youngest, etc. are selected to transmit certain components of social life – titles, land, ritual functions – which are, at the same time, components of the kin group's identity and local conditions of the global reproduction of the society as a whole.

Later, we will discover another proof of the abstract, social character of kinship when we look at marriage systems and kinship terminologies that distinguish between parallel and cross cousins, two categories of individuals of both sexes whom we know (something we have learned recently) to stand at the same genetic and biological distance from Ego but whose social status is basically different and even opposed, since theoretically one may marry one's cross cousins but not one's parallel cousins, because the latter are assimilated to siblings. This remark poses the problem of the relationship between kinship and biology. But to tackle the question, we must start from a universal fact anyone, anthropologist or not, can see when travelling the world: there is no language that does not have a so-called kinship vocabulary. In all languages, whatever the society's descent and marriage rules, there are specific words to designate the positions and relationships of individuals of *both sexes* in at least five generations – two ascending and two descending generations starting with an individual (or a class of individuals in positions equivalent to that of Ego) characterized universally by his or her sex and by the place he or she occupies in his or her generation with respect to others of both sexes born before or after and connected to either the same 'relatives' or to the relatives of these relatives.

In short, all societies are concerned with organizing, on the one hand, the succession of generations – an obvious condition of their physical continuity – and, on the other hand, the relationships between persons of both sexes belonging to a certain number of successive generations (usually five). All cultures attribute meaning to these facts and to these relationships. All languages talk about them. *Individuals of both sexes belonging to different generations, which succeed each other and are linked to each other in the process of reproducing human life, as well as being linked by the place their society attributes to them in this process – these are, to my way of thinking, both the biological and the social underpinnings of kinship relations.* Kinship relations are therefore not just any kind of social relations. They are not, for example, relations springing from the desire on the part of a certain number of individuals or groups to create a hometown football club and who get together to bring it about, finance it, train local players or recruit outside players, and who fight to see their club rise higher and higher in the national and international tables.

Some anthropologists, like Mary Bouquet or Janet Carsten,[32] concerned with ridding the definition of kinship of any reference to the biological process of reproduction, devote considerable time to scrutinizing the word 'relative', which designates any kind of kin and comes from the verb 'to relate', in an attempt to discover the real meaning cleansed of any hint of biology and therefore of kinship. Of course all they found at the heart of the word was the formal notion of a 'tie' or 'link' between two components, henceforth connected by this tie, a notion that can apply to all manner of ties without permitting their distinction. For, as Holy reminds us,[33] one can be connected in a thousand social ways – people can be close friends, come from the same town or the same country, etc. – and to distinguish between these different types of relatedness we need to reintroduce contexts, specific contents that will allow us to distinguish, for example, the relatedness of friendship from the relatedness of ethnicity from the relatedness of citizenship. Eliminating all reference to the reproduction of life in analyzing the domain of kinship, and glossing the etymology and the semantic field of the word 'relative', do not lead to any positive deconstruction of kinship theories, but only to their dissolution in a sea of formal discourses that provide no hold on the realities.

---

32   M. Bouquet, *Reclaiming English Kinship: Portuguese Refractions on British Kinship Theory* (Manchester, Manchester University Press, 1993); J. Carsten, 'The Substance of Kinship and the Heat of the Earth: Feeding, Personhood and Relatedness among Malayo in Palau Lankaudi', *American Ethnologist*, no. 22 (1995), pp. 223–41.

33   L. Holy, *Anthropological Perspectives on Kinship* (London, Pluto Press, 1996).

In reality it is impossible to grasp the domain of kinship relations if one completely separates kinship relations between the sexes from the reproduction of life. The recent appearance in Western Europe and North America of same-sex families, and the legal and ethical debates this continues to arouse, will not contradict us here. For with the appearance of gay or lesbian couples the question is still one of gender, and, with the adoption of children or insemination, it is very much that of the transformation of a couple into a family. Sex, gender, couple and family: we are once more immersed in the universe of kinship.

It is impossible deliberately to disregard, even more so to deny, that – whatever role a society assigns to the man or the woman in making babies, whatever the rule followed by this society to determine who the child will belong to after birth, what groups of adults will have rights and duties with regard to the child (which are liable not to be identical for the father's or fathers' and the mother's or mothers' sides) – in all known societies there are rules (associated with representations and value judgements) that define the conditions under which unions between individuals of the opposite sex (and today of the same sex) will be socially recognized and which set out in advance the social identity of any children that may be attributed to these couples either by birth, by adoption (with or without insemination) or by other means. And it is by putting these rules into practice – or into action if one prefers – that people produce, between themselves and between the social groups to which they belong by birth (families, houses, clans, lineages, etc.), the *specific* social relations that are precisely kinship relations. This is true of all known kinship systems, including that of the Na of Yunnan, where the unions between a woman and the men who visit her at night (or a man and the women he visits at night) almost never result in a 'marriage' and therefore in an 'alliance' between two kin groups, two houses. For in this case, too, the union of the sexes and the status of the children are defined by society, since the sexual permissiveness of the adults is countered by a total taboo on sexual relations within the houses; and within the resident matriline, there is a taboo, on pain of death, on sexual relations between a brother and his sisters, an uncle and his nieces, an aunt and her nephews, and of course between a mother and her sons. The children born of the men's nocturnal visits to other houses belong exclusively to their mother's house and are raised by all of the members – male and female – of their matriline.

It must also be recalled that all societies, even though they may believe that certain births are not the result of a union between a man and a woman but stem from the union of a woman with a spirit or a god, recognize that there is a connection between sexual intercourse between two people of opposite sex and the birth of a new human being. Nevertheless, recognizing this does not necessarily mean that the man and the woman who unite are perceived as the genitors of the children born to them. In many matrilineal societies, for example, the 'father', in other words the mother's 'husband', is not recognized as being the 'genitor' of the children his wife bears. In the Trobriand Islands, as we will see, a woman is not pregnant because she has been fertilized by her husband's sperm. She becomes pregnant when the spirit of a male or a female ancestor of her clan wishes to come back to live with his or her people and leaves Tama, the island of the dead, in the form of a spirit-child who floats over the water to Kiriwina and enters the woman's body. The spirit-child then mingles with the woman's menstrual blood, which coagulates and becomes a foetus. When the woman tells her husband she is pregnant, he multiplies his sexual relations with her to nourish the foetus in her womb and shape it to resemble him. The patrilineal Baruya do not consider the woman to be the genetrix of her children. It is the man who makes the foetus in her womb from his sperm, and it is the Sun that makes the foetus into a human child. The woman's womb is a 'netbag' where the actions of the husband and the Sun, the child's only genitors, work together.

In short, in the Trobriand Islands as among the Baruya, people are perfectly capable of detailing their genealogy over several generations – moreover they have numerous reasons to keep it in mind. But reconstructing their genealogy with them by no means implies, as Schneider claims, that the anthropologist projects Western cultural presuppositions onto the ties being described, namely: that through sexual intercourse a man and a woman become the genitors of the children that will be born to their couple, that children are of the 'same blood' as their parents, that 'blood is thicker than water' and so on. If a married Trobriander is not the genitor of his children, who in all events will not belong to his clan but to that of their mother and their mother's brother, he is therefore not a 'father' in the Western sense of the term; and nothing obliges an anthropologist from the West to project his own cultural representations when he asks people he knows to tell them their genealogy. In fact he is prevented from doing so by what he knows of their culture. The Trobriand example is a particularly convincing demonstration. How can one project the Western notion of consanguinity onto a society where, as Annette Weiner showed much more clearly than Malinowski had a half century earlier, the blood (*dala*) that flows in the veins of all members of a clan is always the 'same' blood, which comes from the blood of the founding ancestress of the clan who one day emerged, alone or with a brother, from a hole in the ground? And the very word that designates that blood also means 'clan', since every child that comes out of a woman's womb is made from its mother's menstrual blood, which the spirit of a clan ancestor in search of reincarnation came to coagulate and inhabit.

Let us travel back, to the Classical China of the Chu. At this time, society was ruled by a warrior nobility, by kings, princes and dukes organized into big patrilineal clans (*tsu*). These clans encompassed all descendants of a common ancestor, with whom they shared not the same blood but the same breath (ch'i). This breath bound them together into a community of feeling (kan-tung), which they shared with the ancestor from whom they were never separated and whom they regularly worshipped at his tomb (tsung). Even if their bodies were separate, the breath that gave life to a father and his sons, and to the sons together, was always the same breath. The Chinese notion of agnation thus has nothing to do with the idea of 'one blood', which the West inherited from the Romans. We also see why the terms used to designate the elder lineages (ta-tsung) or the younger lineages (hsiao-tsung) that make up a clan are constructed with reference to the descendants' obligation to make offerings on the ancestor's tomb (tsung) and to venerate him down through the generations.[34] This viewpoint ignores the woman's reproductive capacities. Life here can be perpetuated and extended only through the breath (ch'i) that dwells in men.

The examples of the Trobriand Islanders and of the ancient Chinese nobility point up another aspect of kinship relations. If, in the Trobriand Islands, it is the same blood that unites a mother and her children, brothers and sisters, uncles and aunts on the mother's side to their nephews and nieces, and connects them all to the founding clan ancestress, and if, in Chu China, it is the same breath that unites a father and his sons and brothers, and connects them to the founding clan ancestor who has a separate body but the same breath, it means that the birth of a child in each of these societies is the result of a gift of essential vital principles stemming from invisible but ever-present and ever-acting ancestors who are transferred to the new human being taking shape through the agency of either men (the fathers) or women (the mothers). We must therefore take careful note that these vital principles are not made by these fathers or mothers, who are merely the chosen, favoured vehicles of their transmission. What is essential is that individuals think of themselves and experience themselves as not separated by part of themselves from certain ancestors.

But there is nothing exceptional about these examples. They simply place us in a particularly clear manner in the presence of the fact that, in all known societies, the making and birth of a baby are the outcome of a series of gifts that human beings, but also ancestors, spirits or gods, have made in order to assemble and unify the components of a new human being. Whether these components appear in the form of what we in the West call bodily substances (blood, bones, flesh, etc.) or of less visible realities (breath, soul, spirit – which, moreover, many societies do not see as totally immaterial realities, since souls are liable to reappear after death), for the child all of these are gifts that beings, which can be human and/or non-human, close or remote, have made so that it can be born.

---

34   See the remarkable article by A. J. Chun, 'Conceptions of Kinship and Kingship in Classical Chou China', Toung Pao, vol. 76, nos 1–3 (1990), pp. 16–48.

For a child (and for its parents) this has two consequences, which take various forms depending on the society. The child will be led to conceive of himself (or herself) (and even to feel) as being identical to or resembling all those of whom he (or she) will learn that he shares some component of his being, by virtue of which he is 'the same' as they. Hence the community of breath and feeling invoked by ancient Chinese authors. Second, as soon as adults have taught the child that he owes his existence and the elements of his being to a certain number of visible or invisible human and non-human donors who have made him what he is, the child will find himself indebted to them for his life and therefore under obligation.

But this feeling of obligation can die out or be called into question if the individual discovers or imagines that the human or non-human beings to whom he believes he owes his birth and being do not act as they should toward him; furthermore there often exists the idea that a child's 'real' parents are not the people who gave birth to him but those who raised him and behaved toward him *as parents should*. One must also be careful about thinking that in all societies a person's identity is constructed from what they received from others at birth. Most societies consider that a person's identity is constructed over their lifetime, both by what they receive from others and which becomes incorporated in them and by what detaches itself from them and becomes incorporated in others. Some societies even consider that what one receives from others after birth counts as much, if not more, in creating kinship ties between oneself and others as what one received from one's parents at birth. This is the case for the Baining of New Britain.[35] As the Anglo-Saxons say, *nurture* is often stronger than *nature*.[36]

In reality, the ancestors' strength and identity are not always transmitted solely through blood, breath, sperm or the soul, which borrow the medium of sexual relations in order to mingle and act. In numerous Melanesian societies, the ancestors and their powers are present in the ground they cleared. It was their flesh that fattened the land, their bones placed in trees that attract game and keep away evil spirits. These beliefs and rites explain why an adopted lost child or an outsider taken in after an unfortunate war can gradually become a relative who can legitimately claim the same ancestors. By working the same land year after year, by sharing and eating the same products of this land impregnated with the ancestors' subsistence and presence, the outsider acquires a new body and with it a new social identity. He becomes one more descendant

---

35   J. Fajans, *They Make Themselves: Work and Play among the Baining of Papua New Guinea* (Chicago and London, University of Chicago Press, 1997).

36   This is the case of the Sulka of New Britain. Cf. M. Jeudy-Ballini, 'Naître par le sang, renaître par la nourriture', in A. Fine (ed.), *Adoptions; ethnologie des parentés choisies* (Paris, Editions de la Maison des Sciences de l'Homme, 1998), pp. 19–44.

of the ancestors of the clan that took him in, a descendant whose identity was not transmitted to him through sexual intercourse, a descendant without gene-alogical ties, direct or indirect, with the other members of his clan.

And yet his age, his sex, the position he will occupy in the kin network of those who took him in and fed him will make the outsider a kinsman – a son for some, an uncle or a younger brother for others, a brother-in-law, and so on. In a word, the kin terms used by others to designate or address him, and to which he responds using the appropriate terms, act in his case as categories devoid of genealogical content but which nevertheless assign him a symbolic genealogical position in the pre-existing network of kin ties between the members of the society that is now his. What is exceptional in this case – the fact that an indi-vidual finds himself related to others without having any genealogical connection with them – is frequent in societies divided into sections (or matri-monial classes), as are a large number of Australian and a few Amazonian societies (the Pano, for example). Belonging by birth or adoption to a particular section gives an individual specific kin ties with all other members of his society, whether they belong to his section or to the three others and even though he has no genealogical ties with most of them.

Let us take a simple example. Imagine a society divided into four sections, of the so-called Kareira type. A man born to section A must marry a woman from section B, and his sister will marry a man from section B. The children of the couple AB belong to section C. The children will in turn marry members of section D, and their children will belong to section A, like their grandfather. For a man from A, all women in B are potential wives, whereas only a few of them will actually be. All children born to women in section B will be A's sons and daughters, whereas he is not their father. We thus see that, in this system, kinship relations coincide only partially with real genealogical ties. But we also see that this does not imply that kinship relations are purely abstract social rela-tionships that have nothing to do with sexuality and the reproduction of life. In reality, kinship relations, in so far as their abstract categorial content is concerned, are structured by a double reference: descent rules and alliance rules, which back onto the prohibition of incest between members of the same section, and the roles played by the men and women of each section in the initiation ceremonies and the rites ensuring the reproduction of plants and animals, and human beings.[37]

It is because kinship relations refer to ties between individuals who provide or have provided members of the new generation with the components of their life, in other words of their physical existence and/or their social identity as new

37   L. Dousset, 'Production et reproduction en Australie. Pour un tableau de l'unité des tribus australiennes', *Social Anthropology*, vol. 4, no. 3 (1996), pp. 281–98.

human beings, and because the individuals have neither negotiated nor produced these components themselves but have received them as a gift, that these ties constitute a separate domain. This domain is initially dominated by the values of gift and debt, by the existence of rights that have not been acquired by the individual himself but with which he finds himself vested by virtue of relations with certain other individuals who appear as his father(s) and mother(s), his brothers or his sisters, his cousins or his affines, and so on. For, in most societies, there is no such thing as descent without alliance, and the exercise of kinship consists in transforming affines into consanguines and ensuring that, after a certain lapse of time, distant consanguines become potential affines.

In short, kinship ties, whether with descendants or with affines, are inseparable from the relations humans must produce with each other so that new generations of men and women may come into being and human life go on, which by no means implies that humans think they are the only ones involved. But I already hear the objections of those who claim that kinship is a purely social relationship, that there is nothing in its content that refers to sex or gender and to the biological process of reproducing life. Every anthropologist faces these objections and must address them.

PARENTS BY ADOPTION

Let us therefore take the case of adoption, that is, of the creation of a non-engendered line of descent. First of all we must distinguish between adoption and fosterage.

Adoption implies the definitive replacement of the ascendants by the adopting parents. Fosterage is merely the momentary replacement of the ascendants by designated guardians. Adoption entails a change of identity for the child, whether this is deep-seated or not. Fosterage offers a means of preserving the child's identity and social status.[38]

It is readily understandable that not just anyone can give his or her child up for adoption, and not just anyone can adopt a child. In ancient Rome, a woman could not adopt a child. Only a male Roman citizen could. But a man was not allowed to adopt a man older than he. There had to be a sufficient age difference, according to 'nature', that is to say, which corresponded to the average age at which a man is able to engender children. And yet in Rome eunuchs and men recognized as being impotent could adopt. In the Middle Ages, eunuchs could not legally adopt a child, while the adopter had to be older than the adoptee by

---

38   Cf. S. Lallemand, 'Adoption, fosterage et alliance', *Anthropologie et sociétés*, vol. 12, no. 2 (1988), pp. 25–40.

a margin that imitated nature. Even in the legal fictions of Antiquity and the Middle Ages, then, where adoption is conceived of as an abstract and not a biological filiation, the reference to engendering and biological filiation is present.[39]

Adoption,[40] when not practised between two sisters, as in Polynesia where two sisters give each other children who were therefore already related to their new parents, makes children (and sometimes even adults, as in Rome) from outside the family into descendants who theoretically enjoy the same attention, the same rights as the other children (if they exist) engendered by the adoptive parents. More generally, adopted children are supposed to enjoy the same status as non-adopted children. So we see that the standard status accorded adopted children does not result from adoption itself but from the rules of conduct set out by the society in question for dealing with *non-adopted* children.

Moreover, unless they appeared by magic, adopted children were themselves engendered and, even if their social parents are absent, they still had genitors. All societies have various reasons for allowing or forbidding the transfer of children between adults and between social groups. And, in most cases, kinship by adoption is a complementary, second kinship. Nevertheless there are extreme cases in which adoption appears as a plus with respect to kinship by filiation, as among the Mbaya-Guaycuru, cited by Lévi-Strauss in *Tristes Tropiques.*

It was a society remarkably adverse to feelings that we consider as being natural. For instance, there was a strong dislike for procreation. Abortion and infanticide were almost the normal practice, so much so that perpetuation of the group was ensured by adoption rather than by breeding, and one of the chief aims of the warriors' expeditions was the obtaining of children. It was estimated at the beginning of the nineteenth century, that barely 10 percent of the members of a certain Guaycuru group belonged to the original stock.[41]

When children were born and survived, they were not brought up by their parents but entrusted to another family, and visited only at rare intervals.[42]

39   Cf. Y. Thomas, 'Les Artifices de la vérité', *L'Inactuel*, no. 6 (1996), pp. 81–96 and 'Le 'ventre', corps maternel, droit paternel', *Le Genre humain*, vol. 14 (1986), pp. 211–36; F. Girard, *Manuel élémentaire de droit romain* (Paris, Librairie Rousseau, 1918), pp. 173–85.

40   In Malaysia as in Polynesia, adoption plays an important role. See J. Massard, 'Engendrer ou adopter: deux visions concurrentes de la parenté chez les Malais péninsulaires', *Anthropologie et sociétés*, vol. 12, no. 2 (1988), pp. 41–62. For Europe, see A. Fine, 'Adoption et parrainage dans l'Europe ancienne', in M. Corbier (ed.), *Adoption et fosterage* (Paris, De Boccard, 1999), pp. 349–54.

41   C. Lévi-Strauss, *Tristes Tropiques* (Paris, Plon, 1955, 1993), p. 206; English translation: *Tristes Tropiques*, translated by John and Doreen Weightman (Penguin books), pp. 181–2.

42   Lévi-Strauss, *Tristes Tropiques*, English translation p. 192.

Without going to this extreme, other societies testify to the importance that may be given to the adoption of captives. Such is the case of the Txicao of central Brazil studied by Patrick Menget.[43] The Txicao are slash-and-burn agriculturalists, hunters and fishers who today live on the left bank of the Xingu River. Their social organization is based on a system of cognatic kindreds organized around uxorilocal residence. The Txicao practise two forms of adoption, one within the group and the other resulting from the capture of enemy children. The term for internal adoption is *anumtxi*, which means to 'lift up'. The usual reason for adopting a child is the death of its mother. The child is then entrusted to one of its classificatory mothers to be raised. This form of adoption never gives rise to the definitive rupture of kinship relations with the paternal and maternal kin. The child enjoys all of these relationships concurrently. Another reason for adoption is the woman's sterility. In this case, her husband's brother or one of his sisters gives a child who will be adopted when it is weaned. This kin tie is not a substitute for filiation but rather a complement.

The adoption of a captured child is entirely another matter. To understand this practice, it must be seen in its cultural context. For the Txicao, death is not a natural occurrence but the effect of another's malice. Following a series of deaths in a village, for instance, the villagers would organize a raid to punish the enemy group they suspected of causing these deaths by means of sorcery. The aim was both to punish these enemies by killing some of their numbers and to capture children to replace the dead Txicao. The adult prisoners were killed on the spot and their bodies used to make a series of trophies, which the warriors displayed upon returning to celebrate their victory.

The status of captured children was complex and they held both a central and an ambiguous position in Txicao social organization. The captured child is called an *egu*, a term that designates at the same time trophies taken from enemy corpses, house pets, the bamboo horns played at initiations or any member of an animal species as it relates to the spirit master of its species. The child's education follows two rules: to root out the child's ethnic origins by making fun of them and to reward the acquisition of Txicao qualities. Gradually, as the alien child acquired more and more Txicao features, he becomes a source of pride for his adoptive kin. As Patrick Menget writes, it is as though the adopted child became a superlative child, adding something to the group's identity. When the adopted child grows up he or she becomes a favoured sexual partner for the Txicao, and as such the object of rivalries. Nevertheless, the union between a Txicao man and an adopted women is never a marriage in the strict sense of the term. The word used to designate this woman is still that used for family pets.

43   P. Menget, 'Note sur l'adoption chez les Txicao du Brésil central', *Anthropologie et sociétés*, vol. 12, no. 2 (1988), pp. 63–72.

But at the same time, captives are considered to be the principal source of proper names for the Txicao, and they thus contribute something of their alien identity to making new Txicao. This practice corresponds to the logic shared by many Amazonian societies, which are constantly on the lookout for elements in outsiders that could be used to constitute themselves, whether in the form of another's flesh (cannibalism), symbolic components (trophies), disembodied entities (spirits of the dead) or finally identities connected with names. But the ambiguous status of the adopted prisoner, who is both more and less than a Txicao, shows that the ultimate reference is still that of the native-born Txicao.

Another, this time more serious, objection: there are a number of kinship systems, the Australian section systems, for instance, in which individuals from different sections are, with respect to each other, as fathers, sons, husbands or wives, without being linked, for the most part, by any real genealogical tie or alliance. Yet an individual will call the child of a woman, of a 'wife' whom he has never married, 'son' or 'daughter'. This is an example of the 'categorial' character of many kin terms and explains the fact that individuals who do not stand in the same genealogical relation to Ego are classified under the same term (the term 'cousin', for example, designates both the son of a paternal uncle or a maternal aunt) and who may even not have any genealogical tie whatsoever with Ego.

We will deal later with this problem, which has continually enflamed debates between the partisans of the two opposing theses. For one side, from Malinowski to Scheffler by way of Murdock, these categorial terms result from the extension of the kin terms used to address the father, the mother, the brothers and the sisters who live alongside the child or to refer to them beyond the nuclear family circle (where children worldwide are supposed to be born and live their early childhood). According to this theory, there is a shift from the real father to the metaphorical fathers (the father's brothers, who also are 'fathers') and from the primary relationships within the nuclear family to the secondary relationships created by the extension of the genealogical links between individuals and between their generations. For the other side, from Hocart to Leach and Dumont, this categorial classification is neither secondary nor derived from a genealogical classification but exists in and of itself, the class of 'fathers' being made up of a number of men in an equivalent relation to Ego one of whom is the mother's husband. It is therefore not by extending the notion of father but by reducing the class to a single individual that one obtains the genealogical father. Extension? Reduction? We favour the reduction thesis, and this is because of the very argument Lounsbury and Scheffler use to combat it.

For what matters are the social values and statuses a society attaches to the fact of being a father, a son, etc., whether we are dealing with a classificatory or with a 'genealogical' father or mother. What matters are the attitudes, obligations and rights that the recognition of these relationships entails for the individual. And the more essential or vital components of their 'flesh-and-blood' existence or their social identity these relations appear to contribute or to have contributed, the stronger the bonds between the individuals.

We would like to show here that the quarrel between partisans of an exclusively genealogical (and in the last analysis biological) theory of kinship and those of a purely social theory (which in the last analysis excludes any reference to genealogical and biological ties) fuels a false debate based – on both sides – in part on real facts but used to ask bad questions. Whatever they may think, both sides have to explain what a father is and what is expected of fathers (or mothers, etc.) in a given culture and in a given kinship system. In each case they are confronted with the various ways societies have come up with to think and regulate the process of reproducing life, which means organizing the succession of the generations and the appropriation of the children born in each through the individuals of both sexes who claim to be their parents.

In short, the quarrel between extensionists and reductionists in no way calls the definition of kinship into question. Both sides miss the point. For however you become a relative – by birth or by adoption, by eating the same food or by living on the same piece of land, etc. – once you are, you have to behave like a member of the family, that is, treat the other members as though they had given you certain pieces of themselves – their blood or their sperm, their breath or their name, their spirit – elements that helped give you life and a social identity and which became part of you and which you can give in turn, can detach from yourself and give to others, who will in turn exist partly thanks to you.

Of course, as we will see later, these representations of the components (sperm, blood, breath, etc.) that are believed to pass from one individual to another and from one generation to the next are partly fictitious, and a society's ethnobiological conceptions are not a matter of biology but of ideology. But beforehand, to show those features of kinship that cannot be explained by biology or ethnobiology, let us recall that it is not the biological ties that explain that two related individuals will (or will not) share the same residence, own (or not own) land together, intervene on the same side or on the other side of a political conflict: all these social behaviours are connected with kinship relations and mean that these are also social relations which can in no way be reduced to biological facts (even though kinship relations are largely underpinned by biology).

Whatever the role each culture ascribes to the man, the woman, the ancestors and the gods in making children, kinship relations attach divers social realities to the relationships that grow up between individuals owing to their (real or fictive) place in the reproduction process according to their sex and generation. Sex and sexuality are at the heart of kinship. And the fact that the taboo on incest, which concerns the exercise of sexuality, is a universal condition[44] for the reproduction of kinship relations is a constant reminder of their existence and importance.

This detour having been completed, we can now resume our study of descent groups. To simplify the task, we will limit ourselves to groups, lineages and clans resulting from the application of a unilineal descent rule. These social groups are constructed with reference to ancestors, and therefore to a memory, and are based on a criterion that selects from among all the descendants of these *male and female* ancestors who share an identity those men and women who transmit it. This criterion can be the fact of coming from the same sperm (Baruya), from the same blood (Trobrianders) or from the same breath (Chinese). In most cases memory of the founding ancestors does not go back more than four or five generations. And if the name of the lineage founder is usually known by his descendants, the name of the most remote ancestor, from whom all of a clan's lineages are believed to descend, is either unknown, legendary or mythic (a supernatural being). But even if the name is unknown, the existence of real ties between the lineage ancestor and the clan ancestor is posited. In some societies – Mandarin China as well as the aristocratic families of Tonga – a written record (ancestor tablets) or an oral account (recitation of genealogies) traces the ancestors back fifteen or more generations. Because they share the same ancestors and the same bodily and social identity, together the members of a lineage make up a sort of collective individual, a 'corporate group', as Meyer Fortes called it,[45] following Maine[46] and Max Weber,[47] that is supposed to act as a single individual, which never dies, not only because its members are replaced by other members but because they own land, titles and rights, all of which must be kept and transmitted intact to the following generations.

We came across analogous phenomena when describing the 'house' system. Let us pause for a moment and examine the fact that all members of a lineage are seen as coming from the same sperm (the patrilineal Baruya) or from the

---

44   For the moment we will leave aside sister–brother marriages in the royal families of certain Polynesian chiefdoms, among the Inca, in ancient Iran, among the Lovedu of Africa and, of course, in the case of the Egyptian pharaohs. However in Iran and in ancient Egypt, marriages between brother and sister were frequent in other levels of society (see Chapter 13). For the Lovedu, see E. J. and J. D. Krige, *The Realm of the Rain Queen* (London, Oxford University Press, 1943).

45   M. Fortes, *Kinship and the Social Order: The Legacy of L. H. Morgan* (London, Routledge and Kegan Paul, 1969), pp. 74–5, 108, 294–302.

46   Sir H. Maine, *Ancient Law* (London, Murray, 1861), pp. 122–3, 181.

47   M. Weber, *The Theory of Economic and Social Organization* (New York, Free Press, 1947), pp. 146–50. In Weber the term *Verband* includes the notion of 'corporate group'.

blood of the same ancestress (the matrilineal Ashanti or Trobrianders). This blood, which is the same from one generation to the next and is transmitted solely by the women, is not a biological reality. It is a fiction. The concept does not stem from empirical knowledge about the body. It is a representation that makes it possible to *exclude* certain individuals (who are kin) from the formation and reproduction of the kin groups – lineages, clans – that as collective rights-holders play a role in reproducing the society as a whole. Blood is not merely a concept that makes it possible to determine the internal composition of a lineage and its boundaries, it is also a criterion that *legitimizes* this exclusion by referring to the presence of a vital component of a person's identity, which some possess and others do not. Furthermore, it is a component that only some of those who possess it (women in the case of matrilineal systems) have the capacity to transmit to the next generation. A lineage, a matrilineal clan in the Trobriand Islands, thus appears as a kin group built on a twofold fiction – namely that blood is constitutive of an individual's identity, it is his or her essential substance which only women can transmit, and therefore that the blood of all of the members of the matrilineage, men and women alike, is *female* blood.

'Blood' is therefore not simply the mental representation of an imaginary identity projected onto concrete individuals, it is a concept that gives social meaning to a vital, concrete component of these individuals, an element of their body which connects them simultaneously with their ancestors who made them this gift and to all those who received it in common. At the same time as their life and their identity, members of a lineage also receive the use, to be transmitted to the following generations, of lands, titles and functions, all of which are also gifts from the ancestors and remain the joint property of the group for as long as it exists.

KINSHIP BISECTED

It was on the basis of such facts, and using almost exclusively examples from Africa, that Meyer Fortes[48] proposed to distinguish between two components of unilineal descent-group structure, one juridical-political and the other domestic. The first would correspond to the lineage and the clan, as the collective owner of the land and other means of production as well as of the political-ritual functions that give this corporate group a rank and an influence in reproducing the society (cf. the eight matrilineal clans of the Ashanti 'kingdom'); the second would correspond to each of the families of the married members of the different lineages. In the matrilineal Ashanti society, married men live with their wives during the day, but in the evening they go home to

---

48   Fortes, *Kinship and the Social Order*, chaps. 7 and 8, pp. 101–37.

their sisters and their mother, who live together under the authority of the oldest women of the matriline. The family is the unit in charge of bringing up the children. But it is also a unit of production and consumption. The relationships between individuals within the family are relations of bilateral filiation, but they are cross cut and marked by the matrilineal descent principle, which stipulates that a man does not transmit his goods or his functions to his own children but to those of his sister, and that his own children will inherit from their maternal uncle, their mother's brother.

To account for the close ties between children in this matrilineal system and their father and the members of his lineage, Fortes proposed the notion of 'complementary filiation'.[49] He was strongly criticized by Leach, who felt that the notion concealed or reduced to purely personal and domestic ties between children, on the one hand, their father's clan and family and, on the other hand, the relations of affinity between two lineages and two clans. As proof of the importance of the father and his lineage in the constitution of the Ashanti person, he cited the fact that, while all members of a matrilineage share the same maternal ancestral blood, called *abusua*, every child receives from its father and his lineage the spirit (*atore*) that animates his or her body.[50] Leach's criticism seems to me altogether founded.

But coming back to the distinction between the two spheres – juridical and domestic – that Fortes saw as being combined in kinship, Fortes has also been criticized for having projected a Western perspective onto the Ashanti and the Tallensi in so far as, until recently in the West, the political-juridical sphere was considered to be the preserve of men and the domestic sphere the preserve of women. In many societies however, there is no such clear-cut separation between these domains. For example, women, in their capacity as sisters, may actively participate in managing the patrimony shared by their lineage. Annette Weiner, discussing gender relations in Trobriand society, showed the essential role played by women as sisters of the deceased in the funeral rites, which are extremely important in this part of New Guinea. During these ceremonies, the sisters redistribute large quantities of female wealth in order to restore to their lineage's patrimony the elements their brother had dispersed over his lifetime by making gifts, for example, to his sons, who in virtue of the matrilineal descent role do not belong to the same *dala*, the same 'blood', the same lineage as their

49   M. Fortes, 'The "Submerged Descent Line" in Ashanti', in I. Shapera (ed.), *Studies in Kinship and Marriage* (London, Royal Anthropology Institute of Great Britain, 1963) and 'Descent, Filiation and Affinity: A Rejoinder to Dr Leach', *Man*, vol. 59, no. 309 (1959), pp. 193–7 and vol. 59, no. 331, pp. 206–12; E. Leach, 'Descent, Filiation and Affinity', *Man*, vol. 60 (January 1960), pp. 9–10 and *Rethinking Anthropology* (London, University of London/Athlone Press, 1961), chap. 1.

50   Cf. M. Fortes, 'Kinship and Marriage among the Ashanti', in A. R. Radcliffe-Brown and D. Forde (eds.), *African Systems of Kinship and Marriage* (London, Oxford University Press, 1950), chap. 6.

father. The gifts presented by his sisters also make it possible to consolidate alliances threatened with extinction by this death. These facts had been ignored or perhaps deemed to be of little interest by Malinowski, which explains the charges of androcentrism Annette Weiner addressed to his work.

But it is not only in matrilineal societies that women in their role as sisters play an important part in managing lineage or clan resources and wealth. Among the Kako of Gabon, an agriculturalist–hunter-gatherer society with an Omaha-type patrilineal kinship system, the eldest sister of the head of the lineage, who is married in another lineage, intervenes throughout her life in her brothers' management of lineage goods. She performs the rites that will ensure him success in hunting and war, but also abundant harvests. She has authority over his wife and can, by magical means, make her fertile or barren, thus depriving her brother of children. In short, although she left her original lineage when she married, she continues throughout her life to play a key role enjoyed by neither her brothers' nor her nephew's wives.

In Polynesia – Tonga but also Samoa – women as *sisters* rank socially *higher* than all their brothers, including their older brothers. They are in fact regarded as being closer to the ancestors and the gods, and play an essential role in the funeral rites. In Tonga, the most sacred, highest ranking person is not the Tu'i Tonga, but his sister, the Tu'i Tonga Fafine, to whom her brother, after having received the first fruits of the harvests from all the *kainga* (descent groups) in his kingdom, presents the best fruits together with other gifts, always of the finest quality. In short, we must not generalize a simplistic conception of gender relations and the possible forms and contents of male domination.

Another aspect of Fortes' distinction calls for discussion as well: what did he mean by the political-juridical sphere within kinship relations? If one means the existence of relations of authority and responsibility within the kin group, lineage or clan, and the fact that the same persons represent the entire group to the rest of society, that they affirm and defend its rights in pieces of land, persons and functions, then we have only part of the political-juridical – or better, political-religious – relations that bring a society to exist as a whole, even if there is no *central power* capable of submitting the reproduction of the society as a whole to its will and power. We have seen this in Baruya society. Each lineage has collective rights in hunting territories, rivers and arable land. The lineage elders manage their distribution and use, and all male members of the lineage take up arms and call on their affines to defend their resources against those who, for instance, have cleared a garden in their forest without permission. But political-religious relations always extend beyond kinship relations and kin groups.

For example, each Baruya clan plays a specific role in the initiation rituals, and it takes the ritual and material cooperation of all clans to make a new generation of warriors that will defend not only their clan lands but the entire tribal territory. Or to take another example from ancient Rome, the *pater familias* at the head of his *gens* (a patrilineal descent group) had the right of life and death over his children and over the other members of the *gens*. He managed its resources. But he and his *gens* occupied particular positions in Rome's political system. They belonged to the senatorial families or to the *equites* (knights). They were able to accede to or were excluded from given functions in the city. But all sons born to freemen, once accepted by their father and presented to the city magistrates, became Roman citizens (*civis romanus*) and enjoyed life-long privileges attached to this status wherever Rome exercised its power and its dominion.

In short, even in 'segmentary' tribal societies like the Nuer and the Bedouins, political relations are not to be confused with the relations of power or solidarity that spring up between clans or lineages in times of conflict. The well-known Arab saying, 'Me against my brother; my brother and I against my cousins; I, my brother and my cousins against the world', is not the last word on political relations in these societies. For even in the event of a scission between the kin groups that make up a tribe or a tribal confederation, the seceding groups associate with others, and the broadest resulting social group once again takes the overall form of a tribe. Furthermore, the Arab proverb is not universally valid. When a conflict arises between two Baruya lineages both of which have given wives to a third lineage (and have received wives in return), the third lineage splits into two groups, each of which goes to the aid of one of the feuding lineages. This practice can be seen as revealing of a concern to balance forces and avoid one of the lineages undergoing such a defeat that it is for all practical purposes doomed to disappear or to abandon its lands and seek asylum in a neighbouring tribe. But it is also the outcome of a marriage rule that obliges brothers to marry into different lineages and is the concrete proof that solidarity between members of a same lineage, of a same blood, comes second to each man's solidarity with the lineage that gave him a wife. In this case marriage alliance plays a direct role in the way the descent reckoning operates. This is perhaps because marriage is based on the direct exchange between two men and two lineages of one of their sisters (or for fathers, of one of their daughters). The marriage alliance does not have the same importance when there is no direct exchange of women and a lineage exchanges wives for bridewealth, which used to be the most prevalent practice in Africa, but also in Asia and certain parts of Oceania.

These facts hardly concord with Fortes' theoretical position on kinship. For above and beyond the question of the division of kinship into two domains, or the distinction between descent and complementary filiation, Fortes is probably the most eminent representative of those theoreticians of kinship for whom the essence of kinship resides in descent and not in alliance. He repeatedly declared that he was drawn to the study of institutions that were indispensable for ensuring the temporal continuity without which there can be no enduring society, and for this process to continue, he stressed, institutional forms of alliance are not essential.[51] This places him in direct opposition to Lévi-Strauss, for whom kinship is first and foremost alliance. For Fortes, however, 'the ways in which the reproductive cohabitation of men and women is regulated are of secondary concern'.[52]

Let us return to the problem of descent groups that persist over many generations. We have remarked on the very small number of rules used to generate these groups and which operate by manipulating the difference between the sexes (unilineal, duo- and bilineal systems) or by cancelling this difference (undifferentiated systems). Why have some societies chosen this principle rather than another? Meyer Fortes always refused to ask this kind of question, claiming that societies are not like individuals, who can over their lifetime 'choose', for example, the languages they want to speak. He is right on this last point. But one day we will have to come up with satisfactory answers to this type of question. Murdock[53] and in his wake Goodenough[54] in effect attempted to explain the appearance of matrilineal systems by change of residence, which in certain circumstances (importance of women's gathering activities), they suggested, switched from virilocal to uxorilocal and entailed substitution of a matrilineal descent rule for the patrilineal rule that had previously applied. But these hypotheses proved unconvincing.

Jack Goody took another tack. Leaving to one side the unresolved and unresolvable question of why certain societies adopted a patri- or matri- or nonlineal descent rule for forming kin groups, and adopting Fortes' idea that descent groups (whatever their principle of organization) are corporate groups, 'moral persons' who act as a 'collective individual', Goody turned to the raisons d'être of these collective subjects that traverse generations and transcend the life and death of their members. He thus advanced the hypothesis that the appearance of these groups had its basis in different forms of *common ownership* of the resources indispensible for the survival, reproduction and development of tribal societies – hunting and fishing grounds, lands cultivated using extensive agricultural or horticultural techniques.

---

51   M. Fortes, 'Primitive Kinship', *Scientific American*, no. 200 (1959), pp. 146–58.

52   M. Fortes, 'Kinship and Social Order: The Legacy of L. H. Morgan', *Current Anthropology*, vol. 13, no. 2 (April 1972), p. 286.

53   G. P. Murdock, 'Correlations of Matrilineal and Patrilineal Institutions', *Studies in the Science of Society* (New Haven, Yale University Press, 1937), pp. 445–70 and *Social Structure* (New York, Macmillan, 1949), pp. 201–19.

54   W. Goodenough, 'Residence Rules', *Southwestern Journal of Anthropology*, vol. 12, no. 1 (1956), pp. 22–37 and *Description and Comparison in Cultural Anthropology* (Chicago, Aldine, 1970), chap. 3.

However Fortes had already rejected Goody's hypothesis in his own explanation of the formation of corporate descent groups in tribal society. '*I maintain that it is a mistake to interpret the model of corporate descent groups to imply that productive or durable or any other form of property is the formative basis of corporate group structure in tribal society*.'[55] His reason for rejecting hypotheses based on the social importance of various forms of property was that 'filiation and descent would probably be accepted as endogenous variables that are predominantly if not entirely independent of exogenous forces'.[56] For him, the relations and institutions entailed in kinship have a sui generis, autonomous status in all societies.

RELATIONS OF DESCENT AS A SOURCE OF DUTY OF ALTRUISM

The formation of these corporate descent groups that transcend the existence of their physical members from one generation to the next would be explained by the fact that, wherever and whenever they are found, kinship relations link people personally, whether or not they love or even like each other. Meyer Fortes called this principle that sums up the obligations engendered by these ties, by their inherent strength, 'the rule of prescriptive altruism', 'the axiom of Amity'. In short, he believed this duty of altruism between kin to be the psychological, moral and religious force that transformed a group of related individuals into a collective individual, a corporate group, which encompassed them all, present in each member while remaining distinct.

I do not deny that the universe of kinship is a place where solidarity, cooperation and sharing often prevail over competition, refusal to help others and egotism, if only because it is into the universe of kinship relations that children are usually born and that they survive only because they are cared for by adults who are related to them and for this reason feel and believe themselves to be obliged to do this. But the 'duty-of-altruism' explanation is too general and proves to be inadequate if one seeks to explain the formation of social groups that exist and develop by placing (and keeping) their material and immaterial resources in common and ensuring that each generation considers itself less as

---

55   Fortes, *Kinship and Social Order*, p. 288. Much later Lévi-Strauss, too, would characterize the descent and residence groups of the Northwest American Indians – which he called 'houses' – as 'corporate groups'. In addition to the economic criterion of common ownership of material resources, he also invoked the joint ownership of immaterial goods, crests, titles, chants, dances, ritual functions, etc. See C. Lévi-Strauss, *La Voie des masques* (Paris, Plon, 1979), p. 175; English translation: *The Way of the Masks*; translated from the French by Sylvia Modelski (Seattle, University of Washington Press, 1982), and *Paroles données* (Paris, Plon, 1984), pp. 192–9; English translation: *Anthropology and Myth: Lectures, 1951–1982*, translated by Roy Willis (Oxford/New York, Blackwell, 1987).

56   Fortes, *Kinship and Social Order*, p. 291.

the owner of these resources than as a 'steward' whose first duty is to transmit them in turn to the following generations. One has only to remember that for hundreds of years, in both the East and the West, in both the Old and the New World, land, whether for growing or for hunting, was excluded from those things a person could buy or sell. There were fundamental reasons for this, which were not only moral or religious but also pragmatic and material. For by holding their material and immaterial resources in common, individuals and families gave themselves the means to survive and grow together, even in hard times. In this common holding and refusal to divide up resources (which by no means implies that they were *exploited* collectively) a material and social force was added to the moral force of the obligations that bound kin together.

I will conclude this point by voicing my agreement with Fortes that kinship relations are specific and that their evolution and their transformations lead to the formation of other types of kinship relations and not to something else, for example class relations. But transformations and evolution are not brought about by internal factors alone. While they are specific, in no case are kinship relations completely autonomous, but neither do they depend mechanically on the transformations and evolutions occurring elsewhere in society. Nevertheless these relations always entail stakes that do not stem from kinship. Before going into this second component of kinship – alliance relations – I would like to give what seems to me a particularly striking example of the material and social stakes entailed in the functioning and reproduction of kin groups, and at the same time an example of the way these groups manipulate the imaginary and symbolic stakes involved in kinship relations to serve their own interests. The example is that of child sacrifice in the Mandak and Barok societies of the South Pacific island of New Ireland.[57] This sacrifice used to enable members of the child's lineage to integrate the lineage of its father and therefore to change clans.

The Mandak and the Barok are matrilineal societies divided into two exogamous moieties each of which has a number of matriclans and matrilineages which own lands, rivers, sacred emergence sites and rights in the making of the carved cult objects known as *malanggan*. These goods were regarded as 'food' that each clan gave in abundance to each of its members and which were an extension of the food received from the mother while in the uterus. Each matriclan has an enclosure where the men of the clan sleep and a burial site for all of the clan members, both men and women. The clan, the male enclosure and the burial site are, in the Mandaks' minds, a sort of vast maternal womb, which contains and nourishes its members and then receives them when they die.

---

57   R. Wagner, *Asiwinarong: Ethos, Image and Social Power among the Usen Barok of New Ireland* (Harvard, Princeton University Press, 1986), pp. 153–4. Concerning child sacrifice among the Mandak, see B. Derlon, 'Corps, cosmos et société en Nouvelle-Irlande', in M. Godelier and M. Panoff (eds.), *La Production du corps* (Paris, Archives Contemporaines, 1998), pp. 163–86.

In certain circumstances, when a matrilineage that is short of land wanted to acquire some of the clan territory of a man who had married one of the women of the lineage or when a woman cut off from her clan and living on her husband's lands was widowed and sought to ensure herself and her descendants the right to go on living in the village she should have left after her husband's death, in both cases the man's youngest child was beaten to death at the funeral by his maternal uncle, 'who then took the child's body to the male enclosure of the paternal lineage and placed it in the tomb where the father's corpse had been laid'.[58] The sacrificed child was supposed to live a second imaginary and symbolic gestation in the same 'maternal container' that gave birth to its father. The child was thereby 'reborn' in death as a member of its paternal matrilineage and automatically became the owner of a usage right in the lands of this lineage. At the same time, this right extended to the child's mother and to her descendants. Paradoxically, it was the son who came to belong to a new lineage after death and transmitted the belonging to his mother and brothers, thus re-engendering them, as it were, in a different lineage from that of their birth. One can measure the imaginary character of all of these transformations, but also the fundamental social importance in this society of a reassignment of kinship acquired in this instance at the cost of child sacrifice.

In other cases, instead of sacrificing one of its children, a lineage desirous of acquiring permanent rights in pieces of another clan's territory would pay a very large compensation in pigs and other valuables. Wealth was substituted for a life, for life, which is the principle of all systems in which women are not exchanged for women or (which also happens) men for men.

---

58   Derlon, 'Corps, cosmos et société en Nouvelle-Irlande', pp. 180–3.

CHAPTER FOUR

Alliance and Residence
(Second and Third Components)

ALLIANCE: FORMS AND RULES

With the analysis of alliances and marriage we enter another zone of scientific turbulence induced by the publication, in 1949, of Claude Lévi-Strauss' *Structures élémentaires de la parenté*. Taking the opposite stand from Radcliffe-Brown's then-dominant thesis, which maintained that descent was the essence of kinship, Lévi-Strauss asserted that, on the contrary, kinship was based on alliance, since, owing to the universal taboo on incest, no descent group, no family, could perpetuate itself alone; all were compelled to contract alliances in order to reproduce themselves. And for Lévi-Strauss, alliance meant that men exchanged women from their own group, whom they were forbidden to marry.

In short, for Lévi-Strauss, if alliance takes precedence over descent, it is because kinship is basically exchange, and, more specifically, the exchange of women between and by groups of men.[1]

We will not go into the foundations of the incest taboo at this time – these will be dealt with later – but merely recall the explanation proposed by Lévi-Strauss in the following passage, which is more than a theory of kinship, since, according to the author, with the incest taboo we are dealing with the very origins of human society, with the decisive moment when humans extracted themselves from the state of nature and entered the state of culture:

> As Tylor has shown almost a century ago, the ultimate explanation is probably that mankind has understood very early that, in order to free itself from a wild struggle for existence, it was confronted with the very simple choice of '*either marrying-out or being killed-out*'. The alternative was between biological families living in juxtaposition and endeavoring to remain closed, self-perpetuating units, over-ridden by their fears, hatreds, and ignorances, and the systematic establishment, through the incest prohibition, of links of intermarriage between them, thus succeeding to build, out of the artificial bonds of affinity, a true human society, despite, and even in contradiction with, the isolating influence of consanguinity.[2]

---

1 C. Lévi-Strauss, *Les Structures élémentaires de la parenté* (Paris, Presses Universitaires de France, 1949), p. 548; English translation: *The Elementary Structures of Kinship*, translated by James Harle Bell, John Richard von Sturmer and Rodney Needham (Boston, Beacon Press, 1969).

2 Cf. C. Lévi-Strauss, 'The Family', in H. L. Shapiro (ed.), *Man, Culture, and Society*

According to this approach, our distant ancestors did not originally live in society but in isolated biological families that perpetuated themselves through incest. The state of nature from which humankind had to extricate itself was that of animal-like promiscuity, of generalized incest. This had been Morgan's vision. It was also that of Freud, in *Totem and Taboo* (1911), before going on to be adopted by Lévi-Strauss (1949).

EXCHANGE OF WOMEN, OR LÉVI-STRAUSS' COUP DE FORCE

Let us take a closer look at Lévi-Strauss' argument, which links the incest taboo, exogamy and the exchange of women by men in a single chain of cause and effect. He posits that the origin of the different marriage rules should be sought in the various forms that this exchange can take.

But this line of reasoning actually conceals a real *coup de force*. For, logically speaking, the incest taboo (and, I repeat, we will not discuss here whether or not it is universal), admits simultaneously of three possible forms of exchange. Either men exchange women among themselves, or women exchange men among themselves, or men and women leave their families to create new ones, and in this case it cannot be said that a brother exchanges his sister or a sister her brother for a spouse. But that is not all. The latter form is no longer a direct exchange of persons but a matter of reciprocal gifts of men and women between families.

Of course Lévi-Strauss was not unaware of the logical existence of these three possibilities, but he retained only one of them – the exchange of women by men – as the sole possibility that fitted reality. And he dismissed the other two as illusions that humans (women in particular) took pleasure in entertaining about themselves.

> The female reader, who may be shocked to see womankind treated as a commodity submitted to transactions between male operators, can easily find comfort in the assurance that the rules of the game would remain unchanged should it be decided to consider the men as being exchanged by women's groups. As a matter of fact, some very few societies, of a highly developed matrilineal type, have to a limited extent attempted to express things that way. And both sexes can be comforted from a still different (but in that case slightly more complicated) formulation of the game, whereby it would be said that consanguineous groups consisting of both men and women are engaged in exchanging together bonds of relationships [kinship].[3]

(London, Oxford, Oxford University Press, revised edition 1971), pp. 333–57, p. 350 (emphasis added).

3   Lévi-Strauss, 'The Family', p. 356.

In point of fact, as we will see, there are societies where the women exchange men among themselves, and many more where families make each other mutual gifts of their sons and daughters. The rules are not the same in each case, even if the basic rule is always that of exchange. In all events, Lévi-Strauss posits male domination as the condition for the emergence of human kinship systems, and one that has continued to be so down to the present day. Male domination is a transhistoric, ontological fact that Lévi-Strauss links to the emergence of the human capacity for speech and symbolic thought. For, if he is to be believed, 'the emergence of symbolic thought must have required that women, like words, should be things that were exchanged'.[4]

Caught up in this logic of the ontological character of male domination, one of Lévi-Strauss' closest disciples, Françoise Héritier, would even try to show, in *L'Exercice de la parenté*,[5] that all kinship terminologies – even those of the Crow type, usually associated with societies having matrilineal descent groups in which sisters treat their brothers like sons – bear the mark of the 'differential value of the sexes', which rates the man more highly than the woman, and the brother more highly than the sister.

Let me be clear. I do not deny that male domination exists; but unlike Claude Lévi-Strauss and Françoise Héritier, I do not think that it is a constituent principle of kinship. What is constituent, owing to the incest taboo, is the obligation to exchange. But exchanging women is not the universal condition for alliance and kinship. There is also the exchange of men by women, and we will give examples. As for the third possibility, it occurs every day in European and Euro-American cognatic societies, where sons and daughters leave their family to live with the one they have chosen, and no one says they have 'exchanged' their brothers or sisters with anyone. While male domination is a reality in numerous areas of social life in Europe, the United States and Canada, it does not play or no longer plays a role in the fact that people choose each other to form a married or cohabiting couple. Moreover, once they reach their legal majority, individuals have no need of their family's permission to marry whomever they wish, with the exception of a small circle of blood relatives and close in-laws, who are forbidden by law. In addition to these taboos, which are the same for all citizens of the same country, there are other prohibitions specific to communities within the society, for example the prohibition for certain groups on marrying outside their own religion.

Let me say a few words about the exchange of men among women, which is an actual practice even if there are few examples. This is the rule among the

---

4   Lévi-Strauss, *Les Structures élémentaires de la parenté*, p. 569; English translation, p. 227.
5   F. Héritier, *L'Exercice de la parenté* (Paris, Le Seuil, 1981), pp. 48–52.

Rhades of Vietnam, the Ata Tana'ai[6] of the Flores Islands, the Tetum of central Timor, the Negeri Sambilan[7] of Malaysia, the Nagovisi of Bougainville, the Makhuwa[8] of Mozambique and a few other groups. All of these societies are matrilineal, and residence is either matrilocal or uxorilocal. Among the Rhades,[9] it is the bride's family that pays compensation to the family of the groom. In place of bridewealth, we have here groomwealth,[10] made up of valuables, jugs, Chinese gongs and livestock. Among the Tetum,[11] the men go from their mother's house to that of their wife, which is built next to the 'big house' of the eldest woman of the lineage. It is she who keeps the lineage's valuables, the cult objects (which are female) and the relics of the male members of the lineage. Each house is divided into two spaces: one inside, which holds the women's quarters, the harvests, and the relics and cult objects; and the other outside, a sort of large platform in front of the house, which is also divided in two, with one side for the husbands and the other for the brothers of the women of the house. The households thus function as brother-exchange groups, the ideal being to repeat these bilateral exchanges from one generation to the next.

Among the Nagovisi,[12] the women control their matrilineal land and act as stewards of its wealth. They play an important role in managing village life and, before the Europeans arrived and people converted to Christianity, women took part in the male initiations.

KINSHIP IS NOT UNIVERSALLY FOUNDED ON THE EXCHANGE OF WOMEN BY AND FOR MEN

The conclusion to be drawn from all this is that the formula: kinship is based on the exchange of women between and by men does not have the universal validity Lévi-Strauss and his disciples attributed to it. And therefore *men's domination of women is not the basis of kinship*. Were this not the case, the feminist struggles of the past decades (which began in the West but have now spread far beyond) to move societies toward ever greater gender equality in the management of public affairs and private life, all these struggles that have brought our societies

---

6   Cf. L. Holy, *Anthropological Perspectives on Kinship* (London, Pluto Press, 1996), p. 36. On the Ata-Tana'ai, see E. D. Lewis, *People of the Source: The Social and Ceremonial Order of Tana Wai Brama of Flores* (Dordrecht, Foris, 1988).

7   M. G. Peletz, 'Neither Reasonable nor Responsible: Contrasting Representations of Masculinity in a Malay Society', *Cultural Anthropology*, vol. 9 (1994), pp. 135–78.

8   Cf. C. Geffray, *Ni père ni mère: critique de la parenté, le cas Makhuwa* (Paris, Le Seuil, 1990).

9   Cf. A. de Hautecloque-Howe, *Les Rhades, une société de droit maternel* (Paris, CNRS, 1987).

10   J. Nash, 'A Note on Groomprice', *American Anthropologist*, no. 80 (1978), pp. 106–8.

11   G. Francillon, 'Un profitable échange de frères chez les Tetum du Sud, Timor central', *L'Homme*, vol. 29, no. 1 (1989), pp. 26–43.

12   Cf. J. Nash, 'Women and Power in Nagovisi Society', *Journal de la Société des océanistes*, vol. 60, no. 34 (1978), pp. 119–26.

so far, would ultimately come up against the need to tear down kinship relations in order to achieve this equality. This is the criticism that Gayle Rubin made of Lévi-Strauss' thesis early on in an article that was to have a considerable impact.[13]

Can we say then that, once rid of the abusive generalization that kinship is based on the exchange of women by and between men, once it is reduced to the proposition that kinship is based on various forms of exchange, Lévi-Strauss' theory has an analytical basis? Roughly speaking, the answer is 'yes'. But we must be aware that this amended theory no longer has anything to do with the first, since the exchanges that found kinship are now analyzed in a different and broader perspective. For even set on new empirical and analytical foundations, the thesis of kinship as exchange can never alone be the general theoretical basis for the anthropological analysis of kinship. It is necessary for analyzing forms of alliance and the marriage rules that express them. But it leaves aside or minimizes the importance of the forms and modes of descent reckoning. Systematically the inverse of Meyer Fortes (who saw alliance as a second and secondary aspect of kinship), Lévi-Strauss demonstrated a lack of interest throughout his work in analyzing the logics of descent, except at one later point when he rapidly explored the concept of the 'house'. It was when studying the art of the Indians of the northwest coast of the United States and Canada, that, after having reconstructed the ties between the different types of masks and the Indians' myths and rites,[14] he tried to situate this corpus in the overall internal workings of societies whose complexity had somewhat disconcerted Boas.

Today claims to the hegemony of one thesis over the other, to the primacy of alliance over descent or vice versa, of one school over the other, are a thing of the past. Moreover, in Europe the institution of marriage is crumbling while descent stands fast. Our era is marked by a theoretical pragmatism that has nothing eclectic about it. It consists in solid knowledge of the theories, in refusing to simplify the facts under analysis to make them fit a given thesis, in knowing how to analyze the hypotheses found in highly divers and opposing theoretical approaches that have proven themselves capable of shedding light on certain facts, and in knowing how to combine them to explain other, even more complex facts without claiming to explain everything. It is in this context that we propose to examine a few forms of exchange and to scrutinize the very concept.

Let us restate the departure point of this examination. It seems well established that, owing to the incest taboo, the reproduction of kinship relations and the perpetuation of families and descent groups (where these exist) demand

13   G. Rubin, 'The Traffic in Women: Notes on the "Political Economy" of Sex', in R. Reiter (ed.), *Toward an Anthropology of Women* (New York, Monthly Review, 1975), pp. 157–210.

14   C. Lévi-Strauss, *La Voie des masques*; English: *The Way of the Masks*; translated by Sylvia Modelski (Seattle, University of Washington Press, 1982).

that individuals of both sexes look 'outside' for partners of the opposite sex with whom to establish the socially recognized forms of union that will ensure the reproduction of these relations and the perpetuation of these groups. This 'outside' can vary from very close to very distant, since the incest taboo can be limited to the closest consanguines and affines of a person's birth family or extend beyond the boundaries of the lineage to all members of the clan, if it is truly exogamous, or even to cousins of the third degree, as in certain cognatic societies of Oceania –Tuamotu,[15] the Cook Islands,[16] Anuta,[17] – or of Malaysia – among the Iban[18] and their neighbours – and, finally, to the seventh degree of kindred (a restriction the Catholic Church attempted to impose on Western Christian societies between the eighth and the thirteenth centuries).

It should be remembered that marriage is one of the forms of socially recognized union, but it is not the only one, even if it is the most frequent. Moreover, when there are several forms of marriage in the same society, they never have the same status. Some may not imply any form of exchange, for example marriage with a captive.

Exchanges that seal a matrimonial alliance usually appear as reciprocal gifts. These gifts can take the form of either the exchange of a person for a person or the exchange of goods and services for a person. In the second case, a certain amount of wealth is collected by the groom's family and transferred to the family of the bride (bridewealth) or assembled by the bride's family and transferred to that of the groom (groomwealth). There can also, as among the Vezo, be two groups, one of which gives a son when the other gives them a daughter, the man and the woman being considered 'equivalent', and their children as mingling inseparably and indistinguishably within themselves what comes from their father and what comes from their mother.[19]

Finally, there are alliances without counter-gifts, as in India, which consist in giving a young virgin to the family of her future husband to which is added the obligation of a gift of wealth, a dowry. The dowry must be as large as possible to show the social status of the bride's family and is often negotiated between the two families.

---

15   P. Ottino, *Rangiroa, parenté étendue, résidence et terres dans un atoll polynésien* (Paris, Cujas, 1972.)

16   J. Hecht, 'The culture of gender in Pukapuka: Male, female and the Mayakitanga sacred maid', *The Journal of the Polynesian Society*, vol. 86, no. 2 (1977), pp. 183–206.

17   R. Feinberg, 'Kindred and Alliance in Anuta Island', *The Journal of the Polynesian Society*, vol. 88, no. 3 (1979), pp. 327–48.

18   D. J. Freeman, 'The Family of Iban of Borneo', in J. Goody (ed.), *The Development Cycle in Domestic Groups* (Cambridge, Cambridge University Press, 1968).

19   Cf. R. Astuti, 'Food for Pregnancy: Procreation, Marriage and Images of Gender among the Vezo of Western Madagascar', *Social Anthropology*, vol. 1, no. 3, pp. 227–90.

THE EXCHANGE OF A PERSON FOR A PERSON

Let us analyze the first case: the exchange of a person for a person, taking the example of direct sister exchange involving real or classificatory sisters (e.g. patrilateral parallel cousins) between two men. Such an exchange seals an alliance between the men's and the women's lineages.

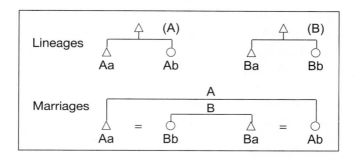

WIFE-GIVERS ARE SUPERIOR TO WIFE-TAKERS

We have already cited an example of this case when analyzing the prevailing form of marriage among the Baruya, *ginamaré*, which is precisely an exchange of sisters between two men and two patrilineal lineages. Here we are in a logic of reciprocal gift and counter-gift. It is important to understand that the counter-gift of a woman in this case *does not cancel* the debt each of the two men or their lineages has contracted with regard to the other by receiving one of his sisters as a wife. At the close of these reciprocal exchanges, the two men and their lineages find themselves in equivalent positions: each is simultaneously the other's creditor and their debtor. Each creates an obligation in the other as a wife-giver and is in their debt as a wife-taker. Each lineage thus finds itself in two opposing relationships with the other, but the sum of these opposite inequalities actually puts them back on an equal footing in the society (which supposes a code of values shared by all members of this society when it comes to assessing this status). This alliance sealed by a double marriage will be the starting point of a flow – between the two brothers-in-law and the two sisters-in-law and their two lineages – of goods and services that will last throughout the couples' lifetime and be continued by their descendants. After several generations, the debts die out and marriage alliances can once more be concluded between the two lineages.

SOME DEBTS ARE NOT CANCELLED BY A COUNTER-GIFT

Why is the debt created by the gift of a woman not immediately cancelled by the counter-gift of another woman? At the close of this exchange, each woman has taken the other's place without ceasing to belong to her original lineage. If the counter-gift does not erase the debt, it is precisely because the person 'given' has not been detached from the lineage that gave her. She has been 'given' without being truly alienated by those who gave her and who continue to have rights in her (and her descendants). Through this exchange, one woman has taken the place of another while keeping her original identity. This reciprocal permutation of persons and places is the act that produces the alliance between the members of the two lineages. These movements of persons, this production of new relations between them and between their birth (or adoptive) groups are induced by the fundamental social pressure that is the prohibition of a man marrying his sister or a woman marrying her brother. The source of sister exchange – but this is just as true in the case of brother exchange – lies in the compelling force of the incest taboo.

A few more remarks are needed to enter more deeply into the logic of these exchanges. The persons who have been 'given' are not alienated. They keep their original identity and are not completely detached from their original lineage. They are separated from it. They are not goods that one can alienate and which pass from seller to buyer, who does what he will with them. What is given, ceded, are the *rights* in the persons, rights to their domestic, sexual and economic services and to their reproductive capacities. But we should not forget that, when it comes to matrilineal societies, a woman's children belong to her own lineage and not to her husband's.

Furthermore, when two persons (two men or two women) are exchanged, this is an exchange of two beings whose 'value' is a priori deemed equivalent by their lineages and their society. Children's socialization and education ensure that boys know how to hunt, clear forest, fight, etc., and that girls know how to cultivate gardens, raise their children, care for pigs, make clothing. And everyone is asked to conduct themselves as responsible adults who do not go about creating conflicts that are a threat to families and society. But even the best upbringing cannot guarantee that a woman will not be barren (or a man sterile), that their children will survive, and so forth.[20]

It needs to be stressed that, by this gift and counter-gift of women, the two lineages find themselves mutually *indebted* to each other and thus feel obligated for the rest of their lives to exchange services, to share the salt-bars they produce, the meat of the pigs they slaughter, to invite each other to clear a new garden in

---

20   Among the Baruya as in many other societies, it is only women who are sterile, never men.

the forest and to work it together. These reciprocal gifts of goods and services, this mutual aid in the event of strife in the village, materialize the debt they contracted by each receiving a wife from the other who would enable them to perpetuate themselves (independently of what, in the child, is supposed to come from its father or mother). These gifts are therefore in no way bridewealth.

It is also important to reiterate that many societies, like the Baruya, who practise direct sister exchange for the most part, abstain from repeating the same alliances before several generations. A son may not reproduce his father's marriage and take a wife from his mother's lineage. Two brothers may not take wives from the same lineage, and even less marry two sisters. These bans prevent the constitution of groups made up of two lineages or two clans that reproduce together and thereby isolate themselves from the rest of the society, at least from the standpoint of the exercise of kinship. These prohibitions thus compel each lineage to multiply its alliances and ensure that each is simultaneously the starting and ending point of several alliance paths, which, despite their possible expansion, can never manage to include all the lineages of all the villages of the society. In order for an exchange system to bring all members of a society into a single network, these individuals must have been sorted from birth into distinct categories which intermarry according to rules that compel each individual, according to his or her category (moiety, section, subsection), to choose their spouse exclusively from another category, the same one every time, thus reproducing the same alliances from one generation to the next. This is the logic underlying the Australian and certain Amazonian systems, which will be examined later.

A final point: the principle of the direct exchange of women – real or classificatory sisters – is always limited by the number of 'sisters' available for exchange, so that, in order for all men to find a wife, there must be a prohibition or a strict limitation on certain men – the eldest, for example – exchanging all of their sisters for their own benefit and thus sentencing their younger brothers to a long bachelorhood and to delaying marriage or marrying widows. But this obstacle to direct exchange disappears when it is no longer persons but goods or wealth that are exchanged for a person. In this case, the character of the exchange and its limits are entirely different. On one side, there is a woman or a man, in other words concrete persons, and, on the other, wealth, valuables (shells, jewellery, etc.), or goods (livestock, pigs, etc.), which can be produced or procured through trade or by some other means. On the one side, there are persons; on the other, different kinds of 'things' that function as substitutes for persons. The equivalence between the two exchange terms takes on a new, much more abstract character than in the exchange of a person for a person. The moment persons (men or women) are exchanged for wealth, there appears a true political economy of kinship. Wealth procures women, and women procure wealth through the bridewealth they bring to their lineage and through their productive activities in their husband's lineage.

WEALTH FOR PERSONS

To illustrate this change of logic in marriage practices and in the way societies function, we will take the example of the Melpa, a widely dispersed set of tribes whose territories lie around Mount Hagan in the heart of the New Guinea Highlands. The Melpa are famous for their system of competitive ceremonial exchanges known as *moka*, in which clans and tribes from an entire region used to face off on the occasion of large-scale redistributions of pigs and goldlip pearl-shells, which would be exchanged for pigs, marsupial furs and so forth with tribes further to the south, who had procured them through exchange with tribes living along the Gulf of Papua. *Moka*, like the Kwakiutl potlatch, consisted in giving more than the other clan could give in return, or returning more than had been given, the aim being to make the others your debtors and force them to recognize their inferiority when it came to accumulating and redistributing wealth. As one might guess, this escalation of generosity was driven by political interests. It glorified the name of the richest and most generous clans, it spread far beyond their tribal boundaries the renown of their Big Men who had managed to amass such wealth by their ability to produce it and/or to convince their kinsmen and their affines to engage their own pigs and shells in the same venture.

In these Big Men societies of New Guinea, direct sister exchange, while theoretically known, was not practised and was even explicitly forbidden by the Mendi. The general rule for concluding a marriage alliance was to exchange wealth for a woman. For example, in the Melpa society, when two lineages agreed to unite two of their children, negotiations to set the amount of the marriage payments were conducted in several stages. We will summarize this process, referring to Andrew and Marilyn Strathern's remarkable analyses.[21]

In the first phase, the bridegroom's lineage presents the bride's lineage with a number of goods they plan to give them. In the second phase, these goods are formally given to the woman's family, which gives other goods in exchange. The men make long speeches, while the pork from a certain number of pigs brought by the groom's family is redistributed and eaten. The woman's family gives the couple a number of live pigs to start the herd they will later raise and which will enable the couple to present the woman's lineage with pigs.

---

21   A. J. Strathern, *The Rope of Moka: Big Men and Ceremonial Exchange in Mount Hagen, New Guinea* (London, Cambridge University Press, 1971) and 'The Central and the Contingent: Bridewealth among the Melpa and the Wiru', in J. L. Comaroff (ed.), *The Meaning of Marriage Payments* (London, Academic Press, 1980), pp. 49–66; A. J. Strathern and M. Strathern, 'Marriage among the Melpa', in R. Glasse and M. Meggitt (eds.), *Pigs, Pearl-shells and Women* (Englewood Cliffs NJ, Prentice Hall, 1969); M. Strathern, *Women in Between: Female Roles in a Male World: Mount Hagen, New Guinea* (London, Seminar Press, 1979).

FOR THE WOMAN'S HEAD AND VAGINA

In the course of these ceremonies, a number of shells are exchanged between the two groups, while others are presented to the bride's family as a one-way gift. Several of these shells are called *peng pokla*, which means 'to cut off the (girl's) head', in other words separate her from her lineage; but this separation is never complete. A number of pigs are also given with no expectation of reciprocity. Several of these pigs are described as *kem kng*, 'for the girl's vagina'. A particularly large pig is called *mam peng kng*, 'the pig for the (girl's) mother's head'. Another is given to the bride's father as a present from the groom's family.

If we analyze these exchanges, we see that they have three components. Reciprocal exchanges of shells and pigs – approximately equivalent in quantity and quality (before the Europeans arrived, a living pig exchanged for two pearl-shells) – between the two parties designed primarily to seal their alliance. A second series of shells and pigs are given to *partially* detach the woman from her own lineage and from that of her mother, and to transfer rights to her sexual services and reproductive capacities to her husband's lineage. Last of all, the woman's family presents the couple with a number of pigs that constitute the beginnings of a herd whose eventual size depends primarily on the labour of this woman, but the product of which will be used by the husband to take part in *moka* and to fulfil his responsibilities in various situations (funerals, initiations, etc.) which require contributions of pork. By endowing their daughter with this 'productive capital', the members of her lineage establish themselves as the future couple's primary *moka* partner.

This third component is not a dowry, in the sense of having been given by the bride's lineage to ensure her material autonomy in her new family and which she could take with her in the event of divorce, as was the case with dowries in societies around the Mediterranean Basin. Lastly, it is to be noted that land never features in these endowments. Lineage land is indivisible. When land is divisible and part of a family's land is detached and included in a daughter's dowry when she marries, we are dealing with an altogether different logic and other marriage strategies, as shown by Jack Goody and S. J. Tambiah in their work on dowry and devolution of goods in Europe and the East[22] as well as by the discussions[23] sparked by their hypotheses.

Two remarks are called for here. It is clear from the Melpa example that the

22   J. Goody and S. J. Tambiah, *Bridewealth and Dowry* (London, Cambridge University Press, 1973); J. Goody, *Production and Reproduction: A Comparative Study of the Domestic Domain* (London, Cambridge University Press, 1977), pp. 6, 13.
23   D. O. Hughes, 'From Brideprice to Dowry in Mediterranean Europe', *Journal of Family History*, vol. 3 (1978), pp. 262–96.

circulation of goods entailed in a marriage alliance can be imbedded in much broader exchange systems based on competition for prestige and renown, in short, on winning status in a political configuration. The intention behind some of these gifts is not only to repay the gift of a woman with wealth, but to make affines into *moka* partners. The Melpa marriage is actually *fully* concluded only when the groups and individuals involved become partners in the *moka* and enter into competition with each other even as they cooperate. Marriage alliances and kinship relations are therefore subordinated to the perpetuation of a far-flung network of competitive political-ceremonial exchanges, following a potlatch logic, and made to serve the expansion of this network, which entails many dozens of clans and thousands of individuals. In short, these relationships are of another order than kinship: they are political.

This example tells us why, with a few exceptions, marriage in potlatch societies cannot be based on the direct exchange of women. Such a system would risk short-circuiting the competition between groups in the exchanges of wealth that give access to titles, ranks and functions – whose number is limited – as well as to power and renown.[24]

More important still, the equivalence between the terms of exchange in the case of wealth for a person has nothing in common with the equivalence postulated when exchanging a person for another person. Even though societies may strive to limit the amount of wealth given for a woman (or a man) and to set an average exchange rate, there is no objective criterion that can justify giving six big pearl-shells and three pigs for a woman's 'vagina' rather than four shells and two pigs. The nature and the quantity of the 'things' given are primarily indicative of the rank and status of the groups contracting a marriage alliance. Today in New Guinea, marrying the daughter of a Big Man or of a regional member of the National Assembly can entail dowries and redistributions of several hundred live or slaughtered pigs (some of which are bought from industrial pig farms with money from the sale of coffee[25]), to which are often added a Toyota or Nissan truck and tens of thousands of kina in cash.

The inflation of dowries, observed not only in Oceania but also in Africa and Asia, is the direct consequence of the growing involvement of these societies in the local and global market economy. This inclusion results in the generalization of the use of money in traditionally non-economic social

---

24 The Mendi, another New Guinea Highland people, forbid the direct exchange of women because it would prevent affines from vying with each other in the large-scale ceremonial exchanges (cf. R. Lederman, *What Gifts Engender: Social Relations and Politics in Mendi* [New York, Cambridge University Press, 1986].) But the Melpa, like the Mendi, keep a mental tally of the number of women they have given other clans and ensure that it more or less balances out over the medium term with the number of women they have received.

25 Cf. C. Gregory, *Gifts and Commodities* (London/New York, Academic Press, 1982).

exchanges (e.g. rituals) and accentuates and multiplies the differences of wealth between individuals and between kin groups, which are still an important component of local territorial groups' social structure. In this shift, we see the development of a genuine traffic of women, a phenomenon that did not exist in the case of sister exchange between two men and their lineages.[26]

A dowry payment at the time of the wedding does not mean that the debt of the wife-taking lineage is extinguished at the end of the ceremony, if there is one. Other 'payments' will come due, for example, each time the couple has a child. This is the case among the Wiru and the Daribi of New Guinea, societies that do not take part in regional competitive systems like the *moka*, but where the bride's father and her lineage are supposed to exercise ritual control over their daughter's fertility *throughout her life*. Each child she bears is seen as a *new gift* made to her husband's lineage, which is added to the initial gift of its mother. Based on this (imaginary) representation of the process of reproducing life, a flow of gifts thus accompanies the birth, marriage and death of all individuals. The dowry in this case is merely the first of a series of gifts inaugurated by a marriage alliance, which will punctuate the life of the individuals that will be born from this marriage, from their birth to their death – and beyond.[27]

THE CASE OF INDIA, WHERE WIFE-TAKERS ARE SUPERIOR TO WIFE-GIVERS

In a great number of societies the wife-takers are superior to the wife-givers. So that the marriage may take place, the givers offer the groom's parents, in addition to their daughter, a dowry (and not bridewealth), the amount or the nature of which the groom's parents can accept or reject. It is often stipulated that the girl must be a virgin. This 'value' attached to women's virginity is not universal, but it prevails in the Euro-Asian zone and can be found in various forms as a principle of Christianity, of Islam, of Hinduism – but also of traditional Chinese society. In this case, the woman's body is the vessel of the family honour and status. We will take the example of Brahmin India.[28]

---

26   It should be noted that, in many parts of the world, Western colonial authorities (French, English, etc.) put a stop to marriage by direct exchange of woman and replaced it with marriage with dowry. They considered that the woman was being treated like an object in the first case and with more respect in the second. Just as they (belatedly) abolished slavery, they were opposed to marriage by sister exchange. The Tiv, a population living in Nigeria and Cameroon, are a clear example. The Tiv practised direct sister exchange, rare in Africa, and abandoned it under pressure from the British administrators (and their wives). Cf. P. Bohannan, *The Tiv of Central Nigeria* (London, International African Institute, 1953) and 'Marriage in a Changing Society', *Man*, no. 14 (1953), pp. 11–14. See also L. de Sousberghe, 'Cousins croisés et descendants: les systèmes du Rwanda et du Burundi comparés à ceux du bas Congo', *Africa*, vol. 35, no.4 (1965), pp. 369–421.

27   R. Wagner, *The Curse of Souw: Principles of Daribi Clan Definition and Alliance* (Chicago, University of Chicago Press, 1967).

28   My analysis of forms of marriage in India is based largely on a rich text by J. Fezas, 'La

In India the superiority of takers over givers is connected with the form of marriage practised by the purest, highest caste in Indian society,[29] the Brahmins. In an ideal Brahmin marriage, a father gives his virgin and richly endowed daughter to a family of superior or equivalent rank to his own. And for this gift to be a source of merit, in the present life and beyond, it must be freely given, with no expectations or reciprocity, with no counter-gift on the part of the groom and his family.

This type of marriage was already described in the *Manava-dharma-sastra*, a set of normative Sanskrit texts known as the 'Laws of Manu', written over a period of several centuries (probably between the second century BCE and the second century CE, in other words, at a time when Buddhism was spreading through India and driving the Brahmins to set their traditions down in writing). This form of marriage – the gift of a virgin with a dowry – subsequently became a norm that spread to other castes as Indian society became Sanskritized,[30] and many local tribal societies adopted Hinduism, little by little entering the caste system or continuing outside it but under its influence.[31]

The *Dharma-sastra* mentions seven other forms of marriage as well, and classifies them into two groups of four. The first are entitled *Dharmya*, in other words 'according to *dharma*', and are therefore virtuous, adding to the merits of those who practise them. The second group uses terms referring to evil spirits, enemies and rivals of the gods to designate four forms of marriage based on *interest* (accepting bridewealth, a marriage payment, for the gift of a girl), or on *desire* (choosing each other without being authorized by the fathers), or on *violence* (abducting the bride), or on *fraud*. In short, eight forms of marriage, ranging from the purest, most virtuous, most disinterested to the most immoral and impure. But even if the last four forms are opposed to the first four, all are regarded as forms of marriage. We will return later to this list and its underlying principles after having attempted to identify the principles, values and representations of traditional Hinduism that ground the tradition of the superiority of wife-takers over wife-givers.

The explanation lies in the representations of the status of son and daughter, and therefore that of husband and wife, in Hindu tradition. According to

dot en Inde: des textes classiques aux problèmes contemporains', *Annales de Clermont*, vol. 32 (1996), pp. 183–202.

29   And therefore the caste most exposed to the danger of pollution.

30   See the remarkable example of the Sanskritization of the cult of the goddess Pattini in Sri Lanka, analyzed by G. Obeyesekere in *The Cult of the Goddess Pattini* (Chicago, University of Chicago Press, 1984).

31   It must be recalled that in Hindu tradition, marriage has three purposes: to accomplish one's *dharma* (religious duty); to have descendants, i.e. for a woman, to give her husband a son; and finally to enjoy lovemaking (*rati*). But sexual pleasure, which is neither denied nor condemned (see the *Kama Sutra*), comes second to duty.

this tradition, a man is born with three debts – to the gods, to the *rsi* (the original sages or seers, who 'saw' the Veda) and to the 'fathers'. A man therefore owes
sacrifices to the gods, owes study of the sacred texts to the seers, and owes
descendants, above all a son, to the fathers. Over his lifetime, little by little,
through sacrifices, study and engendering a son, the man frees himself from his
original debt. In addition, a man must engender a son for himself as well, for it
is a son that must perform the funeral rites when his parents die and thus enable
them to enter the world of the ancestors. It is a son who will then continue to
make offerings to the family ancestors for the rest of his life. In India the birth
of a son is therefore a source of joy and an occasion for rejoicing.

This is not the case for the birth of a girl, for she is a woman, and according
to the classical texts, women have an evil nature. She is inherently evil. Her
insatiable sexual appetite is a danger to men and society. Her body is a source of
pollution through the menstrual blood that periodically flows from it. Furthermore, the woman is considered unfit for reflective thought – and therefore
incapable of independence. She must always submit to men, whose duty it is to
guard her, 'even from herself', to guide her but also to protect her. 'Her father
protects (her) in childhood, her husband protects (her) in youth, and her sons
protect (her) in old age; a woman is never fit for *sva tantra* (independence).'[32]

A father's duty is therefore to keep his sons and to marry off his daughters
as soon as they reach puberty or even before. The Sanskrit word for marriage,
vivaha, contains the idea of dissociation (*vi*) and the transfer of the daughter
from her father's house to that of her husband. But it is also the rule that if a
certain time is allowed to elapse after a girl reaches menarche, she is then no
longer under her father's authority and can choose her own husband – but she
then loses all right to a dowry. Nevertheless, she can choose to go ahead without
incurring any blame, since her father and the members of her group will be
regarded as the ones responsible for not having found her a husband in time.
They will be the ones censured by public opinion and not the woman or her
husband. For the father, this social condemnation will be accompanied by the
ancestors' wrath, since, for a Brahmin, not to marry a daughter in time is
considered to be as serious as murder, the gravest crime one can commit.[33] The
ancestors may even be so angry that they thirst for the girl's menstrual blood as
an offering.

It is with these philosophical-religious representations of the woman as a
potential and constant source of defilement in a social and cosmic order organized around the opposition (at multiple degrees) between pure and impure that

32   Laws of Manu, 9, 3, translated by various and edited by F. Max Müller, Oxford:
Clarendon Press, 1886, p. 328.
33   Reference to a late text, *Parasara-smrti* 7–6–9, cited by Fezas, 'La dot en Inde', p. 190,
who refers to P. V. Kane's *History of Sharma-Sartra* (Poona, 1930–62, 5 vols), vol. 2, p. 444.

we must begin our attempt to understand why, in India, wife-takers are superior to wife-givers, as well as why the gift of a pre-adolescent or an adolescent girl who has never had sexual relations with a man (nor, they add, with a woman) is regarded as a disinterested gift, and at the same time as a religious act. But a piece of the puzzle is missing. For the gift is disinterested in the sense that the wife-takers do not reciprocate with either women or bridewealth. And yet it seems that at another – immaterial, religious and cosmic – level, the wife-takers do reciprocate with a counter-gift. They take upon themselves the *responsibility* of dangerous fertility, source of the pollutions occasioned by this menstruating girl. They, and no longer the girl's father, will be responsible for the 'bad omens' entailed in these occasions for pollution, which the bride carries with her, in her body by her very nature. And it will be up to them to transform this dangerous fertility into a source of life, through marriage and procreation.

To celebrate the marriage of a girl is therefore at the same time to transfer from one family to another – from the givers to the takers – the dangers carried in this girl's sexual body. These dangers are infinitely greater still if she has had illicit sexual relations with men or women before her marriage. A woman thus contains within her body the possibility of 'bearing' her family's rank and status, of bringing them honour or shame. Her virginity is the means and the stake. In addition to being a virgin, she must also testify to her family's wealth, prestige and standing. This she does when she arrives with her dowry, decked in her jewellery and accompanied by the goods given to women when they marry and which are already their inheritance. These are personal goods, for in India real estate such as land and houses is traditionally reserved for the sons and is divided among them on their father's death.

That the gift of a virgin with her dowry has never been entirely a one-way, non-reciprocated gift, and that this counter-gift takes place on a level other than that of women and material wealth, has been largely confirmed by the results of detailed ethnographic studies, such as those conducted by Gloria Goodwin Raheja on marriage rites and payments in the dominant caste of a North Indian village. In an acclaimed book entitled *The Poison in the Gift*,[34] she showed the importance of a set of ritual acts by which the wife-takers act with the explicit intention of ensuring the well-being of the givers by taking responsibility for the inauspiciousness that accompanies the transfer of a woman into their family and which is connected with the fact that the families' ancestors and gods attend the wedding and mingle with the guests to ensure that the rules have been respected. Among the Gujar – but this is not the case everywhere in India – the groom's family in turn, through other rituals, transfers onto the Brahmins who

---

34   G. Raheja, *The Poison in the Gift: Ritual, Prestation and the Dominant Caste in a North Indian Village* (Chicago, University of Chicago Press, 1988).

perform the ceremony for the family some of the impurities and faults engendered by the act of receiving the gift of a virgin woman who has begun to menstruate (*kanya dan*). In the end, all the world's impurities converge on the Brahmin, and for that he receives goods and prestations.[35]

Giving a virgin with dowry to a Brahmin is, according to the *Dharmasastra*, the second of the four forms of *dharmya* marriage that are a sign of virtue and a source of merits for the girl's father and her family. This marriage is called *daiva*, a word derived from *deva*, meaning 'gods', and consists, for a rich man who has embarked upon a cycle of major sacrifices, of giving one of his daughters to the Brahmin who performs these sacrifices for him. The gift of his daughter is added to the material gifts and prestations normally given a priest for fulfilling this role.

Without suggesting in the slightest that the forms of marriage practised in India today correspond to the eight forms listed and ranked by the Laws of Manu, it is still worthwhile examining these forms briefly in an attempt to glimpse a cultural and social world with which we are not automatically familiar. They are listed in descending order starting with the first, which we have described, the so-called *Brahma* marriage, from the name of the great god of all the worlds. The second form is *Daiva*. The third is named *Arsa*, from the term that designates the *rsi*, or seers, the sages of old. In this type of marriage, the father gives his virgin daughter but receives in exchange from his future son-in-law a few head of cattle for ritual use. The fourth form of marriage is called *Prajapatya*, from the name of the god of procreation, Prajapati. It differs from Brahma in that the gift of the girl is solicited.

Next come the four forms of marriage placed under the sign not of the gods but of the demons or spirits inimical to the gods. *Asura* – a term designating spirits that personify evil nature spirits – by which a man requests the gift of a woman and makes a marriage payment (*sulka*) to her family, and gives the woman herself goods which constitute a sort of dowry. The *Gandharva* marriage – from the name of the heavenly musicians who play dance music for the nymphs – is the union of a man and a woman who desire each other and marry without their families' consent.[36] *Rakasa* – from the name of the highly

---

35   It is interesting to recall that Marcel Mauss had the sentiment that India was exempt from this theory of 'the obligation to give in turn'. In his essay on the gift, he wrote 'The cunning Brahmins in fact entrusted the gods and the shades with the task of returning gifts that had been made to themselves' (*Sociologie et Anthropologie* [Paris, Presses Universitaires de France, 1950], p. 243; English translation: *The Gift: The Form and Reason for Exchange in Archaic Societies*, translated by W. D. Halls, foreword by Mary Douglas [New York/London, W.W. Norton, 1990], p. 147). In reality the actions G. Raheja reports seem to show that, on the contrary, in India the gift of a woman does not go without a counter-gift from those who receive her. But this gift is cosmic and spiritual, not material.

36   The Laws of Manu do not discuss another kind of marriage well attested in Indian epic.

dangerous nocturnal demons (*raksas*) – is marriage by the forcible abduction of the girl from her family.[37] And last of all, in *Paisaca* – from the name of the carnivorous demons that haunt cremation grounds – a man has sex with a woman he has found in an inebriated state or asleep and makes her his.

Under the sign of the gods	Under the sign of the demons
1. Brahma	1. Asura
2. Daiva	2. Gandharva
3. Arsa	3. Raksasa
4. Prajapatya	4. Paisaca

Several remarks are called for concerning these 'demoniacal' forms of marriage (it must not be forgotten that demons, though below the gods, share the same nature).

In *Asura*, a woman is exchanged for wealth. This form is encountered in Africa and in New Guinea, among the Melpa, for example. In India, it is also called by the names of local tribes, as though it were still marked by the forms of marriage exchange practised by tribal groups subsequently absorbed into the caste system. But even more interesting is the fact that this marriage has negative connotations in India because it does not appear as a gift but as the sale of a daughter, a materially interested gift, which thereby loses its gratuitous character. The father and mother are held equally responsible for 'selling' their daughter because they subsequently share the goods received in exchange. It is as though giving a woman in exchange for wealth was already, at the time of the Laws of Manu, assimilated to a commercial transaction in which the parties negotiated the price of a commodity. This view partakes of a world vision and a value hierarchy that associates buying and selling, and more generally all commercial activities, with defilement. It is therefore not because the parents decide for their daughter without her consent that this form of marriage is censured. It is because

---

This is *Srayamvara*, which like *Gandharva*, results from mutual choice between the partners. But *Srayamvara* is found in the romances of chivalry in which each of several princes enamoured of the same princess vie in prowess to convince her to marry him. *Gandharva* appears as the 'democratic' form of this princely marriage. Cf. N. Allen, 'Hinduism, Structuralism and Dumézil', *Journal of Indo-European Studies Monograph*, no. 33 (2000), pp. 241–60.

37   The importance of marriage by capture in Indo-European myth and epic traditions was shown by Georges Dumézil in a landmark publication, *Mariages indo-européens* (Paris, Payot, 1979). Dumézil bases his analysis on material taken from Sanskrit, Latin, Greek and Scandinavian literature. He associates marriage by abduction with the exercise of the second function in the varnas, that of the power and strength represented by the warrior caste. See below our analysis of marriage by abduction among the Sioux. Cf. also N. Allen, 'Marriage by Capture', *The Journal of the Royal Anthropological Institute*, vol. 6, no. 1 (2000), p. 135; R. Barnes, 'Marriage by Capture', *The Journal of the Royal Anthropological Institute*, vol. 5, no. 1 (1999), pp. 57–73; P. Sagant, 'Mariage "par enlèvement" chez les Limbu (Népal)', *Cahiers internationaux de sociologie*, no. 48 (1970), pp. 71–98.

this marriage is not a gift but a sale, and a sale can be concluded with whoever offers wealth for a woman – whether he is from the same or, worse, from a lower caste. In short, according to this viewpoint, commercial relations have their place in the logic of caste hierarchy but never beyond. It must also be stressed that, in this view, the parents of a girl who has been abducted or forced to marry always have the right to demand material compensation after the fact. This payment is not bridewealth but atonement for a wrong.

Another interesting fact is the recognition expressed in these texts of the woman's right to marry whom she will if her father has not found a husband for her within a certain lapse of time after her menarche (*Gandharva* marriage).[38] In this case, she is free to marry; however, although she is not at fault she loses her right to any dowry. She *no longer represents her family* and no longer has a right to their support or to their assets. Last and above all, these ancient texts leave room for the love marriage. To be sure, this is considered a bad form of marriage because it does not respect paternal authority, but it is accepted as a possibility. Moreover, it is this form of marriage that for centuries has nourished a whole poetic, lyric, even 'romantic' literary genre. Today its importance in people's imaginary and aspirations has not ceased to grow and it now passes for the 'modern', non-traditional form of marriage, shifting desire and individual wishes to the fore, rather than the authority of one's kin, who continue to pursue their marriage strategies in view of maintaining or raising their position in the caste hierarchy.

Today, too, the extreme monetarization of the dowry, the consequence of a distortion of ancient customs, resulted in a law being passed in 1961 in India which forbids a girl's parents to pay a dowry to the parents of the future husband on pain of as much as six months in prison and a fine. The law also stipulates that, if a brideprice is paid, it should go to the woman or be used by the newly-weds to set up house, but should not be paid to the father of the bride. This now-banned dowry or brideprice is called *vara-dakshina*, from *vara* (future husband) and *daksina* (gift made to the household priest for performing the life-cycle sacrifices). It actually functions as a groomwealth, as a payment demanded by the parents of the groom for allowing their son to marry. The *vara-daksina* is widespread and has taken on a modern form linked to the expansion of commercial and monetary relations. Instead of the young woman arriving at her husband's house decked in her traditional finery (gold, jewellery, clothing, etc.), she now comes bearing several hundreds of thousands of rupees, the sum her future in-laws have demanded to accept her as a daughter-in-law. More than ever in India it is better to have sons than daughters to marry.

---

38   See Francis Zimmerman's fine text, 'Le corps mis en scène: à propos du mariage en Inde', in M. Godelier and M. Panoff (eds.), *La Production du corps* (Amsterdam, Editions des Archives Contemporaines, 1998), pp. 249–68.

Thus in Brahmin marriages, although the givers of a virgin do not receive a woman or wealth in return, on the spiritual level they receive a sort of indirect gift from the takers, since the latter take responsibility for the pollution their daughter bears and bears away with her. But there are also societies in which wife-takers give nothing in return. An example is provided by the former marriage practices of the Sioux Indians.

In Sioux society, where the men divided their time between making war, hunting buffalo and taking part in large-scale rituals, and where all of the material goods belonged to the women, to the wives, the rule was to marry outside the band. The ideal wife was a prisoner of war, and the adoption of children or adults was just as important as descent. Their kinship terminology was Dravidian, but they had no specific term for husband or wife. The word for 'to marry' was 'to abduct', to capture (a woman). Moreover, a man was forbidden to speak to his in-laws, who were treated as, or really were, enemies. Sisters lived under the very strict supervision of their brothers, and it was the latter who made the decisions concerning their marriage and the size of the brideprice (in horses or other forms of wealth) that the suitor was to pay. Warriors gave their sisters enemy scalps, and it was the women who tortured prisoners, sometimes to death. Ideally the brother-in-law should be killed in order to capture his sister. We are at the far pole from the practices and values of the Baruya, for whom sister exchange between two men binds them for the rest of their lives and draws them into a cycle of exchanges of goods and services that ceases only with their death. Ultimately, in Baruya society, two brothers-in-law eventually become closer and more committed to each other than two brothers.

It may be the prime importance of bride abduction, of marriage founded on capture, on predation, that explains why, in a highly unusual manner, Sioux kinship terminology derives the terms for cross cousins from those designating affines, the wife's brother and sister. The outside prevails over the inside, but it is an outside characterized by predation and death. At least this is what Emmanuel Desvaux has tried to show in an article rich in surprising perspectives, devoted to the difficulties of Sioux kinship nomenclature.[39]

WHEN TAKERS AND GIVERS ARE EQUAL

Finally, the last possibility: wife-givers are neither superior nor inferior to wife-takers. Takers and givers are equal. This is the case in many societies, including the Vezo of Madagascar, studied by Rita Astuti.[40] In this possibility, the exchange

---

39   E. Desveaux, 'Parenté, rituel, organisation sociale. Le cas des Sioux', *Journal de la Société des américanistes*, no. 83 (1997), pp. 111–40.

40   Astuti, 'Food for Pregnancy'; see also her *People of the Sea: Identity and Descent among the Vezo of Madagascar* (Cambridge, Cambridge University Press, 1995).

takes the following form. The woman's parents say to the man's parents: 'We give you our daughter, take her.' And the man's parents respond: 'We give you our son, take him.' The two gifts are equivalent. The Vezo have a cognatic kinship system in which a person is linked to the ancestors through men and/or through women, indifferently. There is therefore in this case no exchange of women by the men or exchange of brothers by their sisters. Nor is there any such thing as exchanging a woman or a man for wealth (bridewealth or groomwealth). There are two reciprocal gifts of individuals of different sex by two families, who cooperate to produce a third family whose members will descend from each of the two spouses inseparably. From a certain standpoint, it cannot be said that these two gifts of persons of different sex are an exchange. The gifts are two parts of a single act performed at the same time by two families in order to form a third. In addition, according to Rita Astuti, this society does not discourage sex before marriage and does little to encourage it afterwards. The woman has more rights over the children than the man.

A summary of the various cases of marriage and the status of the partners is shown in the following table:

Wife-givers are superior to wife-takers (anisogamy)
Wife-takers are superior to wife-givers (anisogamy)
Wife-givers and wife-takers are equal to each other (isogamy)

It is clear that the obligation to pay a bride- or a groomprice to seal an alliance places young people of marriageable age in a situation of personal dependence on their parents, their elders, their family or their lineage. Generally speaking, these young people have not yet managed to build up their own means of payment (livestock, shells, gongs, pottery vessels, etc.). They rely on other people to provide these so that they may give them in turn. Yet the fact that elders control the wealth and the means of social reproduction does not mean that they behave like a 'class' which dominates the younger people and exploits their labour in exchange for the payment that will enable them to find a spouse. This thesis was defended in the 1970s by a number of Marxist anthropologists, citing Claude Meillassoux's work.[41] They saw control by the

---

41   C. Meillassoux, 'Essai d'interprétation du phénomène économique dans les sociétés traditionnelles d'autosubsistance', *Cahiers d'études africaines*, no. 4 (1960), pp. 38–67, *Anthropologie économique des Gouro de Côte-d'Ivoire* (Paris/La Haye, Mouton, 1964), and 'From Reproduction to Production', *Economy and Society*, vol. 1, no. 1 (1972), pp. 93–105. See also E. Terray, *Le Marxisme devant les sociétés primitives* (Paris, Maspero, 1969); C. Coquery-Vidrovitch, 'The Political Economy of the African Peasantry and Modes of Production', in P. W. Outkind and E. Wallerstein (eds.), *The Political Economy of Contemporary Africa* (London, Sage, 1976), pp. 40–6. These theses drew strong criticism from other Marxists, in particular B. Hindness and P. Hirst, in *Pre-capitalist Modes of Production* (London, Routledge and Kegan Paul, 1975), pp. 45–78. See also J. Comaroff, *The*

elders as 'the beginning of the transformation of the society with the genesis of hierarchical social classes', the transformation of older–younger relations into patron–client relations.[42]

No one can deny the general fact that younger generations depend on their elders for, according to the context, transmission of land or status, succession to functions, and marriage payments. This dependence also entails a relationship of authority between older and younger generations, and unequal responsibilities. But it does not necessarily mean domination or exploitation. In New Guinea, for example, the young people have duties to the other members of the lineage, but that is not all; they also share rights with the older members – the right later to use lineage lands, the right to the bridewealth they need to get married, the right to be avenged by their lineage in the event of homicide or to count on their armed solidarity in the event of aggression or vengeance.

In societies where the merits someone has acquired or the wealth they have produced, individually or by their capacity to enlist kinsmen, affines or friends, give them authority in their group, authority and prestige do not automatically go to the older men, and even less to the oldest or the 'elders', but to the Big Men (and to certain women, who achieve the status of Big Women through other means). The Big Man is an older man, but not all older men are Big Men, and even less the oldest. This is apparently not the case in the African societies described by numerous specialists, from Meyer Fortes to Meillassoux. But the example of New Guinea shows at least that the fact that the older men control the lineage lands does not automatically result in domination and clientelism. Other conditions – which largely remain to be described – must be present for this to occur.

Another point is worth mentioning: we saw, among the Daribi for instance, that gifts to the wife's lineage continued throughout life because the woman's father is believed to have spiritual and ritual control over his daughter's fertility. The children she bears are therefore further gifts, as it were, from the woman's lineage to that of her husband. This is a cultural dimension based on an imaginary representation of the source of women's fecundity. This representation has serious social consequences, because it makes for a particular configuration of the exchanges between the two groups of affines and between individuals in virtue of the positions they occupy within their group and in these exchanges (husband/wife, father/daughter, father-in-law/son-in-law, etc.). It is important to take note of the social character and the imaginary dimension of the wealth exchanged or given as a one-way gift to seal these alliances and produce new

Meaning of Marriage Payments (London, Academic Press, 1980), pp. 22–6.

42   G. Dupré and P. P. Rey, 'Reflexions on the Pertinence of a Theory of the History of Exchange', *Economy and Society*, vol. 2, no. 2 (1973), pp. 131–63.

social relationships. In New Guinea, the pig is not valued because it is the High-landers' principal source of protein, and to give dead or live pigs is not merely a way of redistributing a certain quantity of pork for consumption or of making a gift of sows that will have piglets. The same is true of cattle in Nuer society. But it also applies to 'inanimate' objects which, in addition to pigs, feature in exchanges – polished and decorated shells worked by the men and women in Melpa society, or decorated mats which circulate by the dozens in Polynesian exchanges, the most valuable, the most sacred of which were used to envelop statues of their gods or the bodies of their dead.

OBJECTS AS SUBSTITUTES FOR PERSONS

All of these valuables act as *substitutes for persons living or dead*. They are given, for example, by a murderer's lineage to that of the victim to compensate this death and to save the murder's life. They must therefore be produced (or acquired) and then transferred into other hands so as to establish not only marriage alliances but also political alliances, and alliances with gods and ances-tors. By means of these objects and their transfer, individuals and groups contract relations with others, and these relationships form part of their iden-tity. The exchanged objects are loaded with both the meaning and the strength of these relationships, vested with cultural meanings and social importance. They are thus mental and social representations materialized in animate or inanimate beings. I purposely say 'beings' rather than things or objects, for these 'things', which are substitutes for persons, are perceived as containing powers for acting on persons and therefore as being in a certain manner persons themselves. That is why, like human or supernatural people, some of these objects (shells, mats, etc. – which are of no use in daily life when it is merely a question of subsistence, but which are necessary for producing a social exist-ence) acquire a name, an identity, a history and powers of their own.

As an example of the complexity of the imaginary and symbolic meanings taken on by some shells, which explain their use in the reproduction of kinship and political relations but also their status as both wealth and symbols of power, we will summarize some findings that Jeffrey Clark presented in his exemplary study of the symbolism of pearl-shells among the Wiru of New Guinea,[43] who exchange them for 'the body' of a wife, for 'the skin' of the children she bears, and so forth.

43   J. Clark, 'Pearl-shell Symbolism in Highlands Papua New Guinea with Particular References to the Wiru of Southern Highlands Province', *Oceania*, no. 61 (1991), pp. 309–39. See also M. Strathern, 'Subject or Object? Women and the Circulation of Valuables in Highlands New Guinea', in R. Hirschon (ed.), *Women and Property, Women as Property* (London, Croom Helm, 1984), pp. 158–75 and *The Gender of the Gift* (Berkeley, University of California Press, 1988).

Here briefly is how the Wiru load a pearl-shell with meaning. The naturally yellow pearl-shell is rubbed with ochre powder and its lower lip is outlined in white sap, which quickly turns black. Several notches are cut into the upper lip, and the whole shell is laid and exposed on a bark support. All of these operations are the outcome of meticulous work which transforms an object that entered Wiru society as a commodity bartered for a pig (or bought with money) into an object not only loaded with a new meaning but also one that has become more beautiful in their eyes – and by their hand. What is this new meaning? For the Wiru, yellow is a *female* colour, associated with a yellowish substance that they say is found in the womb and becomes a key component of the foetus when it is conceived. Ochre is associated with virility and wealth, and for this reason the sacred stones associated with the fertility of the land, human health, etc., are smeared with ochre powder. The white of the sap is associated with semen, and the black, like the ochre, is associated with virility. The cuts on the female lip of the object represent the incision of the glans of a penis. In short, these androgynous objects harbour the attributes of the men's masculinity and the women's femininity – in this case essentially their reproductive capacities. It is in this sense that the apparently *inanimate* objects given in exchanges are not only substitutes for persons but are themselves objects endowed with meaning and power.[44]

The same holds for the Nuer who, according to Evans-Pritchard, define all social relations in terms of cattle. When they are initiated, young men are given the animals that they will tend to throughout life, a life they will spend in a society where the production or maintenance of practically all social relations demand the transfer of cattle in various ways.[45] It is understandable that in these conditions an identification is created between men and their cattle such that, when they give away their animals, they are giving part of themselves. By alienating part of their herd to get a wife, men detach part of themselves from their own lineage and expect that their wives will detach from their own bodies and lineage the children they will bear. But the husband's lineage will not appropriate these children unless he has paid his affines a brideprice. Otherwise they will belong to the man who pays the price in the husband's stead. This man will then become the children's social father, while the husband is no longer the father but simply the genitor.[46]

---

44   In *Argonauts of the Western Pacific* (London, Routledge, Kegan, 1922), Malinowski describes how long it took him to understand why 'ugly, useless' objects were for the Trobriand islanders 'an unfailing vehicle of important sentimental associations' that 'inspire with life and at the same time . . . prepare for death' (pp. 89, 513–14).

45   E. E. Evans-Pritchard, *The Nuer* (London, Oxford University Press, 1940), p. 19 and, *Nuer Religion* (Oxford, Clarendon Press, 1956), pp. 255–60, 279.

46   E. E. Evans-Pritchard, *Kinship and Marriage among the Nuer* (Oxford, Oxford University Press, 1956), Chapter 4; Holy, *Anthropological Perspectives on Kinship*, pp. 162–5.

WHAT IS THE BRIDEPRICE?

Making a marriage payment, paying a brideprice is therefore not 'buying' a woman. Except in very rare cases, such as ancient China, the woman is not completely detached from her birth group and absorbed into the group, clan, lineage or family that has alienated a portion of its wealth to obtain her. Women continue to possess rights in their birth group and have obligations to the members of this group. In addition, a wife acquires rights in her husband's group, together with duties. This is precisely the case in China, where the daughter-in-law's status changes once she has given birth to a boy who will carry on her husband's line and continue to venerate their ancestors after his father's death. When a woman dies, it is not unusual for her name to be included among her husband's ancestor tablets. In short, we are far from the image suggested by Lévi-Strauss' famous formula 'kinship is based on the exchange of women by and for men'. Moreover, the groups that exchange partners are not composed exclusively of men but of men and women who descend from common ancestors and in which women also have a voice.[47]

In matrilineal Minangkabau society, where the husband is called by an expression that means 'borrowed man', the matrimonial prestations give the husband and wife rights in each other and, through them, extend these rights to their groups.

In sum, all these various prestations (bridewealth, groomwealth, dowry, conjugal prestations) establish two kinds of ties at once: conjugality between the spouses and affinity between the groups that become allied through them. In the next generations, the affines are transformed, depending on the type of kinship system, either into consanguines (as in the Western kinship system) or into consanguines and affines (as in the Dravidian system, where the mother's brother and the father's sister are affines for Ego and not consanguines).

To conclude this point, let us say that the exchanges that seal an alliance are always fundamentally exchanges that transfer from one group to the other rights in the persons who are detached from one group and attached to the other. But these detachments and attachments are almost never complete.

Jack Goody, following Leach, drew up a relatively exhaustive list of the various categories or rights that can be transferred by these exchanges and which constitute reciprocal or non-reciprocal obligations between the spouses (conjugal rights) and between the allied groups.

---

47   J. Goody, 'Inheritance, Property and Marriage in Africa and Eurasia', *Sociology*, vol. 3 (1969), pp. 55–76 and 'Marriage Prestations, Inheritage and Descent in Preindustrial Societies', *Journal of Comparative Family Studies*, vol. 1 (1970), pp. 37–54.

- Rights to henceforth officialized sexual relations.
- Rights to domestic services.
- Rights to the men's and/or the women's procreative capacities and rights for the allied groups on the children born of the marriages.
- Rights to cooperation in the production and exchange processes if the family, lineage, etc., are production and exchange units; and rights to a share of the things produced by these units or exchanged between them.
- Rights to mutual assistance and to solidarity in the event of political and social strife.
- Rights to mutual assistance in the performance of rituals and other ceremonies concerning ancestors, spirits and gods.

Of course one party's rights are at the same time the other parties' duties. This is why it is indispensable to distinguish among these rights those that are reciprocal and non-reciprocal, are identical or different, equivalent or non-equivalent, complementary or opposing. For example, the husband's right to demand that his wife join him in living next to or with his father is an obligation, a duty for the wife. In other societies it is the husband who will go to live with his wife or with her parents, either during the first years of marriage or definitively.

Such transfers of rights in persons are often the starting point for transfers of material and immaterial goods[48] to the individuals that are born to these alliances or who will be integrated through adoption. Lands, names and titles will be inherited by all descendants, male and female, of a union, or by only certain men or women. Standards, values and knowledge will be transmitted, social functions will be transferred. Filiation and descent return in force to unite or divide people according to sex and age, and combine with alliance to ensure the transfer from one generation to the next of a share of the conditions of their physical, material and social conditions of existence. For instance, in a society with a matrilineal descent rule, descent groups give other groups the right to their daughters' sexual services but keep the children born of their marriages for themselves. In ancient Roman law, girls were exherited en bloc, and the father would choose a single son to inherit his *potestas*, or authority, and carry on the ancestral cult after his death. For as long as he lived, the father would

---

48   Leach gave a non-exhaustive list of these goods: immaterial goods – names, titles, crests, functions, magic, chants or songs and dances – as well as material goods – techniques, goods, lands or territories and, finally, persons. Mauss had proposed the same inventory a half-century earlier (cf. *The Gift*, p. 46). Leach concluded that his list showed that the concept of property was meaningless because it covered so many different things. He likewise concluded that the concept of marriage was meaningless because there was no definition that applied to all societies, and more broadly, that kinship, which covers very different things according to the society, does not exist either . . .

exercise his *patria potestas*, the absolute right, recognized by the city of Rome, over the members of his family, including his married sons and even his married daughters, if they were still 'under his hand'. And yet the authority that prevailed in the everyday domestic life of this 'family' was not founded, as Yan Thomas showed, on this unlimited *potestas*.[49]

Let us take another look at the notion of *patria potestas*, the absolute right of the *pater familias* over his descendants. To be a *pater familias* in ancient Rome, a man could not be under the control of another, he had to be *sui juris*, under the control of no other, to have been chosen by his father to inherit his *potestas* and have received it instantaneously on his father's death. The *pater familias* was thus an autonomous subject, whereas all other members of the family were *alieni juris*, under the control of another. The *pater familias* thus had control over his wife, his children, his slaves and his goods. It was the fact of inheriting the *patria potestas*, the father's power, that made a man a *pater familias*. Such an heir could be unmarried or be married without children. He was still a '*pater*' *familias*. This power lasted all his life, for his sons, even when they married and had children, remained under the control of the *pater familias* until his death. Daughters too, but in ancient Roman law girls were given in marriage and then passed under 'the hand', the *manus*, of their husband, becoming as a daughter. A wife thus became the sister, as it were, of her sons and daughters. And if her husband was under the control of her father-in-law or an older ascendant, then she came under this man's control also. But alongside marriage with *manus*, usually reserved for patricians, there was a marriage without *manus*, practised for the most part by plebeians. In this case the married woman remained under her father's *patria potestas*.

These laws evolved considerably up to the end of the Republic and over the duration of the Roman Empire. Women became able to transmit their possessions to their children, who had priority over the woman's own brothers and sisters, her agnates. But until a very late date, a Roman woman could not testify in court on behalf of someone other than herself, and she was never able to undertake the defence of someone else, or to represent anyone other than herself. The last function remained a male public prerogative. As Yan Thomas stresses, in the political arena as in intersubjective civil relations, Roman women were always prohibited from providing a service that went beyond the narrow sphere of personal interests. Until the very end, the city-state remained a 'men's club', as Pierre Vidal-Naquet termed it. Never did the Roman woman receive authorization to take on the general nature of an 'office', a male task par excellence.

---

49   Y. Thomas, 'Remarques sur la juridiction domestique à Rome', in J. Andreau and H. Bruhns (eds.), *Parenté et stratégies familiales dans l'Antiquité romaine* (Rome, Ecole française de Rome, 1990), pp. 449–74. See in the same work J-C. Dumont's analysis of the right to command in the private and public spheres, in 'L'Imperium du pater familias', pp. 475–95.

This raises several questions. Are there any matrimonial alliances that are contracted without marriage, without a more or less ceremonial act? Indeed, this is the case in many hunter-gatherer societies and among certain agriculturalists. The man and the woman begin by living together, and then their status gradually changes over time. It cannot be said that they go from being not married to being married, since *marriage does not exist*. What is important is that this union becomes publicly known and no one opposes it, no one finds anything to say against it on either the man's or the woman's side or in their respective communities. This is also the case with the millions of couples who live together without being married in the West and who declare their children with the state representatives near their place of residence. Their children automatically become citizens of the country where they were born, members of a nation whose boundaries are broader than those of their family and their local community. The fact of becoming the parents of legally recognized children gives these unmarried parents the rights and duties that the state confers on all relatives in the direct line, whether or not they are married.

If there are alliances without marriage, are there also alliances that are not marked by the transfer of goods and/or services between the families involved? In Western societies, where young people who are of age can marry without their family's consent, many unions are contracted without an exchange of prestations between the families or between the spouses, except for a few reciprocal gifts. In many nomadic hunter-gatherer societies, which do not amass material possessions – among the Bushmen for instance[50] – the young man moves in with his wife's people until the birth of their second or third child. During this time, he shares the spoils of the hunt with his in-laws and renders them many services. Then, he may, if he wishes, return to his native band where he has kept his rights, taking his wife and children with him. Among the Purum agriculturalists of Manipur Province in India, the husband lives with his in-laws for three years and works off his marriage payment. Then he goes home to his own people.[51]

Lastly, do these alliances, sanctioned by marriage or not, always produce conjugal families? Among the matrilineal Ashanti, we saw that the husband visits his wife in the daytime, but spends his nights with his mother, his sisters and their children. His own children live with their mother. The couple's residence is therefore matrilocal for the woman and duolocal for the man.

The Na are a Tibeto-Birman-speaking group, living in the Himalayan foothills of Yunnan and Sichuan provinces in southern China, who are matrilineal

50   L. Marshall, 'The Kung Bushmen of the Kalahari Desert', in J. L. Gibbs (ed.), *People of Africa* (New York, Holt, Rinehart and Winston, 1965).

51   R. Needham, *Structure and Sentiment: A Test Case in Social Anthropology* (Chicago, University of Chicago Press, 1962).

and matrilocal. Their residence unit is made up of groups of sisters living with their children of both sexes and with their brothers, the children's maternal uncles. They do not have marriage. The men leave their sisters at night to visit the women in the neighbouring houses who have accepted them as temporary lovers. Even in the case of a long-lasting liaison, each man or woman can have other amorous relations at the same time and can separate when he or she chooses. Conjugal families are very rare, and if their number has grown in the past decades, it is due to pressure from the Communist rulers, hostile to the 'furtive visits' and concerned with imposing monogamy, a mark of civilization and of course of the superiority of socialism. Even in this extreme case, though, where there is no marriage or official direct exchange between families, an indirect exchange occurs and an adelphic family is formed in which it is the women who provide the children with their identity. The man is like the rain, a shower that awakens a seed-child in the woman's womb, where it then develops. In Na society, then, there is no marriage, and therefore there are no husbands and no fathers. But the family exists, an adelphic family where the incest taboo between brother and sister is primordial and where any sexual allusion within the walls of the home is forbidden. The mothers and the maternal uncles exercise their authority jointly over the children engendered by the women of the house.[52] The residence pattern is the same for men and for women: matrilocal.

RESIDENCE MODES

A great diversity of family types is engendered by the conjunction of different descent rules and different residence patterns. In matrilineal societies, residence can be matrilocal (Na, Rhades, Tetum), uxorilocal (Hopi), duolocal (Ashanti and Senufo), avunculocal (the family lives with the wife's mother's brother: Trobrianders), virilocal (the wife lives with her husband's family). Patrilineal societies usually have residence patterns that are patrilocal (the family moves in with the husband's father: Melpa, Baruya, Tallensi) or virilocal (the family settles on the husband's land: Wolof,[53] Tamil[54] or Reunion Island). In Dobu,[55] in southeastern New Guinea, a couple alternates residence according to years, sometimes patrilocal, sometimes uxorilocal. Cognatic societies often combine these principles, since one can choose to live with one's maternal or paternal kin. In Samoa, on the other hand, women leave their village for that of

---

52 C. Hua, *Une société sans père ni mari. Les Na de Chine* (Paris, Presses Universitaires de France, 1997).

53 M. Dores, *La Femme village* (Paris, L'Harmattan, 1981).

54 C. Ghasarian, *Honneur, chance et destin. La culture indienne à la Réunion* (Paris, L'Harmattan, 1991).

55 R. Fortune, *Sorcerers of Dubu* (London, Routledge, 1932).

their husband (virilocal residence). Finally, in Western Europe, Japan, the United States, but also among the Inuit, residence is neolocal, the couples choosing their place of residence without reference to their parents. It is easy to see that the various forms of residence have different effects on the children's socialization, as they live closer to their paternal or their maternal kin, or find themselves surrounded by everyone, seeing their father in the daytime, their maternal uncle at night, or their maternal uncle in the daytime but never at night, etc.

RESIDENCE PATTERNS
Matrilocal
Uxorilocal
Duolocal
Ambilocal
Avunculocal
Patrivirilocal
Virilocal
Neolocal
Natolocal

POLYGAMY AND POLYANDRY

Lastly we will mention some other principles that also help determine different family and group structures: polygyny and polyandry (the possibility for a man to have several wives – in Islam he is allowed four, plus concubines – or for a woman to have several husbands). Polygamy is widespread in Africa, among the Muslim populations of Asia, and in Melanesia. However, it is lessening with the Christianization of these populations, which imposes monogamy and restricts (the Orthodox Church) or forbids (the Roman Catholic Church) divorce. Polyandry remains limited to certain regions of the Himalayas, India, Amazonia and Oceania. A very rare and perhaps unique case in North America were the Shoshone, who practised both polygyny and polyandry.[56] Polyandry can be adelphic (Tibet[57]) or not (Guayaki[58]). In the first instance, a woman marries a group of brothers, and the children are attributed successively to each of the brothers,

---

56   J. H. *Steward, Basin-Plateau Sociopolitical Groups*, Bureau of American Ethnology, Bulletin no. 120, 1938. Cf. R. M. Keesing, *Kin Groups and Social Structure* (New York, Holt, Rinehart and Winston, 1975).

57   N. E. Levine, *The Dynamics of Polyandry, Kinship, Domesticity and Population of the Tibetan Border* (Chicago, University of Chicago Press, 1988). See also the special issue of the *Journal of Comparative Family Studies*, vol. 11, no. 3 (1980), edited by Walter H. Sangre and Nancy E. Levine and devoted to polyandry.

58   P. Clastres, *Chronique des Indiens Guayaki* (Paris, Plon, 1972).

beginning with the oldest, or are all regarded as descendants of the oldest brother. The main reason for adelphic marriages is to avoid dispersing family assets. In the second case, a woman has several husbands who are unrelated to each other, and the children are attributed to each man in succession.

Let us mention also the importance of the age of the persons getting married. Among the Siberian Chukchee[59] a young woman can 'marry' a three-year-old boy, whom she will raise along with the children she conceives with her 'authorized lovers'. The young Arapesh girl[60] is betrothed at a very early age, around six or seven, and will go to live with her future husband's family, where she will be brought up by her in-laws. In Australian Aboriginal society, the age difference may be as much as fifteen years or more, and here, too, the husband may raise his wife as his daughter, as it were. Finally, large differences are introduced in the internal functioning of families, in their members' behaviours and in the exercise of kinship in general, depending on whether or not divorce is allowed to end the marriage that brought about the family (divorce or separation, since for co-habiting couples divorce is meaningless because there was no marriage to begin with). Whether or not individuals are allowed to remarry after divorce and on what conditions also has an influence. The question arises, too, of the remarriage of a widow or a widower. In the Christian West, because marriage is a sacrament for Catholics and the spouses are supposed to become 'one flesh' after their marriage, the bond cannot be dissolved and divorce is forbidden. Divorce was also banned among the Incas,[61] and in present-day India it is almost unknown, even if it is permitted by law. The woman who asks for a divorce finds it hard to remarry. And if a man divorces, he runs the risk of having to return his wife's dowry. Divorce is forbidden in Baruya culture. A man can repudiate his wife, but in this case he gives her to a brother or a parallel cousin, who takes her as a second or third wife.

DIVORCE

Divorce exists in numerous societies and is sometimes practised so intensively that an individual marries and divorces several times, which entails the appearance and disappearance of a succession of more or less reconstituted families. Generally speaking, the fate of the children after their parents' divorce or separation is decided by custom. Among the Touareg, custom dictates that the sons go with their father and the daughters with their mother. In matrilineal

---

59 Cf. Lévi-Strauss, 'The Family', pp. 261–85. W. Bogoras, *The Chukchee*, Memoirs of the American Museum of Natural History, vol. 11, 1904–9.

60 M. Mead, *Sex and Temperament in Three New-Guinea Societies* (New York, Morrow, 1935).

61 R. Karsten, *La Civilisation de l'Empire inca* (Paris, Presses Universitaires de France, 1986).

societies, since children belong to the mother's and not to the father's lineage, divorce is much more frequent than in patrilineal societies. This is the case with the Trobriand Islanders, the Hopi and so forth.

BACHELORHOOD

A last word on bachelorhood and the status of bachelors in most societies. In many societies, for example the Baruya, it is unthinkable and forbidden not to marry. All individuals, unless they are gravely handicapped, must marry. Among the Inca[62] all men having reached twenty-five years of age and all women having reached fourteen were supposed to be married or betrothed. The imperial administration took systematic population censuses and forced those who delayed to marry, sometimes even appointing a spouse. Nevertheless, remaining unmarried is valued in many societies when it is associated with the exercise of an important social function – religious or other – that demands partial renunciation of sexuality and the responsibilities of founding a family. This is the case among the Duna of New Guinea and other groups,[63] where the masters of the male initiations remain unmarried for life but secretly marry a spirit-woman, who controls the fertility of the land, the abundance of the game in the forest and who is supposed to be without a vagina. The man is thus a bachelor in his village but a married man in the forest, where he spends most of his time, safe from the pollution and dangers entailed in sexual relations with women. In medieval Western Christendom, after the split between the Roman and Orthodox Catholic Churches, the Roman Church imposed celibacy on priests and monks, who found themselves married with the Church, which was represented as the mystic bride of the crucified Christ. Nuns became the brides of Christ, as attested by the ring on their finger. Like the Duna master of initiations, they were at once virgins among humans and married to a god. This is also the case with the traditional Indian 'renouncers'.[64]

As for those bachelors who had no good reason to forego marriage, their status was usually frowned upon in Oceania and Africa. Given the sexual division of labour, an unmarried man had to depend on women to survive – his sisters,

62   Ibid.

63   A. Strathern, 'The Female and Male Spirit Cults in Mount Hagen', *Man*, vol. 5, no. 4 (1970), pp. 571–85; A. Biersack (ed.), *Papuan Borderlands: Huli, Duna and Ipili Perspectives on the New Guinea Highlands* (Ann Arbor, University of Michigan Press, 1995); P. Wiessner and A. Tumu, *Historical Vines: Enga Networks of Exchange, Ritual, and Warfare in Papua New Guinea* (Washington DC, Smithsonian Institution Press, 1998).

64   Cf. L. Dumont, *Homo hierarchicus: essai sur le système des castes et ses implications* (Paris, Gallimard, 1966); English translation: *Homo Hierarchicus: The Caste System and its Implications*, Complete Revised English edition, translated by Mark Sansbury, Louis Dumont and Basia Gulati (Chicago, University of Chicago Press, 1970).

his mother or other men's wives, for example those of his brothers or his uncles. Not having a wife, he could be tempted to take too much interest in the wives of others. And above all, the choice to remain a bachelor is usually regarded as a refusal to do what one is supposed to do to ensure the continued existence of a lineage, of a family, namely to marry and have children. These criticisms were usually even stronger in the case of a woman who refused to marry.

It is important to recall that in the Christian West, the Church not only promoted the celibacy of priests, proscribed divorce and made it difficult for widows to remarry, it also forbade adoption, which reappeared in the various European legal systems only at the end of the nineteenth century.

The adoption of children from outside (and not children who were orphaned or abandoned by their parents) gives children who have no genealogical ties to their adoptive parents the status of descendants. The status of parent in this case is a purely social relationship, devoid of any biological basis, which rests, as Maine said, on a 'legal fiction'. In forbidding adoption, the Church thus helped promote a model that reduced kinship to essentially genealogical, that is to say biological, ties, even if these 'carnal' ties were made sacred by the sacraments of marriage and baptism. The paradox is that, at the very moment when the Church forbade adoption and its social fictions, it promoted another type of entirely imaginary parenthood, a spiritual one, which grew out of the institution at the end of the sixth century of the baptism of children at birth, which eventually replaced adult baptism. The sixth century also saw the institution of godparents.[65] The child taken into the Church through baptism is accompanied by a spiritual father and mother, is sponsored by a godfather and a godmother. Theoretically a child's godparents are even more responsible than the parents for their godchild's spiritual upbringing. They are supposed to be particularly vigilant that the baptized child acquires the three Christian virtues of chastity, charity (*caritas*, which means more than the contemporary 'charity' and encompasses love of God and one's neighbour) and uprightness. Godfather, godmother, godson, goddaughter: the Church that had banned adoption and its fictions replaced it with the fiction of the rebirth of children in the Church and chose for this imaginary filiation the vocabulary of genealogical filiation. Simultaneously the marriage prohibitions linked with the incest taboo applying to

<hr />

65   See the pioneering work of J. Goody, *The Development of the Family and Marriage in Europe* (Cambridge/New York, Cambridge University Press, 1983), which sparked much discussion but above all new research on kinship at other times in European history. See also A. Guerreau-Jalabert, 'Sur les structures de parenté dans l'Europe médiévale', *Annales*, no. 6 (1981), pp. 1028–49; 'La parenté dans l'Europe médiévale et moderne: à propos d'une synthèse récente', *L'Homme*, vol. 29, no. 110 (1989), pp. 63–93; 'Spiritus et caritas. Le baptême dans la société médiévale', in F. Héritier-Augé and E. Copet-Rougier (eds.), *La Parenté spirituelle* (Paris/Basel, Archives Contemporaines, 1995), pp. 133–204; as well as, in the same volume, A. Fine, 'La Parenté spirituelle: lieu et modèle de la bonne distance', pp. 51–82.

real kin were extended – with a variety of modalities – to spiritual parents and spiritual children. Initially prohibited to the seventh degree and then to the fourth degree of consanguinity, extended to close affines, husband's brother, wife's sister, etc., incest in the Christian West would threaten a second domain, that of the imaginary descent ties between Christians and their God.

Alliance, marriage, simple socially recognized union, with or without exchange, always raises the problem of who one can marry. We already know one can marry persons and into groups that do not come under the incest taboo as it is defined by a given society, or under other taboos which further extend this field: one must not repeat one's father's or one's brothers' marriage, etc. To these taboos within the field of kinship are added others that originate else-where: one must not marry outside one's religion, class or rank. Which means that it is preferable or mandatory to marry someone of one's own caste, rank and religion.

There are also a great many kinship systems where positive rules are added to the prohibitions and indicate whom it is prescribed or preferable to marry, which often entails the exchange of persons or goods. These systems are at the far pole from the Western European and Euro-American systems (which are cognatic with an Eskimo-type terminology), where, with the exception of a small group of consanguines and close affines, no one is prescribed and no one is forbidden – in terms of kinship, though not in terms of wealth, rank, name, etc. We are indebted to Claude Lévi-Strauss for having been the first to try to classify kinship systems in terms of the presence or absence of a positive marriage rule contained within the system as part of its structure. His analysis led to distinguishing three classes of systems:[66]

(1) Systems that make a positive statement about the class and termino-logical categories in which Ego can and must find a spouse, where exchange is forbidden between parallel kin but allowed and even prescribed between cross kin. For Lévi-Strauss, these systems, which he called 'elementary structures of kinship', are based on two types of exchange, depending on whether the wife-givers are or are not takers. In the first case, we are dealing with restricted exchange, in the second, with a generalized exchange, between kin groups.

(2) Systems that multiply marriage taboos and have no positive rule for choosing a spouse. Ego cannot take a wife in his father's, his mother's, his father's mother's or his mother's mother's clan, lineage or line, nor marry a certain number of cognatic kinswomen. However repetition of alliances with these same groups is not only allowed, it is sought, after a certain number of genera-tions, as soon as distant consanguines can once more become affines. As a

---

66   Lévi-Strauss, *Les Structures élémentaires de la parenté*, new preface; English translation: *The Elementary Structures of Kinship*, preface to second edition.

typical example of this category, Lévi-Strauss cites the Crow and the Omaha systems, later studied in more detail by Françoise Héritier.[67] The findings of the latter's analysis led her to object to the general thesis Lévi-Strauss used to characterize alliance.[68] Héritier showed that, if it is true that two brothers or two sisters cannot marry in the same direction, a brother and a sister can do so, which means that in every other generation an exchange of 'real or classificatory sisters is possible without violating any rules'. She thereby showed that elementary forms of restricted exchange are present in Crow–Omaha systems, even if they are concealed beneath numerous tacit prohibitions. Radcliffe-Brown's sacrosanct rule – the genealogical equivalence of siblings – therefore does not apply in this case. Cross-sex siblings can do what parallel-sex siblings cannot; a brother and a sister do what two brothers or two sisters cannot do: marry in the same direction, replicate an alliance.

Alongside Crow-Omaha systems, which many anthropologists, such as Viveiros de Castro, continue with some reason not to regard as genuine, specific 'systems', Lévi-Strauss placed in the category of semi-complex systems and without analyzing them, the Iroquois and Hawaiian systems. And the matter has been left up in the air ever since. We will return to this issue later when we analyze the difference between Iroquois and Dravidian systems. The Baruya, as we will recall, have an Iroquois system, practice direct sister exchange, forbid the repetition of marriages before several generations, and diversify their alliances in each generation so that two brothers do not marry in the same direction or into their mother's or their father's lineages. According to this description, the Baruya should be placed in societies with semi-complex structures. But in their case, it is their 'regime' of 'marriage' that would be 'semi-complex' and not their kinship system or terminology.[69]

(3) Systems that fall into 'complex structures' of kinship, where marriage prohibitions concern 'kin positions defined by their degree of proximity to Ego'. The formula corresponds specifically to cognatic systems with kindred, like the Western European systems and those of the Canadian Inuit. In this case, beyond the more or less narrow circle of prohibited kin, other criteria that have nothing to do with kinship intervene in the choice of a spouse and therefore in marriage strategies, if these exist. With complex systems, kinship,

---

67   Héritier, *L'Exercice de la parenté*.

68   Lévi-Strauss, *The Elementary Structures of Kinship*: 'Each time Ego chooses a line from which to obtain a wife, all its members are automatically excluded for several generations from among the spouses available to Ego's line' (p. xxxvii; *Structures élémentaires*, p. xxvi).

69   Cf. the polemical debate between Françoise Héritier and Elisabeth Copet-Rougier, and Eduardo de Castro, who rightly supports this theory. E. Viveiros de Castro, 'Structures, régimes, stratégies', *L'Homme*, vol. 33, no. 1 (1993), pp. 117–37; E. Copet-Rougier and F. Héritier-Augé, 'Commentaire sur commentaire: réponse à E. Viveiros de Castro', *L'Homme*, vol. 33, no. 1 (1993), pp. 139–48.

according to Lévi-Strauss, 'leaves the determination of the spouse to other, economic or psychological, mechanisms'. We have seen that this was true of the Melpa, who sought to use marriage to make an affine into a *moka* partner or to make a *moka* partner into an affine.

Once again, combining the word 'complex' with the word 'structure' is not the best solution. When it comes to structure, contemporary Western systems, the Canadian Inuit system,[70] or that of the New Guinea Garia are not complex, or much less, in any event, than the Australian or Iroquois systems – like those of the New Guinea Yafar or the Ngawbe in Costa Rica. What is complex is the variety of criteria *other than kinship* that determine the spouse and eventually the marriage strategies these various criteria can inspire in certain social strata or classes. In any event, today we see more clearly that kinship does not suffice to organize any society. For example, whether one considers the Australian Aborigines, the Baruya or the South Indian Pramalai Kallar,[71] one cannot get married if one has not been initiated. In Europe, until recently, a young man did not marry before he had done his 'military service' or reached his majority. Kinship is always subordinated to other social relations, placed in the service of other goals than that of reproducing kinship.

THE ELEMENTARY STRUCTURES OF KINSHIP

Let us come back to this classification of kinship systems in order to illustrate a few examples and point out some of the problems they raise.

As examples of 'elementary' systems, Lévi-Strauss picked the Australian systems that Radcliffe-Brown had classified into moiety systems, section systems or subsection systems. Radcliffe-Brown mentioned a few other, what he deemed 'aberrant', systems, like the Aluridja, Bardi and so on. Elkin, his successor, and later on Lévi-Strauss, espoused this negative view. We will see below that there was nothing aberrant about these systems; they simply obeyed another logic, which came to be called Dravidian.

Let us take the Kariera, whose kinship system was for both Radcliffe-Brown and Lévi-Strauss the epitome of the section system. The members of the tribe are divided into four marriage classes, named Banaka, Burung, Karimera and

---

70   'Inuit' has replaced 'Eskimo', a derogatory term used by the Ojibwa Indians and adopted by Europeans.

71   L. Dumont, *Une sous-caste de l'Inde du Sud. Organisation sociale et religieuse des Pramalai Kallar* (Paris/La Haye, Mouton, 1957); English translation: *A South Indian Subcaste: Social Organization and religion of the Pramalai Kallar*, translated by M. Moffatt, L. and A. Morton; revised by the author and A. Stern; edited with an introduction by Michael Moffatt (Delhi/New York, Oxford University Press, 1986).

Palyeri. A Banaka man can marry only a Burung woman, and a Banaka woman only a Burung man. Owing to their matrilineal descent mode, the children of a Banaka man and a Burung woman are automatically Palyeri. The children of a Banaka woman and a Burung man are Karimera. The children of a Karimera man and a Palyeri woman are Burung, and the children of a Palyeri man and a Karimera woman are Banaka. Radcliffe-Brown sums up these rules in the following diagram.[72]

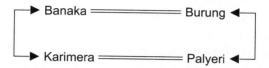

If we replace the section names with the letters A, B, C, D, we obtain the following diagram:

If we let the upper-case letters stand for men and the lower-case for women, as in Radcliffe-Brown's diagram, we obtain the following rules:

A marries b	→	their children are D or d
B marries a	→	their children are C or c
C marries d	→	their children are B or b
D marries c	→	their children are A or a

Children never belong to their father's or their mother's section. The sections are therefore not descent groups or clans or lineages. Clans exist; they bring together fathers, sons, grandsons and so forth, and they ensure religious and ritual functions that depend on kinship for their existence; but they do not play a direct role in the exercise of kinship – and therefore do not exchange women. Their role is to oversee religious and social activities, which take place in the band's territory as a result of the spiritual and ritual links their members have with certain mythical beings that formed the earth and its landscape in the original Dreamtime.[73]

---

72   Lévi-Strauss, *Les Structures élémentaires de la parenté*, Chapter 11, pp. 170–93; English translation, pp. 146–67.

73   A. Testart, 'Manières de prendre femme en Australie', *L'Homme*, vol. 36, no. 139 (1996), pp. 7–57.

The system can be divided into two patrilineal moieties, which contain (A and D) and (B and C), whereas (A and C) and (B and D) are matrilineal moieties. In addition, grandfather and grandson or granddaughter find themselves in the same generational moiety. Sons and daughters of A are D and d, sons and daughters of D are A and a. Sons and daughters of B are C and c, sons and daughters of C are B and b, and so on. In short, in addition to the patrilineal and matrilineal moieties, we have moieties comprised of alternating generations, which put the grandfather and his grandchildren in the same category. The temporal linear succession of generations comes full circle and puts two individuals separated by a generation in the same cosmic time cycle, which encompasses linear time in the succession of times and (metaphysically) cancels it out. For at work behind these moiety and section systems is a dualist rule for classifying not only humans but all plant and animal species as well as the other phenomena that compose the cosmic order (dry/wet, sun/moon, etc.).

Moreover, dividing the moieties in half produces the section systems, and dividing the section systems in half produces the subsection systems, of which the Aranda – another group – have become the prototype in anthropological literature.

A is divided into 2 subsections A_1 and A_2
B is divided into 2 subsections B_1 and B_2
C is divided into 2 subsections C_1 and C_2
D is divided into 2 subsections D_1 and D_2

This subdivision produces the following marriage rules:

$$A_1 \times b_1 \rightarrow D_2 + d_2$$
$$A_2 \times b_2 \rightarrow D_1 + d_1$$
$$B_1 \times a_1 \rightarrow C_1 + c_1$$
$$B_2 \times a_2 \rightarrow C_2 + c_2$$
$$C_1 \times d_1 \rightarrow B_1 + b_1$$
$$C_2 \times d_2 \rightarrow B_2 + b_2$$
$$D_1 \times c_1 \rightarrow A_2 + a_2$$
$$D_2 \times c_2 \rightarrow A_1 + a_1$$

Therefore if a woman is a_1, her daughter is c_1, her granddaughter is a_2, her great-granddaughter c_1, and her great-great-granddaughter will be a_1 like herself. Instead of a woman and her granddaughter being in the same category, as in the Kariera system, this time a woman shares the same category with her great-great-granddaughter. The women's cycle is extended by two generations: $a_1 \rightarrow c_1, a_2 \rightarrow c_2 \rightarrow a_1$. The same does not hold for the men's cycle: $A_1 \rightarrow D_2 \rightarrow A_1 \rightarrow D_2 \rightarrow A_1$. But since A_1 and A_2 belong to the same section, in both the Aranda and the Kariera systems, grandson and granddaughter come back to their grandfather's section.

This division of society into moieties, sections and subsections splits the rest of the society into eligible or ineligible spouses (for instance one cannot marry a brother, a real or classificatory sister, a son, a real or classificatory daughter, etc.), and the incest taboo extends to all members of an individual's section or subsection. Everyone who belongs to a section is automatically forced to take a spouse exclusively in one of the three other sections that make up the society, in the section with which the members of his or her own section must marry. Men and women in section A must marry men and women in section B. The children of the men of A will belong to section D, and the children of their 'sisters' – the women of A – will therefore belong to section C. Since members of D marry members of C, whereas a brother and a sister cannot marry each other, their children can. In genealogical terms this means that cross cousins can marry but parallel cousins (children of two brothers or two sisters) cannot, since they belong to the same section – and therefore come under the incest taboo.

This is exactly what the kinship terminology of these systems says. And here we will anticipate our study of the third component of kinship: terminologies. In a Kareira-type system, in the first ascending generation with respect to Ego, there are only four specific terms for kin. What we translate as 'father' designates not only the (biological) father, but the father's brother, the mother's sister's husband, the father's father's brother's son, the mother's mother's brother's son, and so on.

We can see that, if the same term designates simultaneously father's brother and mother's sister's husband, the father and all his brothers are therefore real or potential husbands for the mother and all her real or classificatory 'sisters'. In other words, all these women belong to the same section. And since we know that children of parallel cousins are in the same section, my father's father's brother's son, i.e. my father's parallel cousin, is also a father for me. We find the same rules at work when we examine the terms used for Ego's kin in the first ascending generation (G^{+1}), namely the terms translated as 'father' and 'father's sister' and 'mother' and 'mother's brother'. We also note that the term for mother's brother (MB) also designates the father's sister's husband (FZH) and Ego's wife's father (WF). We thus have the equation (MB = FZH = WF). Which means: (a) that my father and my maternal uncle married each other's 'sisters', and (b) that the woman I will marry is both my mother's brother's daughter and my father's sister's daughter. In genealogical terms, she is a bilateral cross cousin.[74]

---

74 In the Aranda systems, Ego does not marry cross cousins in own generation but cross cousins born of cross cousins, as well as all women designated by the same term. Instead of

If we were to go back to the second generation above Ego, we would also find four classificatory terms designating 'fathers' fathers' (FF), 'fathers' mothers' (FM), 'mothers' fathers' (MF) and finally 'mothers' mothers' (MM). My mother's mother's brother is classified in the same category as my father's father. As we have seen, the mother of a man belonging to section C and the mother of a woman from C both belong to section A, Ego's section. Ego's maternal grandmother's brother is therefore an A, like his sister and her grandson. This means that in G^{+2}, the women of A marry men from B and that Ego's maternal grandmother's brother married a woman from b. In short, in all ascending and descending generations as well as in Ego's generation (G^0), we find the same principle for organizing marriages.

Two points must be stressed here. The first is that this terminology sorts individuals into categories in which all members are the equivalent (for Ego) of all others. This terminology is therefore classificatory, but it can also be used to trace genealogical ties. As Alain Testart writes,[75] *whether or not* a Kariera marries a given cross cousin, he will call her son by the term he uses to address his own son, and he will refer to the sons of the sons of this woman as grandsons. In other words, kinship terms serve as categories, to be sure, but these categories also translate into genealogical ties. The existence of separate terms for cross cousins (potential marriage partners) and parallel cousins (ineligible as partners) results from the *translation and reduction to 'genealogical' positions* of 'relations between categories' of 'kinship relations'.

And this is our second point. The classification into kin categories applies simultaneously to all members of Ego's society. Each man and each woman finds him- or herself automatically placed at birth in one or several 'kinship' relations with every other member of the society. In this universe, there is no such thing as non-kin. And this universe extends beyond the borders of the local territorial group, of the 'tribe'.

When two Aboriginal people from different tribes meet in the desert, rather than fighting, they lay down their weapons and begin reciting their pedigree, the section they belong to, their father's section, their mother's, and so on. Until each comes to an ancestor who belonged to the same 'type' of section. They can then situate each other in a fictive universe of kinship relations and then conduct themselves according to the code that would govern their respective behaviours and mutual obligations if they belonged to the same tribe. This process is attested by numerous anecdotes.

Kinship, according to Alain Testart's expression, 'saturates' Australian

---

marrying his mother's brother's daughter (MBD), he marries his mother's mother's brother's daughter's daughter (MMBDD).

75   Testart, 'Manières de prendre femme en Australie', part 4: 'La Question de l'échange'.

Aboriginal societies. But the expression could lead us astray if it is true that, as some specialists claim,[76] the primary function of the division of society into sections and subsections is not to govern kinship relations and the exchange of spouses between individuals, but is merely a form of social organization designed to regulate ritual relations with the heavenly and earthly beings that fashioned the earth in the Dreaming, and to ensure peaceful relations with neighbouring tribes and with more distant neighbours of their neighbours. This regulation is necessary because each local group is in charge of part of the itinerary followed by the great beings of the Dreaming, which in the course of their travels and adventures brought forth here a lake, there a mountain and left behind millions of seeds of life of all the plant and animal species. These seeds are reactivated year after year when humans perform the multiplication rites for the plants and animals they use for their food.

Today, however, we know that sections did not exist in many of the groups living in the immense Central Desert of Australia at the time these regions were first explored by Europeans. We also know that some of these groups had only recently adopted the section system, which they had borrowed from their neighbours either at the beginning of the twentieth century, as with the Pintupi,[77] or around 1930, as the Ngaatjatjarra did.[78] And yet the latter groups took just as active a role as their neighbours in the initiations and fertility rites associated with the Dreamtime, and therefore fully shared the mythico-religious universe common to all Australian Aboriginal societies. But until then they had not needed to split into sections or subsections to exercise kinship and regulate their relations with the land and the Dreamtime. So what were their kinship systems like if they did not have sections? To Elkin and Lévi-Strauss they seemed 'aberrant' and 'marginal'. Yet they were hardly marginal, since they covered several hundred thousand square kilometres. Nor were they aberrant, because it has since been shown that these systems were not anomalies but variant Dravidian systems that had never yet been shown to exist in Australia. And these Dravidian systems were particularly well endowed with a distinct terminology for real affines, which is rare in Dravidian systems but general in Iroquois systems.

Mervyn Meggitt,[79] in his work on the Walbiri, was the first to challenge the

---

76   M. Meggitt, *Desert People: A Study of the Walbiri Aborigines of Central Australia* (Chicago, University of Chicago Press, 1975).

77   F. Myers, *Pintupi Country, Pintupi Self: Sentiment, Place and Politics among Western Aborigines* (Washington DC, Smithsonian Institution, 1986), pp. 28–32.

78   L. Dousset, 'Diffusion of Sections in the Australian Western Desert: Reconstructing Social Networks', in *Assimilating Identities: Social networks and the diffusion of sections* (Sydney, Oceania Publications, 2005, Monograph 57).

79   M. Meggitt, 'Understanding Australian Aboriginal Society: Kinship or Cultural Categories?', in P. Reining (ed.), *Kinship Studies in the Morgan Centennial Year* (Washington DC, Anthropological Society of Washington, 1972).

idea that the system of sections and subsections arose from the need to regulate the exchange of women and marriage in Australian societies. He has since been followed by many others, of whom Laurent Dousset is the latest. For Meggitt, sections are a way of classifying society, which is itself part of a general classification of all beings in the universe: the sun, the moon, reptiles, birds, cold-blooded animals, warm-blooded animals and so forth.[80] This classification is based on a dualist principle that at every level distinguishes and opposes elements of the universe or the society, which are both distinct and complementary. It would therefore appear that the division into sections and subsections arose from the need to distribute all members of society into categories playing complementary and opposite roles in the ritual management of the universe: one section would perform rites to the sun, another would have privileged relations with the moon, with the rain, with the plants and the animals that are classified as wet, as opposed to the sun and everything classified as dry. In sum, the sections would have appeared in response to questions other than the organization of the exchange of women and kinship. This division would have appeared necessary for society to exist as a whole differentiated into complementary groups, each with a ritual influence on the portion of nature and the cosmos for which it was responsible. This political-ritual division would have gone on to subsume kinship relations and so restructure them that they were congruent with the functioning of the initiation rites. To the initiations, an instrument by which the men exercised political and religious dominance over women and young people, were added rites ensuring the fertility and multiplication of the plants and animals, also in the possession of the men who owned the *churinga*, the sacred objects and secret formulas indispensable to the performance of these rites. In this organization, the men must of necessity appear as the primary persons responsible for the survival of their group.

It is because the division of society into sections is not rooted in human (or divine) male or female ancestors that it distributes all individuals, without reference to genealogical ties, and that, when applied to the exercise of kinship, it endows kin terms with a categorial dimension. Using these terms then makes it possible to reconstruct, if necessary, individuals' genealogical ties with each other, but also to skip this reconstruction. Incest, marriage and descent, the three basic components of kinship, are thus redefined in terms of kin categories and not of genealogical positions. The other component, 'residence', was not, as Radcliffe-Brown believed, the fact of individuals living together in patrilineal or patrilocal nomadic bands. In reality the bands in question were groups of

---

80   Cf. C. G. von Brandenstein, 'The Meaning of Section and Subsection Names', *Oceania*, no. 41 (1970), pp. 39–49 and *Names and Substance of the Australian Subsection System* (Chicago, University of Chicago Press, 1982).

related individuals who belonged to several sections and moved about various parts of the tribal territory along strings of sacred sites belonging to these different sections. When they came to the sacred sites of one section, the members of a band from this section, if there were any, would give the others ritually, as it were, the right to use the animal and plant resources of the territory around these sites.

There is therefore a congruence of sorts between the existence of sections and kin terms. Some authors, like Scheffler, have claimed that the sections acted as terminological 'superclasses'. We will come back to this point, but beforehand I would like to stress that we can no longer, as Lévi-Strauss did a half century ago, go into raptures over the 'crystalline beauty' of the Australian systems, which we supposedly owe to the possibility of expressing, in an equivalent manner, Australian kinship relations according to a categorial logic, in other words in the language of marriage classes envisaged as equivalent to sections, and according to a genealogical logic. It has since become clear that these two logics do not completely overlap and that the crystal contains some impurities.

THE NOTION OF SUPERCLASS

Before coming back to the exchange of women in Australian societies, let us take a closer look at this notion of superclass with the aid of F. Tjon Sie Fat's analyses.[81] The concept was developed by Lounsbury and Scheffler[82] in the framework of what they called a structural analysis of the 'semantic field' of kinship. Lounsbury had begun, in 1964,[83] by analyzing Fox Indian kin terms from this standpoint. He had shown that the term 'mother' acted as a superclass because it subsumed two subclasses, that of mother in the direct line from Ego, which contains only one individual, and that of mother's sisters, also designated as mothers of Ego but who are mothers in the collateral line. All these women call their children by the same terms, *negwihHA* and *netabensA*, which mean 'son' and 'daughter'. But these terms are also used by those who are said to be the fathers of these sons and these daughters. So that for Lounsbury, over and above the concept of 'mother' as a superclass, there is another, higher superclass, that of 'parents'. To this superclass would correspond the reciprocal superclass of 'children', divided by the sole criterion of sex, whereas the superclass of 'parents'

---

81   I would particularly like to thank F. Tjon Sie Fat for his help in analyzing the concept of superclass as Lounsbury and Scheffler developed it.

82   H. W. Scheffler and F. G. Lounsbury, *A Study in Structural Semantics: The Siriono Kinship System* (Englewood Cliffs NJ, Prentice Hall, 1971).

83   F. G. Lounsbury, 'A Formal account of Crow-Omaha type kinship terminologies', in W. H. Goodenough (ed.), *Explorations in Cultural Anthropology: Essays in Honor of George Peter Murdock* (New York, McGraw-Hill, 1964), pp. 331–43. Reprinted in A. Tyler (ed.), *Cognitive Anthropology* (New York, Holt, Rinehart and Winston, 1969), pp. 212–55.

is built on a twofold distinction, between the sexes and between lineals and collaterals. These relations, which, according to Lounsbury, indicate the presence of a law that he calls 'the coherence of reciprocal terms', are shown in the following diagram:

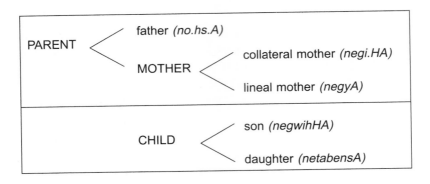

Lounsbury took care to acknowledge that such superclasses are often not designated by a specific term in the language, and therefore in the kinship terminology, of a given society. They are, according to this reasoning, implicit mental realities that individuals may sometimes verbalize by a variety of circumlocutions. But what raises questions is the fact that, for these authors, such terminological classes are derived from an original meaning, from a referent that is the seat and the basis of the class. For instance, some languages have a category called 'father's sisters' (FZ), which includes several subclasses, among which the father's genealogical sisters and all of his classificatory sisters. In some kinship systems (Dravidian, Australian), these father's sisters are potentially or really Ego's wife's mothers (FZ = WM). For Lounsbury, this class of father's sisters is therefore constructed by extension of the genealogical relation between Ego's father and his real sisters. This extension would be accomplished by establishing a series of structural equivalents between certain individuals, all of which can be reduced to genealogical ties.

One can object that, in these systems, the father's genealogical sister is not distinguishable from the father's sisters who are real or potential wife's mothers. And this is because the marriage rule is based on sister exchange between two men, which means that the father's sister is at the same time the maternal uncle's wife. Now if a male Ego reproduces his father's marriage, he marries his mother's brother's daughter, who is at the same time his father's sister's daughter. In these systems there is therefore no father's sister who is not potentially a wife's mother and whose genealogical meaning would thus extend to all wife's mothers.

Going further than Lounsbury, Scheffler, in his book *Australian Kin Classification*,[84] thought he could show that it was possible to move easily from a system of Ego-centric terminological superclasses, in other words genealogies, to a system of classes no longer centred on Ego, a system of socio-centric sections. Scheffler imagined this passage as the product of a series of operations that established the equivalence between agnates and uterine kin in alternate generations. In a section system, for example, Ego's father's father belongs to the same section as Ego, as do Ego's son's children (FF → B); (MM → Z). Or, from another angle, that of systems divided into alternate generational moieties, Ego's father's father is in the same moiety as Ego and Ego's grandsons (FF = SS), and grandparents and grandchildren use reciprocal terms of address. But it can be shown that this supposed equivalence between individuals in non-consecutive generations cannot be explained by the extension of genealogical ties. The continuity is not between the father and the son but between the grandfather and the grandson. The equivalence of alternate generations is not based on genealogical ties but on an idea of time, a cyclical, cosmic time that erases genealogical ties every three generations. What we find behind this dynamic of kin terms is therefore *a philosophical conception of the cosmos and society* and *not an extension of genealogical kin ties*.

It is therefore the socio-cosmic equivalence of a certain category of individuals belonging to different generations that explains that these same individuals can occupy like positions in the initiation and fertility rites whose organization depends directly on the existence of sections.

To sum up my position in this debate: while I acknowledge that superclasses exist, explicitly or implicitly, in many kinship terminologies, to my mind this is not enough to sustain the 'extensionist' explanation of kin terms, which is based ultimately on genealogical ties. A large portion of the equivalence relationship between kin, when it exists, cannot be thought of as forms of the extension of primary genealogical ties to distant, secondary kin.

In this perspective, we can rethink the meaning of the expression 'exchange of women' in Australian systems. For (a male) Ego to marry, three conditions must obtain: the woman must belong to the category of potential wives, but this man must also have acquired certain rights on this woman and – an additional condition which has nothing to do with kinship and *precedes* a man's marrying anyone – he must have been initiated.

Let us come back to the first condition. At the global level of a society divided into, say, four sections, or 'marriage classes' as they used to be called, the marriage in question is therefore 'classified', and this division is the general condition, the

84   H. W. Scheffler, *Australian Kin Classification* (Cambridge, Cambridge University Press, 1978).

preprogrammed framework, as it were, of every potential regular marriage and precedes the fact of any real marriage. This has led certain authors, like Alain Testart, to distinguish two levels of kinship in Australia: classificatory kinship and manipulated kinship. And these authors claim, in a formula aimed at Lévi-Strauss, which may seem surprising, that 'the Australian kinship system is not a marriage-*exchange* system' because, if 'my wife's brother' (WB) is called by the same term as 'my sister's husband' (ZH), it is in virtue of a 'structural property inherent in the kinship system. In this system, all WB are automatically classificatory ZH'. There is therefore at this level no possibility of an alliance strategy:

> From the structural standpoint, nothing changes and there is nothing to give, since my sisters are and have always been, in virtue of the system of kinship, destined to be my wife's brothers' wives (Z = WBW). There is a logical reciprocity at the heart of the structure, but no sister exchange properly speaking.[85]

Testart has the great merit of having shown, by a meticulous study of the principal publications on Australian Aboriginal peoples going back to the work of Fison and Howitt in 1880, that *direct* sister exchange does indeed exist in Australia. But it is *neither a regular practice nor even a major constant of Aboriginal social life* – although it is suggested by the existence of sections and the fact that they serve as 'marriage classes' (which Lévi-Strauss analyzed as such).

Nevertheless, to say as Testart does that classificatory kinship is not basically an exchange system is a paralogism. Because all sections are exogamous (since marrying within the same section is regarded as incestuous and therefore is forbidden), in practice all members of a section must look outside their section for a permissible partner. Here we have the chain of cause and effect (incest taboo–exogamy–exchange), but the exchange does not take place concretely between two persons. It is an abstract, global exchange between groups belonging to different sections. In this way the division of society into sections creates the global, logical and sociological necessity of exchange. But this exchange, which could take the form of an exchange between members of one section and those of the three others, is also limited, since the members of one section are potential spouses for the members of only one of the other three sections.

The original feature of this system is that the children of the two intermarrying sections automatically belong to the two sections into which their parents do not marry. And conversely, the two sections to which the children belong engender through intermarriage the members of the two parental sections. The system is logically and sociologically circular, closed. It is also philosophically circular, since this circularity is conceived as having been preordained from the original

---

85   Testart, 'Manière de prendre femme en Australie'.

Dreamtime, a time that does not pass or change, an eternal time. In such a system, if one considers only the level of classificatory kinship (which is presented as having been based from the beginning of time on a dual division of both the cosmos and society), it is obvious, as Alain Testart writes, that the 'family', and even less the 'nuclear' family if not the biological family, could never be the basis of society.[86] Alternatively, when it comes to the concrete everyday practice of kinship, marriage is truly a question of choice, of decisions to ally oneself with one family or another. It acts as a founding point of departure. Let us add that marriage, among Aboriginal peoples as among the Baruya and in many other societies, is not a religious act. How then is a marriage actually decided in Australian Aboriginal societies?

Real marriages are in fact the result of a man acquiring rights on a woman (which comes as no surprise), and therefore of the creation of ties between this man and a certain number of men and women in the preceding generation. These ties can be, for example, those that exist between this man and the man who initiated or circumcised him and who therefore owes him a wife or has a duty to help him find one. The ties can also bind this man to a woman, often of the same age as he, whom he treats as his mother-in-law, which gives him rights on her children, which rights he can even transfer to other men. The abduction of a wife or a girl promised to another, on the other hand, will prompt reprisals and compensations. Sometimes, as among the Walbiri, the wife or fiancée will be between three and ten years of age, and will be abducted by her husband, etc. Afterwards, the man's obligations to his wife-givers will translate into numerous gifts of game, services, etc. Here we are back in a familiar world.

If we compare the various exchange formulas we have just examined, the differences are clear: in Baruya society, direct sister exchange between lineages is the general marriage rule, but with it goes the ban on repeating the same marriage for several generations. In Australian Aboriginal society, the general rule is sister exchange between sections (which are not clans or lineages). The exchange is reciprocal and is repeated from one generation to the next. But this general formula is not accompanied by generalized practice of sister exchange. Lastly, among the Crow-Omaha, direct exchange is forbidden, the ban on repeating the same marriages extends to many categories of kin and lasts for a certain number of generations. However, as Françoise Héritier showed,[87] restricted exchange is actively present in the system for two complementary reasons. Opposite-sex siblings, a brother and a sister, can in effect marry members of the same lineage, something two brothers or two sisters cannot do. And while an exchange cannot be made with the lineage from which one of them took his wife, it is possible with another lineage in the same clan.

---

86   Ibid.
87   Héritier, *L'Exercice de la parenté*, Chapter 2, pp. 73–131.

The facts are thus much more complex than Lévi-Strauss had supposed a half century ago and today raise new questions that call for new formulations. The same is true for Lévi-Strauss' second class of elementary structures, that of systems engendered by the 'generalized' exchange of women between the kin groups that make up a society. The rule is simple: instead of wife-takers also being wife-givers, as in 'restricted' exchange, and each group being at the same time in the position of taker and giver vis-à-vis another group, this time the givers are not takers. Each group receives women from one or several groups and gives its own women to one or several other groups. In order for this formula to work, the existence of at least three groups is required: the group of Ego (B), that of his givers (A) and that of his takers (C).

$$A \to B \to C$$

For the system to be closed, A, which gives its women to B, must receive women from C.

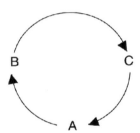

This type of system is common in Indonesia and in Southeast Asia, and Lévi-Strauss thought he had also identified it among the Murngin of Australia as well. It was in fact a Dutchman, Van Wouden,[88] who, although not having done fieldwork in Indonesia but using the ethnographic data collected by Dutch missionaries and administrators working in the archipelago, had worked out the formula in his doctoral dissertation, thus founding the Dutch structuralist school, whose important contribution to alliance theory predated the work of Lévi-Strauss and Louis Dumont by a good ten years.

Van Wouden used the Latin term *connubium*[89] for these intermarriage chains and revealed their asymmetrical structure, which results from the fact

---

88   F. A. E. Van Wouden, *Sociale Structuurtypen in de groote Oost* (Leiden, J. Ginsberg, 1935); English translation: *Types of Social Structure in Eastern Indonesia*, translated by Rodney Needham (The Hague, Nijhoff, 1968).

89   Van Wouden, 'Connubium, relations de parenté par alliance instituées par des mariages répétés', in *Sociale Structuurtypen in de groote Oost*, pp. 11–13, 91–3.

that relations between the groups, when it comes to the circulation of women, are unilateral. In reality, these relations are two-way though, for, opposite the direction in which the women circulate, which goes from givers to takers, goods and services flow from takers to givers.

In this system, givers are superior to takers, but as each group is at the same time giver *and* taker, each ends up being simultaneously superior to its takers and inferior to its givers. Unlike the Baruya, where takers and givers exchange wives reciprocally and, at the close of the exchanges, find themselves on an equal social footing, since each group is simultaneously superior to its allies as a giver and inferior as a taker, here the groups are also both givers and takers, but their status vis-à-vis their takers and their givers is *permanently* unequal.

While these systems imply at least three descent groups from Ego's standpoint, they actually have only two sides (two lines): the mother's side (the givers) and the father's side (the takers). The system is not based on exchanging persons for persons but goods and services for persons, as among the Melpa, etc. Why then did Lévi-Strauss include these systems in the elementary structures when they forbid the exchange of women? It would appear to be because the repetition of marriages between the same groups means that a man will take a wife in his mother's line and marry his mother's brother's sister, his matrilateral cross cousin, while his sister will marry her father's sister's son (her patrilateral cross cousin). It is therefore because the spouse's position is inscribed in a pre-existing kin tie – with the mother's brother for a male Ego, with the father's sister for a female Ego – that Lévi-Strauss classified this form of marriage among the elementary structures of kinship, whereas it actually *excludes* the direct exchange of women.

In Kachin society, the giver–taker relationship is designated by a specific term, it is the *mayu–dama* relationship. Leach goes on to explain that marriage rarely (or never) takes place with a genealogically close matrilateral cross cousin but rather with a classificatory cross cousin.[90] He also points out that, in practice, the Kachin *are not aware* that their system comes full circle at either the local level (their individual group) or the global level (that of their society as a whole).[91] They know only that there are, on one side, a certain number of giver-groups and, on the other side, a certain number of taker-groups. And they are not tied to their givers or their takers for life. They can add new ones and eliminate old ones. In short, marriage alliances are repeated with the same groups over a certain number of generations, and in this sense, as Louis Dumont said, they are 'inherited'[92] (as one inherits goods or titles in a descent group). But not forever.

---

90   E. Leach, 'Aspects of Bridewealth and Marriage Stability among the Kachin and the Lakher', *Man*, nos. 276–9 (1987), pp. 179–80.

91   F. K. Lehman, 'On Chin and Kachin Marriage Regulation', *Man*, vol. 5 (1970), pp. 118–25.

92   L. Dumont, *Affinity as a Value: Marriage Alliances in South India with Comparative Essays on Australia* (Chicago, University of Chicago Press, 1983), p. 72.

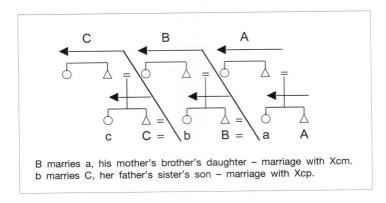

B marries a, his mother's brother's daughter – marriage with Xcm.
b marries C, her father's sister's son – marriage with Xcp.

There are even societies that take generalized exchange further, up to the point of including in their terminology their givers' givers and their takers' takers. In this case, the kin terms are distributed along five lines and not three. The Kachin have an asymmetrical prescriptive terminology: the term they use for father is the same as for father's brother: F = FB, which is different from the term for mother's brother (MB), which in turn is different from the terms for father's sister's husband (FZH). This gives us (F = FB ≠ MB ≠ FZH), whereas in a Dravidian-type symmetrical system, we have (F = FB) ≠ (MB = FZH).[93]

A word about the wealth, goods and services that circulate at the same time as women, but in the opposite direction. Among the Purum, an Indian tribal people with a patrilineal descent rule and patrilocal residence, marriage entails two types of circulation of goods: a movement of 'male' goods that flows from takers to givers, completed by a multitude of services the son-in-law will render to his father-in-law's family;[94] and an opposite movement of 'female' goods which completes the gift of the women – household utensils, clothing, jewellery, etc. – that flows from givers to takers. Needham stresses that the oppositions between takers and givers and between male goods and female goods extends to the universe as a whole, to things, individuals, colours, and so forth, all classified according to the same dualist principle which repeatedly both brings together and opposes pairs of opposites.[95]

---

93   The same type of equation can be found in the Kariera system, which is both symmetrical and prescriptive.

94   He owes him his labour for the first three years of the marriage, after which he can bring his wife home to live in his lineage.

95   Needham, *Structure and Sentiment: A Test Case in Social Anthropology*, pp. 95–6.

THE SEMI-COMPLEX STRUCTURES OF KINSHIP

We will now move on from the 'elementary' structures of kinship, that is to say those based on the restricted or generalized exchange of women, to examine what Lévi-Strauss called the 'semi-complex structures' of kinship. A reminder of their definition: we call 'semi-complex' systems those that multiply the prohibitions on reproducing past marriage alliances for a certain number of generations and which do not have an explicit positive rule for choosing a spouse. The outlines of this category of systems remain vague. It seems that Lévi-Strauss included the Hawaiian and Iroquois systems, but without analyzing any examples, and he always cited the Crow and Omaha systems as a reference.[96]

This system forbids direct 'sister' exchange between two men and two lineages. The form of exchange practised is that of goods and services for a wife. Repetition of marriage alliances is allowed on the condition that the lineages alternate their exchanges in each generation as follows: a man having married two women from different lineages will in the following generation give each of these lineages a woman, taking a daughter he has had with the wife from the first lineage and giving her to the second lineage, and vice versa. Sometimes he will wait even longer and give one of the lineages a daughter from one of his sons. In Ego's generation, the marriage is therefore accomplished without the exchange of persons but by the exchange of goods and services.

The Samo of Burkina-Faso, studied by Françoise Héritier, have a patrilineal kinship system of the Omaha type. They, too, give the lineage of one of the wives a daughter born to another wife from another lineage And since, in this patrilineal system, a son cannot take a wife in his own lineage nor in his mother's or father's lineage, in every generation each lineage finds itself linked with several other lineages but must turn to yet other lineages to marry its sons and daughters. The lineage thus finds itself part of several generalized exchange cycles, as in Kachin society, but has the possibility of transforming former takers into givers and vice versa after a few generations, a possibility that does not exist for the Kachin. In addition, the Samo contract one-off secondary marriages with lineages in distant villages for which they simply pay a high bridewealth. These marriages bring them sons and daughters to exchange in order to create new exchange circuits with the local lineages, since their mother does not come from any of them.[97]

---

96   Françoise Héritier, on the other hand, rapidly analyzed an example of an Iroquois system with some Hawaiian features, found among the Tanebar-Evav on Kei island in the Moluccas (cf. C. Barraud, *Tanebar-Evav, une société de maisons tournées vers le large* [Cambridge, Cambridge University Press and Paris, Maison des Sciences de l'Homme, 1979]) in *L'Exercice de la parenté*, pp. 129–31.

97   Héritier, *L'Exercice de la parenté*, p. 125.

We are thus in the presence of systems which, in practice, have not fore-gone the principle of 'sister' exchange but which have made it a silent, implicit rule that applies in that space of kinship relations left open by the many prohibi-tions on the repetition of marriage alliances. But since these communities are relatively small and were formerly wary of outside relations, owing to the many conflicts and feuds between villages, repetition of marriages is a social necessity that can be deferred for no more than two or three generations. Consequently the multiplication of prohibitions elicits a multiplication of new alliances in each generation, and the obligation to give a woman for a woman received continues in force as well, if only to ensure that the gifts of women between line-ages and clans balance out over the middle term.

The example of Tanebar-Evav, a small Indonesian society of some one thousand people living in the Kei islands, is a perfect illustration of how it is possible to juxtapose and combine several marriage rules, one of which forbids exchanging women, while the other allows it but forbids reproducing this exchange for several generations. Tanebar-Evav society is organized as a system of exogamous, ranked 'houses' (like Kwakiutl society). Each house has two opposing 'sides', right and left, elder and younger. Pre-eminence goes to the right and the elders. Each side is occupied by a patrilineage (*rin*). It is forbidden to marry either in one's lineage or into another lineage in the same house.

Two different rules are at work in the organization of marriages.[98] The oldest son in each *rin* must marry his mother's brother's daughter (MBD), in other words his matrilateral cross cousin. In doing so he repeats his father's marriage and reproduces the hierarchical relationship between the two houses, since as 'takers' his lineage and his house are inferior to the lineage and the house of their 'givers'. However this marriage of the eldest is regarded almost as incest and requires sacrifice to a special god.

The younger sons of noble lineages and 'commoners' marry in an 'egalitar-ian' fashion by exchanging women directly between houses. These exchanges cannot be repeated before three generations, and two brothers are prohibited from taking wives in the same *rin* or in the same house. When three generations have elapsed and the alliance is repeated, the sister exchange takes place with the other *rin* of the house with which an ancestor had formerly contracted an alliance or with another segment of the same *rin*, as with the Samo of Africa, the Omaha of North America and perhaps the Mekeo of New Guinea. This system thus combines an asymmetrical marriage rule, as in Purum society, who marry their matrilateral cross cousin, and a rule of direct exchange that is not renew-able for several generations, like the Baruya or the Omaha.

In the final analysis, the first rule is one of the exchange of goods and

---

98   Cf. ibid., pp. 129–30.

services for a person within a hierarchical relationship between social groups (houses) that reproduce the same unilateral alliances generation after generation and in so doing reproduce their superior–inferior relations within a social ranking between noble and commoner houses. The younger sons of the noble houses are assimilated to commoners because they do not inherit their father's house and do not represent its status. The second rule is based on direct sister exchange but, by forbidding repetition of the alliance for several generations, it forces each house to change the direction and the circle of its alliances at each generation, thus producing a complex generalized exchange that contains, on the one hand, the possibility of cycles which come full circle in the same generations (A → B → C → A), but which also gives rise in each generation to branching, interlinking networks. A is linked with (B, E, F) while D is linked with (A, B, C, F) and E with (G, A, C, H), and so on.

In short, in all these societies, the kinship systems have opened up because the many prohibitions compel the kinship units (clans, houses, lineages, etc.) to multiply their alliances and to delay their repetition for one or two lifetimes (i.e. two or three generations). Since these alliances will have to be repeated sooner or later, in so far as these societies are small communities and relatively closed to other societies, when that time comes, the principle of the direct exchange of women comes to the fore once again, but reshaped so as to comply with the marriage taboos.

THE COMPLEX STRUCTURES OF KINSHIP

The openness and fluidity of marriage alliances are even greater in the 'complex' structures of kinship. There are two reasons for this. First of all because two things have disappeared (or never existed) from the field in which kinship is exercised.

On the one hand, in these societies, there are no descent groups recruited on a unilineal or other basis, and therefore no lineages, clans, 'houses', and so forth obliged to ensure their existence by manipulating their alliances and repeating them advisedly when it once again becomes possible and useful.

On the other hand, in 'complex' systems, there is no positive rule that prescribes or recommends that individuals marry a given class of kin. Alternatively, a certain number of kin are forbidden as marriage partners, usually consanguines and close affines in Ego's generation as well as in the ascending and descending generations. If Ego is a man, he cannot marry his great-nieces and his great-aunts, nor his father's or mother's mother or sisters, nor his father's and mother's brother's and sisters' sisters or daughters, nor his or his brothers' and sisters' daughters, nor his granddaughters and great-nieces. Some of these prohibitions are set out explicitly in civil law. In France, for instance, until recently a man could not marry his wife's sister, even if the former had died or had divorced. Today, however, a man can divorce his wife and marry his sister-in-law.

The number of persons it is forbidden to marry in the twenty-first century is paltry compared with other periods in Christian Western Europe. In the Early Middle Ages, the Church had multiplied the number of degrees of kinship that prohibited marriage to the point that, in the thirteenth century, marriage was forbidden between kin to the seventh degree. Faced with the difficulty of applying this norm in many village or urban communities, where people married both within their condition and in their own neighbourhood (where families were often related – close or distant cousins),[99] the Church found itself obliged to reduce the distance to the fifth degree of kinship, at the Lateran Council (1215), and then finally to limit itself to the second degree, which is today's norm.[100]

Since the end of the eighteenth century, the social makeover that accompanied the rise of industrial capitalism and the appearance of new urban zones drew segments of the rural and small-town populations to the new urban industrial centres and the big cities of Western Europe. In the wake of these population flows and mingling, people more or less rapidly fell out of touch with their kindred and, among them, with their collateral kin. And since many of them, as well as their direct descendants, had changed their social condition and even class over their lifetime, social distances were added to genealogical and geographical distances, further fragmenting families and kindred. For the majority of people, marriage is no longer associated with perpetuating a family line or name, or with transmitting land or other forms of wealth. It has to do more with the desire to live with the person one has chosen and thus with the desire to found something new rather than to ensure continuity with the past. Nor is marriage necessary to fulfil these desires – hence the multiplication of couples simply living together, for whom what matters is social recognition not of their union but of their children, recognized by the civil authorities who provide the children, and through them their parents, with a status and social advantages.

When there is a divorce or a cohabiting couple separates, new families or new unions are formed, composed of adults and children either from former unions or born to the new couple. By exerting pressure on the parents, whatever the nature of their union, to recognize their children, the state partially protects them from the upheavals occasioned by their parents' lives. From this global standpoint, the

---

99   See T. Jolas, M.-C. Pingaud, Y. Verdier and F. Zonnabend, *Une campagne voisine* (Paris, Editions de la Maison des sciences de l'homme, 1990); M. Segalen, 'Parenté et alliance dans les sociétés paysannes', *Ethnologie française*, vol. 11, no. 4 (1891), pp. 307–29.

100   As imposed by the Catholic Church.

developments in marriage, the family and the other forms of union we see in our societies – as well as the example of the Baruya or the Melpa – clearly show that the family and kinship are not the 'foundation' of society. Other social relations – political, economic and juridical – associated with the existence of the state, ensure that all children recognized by their parents enjoy the same rights in their society, whatever the nature of the bond between their parents.

Last of all, recently, in certain Western European countries (Holland, Great Britain), homosexual couples have been authorized by law to make their couple a family by allowing them legally to adopt children. This is a radical change in human kinship relations, in so far as it makes adoption a founding principle of descent fully equal with biological reproduction and completely excludes sexual relations from the criteria for founding a family. One of the consequences will be that heterosexual relations, which engender children 'naturally', will now be placed at the service of homosexuals' desire to have children, a desire that moves them to claim the right also to found families. One portion of humanity will therefore now provide the other with the means to have children without recourse to the union of the two sexes. Heterosexuality will thus be globally pressed into the service not of the homosexual desire of these couples (or of the communities comprised of several homosexual couples) but of the desire of homosexuals to have children, descendants, without themselves having to bow to the fact of sexual difference. But until we can produce children outside the womb by purchasing male semen, until the babies engendered by a cutting-edge technology are available to all individuals – homo- or heterosexual – who want to have a child without having to engender or adopt it themselves, heterosexual relations will remain the general condition for the perpetuation of human kind.[101]

---

101   It goes without saying that this radical revolution in kinship and parenthood demanded by some homosexual groups has nothing in common with Baruya ritual homosexuality, which is an instrument of the male political and social domination of women in society as in the family. And it has nothing in common either with the marriage between women in the Nuer society. In this south Sudanese society, when a wealthy woman is sterile, it is possible for her to marry another woman, providing she pays her family a brideprice as a man would normally have done. In so doing, she gains the right to appropriate the children that this woman she has 'married' engenders with authorized lovers. And these children will become members of the first woman's patriline. In other cases, the widow of a man who has died without issue can marry a woman in order to procure descendants for her husband's lineage. (See Evans-Pritchard, *Kinship and Marriage among the Nuer*, pp. 144–5.) This text is sometimes used as anthropological evidence by certain supporters of civil marriage in the juridical context of the constitution of a homosexual family by adoption or insemination. (See also our Conclusion.) However the marriage of a sterile woman or a childless widow with another woman has nothing to do with founding a homosexual family. The two women do not have homosexual relations with each other, and the children conceived by one of them with an authorized lover (who is not the father but the genitor) belong to the patrilineage of the husband of the sterile woman or the widow. Marriage between two women is thus a way around, a flexible (and sociologically rare) means of perpetuating the patrilineal descent rule that is central to the Nuer kinship system and is based on heterosexual relations.

CHAPTER FIVE

Kinship Terminologies
(Fourth Component)

An overview will enable us first of all to show how representations of consanguinity, affinity and cognation differ according to the major kinship terminologies and forms of alliance. We will then have a general view of the functions of kinship. Knowledge of the various descent and alliance rules is the prerequisite for reconstructing and understanding what, in various societies, is meant by what we call fatherhood, motherhood, siblings, ascendants, descendants, affines, and close or distant relatives. In each case, the functions of kinship are distributed differently among persons occupying distinct positions in the network of kin ties. We will end the chapter with an example of what a child is for its parents in Inuit society, a society whose kinship terminology belongs to the same category as that of Western societies, but which puts it to a very different use and continues to do so in spite of 150 years of subordination to the West.

Morgan's discovery of the scientific interest of kinship terminologies and their systematic study laid one of the building stones of anthropology and established it as a new social science. For over a century (until the 1970s), the study of kinship was one of the main objects of anthropologists' efforts. One of the first things young anthropologists were advised to do when going into the field was to collect kin terms and marriage rules. Hundreds of terminologies from societies with a wide variety of languages and structures were thus gathered and compared. It quickly appeared that, once the principles of construction had been isolated, the great majority of nomenclatures fell into one of the major types of kinship terminology that Morgan had identified and described in his *Systems of Consanguinity and Affinity of the Human Family* (1871) after having processed the worldwide survey he had organized and administered in the 1860s. All turned out to be more or less complex variants of one of his types or combinations of components of several types. In the latter case, the terminologies appeared as hybrids of two types or as systems in transition from one type to another.

Morgan identified six types because he had not made a distinction between the Iroquois and the Dravidian terminologies. This distinction was definitively established following the work of Lounsbury and Trautmann, and Dravidian systems are now a separate type from Morgan's Sudanese, Australian, Crow-Omaha, Hawaiian and Eskimo systems. One problem that remains unresolved is that of the Crow-Omaha systems, which certain authors refuse to consider as a type in its own right.[1]

A small number of other types have recently been identified, but, as we shall see, they occupy a position between two of these seven because their structure is a stable combination of components of the two types in question. For example, the terminology used by the Yafar of New Guinea, which was subsequently found to be used by the Aguaruna of Amazonia and the Red Knife Indians of North America, is a variant of the Iroquois-type but halfway to being a Dravidian terminology.

KINSHIP TERMINOLOGIES ARE INDEPENDENT OF DESCENT RULES

Two facts of major historical and theoretical importance need to be underscored before proceeding further with the details. First, when all is said and done, there are *very few types* of kinship terminologies (only ten or so), into which can be placed the hundreds of terminologies collected in societies having completely different languages, cultures, modes of production and political regimes. And, second, all these terminologies are *independent* of the descent rules (patri- or matrilineal, bilineal or non-lineal) found in these societies. The Baruya thus have an Iroquois-type kinship terminology and a patrilineal descent rule, whereas the Iroquois mode of reckoning descent was matrilineal. Terminologies serve to situate an individual known only by his or her sex, a male or female Ego, with respect to relatives (consanguines and affines) connected to him or her by categorial and/or genealogical ties. Some of these terminologies are associated with positive marriage rules (Australian, Dravidian and, up to a certain point, Iroquois), others are not (Crow-Omaha, Hawaiian, Eskimo, Sudanese).

Let us take the example of the kinship terminologies in use today in most western European societies and among Euro-Americans. These are what we call Eskimo-type terminologies, in which the same term, 'uncle', is used for both father's and mother's brothers, and another, 'aunt', for both father's and mother's sisters, while the term 'cousin' designates the children of both maternal and paternal uncles and aunts. This type is called 'Eskimo' because Morgan had found it among the peoples of the American Great North, which were called Eskimos at the time, but today prefer the term 'Inuit'.

The existence of this type of linear terminology – so named because it clearly distinguishes and opposes kin in the direct line and those in the

---

    1   R. Needham, 'Remarks on the Analysis of Kinship and Marriage', in R. Needham (ed.), *Rethinking Kinship and Marriage* (London, Tavistock Publications, 1971), pp. 14–16; R. Barnes, *Two Crows Denies It: A History of Controversy in Omaha Sociology* (Lincoln/London, University of Nebraska Press, 1984).

collateral line – is attested in Rome from at least the second century CE in various texts, among which those by Aulus Gellus. And we know that this terminology is itself the result of a series of changes in an older nomenclature used by the archaic Latins.[2] This older terminology was of the Sudanese type, so called because it is found among certain populations of the Sudan. But it also existed in medieval Russia, Poland, China, etc.

Unlike the Eskimo system, ancient Latin terminology (of the Sudanese type) uses different terms for direct and collateral lines. It distinguishes father (*pater*) from father's brother (*patruus*), mother (*mater*) from mother's sister (*matertera*), mother's brother (*avunculus*) from father's sister (*amita*) and so forth. Toward the end of the Roman Republic, and for no known reason, the term *patruus* disappeared and the term *avunculus* began to designate both mother's brother, its original meaning, and father's brother, a new meaning. At the same time and in a symmetrical fashion, the term *matertera*, for mother's sister, disappeared, and the term for father's sister (*amita*) came to designate mother's sister as well, with the word *cosobrinus* now designating all of Ego's uncles' and aunts' sons. In English (as in French), the word has become 'cousin', *avunculus* became 'uncle' ('oncle' in French and 'Onkel' in German), etc. By the time these changes were complete, the Sudanese system had become an Eskimo system.

The fact that these changes affected several terms at once – those designating the maternal uncle and the paternal aunt, the cousins on both sides, etc. – proves that the relationship between these terms constituted a specific configuration, that it possessed a *structure*, one of whose terms could not be changed without affecting all of the other terms connected in a network of complementary relationships.

In the end, it is this second Latin terminology that spread through Europe with the expansion of the Roman Empire and replaced the terminologies in use among the local peoples brought under Rome's domination or influence. The expansion of the Latin system must have been greatly influenced by the fact that many local groups spoke Indo-European languages from the same linguistic family as Latin or Greek. These facts, this particular history, already give us an idea of how illusory it is to look for a direct cause-and-effect relationship or even for a structural correspondence between types of terminology and modes of production or political systems.

Let us examine the problem of the possible relationship between Eskimo terminologies and the different ways in which societies organize production. This is a question many Marxian anthropologists put to themselves in the 1970s and 1980s. Before their contact with Europeans and the intense development of

---

2 Cf. L. H. Morgan, *Systems of Consanguinity and Affinity of the Human Family* (Washington DC, Smithsonian Institution, 1871), Chapter 3, pp. 22 ff.

the fur trade that ensued, the Inuit economy was based on hunting, fishing and gathering, done by bands of a few hundred (or even a few dozen) individuals moving over vast territories. Their nomadic life was bound up with the cycle of the seasons and the available animal and vegetable resources, which led them to disperse during the winter and to regroup in the summer. Their economy had nothing in common, then, with those of Roman Europe or even with that of medieval Europe, with its seigniorial economy and feudal, monarchical politi-cal regime. Yet this so-called Eskimo terminology is still in use in Europe, whereas the seigniorial economy and the feudal system have disappeared, grad-ually giving way to merchant and industrial capitalism and to parliamentary and democratic political regimes. The fact that variants of the same type of terminology can be found in societies with such different structures and cultures, and can persist despite major changes in the social organization, attests to the relative *autonomy* of kinship relations and systems with respect to the appearance and disappearance of other features of social organization.

This *relative* autonomy of kinship relations rests, as we have said, on the fact that their primary raison d'être is not to organize hunting, industrial produc-tion or trade. Nor is it to select those who will lead the society and represent it on the political-religious level. It is, rather, to regulate the forms of descent and marriage alliance authorized in a society. It therefore concerns all individual members, including slaves where they exist. Kinship relations define each indi-vidual's place with respect to individuals of both sexes belonging to (genealogically or categorially) ascending generations and who have rights and duties with regard to Ego in virtue of his or her having been born or adopted. Following the same logic, these relations also define this individual's rights and duties with respect to his or her 'descendants' or relatives. And lastly, they define who this person may (or must) marry and whom he or she may not (or must not) marry, and if Ego can marry relatives, what their degree of kinship must be.

These are the raisons d'être of kinship and, as its functions cannot be confused with any others (organizing hunting, power, etc.), it is kinship's particular func-tions that give these relationships a basis and their own structures capable of ensuring their relative autonomy and their permanence with respect to the more or less rapid succession of forms of production and power. It is for the same reasons that kinship terminologies are a specific linguistic fact, a separate vocabu-lary within a language, whose nature and importance were discovered in the nineteenth century, not by linguists (and particularly not by philologists, who had, at the time, just discovered the existence of the Indo-European, Semitic, etc., language families), but by an attorney-turned-anthropologist, Lewis Henry Morgan.[3]

---

3   T. Trautmann, 'Kinship as Language', in P. Descola, J. Hammel and P. Lemonnier (eds.),

WHAT IS A KINSHIP TERMINOLOGY?

A kinship terminology is a set of a very few *words* (usually between twenty and thirty) that designate the relations of what we call 'consanguinity' and 'affinity' that a person of the male or female sex entertains with other individuals, living or dead, belonging to this person's generation or to a certain number of generations above or below him or her. Kin terms are thus linguistic phenomena that allow individuals (and the groups to which they belong) to position themselves with regard to others in the kinship relations that characterize their society. They provide individuals with a self-representation and enable them to communicate to others their place within a set of particular social relations, and to have a representation of the place others occupy in this network without their having necessarily to be related to the speaker. Hence the two series of terms always found in kinship terminologies: one used to address a given relative and the other to designate kin ties. A is the 'father' (reference) of B, and B addresses him saying 'Papa'. A kinship terminology thus combines two types of vocabulary, a vocabulary of *address* terms and a vocabulary of *reference* terms. Social anthropologists generally prefer analyzing reference terms because these designate relationships. But they also need to consider the address terms because they are often the first to register changes in kinship relations when these are confronted with new socio-economic contexts.

By *type* of terminology, we mean the principles of construction underlying the particular configuration of the terms used in a language to designate consanguineal and affinal relations. By comparing the principles that organize a specific terminology with those underlying other terminologies (whatever the languages in which these are found), it is possible to decide whether the varieties in question belong to the same type or to different types (Sudanese, Eskimo, Dravidian, etc.). We will return to this point later.

But first, a few important remarks. It is impossible to understand the way certain types of terminologies are constructed without having a clear view of the marriage rules, and of the forms of alliance they implicitly suppose and about which the terminology informs us directly. This is the case with the Australian and Dravidian systems. In a Dravidian system, for example, the same term (x) is used for both mother's brother (MB), father's sister's husband (FZH) and Ego's wife's father (WF), which we represent by the equation $x = (MB = FZH = WF)$. This equation makes sense only if, in the preceding generation (G^{+1}), Ego's father and maternal uncle exchanged 'sisters'. This is confirmed by the fact that the term (y) used for father's sister (FZ) also designates the

La Production du social (Paris, Fayard, 1999), pp. 433–44.

mother's brother's wife (MBW) and Ego's mother-in-law, his wife's mother (WM). From this we deduce the existence of a rule that dictates marriage with the bilateral cross cousin, which organizes the kinship terms and constructs their semantic field. A man's wife is therefore at once the daughter of his maternal uncle (MBD) and the daughter of his paternal aunt (FZD), and therefore (W = MBD = FZD). This does not mean simply that the marriage rule comes down to simple direct 'sister' exchange between two men, two lines or two groups who are in the position of reciprocal wife-givers and -takers, it also implies that this exchange is repeated from one generation to the next.

On the other hand, some types of terminology do not contain any direct indications about the marriage rules practised in the society where they are found. This is the case with the Eskimo, Hawaiian, Sudanese and Crow-Omaha systems. All of these have a special vocabulary for affines, such that the term for wife's father (WF) is distinct from that used for mother's brother (MB), hence the equation (M) $\neq$ (WF). This is also true of Iroquois systems, for example. However, while these types make a distinction in Ego's generation (G°) between cross and parallel cousins, they admit the possibility of (without prescribing) marriage with cross cousins, so that mother's brother and father's sister, who engender Ego's cross cousins (sometimes potential spouses) are not identified in the vocabulary with Ego's wife's father and mother (MB $\neq$ WF; FZ $\neq$ WM).

Many terminologies contain indirect indications of the marriages that are forbidden. This is the case with Dravidian and Iroquois systems, where the terms used for Ego's brothers and sisters, his siblings, are sometimes also used for the children of Ego's parents' brothers and sisters, his parallel and cross cousins to a certain number of degrees. In these systems, the distinction between siblings and parallel and cross cousins is therefore cancelled in G°, Ego's generation (Sb = // = X). In this case, the terminology is said to be 'generational in G°'. This makes the terminology comparable, but *only for this level*, with Hawaiian-type terminologies, which cancel this distinction on the other genealogical levels. Such facts give indirect indications about the forms of marriage practised in these societies. The extension of the terms for brother and sister to all parallel and cross cousins close to Ego is, for instance, an indication that it is forbidden to marry these relatives because it would be tantamount to brothers and sisters marrying and therefore committing incest. It also tells us indirectly that, if the same marriage were to be repeated, at least two generations would have to elapse before it was.

Another important fact: all kinship terminologies start from a reference Ego, and extend to several ascending and descending generations, usually two above (G^{+1}, G^{+2}) and two below (G^{-1}, G^{-2}). This implies that everyone is supposed to memorize all information concerning five generations, their own included, a span that covers nearly a century, if one calculates an average of twenty-five years between two generations. The notions of Ego and generation do not have the same meaning in all kinship systems, however. In the European system, Ego designates *one* abstract individual designated only by his or her sex. Likewise, in this system, Ego has only one father and one mother, but can have several uncles, aunts, cousins, sons, nephews, etc. Some of these terms are constructed on a purely genealogical model, and others on a model that is both genealogical and categorial.

But in other systems, the Australian systems with their sections and subsections, for example, Ego is not a single individual but a *set of individuals* of the same sex who stand in the same or in an equivalent relationship with other sets of individuals designated as his or her fathers, mothers, spouses, sons or nieces, etc. In short, here Ego refers to a category of individuals of the same sex occupying the same position with regard to individuals of both sexes classified in other categories.[4] This explains the fact that, in some kinship systems, Ego may call 'father' or 'mother' individuals who are much younger than him or herself but that the system classifies in the category of Ego's fathers and mothers. In this case, the notion of generation no longer corresponds to the average span of time separating two generations, one of which engendered the other. It no longer corresponds to a relationship or to a chronological and genealogical distance. This is the case of the Australian systems, whether they are divided into sections, like the Aranda, or are without sections, like the Aluridja.

SO-CALLED 'ABERRANT' SYSTEMS

It is worth taking the time to examine more closely the so-called 'Aluridja' systems. Until a few years ago, the best Australian specialists regarded these kinship systems as aberrant cases. This was the opinion of Elkin,[5] who studied them on location and considered them to be incoherent and probably on the way to becoming something else. In 1949, Lévi-Strauss, in his *The Elementary Structures of Kinship*, declared that they were lacking the precision and clarity of the Australian systems characterized by sections and subsections.[6] And again in 1980, in a review of Scheffler's *Australian Kin Classification*,[7] Lévi-Strauss evoked the 'obscurity that continues to envelop these systems'. When it comes to matters

---

4   Two same-sex siblings (brother/brother, sister/sister) will produce parallel cousins who will reproduce their own relationship. Two opposite-sex siblings will produce cross cousins who will be classificatory affines and therefore allowed to marry each other.

5   A. P. Elkin, 'Kinship in South Australia', *Oceania*, vol. 8, no. 4 (1938–40), pp. 423–4.

6   C. Lévi-Strauss, *Les Structures élémentaires de la parenté*, Paris, Presses Universitaires de France, 1949, pp. 231, 238, 251, 253; English translation: *The Elementary Structures of Kinship*, translated by James Harle Bell, John Richard von Sturmer and Rodney Needham, Boston, Beacon Press, 1969.

7   H. W. Scheffler, *Australian Kin Classification* (Cambridge, Cambridge University Press, 1978).

of science, of course, it is always a bit odd to declare that something is 'aberrant'. Today, after the work done by Fred Meyers,[8] Annette Hamilton,[9] and especially by Laurent Dousset,[10] the key to the enigma seems to have been found – and the Aluridja mystery solved.

Why did these systems appear to be abnormal, and even incoherent? In the first place, because they have no sections, subsections or exogamous moieties, unlike most Australian systems. Alternatively, they have endogamous generational moieties. In the second place, it seems that they do not make a distinction between siblings, parallel cousins and cross cousins. And finally, they allow marriage between classificatory brothers and sisters, in spite of the prohibition of incest. But what really goes on? To find out, we need to do a long field study, make an inventory of the hundreds of genealogies, record all marriages since the end of the nineteenth century and look at the dynamics of these systems in a historical perspective.

These systems are typical of the societies living in the Great Western Desert of Australia, one of the most arid regions on the continent. The societies carry names that correspond to dialects: the Ngaatjatjarra, the Pitjantjatjara, etc. Laurent Dousset lived and worked among the Ngaatjatjarra for a number of years. This group of some 500 persons is divided into seven bands, which lead a nomadic life confined to different hunting zones. Part of the Ngaatjatjarra emigrated to the towns around 1950, but most of them have since returned to the desert. Around 1930, their neighbours, the Pitjantjatjara, discovered the existence of sections, and around 1940 came the turn of the Ngaatjatjarra. The latter adopted the section system for several years and attempted to apply it to their kinship system. But they finally let it drop, and simply used it for their contacts with certain aboriginal groups whose own organization was traditionally based on sections.

Laurent Dousset's field research finally enabled us to understand the operating rules of the traditional Ngaatjatjarra, Pitjantjatjara, etc. kinship systems. First of all, these groups distinguish in G^{+1}, mother's brother from father and from father's brother, who are grouped under the same term (FB = F). Likewise a single term is used for mother and mother's sister, and this term is not the same as the word for father's sister (MZ = M) ≠ FZ). In G+1 we thus have a bifurcation which, in principle, is also found in the Australian, Dravidian and

8   F. Myers, *Pintupi Country, Pintupi Self: Sentiment, Place and Politics among Western Aborigines* (Washington DC/London/Canberra, Smithsonian Institution Press, 1986).

9   A. Hamilton, *Timeless Transformation: Women, Men and History in the Australian Western Desert* (Sydney, University of Sydney, 1979).

10   L. Dousset, 'On the Misinterpretation of the Aluridja Kinship System Type (Australian Western Desert)', *Social Anthropology*, vol. 12, no. 1 (2003), pp. 43–61, and 'Accounting for Context and Substance: The Australian Western Desert Kinship Systems', *Anthropological Forum*, vol. 12, no. 2 (2002), pp. 193–204.

NGAATJATJARRA TERMINOLOGY BEFORE MARRIAGE

		X	//	//	X
G+2		*tjamu*		*kaparli*	
G+1		*kamuru* MB, FZH	*mama* F, FB	*ngunytju* M, MZ	*kurntili* FZ, MBW
G0	e	alternative *watjirra* (and others)	*kurta*	*tjurtu*	alternative *watjirra* (and others)
G0	y	MBS, FZS	*marlanypa* FyBS&D, MyZS&D, MyBS, FyZS, MyBD, FyZD, yB, yZ		MBD, FZD
G-1		alternative *yukari* mZS	*katja* S, BS, ZS	*yurntalpa* D, BD, ZD	alternative *yukari* fBD
G-2		*tjamu*		*kaparli*	

(ego box located at center of G0)

NGAATJATJARRA TERMINOLOGY AFTER MARRIAGE

		Male				Female		
		x distant	x close	//	//	x close	x distant	
G+2		*kurri* (f MF)	*tjamu*		*kaparli*		*kurri* (m FM)	
G+1		*waputju* mWF *mingkayi* fHF	*kamuru* MB, FZH	*mama* F, FB, MB, FZH	*ngunytju* M, MZ, FZ, MBW	*kurntili* FZ, MBW	*yumari* mWM *mingkayi* fHM	
G0	e	*watijirra* (and others) MBS, FZS	*kurta*		*tjurtu*		*watjirra* (and others) MBD, FZD	
G0	y	*kurri* H *marutju* WB, mZH	*marlanypa* FyBS&D, MyZS&D, MyBS, FyZS, MyBD, FyZD, yB, yZ				*kurri* W *tjuwari* HZ, wBW	
G-1		*waputju* mDH *mingkayi* fDH	*yukari* mZS	*katja* S, BS, ZS	*yurntalpa* D, BD, ZD	*yukari* fBS	*mingkayi* SW (sometimes also *yumari*)	
G-2		*kurri* (f SS)	*tjamu*		*kaparli*		*kurri* (m DD)	

(ego box located at center of G0)

Iroquois systems, and which introduces a distinction in G° between cross and parallel cousins, the latter usually being assimilated to siblings. The Ngaatjat-jarra were not thought to make a distinction between siblings and cross cousins. But Laurent Dousset discovered that they did indeed have a specific term for cross cousins: *watjirra*. Furthermore, they never marry their classificatory brothers or sisters, or their parallel cousins. Alternatively, they do marry genea-logically and geographically very distant cross cousins, cross cousins in at least the third degree.

So what was the basis for the claim that they married their brothers and sisters? It is in fact connected with the presence in their system of endogamous generational moieties. What does this distinction conceal? It means that the totality of the members of a person's society are divided into two groups: Ego's moiety, and the opposite and complementary moiety. Ego's moiety (moiety A) contains all those who belong to Ego's grandparents' generation (G^{+2}) and all those in that of Ego's grandchildren (G^{-2}) plus those in Ego's own generation ($G°$). All of these individuals belong to chronologically and biologically differ-ent generations, but they call each other brother and sister in the context of their common membership in this moiety. This membership is marked by the reciprocity of the kin terms they use with each other. The grandfather calls his grandson by the same term the grandson uses for his grandfather, and so on. The identification between (real and classificatory) grandparents and grand-children is not merely a mental abstraction, a classification. Relations between grandfather and grandson are exceptionally close and free. A continual flow of goods, services, attentions and emotions circulates between them. This contrasts with the hierarchical relations and non-reciprocal flow of goods and services between a man and his father- and mother-in-law. The system operates over five generations. Then the cycle starts over, and Ego's great-grandson is classified in the same category as Ego's father.

In the opposite moiety, B, are all those in generations G^{+1} and G^{-1}, those of Ego's parents and Ego's children. While in Ego's moiety, G^{+2} and G^{-2} are merged and the identity of all their members is posited as the same, in the opposite moiety, the generations are distinguished and correspond to the distinction between engenderers (G^{+1}) and engendered (G^{-1}). When addressing members of this moiety, Ego uses the terms 'father' and 'mother' for G^{+1} and 'son' and 'daughter' for G^{-1}. We see that in the workings of generational moieties, and *in this context only*, cross cousins belonging to Ego's moiety are called 'brothers' and 'sisters', and real or classificatory cross kin in generation G^{+1} (mother's brother or father's sister) are referred to as 'fathers', 'mothers', etc. It is there that the picture blurred for anthropologists, because they had (mis)taken the endog-amous generational moieties for 'marriage classes'.

MOIETIES	MEN	WOMEN	KIN CATEGORIES AND TERMS USED
	TERMS USED IN THE SOCIOLOGICAL CONTEXT OF RITES		
B	F, MB, WF	F, FZ, WM	*Kin categories named*
	Mama (F)	Ngunytju (M)	*Terms used*
A	B, Cc, ZH, WB	Z, Cc, BW, WB	*Kin categories named*
	Kurta (B)	Tjurtu (Z)	*Terms used*
	MF, FF, SS, DS	FM,MM, DD, SD	*Kin categories named*
B	Katja (S)	Yurntalpa (D)	*Terms used*
	S, ZS, DH	D, ZD, SW	*Kin categories named*

☐ Persons in Ego's generational moiety
▓ Persons in opposite generational moiety

Among the Ngaatjatjarra, the moieties correspond to a social division that serves basically to organize ritual practices: one of the moieties, Ngumpaluru, means 'shady side' (facing west), the other, Tjintulkutkultul, means 'sunny side' (facing east). These terms designate the place where the individuals stand in the rites. The ties between individuals in virtue of their belonging to one or the other moieties are not determined by alliance or descent rules, as is the case in Australian systems, where the moieties are exogamous.

But what happens when a Ngaatjatjarra gets married? Here we are no longer in the social context of ritual ceremonies and political-religious practices, but in the field of relations between individuals and between families, of potential and even preferred marriages (or on the contrary forbidden and censured marriages). In choosing a spouse, a Ngaatjatjarra man or woman must respect two rules, one prescriptive and the other proscriptive. It is prescribed to marry a cross kinsman or -woman, but it is forbidden to marry a genealogically or geographically close cross kinsman. The rule then is that the spouses should be born in distinct geographical sites, that they have no claim to a common territorial belonging, and that they have never resided together for any length of time in the same place. We see that this proscriptive rule forbids repeating past alliances before a certain lapse of time and encourages extreme exogamy and the constant openness of each group, which thus wends its way toward new alliances.

The result of combining these two rules is that a Ngaatjatjarra will marry a same-generation cross cousin of at least the third degree.[11] But the rule also says that this cross cousin must be at the same time the daughter of a brother of a classificatory mother (MBD) and of a sister of a classificatory father (FZD). A

11 L. Dousset, 'L'alliance de mariage et la promesse d'épouses chez les Ngaatjatjarra du désert de l'Ouest australien', *Journal de la Société des océanistes*, vol. 108 (1999), pp. 3–17.

Ngaatjatjarra must therefore marry a bilateral cross cousin, which is the basic rule of Dravidian systems. But taking into account the proscriptive rule, this bilateral cross cousin must also be a cousin in at least the third degree. From the standpoint of kinship terminology, this woman, who before marriage was designated by the term *watjirra* (female cross cousin), once married becomes a wife, *kurri*.

But the existence of endogamous moieties also comes into the choice of a spouse. Ego can also marry two other cross relatives belonging to generations G^{+2} and G^{-2}, which, together with his own generation G^0, make up the endogamous moiety to which he belongs. A man may therefore marry not only a bilateral cross cousin in his own generation, but also a mother of a 'classificatory' father, on the one hand, or a daughter of a classificatory daughter, on the other. These two women, normally designated by the term *kaparli* before their marriage, also become *kurri* afterwards. Note that the term *kurri*, which is used for a husband as well as a wife, has no sexual connotation and designates, for a man, three categories of women: female cross cousins, classificatory father's mothers and classificatory daughter's daughters.

Another consequence of applying the proscriptive rule forbidding marriage with close cross cousins – in the first and second degree – is that these ineligible cross cousins are treated like consanguines, like brothers and sisters. This is a second reason for the metonymic use of the terms 'brother' and 'sister' when addressing cross cousins in the first and second degree, who are prohibited spouses. The difficulty anthropologists had in understanding how this system worked stemmed from the fact that they saw that a certain number of cross cousins were treated like siblings and that one nevertheless was enjoined to marry a cross cousin.

We will take several examples by way of illustration. In this system, how is Ego going to address his mother's brother, who for him is a real or classificatory cross kinsman and whose daughter in theory he can therefore marry.

- For a male Ego, the mother's brother (MB) is a *kamuru* before his marriage. The term designates him as a cross kinsman.
- But the same MB can also be called 'father' (*mama*) in the sociological context of the generational moieties, since all men in G^{+1} in the alternate moiety to that of Ego can be called 'fathers'.
- When a classificatory MB becomes a real (or desired) father-in-law, instead of being merely a *kamuru*, he is called *waputju*.

The same logic is at work in designating a male Ego's male cross cousins.

- Ego calls all male cross cousins *watjirra* in the interrelational context of marriage alliances.

- But he will call the same cross cousin 'brother', *kurta*, in the socio-logical context of ritual practices. He thus becomes a generational 'brother'.

- However if Ego marries the sister of this cross cousin, who becomes a real brother-in-law instead of a classificatory one, instead of calling him *watjirra*, a classificatory term, he will call him *marutju*, 'brother-in-law'.

If we were to take the terms of this nomenclature one by one, we would see that the same process is always at work. This is shown in the following tables, which present Ngaatjatjarra terminology before and after marriage.

It is clear that there is nothing aberrant about the system at all, that it follows a Dravidian logic, but that, unlike most Dravidian systems, which have no specific terms for affines, this system has a minimal affinal terminology for spouse's kin. These specific terms thus make it possible to distinguish within the global category of classificatory in-laws (MB + FZ, i.e. classificatory mother's brothers and classificatory father's sisters), those individuals who have become real in-laws.

The example of the Aluridja systems would need further discussion, and we will come back to them later. Indeed, they raise the question of the sociological and historical conditions[12] in which specific vocabularies appeared for affines (for example in the Iroquois, Eskimo, etc. systems) or vocabularies that cancelled distinctions between parallel and cross kin and kept only the generational distinctions (Hawaiian system).

---

12 The Australian societies characterized by the 'Aluridja' system are fluid, open to the surrounding groups, which partially overlap when families split to join another. There is no rule that mechanically encloses them within territorial boundaries. Unlike the Baruya, these 'societies' are not 'tribes'. The only limit they have seems to be *the refusal of other societies* to open up to them. In order to understand their structure, we probably need to look at the living conditions in the Australian Western Desert, and at the cooperation and fluid residential pattern materially and socially necessary to survival – which may explain the systematic will constantly to be open to new alliances with distant affines and to make close affines into quasi-consanguines. This was one way of multiplying, within their own group and in other groups, obligations to share and redistribute erratic resources. Alternatively, outside this great desert, Aboriginal groups live in regions much richer in water and in plant and animal resources. These groups often defended their territory jealously against the arrival of others and their organization was more strongly territorial.

In the interior of the desert, bands were exogamous and always included one or two persons connected by religious ties with the ceremonial sites around which the groups moved. Each group took charge of the rituals that had to be performed on these sites and which usually concerned the reproduction and multiplication of the plant and animal species but also the male initiations. No territory was the exclusive property of any one group. People who did not belong to the band could also be connected with these sites, by birth, for example, and therefore have the right later to use the territory. In short, the social organization of the nomadic groups in this great desert had little in common with a tribal organization. Nevertheless, in the Australian desert as among the Baruya of New Guinea, it is the rites and the sacred objects that structure the local group.

A terminology type thus designates, as we now know, the principles of construction, in other words the structure, of a particular configuration of kinship relations, or at least those that are explicitly designated in a language. Once this structure has been isolated in the language, it can then be studied independently, without reference to the language or the society, and be represented by the abstract symbols of a metalanguage, which is not spoken by a human group but belongs to the sphere of those things produced by scientific research. For example, the Baruya term *noumwe* designates the father and all of the father's brothers, as well as the sons of Ego's father's father's brothers. It can thus be represented by an equation subsuming these equivalences, which would read: *noumwe* = (F = FB = FFBS, etc.). By using such equations, we can now compare the Baruya system with all systems containing the same equation, whatever the society, language or time in history. When we do this, we see that they all belong to a single class of systems built on two principles, a merging rule, which states that F = FB, M = MZ, and a principle of collaterality, which says that: F ≠ MB, FZ ≠ MZ.

We are indebted to Kroeber for having shown (and with what precision!) how the kin terms in different languages reflect the nature of the relationships they express. His first aim was to criticize the overly rigid distinction that Morgan made between classificatory and descriptive terminologies. Kroeber showed that all systems contain some classificatory terms, owing to which hundreds of kin positions can be understood and expressed by a small number of words – twenty-one in English, or twenty-seven if one adds to the vocabulary of consanguinity (father) and that of affinity (father-in-law) the words used for the positions of persons in a family reconstituted after a divorce or the death of a spouse (stepfather). In French, the latter corresponds to the word *parâtre*, which once existed (cf. *marâtre*, which still exists) and which was replaced by *beau-père*, which now subsumes two very different types of kin ties: on the one hand, true affines by marriage (in-laws) and, on the other, previously un-related persons who have become relatives by remarrying persons who, after having divorced or lost their spouse, reconstituted a family including their children from a previous marriage (step-s). The English word 'cousin' designates all of the sons and daughters of Ego's mother's and father's brothers and sisters, whether they are younger or older than Ego, born of parents themselves younger or older than Ego's parents, etc. This single word merges thirty-two different relations. And if we go beyond the level of first-degree cousins, the number of different relationships the term could express would be much higher than thirty-two.

KIN TERMINOLOGIES AND KINSHIP RELATIONS

Ultimately Kroeber[13] distinguished eight categories of relationships that could be translated into kin terms. All eight categories (or only some of them) can be present in a particular kinship terminology.

1. *Difference of generations*: father, grandfather, etc., present everywhere but cancelled in part for certain maternal or paternal relatives in the Crow and Omaha systems.

2. *Difference between lineal and collateral kin*: this difference is cancelled when father and father's brother are merged under a single term, etc.

3. *Age difference within a generation*: e.g. the Baruya language uses different terms for older brother (*dakwe*) and younger brother (*gwagwe*). The English word 'brother' does not reflect such a difference.

4. *Sex of the relative named*: the word cousin in English does not distinguish between a male and a female cousin, whereas the French does (*cousin/cousine*). Many languages use the same term for son and daughter, for grandfather and grandmother, and so forth.

5. *Speaker's sex*: in many languages a son uses different terms for his father and his mother than a daughter does. This is not the case in European languages, where a brother and a sister use the same terms.

6. *Sex of the person through whom the relationship is traced*: in French or English, one must stipulate whether 'uncle' means the father's brother or the mother's brother. In many languages, the terms for a cousin who is a father's brother's son and a cousin who is a father's sister's son or a cousin who is a mother's sister's son or another who is a mother's brother's son are not the same. The terms bifurcate when the relationship goes through two brothers or through two sisters or through a brother and a sister or a sister and a brother. This is the principle that engenders the distinction between parallel and cross cousins, and more generally between parallel and cross kin. The distinction does not exist in European or Polynesian languages, for instance,

---

13   A. Kroeber, 'Classificatory Systems of Relationship', *Journal of the Royal Anthropological Institute*, no. 39 (1909), pp. 77–84. See F. Héritier, *L'Exercice de la parenté* (Paris, Gallimard/Le Seuil, 1981), p. 17, and F. Zimmermann, *Enquête sur la parenté* (Paris, Presses Universitaires de France, 1993), pp. 106–8.

which code for terminologies of the so-called Hawaiian and Eskimo types. The consequence of this principle is that father's and mother's sides are not the same. On the father's side there will be no uncles because FB = F; on the mother's side there will be no aunts because MZ = M.

7. *Distinction between blood relatives (consanguines) and relatives by marriage (affines)*: for example 'père' and 'beau-père' in French and 'father' and 'father-in-law' in English. In some terminologies, however – Australian and Dravidian – the same term designates both mother's brother and wife's father, two distinct kinship ties in Western society, one of which is consanguineous (MB) and the other affinal (WF). In Dravidian systems, the two relationships are merged into one person. This does not mean that in these systems the maternal uncle is both a consanguine and an affine. The logic of these systems makes him fundamentally an affine.

8. *Life situation of the person through whom the kinship relation passes*: For instance, if the person who acts as the link between two other individuals is living or dead, married or divorced, etc. In some North American Indian languages, after the wife's death the terms formerly used for the father- or mother-in-law are banned and replaced with others.

Western European languages make use of only four of these criteria: (1), (2), (4), and (7). North American Indian languages add criteria (6) and (8).

Obviously what is most important for distinguishing terminology types is the role played by criteria (2) and (6): (2) enables the distinction between direct and collateral lines, and (6) the sex of the person through whom the kin ties pass. Using Kroeber's distinctions, Lowie[14] suggested classifying all terminologies by distinguishing those that use either (2) or (6) and cancel the other, those that combine the two, and those that cancel both. He thus obtained four categories of kinship terminologies, which are still used today as a reference frame for studying these nomenclatures. We are indebted to Murdock[15] for the most complete presentation of this classification:

- Systems that combine the two criteria, collaterality and bifurcation, called *bifurcate collateral systems*, represented by what are known as Sudanese-type terminologies.
- Systems that are bifurcate but not collateral. These systems merge F

---

14   R. Lowie, 'A Note on Relationship Terminologies', *American Anthropologist*, no. 30 (1928), pp. 263–7.

15   G. P. Murdock, *Social Structure* (New York, The Free Press, 1949), p. 142.

and FB, M and MZ. They correspond to the Australian, Dravidian, Iroquois and Crow-Omaha type systems.

• Systems that are collateral but not bifurcate. These are terminologies of the Eskimo type, characteristic of, among others, the European and North American systems.

• Systems that use neither (2) nor (6) but simply stress the difference between generations (1). This is the case of the Hawaiian-type systems, which include the Polynesian systems, certain systems in the Malayo-Polynesian zone and a certain number of societies in North and South America, Oceania and Africa.

CATEGORIES	COLLATERAL	BIFURCATE	TERMINOLOGY TYPES
Bifurcate collateral	+	+	Sudanese
Bifurcate merging	–	+	Australian Dravidian Iroquois Crow-Omaha
Lineal	+	–	Eskimo
Generational	–	–	Hawaiian

We can now identify the formal structures of the terminologies in each of the four categories and represent them by equations translating the effects of the presence or absence of one or another of these principles.

1. In a Sudanese-type terminology (bifurcate collateral):
   $F \neq FB \neq MB$
   The term for father is different from the term for father's brother and from the term for mother's brother. By the same logic:
   $M \neq MZ \neq FZ \neq FBW \neq MBW$
   $B \neq FBS \neq MBS$
   $Z \neq FBD \neq MBD \neq FZD \neq MZD$
   $D \neq BD \neq ZD \neq WZD \neq WBD$

2. In an Iroquois-type terminology (bifurcate merging):
   $(F = FB) \neq MB$
   Father and father's brother are designated by the same term, which is different from the term for mother's brother: By the same logic:
   $(M = MZ) \neq FZ$
   $(M = FBW) \neq FZ$
   $(Z = FBD = MZD) \neq (FZD = MBD)$
   $(D = BD) \neq ZD$

3. In an Eskimo-type terminology (lineal):
F ≠ (FB = MB)
M ≠ (FZ = MZ)
D ≠ (BD = ZD)
S ≠ (BS = ZS)

The term 'father' is distinct from the term 'uncle', which designates both father's and mother's brother. The term 'mother' is distinct from the term 'aunt', which designates both father's and mother's sister. Sons and daughters are called by different terms from those used for sons and daughters of brothers and sisters (nephews and nieces).

4. In a Hawaiian terminology (generational):
F = FB = MB
M = MZ = FZ = FBW = MBW
D = BD = ZD = WZD = WBD
S = BS = ZS

All of the kinship terminologies[16] thus make up a group of four possible permutations, since, with two criteria – collaterality and bifurcation – one can account for one but not the other (two possible permutations), for one and the other (third permutation), or for neither of the two (fourth permutation).

As early as 1949, Murdock had already pointed out a fifth logical possibility, but he had never encountered it in reality. It would consist in positing the equivalence between father's sister (FZ) and mother (M) and distinguishing these two women from mother's sister (M = FZ) ≠ MZ, or 'an equivalent grouping in other trios'. This very important remark was not pursued, and it was thirty years later that Françoise Héritier called attention to this absence as well as to that of other formulas constructed on the same pattern, for example (F = MB) ≠ FB, where the father would be the equivalent of the mother's brother, but both would be differentiated from the father's brother (FB).

Héritier suggested a theoretical explanation for the fact that this combination was not found in practice although it was logically possible and structurally feasible. She suggests that to put it into practice would be 'socially unthinkable'. In effect, it would be unthinkable to draw a dividing line between two male siblings, father and father's brother (Héritier does not mention the symmetrical case of a dividing line between two female siblings), coupled with assimilation

---

16   With the exception of the terminology used by the Na of Yunnan, which has no term for father, father's brothers or father's sisters, nor does it have any terms for affines. The Na terminology is not the only one of its kind, either.

between two cross relatives (F = MB). 'It is unthinkable that the relationship between two men via a woman, sister for one and wife for the other, should be classified in a category of greater proximity than the relationship between two brothers.'[17]

Generalizing this remark, Héritier posits that, in human societies, there can be equivalence between parallel kin but never between cross kin. Symmetrical relationships (brother/brother), (sister/sister) differ profoundly from the (brother/sister) or (sister/brother) relationship. In the latter kind we in effect find sexual difference, and with it the possibility of contracting alliances by the exchange of one sex by the other, of the sister by the brother or the brother by the sister, as well as the choice between descent being traced through men (patrilineal), through women (matrilineal), through both (bilineal) or through either one (non-lineal). In short, the existence of this logically possible but socially unthinkable combination shows that the difference between the sexes and the difference between parallel and cross kin are the basis of all kinship systems. Here the asymmetrical relationship (brother/sister or sister/brother) appears pivotal for the production of kinship relations.

If we take the standpoint of Ego's generation and consider the way a kinship system names Ego's brother's and sisters, his/her cousins born of father's same-sex collaterals and mother's same-sex collaterals (parallel cousins) and those born of opposite-sex collaterals (cross cousins), we see, as Murdock observed, that the four terminological categories (bifurcate collateral, bifurcate merging, lineal and generational) classify siblings (Sb), parallel cousins (//) and cross cousins (X) in the following ways, each of which agrees with their principles of construction.

TERMINOLOGICAL CATEGORIES			TYPES
Bifurcate collateral	Sb ≠ // ≠ X	Siblings ≠ Parallels ≠ Cross	Sudanese
Bifurcate merging	(Sb = //) ≠ X)	(Siblings = Parallels) ≠ Cross	Australian, Dravidian, Iroquois, Crow-Omaha
Lineal	Sb ≠ (// = X)	Siblings ≠ (Parallels + Cross)	Eskimo
Generational	Sb = // = X	Siblings = Parallels = Cross	Hawaiian

One formula is missing:

(Sb = X) ≠ // (Siblings = Cross) ≠ Parallels

---

17 Héritier, *L'Exercice de la parenté*, p. 42.

Two facts must be emphasized. The first is that using Ego's generation as a reference does not show the fundamental difference between Dravidian and Iroquois systems when it comes to the definition (and the role) of parallel and cross kin. The definition is the same in the two types of system in Go, but it differs in the ascending and descending generations.

The second is the fact that Crow-Omaha type systems have a particular position in this table, since siblings and parallel cousins are equivalent, as in the Iroquois, Dravidian and Australian systems (Sb = //), but the status of cross cousins in the Omaha and in the Crow systems differs. In Omaha systems (for the most part patrilineal) matrilateral cross cousins (mXc) are classified in the generation above Ego, and patrilateral cross cousins (pXc) in the generation below Ego. In Crow systems (for the most part matrilineal) the opposite is true, patrilateral cross cousins are raised a generation and matrilateral cross cousins are lowered. The generation difference present in other kinship systems is here partially cancelled in the case of cross cousins. In an Omaha system, Ego's father's sisters son, his patrilateral cross cousin, is a 'son' for Ego (FZS = S), his mother's brother's son is a maternal uncle (MBS = MB) and his maternal uncle's daughter is a mother (MBD = M). In a Crow system it is the reverse. My father's sister's son is a father for me (FZS = F) and my mother's brother's son is a son for me (MBS = S).

Omaha System	Crow System

G^{+1} MB   cXm
G^0 (G = P) ≠ $\nearrow$
      $\searrow$ cXp
G^{-1} S
	F cXp
	(G = P) ≠ $\nearrow$
	      $\searrow$ cXm
	S

In short, in these systems, the father's and the mother's side hinge on Ego like a see-saw, raising or lowering the cross kin in one, and sometimes several, generations. As a result, a whole series of individuals belonging to biologically and chronologically different generations are subsumed under a single term. All become 'sons' or 'mothers' or 'maternal uncles', and so forth. The system is governed by what is called a 'skewing principle', which poses the formal equivalence of two types of relatives belonging to two generations, thus neutralizing the difference between generations for a certain number of kin positions. It should be added that, in spite of efforts on the part of numerous kinship theorists using different formal, linguistic or mathematical approaches, no one has yet arrived at a satisfactory explanation for the existence of this principle, which does not seem to depend on the fact that Crow-Omaha systems forbid, for example, a man to take a wife in the lineages of his father, his mother, his father's mother and his mother's mother (F, M, FM, MM), and imposes a lapse of several generations before repeating a marriage.

As a matter of fact, other systems too (Dravidian, Iroquois) forbid in certain cases repeating the same marriages before several generations, but in none does this result in a 'skewing' of the generations. It is true, though, that there are often fewer prohibitions than in the Crow-Omaha systems, which proscribe marriage with the four ascending lines (F, M, FM, MM), to which are often added a certain number of cognatic relationships. On the other hand, fragmentary evidence of skewing can be found in certain Iroquois terminologies – Sudanese (Latin system) and Hawaiian (as among the Fanti, analyzed by David Kronenfeld[18]). The Fanti are interesting in that they have two kinship terminologies, one of the Hawaiian type without skewing and the other of the Hawaiian type with some Crow features. They use one or the other, depending on the context. What is striking is that they use the Crow terminology to designate individuals in several consecutive generations who will succeed each other in the same function.

In short, the question is open, and the answer does not seem to lie with the philosophical explanation proposed by Françoise Héritier, for whom generational skewing would be an 'extreme' consequence of the 'universal' exchange of women by men and therefore of the universal fact of male domination, two facts that she sees as being at the root of all kinship systems. These theses, which originated with Lévi-Strauss, lead her to minimize or block out the realities that challenge their universal validity, such as the fact that, in Crow systems, a woman's brothers become 'sons' for her, a feature that cannot be neutralized, but also the existence of a number of matrilineal societies in which it is the women who exchange their brothers.

The analysis of Crow-Omaha systems thus needs more work. Today it is F. Tjon Sie Fat who seems to have made the most progress.[19] Tjon Sie Fat advances the hypothesis that if, instead of linking a child to both of its parents, the choice is made that Ego – and his/her brothers and sisters – be linked exclusively to one parent, the father or the mother, a binary mode of classification results that would correspond to the Australian moiety systems and thus be compatible with the principle of the symmetrical exchange of spouses and cross-cousin

---

18   See the Introduction to M. Godelier, T. R. Trautmann and F. E. Tjon Sie Fat (eds.), *Transformations of Kinship* (Washington/London, Smithsonian Institution Press, 1998), pp. 1–26 and D. B. Kronenfeld, 'A Formal Analysis of Fanti Kinship Terminology (Ghana)', *Anthropos*, no. 75 (1980), pp. 506–608.

19   Godelier, Trautmann and Tjon Sie Fat (eds.), *Transformations of Kinship*.

marriage. If a rule of lineal invariance were to be added to this unilineal principle of consanguinity, if, for instance, MBC were to be classified as MB, whereas FZC continued to be classified as nephews and nieces, skewing would result, together with the different Crow-Omaha kinship structures as they were described by Lounsbury.[20] This suggests the existence of a closer connection than specialists usually admit between Crow-Omaha terminologies and the presence of a unilineal descent principle in societies where these terminologies are found. Yet Crow-Omaha structures are also found in societies with cognatic systems, while, in societies with patri- or matrilineal unilineal descent rules and Crow or Omaha structures, some of the marriage prohibitions bear on cognatic relationships, as Françoise Héritier and Elisabeth Copet-Rougier have shown, whereas these are not usually named in the terminology. On this point, too, the debate is still open.

LATIN KINSHIP TERMINOLOGY

Now a few words about the Sudanese systems. We will take the example of the ancient Latin system, which distinguished all kin in the direct or collateral lines by different terms, according to the following formula:

– in generation (G^{+1}) F ≠ FB ≠ MB; M ≠ MZ ≠ FZ
– in Ego's generation (G^0) Sb ≠ // ≠ pXc ≠ mXc

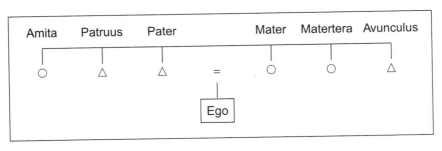

The father and the father's brothers are designated by distinct but closely related terms. Likewise the mother and the mother's sisters. The father's sister and mother's brother are designated by specific terms. *Avunculus* is close to *avus*, which designates the grandfather, a feature found in certain Omaha systems. *Nepos* is the reciprocal of two other terms, *avus* and *avunculus*, and designates both the grandson and the nephew.[21]

---

20   F. Tjon Sie Fat, personal communication.
21   *Avus* became *aïeul* in French, a term that designates a distant ancestor but which used

Toward the end of the Republic and in the very first centuries of the Roman Empire, the term *avunculus* began to be used for the mother's brother as well as for the father's, and *patruus* disappeared. At the same time, the difference between father's sister and mother's sister was cancelled, and the term *matertera* disappeared. The word 'cousin', which comes from the Latin *consobrinus* and designated the children of two sisters (*con-soror*), came to mean the four categories of cousins: the children of the father's and the mother's brothers and sisters. When these changes were completed, the whole structure of the kinship terminology had been transformed and turned into another terminology governed by a different (but just as coherent) logic. A Sudanese-type terminology had turned into an Eskimo-type terminology, which is still used in Europe at the start of the twenty-first century.

We are unable to describe the stages this process went through or to determine the underlying causes. All we can say is that an Eskimo-type terminology is perfectly suited to kinship relations centred on the nuclear conjugal family in a society where clans and lineages do not exist or are disappearing, where bilateral filiation has crowded out other ways of tracing descent – bringing with it the configurations open to related individuals and families that we call kindreds. We thus need to unearth the social forces, the historical factors that stripped both the Germano-Anglo-Saxon cognatic descent groups[22] and the agnatic groups of the Latin or Latinized societies from the European social fabric. The generalization of monogamous marriage, the multiplication of the number of degrees of kinship within which the Church allowed marriage – which had become a sacrament, a mystery, a union in God – the creation of seigniorial domains parcelled out to nuclear families in the peasantry, all certainly moved society in this direction or hastened an evolution begun before the end of the Roman Empire. It will be up to historians interested in these problems and to specialists in these areas to decide.

It must be said that anthropological studies on the Sudanese systems (Latin,

---

to be used for father's father. When the term *aïeul* was replaced by the French *grandpère*, the term derived from *nepos* ceased to designate grandchildren and was reserved for nieces and nephews – children of a brother and a sister, at least in French, German, Flemish and English, but not in Spanish, Italian or Portuguese, where it designates the grandson, or in Dutch, where it continues to designate both the grandson and the nephew. See T. Trautmann, 'The whole history of kinship terminology in three chapters: Before Morgan, Morgan and after Morgan', *Anthropological Theory*, vol. 1, no. 2 (2001), pp. 268–87, and Héritier, *L'Exercice de la parenté*, pp. 101–2. Cf. also E. Copet-Rougier, 'Tu ne traverseras pas le sang. Corps, parenté et pouvoirs chez les Kako du Cameroun', in M. Godelier and M. Panoff (eds.), *Le Corps humain supplicié, possédé, cannibalisé* (Amsterdam, Editions des Archives Contemporaines, 1998), pp. 87–108; p. 98.

22 The term 'clan', which the anthropological literature uses to designate unilineal descent groups, comes from the Scots *Klann* and probably originally designated a large cognatic descent group similar to those found in the Polynesian chiefdoms. See B. S. Phillpots, *Kindred and Clan in the Middle Ages and After* (Cambridge, Cambridge University Press, 1974 [1913]).

Chinese, ancient Russian) and the Eskimo or Hawaiian systems are scarce compared with work on the Australian, Dravidian, Iroquois and Crow-Omaha systems. Much therefore remains to be done.

I would now like to call attention to another, fundamental aspect of kinship terminologies, and that is the fact that some have a specific vocabulary for relatives by marriage while others do not. This difference sheds light on the distinct contents of the notions of consanguinity and affinity in the different kinship systems.

In the terminologies without a separate vocabulary for relatives by marriage, we find the Australian and Dravidian systems (with some exceptions we will not dwell on).[23] Alternatively, the other terminologies have a distinct vocabulary for affines.

KINSHIP TERMINOLOGIES	
NO DISTINCT TERMS FOR AFFINES	DISTINCT TERMS FOR AFFINES
Australian	Sudanese
Dravidian	Iroquois, Crow-Omaha
	Eskimo
	Hawaiian*
* The terms for affines are often reduced to those designating real brothers-in-law and real sisters-in-law.	

It is vital to understand this distinction because it is the only thing that makes it possible to show differences in the importance of the distinction between parallel and cross kin, when it exists. It also makes it possible to measure the effects of the sister-exchange rule depending on whether it is permissible to repeat this exchange in the following generation or necessary to delay for a given number of generations. Lastly, it points to a difference between societies whose members are either consanguines or (real or potential) affines for Ego (Australian and Dravidian systems), and the rest. In the latter case, all members of the society are divided into three categories with regard to Ego: real consanguines, real affines, and the rest of society (composed of non-kin who are potential spouses).[24] Once married, these non-relatives

<hr>

23   Certain Dravidian systems (the Aluridja) have a few terms for close affines – father-in-law, mother-in-law – while other Iroquois systems have equations of the type (MB = FZH = WF), meaning my mother's brother can also be my father's sister's husband as well as my wife's father, which implies an exchange of sisters in G^{+1} by Ego's father which is repeated by Ego in G^{0}.

24   The question of the inexistence or negligible importance of marriage among the Na remains open. For an opinion contrary to that of Hua Cai, see Chuan-Kang Shih, 'Tiese and Its Anthropological Significance: Issues around the Visiting Sexual System among the Moso', *L'Homme*, no. 154–5 (2000), pp. 697–712.

become close consanguines in the following generations and then gradually grow more distant until they are once more potential affines. And beyond all of the non-kin members of Ego's society, there are outsiders and foreigners from the neighbouring friendly or hostile societies whom one is free to marry or not.

To show what is at stake in the difference between terminologies with a special vocabulary for affines and those without, which merge consanguines and affines, we must make a rapid comparison between the rules for constructing Iroquois-type terminologies (which make the distinction) and those of Dravidian type (which do not). Then we will compare these two so-called 'ego-centric' terminologies with the Australian so-called socio-centric types.

The Dravidian terminologies are sets of terms resulting from the intersection of four parameters: sex, generation, relative age (older/younger) and the bifurcation of relatives into two categories – parallel kin and cross kin – which extends over the three central generations (G°, G^{+1}, G^{-1}) and sometimes even over five (up to G^{+2}, G^{-2}), and in this case produces terminologies very close to those found in the 'Kariera' systems.[25] Two principles account for the particular definition of cross kinship used in these systems. The first is what Lounsbury[26] called 'the rule of same-sex sibling merging'. Father and father's brothers are fathers, mother and mother's sisters are mothers, etc. The second is the 'semantic' equivalent[27] of a cross-cousin marriage rule, which determines the nature and extension of crossness. For instance, for a male Ego, the children of a female cross cousin are his 'sons' and his 'daughters', since she is his presumed wife. But the children of a male cross cousin are his nephews and nieces, since as a male cross cousin this man is the presumed husband of Ego's sister. For her, this man's children are therefore 'sons' and 'daughters'.

This rule accounts for the second structural feature characteristic of Dravidian systems, namely the lack of a specific vocabulary for affines. The term for

25   We owe the discovery of the Dravidian terminologies close to the Kariera systems to T. Trautmann, *Dravidian Kinship* (Cambridge, Cambridge University Press, 1981), pp. 141–2, 144, and to E. Viveiros de Castro, 'Dravidian and related systems', in Godelier, Trautmann and Tjon Sie Fat (eds.), *Transformations of Kinship*, pp. 348–52. It alters the vision that had been ours since the pioneering work of L. Dumont, *Dravidien et Kariera. L'alliance de mariage dans l'Inde du Sud et en Australie* (Paris, Mouton, 1971). In North America, the Eyak of Copper River used this type of terminology. Cf. Godelier et al., *Transformations of Kinship*, pp. 106, 123. See also J. W. Ives, *A Theory of Northern Athapaskan Prehistory* (Boulder, Westview Press, 1990), pp. 248–53.

26   P. G. Lounsbury, 'A Formal Account of Crow-Omaha Type Kinship Terminologies', in W. H. Goodenough (ed.), *Explorations in Cultural Anthropology: Essays in Honor of George Peter Murdock* (New York, McGraw-Hill, 1964), pp. 331–43.

27   The formula was coined by T. Trautmann, in 'Dravidian Kinship as a Cultural and as a Structural Type', Paper presented at the symposium 'Kinship in Asia: Typology and Transformation', Moscow, 1992.

mother's brother thus also designates my father's sister's husband, my father's wife's brother and my wife's father, hence the equation MB = FZH = FWB = WF. Furthermore, this equation implies the existence of a marriage by sister exchange in the generation above Ego, since MB = FZH, a marriage that Ego can or should repeat, since his maternal uncle is designated as the father of his potential wife (MB = WF).

In short, Dravidian systems are explicitly associated with a rule of cross-cousin marriage. This rule can take three forms, depending on whether one is supposed to marry a bilateral cross cousin, a patrilateral cross cousin or a matrilateral cross cousin.[28] Marriage with the bilateral cross cousin is usually associated with undifferentiated, cognatic descent modes. The other two forms of marriage, as Louis Dumont noted, are more frequent in Dravidian-type societies with patrilineal and patrilocal[29] or matrilineal and patrilocal descent groups,[30] which leads these groups to prefer unilateral marriage with either the patrilateral or the matrilateral cross cousin. The Purum are a good example of a patrilineal, patrilocal society with a Dravidian terminology. They are found in India, and their system prescribes marriage with the mother's brother's daughter but forbids marriage with the father's sister's daughter. Of the three forms of cross-cousin marriage, that with the bilateral cross cousin seems to predominate. Because it implies the repeated exchange of spouses between two 'lines' from one generation to the next, Louis Dumont spoke of this transmission from generation to generation as a 'marriage alliance', as an alliance relationship concluded between two individuals of the same sex and inherited by their children of both sexes.[31]

We can therefore see why the existence of terms for affines would in, Dravidian systems, be redundant with respect to the basic distinctions underlying these systems, in particular that between parallel and cross kin. The following table illustrates the differences between an Eskimo terminology, like the French system, and a Dravidian terminology.

----

28   In some Dravidian regions of India and America, there also exists the rule that one should marry the daughter of an older sister.

29   E.g. the Pramalai Kallar. Cf. L. Dumont, *Une sous-caste de l'Inde du Sud. Organisation sociale et religieuse des Pramalai Kallar* (Paris/La Haye, Mouton, 1957); English translation: *A South Indian Subcaste: Social Organization and Religion of the Pramalai Kallar*, translated by M. Moffatt, L. and A. Morton; revised by the author and A. Stern; edited with an introduction by Michael Moffatt (Delhi/New York, Oxford University Press, 1986).

30   E.g. the Kondaiyan-kottai Maravar. Cf. Dumont, *Une sous-caste de l'Inde du Sud.*

31   This kind of 'inheritance' of a marriage alliance is not found in certain societies having a Dravidian-type kinship system, such as the Ojibwa of North Canada, who are organized into fluid bands which can disappear after a generation. Cf. John W. Ives, 'Development Processes in the Pre-contact History of Athapaskan, Algonkian and Numic Kin Systems', in Godelier et al., *Transformations of Kinship*, pp. 94–139. See Also E. Desveaux and M. Selz, 'Dravidian Nomenclature as an Expression of Ego Centered Dualism', in ibid, pp. 150–67.

ESKIMO TERMINOLOGY		DRAVIDIAN TERMINOLOGY	
KIN		KIN	
Direct	*Collateral*	*Parallel*	*Cross*
Father, mother	Uncles, aunts	Father, father's brother	Father's sister, mother's brother
Brother, sister	Cousins	Mother, mother's sister	Father's sister's children
		Brother, sister	
Son, daughter	Nephews, nieces	Father's brother's children	Mother's brother's children
		Mother's sister's children	Sister's children (for a man)
		Sons, daughters	Brother's children (for a woman)
		Brother's children (for a man)	
		Sister's children (for a woman)	

The following is an example of Dravidian terminology as used by the Nanjilnattu Vellalar. We have simplified by eliminating all terms which designate relationships between older and younger individuals: father's older brother/ father's younger brother; mother's older sister/mother's younger sister; Ego's older/younger brother; Ego's older/younger sister.

In the Nanjilnattu Vellalar language the terms corresponding to this classification and to these rules are the following:

G^{+2}	Pattan / Patti			
	Parallel		*Cross*	
G^{+1}	Appa (F)	Amma (M)	Mamou (MB)	Attai
+ G^{0}	Annan (B$^+$)	Akka (Z$^+$)	Attan (MBS$^+$ FZS$^+$)	Mayni Kokunti
−	Tampi (B$^-$)	(Tankacei Z$^-$)	Maccinan (MBS$^-$ FZS$^-$)	
G^{-1}	Makan (S)	Makal (D)	Marumakan (ZS(m) BS(f))	Marumakal (ZD(m) BD(f))
G^{-2}	Peran / Patti			

Here now are the English descriptive terms for the kinship relations expressed above using abstract symbols:

	Parallel kin		Cross kin	
Generation	Men	Women	Men	Women
G^{+2}	Grandfathers / Grandmothers (FF / MF / FM / MM)			
G^{+1}	Father, father's brothers, Mother's sister's husband	Mother, Mother's sister, Father's brother's wife	Mother's brother, Father's sister's husband, Wife's father	Father's sister, Mother's brother's wife, Wife's mother
G^0	Brother	Sister	Mother's brother's son	Mother's brother's daughter
Ego	Father's brother's son	Father's brother's daughter	Father's sister's son	Father's sister's daughter
	Mother's sister's son	Mother's sister's daughter		
G^{-1}	Son	Daughter	Sister's son (m)	Sister's daughter (m)
	Brother's son (m)	Brother's daughter (m)	Brother's son (f)	Brother's daughter
	Sister's son (f)	Sister's daughter (f)		
G^{-2}	Grandsons / Granddaughters (SS, DS, SD, DD)			

The same thing can be expressed by means of conventional formal symbols (Sp = Spouse).

	Parallel kin		Cross kin	
Generation	Men	Women	Men	Women
G^{+2}	FF / MF – FM / MM			
G^{+1}	F, FB, MZH	M, MZ, FBW	MB, FZH, SpF	FZ, MBW, SpM
G^0	B	Z	MBS	MBD
Ego	FBS	FBD	FZS	FZD
	MZS	MZD		
G^{-1}	S	D	ZS (m)	ZD (m)
	BS (m), ZS (f)	BD (m), ZD (f)	BS (f)	BD (f)
G^{-2}	SS/DS // SD/DD			

The last two tables express, one in descriptive terms (father, mother, etc.), the other in conventional symbols (F, M), the formal structure of this terminology, the grouping of several kinship relations under a single term and the marriage rules which explain the distribution (MB = FZH = SpF) (FZ = MBW = SpM).

We see in this system that a brother and a sister cannot marry each other but that their children can. Opposite-sex consanguines (B, Z) produce affines in the following generation. Opposite-sex affines, spouses (H, W) produce consanguines in the following generation. Same-sex consanguines produce consanguines in the following generation. And same-sex affines produce affines in the following generation. For a man, his sister is a consanguineal relative who produces affines; and his cross cousin, an affine who produces consanguineal kin. It is the opposite for a woman. This confirms the fact that the brother–sister (B–Z) relationship is the place where sibling identity 'tips over into difference' – according to Françoise Héritier's expression, adopted by Eduardo Viveiros de Castro – and opens siblingship up to alliance.

Because of these rules, which dictate marriages and the reproduction of the same alliances generation after generation, we arrive at the following global rule characteristic of Dravidian – but also Australian – systems:

1. My consanguines' consanguines are consanguines: CC = C
2. My consanguines' affines are affines: CA = A
3. My affines' consanguines are affines: AC = A
4. My affines' affines are consanguines: AA = C

In societies with Dravidian-type terminologies, 'sister' exchange and cross-cousin marriage, the entire society is split, from Ego's standpoint, into potential and forbidden spouses, and whether or not Alter is a potential spouse depends on whether or not he or she belongs to one or another of these four categories which, two by two, define the difference between consanguines (CC + AA) and affines (CA + AC) typical of Dravidian systems. Consanguinity thus associates two kin categories C = (CC + AA) and affinity the two others A = (CA + AC). We could show that the same formula is applied even more strictly in the Australian section and subsection systems. Alternatively, this associative formula does not (or almost not) apply to Iroquois systems. We therefore observe that the formula is compatible only with the following ways of functioning:

1. Sociocentric dualist systems (Australian)
2. Systems practising 'sister' exchange and marriage with the bilateral cross cousin (symmetrical Dravidian systems)
3. Systems applying an asymmetrical marriage rule with one of the two cross cousins within a closed circle of exchanges (asymmetrical Dravidian systems)

We also see something that is harder to understand for people who think and act with respect to kinship categories of the Eskimo type, ourselves, for instance: the definitions of consanguinity, affinity and cognation in the Dravidian systems do not have either the same conceptual or the same sociological content as these same categories in the Western Euro-American systems. In Western Europe and America, a person's cognates are all of his or her relatives in the agnatic and uterine lines. Cognation and consanguinity coincide. In the Dravidian systems, the father's brother and the mother's brother are both Ego's cognates, but the father's brother is a consanguine whereas the mother's brother is an affine. The opposition between father's brother as mother's sister's husband (FB = MZH) and mother's brother as father's sister's husband (MB = FZH) does not mark an opposition between consanguineal kin in the sense of relatives-by-birth and affinal kin in the sense of relatives-by-marriage. The opposition is based on category difference and marriage, and does not correspond to the opposition between relatives with whom one already shares substances (e.g. blood) and relatives by marriage with whom one shares nothing in advance.

Schneider's criticisms are therefore groundless. Using the concept of consanguinity after having reconstructed it according to the rules of a Dravidian logic does not mean simply projecting Western representations of consanguinity and kinship onto a different sociocultural universe. The opposition between consanguines and affines made in Dravidian systems does not coincide with the distinctions we in Western Europe make between relatives and non-relatives, between agnatic kin and uterine kin, and so on. The opposition is between categories and structures, and says nothing about concrete cultural content or about real sociological content, in other words the real social relationships between, for example, Ego and his (real or classificatory) maternal uncles, etc.

CROSS KIN AND PARALLEL KIN

We are now prepared to understand the relationship between the distinction between consanguines and affines and that between parallel and cross kin. The first encompasses the second. But they must not be confused. The opposition between parallel and cross kin translates the categorial opposition between consanguines and affines and its reduction to genealogical relationships. The category of cross kin is the genealogical manifestation of the existence of a general marriage formula based on sister exchange and the possibility of repeating this marriage under certain conditions. But it is not the distinction between parallel and cross kin that explains the form of marriage, it is the marriage alliance that explains the distinction. Moreover, it is because the distinction between consanguinity and affinity encompasses that between parallel and cross kin, without being reduced to it, that it can operate independently of real genealogical ties, as can be seen in certain Dravidian societies in the Amazon.[32]

---

32   Here we see the emergence of a category that Viveiros de Castro calls 'pure affines', in other words affines who are not cross kin and who have no genealogical link with Ego; they may

I would add that the opposition between consanguinity and affinity can be overdetermined by other factors – residential, political, etc.

It was important to emphasize the logic of the Dravidian systems because it is harder to grasp than that of the Iroquois systems. Nevertheless we must pause for a moment to consider these as well. Like the Dravidian and Australian systems, the Iroquois terminologies belong to the bifurcate merging category. Here we find merging of same-sex siblings (FB = F) (MZ = M), as in the Dravidian systems, but the nature of the bifurcation is different: *it does not merge cross collaterals with affines*. To determine if Alter is a parallel or a cross relative for Ego, it uses a very simple principle: it is the sex of the person who is the last link in the chain connecting Ego to Alter that determines whether this person is a cross or a parallel kinsman. Because cross collaterals are no longer automatically real or potential affines, the terminology *must* contain special terms for designating (real) affines. The existence of a specific set of terms for relatives by marriage thus indicates a profound change in the nature of consanguinity and affinity. Ego can now choose to marry a non-relative or a relative.

The distinction between cross and parallel cousins still exists, since it is engendered by the merging of same-sex siblings. But it no longer extends to three generations (G^{+1}, G°, G^{-1}) or to five, as in Dravidian systems. Hence the simplified formula for determining crossness, in other words the sex of the person who is the final link between Ego and Alter, whereas in Dravidian systems the sex of all of the links in ascending generations is involved in determining Alter's crossness.

This means that the two types of bifurcation – Dravidian and Iroquois – classify first cousins in the same manner, but classify these cousins' children differently. In a Dravidian system, the children of a male Ego's female cross cousins are 'sons' and 'daughters' because Ego and Alter are virtually spouses owing to the cross-cousin marriage rule, whereas the children of Ego's male cross cousin are 'nephews' and 'nieces', because this cousin is virtually Ego's sister's husband, and so are therefore 'sons' and 'daughters' for her.

In an Iroquois system, on the other hand, the children of a male Ego's female cross cousin are his 'nephews' and 'nieces', as are the children of his sister (in both systems), and the children of his male cross cousin are 'sons' and 'daughters'. The key here is the fact that Iroquois systems have a form of cross and parallel kinship, but it is *not* associated with a cross-cousin marriage rule. This type of marriage can exist on occasion but it does not correspond to a rule present in the terminology. The existence of a distinction between parallel and cross cousins in G° attests that the principle of sister exchange, which is

---

belong for example to a neighboring society and are regarded as enemies. Concerning all these distinctions, see Viveiros de Castro, 'Dravidian and Related Kinship Systems', pp. 364–9.

central to Dravidian systems, is also present in Iroquois systems, whether Ego marries a distant relative or someone unrelated. This is perfectly illustrated by the Baruya. What has disappeared from Iroquois systems is the principle of repeating this exchange with the *same* partners from one generation to the next. Which explains the absence of a preferential or prescriptive cross-cousin marriage rule in Ego's generation. Ego may marry a cross cousin, but this becomes an exception, as we saw in the Baruya example. When a Baruya man gives his sister to a lineage that has not given a wife in return, this man's son has a right to receive the daughter of his father's sister, his patrilateral cross cousin, for a wife.

The existence of different rules allowing or forbidding the repetition of the same marriage before a certain number of generations gives rise to several variations of the Iroquois terminology. This is reflected in the greater or lesser extension of the category of siblings. Several formulas can be found: either siblings (Sb) and first-degree cross cousins (X_1) are distinct (Sb ≠ XI), or first-degree cross cousins are merged with siblings ([Sb = X_1] ≠ X_2 ≠ X_3)], or first- and second-degree cross cousins are merged with siblings ([Sb = X_1 + X_2] ≠ X_3) or all cousins up to the third degree are treated like siblings and are therefore forbidden to marry (Sb = X_1 + X_2 + X_3). Marriages can therefore be repeated, depending on the case, only after two, three and even four generations. These different formulas affect the terminologies in Go, since, in the end, all that is left on either side in Ego's generation are forbidden siblings. That is why the 'Hawaianization' of these terminologies – a picturesque but erroneous term – is often evoked, whereas the only thing Hawaiian about these systems is the extension of the sibling category in Go. It would be better to speak, as Tjon Sie Fat has suggested, of an Iroquois terminology that is generational in Go. This is the case of the Ngawbe of Panama,[33] of the Kiowa-Apache of North America, of the Kandoshi of Amazonia, of the Yafar and the Umeda of New Guinea, etc. We are somewhere between so-called 'elementary' systems and 'complex' systems.

Descent reckoning is cognatic among the Ngawbe of Panama. Their terminology is of the Iroquois type in $G^{\pm 1}$ and generational in G^0. First-degree cross cousins are merged with siblings ([Sb = X_1] ≠ X_2, X_3). Their marriage rule is direct exchange of women who are second- and third-degree cross cousins. Two types of marriage are preferred for a renewed alliance. A man can choose to marry his father's father's sister's daughter's daughter (FFZDD) or look to his mother's side and marry his mother's mother's brother's daughter's daughter (MMBDD). Both types imply the existence of at least four lines (in reality four

---

33 M. Young, *Ngawbe: Tradition and Change among the Western Guaymi of Panama* (Urbana, University of Illinois Press, 1971).

groups of men related on the paternal side) who, in the first case repeat their marriage every three generations, and in the second case every two.

The Umeda of New Guinea[34] have an Iroquois-type terminology. Marriage is based on exchanging women with unrelated groups. There is no preference. Here again the exchanging groups are divided into four concentric zones encircling Ego:

Group I: that of Ego.

Group II: groups with which Ego can or has exchanged a wife or wives in his own generation (Go).

Group III: groups with which Ego's group has exchanged women in the preceding generations; therefore forbidden female cross cousins.

Group IV: groups of latent affines in the process of becoming potential affines.

The Yafar terminology[35] is of the Iroquois type: the guiding rule is the direct exchange of women with repetition of marriages every four generations with the third-degree cousin on the mother's side. Their terminology lies structurally midway between the Dravidian and the Iroquois terminologies. This example reveals the existence of terminologies reflecting forms of *transition* between the Dravidian and the Iroquois systems, forms of passage from 'elementary' to 'complex' structures. Or more specifically, with these terminologies, we move from systems of restricted exchange, which contain a rule for repeating the exchange in the following generations, to systems that are still compatible with the formulas of restricted exchange but which are associated with more or less numerous marriage prohibitions that forbid repeating marriages for a certain number of successive generations. After a shorter or longer lapse of time, they once again allow the marriage, which gives rise to very different exchange cycles. The Crow-Omaha systems are merely a special case of these restricted exchange systems with numerous prohibitions and a long cycle. They are perhaps the result of a particular change in certain Iroquois-type systems (patri-/matrilinear or cognatic), and perhaps even asymmetrical Dravidian types.[36]

---

34   A. Gell, *Metamorphosis of the Cassowaries: Umeda Society, Language and Ritual* (London, Athlone, 1975).

35   B. Juillerat, 'Terminologie de parenté yafar. Etude formelle d'un système dakota-iroquois', *L'Homme*, vol. 17, no. 4, p. 5–34, and *Les Enfants du sang. Société, reproduction et imaginaire en Nouvelle-Guinée* (Paris, Maison des sciences de l'homme, 1986); English translation, *The Children of the Blood*, translated by Nora Scott (Oxford/New York, Berg International, 1996).

36   Concerning the existence of transformations of Dravidian systems into systems of generalized and therefore asymmetrical exchange, see Chapter 13 in this volume, the example of the Lolo societies.

In the case of the Australian and Dravidian systems, we were dealing with systems in which kinship relations circle back to Ego, and saturate the society. With the Iroquois (and Crow-Omaha) systems, owing to the fact that it is possible for Ego to marry either someone who is not a relative or a relative who is not forbidden, we are dealing with societies in which kinship relations are open and which close only intermittently upon themselves and upon Ego. Formulas such as C = (CC + AA), A = (CA + AC) are excluded. In these systems there is no marriage principle, no rule that states that my affines' affines are consanguines. Eskimo terminologies, such as our own, are even more open, since the principle of the direct exchange of women (and men) has completely disappeared, and there is no reason, as far as the kinship system goes, for alliances to come full circle. Where we find closure, it is for reasons that have nothing to do with kinship, but instead with belonging to a given religion, a given class, or recovering lands given in bridewealth a few generations before, and so on: social factors which orient the alliances or weigh on them directly.

In the end, what Australian, Dravidian and Iroquois systems have in common is the presence of an opposition between consanguines and affines stemming from a symmetrical exchange in the generation immediately above Ego and which has repercussions on repeating or not repeating this same alliance in the following generations. To conclude the analysis of the relationship between consanguinity and affinity, and between parallel and cross kin as defined in the Australian, Dravidian and Iroquois systems, we will summarize the key points of Eduardo Viveiros de Castro's remarkable analysis.[37]

We saw that only the Australian sociocentric systems (those with sections and subsections) are fully associative. The formula (C = CC + AA), (A = CA + AC) applies fully. This means that an individual's position in the kinship system with regard to anyone else can be calculated without referring to genealogical ties. Dravidian systems, in which the distinction between parallel and cross kin extends over five generations ($G^{\pm 2}$) (Trautmann's type-B Dravidian), are almost as associative as Australian systems, whereas those more numerous systems in which the distinction extends to three generations ($G^{\pm 1}$) (Trautmann's type-A Dravidian) associate fewer. Alternatively, associativity disappears in the different varieties of Iroquois systems, some of which nevertheless contain a few Dravidian-type equations (MB = FZH) and are probably transitional forms situated between Dravidian and Iroquois terminologies.[38] Finally, as Viveiros de Castro demonstrated, comparison of the three types of terminologies shows that:

---

37   Cf. Viveiros de Castro, 'Dravidian and Related Kinship Systems'.
38   Of course associativity is not a property of Sudanese, Hawaiian and Eskimo type terminologies. On degrees of associativity, see F. Tjon Sie Fat, 'On the Formal Analysis of "Dravidian", "Iroquois" and "Generational" Varieties as Nearly Associative Combinations', in Godelier, Trautmann and Tjon Sie Fat (eds.), *Transformations of Kinship*.

- The *content* of the parallel/cross opposition is the same in the Australian and Dravidian systems, but the *form* is different.
- The *form* of the parallel/cross opposition is the same in the Dravidian and Iroquois systems, but their *content* differs since, in the Iroquois systems, the distinction between consanguines and affines does not coincide with that between parallel and cross kin.

From the moment cross kin and real or potential affines are no longer merged but belong to partially or even totally separate (social) categories, it becomes practically and intellectually *pointless* to apply rules for constructing parallel and cross relationships extending over the three median generations and terminologies (and sometimes more, as with Dravidian terminologies).[39] That is exactly what happens in the Iroquois systems, which have special terms for affines; this implies that they are not merged with cross kin, or, more precisely, that affines may not be cross cousins. But at the same time, while Iroquois systems distinguish between parallel and cross kin, this distinction concerns only Ego's generation ($G°$) and is limited to the distinction between parallel and cross cousins, without giving rise to other categories of cross kin.

The reduction of the parallel/cross distinction to Ego's generation attests that Iroquois systems have retained the rule of marriage by the symmetrical exchange of spouses between two groups but do not allow this alliance to be repeated before a certain number of generations. In the meantime, each group must look elsewhere, must marry into other groups so as to ensure new affines. This explains the existence of specific terms for affines, since these new in-laws will not be parallel or cross kin. It also explains the fact that the Iroquois method of reckoning the crossness of a relative contents itself with a simple criterion: that of the sex of the last kinsman or woman between Ego and Alter in G^{+1}, that of Ego's parents, the generation in which, precisely, a symmetrical exchange of spouses took place.

Finally, as Viveiros de Castro pointed out, the three bifurcate merging terminologies – the Australian, Dravidian and Iroquois systems – contain a non-cancellable opposition in Go that results from a symmetrical exchange of spouses in the generation above Ego and which concerns the following generations in so far as this marriage can (or must) be repeated either immediately or not before an interval of two or more generations. Depending on whether the repetition is immediate or deferred, and whether it is cyclical or not, there would be a shift from what Lévi-Strauss called elementary structures of kinship to semi-complex structures, structures therefore engendered by different

---

39   Three in type-A Dravidian terminologies, five in type B, according to T. Trautmann's distinction.

marriage *regimes*.[40] Lévi-Strauss' hypothesis, following Morgan, that kinship *terminologies* can be explained by marriage rules thus seems to us to be confirmed, at least for these three types of system, to which can be added those known as Crow-Omaha. Further analysis should thus concentrate on the systems neglected by Lévi-Strauss and most kinship theorists – the Sudanese, Hawaiian and Eskimo systems. We know that, as Lévi-Strauss pointed out, aside from some negative rules which set the degrees of incest and therefore the forbidden marriages, these systems have no positive rules prescribing marriage with a given category of kin.

At the close of these analyses,[41] which we felt were needed to give some idea of the logical character of kinship terminologies and the reasons for the different logics behind these systems, the reader will have come to understand that, in order to gain a perspective, a comparative scientific and not ideological idea of what can be meant by fatherhood, motherhood, consanguinity, affinity, marriage, family and so on, one must not project onto all societies the notions one carries around because one has received them unconsciously or didactically from one's own culture. Each time, these notions inherited from a particular culture must be deconstructed by confronting them with other concrete sociological and historical realities, and then one must go on to reconstruct them in the context of a theoretical analysis capable of detecting, behind the complexity and the diversity of the facts, the action of a certain number of principles and rules which explain this infinite diversity but which themselves are not infinite in number. It is by taking this two-pronged approach, by deconstructing and then reconstructing, that the anthropologist, the historian, the sociologist or the psychologist will be able to decentre him- or herself with respect to the cultural and social assumptions of the society in which they were born (which is not necessarily a Western society) and/or the society in which they learned their trade.

No doubt the hardest thing for a non-specialist to understand is the distinction between cognation, consanguinity and affinity. To my mind, it is Viveiros de Castro who has made this the clearest. For him the notion of cognation is synonymous with *relatedness*,[42] in other words it refers to the existence of a connection

---

40   See the vigorous discussion between F. Héritier and E. Copet-Rougier, on the one hand, and E. Viveiros de Castro, on the other, spanning two issues of *L'Homme*: E. Viveiros de Castro, 'Structures, régimes, stratégies', *L'Homme*, vol. 33, no. 1 (1993), pp. 117–37; E. Copet-Rougier and F. Héritier-Augé, 'Commentaire sur commentaire: réponse à E. Viveiros de Castro', *L'Homme*, vol. 33, no. 1 (1993), pp. 139–48; and E. Viveiros de Castro, 'Une mauvaise querelle', *L'Homme*, vol. 34, no. 1, (1994), pp. 181–91.

41   Analyses which have left aside a huge number of problems, for instance the endogamous or exogamous nature of marriage alliances.

42   For Viveiros de Castro, the notion of relatedness is not emptied of all references to the different kinship relations, as it is for Mary Bouquet in *Reclaiming English Kinship: Portuguese Refractions on British Kinship Theory* (Manchester, Manchester University Press, 1993).

between two individuals starting from any kinship relation, whether descent, filiation, siblingship or marriage. From this standpoint, a cognate is any relative, whatever the nature of their tie with Ego. In Western European kinship systems (Eskimo type), the field of consanguinity and that of cognation coincide. This is not the case, however, in Dravidian systems, where many cognates are real or potential affines. Thus MB and FZ are cognates but are not consanguines in the Dravidian sense of the term. As far as categories go, they are affines. Mother's brother is 'as much' a cognate as father's brother, but in a Dravidian system, mother's brother is an affine and father's brother a consanguine. Mother's brother's daughter is a real or potential wife, father's brother's daughter is a sister. And vice versa, many people classified as consanguines in a Dravidian system are not cognates, since the predominant formula in Dravidian systems is ideally that:

– CC = C: my consanguines' consanguines are consanguines
– AA = C: my affines' affines are consanguines
– AC = A: my affines' consanguines are affines
– CA = A: my consanguines' affines are affines

In Dravidian systems we therefore find non-cognates classified as consanguines or affines. The notion of consanguinity, in the European and Euro-American sense of the term, is totally different from that implied by the Dravidian systems. In the latter, the existence of a tie of consanguinity between individuals does not necessarily mean they are related genealogically by what we call 'blood' ties. In these systems, consanguinity and affinity are categorial definitions that partially coincide with genealogical ties. The opposition of the notions of consanguinity and affinity concerns primarily the fact that the individuals can or cannot marry each other. With respect to this opposition, the notion of cognation is neutral. Finally, a very important hypothesis advanced by Viveiros de Castro: cross and parallel kin are, with respect to Ego, two subcategories of two categories of kin, consanguines and affines, which correspond to those persons in these categories who have genealogical ties with Ego. Yet however clear the category distinctions in the Dravidian kinship terminologies may be, we must not forget that, when it comes to actual practice, to social and cultural realities, there is some ambiguity concerning the status of close affines. Cecile Busby, for example, observed in South Indian societies that Ego will treat his father's sister like a consanguine before she marries his mother's brother, but afterwards will treat her like an affine.[43]

---

43   See Cecile Busby's analysis of South Indian Dravidian systems, 'On Marriage and Marriagibility: Gender and Dravidian Kinship', *Journal of the Royal Anthropological Institute*, no. 3 (1997), pp. 21–42.

Another important hypothesis put forward by Viveiros de Castro is that, if consanguinity and affinity are opposed as categories, the opposition is such that, in certain contexts, one may at the same time *encompass* the other. Using examples from Amazonia, he also shows that, in certain cases, the categories of consanguinity and affinity can be radically disjoined from any genealogical tie or support. In these societies, the 'pure', the ideal affine, is ultimately the distant outsider, the enemy with whom one will never exchange women. The real, close affine, who lives in one's own highly endogamous local group, tends, on the other hand, to be treated like a consanguine.[44] We thus see a double shift occurring in these societies: one toward a consanguinization of all affines living with the consanguines in strongly endogamous local groups with a cognatic descent mode, and the other toward an affinization of outsiders and enemies living on the periphery of these societies but which are virtually encompassed within them by the extension of an affinity entirely disconnected from matrimonial exchanges, from alliances. In short, this disconnected affinity becomes a way of fictitiously entering into the kinship world of persons and groups who are neither affines, nor consanguines, nor cognates; in short, non-kin, strangers and even enemies. In this case affinity becomes a pure representation and exists only in the words used to talk about it. It is a language, but one borrowed from kinship.

We are at the far pole from the vision of Dravidian systems elaborated by Louis Dumont using data collected on the castes of India. In India, Dravidian classifications oppose consanguinity and affinity, and are symmetrical with respect to Ego. In the closed universe of castes, it is as though individuals and lineages transmitted an affinal relationship from one generation to the next, like an inheritance. In certain Amazonian societies, instead of individuals finding themselves faced with two symmetrical categories – consanguines and affines – according to Viveiros de Castro, they are confronted with *three* concentric categories – consanguines, real and potential affines, and pure affines with whom one does not contract marriage alliances.

It is possible that this transformation originated outside the field of kinship, in the political domain, for example, in the sphere of relationships between the inside and the outside of a society and in the cultural representations of the relationships between one's own people (consanguines, affines) and others (especially the stranger, the enemy other). We find ourselves here in the presence of societies where one was supposed to kill and to take the flesh, the soul or the name of an enemy into oneself so as to construct one's own identity and raise one's prestige within one's own group, which was at the origin of

---

44   A. C. Taylor, 'Jivaro Kinship. A Dravidian Transformation Group', in Godelier, Trautmann and Tjon Sie Fat (eds.), *Transformation of Kinship*, pp. 187–213.

cannibalistic practices or headhunting. From a certain standpoint, this 'pure' affinity without marriage is not thinkable without a cosmic and sociological vision of human identity in virtue of which war and the absorption of the outside enemy become the *equivalent* of marriage and birth in constructing the individual and collective identity.

Here we are no longer in the domain of kinship, but in that of political-cosmic relations, in the relationship a society entertains with surrounding societies. And yet a kind of affinity that would make it possible to think relationships with strangers – with enemies in so far as fighting and absorbing them was indispensable to individual self-fulfilment and to the reproduction of one's natal local group – would indeed fall into the domain of kinship. Is not such an enemy – who is indispensable if one is to exist fully and one's society is to continue to exist and who gives his life and his flesh so that this may come about – even more than the affine who gave you a wife and to whom you gave a sister? In this culture and according to this logic of permanently hostile relations between neighbouring groups, this enemy is ultimately sublimated by being transformed into a pure affine and one day being cannibalized.

It should now be equally clear that the notion of fatherhood and the status of father will not be the same if descent is traced through men or through women or through both sexes. Indeed, it is obvious that the notion of father is not the same if all of a man's brothers are also fathers for his children and must conduct themselves as such. Nor is it any less obvious that the status of a brother and a sister will not be the same depending on whether it is the sister or the brother who ensures the continuation of a lineage, etc. And, of course, the notions of close or distant 'cousins' on the father's or the mother's side will not be the same depending on whether certain ones are potential spouses or on the contrary brothers and sisters, and therefore ineligible siblings.

In Chapter 7, we will show how these different types of kin relations are stamped into the body and the consciousness of individuals through the different representations societies have of the process of procreation and through the different ways children are socialized according to the sex they were born with. We will thus see that it is never simply kinship relations that are stamped into bodies and consciousness. For, at the same time, the same bodies and consciousness are imprinted with the political and religious power relations that prevail in the society. These power relations, which are very different in nature, in fact lurk behind the positions of authority and the forms of domestic and social power that parents exercise over their children according to their sex and their generation.

The *family* (whether conjugal or not, nuclear or extended, etc.) or the groups based on kin ties that go beyond the family thus cannot be the ultimate basis of human society, its universal foundation. The idea that the family is kin-based is an unfounded theoretical affirmation, and yet it has been propagated from Aristotle to our day, especially in political and religious discourses, and has been maintained by social anthropologists (with Malinowski, Murdock, Lounsbury or Scheffler's theses on the primacy of the nuclear family). Nevertheless, many of them – such as Lévi-Strauss – have never espoused this theory.

CHAPTER SIX

The Functions and Field of Parenthood

We will now pause in our exploration of the issues connected with kinship in order to consider the notion of parenthood and what it covers.[1] We will limit ourselves to listing the different roles ensured or that can be ensured, with regard to the children born to or adopted by them, by individuals of both (or either) sexes and different generations who are with respect to these children and according to norms defined by their society their paternal or maternal relatives by marriage or by adoption, etc. We have expanded a version of the roles proposed by Esther Goody,[2] adding to them the right of certain kin categories to exercise socially accepted forms of authority over children together with the right to punish them (role 6, below) and the obligation of certain (usually close) relatives to abstain from sexual relations (hetero- as well as homosexual) with certain categories of children (role 7). These roles are actually implicit in Esther Goody's list, but it is worthwhile making them explicit.

The term 'parenthood', as it is used here, designates the set of culturally defined obligations, prohibitions, behaviours, attitudes, sentiments and emotions, acts of solidarity and acts of hostility expected or excluded by individuals who – in a society characterized by a particular system of kinship and reproducing itself in a given historical context – find themselves in a relationship of parent to child with other individuals.[3] Depending on whether the adults are related to the children in the direct or the collateral line, are parents by marriage or by adoption, this relationship is entirely different. The obligations and prohibitions, the expected or excluded behaviours and sentiments on the part of the individuals in the role of parents, are therefore closely bound up with the very

---

1   D. Houzel, *Les Enjeux de la parentalité* (Paris, Erès, 1999).
2   E. Goody, *Parenthood and Social Reproduction: Fostering and Occupational Roles in West Africa* (Cambridge, Cambridge University Press, 1982). Concerning the concept of parenthood, see also the little-known text by B. Malinowski, 'Parenthood: The Basis of Social Structure', in V. F. Calverton and S. D. Schmalhausen (eds.), *The New Generation: The Intimate Problems of Modern Parents and Children* (New York, The Macaulay Comp., 1930), pp. 113–68. Using an analysis of the role of fathers in the Aka Pygmy society, Barry Hewlett briefly compared some twenty societies. See B. S. Hewlett, *Intimate Fathers: The Nature and Context of Aka Pygmy Paternal Infant Care* (Ann Arbor, University of Michigan Press, 1992), Chapter 7, 'Intracultural and Intercultural Variations in the Father–Infant Relationship', pp. 121–50.
3   J. Commaille and F. de Singly (eds.), *La Question familiale en Europe* (Paris, L'Harmattan, 1997); Houzel, *Les Enjeux de la parentalité*; D. Le Gall and Y. Bettachar (eds.), *La Pluriparentalité* (Paris, Presses Universitaires de France, 2001); C. Castelain-Meunier, *La Place des hommes et les métamorphoses de la famille* (Paris, Presses Universitaires de France, 2002). See also the special issue of the journal *La Pensée*, no. 327 (July/September 2001), 'Quelle place pour le père?' (articles by Françoise Hurstel, Anne Thevenot, Marie-Thérèse Meulders-Klein, Patrick de Neuter).

nature of the parent–child relationship that these individuals represent and reproduce, and depend on the position of each of these individuals within this relationship, a position that changes over their lifetime. For although not all children become parents in their turn, when they do, they make their own parents grandparents. Furthermore, kinship, like all other social relationships, is vested with interests that go beyond the field of parenthood and kinship, and these include relations of cooperation as well as relations of power and authority.[4]

Standards of behaviour, and the positive or negative values attached in all societies to the various kin positions, are the basis for the figures of the ideal father, the model daughter, the exemplary (cross) cousin and their negative counterparts: the bad mother, the ungrateful son, the maternal uncle who refuses his duties toward his nephews. A step further would land us in the realm of fairy tales or at the heart of the Bible – for example, in the episode where Cain, consumed with jealousy because Abel's gift was accepted by God whereas Cain's was ignored, kills his brother Abel, the obedient son and therefore the father's favourite.[5] In the end, however, all of these figures enjoy exemplary value – positive or negative – only because they have perfectly accomplished or on the contrary monstrously refused to do what society expected of them, namely to fulfil their roles, their functions, as parents and children. What are these roles?

1) *The first role, which establishes these individuals as the parents of a child, is the role they play – according to sex, age, position in the kinship network or other types of social relations (e.g. religious) – in begetting and bearing this child.[6] Thus stated, kin ties concern not only living persons but ancestors as well, the deceased who go on living in one way or another and, beyond the domain of living and dead humans, non-human actors: gods, spirits, etc. We will return to this subject in more detail in the next two chapters.*

2) *A second role played by parents, or which can make 'parents' of individuals who have not actually given birth to the child, is that of raising, nurturing and protecting the child and thus raising it to adolescence and*

---

4   An extreme example is the right of life and death exercised over his children by a Roman citizen in the name of *patria potestas*. He had this same right over his slaves.

5   Cf. Y. Thomas, 'Parricidium', *Mélanges de l'Ecole française de Rome* (MEFRA), vol. 93 (1981), pp. 643–715, and 'A propos du parricide. L'interdit politique et l'institution du sujet', *L'Inactuel*, no. 4 (1996), pp. 167–87.

6   In certain societies, the man takes to his bed when his wife is in labour with the idea that he is thus taking part in bearing the child. This is the practice known as couvade. The interpretation of such practices entails imaginary and symbolic constructions of fatherhood and not, as some sociobiologists have suggested, for reasons having to do with the biological process of natural selection. Cf. B. I. Strassmann, 'Sexual Selection, Paternal Care, and Concealed Ovulation in Humans', *Ethology and Sociobiology*, no. 2 (1981), pp. 31–40.

even adulthood (the age differs with the society and is not necessarily the same for boys and for girls).

3) *A third role, linked through its very performance to the preceding, is that of educating or bringing up the child, including imparting certain knowledge and skills and training in social skills (at least up to a certain age, when other institutions – groups of initiates, schools – take over or add what they have to add to the earlier parental training).*

4) *In virtue of their kin tie with a given child and depending on the nature of this tie, relatives can or must endow the child, from birth or later in life, with a name and a social status (that they themselves possess or have the ability to confer). They can also endow the child with potential rights in certain tangible and/or non-tangible assets as well as in persons. This endowment with a status and with rights takes place simultaneously within kinship relations and groups to which both the parents and the child belong, as well as within other relationships and social groups to which these individuals and their kin groups also belong – a caste, a class, a religion. One is born a Brahmin and cannot acquire the caste by merit or by competitive examination, as one would in becoming, for example, an electronics engineer.*

5) *A fifth parental role, whether parenthood is acquired through birth, adoption or nurturance, is the exercise of certain rights (usually distinct and unequal according to the parent's sex, that of the child and the distance between these parents and these children) over the person of this child, including the right to put the child to death, to sell it into slavery or to give it away. These rights are obviously inseparable from the existence of duties toward the child. But they also imply that, until the child has reached a certain age, some of its kin (father, mother, uncles, aunts, older brothers and sisters, but also the broader group of paternal and maternal kin, etc.) will be considered to be responsible for what this child does or fails to do and will take responsibility for what it does or is supposed to do.*

6) *Although this sixth role is implicit in the exercise of (2), (3),(4) and (5), it must be recalled that certain categories of kin have the right and the duty to exercise certain forms of authority and repression over a child and to expect behaviours that range, depending on the society and the time, from unquestioning obedience to respect without submission, or reciprocal and shared affection.*

7) *Last, depending on the degree of kinship, generation and sex, certain categories of kin, usually but not necessarily the child's close relatives, are supposed to*

observe a prohibition on having sexual (homosexual or heterosexual) relations
with this child or other forms of intimate behaviour touching in various degrees
on the prohibition of incest or more generally improper sexual conduct.

THE FIELD OF PARENTHOOD						
Begetting and/or bearing.	Nurturance, upbringing, protection.	Training, teaching, educating.	Having rights and duties toward the child. Being considered by society as responsible for the child's acts and accepting this responsibility.	Endowing the child at birth with a name, a social status, rights, etc. In the framework of kinship relations as well as in other social relations (son of a Brahmin, a peasant, etc.).	Having the right to exercise certain forms of authority over the child and to punish. Expecting certain forms of obedience, respect, even affection.	Observing a prohibition on (homo- or hetero-) sexual relations with the child. Applies to those kin for whom this would be incest or improper sexual conduct.

Reading this list of positive and negative roles that those considered as 'parents' of a child should or may assume, it is clear that the roles can in the main be divided up and shared, and can therefore be parcelled out in many different ways, but always according to socially and culturally grounded norms, between the father and his relatives, the mother and her relatives, the in-laws, etc., according the sex and age of these individuals and their distance from the child in terms of kin ties.[7] It is clear, too, that not all of these roles have to be present in the field of parenthood in a given society and at a given time. What is important here is that all of these roles, in so far as they are present, have a form and an outline that are bound up with the nature of the kinship system and the forms of power existing in the society, and always go beyond the sphere of kinship.

In contemporary Western societies, where kin groups such as clans and lineages that contain and encompass the conjugal family do not exist, where

7   S. Lallemand, 'Génitrices et éducatrices mossi', *L'Homme*, vol. 16, no. 1 (1976), pp. 109–24.

marriage is no longer a condition for having a family, where the family itself may have only one parent, etc., all of these roles tend to be concentrated in a small number of persons; but this does not mean that they disappear. This is borne out each time society finds itself confronted with the case of an orphan with no relatives – close or distant – to whom it may be entrusted, or with the case of a child who must be quickly withdrawn from the home to protect it from abuse or incest on the part of the father or the mother or the step-father, etc.

In this event, society, through the state, which represents it and acts in its name, deprives the parents of some of their rights over their children because they were incapable of fulfilling their duties. But it then falls to the state to find an institution or a foster family to care for the children, to assign a social worker (or a psychologist) to supervise the institution or the foster family, to set the times and the duration of the parents' visits or vice versa the time the children spend with one parent or the other. In short, in such painful circumstances, we see a whole network of people unrelated to the child set in place to care for it: civil servants, members of charitable organizations, foster families, all paid for their services and who act as partial surrogates for the parents who have disappeared or failed in some way. Together or separately, these persons will take on a number of parental roles, usually those of upbringing, nurturance, protection, education, but also (often) of giving the child a name.

In these conditions it is understandable that it is impossible to reduce, as a number of family sociologists and psychoanalysis in the West do today, the notion and field of parenthood to 'the desire for a child', which a great number of people feel and which is translated by the desire to make a baby or to adopt a baby that has been made by someone else. It is in order to satisfy this desire to be a 'father' or a 'mother' that some Western European countries, like Holland, have changed their laws to allow adoption by a single person or by a homosexual couple, thus creating different kinds of families – single-parent, homosexual. In this case, parenthood comes down to acting affectively and socially 'as a parent' with regard to a child.

Ultimately the desire to have a child is no longer connected with the biological sex of the person seized by it. Parenthood in this case comes down to 'parenting', to wanting to be a parent and acting like one.[8] However one does not dream of being just any parent but the equivalent of the 'ideal' father or mother. The individualistic desire for a child thus runs up against the traditional models of parenthood, which continue to operate in our society by idealizing those persons who, having begot a child, raise it themselves, lavishing on it all of the attention and protection 'expected' of them. Tomorrow new figures of the 'ideal' parents will probably arise if homosexual families are legalized and their numbers grow. But will the brother of a man who has founded

---

8   I am indebted to Irène Théry for having called my attention to the ongoing evolution in our societies and for having suggested an extremely helpful analysis. See I. Théry, *Le Démariage: justice et vie privée* (Paris, Odile Jacob, 1999).

a homosexual family by adoption act like an 'uncle' toward the child adopted by his brother? In all likelihood he will if homophobia declines in his society.

Of course the desire for a child, this 'parental project', is not confined to the West. In all societies it exists in a large number of individuals, but not all. Nearly everywhere, the desire to have or not to have a child must nevertheless face up to the social obligation incumbent on all adults to have children, to make babies. The guiding force behind the desire, which gives it a social form and content, is not only to have 'a child', but to have 'a son' to carry on a name, a clan, a land; or a 'daughter', so that, for example, her natal matriline, that of her mother and her mother's brothers (but not her father), will live on. In most societies the desire to have a child is therefore not an 'individualistic' desire, in so far as it is almost never the desire to have a child for oneself alone. Depending on the kinship systems, and more broadly depending on the political and economic relations characteristic of a society and which differentiate individuals and social groups, the desire to 'have' a child, to 'make' a baby, does not mean the same thing for a man and for a woman, for a Brahmin and for an Untouchable.

Returning to the field of parenthood, let us take a few examples to illustrate the variations that may occur in these roles, depending on the descent and marriage rules and the forms of power and hierarchy found in a society at a given time.

Looking at the first role: Among the patrilineal Baruya, the father is represented as both begetting and nourishing (with his sperm) the child, and he is both the child's genitor and its social father. Among the matrilineal Trobrianders, the father is not regarded as the genitor of the child. It is the mother who conceives the child when an ancestral spirit-child enters her body and mingles with her menstrual blood to form the embryo. The father nourishes the embryo with his sperm, as among the Baruya, and then when the child is born nourishes it with the products from his gardens. He is thus both the nurturing father and the social father of the child, but he is not the genitor.[9]

Two opposing examples, both from patrilineal systems, illustrate differences in the attribution of parental rights over the person of the child. In Ancient Rome, the newborn child was laid at the father's feet.[10] At this time, he could either pick up the child and raise it in the direction of the alter of the ancestors and the gods, which meant he granted the child its life and that, if it was a boy, he gave the city of

9   See the important article by T. Monberg, 'Fathers Were Not Genitors', Man, vol. 10, no. 1 (1975), pp. 34–40, on the beliefs of the Bellona islanders, in the Solomons. For them, children exist as spirits before being implanted in the woman's uterus by the gods, with the help of the woman's husband's ancestors.

10   Y. Thomas, 'A Rome, pères citoyens et cité des pères (IIe siècle av. J.-C.-IIe siècle ap. J.-C.)', in A. Burguière, C. Klapish-Zuber, M. Segalen and F. Zonnabend (eds.), Histoire de la famille (Paris, A. Colin, 1986), vol. 1, pp. 193–229; L. Hiatt, 'Towards a Natural History of Fatherhood', The Australian Journal of Anthropology, vol. 1, nos. 2–3 (1990), pp. 110–30; P. L. Assoun, 'Fonctions freudiennes du père', in Le Père. Métaphore paternelle et fonctions du père: l'interdit, la filiation, la transmission (Paris, Denoël, 1989), pp. 25–51.

Rome a new citizen, or he could leave the child on the ground, thus abandoning it to be exposed and let starve to death (unless some charitable person were to take it in and adopt it). Among the equally patrilineal Baruya, men never attend the birth for fear of becoming polluted and being killed by contact with the blood and the substances that issue from the woman's body during the birth process. For the next three or four weeks – spent isolated in a temporary shelter built in a space off limits to men, at the bottom of the village – the woman has complete freedom to kill her child. And many do, not only when the child is sickly or deformed, but also when they do not want to give their husband another child because he beats them, mistreats them – or because he has taken a second wife despite the first one's protests. But once they leave the birthing hut and return home to their husbands carrying the new baby in their *bilum* (the netbag in which women in New Guinea carry everything), they loose this right of life and death over their child.

Nevertheless, as we will see in the following chapter, there is nothing mechanical about the correspondences between kinship relations, forms of power and representations of what makes up the identity of a gendered individual. Today we know of many examples of matrilineal societies where the man's sperm is considered to play an important role in conceiving a child as well as examples of patrilineal societies in which the same sperm plays only a minor role. Later we will seek out the reasons for the correspondence, or lack of it, between descent rule and the representation of the process of begetting a gendered individual. And we will see that these are found by looking at the forms and figures of power and not at kinship.

Having suggested, in the form of a list of roles, what parents can be for a child, we will now give an example of what a child can be for its parents. We have chosen the Inuit society because, thanks in particular to the quality and the detail of Bernard Saladin d'Anglure's work, we can see how the arrival of a child in the Inuit's world could be experienced emotionally and socially by its parents and by the members of the little community in which it would grow up.

We know that, before contact with Europeans, the Inuit (a name that means the 'true' humans), formerly called Eskimos (a derogatory term now rejected by the Inuit, which the French had taken over from the language of the Algonquin Indians, neighbours of the Inuit), made their livelihood from hunting, fishing and gathering in the Arctic and sub-Arctic regions of North America. They survived in this harsh environment thanks to their vast knowledge of the natural environment and its resources, their invention of remarkable tools, weapons and techniques, and finally their fluid social organization, which allowed them to alternate seasonally between dispersal into small nomadic bands and regrouping, when the season and the resources allowed, in order to perform weeks-long rites and conclude alliances.[11]

---

11   Cf. B. Saladin d'Anglure, 'Violences et enfantements inuit, ou les nœuds de la vie dans

Their descent rule was cognatic, with no clans or lineages. Their terminology was of the type we continue to call Eskimo, precisely, and which resembles the system used by the French, the English, and so forth. As far as their relationship with children goes, several things struck outside observers: an intense practice of giving and adopting children between relatives or friends (a woman would give one of her children to her sister, or to her mother; a niece to her aunt; a brother to his brother), creating an extraordinary circulation of children within local groups.[12] Giving a child was also a way of honouring blood debts contracted with the relatives of a murder victim or someone sacrificed by his starving companions because they had been caught in a snowstorm and could not leave their shelter for days to hunt or return to their camp. Another fact that weighed heavily on an Inuit's personal identity and the status of a child was the custom of giving this newborn child the name of a close relative or someone closely associated with the life of its parents and who had recently died. In Inuit culture, to name a child after someone recently deceased was immediately to allow this person to live once again in their namesake and to extend his or her 'real' presence among his close relatives and friends. This belief led to the appearance in Inuit culture of individuals belonging to what Bernard Saladin d'Anglure has called a kind of 'third sex'.[13] Frequently a mother would name her daughter after her father who had just died so that the spirit and the personality of the grandfather would be reborn in the body of his granddaughter. Or she could give a daughter the name of a brother who had died in a snowstorm. Throughout childhood this girl would be dressed and raised as a boy – including being taken hunting. This would go on until menarche when she would have to give up dressing like a boy. She would often refuse for a time and then give in. The same was true for boys raised as girls: at puberty they would, like all other boys, go out and kill their first animal.

Another important fact: during all the years when these children belonged to the other sex, their parents would address them as though they were the person they embodied. Their mother would call them 'father', their brothers and sisters, 'grandfather', for example, and their cousins, 'uncle'. They thus lived in two universes of genealogical ties at once, real and imaginary. Practices of this sort ultimately neutralized or gave a very different meaning to a kinship terminology

le fil du temps', *Anthropologie et sociétés*, vol. 4, no. 2 (1980), pp. 65–99, special issue devoted to 'L'usage social des enfants'.

12   B. Saladin d'Anglure, 'L'Election parentale chez les Inuit: fiction empirique ou réalité virtuelle?', in A. Fine (ed.), *Adoptions: ethnologie des parentés choisies* (Paris, Editions de la Maison des Sciences de l'Homme, 1998), pp. 121–49.

13   B. Saladin d'Anglure, 'Nom et parenté chez les Eskimaux Tarramint du Nouveau-Québec (Canada)', in J. Pouillon and P. Maranda (eds.), *Echanges et communications. Mélanges offerts à Claude Lévi-Strauss* (The Hague, Mouton, 1970), pp. 1013–38; 'Du fœtus au shamane, la construction d'un troisième sexe inuit', *Etudes/Inuit/Studies*, vol. 10, no. 102 (1986), pp. 25–113; 'Le "troisième sexe"', *La Recherche*, no. 245 (1992), pp. 836–44.

on the whole formally similar to our own, which by contrast proceeds from one 'real' genealogical position to the next and does not take imaginary byways through a universe of purely spiritual kinship ties and descent reckoning.

So, in the end, what is an Inuit child for its parents?[14]

1. A child is a *bubble of air*, taken from the air in circulation around it the day it is born and which enters its body and lodges near the groin. This air becomes breath, the life force (*inuupiq*). This breath is a small fraction of Sila, the cosmic breath, Sila, the master of the order of the universe and its workings, as well as of all the creatures in it. Sila is also the mind of the world, the power of reasoning that develops in each person, their mana. In reality Sila is a gigantic child, Naarjuk, called 'Little Belly', who fled to heaven after a giant killed his father and mother, and laughed at the child's huge penis, which he had challenged to support the weight of four women. Since that time, it is Little Belly who commands the snow, the rain, the heat and the cold, the wind and the air.

2. A child is a *soul* that is at the same time its double, a duplicate soul (*farniq*). This duplicate soul is housed in the air bubble that from the time of birth connects the child with the universal breath, Sila. This soul looks like an homunculus, which is the exact copy of the child and will grow with it until it dies. The soul will then leave the body in a non-tangible but sometimes visible form to travel to the dwelling places of the souls of the dead, under the sea or in the sky.

3. A child is some of its *father's sperm*, which has become bone, skeleton, structure.

4. A child is some of its *mother's blood*, which it shares with its siblings.

5. A child is a *face*, a physiognomy created by either a subtle balance of its genitors' features or by an excessive dose of life force from one of them.[15]

6. A child is a *name that is also a soul* (*atiq*), the soul-name of a relative or a friend, or of a neighbour of either one of the parents, who died shortly before

---

14   B. Saladin d'Anglure, "'Petit-Ventre", l'enfant géant du cosmos inuit. Ethnographie de l'enfant dans l'Arctique central inuit', *L'Homme*, vol. 20, no. 1 (1980), pp. 7–46.

15   Concerning the problem of resemblance between parents and children, see B. Vernier, *Le Visage et le nom: contribution à l'étude des systèmes de parenté* (Paris, Presses Universitaires de France, 1999), in which the author revisits and develops a topic previously dealt with by Malinowski and by Leach, but which subsequently received little attention from anthropologists.

the child's birth. By giving the child this name, its parents have allowed the deceased to relive in the child's body and once more have him or her with them. Furthermore, it often happens that when a person is old or feels on the verge of dying, they express the desire to live again in the next child that is born to a given set of relatives or friends, who will not necessarily be of the same sex. The child will live according to two genders at the same time because, from the outset, he or she will be him- or herself as well as another. The soul-name envelops the child's body like a sheath and transmits to it all of the experiences lived and accumulated by its deceased homonyms. For it often happens that a child receives, at birth or later in life, several names, and therefore several souls, each of which in turn envelops the child and transmits its experience and its force. A child is thus the product of the desire of others, of deceased persons who want to come back to life and of living persons who seek to be reunited with their dead. Sometimes a shaman who has saved the child's life or has cured a serious illness will give it the name of one of his own protecting spirits to provide it with lifetime protection. The child is thus merely a moment in the ongoing cycle of the reincarnations of soul-names in different human forms. Hence the importance of the rite for naming newborns for all of their parents, grandparents, etc., and their neighbours and friends.

7. A child is thus a *problematic sex* that differentiates itself – and even multiplies at the will of the living and the dead.

8. A child is a *potential productive force*, which contains the forces acquired and accumulated by the long line of his or her eponymous ancestors, who have bequeathed them to him or her along with their name.

9. A child is made of *animal flesh*, of the game recycled from food to excrement.

10. A child is the *otherness* present in one's identity, a 'self' and an 'I' developed on several levels, which changes with each stage of life.

11. A child, according to Saladin d'Anglure, is 'a knot of life in the ball of string unrolled by time'. A way of living life by constantly reproducing it through imaginary or real means.[16]

---

16   Saladin d'Anglure stresses the fact that 'the distinction between the imaginary and the real is relative in Inuit culture, whereas it tends to coalesce into an absolute opposition for Western minds, which live in a world largely disenchanted by their own history, by their initiatives which have created a universe reproduced by scientific and industrial means in which the individual is posited as an absolute for himself and for others, even if he is still attributed with a soul capable of an afterlife'. See Saladin d'Anglure, 'Violences et enfantements inuit, ou les nœuds de la vie dans le fil du temps', pp. 65–99.

Begetting Ordinary Humans
(Fifth Component 1)

ANOTHER LOOK AT THE INUIT

Let us take again the example of the Inuit to complete it and to introduce the analysis of a few other representations of what it is to 'make a baby'. For the Inuit, to make a baby, the parents must have sexual intercourse. The father makes the child's bones, its skeleton, with his sperm. With her blood, the mother makes its flesh and its skin. The child takes shape in the mother's womb. It will resemble its father or its mother, depending on the strength of the life force of each. Its body will be nourished by the meat from the game killed by its father and eaten by its mother. At this stage of intrauterine life, the child is a foetus with no soul.

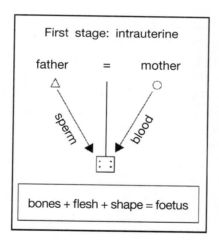

The foetus is still not a human being. The child becomes human on the day of its birth when Sila, the master of the universe, introduces a bubble of air into the child's body that will become its breath, its life principle. This bubble of air connects the child with the cosmic breath. It contains a soul, another gift from Sila, which will grow with the child's body and be its double, a double that will leave only at the person's death and travel to the world of the dead. This inner soul is endowed with intelligence and partakes of Sila, who is the mind of the world. A human child is born.

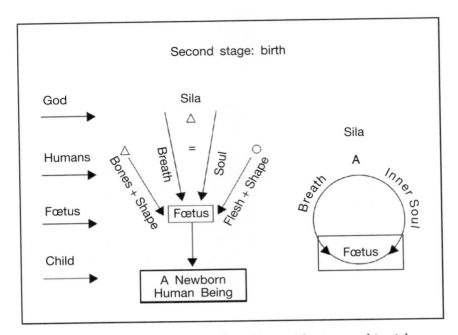

But the newborn baby is not yet a social being. This is something it becomes when it receives one or several names from its parents in a ceremony attended by all of the relatives together with the neighbours and the parents' friends. For the Inuit, names are not merely labels. They have a soul. They are souls themselves, since they harbour the identity and the life experience of those who have carried the same name. Unlike the inner soul that animates the body and grows with it, the child's soul-name completely envelops it and transmits the identity of all those who form the chain of its homonyms. And since an Inuit child usually receives several names over its lifetime, it will experience itself as both one and many, in so far as it knows that it is the meeting point of the reincarnation cycles of several soul-names, which live again each time they are given, in a different form and with a different human face.

Who are these soul-names and who chooses them? They are chosen by the child's parents and are the names of relatives or close friends of the father or the mother, deceased during her pregnancy, or even before, and whom the parents want to bring back to live with them by attaching them to the body of their child. Sometimes these are close relatives or friends who, feeling the end draw near, ask the man and/or the woman to give their name to their next child.

These (imaginary) representations of the process of begetting a child and the ingredients of its inner identity are what underpin the Inuit practice of raising a boy as a girl or a girl as a boy, depending on the sex of the person whose name was given at the child's birth. Nor should it be surprising to hear an

Inuit woman address her son as though he were his own prematurely deceased father. But it is noteworthy that these practices, which separate social gender and physical sex, cease when the child reaches puberty. The son goes back to being a boy and the daughter ceases to be one. This occurs precisely at the moment when each is going to have to take part in reproducing life by assuming the role designated by his or her biological sex.

What are the theoretical assumptions inherent in the Inuit representation of begetting children?

1. For the Inuit, sexual intercourse between a man and a woman is necessary to make a foetus but is not enough to make this foetus into a child.

2. The father and the mother, as the child's genitors, take part in producing and giving form to the foetal body through distinct and complementary contributions. Each partakes in the child by giving it matter and form, but they do not give it life.

3. Life begins when Sila, the supernatural power, introduces a bit of his breath into the child's body, which connects the child to the fabric and the movement of the universe into which it has just been born and where it will grow up. But this breath is also connected to a soul that will later enable the child to understand the world around it and which will survive after the person's death. This soul is singular and sets the newborn baby apart from all other humans who have ever been born, but it is not enough to make the child a complete human being, with its place both in the cosmos and in society. The soul gives the child life and the capacity to learn from its own experience. However the child still does not have a name that will connect it to the whole chain of human beings who have carried the name since time immemorial.

4. When the newborn child receives one or several names, in the course of a public ceremony, it brings to life in itself members of its kindred and, more broadly, members of its community who have gone before. By receiving these persons into itself, the child gives both them and its community a new future. These soul-names were not thought up by the child's parents: they existed before the parents and will live on through the child. They are thus spiritual components of a child's identity, which do not depend on the matter that comprises its body or on its shape. Because of these soul-names, an individual in Inuit society is never an absolute point of departure: he or she does not face life with his or her own experience alone, but with that of all of the homonyms who have gone before

and who, thanks to the parents, now accompany him or her for the rest of his or her life. Lastly, it should be noted that names have a life of their own and are not attached exclusively to a paternal or a maternal side, or even to the kindred of the child's parents, which is very different from the case in most kinship systems, especially uni- or bilineal ones.

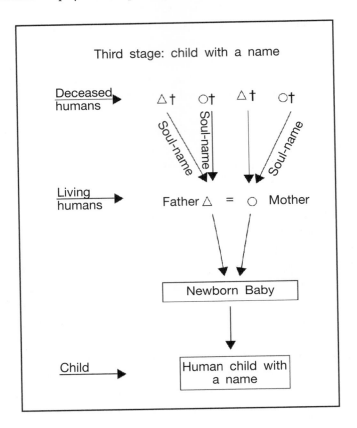

We can thus sum up the main points of this theory. For the Inuit:

- Sexual intercourse between a woman and a man is necessary to make a child but it is not sufficient. Other actors also play a role: gods, and deceased relatives or friends who want to live again and whose intervention is just as indispensable to completing the child and endowing it with an identity that is known and recognized in its society.

- By mixing his sperm and her blood, the man and the woman produce the raw material that makes up the child's body and provides its shape. In this, the child is indeed 'their' child, and therefore belongs to their 'kindred'. The contribution of sperm and blood 'legitimizes', as it were, the child's appropriation by its parents. After the birth, the parents can either keep the child and raise it or give it, for instance, to one of its father's sisters who is childless or whose children have all died, or to its maternal grandmother so that it will take care of her and keep her company.

- The parents' role is not limited to making the child's body. They also give it one or several names and, along with the soul-names, transfer to their child the experience of the deceased who have already carried the name and to whom they wish to give new life. These names are not transmitted exclusively in the paternal or maternal line and are not necessarily those of the child's relatives.

In emphasizing the parents' bilateral contribution to making their child and the undifferentiated transmission of its names, these representations of conception correspond to the Inuit kinship system, which is cognatic.

But we also observe that these representations bring into play forces that lie well outside kinship relations, reaching into the universe of the deceased and the gods. For Sila and the other supernatural powers that control the universe – the masters of the wind, the rain and the game – do not belong to one family or band rather than another. These powers hold sway over all Inuit, and Sila places in each of their children, whoever their father and their mother may be, whatever band they may belong to, whatever camp they are about to be born into, a bit of his cosmic breath and a soul that will grow with the child and become its double.

So Inuit representations of conception not only insert a child beforehand into a network of kinship relations and a kindred, they also give it a place in the overall society and in a particular cultural universe shared by all. The society and the culture that produced these beliefs, which will be self-evident for the child, will also offer it at birth a 'self-image' that will ground its own experience of itself and of others.

THE TWICE-BORN MEN OF THE BARUYA SOCIETY

Let us leave the Inuit now and look at the representations other societies have developed of what a child is. We will begin with the Baruya. The Baruya kinship system, it will be recalled, is patrilineal; their marriage is based on the direct exchange of women between two lineages; and their society is characterized, at the political-religious level, by the existence of large-scale male (and female) initiations, whose explicit aim is to grow boys and legitimize their right to govern society and exercise various forms of power and domination over women and young men.

The Baruya too believe that, in order to make a baby, a man and a woman must have sexual intercourse. The man's sperm (called 'penis water', *lakala alyeu*) produces the child's bones, its skeleton, whatever endures after the body's death, but also the child's flesh and blood, which increase as the embryo develops. The woman makes no contribution whatsoever. Her womb contains a sort of sack or bag (*tandatta*), which the sperm enters and where the child develops. Sometimes, if some of the woman's blood stays in her uterus, the child will look like its mother or someone in her family.

As soon as the woman ceases having periods, which tells her she is pregnant, she informs her husband, and from that day on the couple increase their sexual relations because the man's sperm is believed to nourish the foetus the woman carries in her womb. The Baruya woman can thus scarcely be regarded as her child's genetrix, since nothing passes from her body into that of the child, and her womb is merely a container for a body engendered and nourished by the man, who is thus both the genitor and the nurturer of the unborn child.

Yet the man and the woman are not enough to make this child, for, despite the father's repeated contributions of sperm, the foetus still does not have a nose, eyes, a mouth, or fingers and toes. In short, this being could not see or speak or breathe or walk or hunt, etc., if the Sun did not intervene in the mother's womb to fashion the missing organs and give this now-human body his breath.

The baby breathes when it is born, but it still has no soul, no spirit. It seems that, for the Baruya, the spirit-soul (*kourie*) enters the child's body and lodges in its head, near the top of the skull just under the fontanel. The nose that will be pierced during the initiations links the breath to the soul. The soul-spirit comes from an ancestor in the child's patriline or its clan and reincarnates itself in one of his or her male or female descendants. Apparently the spirit soul takes possession of the child's body only when its parents give the child its first name, the one it will carry until its nose is pierced and it receives its 'big' name, the name carried by all initiated men and women. The other name, the little name, will become taboo, forbidden to pronounce, cast into oblivion.

But before giving the child its first name, the parents wait a year or so to be certain that it will live and that the father has the time to make the child's maternal kin, its mother's side, a series of ritual gifts that detach the child from their lineage. During all this time the father is forbidden to even glimpse the face of his child, which the mother keeps concealed in a loosely woven net. If the child should die in the interval, it is buried without ceremony by its mother, in a remote spot (and not on land belonging to its father's lineage).

The two names given to the child – one before and the other after its

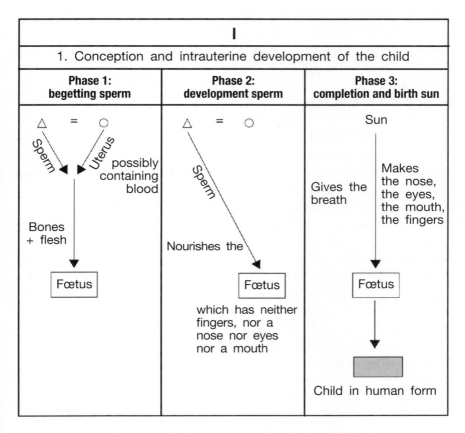

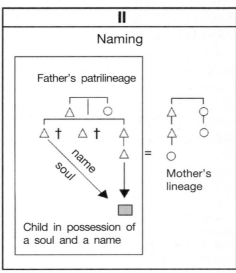

initiation – are always clan names. Each clan has a pool of names proper to it. Gwataye, for instance, is a 'big' (post-initiation) name that can only belong to an Andavakia man, but he could not be called 'Maye', a name reserved for the Baruya Kwarrandariar clan, which always provides the most important master of the male initiations. The Baruya carefully avoid giving the same name to two people from the same clan.

The two names given to a child are thus those of one of its male or female ancestors, on the father's side, in the direct or collateral line, belonging to the generation of its grandparents or great-grandparents. Inasmuch as a child's soul is believed to enter its body at pretty much the same time as its parents confer its name, and inasmuch as this name is that of one of the child's ancestors, it can be surmised that the soul which enters the child is that of the ancestor whose name it will carry from then on. But I have never had a firm confirmation of this hypothesis. When questioned, the Baruya would answer only that it was possible or that it was likely. What seems certain is that the soul that enters a child's body is always that of a male or a female ancestor. What is not certain (for me) is that this soul is that of the ancestor whose name the child will carry.

How can we describe the different stages involved in the process of conceiving a Baruya child? We will distinguish three moments in its intrauterine life: begetting, intrauterine development and finally, in the last weeks before the birth, the intervention of the Sun, to complete the child's body. Later, after its birth, the child will receive a name and a soul. Summing up:

1. For the Baruya, sexual intercourse between a man and a woman is needed to make a child, but it is not enough, for this only produces an unfinished foetus. That the union of the sexes is necessary is borne out by Baruya mythology. According to one of these myths, at the dawn of time, the man and the woman both had sexual organs and an anus, which were not pierced and could therefore not be used. One day Sun took pity on them and threw a flintstone into a fire. The stone exploded and pierced the man's and the woman's sexual organs and anus, and humans have been able to copulate and have children ever since.[1]

---

1   During one of the rituals before the initiates enter the big ceremonial house, the *tsimia*, all of the fires burning in the villages were extinguished and the 'first fire' was lit in the *tsimia* by striking sparks from two flintstones. These flintstones are among the sacred clan objects held by the master of the initiations and the shamans, whose ancestor received them as a gift from the Sun (together with the magic to make them work). In everyday life, the Baruya make fire by friction and not by striking.

In another version, it is Moon,[2] Sun's wife, that pierces the girls when they reach puberty and causes their first menstrual flow.[3] Or, it is not the Sun but the first woman who indirectly pierced the man's penis. She stuck the wing-bone from a bat into the trunk of a banana tree at the height of a man's penis, and the man inadvertently impaled himself. Maddened by the pain and having guessed who had put the bone there, the man grabbed a bamboo knife and slashed open the woman's genitals.

2. The existence of two versions, one in which the gods act on the first humans and another in which it is the first woman who takes the initiative, correspond to the deep structure of the Baruya's view of the world and the origin of things. According to the Baruya, women were the ones who invented bows and arrows, cultivated plants and who made the flutes, etc. But they used their creativity in a way that would have reduced the universe to chaos, for instance by holding their bow backwards and killing too much game. The men were therefore obliged to intervene and, by stealing the sacred flutes, the source of life, they brought about the order that still reigns in the world and which they continue to guarantee, as it were.

The man has the preponderant role in making the foetus, as we have said. His sperm makes the child's body, its bones and its flesh, and nourishes it. The mother appears as a passive vessel. Even the milk the young mother will give her child after its birth comes from the man, since it is a transformation of his sperm. When a young man and woman get married, it is customary for the couple to refrain from making love before the walls of the house, built for them by the men of the husband's lineage, have been blackened by the smoke from the fire burning in the stone fireplace, made by the same men. For days, and sometimes weeks, the young man merely strokes his wife's breasts and gives her his sperm to drink. This sperm is

---

2   According to certain myths known by all men and women, Moon is the wife of Sun. But in the esoteric stories the master of the shamans tells apprentice shamans, Moon is Sun's younger brother.

3   For the Baruya, menstrual blood means just the opposite of its significance for the Kavalan of Taiwan. The Kavalan are an Austronesian-speaking, matrilineal and matrilocal society. The women own the land, the family assets and the children. As shamans, they have the monopoly on access to Muzumazu, the mother goddess of all the Kavalan and source of fertility. Menstrual blood has no negative connotations and comes from Muzumazu. In this society, men are considered to be unstable and lazy as well as destroyers of life because they hunt game and heads. Young men can take a wife only after having brought back an enemy head, which signifies that they now have the capacity to procreate. Finally, men are regarded as human beings to be 'domesticated' by women and are exchanged between matrilines. Cf. Liu Pi-chen's highly interesting analysis, in 'Les Mtiu, femmes, chamanes, genre, parenté, chamanisme et pouvoir des femmes chez les Kavalan de Taiwan (1895–2000)', Doctoral thesis (Ecole des Hautes Etudes en Sciences Sociales, Paris, 2004).

believed to nourish the young woman and make her strong. Some of it is believed to build up in her breasts and change into milk when she becomes pregnant and later nurses her child. Thereafter, each time she gives birth, her husband will once more give her his sperm to drink and will nourish her with the game he has killed so as to build up her strength, which has been sapped by the birth and the loss of blood that goes with it.

3. Not only does the father play the more active of the human roles involved in making the child's body. It is also he who connects the child with his own ancestors by giving it a name and prompting a soul, a spirit, to enter the child. This name has been carried by men and women of his clan from a time so distant that its memory has been lost. But what the man does know is that his children – sons and daughters – will be made of the same sperm and the same blood as he, and that he shares with his brothers and sisters the self-same sperm and the same blood, which came from their father. But it is only the men who are capable of transmitting this blood, since women do not have sperm.

In the Baruya kinship system, the role of the father, as principal genitor of the child, nurturer of the foetus, giver of milk and of names, and transmitter of the soul, concords with a key component of this system: the fact that descent ties are traced exclusively through men, that their principle is strictly unilineal, patrilineal. This does not contradict the great importance the Baruya accord their maternal relatives. Mother's sisters are like mothers for them, and they can always look to their maternal uncles for help, protection and indulgence.

Living with the Baruya brought me to understand that all of the ingredients of kinship relations do not necessarily find expression in the body or in the representations of the body. As we saw in Chapter 2, Baruya kinship terminology is of the Iroquois type, which means that father's brothers are all fathers for the child, and that their children are brothers and sisters. All mother's sisters are mothers, and their children are brothers and sisters. Whereas father's sisters' children and mother's brothers' children are cross cousins.

What the Baruya theory of conception tells us is that all of a man's children share the same blood because they come from the same sperm. Therefore they cannot marry each other. And since all of this man's brothers also share the same blood, because they too come from the same sperm, which they alone (and not their sisters) can transmit, all of the children of this man and his brothers are as brothers and sisters and cannot marry each other. The Baruya's kinship terminology and their theory of conception thus correspond.

But this does not hold for the mother's side. On this side, too, Ego is faced with a group of people of both sexes whom he calls brothers or sisters. These are the children of his mother's sisters. But they do not have the same blood as his mothers and her sisters, since they come from the sperm of their own fathers, who belong to distinct lineages, since the Baruya rule is that two brothers or two sisters never marry into the same lineage and that sons do not repeat their father's marriage by taking a wife from their mother's lineage. Combining the patrilineal descent principle and these (negative) marriage rules gives the following situation. I call brothers and sisters people on my mother's side with whom I do not share the same sperm or the same blood and who, if they are the children of two sisters married to men from different patrilineages, do not even share the same sperm or the same blood with each other. I therefore call brothers and sisters people on my mother's side whom I could marry – and who can marry each other.

Three theoretical conclusions can be drawn from these facts: Once again we have confirmation that kinship terminologies are independent of the descent principles at work in a society. Next, we see that the representations of conception are linked with the principles and forms of descent at work in a society and also act to regulate marriage, if marriage is prohibited, for example, between those who share the same sperm or the same blood, etc. Lastly, we see that the representations of conception do not say everything about the nature of the kinship relations in a society. However they do express certain aspects essential for understanding the meaning of a child's social production and identity.

4. We observe with the Baruya, as in Inuit society, that whatever role the man and the woman play in the making of the child, they do not suffice in themselves. Supernatural forces – Sun and Moon – intervene to do what humans cannot. And they do this for all Baruya children, whatever their sex or their clan. That is why the Baruya say they are sons and daughters of the Sun, whom they call Nouwme, 'father', in their invocations and their prayers. Therefore not all Baruya are children of the same sperm, of the same human father, but all are children of the same divine father, who fashioned them in their mother's womb and gave them breath.

5. But the breath is not the spirit-soul, which comes to reside in the body and leaves it momentarily at night during sleep, or definitively at the time of death. In the latter case the soul returns to the land of the dead, which is located in two places for the Baruya. Some souls go underground, where

they live in villages that can be seen through a big crevasse that cuts deep into the mountain; the others go up into the stars, far from the everyday life of humans. Every human being thus has within himself something that does not die with him and which perhaps lived before him in other bodies and at other times. Where do these souls come from? The Baruya did not tell me. They only know that they come from the primal times, from the time of the first men and women, the *wandjinia*, the dream people. The souls were not made by men and women. Were they made? And by whom? At any rate not by Sun and Moon, for the first man and the first woman with their closed genitals were their contemporaries.

Let us now look at the Baruya boys' fate. Unlike their sisters, boys are twice born, begotten first by their father and mother, and engendered a second time by the adult men of the group, those who are married and/or initiated, who give them a second birth in secret initiations apart from the women and even in opposition to them. Around the age of nine, little boys are separated from their mother and sisters. This separation is brutal: the child is torn from his mother and loaded onto the back of a young fourth-stage initiate, usually one of his maternal kin, who runs quickly a hundred or so metres through facing lines of men, who lash the two bodies with thorny branches. The blood runs down their skin. At the end of this sprint, the child is deposited on the ground, and two or three blood-covered men threaten to shoot arrows into his legs and thighs. Sometimes they even do it. The terrified child then joins the other children, huddled against their 'sponsors', who soothes their wounds by smearing them with cooling yellow mud. For years the young initiate will not to be able to speak or to eat in front of this man, who, in the all-male world in which he will now live, acts as a surrogate mother to him. The maternal role, then, also deserts the women's world to resurface in the world of men.

The initiation cycle spans more than ten years, during which time the initiate will go through four stages. In the first stage he is still dressed partly like a boy and partly like a girl, and his buttocks are deliberately left bare so that he will not dare show himself in front of women. Then begins a long process designed to rid his body of everything that still has a female content, so as to purify him of all the pollutions that women bear in and on their bodies. Some foods are forbidden and others prescribed. He is not allowed to pronounce certain words. But above all, he discovers homosexual relations. He is forced to take the penis of the third- and fourth-stage adolescents into his mouth and to swallow their semen. And if he resists and takes too long, his neck is broken and the men then tell the mother that the child fell out of a tree pursuing an animal in the branches. But these first homosexual relations rapidly become a source of pleasure, and the new initiates seek them out. Inside the 'men's houses' couples form, bringing together for a time an older and a younger boy, the older boy having chosen the younger. A great deal of tenderness can be observed between them, as well as reserved and delicate gestures. There is room here for desire, eroticism and affection.[4] First- and second-stage initiates are thus regularly nourished with the older boys' sperm. These third- and fourth-stage initiates are young men who already fight alongside the married men but who have never had sexual relations with a woman, since they themselves are not yet married and still live in the *kwalanga*, the 'men's house'. Their sperm is therefore pure, free of the defilement entailed in sexual relations with women, since a flow of menstrual blood issues regularly from their vagina. So it is that from one generation of boys to the next, a flow of sperm free of all female pollution circulates and re-engenders them as even more masculine and stronger – and nourishes them.

These gifts of sperm circulate in one direction only. Whereas marriage rests on the exchange of sisters between two men, an exchange which involves a wife-giver and a wife-taker, in the gifts of sperm, the takers (the young initiates) will not be able to give their sperm in turn to their givers when they reach adolescence. Givers are not takers. The takers incur a life-long debt to the older boys. It should also be said that masturbation is forbidden in Baruya culture. Your sperm does not belong to you. It belongs to others, and vice versa, the sperm of others belongs to you. But precisely who can give his sperm to a young initiate? Any unmarried young man who does not belong to the initiate's lineage, for if he did, he would be committing a sort of homosexual incest. Furthermore, when a young man marries, because his penis has entered the mouth and vagina of a woman, he is forbidden to try to put it into the mouth of a boy who has just been separated from the women's world. This would be committing the worst kind of violence and humiliation.

Through these repeated ingestions of sperm, which transform his body into the body of a man, filled with purely male substances and forces, the boy is engendered a second time, no longer by his father, but by the group of young men who have been living for years apart from the women's world and have already rid the boys of every trace of their mother. It is they, and not his father, who will re-engender the boy and then bring him up. The father has practically nothing more to do with his upringing and disappears behind the Great Men, the great warriors, the great shamans, and especially behind the masters of the rituals, in short all the men who fulfil functions in the general interest and regularly visit the men's house to teach the initiates the legendary history of their ancestors and the events that founded the world order, beginning with the famous theft of the flutes by the men.

---

4   Cf. Gilbert Herdt's work on the Sambia and ritualized homosexuality in Melanesia.

For, as I have said, the secret name of the flutes is associated at the same time with the vagina and with the pollywogs that became the first men and which resembled foetuses.[5] It was in these flutes that the women's reproductive powers were originally concealed. When the men stole the flutes, they separated the women from their powers and confiscated their use. The men now have these powers in their possession, but they know that the women still own them and that chaos would be unleashed anew if the men relaxed their control over the women, in other words, their dominion. That is why, generation after generation, boys must be initiated and men's power reaffirmed. But this power is ambiguous, because it is based on the explicit denigration of women and on the secret knowledge of the existence of female powers that men can imitate and reroute but can never fully appropriate for themselves. That is why the Baruya's most sacred objects, the *kwaimatnie*, come in pairs, the more powerful, the hotter of the two being the female *kwaimatnie*, something no woman must ever learn.

During the many rituals that take the initiates from one stage to the next, the Sun is constantly invoked and present. Called upon by the master of the shamans at the beginning of the initiations, it draws close to the humans present and floods them with its light and its force. The masters of the initiations then mutter the secret name, *Kanaamakwe*, each time they brandish their *kwaimatnie* in the direction of the Sun before striking the object on the chest of the initiates so as to penetrate them with the Sun's power and light.

After having pierced the noses of the new initiates, with which the Sun endowed their face when they were still a foetus in their mother's womb, the masters of the initiations squeeze their elbows and their knees to strengthen the boys' body. Finally they jerk both of their arms upward to make them grow faster and stronger. Now, the magic bundle they brandish at the Sun and with which they strike the initiate's chest was a gift from the Sun himself to the ancestors of each clan, and the name *kwaimatnie* comes from *kwala*, 'men' and *yimatnie*, which means 'to make grow'. For it is without the women, but once again with the help of the Sun, that the men, as a group, re-engender their sons. Moreover the Baruya make a connection between the word *yimatnie* and *nyimatnie*, which means 'foetus' or 'novice'.

We are therefore in presence of a sort of collective begetting, which is at the same time a cosmic event, since the Sun takes an active part, as does the surrounding forest. Indeed, one of the most secret rites that follows the piercing of the boys' nose takes place deep in the forest, at the base of a tall, very straight

---

5   M. Godelier, *La Production des grands hommes. Pouvoir et domination masculine chez les Baruya de Nouvelle-Guinée* (Paris, Fayard, 1982), pp. 118, 227–8; English translation: *The Making of Great Men: Male Domination and Power among the New Guinea Baruya*, translated by Rupert Swyer (Cambridge, Cambridge University Press, 1986), pp. 70, 145.

tree whose trunk has been decorated with feathers and lengths of cowries similar to those worn by the men. The little boys are lined up facing the tree, which rises up into the sky, toward the Sun. Nearby stands another tree reputed for producing an abundance of thick white sap. The initiates' sponsors gather this sap in their mouths and come back to deposit it on the boys' lips. For the Baruya this sap is at once sperm and the milk of the tree, and by this gesture, a chain of life forces links the Sun to the tree, the tree to the young virgin men, and these to the young boys who have just been torn from their mother.

During this time, these boys' relationship with their mother and their sisters undergoes a thorough transformation. In the men's world, they had already become foetuses, nourished this time by the sperm of young men who had not yet known a woman and had been fashioned anew by the Sun's power, which entered their chest when the *kwaimatnie* struck them; now they have become older brothers for their sisters, including their older sisters. *The world of men rises definitively above that of women.* Genealogical ties are reshaped by power relations, the relations of domination that give initiated men authority over women, over all women, including the 'Great Women', those who have borne many living children, those who are hard workers, who cultivate big gardens and raise many pigs, and even those who are renowned shamans. The order between the sexes is a political-religious and a cosmic order. This social and cosmic order furthermore establishes an order between the sexes, a sexual order. And in building this social and cosmic order, male homosexuality is one of the means chosen by the Baruya to establish and legitimize the relations of power and force that are supposed to obtain between men and women, and between the generations. The Baruya's homosexuality is thus what in the West would be called a 'political-religious' practice, with a cosmic dimension, before being an erotic practice (which it is as well). Men are taught to be proud of having suffered in order to be initiated into secret knowledge that the women ignore, proud of having a new body, different from women's bodies and stronger, proud of being designated to take on functions, responsibilities in the general interest of which women are incapable and from which they are excluded.[6]

It is this male image that is made visible to everyone – to men, to women, to the children of friendly and hostile tribes alike, with whom hostilities have been called off for the space of the ceremonies – by the *tsimia*, the big ceremonial house built for each initiation in a location somewhere between the villages. Each post of the *tsimia* stands for a new initiate. The posts are planted in the ground (all at the same time) by the initiates' fathers at a signal from the masters of the initiations and the shamans. The fathers are lined up side-by-side,

---

6   Note the ambiguity: incapable because they are excluded, or excluded because they are incapable? For the Baruya the second formulation is obviously the correct one.

244 THE METAMORPHOSES OF KINSHIP

grouped by village and not by lineage, facing away from the circle they form and which outlines the place where the *tsimia* walls will be erected. A war cry rises from the throats of all of the men present when the fathers sink the post that represents their son. For the Baruya, these posts are 'bones', which, taken together, make the skeleton of the *tsimia* (which represents the 'body' of the Baruya tribe, a body whose 'skin' is provided by the women, who gather and transport the hundreds of bundles of thatch the men will use to make the roof). But women cannot enter the *tsimia*. At its centre stands a huge post that supports the edifice. It was sunk in the ground by the fourth-stage initiates. This post is the 'ancestor' of the tribe and it is called 'grandfather'. Before the roof is made, a dangerous animal, captured earlier, is thrown down from the top of the pole and smashes to the ground. Its body is then presented to the oldest man in the tribe, who will eat it and will then be expected to die before the next cycle of initiations. Time has come full circle, the cosmic and social order has been reproduced.

At the close of these rites, which go on for days inside the *tsimia*, the old and new initiates appear outside and dance around the edifice for hours. The women applaud at the sight of them, proud to see their sons adorned with feathers, their body painted, their face discreetly concealed behind a quiver of arrows when they pass before them. The force that sustains this unequal social order, founded on the domination of one sex over the other, is not so much the violence – in all its forms, physical, social, psychological – that the men inflict on the women as it is the belief shared by both sexes that women are a constant source of danger, not only for men but for the social and cosmic order as a whole, and that this is due to their body, to the menstrual blood that flows from their vagina.

The Baruya language has two words for blood: *tawe*, the blood that circulates in the bodies of people and game; and *ganie*, menstrual blood. Baruya men have an almost hysterical reaction when they talk about or when someone else talks to them about menstrual blood. And yet they know that this blood, when it flows for the first time from the body of an adolescent girl whom Moon has pierced, is the sign that she is now a woman and able to bear children. But like all of the fluids that flow from a woman's body, this blood is a permanent threat to men's strength, to their superiority. The menstrual blood produced by women's bodies is the force that destroys the men's own strength. In a sense it is the rival substance to their sperm, a kind of *anti-sperm*, as we saw in Chapter 1. The initiates are told that the man who stole the flutes had watched the women putting them away in a hut. When the women left, he went in, searched the hut and found the flutes hidden beneath a skirt soiled with menstrual blood. He took the flutes, played them and then put them back. When the women returned, one of them tried to play a flute, but no sound came out, and so she threw it down. The men picked up the flute and, ever since, the flutes have obeyed the men and sung for them.

The Baruya's fear of menstrual blood and vaginal fluids is so strong that, when they make love, the woman must not straddle the man, for the fluids from her vagina might run out onto his belly and sap his strength. She is also forbidden to step over the hearth where she cooks the family's food, for fluids from her sex or impurities from her skirt might fall into the fire and mix with the food that will go into the man's mouth. In a word, heterosexual relations are regarded as dangerous by nature, not only for men but for the reproduction of the universe and the conduct of society as well. And it is the woman who is the prime source of all these perils. Sexuality in all its forms must be brought under control if it is to aid in reproducing the social and cosmic order. And if this order is hard on women and subjects them to violence, it is in a way their own fault, due to their nature. Ultimately, inasmuch as they share these imaginary representations of men, women and life, Baruya women cannot help feeling at the same time victims of these acts of violence and responsible for their existence. Fundamentally, victims are guilty. And their only way out is to accept their fate in silence. These imaginary representations are not only mental concepts. For women the consequences are very real.

Indeed there is a social, material and conceptual gulf between the two genders. Girls, because they are women and do not have sperm, do not inherit land from their ancestors. They do not have the right to own or use weapons and are thereby excluded from hunting, making war and using armed violence, which is an attribute of power. They do not have the right to produce 'salt money' (but their husband or their brother gives them salt so that they can buy what they want). They do not control the fate of their daughters, even though their opinion counts heavily when their husband and his people discuss what lineage the girls will be exchanged with. Last of all, they are obviously excluded from owning and using *kwaimatnie*, and therefore forbidden direct access to the Sun and the gods, since it was their life-giving powers that were stolen and enclosed in the *kwaimatnie* that the Sun himself gave to the male ancestors of their lineage.

At the end of this long analysis, which does not do justice to the richness of Baruya representations of conception, we would like to stress the fact that this theory describes two different processes. One concerns both girls and boys (until they reach the age of nine or ten). The other concerns only boys after this age and causes them to be re-engendered by the men in order to become men in their own right.

The idea that sperm plays a twin role in making a child, thus making the father both the genitor and the nurturer (as well as the source of the milk the mother will give her baby when it is born), corresponds to the Baruya's descent rule and legitimizes the fact that the children are appropriated by the father's lineage in accordance with the patrilineal principle. The same goes for the name the father gives the baby and for the ancestor soul that re-embodies itself in the child. But the role played by the Sun in making a foetus into a human child expresses a distinct relationship between the descent and filiation principles, which are conveyed through the father and through the mother. It means that the child, whatever its sex and clan, belongs to the Baruya tribe and at the same time to the group of tribes that recognize the Sun as their common superhuman father and recognize the sperm of the human father as the primary origin of the child. The Sun here is simultaneously a cosmic power, a tribal god and (in so far as he is a god recognized by several tribes sharing the same origin) an 'ethnic' god.

But the primacy assigned to sperm is not based uniquely on the patrilineal descent principle that governs the kinship relations. It refers at the same time to the sperm of all of the young men who inseminate the boys without this time going through a woman's womb. For the Baruya, sperm is a substance that is 'overdetermined'. It acts on behalf of kinship, but at the same time it serves another purpose: to construct and to legitimize the men's claim, both collective and individual, to represent society and to govern it on their own. Sperm, in this case, is therefore not merely an 'argument' for appropriating the children born of legitimate sexual unions and assigning them to a particular kin group. It is also the argument alleged by one part of society, the men, for dominating the rest of the society – the women and children. It legitimizes the general domination, namely political and religious, of one part of society by another. That is the object of the opposition between sperm and menstrual blood, of the positive overdetermination of one and the negative underdetermination of the other. The human body thereby finds itself at the intersection of kinship relations and political-religious relations, marked by all manner of everyday or ritual power, exercised in public and in private life.

Yet another remark. In Baruya society, what we would call the political-religious domain, in other words the sphere of those practices intended to affect society as a whole, encompassing and transcending the differences created between individuals by the kin group they belong to and their distinct places of residence, this almost exclusively male-dominated domain is constituted outside and beyond kinship relations. It is organized around the project to re-engender men through men, an act that at the same time denies, supersedes and imitates that which is at the heart of kinship relations: the begetting of a child by a man and a woman. Without being the same as kinship, the political-religious domain is constructed within the domain of kinship by transposing elements of kinship into another ritual sphere and then eliminating everything these relations owe to women.

THE CASE OF THE TROBRIAND ISLANDERS

The example of the Trobrianders, who live on a chain of islands to the southwest of New Guinea, is probably the best known in all of anthropological literature. Their fame is due primarily to the nature of some of their institutions, but also to the remarkable analyses and publications of an anthropologist, Bronislaw Malinowski, who spent several years of his life with them.[7] He chose to devote his attention to three Trobriand institutions: (1) their kinship system, which is matrilineal, and the representations of the process of begetting children associated with it; (2) their political-ritual system, which – rare for Melanesia – rested on a distinction between 'chiefly' lineages (at the head of hamlets, villages or districts) occupying different functions and ranks, and the rest of the population; and, finally (3) the participation of these chiefs and other important men in the Kula, the vast network of ceremonial exchanges covering hundreds of miles and involving ten or so societies (often with different languages and cultures).[8]

But let us turn to what interests us here, namely, the ideas the Trobriand Islanders' had about child conception before the arrival of missionaries and other representatives of the Western world (who immediately set about combating these ideas so out of tune with scientific knowledge and the principles of Christianity). We will base our discussion on the information gathered personally by Bronislaw Malinowski and on studies by a string of brilliant researchers who, starting in the 1960s, did their fieldwork in the Trobriand Islands and in

---

7   Malinowski was born in a region of Poland that was at the time part of the Austro-Hungarian Empire. He had been considered an Austrian subject during the Second World War and was placed under house arrest in Papua New Guinea, then a British colony, for the duration of the conflict.

8   These exchanges take the form of gifts and counter-gifts of valuables, armbands, shell necklaces and polished stone axes, which circulate in opposite directions. The aim is to attract, through giving, and to retain for a few years one of the finest objects in circulation on the Kula roads and to add one's name to those who have already owned the object and whose names are henceforth attached to it. Those who are successful at this game (which held such fascination for Mauss) see their fame spread throughout the region and even to places they have never visited. And this fame achieved outside their own society is added to the prestige they already enjoy within it.

For information on the Kula, see B. Malinowski, *Argonauts of the Western Pacific* (London, Routledge and Kegan Paul, 1922); M. Mauss, 'Essai sur le don. Forme et raison de l'échange dans les sociétés archaïques', *L'Année sociologique*, new series, 1 (1925), in M. Mauss, *Sociologie et anthropologie* (Paris, Presses Universitaires de France, 1950), p. 258 (English translation: *The Gift: The Form and Reason for Exchange in Archaic Societies*, translated by W. D. Halls, foreword by Mary Douglas [New York/London, W.W. Norton, 1990]); M. Godelier, *L'Enigme du don* (Paris, Fayard, 1996) (English translation: *The Enigma of the Gift*, translated by N. Scott [Chicago/Cambridge, University of Chicago Press, Polity Press, 1998]). Concerning chiefdoms, see B. Malinowski, *Coral Gardens and Their Magic: Soil Tilling and Agricultural Rites in the Trobriand Islands* (New York, American Book Company, 1935), 2 vols.

other islands in the same part of the world. This work has both completed and corrected Malinowski's analyses and conclusions on child conception as well as on the two other institutions he had worked on: chiefdoms and the Kula.[9]

The Trobriand kinship system has a matrilineal descent rule. A married couple's children belong to the lineage of the mother and the mother's brother. A father and a son therefore do not belong to the same clan and do not have the same totem. All of the lineages in the island are divided into four matriclans, whose ancestors emerged from their subterranean dwelling place in the form of four brother–sister couples. All Trobrianders are descendants of these four female ancestors through the women.

Residence after marriage is virilocal, though. When a woman marries, she goes to live with her husband, and their children will be raised by him and will continue to live with him, with the exception of the oldest son. At puberty, this son will go to live with his maternal uncle, who lives on the lands of his own matriline, which controls their use. This boy will be his uncle's successor. The village headman is usually the eldest man in the matrilineage, whose ancestors are believed to have emerged from underground and been the first to occupy these lands.

How is a child conceived according to the Trobrianders? Not through sexual intercourse between a man and a woman, but by the encounter and mingling of a spirit-child (*waiwaia*) and a woman's menstrual blood. These spirit-children are spirits of the dead (*baloma*) that live on Tuma, a little island off Kiriwina, and who from time to time are gripped by the desire to be reborn in the body of one of their descendants. In effect, the dead are immortal and live a pleasant existence on their island under the authority of a god, Topileta, who is their 'chief'. When they grow old, they recover their youth, as was the case for humankind before emerging from their primal subterranean dwelling place. A soul who desires to come back to life in human form thus changes into a spirit-child and floats across the water to the island of Kiriwina. There it must make its way to the body of a clanswoman and enter it either through her head or through her vagina. But the spirit-child cannot find its way alone. The spirit of the woman's mother or that of another maternal kinsman, sometimes even that of the woman's father, transports it and introduces it into the body of the woman, who soon finds herself pregnant. When the spirit-child enters by way of the head, the woman's blood goes to her head and as it descends carries the spirit to her uterus. The spirit-child usually enters by way of the vagina, however,

---

9   We can cite F. Damon, *From Muyuw to the Trobriands: Transformations along the Northern Side of the Kula Ring* (Tucson, University of Arizona Press, 1990); N. Munn, *The Fame of Gawa: A Symbolic Study of Value Transformation in a Massim Society* (Cambridge, Cambridge University Press, 1986); A. Weiner, *Women of Value, Men of Renown* (Austin, University of Texas Press, 1976).

and becomes a foetus when it mingles directly with the menstrual blood that fills the womb.[10]

All of Malinowski's informants agreed that (1) all spirits of the dead recover their youth periodically; (2) all children are reincarnated spirits of the dead; (3) the child has no memory of the life led by its ancestor either on earth or after death in the island of Tuma; (4) the spirits that reincarnate return to the body of a woman of their clan and their subclan; (5) and lastly, the decision to be reincarnated is made by the spirits and not by humans, it belongs to the dead and not to the living.

The appearance of a new human being is thus the outcome of a process that takes place entirely between the spirit world and the woman's body. Two kinds of spirits play an active role: the spirit of a deceased ancestor and the spirit of someone living, both from the same clan and who collaborate to get a clanswoman with child. The woman is entirely passive throughout the process. No man is involved, and the woman's husband, though he contributes to making the child, does not do so as a genitor. The woman is the sole genetrix of her child.

Malinowski of course questioned the Trobrianders on many occasions about what they saw as the role of sperm; this is all the more interesting since, in the Trobriand Islands, people have sexual relations at an early age and lead an intense premarital sex life. Invariably the answer was that it is not enough to make love to make a child. It is the spirits who bring the children during the night.[11] Sperm and vaginal fluids come from the kidneys. Testicles are an 'ornament' of the male sex. The penis and the vulva have two functions: pleasure and excretion.

It should be added that for the Trobriand Islanders, a woman should not have a baby before getting married. A baby needs to have a *tama*, a 'father'. What then, for the baby, is the man who has married the mother and has sexual relations with her? Malinowski's answer came as a bombshell. This man, the mother's husband, is obviously the child's father (*tama*), but he is a 'purely social' father. Whereas the child is of the same substance, the same blood (*dala*) as its mother, 'between the father and the child, there is no bond of union whatever'.[12] Malinowski stresses that the word *tama* 'must take its definition, not from the English dictionary, but from the facts of native life described in these pages'.[13] For the child and its clan, the father is a *tama kava*, an 'outsider'. But this

---

10   Malinowski notes that, in the Trobriand Islands, there are several very different representations of these spirit-children. For some they resemble a sort of little mouse, for others a tiny child, an homunculus.

11   B. Malinowski, *The Father in Primitive Psychology* (New York, Norton & Company, 1927), p. 62.

12   Ibid., p. 12.

13   Ibid., p. 15–16.

'outsider' behaves like the most affectionate of fathers. Malinowski and the observers who followed him all stress the tender care and the affection fathers lavish on their children. The man children fear is not their father but their *kadagu*, their mother's brother.[14] In fact the father tries to retain his sons by giving them land and the means to participate in exchanges, including the Kula.

In short, in a society where kinship relations are governed by a matrilineal descent rule, the fact that children are not engendered by the father but by the mother alone, the fact that they do not share any substantial or spiritual link with their father but are of the same blood as their mother and her brother, and the fact that they re-embody one of their maternal ancestors, all correspond perfectly to the logic of their kinship system. Ignorance of the father's biological role is not a sign of inferior intellectual development, mental deficiency or lack of knowledge. It is part of the beliefs that play a positive active role in organizing a society and reproducing its structures. In 1929 Malinowski writes that,

> In 1916 [he] was still interested in the question 'Is this state of ignorance primitive, is it simply the absence of knowledge due to insufficient observation and inference or is it a secondary phenomenon, due to an obscuring of the primitive knowledge by superimposed animistic ideas?' Now this problem and problems of this type have become meaningless to me.[15]

And elsewhere he warns: 'in future we should have neither affirmations nor denials, in an empty wholesale verbal fashion of native "ignorance" or "knowledge", but instead, full concrete descriptions of what they know, how they interpret it, and how it is all connected with their conduct and their institutions.'[16]

The example of the Trobriand Islanders convinced Malinowski that humans did not need to know or recognize the role of sperm in making children in order to develop kinship relations and forms of family in which men fulfil their role as 'fathers', protecting and loving their children, caring for and cherishing them. He saw the invention of the father as the consequence of the invention of marriage, which attached to a married man the children his wife brought into the world.[17]

Here Malinowski was taking a stand in a debate that had been raging since

14   Ibid., p. 17.

15   B. Malinowski, *The Sexual Life of Savages in North-Western Melanesia: an ethnographic account of courtship, marriage, and family life among the natives of the Trobriand Islands, British New Guinea*, with a preface by Havelock Ellis (London, G. Routledge & Sons, 1929), p. xxiii.

16   B. Malinowski, *The Sexual Life of Savages in North-Western Melanesia* (London, Routledge & Kegan Paul, 2002 [1929]), p. xxviii.

17   B. Malinowski, *Sex and Repression in Savage Society* (London, Routledge and Kegan Paul, 1927), Chapter 10, pp. 253–80; *The Sexual Life of Savages in North-Western Melanesia*, Foreword to the third edition (1932), pp. xix–xliv.

the last third of the nineteenth century, when Spencer and Gillen discovered that Australian Aboriginal peoples attributed the birth of children to a spirit-child, which lived in the vicinity of the sacred sites belonging to the husband's kin group and which entered a woman's body. For these societies, too, sperm did not 'make' the baby. It must be said that, at the time, Australian Aborigines were regarded as specimens of the most primitive state of humanity, still living in the first stages of savagery, in which humans had just emerged from their animal-like condition. For Victorian evolutionism, humanity emerged from its animal state when it put an end to the sexual promiscuity that had formerly prevailed and invented kinship. From this perspective, since, at this stage of ignorance, the only thing that was certain was that children came out of the woman's womb, the first form of kinship could follow no other rule than to trace descent uniquely through women. Matrilineal systems were therefore the first to develop, and with them, *Mutterrecht*.[18] But men still had no status. This came with the invention of the father. But then other systems came into being, patrilineal this time, leaving behind them on the path of progress the matrilineal systems, now mere attestations and relics of a bygone stage of evolution.

Thirty years later, Leach revived the debate with his famous essay on Virgin Birth.[19] Leach had two criticisms of Malinowski. First, he reproached everyone who, from Frazer to Malinowski, took their informants' claims at face value, for not thinking that they could know more or something else than what they chose to tell the anthropologist. In other words, they might know what they claimed not to know or what they denied. But, in a certain sense, that was not the problem. It was, according to Leach, the fact that anthropologists had not seen that the informants' statements corresponded to the ideological position they were obliged to hold regarding the 'structural place' occupied by a child in their society. In short, despite the grand declarations that deliberately exaggerated his differences with Malinowski, Leach entertained more or less the same opinions, but he couched them in the language of his time. Instead of 'culture', he used the word 'ideology', and instead of ties between the culture and the institutions, he spoke of 'dogmas' connected with the position of individuals and groups in the social structure.

Whether or not Leach's theses were new, they had a very positive theoretical impact and sparked the publication of numerous articles and books as well as new fieldwork. Fairly rapidly, thanks especially to Annette Weiner, who revisited the same places Malinowski had worked in, but also thanks to Suzan

---

18   Cf. J. J. Bachofen, *Das Mutterrecht: eine Untersuchung über die Gynaikokratie der alten Welt nach ihrer religiösen und rechtlichen Natur* (Stuttgart, Krais und Hoffmann, 1861).

19   E. Leach, 'Proceedings of the Royal Anthropological Institute', 1966, pp. 39–50; reprinted in Genesis as Myth and Other Essays (London, 1969) and as 'Virgin Birth, Correspondence David M. Schneider, E.R. Leach', Man, vol. 3, no. 1, pp. 126–9.

Montague,[20] who worked in Kaduwinga, an island near Kiriwina, Malinowski's picture of the representations of conception in the Trobriand Islands was to be completed, but also amended.

For Malinowski, two of the Trobrianders' assertions posed a problem. The fact that a young woman had to be no longer a virgin in order to have children, and the fact that – they stressed – children could look only like their father, never their mother, whereas they had no substance in common with their father. To say that a child looks like its mother is a serious insult for the mother and for the child, for it is impossible. To say that a boy looks like his sisters is to insinuate that they have made love, that they committed incest. People explained to Malinowski that the father 'coagulates' the foetus, gives it a form (*kuli*). They also told him that if a woman's sexual organ was not open, the 'spirits realized this and did not give her children'.[21] Of course it was not her husband's penis that opened her vagina, since girls begin having sexual relations well before they marry. But it was indeed the penis of a man.

In short, barring unusual circumstances,[22] there is need of a man's penis for a woman to become a mother. But she does not become a mother through the sperm the man deposits in her womb. She becomes a mother through the intervention of spirits, which discover that she has been opened and send her a spirit-child. But this spirit-child, mingled with the woman's menstrual blood, is not yet a human child. It is only a foetus, a runny blob. How does it acquire, inside its mother's womb, the form it presents at birth and a face that makes it look like its father?

The answer was supplied years later by Annette Weiner.[23] What Malinowski omitted to say – either because he had not been told or because he had been told but had not really understood – was that, as soon as the woman tells her husband she is pregnant, he multiplies his sexual relations with her. His penis strikes, hammers on, the shapeless foetal mass and shapes it, giving it a form that makes it resemble its father. The ejaculate participates in this undertaking and further serves to nourish the foetus. In a word, the picture was changing. Although the man's sperm had no role in the child's 'conception', it was indispensable if the woman was to give birth to a child endowed with a human form

---

20   S. Montague, 'The Trobriand Gender Identity', *Mankind*, vol. 14 (1993), pp. 33–45; 'Trobriand Kinship and the Virgin Birth Controversy', *Man*, vol. 6, no. 3 (1971), pp. 353–68.

21   Malinowski, *The Father in Primitive Psychology*, pp. 47ff.

22   There is a myth which tells that Bolutukwa, mother of the legendary hero Tudara, became pregnant when she shut herself up in a cave on the seashore under a stalactite that dripped water drop after drop, and thus pierced her hymen.

23   A. Weiner, 'The Reproductive Model in Trobriand Society', *Mankind*, vol. 11 (1978), pp. 175–86; 'Trobriand Kinship from Another View: The Reproductive Power of Women and Men', *Man*, vol. 14, no. 2 (1979), pp. 328–48; *The Trobriand Islanders of Papua New Guinea* (New York, Holt, Rinehart & Winston, 1988).

and not to a shapeless foetus, and to a child that looked like its 'father' as well. The following diagram shows the different phases of conception and intrauterine development.

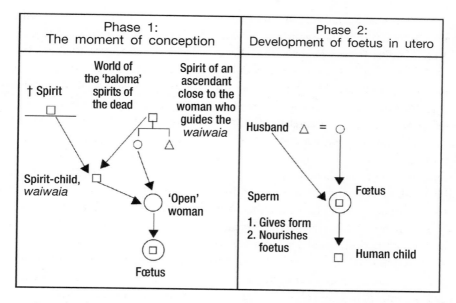

Phase 1: The moment of conception	Phase 2: Development of foetus in utero

Sexual relations and male sperm, which in Malinowski's understanding were believed to have no role in making a child, were, in fact, in the eyes of the Trobriand Islanders, necessary if the foetus conceived by the woman and her ancestral sprits was to become a human child, a child whose facial features would resemble those of a man, its father.[24]

In short, in the Trobriand Islands, too, it is necessary to make love in order to have children. But what happens next has nothing in common with what Europeans think, having derived their ideas from Christian tradition or the study of biology. Malinowski was therefore right to say that, in the Trobriand Islands, sexual relations and sperm have nothing to do with *conceiving* a child, but he was wrong to claim that for the Trobrianders sexual relations had nothing to do with *making* a child.[25] For, while they do not contribute to making the

---

24   It would be interesting to compare the Trobrianders' representations with those of the Baruya. We see that, in each case, the man nourishes the foetus in the woman's womb. In both societies, the foetus needs to be given a human form. For the Baruya this is done by the Sun, for the Trobriand Islanders it is the husband who does this by repeated intercourse during the pregnancy. In Trobriand culture, the flesh, the bones and the skin of the foetus are made from the woman's blood, while for the Baruya these are made from the man's sperm. And in both societies the spirit that imparts life to this matter is that of an ancestor.

25   Cf. Malinowski, *The Father in Primitive Psychology*, p. 12: 'The idea that it is solely and exclusively the mother who builds up the child's body, while the man does not in any way

foetus, they are indispensable for fashioning the foetus to look like a human child. In the final analysis, a child is always a gift from the spirits; in other parts of the world, in Polynesia for instance, it would be a gift from the gods, or in the West, a gift from God.

So we see that, in the Trobriand Islands, the woman and the man, the mother and the father, each make a distinct but complementary contribution to their children's identity. The mother gives them her blood and her flesh, their inner identity. And, through the blood received from its mother, each child is connected to the uninterrupted flow of blood that comes from the ancestral woman who emerged from the underworld and, together with her brother, founded the child's clan. The father gives the child its external identity, according to Annette Weiner's expression.[26] He gives it a face, a name, body ornaments and, if the child is a boy, the right to use part of his lands. But the father also nourishes the child, first in its mother's womb and then by working hard in his yam gardens to feed his wife and his children – but also his sisters, who have married out of his clan. Later on the sons will make gardens for their father, and he himself will make a garden for each of his daughters when she marries. Finally, he will encourage his sons, who belong to their mother's clan, to take a wife in his own clan.

The blood of women and the ancestors reincarnated in their bodies thus defines the relationship between the people belonging to the different lineages of the same clan, while all of the gifts and the acts by which fathers 'nourish' (*kipai*), shape and mould (*kuli*) their children form ties between people belonging to different clans. The father nourishes his wife and children by placing at their disposal his labour and all of the magic inherited from his ancestors, which give him plentiful yam crops and success in his expeditions to distant islands, etc. For, while men do not store up menstrual blood in their bodies, they do store up knowledge and magical powers (*meguwa*) in their bellies. Using this knowledge, they communicate with the spirits (*baloma*) of their ancestors and in turn receive the power to nourish others – or on the contrary to kill them with sorcery or drive them to starvation by casting a spell on their gardens. Interestingly, it is through their father, who is not from the same clan as they, more than through their mother's brother, that men gain access to the world of political relations and the Kula. If we want to understand the connections between the body, kinship and powers in the Trobriand Islands, we must therefore explore their political-ritual universe.

This universe is a hierarchical world: hierarchy between the chiefly lineages with their hereditary ranks (*guyau*) and commoner lineages; hierarchy among

---

contribute to its production, is the most important factor of the social organization of the Trobrianders.'

26   Weiner, 'The Reproductive Model in Trobriand society', p. 182.

the chiefs between those who wield power and influence over a hamlet (*tumila*), over a village (*ralu*) made up of several hamlets, or over a district formed of several villages. Each hamlet, village and district is under the authority of the eldest man of the clan, whose mythical ancestors are supposed to have emerged from or settled in this place. Sometimes another brother and the oldest son of his sister – who will succeed him – live nearby. All of his other brothers live with their father, and his married sisters live with their husbands. Alternatively, he is surrounded by men from other lineages to whom he has granted the right to use part of his lineage lands and who are therefore indebted to him. He is all the more influential because it is he who invokes his ancestors when performing, for himself and for those living on his lands, the rites to ensure successful crops of the yams and other solid foods with which they nourish their families.

This is why the representative of the hamlet's founding lineage is entitled to a share of all of the resources that the other lineages grow on his lands – yams, betel nuts, pigs, etc. These resources he places in his storehouses and periodically redistributes them on the occasion of events involving the whole community (rituals and dances that accompany harvests, building houses or yam silos, making canoes, preparing a trading or war expedition, etc.). And since it is the chief's privilege to take several wives, four times a year he is presented with a share of the produce from the gardens of his affines – fathers-in-law, brothers-in-law, maternal uncles and other members of each wife's lineage. The chief is thus, as Sahlins wrote about Trobriand chiefs, the glorious brother-in-law, glorified by a whole community.[27] But he is also, as Leach suggested, like a father who gathers in, feeds and grants the protection of his magical powers to the lineages to which his clan gave the right to live and to reproduce on its lands. Leach's suggestion was adopted by Mark Mosko, who, in an important article,[28] attempted to rethink chieftainship in the Trobriand Islands as the co-creation by a chief and those who follow and serve him of a relationship analogous to that between a father and his children, whom he nourishes and shapes in his image. The author's demonstration is almost convincing, but he carried it too far and ultimately neglected the interplay of authority relations within the clans subject to the matrilineal principle and the interplay of the brother–sister relationship as placed in the service of each clan's alliance policy.

In the end, it is in the body that the reason for each person's place (men and women) in the process of begetting children and in the political-ritual relations that organize the reproduction of the clans and of society as a whole can be

---

27   M. Sahlins, 'Poor Man, Rich Man, Big Man and Chief: Political Types in Melanesia and Polynesia', *Comparative Studies in Society and History*, vol. 5 (1963), pp. 285–303.

28   M. Mosko, 'Rethinking Trobriand Chieftainship', *The Journal of the Royal Anthropological Institute*, vol. 1, no. 4 (1995), pp. 763–85.

found. According to the Trobrianders, women's bodies are soft and runny on the inside. Men's bodies are hard and solid (*kasai*) on the outside. Through their work and their magic, men produce solid food (*kasai*) that keeps their bodies alive and hardens those of the women. But men's bodies are too hard to carry children, and women's bodies are too soft to shape them. Only the man's penis, when it is hard, can, by repeated acts of intercourse, give the shapeless foetal mass a form.[29]

But women, who are passive when the spirit of an ancestor desiring to live again enters their body, assume the most active role in ensuring the afterlife of deceased members of their lineage. It is the women who organize the large-scale funeral rituals (*sagali*) that will allow their dead brother or sister, or son or daughter, to leave the human world and take their place in Tuma alongside the ancestors of their lineage.

In order to do this, the women must redistribute to everyone (individuals and lineages) who was connected with the deceased during his or her life an enormous amount of female wealth – skirts made of red leaves and bundles of banana fronds (*doba*: skirts; *manuga*: banana leaves) – which the women amass over their adult life, either through their own production or purchased with the yams their fathers, husbands and brothers give them. It is thus women, acting in their capacity as sisters, mothers or daughters, who, by distributing their own valuables, enable the deceased of their lineage to live once more in Tuma and allow the living, whose ties were interrupted by death, to renew them through these exchanges. Women are the only ones able to 'de-conceive' and to ensure those they conceived a new life. And since for Trobrianders death draws all mourners into a sort of 'living death', it is the women who restart the wheels of social life. In so doing, they exercise a real power in society,[30] one that Malinowski had already underscored heavily and which Annette Weiner described in detail:[31]

> In the Trobriand Islands, we find a matrilineal society, where descent, kinship, and all social relations are reckoned by the mother only, and where women have a considerable share in tribal life, in which they take the leading part in certain economic, ceremonial, and magical activities. This influences very deeply the erotic life as well as the institution of marriage.[32]

---

29   Montague, 'Trobriand Gender Identity', pp. 33–45.

30   Weiner: 'Nothing is so dramatic as a woman standing at a Sagali surrounded by thousands of bundles. Nor can anything be more impressive than watching the deportment of women as they attend to the distribution. When women walk onto the center to throw down their wealth, they carry themselves with a pride characteristic as that of any Melanesian Big Man' (A. Weiner, *Women of Value, Men of Renown*, p. 118).

31   A. Weiner, *The Trobriand Islanders of Papua New Guinea* (New York, Holt, Rinehart & Winston, 1988).

32   Malinowski, *The Father in Primitive Psychology*, pp. 11–12.

We will end the analysis of this case by a comparison with our two earlier analyses of what a child is for a society, that of the Inuit and that of the Baruya. In all three cases, the scenario of child conception entails:

1. The presence – active (Inuit, Baruya) or passive (Trobriand) – of a supernatural power that lives far removed from human society but has placed humanity under its protection.

2. The intervention of ancestors, of the deceased who are close and known (Inuit) or remote (Baruya, Trobriand), who want to come back to life (Baruya, Trobriand, Inuit) or whom humans want to bring back to life in a child (Inuit). The child has (Inuit) or does not have (Baruya, Trobriand) a memory of the deeds and gestures of the person reincarnated in him or her.

3. The roles of the woman and the man in the conception process are, in all events, in accord with the descent principle, and ground the children's appropriation by one or the other of the two sides of the family – the father's (Baruya), the mother's (Trobriand), or both in the case of a cognatic system (Inuit). In the latter case, the man's sperm mingles with the woman's menstrual blood to produce the body of the foetus and in the end that of the child that issues from its mother's womb. In the case of the patrilineal system, it is the sperm that makes the foetal skeleton and flesh and nothing is said about the mother's blood, especially not about her menstrual blood, regarded as destroying men's strength, like an anti-sperm. In the case of the matrilineal system, nothing is said about the man's sperm, and the woman's menstrual blood moves to the fore.

4. In two out of three cases, sperm also nourishes the foetus, and the father, even if he is not the child's genitor (Trobriand), is a nurturing father who begins nourishing the foetus before its birth as a child. In all three cases, the husband nourishes the mother and the child with strong foods – game for the Inuit, game and tubers for the Baruya, yams and other 'solid' foods for the Trobrianders.

5. In all of these cases, human labour is not enough to make a child, which is always the result of cooperation between the invisible world of the gods and the ancestors, and the visible world of men and women.

6. All three societies recognize the possibility of births stemming from the intervention of gods or other supernatural entities, without the help of humans.

The fact that, for the Trobrianders and for Australian Aboriginal peoples, children exist even before they are begotten by their parents makes us wonder whether this vision of life might exist outside of Oceania. In fact, one can actually find a great number of examples, especially in Africa. We have chosen to present the case of the Nzema as an example.

THE NZEMA OF SOUTHERN GHANA

The Nzema of southern Ghana are a section of the greater Akan people.[33] Nzema society is divided into seven matrilineal clans (*abusua*), but residence is patrilocal, two principles we already encountered in the Trobriand Islands. Villages and small towns are under the authority of ranked chiefs.

For the Nzema, children are deceased persons who wanted to live a new life in the body of a child. The dead live underground in a place called Ebolo, which lies on the other side of a subterranean river that the dead cross by paying a few coins to a boatman, who ferries them to the other shore. There they are welcomed by all of their deceased fellow clansmen, who take them to their chief, to whom the dead must render a detailed account of the life they led on earth. Afterwards begins a life very similar to the previous one, but more pleasant. The deceased eat, drink, go walking. They enjoy their death.

The dead exist in the form of a soul (*ngomenle*) but also have a body of sorts (*funli*), which is not the body (*ngonane*) they had when they were alive. Some of the dead decide to return to earth to live another life, but far from their relatives and friends for fear of being recognized. In this case, their body once more dons its previous form. Others want to be reincarnated in a child. In this case, the spirit of the deceased changes into a sort of 'grub', which is the body of a spirit-child. The spirit-child then takes up residence in the uterus of a woman, usually but not always a fellow clan member. The human child that will be born will belong to this woman's clan and not to that of her husband.

Once inside the woman's womb, the spirit-child turns into a foetus as a result of the sexual relations between the father and the mother. With her menstrual blood, the woman will produce the child's flesh and bones. With his sperm, the man will produce the child's blood. The man's blood carries a life force (*mora*), which, if it is 'accepted' by the life force contained in the woman's blood, will give the gestating child the ability to move and later to breathe. Without this 'acceptance' by the woman's blood, the child will not be conceived.

---

33   V. L. Grottanelli, 'Pre-existence and Survival in Nzema Beliefs', *Man*, vol. 61 (1961), pp. 1–5.

At birth, the child receives two names: one given by the father and the other a soul-name (*ekela*) which indicates the day of the week the child was born and connects it to the gods, in particular the great god Nyamenle. This name will not survive the person, just as the life force carried in his or her blood will disappear at death. This name will return to the gods, while the soul will set out on the journey to Ebolo, taking with it the *funli* body. The deceased's bones are then returned by the paternal kin to the maternal clan. This clan organizes the funeral rites, performs the rituals that dispatch the deceased to the land of the dead and settles the problems entailed in the inheritance of the deceased's goods, the transfer of his functions, his titles, and so on.

As we see, in this matrilineal society, the father's role in kinship relations, in the definition of the children's identity, in the phases of their life, and so forth, is very important and is expressed in the theories of child conception in a number of ways. The blood that flows through the child's body and the life-giving breath also come from the father's sperm. The name carried by the child was chosen by the father. The qualities identified in the child also come from the father, from the *mora* carried in his blood. The father surrounds the child with his care and his spirit, and protects it so that, it is said, if a child is separated from its father, it will not grow. In effect, the child nourished by its father must observe all of the father's food taboos and seek the protection of the gods worshipped by the father as he respects these taboos.

The example of the Nzema, who are matrilineal but whose residence is patrilocal and where the father's social role is extremely important, concords with the Trobriander example. In both cases, the fathers give their children a name, assets, and protection and affection. In the case of the Trobrianders, the father's role is to shape the foetus and to nourish it with his sperm, but not to make its substance. In the case of the Nzema, the man's sperm makes the child's blood and its breath. Here, too, sexual intercourse between a man and a woman is necessary for there to be a child, but it is not enough. Other actors come into the picture, and once again these are ancestors and gods.

The Nzema case presents two specific features which must be stressed. The spirit-child that lives in the land of the dead is not safe from malevolent aggressions and influences on the part of the gods and evil spirits (*asongu*). This will manifest itself after the child is born (it has no memory of these events) by various symptoms, including diarrhoea and vomiting, which will be treated by prayers, potions and magical charms. But sometimes that is not enough. For example, in the case where the children in a family die one after the other, a diviner is asked to discover which ancestor or deceased clansman was reincarnated in these children who died or fell seriously ill and what he or she wants. When the diviner has found the identity of the reincarnated soul and the reasons for his or her anger, he tells the parents and offers a sacrifice to the angry spirit. Finally, he gives the parents a series of prescriptions and – of course – expects a reward for his services.[34]

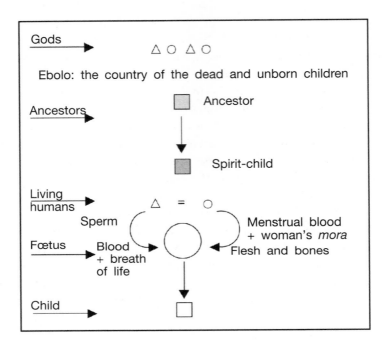

---

34   In many West African societies one finds the idea that the birth of a child means 'the return of an ancestor', and that the identity of this ancestor is initially unknown by the child's parents (and of course by the child itself, who has no memory of its life in the land of the dead). But, as among the Nzema, the successive deaths of infants, miscarriages, etc., lead people to try to identify the ancestor and offer him or her propitiatory sacrifices. Among the Mossi, the process by which an ancestor 'comes back' to one of his or her descendants is called *segre*. What the deceased transmits to the child is a breath, a life principle (*siga*), which leaves the nostrils at the person's death and wanders in the bush before returning to live anew in the body of one of his or her descendants. The soul of the deceased (*kilima*) is believed to depart and go to live in the ancestors' village, in a place called Pilimpiku. When a child is born, the father – or the man in the lineage who is qualified to make sacrifices on the ancestors' altar – goes to a sorcerer and asks him to identify the ancestor who has come back to life in the child. The diviner identifies the ancestor, whose lineage name the child will carry thereafter. The child then receives another, personal name (*yure*). The many childhood illnesses or deaths are explained, according to the Mossi, by the fact that two ancestors are fighting to come back in the same child. Doris Bonnet's list of the ancestors who can come back in a newborn child concords with the patrilineal character and the Omaha nomenclature of their kinship system. The most frequent incarnations are the child's father's father and the father's brother, who is also regarded as Ego's father, and so on. Finally, it is interesting to note that, among the Mossi, what is reincarnated in a child is not the ancestor's soul but his or her breath, which imparts life to one of his or her descendants. See D. Bonnet, 'Le retour de l'ancêtre', *Journal des africanistes*, vol. 51, nos 1–2 (1981), pp. 149–82.

Next is a final example of a society in which the descent rule is also matri-lineal, as among the Trobrianders and the Nzema, but where the father's social importance is even greater than in these two societies, and where the *mother no longer shares any bodily substance* with the child she bears, which belongs to her matrilineage.

THE MAENGE OF NEW BRITAIN

The society of the Maenge, who live in the eastern part of the South Pacific island of New Britain,[35] is divided into two exogamous moieties each of which is divided into exogamous clans and subclans. The clans and subclans are geographically dispersed, and their members live in places where their ances-tors emerged. Neither the moieties nor the clans function as true social groups. They do not have chiefs or leaders to represent them and they operate merely as classification categories. The true political, economic and ceremonial units are the subclans, whose members live in the same village or in one of the hamlets that compose a village. These descent groups share rights in the lands adjoining the village. They possess a common treasure of valuables, shell money, stone axe blades, etc., whose management is entrusted to one of their Big Men. And they act as a whole in various circumstances: planting ceremonial gardens, perform-ing rites concerning the land, and especially going to war.

Each village or hamlet is under the authority of a Big Man, who in principle belongs to the founding matrilineage or one of its subclans. This man is called *maga tamana* ('village father'). Among the Maenge, polygamy is widespread, so that the children of a man who has several wives belong to different matriline-ages. Unlike the Trobriand residence rule, here residence after marriage is not necessarily virilocal. A third of new couples live with the wife's people, a third with the husband's family, and the rest live in the couple's natal village.

Within matrilineages and villages, there is vigorous competition among male members of the same descent group for recognition both as the repre-sentative of their group and as the 'village father'. The village father is not necessarily the oldest man in his lineage. And it is not necessarily the nephew who succeeds his maternal uncle. This is because the 'village father' usually does everything in his power to ensure that it is his eldest son, or at least one of his sons, and therefore someone from another matrilineage, who succeeds him. Of the twenty-nine successions analyzed by Michel Panoff, fifteen featured a nephew who had succeeded his maternal uncle, and fourteen a son who had succeeded his father.

35   Cf. M. Panoff, 'Patrifiliation as Ideology and Practice in a Matrilineal Society', *Ethnology*, vol. 15, no. 2 (1976), pp. 175–88.

All of these details together with the words 'village father' point to the existence, in Maenge society, of a second kinship principle that this time classifies
people on the basis of their shared descent from a common male ancestor, or
from several brothers by the same father, even though, through their mother,
they belonged to different matrilines. These kin groups have a name, and the
term for them, *malo tumana*, translates as 'that which is wrapped in the bark
strip that encircles a man's loins', a metaphor for the man's penis. Michel Panoff
translates this by an Old French legal expression 'relative by the rod', as opposed
to 'relative by the belly', in other words uterine kinship.

Malo tumana is an institution that encompasses:

1. Children of the same father but different mothers.
2. Children of two or several full brothers, but not half-brothers.
3. Children of men from the two preceding groups. Beyond these groups it
   is considered that the blood of these men's children is too mixed.

It is worth noting that children of the same father and the same mother,
full-blooded siblings, are not included in the *malo tumana*, nor are half-siblings
of the same mother, which clearly distinguishes the *malo tumana* from a matrilineage. It is expected that all persons belonging to the same *malo tumana* will
demonstrate solidarity in all sorts of contexts, such as trading expeditions, war,
etc. This solidarity is called *piu*, which means 'to bind or tie'. It is not based on a
shared interest of which it would be the sublimated face, as in rights in the same
piece of land. It is founded on individuals sharing the same male blood, which
forbids them marrying each other, even if the fact of belonging to two different
moieties would make it possible. It is therefore founded on shared descent through
men, in other words on the implementation of a principle of patrifiliation. What
is interesting here is that the coexistence of the two principles – patrifiliation and
matrilineal descent reckoning – is expressed in the way the Maenge represent
the conception of a child.

For the Maenge, it is the father's sperm, and it alone, that makes the child's
body, that turns into its blood, its flesh and its bones, and endows it with the
ability to move and breathe. The woman shares no substance with her child, but
she holds it in her uterus and gives it an inner 'soul' (*kamu e pei*), which will take
up residence in the blood transmitted by the father. The Maenge believe that
every person has two souls, an inner soul and an outer double (*kamu e soali*).
The inner soul permeates the body's substance and gives it its strength and
beauty. The outer soul is a sort of double self, normally invisible, which
completely envelops the human body, hugging its curves and features. Both
souls can leave the body in various circumstances – at night during sleep, or
during the strenuous physical ordeals undergone by boys and girls during their

initiations and, of course, after death, when both abandon the cadaver that has begun to decompose. At this time, the two souls, still conjoined, change into a 'ghost' (*soare*), which, after several days and diverse rites, leaves its village where it still mingled with the living and sets out for the submarine village of the dead from which the clan ancestors originally emerged.[36] With them, the deceased take the souls of the taros and other cultivated plants that the members of their lineage gave as an offering to appease any evil spirits that might attack.

Whereas for the matrilineal virilocal Trobrianders, male sperm had no part in making the child but shaped it, whereas for the matrilineal patrilocal Nzema, sperm makes the foetus' blood and imparts breath, for the Maenge, sperm makes the child's whole body; but it is the mother who provides an inner soul and (probably) its outer form, which leaves the body of the deceased and, still attached to the inner soul, sets out for the land of the dead.

But a father's relations with his children are not limited to providing them with a body. He also gives them his affection and protection. He gives them shell money and, to his sons, tracts of his lands (which are lands of his own matrilineage, to which his children do not belong). He also transmits to them pieces of his ritual knowledge. And he makes a heavy contribution to the expenses involved in organizing their initiations. His brother-in-law, the children's maternal uncle, also contributes, but less. The father brings the greatest share when it comes time to assemble the payment each of his sons will have to make in order to get married. As in the Trobriand Islands, a man usually encourages his sons (or at least his eldest son) to marry in his own matrilineage, to choose one of his 'sister's' daughters. Here, too, the mother's brother makes a contribution, but again it is less. Yet a man is not allowed to train his own son for war, for he might hurt him or be hurt, and for all concerned this would be tantamount to attacking their own blood. It is therefore the men of the child's matrilineage who will teach him to use weapons and to kill. It is with them that the son will work the big gardens cultivated for the religious ceremonies, and with them that he will manage the lands held in common. This institution,

---

36   Cf. M. Panoff, 'The Notion of Double Self among the Maenge', *Journal of the Polynesian Society*, vol. 77, no. 3 (1968), pp. 275–95. The 'land of the dead' lies on the other side of a first river, called 'Sorrow', and is guarded by a hideous supernatural being, Kavavaleka, who forces the dead souls to lick an infected, oozing sore that covers one of his legs if they wish to cross to the other side. Those souls that refuse are sent away and become the 'bad/evil dead' doomed for all eternity to wander the earth, where they take pleasure in assaulting the living. Those souls that cross the river are welcomed by a god, Notu, who washes them and rids them of whatever dirty malodorous remnants of their outer double may still cling to their inner self. The deceased thus becomes 'like a beautiful light', and it is then that the god Noti takes him or her across a second river, called 'Oblivion' – as in Lethe, the river of the ancient Greeks. There, on the other side, he or she is welcomed by the deceased members of the matriclan. The soul is now rid of all earthly ties, and ready to begin a blissful life free of labour or suffering of any kind. The human being once again becomes what he was in the beginning: immortal.

which groups people on the basis of their maternal ties, is called *galiou*, 'shield'; it is the opposite and the complement of *malo tumana*.

Bearing in mind this dual social organization, we can now understand both the fathers' attitudes toward their children but also the fact that the leader of each village is called the 'village father' (*maga tumana*), a term borrowed from the universe of kinship and used to designate a political-ritual relationship. In effect, the 'father' of a village is much more than the leader of a local clan segment. He wields his authority over all of the other lineages living on his lands and which he feeds and protects through the rites he performs on behalf of everyone. A man does not become a Big Man until in the first place he has managed to organize and finance, from his own resources and those of the fellow members of his matrilineage willing to help, the initiation rites designed for his own children. Another challenge he must face if he wants to show his influence and his wealth (for every ceremony demands the sacrifice of pigs and the distribution of shares of the meat together with shell money and other valuables) is the building and the upkeep of a men's house. He usually names this house after his eldest son. Furthermore, the *maga tamana* has the privilege of organizing for his (male or female) firstborn a complicated cycle of costly ceremonies (*alangapaga*) that begins with the birth of the child and ends with his or her marriage. These ceremonies are designed to 'lift up' the person of this child, to raise his or her name higher than that of all the other children born in the village at the same time.

With the Menge we are looking at a matrilineal society that made the principle of patrifiliation the basis of a whole series of practices necessary to the society's reproduction. The coexistence of these two principles, which in part pull in opposite directions – sons succeeding their father and/or nephews succeeding their maternal uncle – creates a permanent tension, but one that does not abolish the ultimate pre-eminence of the matrilineal principle. The predominant role of sperm, which corresponds to the social patrifiliation principle, is complementary to the mother's contribution of the inner soul and the child's outer form. Last of all, it is to the land of the mother's ancestors that a soul returns after death, to live a life without suffering or labour: the maternal paradise.

A final remark. The Maenge once again provide a good example of recourse to the vocabulary and representations of kinship relations – in the present case the figure of the 'father' – to designate a person exercising political-ritual functions that go far beyond the strict domain of kinship. The relations of affection, protection and sharing connected with kinship in the context of the family and the household are thus projected onto other social relations, which are conceived in their image, transformed by and wrapped in the vocabulary of kinship. But here too, political relations are neither the extension of kinship relations nor analogous to them. Here as elsewhere, kinship is not the ultimate basis of society.

THE KHUMBO OF NEPAL

Up to this point we have assumed that, in a given society, there is only one system for representing the process of child conception and only one dogma. In reality, many societies have several coexisting systems, which do not necessarily concur or which agree on some points and disagree on others. In still other societies, we discover systems that have combined several traditions stemming from periods and historical facts located at a greater or lesser distance in the past. These systems imprint themselves in the body unbeknown to the child (and often unbeknown to the child's parents, who have no memory of these facts). We will begin the discussion of these historical syncretisms by citing the case of the Khumbo, a Tibetan-speaking group of pastoral agriculturalists living in the heart of the Nepalese Himalayas, in the 'hidden valley' of Arun at the foot of mount Makalu.[37] This society emerged from the encounter and association of several clans that came from Tibet at different epochs. While the clans still exist, their social role has disappeared behind the now-more-important fact of belonging to the same territorial community, which lives in Sepa under the protection of their mountain deities and of the mountains which are themselves gods, sacred beings.

For centuries the Khumbo have lived at the periphery of the space admin-istered by the Tibetan state as well as on the fringes of the zones of influence of the large Buddhist monasteries. Their society has thus retained certain pre-Buddhist religious beliefs characteristic of the time of the first Tibetan kings. Two kinds of priests preside over worship: *lhaven*, married priests who serve the clan gods and the territorial deities; and *lamas*, who belong to the Nyim-mapa Buddhist tradition and who also are married. They are the Khumbo's 'great men'. Their ritual functions and their knowledge raise them above the other men who head the big households. A few women, known as *lhakama*, 'she who allows the gods to speak', also play a large role. These women undergo possession by the gods and the spirits of the dead, and are subjected to terrify-ing experiences when they confront devils from the impure part of the universe. They act as oracles and give voice to that which everyone would like to hide, hence their power.[38]

The notion of impurity plays an important role in Khumbo society. The birth of a child is an impure event, which harks back to the primordial incest

---

37   H. Diemberger, 'Blood, Sperm, Soul and the Mountain', in T. Del Valle (ed.), *Gendered Anthropology* (London, Routledge, 1993), pp. 88–127, and 'Montagnes sacrées, os des ancêtres, sang maternel: le corps humain dans une communauté tibétaine du Népal', in M. Godelier and M. Panoff (eds.), *La Production du corps* (Paris, Archives Contemporaines, 1998), pp. 269–80.

38   These women's functions associate them with a Tantric tradition founded in the twelfth century by a Tibetan woman, certain components of which can be found in Khumbo culture.

between the son of the Earth mother who, upon being born, immediately tried to return to his mother's womb. And therefore humans, who were supposed to be immortal, are now mortal. For the Khumbo, the father is the one who rids the mother and child of the birth impurity by giving the child a name, which makes it a member of his clan, and then by presenting it to the mountain gods as being their child as well.[39] Khumbo kinship relations are governed by a patrilineal descent rule. People belong to their father's clan, which is exogamous. Residence after marriage is usually, but does not have to be, patrivirilocal. Sons are forbidden to marry a woman from their mother's clan. Every generation is obliged to marry into new families.

How is making a child seen in this universe?

The child's conception begins with sexual intercourse between a man and a woman, who will become its father and its mother. The woman's vagina is regarded as a red flower that blooms every month and closes once again if no sperm has entered her in the ten to twelve days following her menses. When sperm enters this flower, it closes and, as soon as the woman's blood mixes with the sperm, an embryo begins to develop in the her womb.

The man's sperm makes the child's bones and brain, and that is why the child belongs to its father's clan. In fact, the word for 'clan' is the same as that for 'bones'.[40] The bones are the hard part of the human body, transmitted from one generation to the next by the men (and not by the women), since the bones make the sperm and the sperm makes the bones. The child is attached by its bones to a 'bone line', which connects it to the male clan deity (which is thus present in the child). This god is attached to the clan and is worshiped by all members of this clan. The deity's name is associated with a sacred mountain in Tibet, which was the home of the clan ancestors before they migrated. But today these ancestral clan gods all live together in the mountains of Beyul Khenbalung, their new abode. They have become the gods and ancestors of the new community formed at the conclusion of the various migrations.

The woman's blood gives the child its flesh and its own blood. Through its blood the child is connected to its mother and to its mother's mother, etc. Whereas bones distinguish and separate the clans, the women's blood circulates among the clans and brings them together. For the Khumbo, women's blood is

39   On the birth of their first child, girl or boy, its parents are no longer called by their name but by the name of the child.

40   The term meaning 'clan' is *rus* (bone), a widely spread word in central Asia. In his *Elementary Structures of Kinship*, Claude Lévi-Strauss alluded to the existence of 'relatives by the bone' and 'relatives by the blood' in these societies. More recently, 'bone' relatives and the concept of *rü* have been the object of new research, among which the particularly enlightening study by Nancy E. Levine on the Nyinba of Nepal: N. E. Levine, 'The Theory of Rü Kinship, Descent and Status in a Tibetan Society', in C. von Fürer-Haimendorf (ed.), *Asian Highland Societies in Anthropological Perspective* (New Delhi, Stirling, 1981), pp. 52–78.

positive, since it is the source of the flesh, the blood and the shape of the body of everyone. But their menstrual blood also bars women from approaching the sacred weapons, which are kept in every house, near the altar facing the mountains and dedicated to Dabla, the god of war and defender of the territory.

During the woman's pregnancy, the couple does not stop having sexual relations, quite the contrary, for sperm is believed to nourish the foetus and add to the food eaten by the mother. Later the woman will feed her baby with the milk from her breasts, considered to be full of grain, which changes into milk. But the man's sperm and the woman's blood are not enough to make a child. It is still lacking a soul – or rather two souls. Here is where we will see the bodily mark of the historical encounter between a pre-Buddhist religion and a branch of Buddhism.

The first soul (*la*) is a life force that connects the child to all of nature and to the surrounding mountains. If this principle leaves the body and departs, or if it is stolen by devils, it can be brought back to the body by means of specific rituals. It is this soul that gives the person his or her energy and breath. When the person dies, this soul leaves the body for good and takes up residence in the sacred mountains of Khenbalung. Priests' souls dwell near the summits; the other souls at the base. These mountains are the 'owners of the land', the 'masters of the territory'. For they have a soul (*la-ri*) which provides the land and the Khumbo community with their energy.

In addition to this first soul, which connects each Khumbo to the sacred mountains, there is the *namsche*, the 'consciousness', which in the Buddhist tradition is the organ of the (illusory) perception every person has of the world and of the self. It is the organ of the actions that will keep the individual a prisoner of the cycle of reincarnations, of the *samsara* in which, from one reincarnation to the next, all living beings have already been the fathers and mothers of each other. This 'consciousness-soul' detaches itself from the interspace of the reincarnation cycles (*bardo*) and enters the woman's vagina when she makes love. If the *namsche* is drawn to the mother, the new being will be a boy; if it is drawn to the father, it will be a girl. When a person dies, the *namsche* leaves the body and, propelled by the nature of its past actions (*karma*), is soon reincarnated in another living being.[41] In short, sperm and blood connect the child with the clan of its fathers and with those of its mother, its mother's mother, etc. One of these two souls is connected with the deities and the ancestors that protect its community; the other is linked to the universe of Buddhism, to which the Khumbo also belong. This double affiliation explains the two kinds

41 According to the famous Book of the Dead, which the Khumbo, like all other Tibetans, read at funerals. Cf. F. Fremantle and C. Trungpa, *The Tibetan Book of the Dead* (Berkeley, Shambala, 1975), p. 84.

of priests who preside over worship and stand on either side of the altars: the *lhaven*, whose name is reminiscent of the *lha-bon*, the priests of pre-Buddhist Tibet, and the *lama*.

Below is a diagram of the process of conception as seen by the Khumbo.

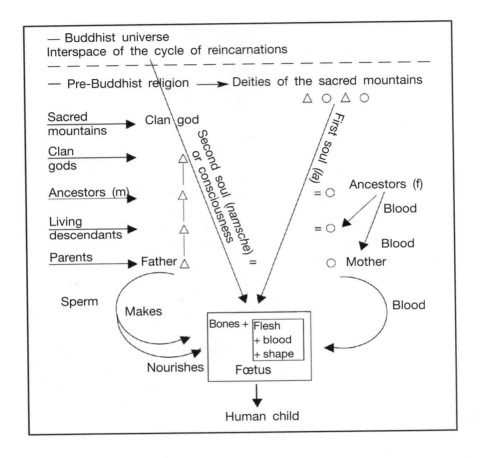

Once again we are confronted with the same fundamental fact. *The parents of a Khumbo child do not suffice to produce the whole child, to make a human child.* More powerful spiritual agents must intervene: ancestors, deities and, permeating the whole configuration, the invisible world of the Buddhist cycle of reincarnations. The child is not only included in a network of kin relations and groups (its paternal clan, etc.), but it is also closely connected with realities that transcend the boundaries of these relations and of the division of the society into clans and so forth, which address each person as a member of the same territorial community that protects them and which all must reproduce. At the same time, all members of this community belong to a religion that does not recognize boundaries between clans and communities, but instead is addressed to all human beings who desire to free themselves of the world of illusion in which they live and, through enlightenment, like the Buddha, end the cycle of reincarnations and enter nirvana.

To the north, in another valley that was a part of Tibet for centuries, live the Kharta, a group with whom the Khumbo trade and occasionally marry. We learn a great deal from a comparison between the Kharta and the Khumbo. The Kharta kin system and terminology are roughly the same as those of the Khumbo. But there are some deep-seated differences between them. The Kharta no longer have named clans. People define themselves with respect to their family and their village. The terms 'bone' and 'flesh' designate the person's paternal lineage and their maternal ties. The Khumbo clan deity (*pholha*) has become a family god, and the mountain gods have been 'Buddhified'.[42] For the Khumbo, who have been living on the edge of the Tibetan state for centuries, the changes never reached this magnitude, and this is attested to once again by the bodies and souls of their children.

But Buddhism did not try to drive out the old gods, as other religions did and continue to do in their endeavour to convert the whole of humanity to their faith, to their 'true' god.[43] For Buddhism, the gods are part of the illusion that

---

42   The contrast between the Khumbo and the Kharta harks back to a process that began in central Tibet well before the thirteenth century. The formation of the old kingdom of Tibet had already weakened the clan confederations and replaced them with a new military and civil administration, dividing the society into 4 rü (horns), each of which was split into 8 districts. But the clans continued to exist, even if their functions had been redefined by the new social structures that served as a power base and an instrument of a new hereditary aristocracy and the royalty. By the twelfth century, with the recognition of Buddhism as the official religion and the decline of the royal family, a new social order was created, featuring the emergence of large religious centres and monasteries, which became the new sites of political and religious power. The clans and clan names began to disappear. People were increasingly defined by their place of birth and residence, and by their affiliation with one or another form of Buddhism and a given religious centre. The patrilineal descent rule and genealogical memory became the marks of priestly or aristocratic families. As Diemberger writes: 'With the 13th century, the idea of the reincarnation of a conscious principle independent of kinship became the conceptual basis for thinking the reincarnation of political-religious figures, the *tulku*, lines of hierophants the most famous of which is the Dalai Lama. This transpired at the time when Buddhism came to structure society. Then, generally speaking, clan names yielded to place names and names of religious communities of belonging as indicators of identity' (Diemberger, 'Montagne sacrées, os des ancêtres, sang maternel', p. 281).

43   In various passages of his work, Malinowski mentions the Trobrianders' exasperation with the preaching of the Protestant and Catholic missionaries, who criticized their sexual practices and their beliefs about the way babies are made. Here is what he says: 'The whole Christian morality is strongly associated with the institution of a patrilineal and patriarchal family with the father as progenitor and master of the household. In short the religion, whose dogmatic essence is based on the sacredness of the Father to son relationships and where the moral stand or fall with a strong patriarchal family, most obviously proceeds by making the paternal relation strong and firm, by first showing that it has a natural foundation. Thus I discovered that the natives had been somewhat exasperated by having preached at them what seems to them an absurdity, and by finding me, so 'unmissionary' as a rule, engaged in the same futile argument' (Malinowski, *The Father in Primitive Psychology*, p. 59).

humans entertain about the world and themselves. Buddhism does not try to expel them because they are among the illusions that are dispelled as the person advances along the path of 'illumination'.

We now come to the second type of situation, that in which two or more models of the process of child conception exist side by side in the same society and are more or less incompatible with each other. The different models do not appear, as in the case of the Khumbo, as a native model plus another one imported into or imposed on the local society from outside. In the two cases discussed below, we are dealing with distinct models which developed in the same society and which express, by their very existence and differences, the views of two social groups standing in an unequal relationship with each other, one being dominant and the other subordinate, in a word: engaged in power relations that express and imprint themselves in the bodies of the children.

THE TELEFOLMIN OF NEW GUINEA

The first case is that of the Telefolmin,[44] a group of intensive horticulturalists and hunters living in the New Guinea Highlands near the headwaters of the Sepik river. The Telefolmin have two models of conception: an 'official' model shared by both the men and the women, and a 'secret' model known to the women and which partially contradicts the 'official' version. Their gardening and hunting activities disperse the families around the villages, which serve as a home base. These villages are strongly endogamous and are organized around a big men's house, which is at the same time the place where the relics are kept – these are the bones of male ancestors that only the men are allowed to venerate. The ancestor cult is marked by a series of initiations for the boys, who are split into two moieties that act as two ritual spheres: the 'Taro' moiety and the 'Arrow' moiety. The Taro moiety rites concern life-giving powers: the powers to grow good crops in the gardens, to raise pigs, to feed people; its colour is white. The rites of the Arrow moiety concern death-dealing powers: the powers to kill, and to be a successful hunter and warrior; its colour is red.

Dan Jorgensen, who worked among the Telefolmin, stressed the difficulties he had collecting information on the way children are made there. The men considered it a disgusting and unworthy topic of conversation, something to ask women about because it is their affair, whereas men's business is the domain of religion and esoteric rituals, and the governance of society. At long last, the men agreed, for friendship's sake, to give him the following account.

---

44   See the important article by D. Jorgensen, 'Mirroring Nature? Men's and Women's Models of Conception in Telefolmin', *Mankind*, vol. 14, no. 1 (August 1988), pp. 57–65.

Children are made by combining 'penis water' and 'vaginal fluids', which meet and mingle in the woman's womb when a man and a woman make love. The men did not make a difference between the man's and the woman's contribution. The sperm mixes with the vaginal fluids and the mixture makes the baby's body. But the foetus is not made at one go. One must make love often so as to accumulate sperm and the woman's fluids. Once the woman realizes she is pregnant, the couple must stop making love in order not to make twins.

But the foetus is not yet a child. It still needs a soul and a mind, and a shape that will distinguish it from other people. All of that is tied to the presence in the body of *sinik*, a component of the human being, the origin of which the Telefolmin admitted ignorance. They said that, as a baby grows, it becomes capable of understanding and talking. That is because the *sinik* is growing inside him. As for a child looking like its father or its mother or someone else, no one really had an explanation.

This male version of procreation fits their kinship system, which is fundamentally cognatic and makes no reference to the existence of clans, lineages, etc. People belong to different kindreds, but there is no visible inclination toward ties with the father's or the mother's side. The Telefolmin stress the care given a child, in the form of feeding, raising and protecting it, rather than the circumstances surrounding its birth. The great hunters are like 'fathers' to their village because they feed everyone with the game they bring home.

But none of this explained why women retired to a hut, either to wait out their menstrual periods or to give birth, and why the men regarded menstrual blood as a great danger for themselves. And so Dan Jorgensen decided to ask the women and, to his great surprise, they showed no repugnance or reluctance to talk about these matters. Indeed the women knew the version the men had given Dan. They agreed with the idea that the foetus is formed from the mixture of sperm and their vaginal fluids. But they diverged from the men on one point: the role of menstrual blood, of uterine blood (*nok ipak*), a subject on which the men had remained silent. For the women, it is this blood that makes the child's bones. The sperm and the vaginal fluids have an equal part in making the child's blood, but not its bones. As we see, this representation is in total opposition to that of the Khumbo, and it is very unusual for New Guinea. While the men's representations, for whom the man's and the woman's contributions are equivalent and complementary, fit the thoroughly undifferentiated character of the kinship system, where did the women's representations come from? What was at stake?

To understand better, we need to look at the men's world and the rituals they are responsible for and which are closed to women. One of the aims of these rituals is to slow the gradual drift of the universe toward nothingness. And the rites that permit this entail the manipulation of the bones of the most prominent male ancestors of each village, which are kept as relics inside the spirit houses. Here we in fact discover that, according to the women, the sacred relics that lie at the heart of the male rituals – from which, I repeat, they are systematically excluded – come from the very substance that the men abhor most: menstrual blood. The women's theory thus overspills the sphere of kinship relations and the domestic world. It asserts that women are present at the very heart of the *political-ritual sphere*. Once again, as we saw in the case of the Baruya, the men's powers appear as powers they appropriated from the women, who are their primal and permanent source, thus sentencing them to be passive onlookers of the actions performed by the men in order to act on the cosmos and reproduce their society. Whereas the men do not claim any priority in the conception of children and accept the idea that the women play a role equal to theirs, the women, on the other hand, claim a priority that gives them virtually, mentally, a central position in the secret rites performed by the men. In so doing they reject the disjunction between the spheres of kinship and politics, and contest their relegation to the sphere of domestic life.

Jorgensen was later to learn from the men that menstrual blood, which in public prompts their disgust and their fear of women, is secretly used to 're-engender', without the help of women, the boys whom they have separated from their mother in order to initiate them. The boys' faces are smeared with yellow clay, whose secret name is 'menstrual blood', and which contains some blood from a woman who was menstruating at the time the rituals were about to begin. This is also the blood of Afek, the Old Woman, the primordial woman who made her brother the first man. She cut down his penis, which was too long, tried it out in her own vagina to see if it was the right length for copulating, and after this founding act of incest, told her brother the secrets of the initiations, of hunting and of growing taro, and then taught him to decorate his body for his initiation. Ultimately it is thanks to Old Woman, then, that men dominate women, for, in the beginning Afek gave them her bones, which they keep secretly in a cult house located in the centre of the country in the village of Telefolip,[45] the most sacred place of all. Knowing this, it will come as less of a surprise that it was women who, in Telefolmin in 1978 and 1979, played such an important role in the destruction of the relics and the abolition of the male cults encouraged by some Protestant preachers announcing Christ's return and the revival of humankind.

It should be quite clear that the men's model is no more 'true' than the women's – or vice versa. Each of these models expresses the different and unequal position of the two sexes in the society; each is simultaneously the expression of this inequality and a means of imposing it (for the men) or of mentally refusing it while submitting in practice (for the women).

---

45   Concerning Afek, see Godelier, *L'Enigme du don*; B. Craig and D. Hyndman (eds.), *Children of Afek: Tradition and Change among the Mountain-Ok of Central New Guinea* (Sydney, Oceania Monograph, 1990).

THE KINGDOM OF TONGA

The second example of a society with two coexisting models of procreation is that of the Kingdom of Tonga. The kingdom is composed of sixty-nine islands and, together with Hawaii and Tahiti, was one of the most stratified societies in Polynesia.[46] There was an absolute separation between the masses of *tu'a*, commoners, and the *eiki*, those endowed with titles and ranks. A distinction was made among the *eiki* between the *toa*, the 'little chiefs', or plebian chiefs, and the *eiki sii*, whose ancestors had received their title from the *Tu'i Tonga*, the representative of the royal line or high-ranking nobles. *Toa* means 'brave', and goes back to the time when warfare was endemic and feats on the battlefield and physical strength raised a commoner above the masses and earned him a title – but a title that could be taken away from him or his descendants. It was his *mana* that had distinguished him, and his *mana* could leave him. True nobles, on the other hand, the *sino'i eiki*, those who are 'chiefs in their body', who derived their rank from their proximity to the royal lines, possessed inborn *mana*; it was consubstantial to them and attested to their divine essence. Everyone with a title had authority over a portion of the territory and its inhabitants. But this authority was always delegated, and emanated ultimately from the person of the paramount chief, the Tu'i Tonga. In the past, a title was transmitted either adelphically, from older to younger brother, with the title returning to the eldest son of the eldest line, or patrilineally, from father to son, as has become the case in the line of the Tu'i Tonga.

A chief was therefore the head of a *kainga*, a group composed of kin but also of clients and protégés residing on the same land. The term kainga has several meanings. It designates first of all a person's kindred, all relatives on both the father's and the mother's sides. It also designates the territorial group made up of people who are related or have been allowed to live on the land ruled by a chief and are under his authority. Sexual relations – and even more, marriage – between members of the same kainga were strictly forbidden. The group was therefore exogamous. Members of a kainga shared the same bodily substances if they were related, and all, related or not, ate the same products of the land baked in the same oven. Now, for Tongans, the land was *fonua*, a word that also designates the womb, the place where the child receives its blood. The fact of sharing the same food as the other members of a kainga meant that those who were not originally related became kin.[47] All members

---

46   Cf. F. Douaire-Marsaudon, 'Le Meurtre cannibale ou la production d'un homme-Dieu', in M. Godelier and Michel Panoff (eds.), *Le Corps humain. Supplicié, possédé, cannibalisé* (Amsterdam, Archives Contemporaines, 1998), pp. 137–67.

47   Food and feeding others played an important role in constructing Tongan social identity. It must also be remembered that in Tonga, women did not traditionally work the land and did not usually do the cooking. These were male tasks. The women devoted a large part of their time to the production of big mats made of beaten bark, *tapas*, which were distributed or exchanged on all ceremonial occasions. The men thus had a very important nurturing role. It was they who

of a kainga owed tribute to their chief in the form of products and services, the *fatongia*.

When the Europeans arrived, the term kainga designated a sort of 'seigniorial domain', on which the kainga of the commoners were gathered around those of the noble families. Their chiefs were called *tamai*, 'fathers', and had almost absolute power over the possessions and the life of all members of their kainga. Every year, all of these chiefs presented the Tu'i Tonga with the first fruits of all of the crops of the kingdom in the course of a huge cosmic-political ritual called *inasi*. For the Tu'i Tonga, the whole kingdom was his kainga, of which he was the paramount chief and the nurturing father. Finally, the Tu'i Tonga himself presented his sister, the Tu'i Tonga Fafine, with a share of these first fruits, made up of the finest specimens, thereby recognizing her superior status, since she was even closer to the gods than he was.

In effect, in Tonga, as in Samoa and other parts of Polynesia, the sister outranks the brother, regardless of their respective ages, and elder outranks younger.[48] As a consequence, lines descending from sisters outrank lines descending from brothers, and lines descending from older siblings outrank lines descending from younger siblings. A person belongs to a local group, a kainga, either by their father or by their mother, and membership of this group gives them the right to the use of its land and its resources. However, the strongly virilocal residence pattern gives local groups a strongly patrilineal bias, whereas the kinship system as reflected in its terminology and its structure is cognatic. With these sociological indications in mind, we will now look at the two theories of procreation found in Tonga before the Europeans arrived and introduced Christianity.

According to the first, and probably oldest, theory, the father makes the child's bones with his sperm, which mixes with the woman's menstrual blood to form a clot. The woman's blood makes the child's flesh and its blood. And the clot becomes a foetus. Then a soul, which is a gift from the ancestors or the gods to the living, takes possession of the foetus. In this model, the father and the mother are the genitors, but their action alone is not enough to make the child.

---

grew the yams and prepared the ground for the cuttings. But it was the earth that made the cutting into a tuber. The earth thus acted like the women. In the Tongan language, womb, land and grave are all the same word, *fonua*. And it is on the maternal relatives' land that the newborn child's umbilical cord is buried. It is in this sense that non-relatives who live together and regularly eat the products of the same land end up sharing the same substances and becoming quasi-relatives, between whom marriage is forbidden. In Tonga, the fact of sharing or not sharing the same substances made people relatives or subjects. Cf. F. Douaire-Marsaudon, 'Je te mange, moi non plus', in M. Godelier and J. Hassoun (eds.), *Meurtre du père, sacrifice de la sexualité. Approches anthropologiques et psychanalytiques* (Paris, Arcanes, 1995), pp. 21–52.

48   In a kainga, the 'father', *tamai*, wielded and transmitted authority over the land and the people on it. The father's sister, *mehekitonga*, played a crucial role in the rites of passage. She was believed to control the fertility of her brother's wife, whom she could make barren at a whim. She also controlled all transactions concerning her ancestral lands and the marriages of her brother's children.

A child is always a gift from the ancestors and the gods. At the beginning of the twentieth century (despite a century of Christianization) the hair of the newborn child was still called 'the hair of the god'. And when a person dies, their bones retain something of the deceased's essence. It should be added that the female substances – saliva, blood and the mysterious 'water of life', *vaiola*[49] – are believed to be endowed with procreative capacities capable of giving (or restoring) life. Many myths feature women who have become pregnant after having been penetrated by the sun's rays or by the wind, or by water, all natural elements suffused with divine power, *mana*.

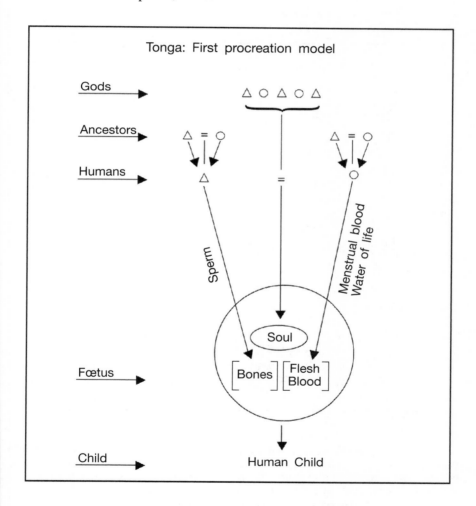

---

49   Perhaps the amniotic fluid. The chiefs used to bathe in ponds also called *vaiola*. Today this is the name of the hospital in the kingdom's capital city.

But a second model existed in the former culture of Tonga, according to which the child's substance, its flesh, blood, bones, skin, hair, etc., came from the mother.[50] The man's sperm had only one role: to stop up the menstrual blood in the woman's uterus. To this end, a clot forms which turns into an embryo through the intervention of the *mana* of the gods or of the Tu'i Tonga.[51] In this version, the father disappears as genitor. He is merely the mother's sexual partner. His role is to prime the woman to be fecundated by a god or by a man-god, the Tu'i Tonga. Like the gods, the Tu'i Tonga impregnates the woman with his desubstantified seed, a fecundating breath, a sperm *pneumatikos*, as Françoise Douaire-Marsaudon termed it.[52]

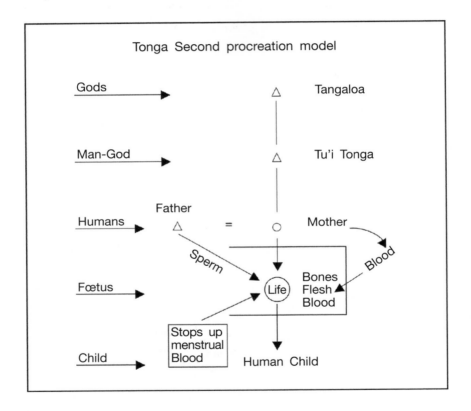

---

50   This version was collected and discussed by the Tongan historian and philosopher Futa Helu-Aite, in 'The Herda', *Phyllis* (1975), p. 63, and 'Gender, Rank and Power in the 18th-Century Tonga', *Journal of Pacific History*, 22 (1987), pp. 195–208, and by F. Douaire-Marsaudon, 'Le Meurtre cannibale', p. 140; see also G. Rogers, 'The Father's Sister Futa-Helu is Black: A Consideration of Female Rank and Power in Tonga', *Journal of the Polynesian Society*, vol. 86 (1977), pp. 157–82.

51   The ancestor of the Tu'i Tonga, the god Tangaloa, is also called Eitumatupua. *Aita* = god, *tupua* = ancestorhood. The god Tangaloa is thus the ancestor par excellence, *Aitu*.

52   Douaire-Marsaudon, 'Le Meurtre cannibale', p. 142.

This second model is clearly a transformation of the first, by virtue of combining two complementary operations. The woman's role in procreation, already important in the first model, is even greater here, while the man's role disappears and is replaced by the fecundating power of the Tu'i Tonga. The woman's blood now makes the child's entire substance. However, in Tonga, a woman transmits not only her blood, but her rank as well. Thus in the old kingdom of Tonga the quality of being a noble, of being a 'chief in the body', was transmitted only by women. The child of a high-ranking noble man and a female commoner was a commoner. The child of a commoner and an aristocratic woman was considered to be an aristocrat.

This model is thus a reworking of the first, but while it uses the traditional representations of the woman's role in conception, it is not, as one might think, in order to exalt the woman's procreative powers, but to *completely exclude ordinary men* from the process and to exalt even more the power of the *mana* of the paramount *eiki* and the members of the royal lines. The origin of the second model seems to be linked to the profound social and ideological changes that occurred in the Tongan political system in the wake of attempts – semi-successful and always challenged – on the part of one chiefly line, the one that would take the name-title of Tu'i Tonga, to raise itself definitively above the other royal lines. It was in this royal line moreover that the transmission of the paramount title would cease to be adelphic and pass in direct line from father to eldest son. At the same time, too, the gap between the social standing of nobles and that of commoners widened. At the outset, commoners, who were members of younger branches of kainga that had lost track of their old genealogical ties with the chiefly families, became less and less relatives and more and more subjects, over whom the nobles and the Tu'i Tonga had right of life and death. Closer to the ancestors and therefore closer to the gods, the chiefly families claimed to have a different origin and a different destiny than the common people.

By identifying himself as the one who impregnates all of the women in the kingdom (without actually having sexual intercourse with them) and as the one who fertilizes all of the lands (without actually working them), the Tu'i Tonga became the 'father' of all Tongans, their common ancestor, who were connected to the gods through him. Deprived of their own ancestors, the commoners were thus also deprived of survival in human form after death. Their spirit left their corpse and turned into an insect in danger of being swallowed by an animal or a god.[53] For in Tonga, the gods ate people. By this reasoning, it was the exclusive privilege of the chiefs (and sometimes the bravest warriors) to eat human flesh, for to eat another human was considered to be the way to prevent them

---

53 Certain accounts collected by Europeans at the start of the nineteenth century show that not all commoners shared this aristocratic representation.

surviving and becoming an ancestor. It was to annihilate them completely. To eat another person was the surest sign of power. Already having the gods as ancestors, having the right to have several wives, and to eat human beings, Tongan aristocrats had, after this life and such an exceptional destiny, the perspective of being the only ones to have access after death to Pulotu, the Tongan 'paradise'.

In short, the presence of two models of conception in Tonga reflects transformations of the (mental) universe of representations, ideological transformations, that were part of the process of the emergence of a dominant 'class' or 'caste', which concentrated in its membership all of the major political and religious functions, controlled access of the rest of the population to both the land and the gods, and claimed right of life and death over all who were not noble.

As the functions and ranks of the eldest lines progressively separated them from the younger lines, the kinship relations between the chiefly families and the rest of the population gave way to relations between masters and subjects. As this tribal aristocracy concentrated rights in the land, the labour, the services and finally the life of the rest of the population, these powers separated it definitively from other human beings and raised its members higher, bringing them closer to the gods so that they ultimately came to claim them as their direct ancestors. This is why the Tu'i Tonga Fafine, the sister of the Tu'i Tonga, had to marry her brother and unite with him as the gods do among themselves, for there was no blood in her own society that was equal to hers; the only alternative was to marry the paramount chief of another society, far away, in the Fiji Islands.

The example of Tonga shows us once again that political-ritual relations go far beyond the sphere of kinship, while at the same time using the images and values connected with this domain for their own representation. After all, is not the paramount chief, the Tu'i Tonga, at the same time both the chief and the 'father' of all Tongans, the *tamai*, just as the chief of a small Maenge village is also called 'father' (*tamai*)? In Tonga, as in New Britain, thousands of kilometres away, we see societies with Austronesian languages and cultures where, following very ancient patterns, the notions of father and chief are conjoined. This was not the case for the New Guinea Highland societies with non-Austronesian languages and cultures that belong to a much older population stock than the Austronesian-speaking groups. The Baruya do not have chiefs, they have Great Men, and the 'fathers' are no one's subjects.

To conclude, we will now leave the societies of Africa and Oceania and pay a visit to two great civilizations: Europe, fashioned by Christianity, and China, where ancestor worship has been an essential aspect of both the religious and state workings for centuries. In Europe, Christian theologians have represented the sexual union of a man and a woman united by the sacrament of marriage as forming one flesh, *una caro*, which they transmit to their children. But here too, the union of a man and a woman are not enough to make a child. What they make is a foetus, which needs a soul in order to become a child. It is God who introduces this soul while the child is in the womb. Apparently we are not so far from the Tu'i Tonga man-god, whose spermatic breath fecundates all of the women of his kingdom. And yet, as we will see when we visit China, the difference is radical.

From Chinese Antiquity up to the twenty-first century, one of the fundamental institutions of society and the state has been ancestor worship. Even the onslaught of the Red Guards was unable to eradicate it. The rites are celebrated in the family and the lineage on the house altar, which holds the tablets of the male ancestors, each accompanied by his wife's tablets, going back four generations. These rites reflect the way the Chinese represent the individual, his birth and his death, the central idea being that the ancestors are reborn in their descendants every five generations.

For the Chinese, a person has two souls, a body-soul, whose presence is indicated by the breathing that shows a person is alive; and a breath-soul, which, unlike the body-soul, does not disappear at the time of death but subsists for several generations before being born again. At the time of death, while the body-soul disappears into the ground, the breath-soul takes up residence in the tablet that will henceforth represent the deceased and will be placed, in accordance with his rank, on the home altar. This tablet, on which are marked the deceased's name and a few salient details of his life, accompanies the body to the graveside and is then brought back to the family altar, now containing the disembodied soul of the deceased. Four generations later, this tablet will be either buried or burned, and the soul of the deceased will be reincarnated in one of his descendants, ideally the son of his great-great grandson.[54]

Here the incompatibility between the Christian and Chinese religions becomes evident. For Christians, each soul is unique and is a gift from God. But the soul that was introduced into the body before birth will be immediately defiled by the original sin committed by Adam and Eve, the ancestors of humanity, and this sin is transmitted from one generation to the next by the carnal union of a man and a woman. It is therefore the Christian's duty to live in such a way that he will be able to erase the sin that marked his birth and which he will confront after death when he is called before the throne of God. The idea that a person's soul could be the reincarnation of another person, of an ancestor, is for

54 M. Granet, *Catégories matrimoniales et relations de proximité dans la Chine ancienne* (Paris, Félix Alcan, 1939), pp. 86–7. Granet is referring to aristocratic traditions dating to the so-called 'feudal' period, i.e. before the first Chinese Empire (221 BCE).

Christian theologians a heretical idea in so far as it denies God's systematic intervention in the 'animation' of bodies. This allows us to understand why Christianity, wherever it has been present, has always fought with all its might against ancestral religions that entailed the idea of reincarnation (from Roman Antiquity, with the veneration of the *manes*, the ancestors and the house gods, *lares*, to the ancestor cults encountered in Africa, Asia or Oceania).

But to attack the veneration of ancestors was at the same time to attack the existence of the social forms that organized kinship, such as lineages, clans, etc. Such an assault was particularly unacceptable to the Chinese, since it challenged not only the universe of kinship relations, but also one of the basic pillars of the state (filial duty). This explains why, when (after an initial period in which the Jesuits tolerated ancestor worship) the Dominican missionaries demanded that their flock renounce veneration of the ancestors and destroy the home altars, not only did the people resist, but the Emperor immediately ordered the European missionaries to be expelled.

CHAPTER EIGHT

Begetting Extraordinary Humans
(Fifth Component 2)

Incest, cannibalism, right of life and death over others: the dominant are sometimes distinguished from the dominated by what they do (what is forbidden the
others to do) and sometimes by what they eat. Power differentiates bodies.

THE KAKO OF GABON

The Kako of Gabon are a striking example of such differentiation. In this society
divided into exogamous patrilineal clans, where a person was forbidden to marry
with a member of the clans of his four grandparents as well as anyone from his
kindred within a distance of four generations (Omaha-type prohibitions), the basic
social unit was the village under the authority of a chief. Hunting, warfare, agriculture and the production of weapons and iron tools were the main activities of this
society for which blood was the prime substance, the basis of the human being.

For the Kako,[1] blood makes everything: flesh, blood, bones, breath. Blood is
an ingredient of even the soul, and it goes with it back to the village of the dead. But
the soul is introduced into the foetal body only toward the end of the pregnancy,
and this is done as a gift from the spirits to humans. The soul leaves the body
shortly before death and wanders in the bush in the form of an animal. At this
point it can be killed and, in this event, turns into a spirit that wanders among the
nature spirits for all eternity. If it is not killed, it reaches the village of the death.
Two fluids actually coexist in a human body – male or female – and keep it alive;
these are: blood, a male fluid, and water, a female fluid that tempers the blood's
heat and strength. The blood and water descend from the head along parallel paths
and meet in the man's testicles or the woman's lower back. There they mix with fats,
which thicken them and make them into male and female sperm.

In order to make a child, the man and woman unite sexually. The 'female
sperm' facilitates the entry of the male sperm, which makes its way to a place where
it encounters menstrual blood. The foetus is formed from these 'pieces of blood'.
During the pregnancy, the couple makes love in order to nourish the foetus, the
man with his sperm and the woman with what she eats. The child's sex is

---

1   E. Copet-Rougier, 'Tu ne traverseras pas le sang. Corps, parenté et pouvoirs chez les
Kako du Cameroun', in M. Godelier and M. Panoff (eds.), *Le Corps humain. Supplicié, possédé,
cannibalisé* (Amsterdam, Archives Contemporaines, 1998), pp. 87–108.

determined as soon as the man's and the woman's blood-sperm meet. If the man's blood is stronger than the woman's, the child will be a boy, if the contrary, the child will be a girl. Sex is thus transmitted in two gendered, parallel and exclusive lines. Men always beget men, and women, women. From the first sexual encounter, too, the blood of the father and that of the mother (who themselves result from the mixing of their own father's and mother's blood) combine into a single blood, which will give the child its very own substantial identity. As the child is supposed to be made 'in equal parts' from its father's and its mother's blood, this blood contains the cognatic relations that link each individual to all of his or her ascendants.[2]

But the bloods that mingle in the child do not have the same weight. Women's blood is much lighter. Beyond the fourth generation, all traces of uterine blood have disappeared and only the stronger agnatic blood subsists. These representations correspond to the Kako's patrilineal descent principle. Men keep their clan's blood forever, women lose it. At the same time, because each person contains the four grandparents' bloods and since the uterine bloods disappear after four generations, it becomes possible once more to contract marriages with these clans in the fifth generation. These representations of blood thus also correspond to the Omaha character of their kinship system, to the prohibition on marrying in the four clans of the grandparents and in one's own kindred.

But why is women's blood of a lighter colour and weight and why does it disappear after a few generations? It is because women do not fight or hunt and are banned from consuming the meat and blood of 'cruel animals', whose blood is like that of men, and they are even more strictly excluded from eating human flesh. Since, for the great hunters and warriors, humans are the game of choice, the 'meat' par excellence.

But in order for a man to have the right to eat human flesh, he must have killed many men. Those having fought, killed and eaten human flesh were called 'the cruel ones' and they 'held the village', whose chief could be nothing other than a great hunter, a great warrior and a great eater of human flesh. Humans, the prime game, are one of the cruel animals, even the cruelest of all. The trail of blood thus traces a continuity between the human and the animal states. Each time an animal or a man was killed and eaten, the same rite, *simbo*, was performed so as to ward off the victim's vengeance. His flesh and blood were consumed, while the fat (the female part of the body) was carefully conserved. Only the 'very great' men, those who 'held' the village, had the right to keep human fat. This fat was used ritually to coat the iron lode from which the smiths extracted the iron they used to make weapons, tools and 'dowry money', the iron objects that formed part of the bridewealth.[3]

---

2   It should be remembered that cognatic relations are present in all kinship systems, even though they may not be named.

3   Warriors cut off the enemy heads, for the head is the source of blood, strength and life. By eating the bodies, they made sure they could not become ancestors, protectors of their

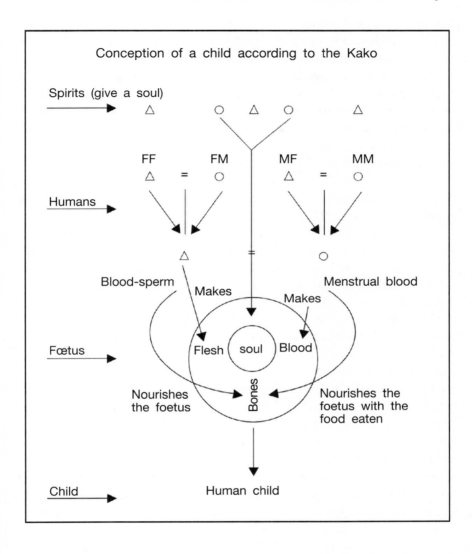

Conception of a child according to the Kako

Spirits (give a soul)

Humans

Foetus

Child   Human child

Women and children are excluded from eating the flesh of all cruel animals and of humans. For all other game and domestic animals, additional taboos (*mkire*, from *mkiyö*, 'blood') also apply. These taboos concern the heart, head, sexual organs, gizzard, in short everything associated in Kako representations with the organs and substances connected with sex and the reproduction of life.

When it comes to children, boys' bodies are going to be little by little made

---

descendants. The enemy blood and fat became tools for the Kako's material and social reproduction by thickening their blood and ensuring the continuity of the patrilineal clans (dowry) and enabling them to augment their means of production (tools) and destruction (weapons).

different from girls' bodies. A father will perform rites to gradually lift the prohibitions preventing his son from eating certain animals, until one day when he has become a hunter and warrior and has killed many men and animals, the young man receives from the Tumba – the Great Men – the right to eat real 'meat', human flesh. He is now considered to be a complete man, with heavy, thick, hot and powerful blood. The complete man thus possesses power within and by means of his body. His body is the incarnation of power – physical strength; political, military and economic power; and the power to make dowry money and to exchange it for wives. The reproduction of society thus appears to lie entirely in the hands of these cruel men. And blood symbolizes the unity of this society, since the Kako are formally forbidden to eat not only a relative but any member of their tribe. A tribe is the same blood shared.[4]

And yet the power is not entirely in the men's hands. In this society, where, owing to the Omaha character of the kinship terminology, sisters are designated by their brothers and regarded as their 'daughters', women have a great deal of spiritual (and therefore social) power, which stems from the brother–sister relationship. For marriage does not separate women from their patriclan, and when they die they are buried beside their brother on their clan lands. And among the sisters, the eldest enjoy an exceptional status. They have pre-eminence over their brothers' wives. Like the father's sister in Tonga, the *mehekitanga*, they ritually ensure the fecundity of their sisters-in-law. But they can also cast an evil spell on them and deprive their brothers of descendants, thus endangering the continuation of their own clan. They dispose of other rites to ensure the fertility of their brothers' fields. And it is especially they who are called upon when a village is founded. They perform the rite that ensures that the spirits of the place will look favourably on the humans there. This rite must be renewed each year at the start of the dry season, and it is supposed to 'bind' people together, to bring harmony and to renew the ties between the living and the dead. Last of all, women also play a role in the two activities that are the source of the men's strength and their privilege: hunting and warfare.

In the past, when the men set out for war or to go hunting, the eldest sisters would lie across the trail and all the men had to step across them too ensure a successful outcome. Women thus had a real social and spiritual power. And they wielded it from time to time by refusing to perform the rites for the start of the dry season, thus threatening the village with famine. In this event, discord

---

4   'The blood of the body, of sperm, of the foetus, blood souls, blood-thirsty spirits and blood-drinking warriors: it is around this essential notion that representations, discourses and practices are elaborated. Whether we are talking about the body, procreation, the kinship system, animal categories, cannibalism, sorcery or leadership, we must follow the blood trail if we want to understand both the symbolic and ideological logics, and the orders and disorders of social life' (Copet-Rougier, 'Tu ne traverseras pas le sang', p. 89).

became entrenched, accusations of sorcery flourished, the village chief's authority was threatened. In short, although their lighter blood fated them to submission to male power, women not only provided another clan with children and ensured its continuity, through their ritual activities and privileged access to the ancestors, they also contributed to ensuring that their own clan would enjoy equilibrium, concord and longevity.[5] Women gave their blood to the other clans so that they might reproduce themselves. But they kept their spiritual powers for their own clan, which were enabled to reproduce by the blood of women from other clans. There was one law for all: 'You must not cross blood'. You must never eat a member of your own tribe. The Kako example clearly shows how the body, the gendered body differentiated by its sex, is vested with power relations – political, religious but also economic – and witnesses to and implements them.

THE PAICI OF NEW CALEDONIA

Comparable to the Kako example, but differing on a crucial point, endocannibalism on the part of chiefs, as in the case of the Paici of New Caledonia, also highlights the social and symbolic importance of differentiating, through kin ties and food, the body of chiefs from the bodies of those who follow and obey them. The Paici are particularly interesting because, as is often the case in New Caledonia, the chief has been brought in from outside, 'from the bush', and he must then be made into a native and, furthermore, must be made into an ancestor in his own lifetime. How to make a native and an ancestor of an outsider so that he may become your legitimate chief: this was the problem facing the Paici each time internal power struggles for the succession to chiefdom drove the clan elders to seek a new chief outside their group.

A Kanak chiefdom is a political-military organization led by a group of older, high-ranking (*ukai*) men grouped around a central figure, *pwi ukai*, who wield their authority over a majority of commoners called 'gens petits' (small people) or servants.[6] The high-ranking men who surround the chief – and manifest, in highly coded forms, their respect and support – are called his 'fathers' (*caa*) and 'grandfathers' (*ao*). The chief alone embodies and manifests the might of the territorial group. The chief and the prominent figures are considered as 'older brothers', while the commoners and their lineages are regarded as 'younger brothers and sisters'. Certain lineages provide the chief's

---

5   Elisabeth Copet-Rougier notes a very important fact, which is that for women 'the brother is *not really* like their father', and at this point the terminology they use 'switches to the Hawaiian type' (ibid., p. 97).

6   A. Bensa and A. Goromido, 'Contraintes par corps: ordre politique et violences dans les sociétés kanak d'autrefois', in Godelier and Panoff (eds.), *Le Corps humain*, pp. 169–97.

household with meat and fish, help in the fields, etc. They are called 'servants' but also hold rights in the land and customary functions. The divisions are a function of the order in which groups and people arrived on a territory and, for individuals, of birth order in their lineages and clans.

The first occupants of a site are considered to be the 'masters of the land', and all firstborn of these clans and families are, like them, *ukai* because they are closer to the ancestors and the origin of the sites. Each patrilineal lineage carries the name of a dwelling site, a 'mound' founded by its ancestors, a name that is also a title borne by the descendants. From the standpoint of wealth and exchanges, there is no basic distinction between nobles and commoners. It is the title-names that make the difference. These title-names are ranked. However, while the ranking of the titles is quite stable and shows little variation over time, the same is not true of the title-holders. Title-names are lost and won, and the lineages and clans, long established or newcomers to a territory, are in permanent competition to conserve their status or to acquire a more prestigious one. Even the chief is not considered to automatically inherit his father's title and position, nor is he supposed to leave them to his son. In all circumstances, the chief must be chosen by the masters of the land, who will lend him their support. As Alban Bensa stresses, the genealogical vocabulary used to speak of the chief can lead one to think that chiefdom is hereditary, but this kinship vocabulary 'is only a veneer'.

How do kinship and the representations of how a human is made function in Paici society? Their kinship system is based on clans and lineages organized by a patrilineal descent rule, but in which maternal kin play an extremely important role.

The Paici assimilate sperm to blood, and two coexisting theories ascribe different roles to this male substance and therefore a different role to the father in making the child.[7] According to one of these theories, the man's blood-sperm mixes with the mother's blood, which plays a preponderant role in making the foetus. According to the other, the man's blood-sperm stops the menstrual blood from running out of the womb and in this case it becomes a foetus. In the second theory, the mother's role and the debt to the maternal kin are even greater than in the first. This explains the extreme importance of the mother's brother in Kanak societies. It is he who, through the medium of his sister and

7   Maurice Leenhardt's thesis, which says that the role of the Kanak father is merely to fortify because sperm plays no role in conceiving the child, is not sustained by later ethnological studies. But the existence of two conceptions of the role of sperm, one of which sees it as a plug, points in this direction. The debate is open and has been renewed by the publication of Christine Salomon-Nekiriai's work, which criticizes certain aspects of Alban Bensa's analyses. It is up to the Kanaks and to those working with them to reconstruct their traditions and to take a stand. Cf. C. Salomon, *Savoirs et pouvoirs thérapeutiques kanaks* (Paris, Presses Universitaires de France, 2000), p. 43.

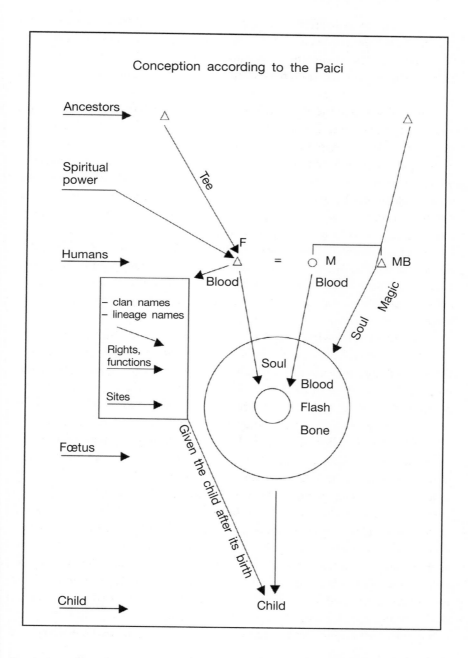

Conception according to the Paici

Ancestors

Spiritual power

Tee

Humans

F
=   M   MB

Blood   Blood

Soul   Magic

- clan names
- lineage names

Rights, functions

Sites

Soul

Blood
Flash
Bone

Given the child after its birth

Fœtus

Child   Child

her spiritual powers, transmits their blood, flesh, bones and skin to his nephews and nieces. The maternal uncle also gives the child its soul, which comes from the ancestors who live in a place under the sea. The soul takes up residence in the body of the foetus and gives it breath and life.

It is from its father's lineage and from its father himself that the child receives a clan name, a lineage name, rights in the land and sites to live on. The child also receives its ancestors' spiritual force (*tee*) through the agnatic line. This force is present in certain plants, animals and rocks, which are specific to a clan. Leenhardt called these supports of ancestral power 'totems'.

Throughout their life, the child's maternal uncles will make repeated propitiatory acts and sacrifices to win their nephews and nieces health, strength and success in their endeavours. When a person dies, the paternal kin return the body to the maternal side. The soul remains in the vicinity of the deceased's home until the end of the mourning period. The uterine kin of the deceased then conduct rites by which they accompany the soul they transmitted to the entrance of the undersea country of the dead. When the body has decomposed, a second funeral is held, and the deceased's maternal uncles come and lay the bones of the deceased in the cemetery of the paternal kin. These bones become relics and draw down and concentrate all of the ancestors' spiritual power, which constantly radiates from funeral sites and mounds. From this time on, the deceased's maternal kin no longer have access to the resting place of their nieces' and nephews' skulls and bones.

How, in a society which lays such emphasis on the ancestors' power, on the exceptional status of the elder lineages and on the eldest children in all lineages, precisely because they are closer to the ancestors, closer to the relics, to the old mounds, etc., I repeat, how in such a society, when a chief has died or been ousted and the clans are unable to agree on a local successor, will they go about *making an ancestor of the outsider* they have brought in to be this successor?

This outsider is henceforth cut off from his natal group and is no longer surrounded by his agnatic or his uterine kin. The clans that receive him will give him a clan name and affiliation. This affiliation will link him with the oldest mound-name in their territory. They will also provide him, like maternal kin, with a *new body* full of health and force. In short, the body of the chief will be re-made both ritually and physically, so that he may be inserted into the lineage of the chiefdom's most prestigious ancestors. The 'prominent' families who will be his support-system and his advisors will become his 'fathers and grandfathers' (*caa ao*), and one of the terms used to address him, 'older big brother' is the same as the one used to designate the paternal great-grandfather. The chief thus becomes at the same time their son, their grandson, their older brother and their great-grandfather; he becomes both an ascendant and a descendant of those who chose him.

In order to provide the chief with a new body produced on site this time, he is fed with special food. He is served yams considered as very 'old'. Periodically he is served the flesh of a high-ranking man from his adoptive lineage. Before the sacrifice, a mourning ceremony had already been held for the victim, in which the person making the sacrifice had asked the future victim's maternal uncles to reclaim their share, namely: his soul. Only the chief could eat this meat designed to make him strong. The sacrificial victim's heart and liver, the seats of life in Paici culture, were offered to the 'war stone', inhabited by the spirit of an ancestor who had been a great warrior and a great eater of human flesh, to which was regularly served up pieces of slain enemies.

It therefore goes without saying that the lineage providing the chief with a victim had considerable political weight. No decision could be taken without it. The chief's flesh was also their flesh. They acted in a way as maternal relatives of the chief, while he played the role of container and them of contained. Because of this, the victims became ancestors in his body and in turn made him an ancestor. But the chief was also allowed (and even obliged) to eat the flesh of one of his 'father's sisters' – sisters of his real father or those of his 'fathers' in the sense of political backers. His fathers, therefore, instead of exchanging their sisters for wives and widening their network of alliances, devoted certain sisters to making the most important man of the chiefdom, its chief, even more powerful.

Having become an autochthon through endocannibalism, the chief could then perform his tasks to the full measure: destroy enemies, put them to flight or massacre them, take their women and children for adoption or exchange, eat the bodies of enemy warriors in order to annihilate them by depriving them of the means of becoming protecting ancestors for their own group and hiding their bones so that they might not be used as relics and draw down the strength of their ancestors.

Ultimately, the chief, made by others and raised by them above themselves, was nothing without his *caa mä ao*, his support-system. When this chief died, the problem of his succession arose again, and his formers supporters, as masters of the land and local elders, could recover the title to bestow on one of their own. But the internecine conflicts could be such that, even before his death, a chief's legitimacy could be contested by some of those who had supported him. In this event, instead of waiting to be exiled or killed, he could offer himself in sacrifice in order to force the warring factions to put an end to their conflicts and oblige them to go on living together: in short, sacrifice himself in order to save the chiefdom.

The day of the sacrifice, the chief walks to the ceremonial hut decked in his costume and his weapons, which he hands over to the man who is to carry out the sacrifice. The latter smashes his skull with a blow of his club. Before burying the body in the clan cemetery, the man charged with the sacrifice removes the liver, which is then cooked. Part is then symbolically shared out and eaten, and the rest is offered to the ancestors whose blessing is sought. This offering was designated by the same name as the gifts (*pwö*) made to the maternal uncles, who were present when the chief was killed and were given a gift, as was the sacrificer.

By sacrificing himself, by offering his life and his flesh to be consumed, the chief was supposed to restore peace to the chiefdom. Thereafter it was impossible for those who had been fighting and wanting to separate to do so. The chief's sacrifice had sealed a new *social covenant*. But it had also made his sons outsiders once again. His family was therefore forced into exile, together with those of the chief's most ardent supporters who had attached themselves to him. The title reverted to the masters of the land, who had originally conferred it on the sacrificed chief. The cycle could now begin all over. There was, then, nothing hereditary about this power, which nevertheless could be established only in the name of the ancestors and was compelled to make an ancestor during his lifetime of someone who had no former descent ties with the living and the dead whom he governed.[8]

THE TU'I TONGA, A LIVING MAN-GOD

Let us come back from the ancestor-man living among humans that is the Kanak chief to the living man-god that is the Tu'i Tonga. According to mythology, his divine essence comes from the fact that his ancestor was *twice begotten*: once when a human woman united with a god and once when his divine father brought him back to life after the other gods, his brothers, jealous of his looks, had killed and devoured him. The myth tells that

> one of the great gods fell in love with a chief's daughter and got her with child. The god went back up into the sky and sent down to the mother a piece of land and a yam to feed the child, whom he named Aho'eitu (the dawn god, the 'new' god). When he grew up, Aho'eitu asked his mother who his father was, and having been told he was a god who lived in the sky, he decided to join him. When he got there, the father presented him to his other sons, his divine brothers. The brothers, jealous of his looks, killed him and threw his head into a bush and ate his body. The father discovered the infamy and ordered his sons to find the head of Aho'eitu, which he placed in a wooden bowl, and then to vomit up the remains of their brother into the

---

8   Alban Bensa rightly draws a parallel between the example of the Kanak chiefdom and the great Melanesian chiefdoms of the Fiji islands, with which, as we have seen, the Tongan aristocracy intermarried. In Fiji the chief was also an outsider, a heavenly god received by the people of the land where he was supposed to have appeared one day. In order to become one of them, this foreign chief had to drink *kava* made from a plant that had grown atop the corpse of a local child. Later, the chief would lead his warriors to raid human victims beyond his borders and share their flesh with them. Cf. M. Sahlins, *Islands of History* (Chicago, University of Chicago Press, 1985), pp. 75, 97–8.

bowl. Then he restored Aho'eitu to life and sent him back down to earth, giving him the office and title of Tu'i Tonga, and he ordered his other sons to help their brother govern without ever laying claim to his office.[9]

Let us review the steps in this double birth, which changed Aho'eitu into Tu'i Tonga, a unique individual at the same time human and divine, who became the paramount chief and god after a series of initiatic ordeals. First, his birth, the result of copulation between a human woman and a god who fertilized her by his power, his *mana*. Then his growth, facilitated by a twofold food, divine through the yam and the land that his father sent, and earthly through his mother, who nourished him. Moreover his good looks are a sign of the *mana* that inhabits him, and it is this beauty that provokes the jealousy of the gods, his brothers. The brothers devour him, which fits with the fate of mortals who, in Polynesia, were always in danger of being devoured by the gods or by the chiefs. The father obliges his sons to vomit their brother's remains into a *kava* bowl. In Tonga, saliva and vomit are life-restoring substances. His human body thus becomes a divine body since it now possesses his divine brothers' lifeforce, their saliva. Then Aho'eitu returns to earth, having undergone a double birth, one on earth, the other in the sky. The myth ends by presenting as a divine decree that the Tu'i Tonga, last-born of the Great God's sons, will reign over the earth and that none of his brothers must ever attempt to govern in his stead or to take away his title.

Now this is exactly the policy followed by the line of the Tu'i Tonga, when it broke with the adelphic mode of succession that had been the rule in the royal lines and brought in a patrilineal mode of transmission, from father to son, thus creating a 'dynasty'. It is understandable, in this case, that, born directly from the fertilization of his distant mythic ancestor by a god, the Tu'i Tonga claimed to be the great, the unique fertilizer not only of all of the women in his kingdom, but of the land and its crops, as a result of the land and the yam given by a god to the woman he had fertilized so that she might nourish their child. Invented in the context of the Tu'i Tonga's court, the myth had all of the qualities ascribed to the discourse of dominant castes or classes. It aggrandized and divinized in the imaginary the members of this caste, which legitimized in their own eyes and in the eyes of those under them the forms of domination they wielded over the rest of the population.

After the example of the Kanak twice-born ancestor-man, born the first time in the same way as other humans and the second time in a mystical and symbolic way through endocannibalism, and the example of the man-god, also

---

9   See Françoise Douaire-Marsaudon's analysis in 'Le Meurtre cannibale ou la production d'un homme-dieu. Théories des substances et construction hiérarchique en Polynésie', in Godelier and Panoff (eds.), *Le Corps humain*, pp. 137–67; pp. 152–7.

twice born, but both times in a 'spiritual' manner, the first on earth and the second in the sky, being eaten and reborn through the mana of a god, his father, we find ourselves in the presence of two cases where some 'men' set themselves apart from and raise themselves above humans by having been conceived several times. Ultimately the others exist only as fragments of themselves, fragments to which the gods give life and from which they can take it back.

DE-CONCEPTION OF THE MEKEO CHIEFS OF PAPUA NEW GUINEA

With our final example, that of the Mekeo chiefs, we have the opposite case. Instead of being twice-conceived, in order to attain their divine essence and manifest it to one and all, the Mekeo chiefs must be twice-de-conceived.[10] The Mekeo are an Austronesian-speaking group that live along the Biaru river, which empties into the sea in the middle of the Gulf of Papua. Their society was divided into two exogamous moieties, which were in turn split into two patriclans. Each person was supposed to marry within the tribe but into the other moiety. Furthermore, a man could not marry a woman from his mother's clan. He could not repeat his father's marriage. He would therefore marry a woman from the alternate clan in the other moiety, thus marrying a second-degree cross cousin (see diagram).

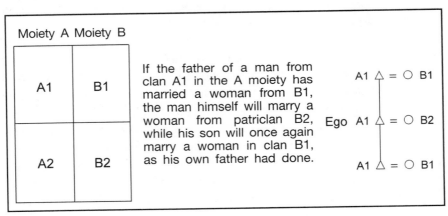

In the Mekeo society, the political-ritual functions belong to the hereditary chiefs of the four clans and are distributed according to the rule of both opposing and complementary moieties.[11]

10   M. Mosko, 'Conception, De-conception and Social Structure in Bush Mekeo Culture', *Mankind*, vol. 14 (1983), pp. 24–32; *Quadripartite Structures, Categories, Relations and Homologies in Bush Mekeo Culture* (Cambridge, Cambridge University Press, 1983); 'Motherless Sons: "Divine Kings" and "Partible Persons" in Melanesia and Polynesia', *Man*, vol. 27 (1992), pp. 697–717.

11   M. Mosko, 'Peace, War, Sex and Sorcery: Non-linear Analogical Transformation in the

Before Europeans arrived				After Europeans arrived		
	Internal relations	External relations			Internal relations	External relations
Secular authority	Lopia Peace chief	Iso War chief		Secular authority	Peace chief	Regional represent-atives + village police
Ritual authority	Unguanya 'Peace sorcerer'	Falka 'War sorcerer		Ritual authority	'Peace sorcerer'	Catholic Church

There were thus four chiefs: one for war, one for peace, as well as a 'war sorcerer' and a 'peace sorcerer'. The war chief led the warriors into battle and carried out all the rites that had to do with killing. He was assisted by the 'war sorcerer', who possessed the powers to magically sap the enemy's strength. In intertribal fights, the death of a Mekeo warrior was repaid by the death of an enemy warrior. There was also a reciprocal 'exchange' of male blood between the groups. Men made ready for war by 'closing' their body through fasting and sexual abstinence, to make them strong, swift and impenetrable to enemy war magic. War and sex were incompatible.

The peace chief had an equally fundamental role within the tribe. He presided over the de-conception ceremonies for the deceased during funeral rites and festivities. He was aided by the 'peace sorcerer', who ensured that the Mekeo rules of marriage and clan exogamy were respected. He also saw to it that everyone cooperated with the 'peace chief' to carry out correctly the recip-rocal exchanges of special-food gifts between the deceased's paternal and maternal kin.

Before trying to analyze what it means to de-conceive someone for the Mekeo, we need first to know how the person was conceived. Every person belongs to a moiety and to a specific clan, and people from different clans, and

Early Escalation of North Mekeo Sorcery and Chiefly Practice', in M. Mosko and F. Damon (eds.), *On the Order of Chaos: Social Anthropology and Science of Chaos* (New York, Berghahn, 2005). The Mekeo were 'pacified' in 1890 by William MacGregor at a time when Papua was still a British colony. Between 1890 and 1940, eighty per cent of the population died from a series of diseases introduced by the Europeans and for which the Mekeo had no immunity. With the end of war and these mass deaths, initially blamed on the peace sorcerers, internal strife and accusations of sorcery multiplied. The role of the peace sorcerers became increasingly important. Representatives elected by the Kairuku regional administration replaced the war chiefs and at the same time the Mekeo were converted to Christianity by French Catholic priests.

from different moieties, are therefore from different 'bloods', agnatic bloods, since Mekeo descent reckoning is patrilineal. For two people to marry, they must be from 'different' bloods. They conceive a child when they unite sexually and their sexual 'bloods' – the man's sperm and the woman's womb blood – mix in equal proportions in the woman's uterus.[12] The mixing of the father's and the mother's blood inaugurates the life of the foetus, its conception.[13] At the same time as this act mingles the two bloods and makes them one, it transmits this blood to the child.

The man's sperm-blood is believed to coagulate and solidify the woman's liquid, shapeless menstrual blood. It shapes the foetus and then nourishes it. For this to happen, the couple increases their rate of sexual intercourse for the first three months of the pregnancy. During this time, the future mother is fed with huge quantities of boiled plants in order to increase the amount of 'blood' in her womb and make the foetus grow. From this moment on, the woman ceases to work in order not to cause the blood to leave her womb. After the first three months of the pregnancy, the man refrains from all sexual relations, so as to 'close' his body back up and again be ready for war. The abstinence will last until the child is weaned, around a year and a half after its birth.

For the Mekeo, parents and children are thought to share the same blood, and this blood stems in particular from the fact that they have shared the same cooked foods, for they believe that cooked food makes blood and raw food separates bloods. Since marriages are repeated from one generation to the next, alternating between the two clans of the other moiety, the Mekeo see themselves, with regard to the other tribes, as having 'a single blood'. But when it comes to their representations of themselves within the tribe, they see each other as being of different bloods, and it is on this condition, they say, that they can marry each other. When the men of one clan marry, they *receive* the blood of other clans, whereas their sisters and daughters *give* the other clans part of their blood. The Mekeo say that the clans 'open themselves' to others by exchanging their women, and the tribe thus reproduces itself through the reciprocal exchange of female blood between the two moieties and the four clans. The women are a clan's 'skin', the part of its body turned toward the outside. When a couple marries, the representatives of the four clans are present, and the ceremony begins with the de-conception of the bodies of the future spouses, which rids them of two of the four bloods they carry in them.

---

12   The word for 'womb', *ina*, is also the word for 'mother'.
13   *Engama*, in the Mekeo language, means 'beginning' and 'conception'.

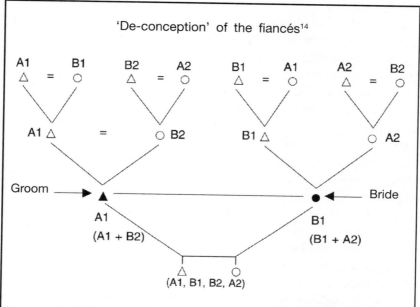

'De-conception' of the fiancés[14]

The groom (A1) will be de-conceived of the bloods of his two grand-mothers, his father's mother (B1) and his mother's mother (A2)

The bride (B1) will be de-conceived of the blood of her two grand-mothers, her father's mother (A1) and her mother's mother (B2)

The de-conception rite is celebrated by the 'peace chief' and his assistant, the 'peace sorcerer'. It consists in exchanges of valuables – lengths of cowry shells, necklaces of dogs' teeth, bird-of-paradise feathers, raw pork from domestic pigs. The clan of the groom's father (A1) gives a certain number of valuables and an amount of raw pork to the clan of the bride's father (B1), and the groom's mother's clan (B2) gives the same amount of valuables to the bride's mother's clan (A2). The two clans (B1 and A2) that receive these gifts in turn present their givers with raw pork. To give raw rather than cooked meat is to deny or reject the existence of kin relations between givers and receivers that go through the married couple. This exchange is called *ifa kekapaisa* (to manipulate the blood). By 'manipulating' their bloods, the relatives affirm symbolically and fictively that they are not relatives.

Thus, in the reciprocal exchange of raw pork, the clan of the groom's father (A1) de-conceives the former of the blood of his father's mother (B1), which is

---

14   Looking at this diagram, we immediately see that the blood (A1) the groom has received directly from his grandfather's clan (his own) is the same as the blood the bride received from her father's mother, and so on.

precisely the blood of the bride's father's clan (B1). Alternatively, the bride's clan (B1) de-conceives her of the blood of her father's mother (A1), which is precisely the clan of the groom's father. When clans A2 (the groom's mother's clan) and B2 (the bride's mother's clan) exchange pork, they thereby de-conceive the future spouses of the blood of their mothers' mothers (A2, B2). At the close of these de-conceptions, each spouse has only the blood of their two grandfathers. They are rid of the blood of their future spouse's clan, which they also carried, and are now free to marry. Through these 'manipulations' of their blood, they are reborn as new social persons. This transformation is indicated by the word used to designate the de-conception of the newlyweds: *engama*, which also means 'conception'. Nevertheless, these manipulations, which simultaneously de-conceive and 're-conceive' the people involved, are considered by all parties as a 'fiction'. And the newlyweds often behave toward their new affines as though they were still 'a single blood'. For, in the Mekeo's thinking, a person's 'true' 'de-conception' occurs when they die.

The funeral rites and festivities are the most important social institution in Mekeo culture, and their performance is extremely complex. The 'peace chief' of the deceased's clan gives, on behalf of the mourning clan, a quantity of various raw foods to the chiefs of the two clans in the other moiety. Those who helped collect these foods are: members of the deceased's clan, but also all of the children that the women of these clans have given to the two clans of the other moiety. The clan chiefs who receive these gifts redistribute them to those clansmen whose mothers are not from the deceased's clan and to the children of the clanswomen married into the clan of the other moiety which is not that of the deceased.

The mourners give three categories of food: tubers from the deceased's garden, which provided part of his blood; meat of game and wild pig; and pork from domestic pigs. These two kinds of meat – bush meat and village meat – represent the deceased's flesh and blood, and his fellow clansmen may not eat of this meat at any cost: it would be tantamount to autocannibalism. The wild meat has been smoked. It is dry and represents 'male' blood; while the domestic pork is 'female' blood. These meats represent the bloods of the deceased's two grandmothers: his father's mother and his mother's mother, two bloods that the feast givers 'return' to the clans that have given them women. The clans that give these meats are thus *rid of the foreign bloods that entered into the process of conceiving their members*. By the same token, the clans that receive and eat these meats reappropriate the bloods they have lost over the previous generations by giving their women to the other clans so that they might provide them with descendants.

What had been partially or fictitiously done at the time of the marriage is brought to fulfilment at the time of death. In the end, all clan members are once again connected by a single, 'strictly' male blood. The clans that had 'opened themselves' to others in order to conceive, 'close back upon themselves' by de-conceiving their members. New alliance ties can be created, non-relatives can once again become relatives. The (apparent) contradiction between clan exogamy and tribe endogamy is resolved. All Mekeo are a single blood, which is divided into four different bloods, and so on.

But this 'ordinary' de-conception of commoners, which happens only when they die, is not the same as the 'extraordinary' de-conception practised among the chiefs *during their lifetime*. They perform this de-conception at each instal-lation of new 'sons of Akaisa', the god that gave the Mekeo ancestors everything: fire, domestic plants, game, their own daughters, and who vested the ancestors of the hereditary chiefs with the political-ritual offices that their descendants still hold. But they also do this each time a funeral is celebrated by the 'peace chief', in so far as this chief must at this time also perform his own de-concep-tion and that of the other chiefs. He does this by giving them portions of sacred food, *ikufuka*. These portions of *ikufuka* (which can be translated as 'magic-power mountain') are composed of the whole carcass of a dog and certain special parts of the skin and certain organs of a pig. This sacred meat can and must be eaten by the commoners, but in no event by the chiefs. The latter redis-tribute their own share of the *ikufuka* to their fellow clansmen but do not eat any. That would be tantamount to eating the flesh of the god Akaisa, and eating their own flesh, since all chiefs descend from the sons of this god, who were born at the beginning of time, without a mother, without female blood in their bodies. In short, by de-conceiving themselves while they are still living, the chiefs purge themselves of that which came from their mother. They detach this part which made them androgynous beings, and with it all of the attendant social relations, and in so doing recover their ancestral, divine and purely male essence.

Chiefs thus are reborn during their lifetime, without the mediation of women to bring them into the world and, in the process, recover the primal condition enjoyed by humans at a time when there were only men who never died and who, when they grew old, shed their skin like snakes and became young once again. It was in those times that Foikale, chief of the first men, who had always lived underground and had no wives, emerged and appeared in the garden of the god Akaisa. The god gave him a warm welcome and told him to go fetch his companions. These first men did not know how to hunt, or work the land and did not drink water. Later, Akaisa gave them fire, the edible plants, meat and his own daughters so that they might have sexual intercourse and procreate. Akaisa then lived among his protégés in the guise of a young boy, who soon made the humans jealous because of the game that ran into his nets and which he shared generously with everyone. One day the men beat him and drove him away. In revenge, Akaisa drove the men, through his magic, to kill each other. Death had made its appearance. Three times Akaisa drove them to fight each other, and three times he brought them back to life. At last, he sent the men down to earth after having distributed to certain of them the four polit-ical-religious offices, which have since become hereditary. At the same time he sent down the chiefs' wives, whom he had made pregnant, and it was the first-born sons of these women who were later to hold the offices and titles.

According to another myth, Akaisa challenged his young brother Tsabini to kill his mother and eat her, telling him that he had already killed his own and that they were going to share her. Tsabini discovered that he had been tricked by Akaisa, who had substituted a pig for his mother. He killed Akaisa's son. Akaisa carried his son's corpse to the top of a mountain and laid it on a platform for the bones to dry. But each night, his son's bones changed into game animals. So Akaisa called together the Mekeo's ancestors and told them to catch the game and to organize a funeral feast for his son. He showed them how to do this and gave the chiefs the pieces of the boy's body changed into game to be distributed to all the members of their clans but without eating any themselves.

It is these founding myths that assert the chiefs' divine essence and which the peace chiefs and the other clan chiefs reactivate each time a Mekeo dies and his clan performs the (ordinary) de-conception of the deceased.

In contrast to the Kanak chief or the great Tu'i Tonga, who become a human-ancestor or a man-god by eating human flesh and thus raising them-selves higher, here we are dealing with chiefs who assert their divine essence and their legitimate right to govern others by detaching from their body every female ingredient that might subsist there and having others consume it. It is by reducing themselves that they raise themselves.

In the West we are familiar with another god who shared his flesh and his blood with his followers, and who is said to have been born of a human woman who had conceived him without having had sexual relations with her earthly spouse. For Christ is a god, son of another god and of the Holy Spirit. A god without a heavenly mother, a purely male god conceived of a woman who had never had intercourse with the man she married, Joseph. A god born immacu-late of a virgin herself born of an 'immaculate conception'.

But whether one is a man-made god (Tu'i Tonga) or a god-made man, whether one 'raises oneself up' by eating others or by giving oneself to be eaten by others, this exceptional human or superhuman being then must prove that he is entitled to veneration and to the submission of ordinary humans by providing them with abundance, health, strength, in short, life; or on the contrary by depriving them of strength, health and life by annihilating them by his wrath. He will have to either give life or take it away in order to manifest his divine essence and power.

CHAPTER NINE

The Sexed Body

A Ventriloquist's Dummy That Gives Voice to the Order or the Disorder of Society and the Cosmos

Having come to the end of this journey through some twenty societies and listened to what they have to say (or recently had to say) about the way babies are made, and having observed that ordinary humans and superhumans are not necessarily conceived in the same way, we must now disentangle from the mass of details a series of general theoretical propositions.

First of all we are obliged to say that *nowhere, in any society, do a man and a women alone suffice to make a child*. What they make together, in proportions that vary from one society to the next and with a diversity of substances (sperm, menstrual blood, fat, breath, etc.), is a foetus, but never a complete, viable human child. For this, other agents are needed, who are more powerful than humans, present in the vicinity but normally invisible, and who add what is lacking for the foetus to become a child. What is lacking is what we customarily call a soul, a spirit, in short a usually invisible component but one which is not necessarily immaterial, since the soul can reappear after death in the form of a 'ghost', which has a material, visible form but is usually intangible.

The agents cooperating with humans to make a child are of several kinds: deceased persons, ancestors, spirits, deities. The ancestors are deceased humans who continue to live another life beyond death and who choose to be re-embodied in one of their descendants. These ancestors are either known by name to the child's parents (Inuit), or are one of a stock of ancestors who carry clan names. Naming the child after a clan ancestor connects it with all those who have previously carried the name. Generally speaking, the child who bears the name of an ancestor does not start out in life with the memory of these existences, of all the experiences undergone by those who have borne the name. Alternatively, for the Inuit, because they are dealing with people who, prior to dying, designate the child in whom they wish to live again and to whom the child's parents, for various reasons, have promised to carry out their wish, the child is constantly reminded of the episodes in the life of the reincarnated person and is thus permeated by their experiences. In short, in many societies, the birth of a human being is not an absolute beginning, and death is not the end of life.

But the ancestors, too, are often not enough to make the foetus into a human child. Deities take a hand: for the Inuit, it is Sila, the master of the universe, who gives the child its breath and a soul; for the Baruya, it is the Sun, who adds the child's nose, eyes, fingers and toes. For the Mandak of New Ireland[1] – a society in which the descent rule is matrilineal and which is divided into two exogamous moieties, one under the sign of the Sun, the other under the sign of the Moon (who are both cross cousins and husband and wife) – when a human couple makes love, the two deities take part in the coupling. Moroa, the Sun, renders the man's sperm effective by depositing his own supernatural seed in the woman's womb at the same time. Sigirigem, the Moon, for her part, makes women fertile by bringing on their periods, and she accompanies the gestation of the foetus in the womb. Each of the supernatural parents then leaves its mark on the child's body, in the lines of its hand and in its gait. By these signs, everyone knows which moiety the person belongs to.

Finally, in all societies the child is a gift from the ancestors and/or the gods. The role of human beings is first and only to make a foetus. Among the Amazonian Canela, as soon as a woman realizes she is pregnant, she chooses several men as lovers to help her husband, by means of their sperm, make the foetus. Their sperm does not nourish the foetus. It makes the substance of its body. Generally speaking, the woman chooses her partners among the good hunters, who will later look after the child, bring it (and its mother) game and ensure them material and religious protection.[2]

Among the Cashinahua, another Amazonian society, the pregnant woman multiplies her sexual relations with several men, this time in order to nourish the foetus. When the child is born, the father is recognized as its father in the course of a big public ceremony.[3] The foetus becomes a child when it is brought to life by a soul, which comes from the child's ancestors. It is 'kinship', accumulated in the past and always ready to be put to new uses.

Quite often the life-breath is distinguished from the soul because it ceases after the person's death while the soul lives on. Furthermore, the breath is tied

---

1   The Mandak are another case of a matrilineal society in which sperm is believed to make the child's whole body substance (as for the Maenge), while the mother nourishes the foetus at the same time as she nourishes herself. She does not 'conceive' the child but nourishes and develops the foetus. In this society, children always look like their father, as in the Trobriand Islands.

2   See W. Crocker, 'Canela Other Fathers: Multiple Paternity, Its Changing Practices', Paper presented at the 49th international meeting of Americanists, Quito, 1997. Since the Canela became Christians, these practices have disappeared and monogamy has become the rule. See W. and J. Crocker, *The Canela: Bonding through Kinship, Ritual and Sex* (New York, Harcourt Brace, 1994).

3   K. Kensinger, 'The Philanderer's Dilemma', Paper presented at the 49th international meeting of Americanists, Quito, 1997; 'Hierarchy Versus Equality in Cashinahua Gender Relations', paper presented at the Wenner-Gren symposium 'Amazonia and Melanesia: Gender and Anthropological Comparison', Mijas (Spain) 1996. For the Cashinahua, the ideal marriage unites a man and two sisters; incest of the so-called second type therefore does not exist in this society, and the notion would be meaningless for them. Cf. K. Kensinger, *How Real People Ought to Live: The Cashinahua of Eastern Peru* (Prospect Heights IL, Waveland Press, 1995).

to the body, whereas the soul can leave the living body at night and wander at large before returning to the sleeper the next morning. For the Shuar, a Jivaro group, life-breath is a property of all living beings. For the Nzema, the man's sperm contains a life force (*mora*) which is distinct from the soul (*ngomenle*) and which goes back after the person's death to live with the ancestors in Ebolo, the land of the dead, before being reincarnated once more in a child. But the woman's blood also contains this life force (*mora*), and the child is not really conceived unless the life force contained in the man's sperm suits that of the woman. If it does not, the woman will miscarry.

According to the Azande, sperm and vaginal fluids, both designated by the same word, *nzira*, contain life forces placed in them by Mboli, a great god responsible for the birth of children. These life forces are linked to corporal substances, but the person also possesses a soul, which can detach itself from the body and which leaves it at the time of death.[4] The life force, source of movement, is thus rather a property of living human substances – sperm, blood – which combine to make a child. But, as in the case of the Azande, it can have been placed in these body substances by a deity.

As for the distinction between the soul (*anima*) and what the ancient Romans called *mens*, 'mind' (the intellectual part of the soul, the part that thinks and reasons), it is present in certain forms in the cultures that have been analyzed, but they usually have no theory about it. The Telefolmin, as we heard, were content to say that when a child grows up it is normal that he learns to talk and think. The difference between people and animals is that, although animals think, since they understand what we say, like the dog or the pig, they do not talk.[5] And yet some societies also offer an explanation for the origin of the human intellectual capacities that are called 'thinking' in the West. We will illustrate this point with an example from the Melpa, a group of tribes living in the New Guinea Highlands, which have been remarkably documented by Andrew Strathern.[6]

For the Melpa, the seat of thought is not in the brain but in a spot in the chest cavity near the trachea, the passageway of speech. It is a material entity called *noman*, but which remains invisible even if one opens the chest. It is also the seat of the desires and emotions connected with relations with others, with members of the community in which the person lives. The *noman* is in relation

---

4   E. E. Evans-Pritchard, 'Heredity and Gestation as the Azande See Them', originally published in 1932 in *Man* and reprinted in E. E. Evans-Pritchard, *Social Anthropology and Other Essays* (New York, Free Press, 1962), pp. 243–56.

5   The same idea can be found among the Melpa of New Guinea, but also among the Ashuar, a Jivaro group living in Equatorial Amazonia. Cf. A. C. Taylor, 'Remembering to Forget: Mourning, Memory and Identity among the Jivaro', *Man*, vol. 28 (1993), pp. 653–78.

6   We are summarizing the analyses proposed by A. Strathern in 'Keeping the Body in Mind', *Social Anthropology*, vol. 2, no. 1 (1994), pp. 43–53.

with the skin, the outside of the body, for emotions and desires mark themselves on the body, on the skin. Animals too have a *noman*, but they do not have the power of speech. The *noman* appears and goes on to develop throughout a person's life, but it does not survive after their death. In life, it is the most active part of the person, their 'prime mover' and the source of their self-control. But the *noman* receives its power from the *min*, a life force implanted in the foetus by the ancestor-spirits of the child's patrilineal clan and which remains tied to them by invisible threads that terminate in the child's head.

The *min* is not a reincarnated ancestor. It is an ancestral life force that changes into a soul when it is implanted in the body of one of their descendants. The soul then permeates the body.[7] The soul is also the person's shadow, their double, and can often leave during sleep or when the person is in the grip of a strong emotion. But the soul remains 'passive' with respect to the *noman*, for it is the *noman* that allows the individual to act on others and on him- or herself, and causes them to suffer the consequences of their decisions and actions.

Upon the person's death, everything changes: the *noman* vanishes, and the 'passive' soul becomes active. It changes into a *kor*, a spirit-soul, an ancestor, and begins a new, this time highly active life, mingling in itself the *min's* life force and something of the deceased's intelligence. The *kor* then connects itself with the still-living relatives. It sees into their *noman*, it knows their intentions, good or bad, and it sends them sickness or good fortune. In effect, the ancestors watch over, protect or punish their descendants, to whom they are permanently attached by the invisible threads of their *min*. The power of a deceased's soul is greater then than the power of this same soul when it was present, incarnated, in a living body.[8] The Melpa thus make a distinction between the soul and the mind without separating them completely, whereas their neighbours, the Daribi, use a closely related term, *noma*, to designate both the soul and the mind or thought. The soul can detach itself from the body, and at the same time it is the body's shadow. It is the source of thought, whose seat is mainly in the liver.

Andrew Strathern interestingly posits that the Melpa may have been led to distinguish action-thought (and emotion) from the soul (*noman* from *min*) because their life is strongly linked to the existence of a far-flung network of competitive ceremonial exchanges, *moka*, a fundamental institution that regulates matrimonial as well as military-political alliances throughout an entire region. People are thus involved in practices that require them to make *multiple political and ethical choices*, which is not the case of the Daribi or the Wiru, who live in much more inward-looking communities. From a certain standpoint, the

---

7   The first sign that the life force *min* is present is the kicking of the foetus.

8   See R. Wagner, *The Curse of Souw: Principles of Daribi Clan Definition and Alliance* (Chicago, University of Chicago Press, 1967), pp. 42–4.

Melpa *noman* represents that which is invisible in people, that which makes them responsible for their acts, unlike the substances that make their body, the bones and skin they share with their paternal and maternal relatives. Because substances are divisible, they can be shared, but at the same time, because they are divided and, coming from different sides, are found in the same individual, they make him or her partible and interlinked with those who contributed them. One thing should be made clear: for the Melpa, men and women, both sexes therefore, possess *noman*, but men's *noman* is 'stronger' than women's.

It would be interesting to compare these theories about the body, the soul, the mind and, finally, the person, with the Christian tradition that developed in the West, reshaping the Greco-Latin legacy. The topic is both vast and complex. Let us merely say that the Latins made a distinction between *anima* (the soul) and *mens* (the mind), and that they linked the *mens* to *anima* (life force and soul). Christianity would separate the mind from the soul and attach it to the spirit (*spiritus*). But the soul itself would become the work of the Holy Spirit.

As we have seen, the Christian body is born of the sexual union of a man with a woman, who become one flesh (*caro*). But the man and the woman only make a foetus. For this foetus to become a child, it needs a soul. The soul is introduced into the foetal body directly by the action of the Holy Spirit. How do Christian theologians see this action? I am indebted to Jean-Claude Schmitt for having indicated the existence of a twelfth-century miniature representing the vision that Hildegard of Bingen, a nun and great mystic, had of this sacred mystery.[9] For Hildegard, the soul is created by the Holy Trinity and comes down from heaven into the body of the foetus and enters its heart as a ball of fire: 'The foetus . . . she comments . . . is like a complete man who, by the secret command and hidden will of God, receives the Spirit in the mother's womb when something resembling a ball of fire, presenting no features of the human body, takes possession of the heart of this form.'[10] Hildegard then describes the struggles of this new soul against the devils that assail it, and its victory with the help of the angels. When a Christian dies, his or her soul is called back to God, its creator, and cannot be reincarnated in the body of a descendant. The soul will await the Last Judgement, when all flesh will be raised up and all souls will be reunited with their body before being admitted to Heaven or cast into Hell for all eternity. For Christianity, then, as for the religions of so-called 'primitive' societies, a man and woman do not suffice to make a human child. God must intervene, a god in three persons: the Father, the Son and the Holy Spirit. It was the Holy Spirit that created the

---

9   J.-C. Schmitt, 'Le corps en Chrétienté', in M. Godelier et M. Panoff (eds.), *Le Corps Humain. Supplicié, possédé, cannibalisé* (Paris, Editions du CNRS, 2009), pp. 339–53.

10   H. de Bingen, *Liber Scivias* (A. Fuhrkotter, 1978), p. 78; quoted in J.-C. Schmitt, 'Le corps en Chrétienté', p. 340.

304 THE METAMORPHOSES OF KINSHIP

body of a god become man in the womb of a human woman, Mary. Mary, dogma stresses, remained a virgin who had never had carnal relations with her husband Joseph or with God, her divine spouse. But for simple humans this is not how things work. They must have sexual intercourse in order to make a child, and therefore commit the 'sin' of the 'flesh'. In so doing, they unwittingly transmit the stain of Original Sin, committed by Adam and Eve when they disobeyed God and were driven out of the Garden of Eden where they had been immortal. Eve, who was made from Adam's rib, thus united with him, adding to her disobedience the sin of original incest. Condemned to unite in order to reproduce and to live only to die, the future of humankind lies in human hands: one day to return to Heaven or be sentenced to Hell. Henceforth the outcome now depends on their struggle with themselves against the flesh, in the name of the spirit, of reason. As in the case of the Melpa, the spirit has pride of place in the person, but instead of being content with bringing earthly success and happiness, it has the prodigious power to provide humans with eternal peace and happiness – but only after death.[11]

Another theoretical consequence we can draw from the above analyses is that, everywhere, even in societies where sperm does not enter into the child's conception (Trobriand) or, on the contrary, in those where the woman is simply a nourishing container for the child (Mandak), procreation implies that a man and a woman have sexual intercourse, whether in order for the sperm to keep the menstrual blood in the womb, or to open the way for a spirit-child, or to nourish the foetus: men and women must have sexual relations (and they expect them to have certain consequences for the making of the child that is in the woman's womb). *Making ordinary humans therefore in all societies normally supposes sexual relations*, whatever role the society attributes to given male or female substances in this process.

Of course, all societies accept the idea that certain children can be born without the woman having had sexual relations with another human being. These are exceptional births and they play a large role in the construction of these societies' political-religious universe, but they are not daily occurrences, not the general rule. Likewise, if, in the beginning, men could beget other men without the help of women (Mekeo), or women could, without the help of men, give birth to boys they would kill one after the other at birth (Trobriand), these

---

11 It is a caricature to say that the West is typified by a dualist vision of the person, opposing mind and body, and generally adducing Cartesian dualism as proof. In the West, the person is actually conceived as being composed of a body, a soul and a mind. Christians worry about the fate of their soul after this life, but its fate is dictated by the way people conduct their struggle between the flesh and the spirit. The spirit is that part of ourselves that accepts or rejects the word of God and his commandments. The soul seems to be relatively passive in this struggle, but in the end it is the soul that 'pays' forever.

times are past and can only be represented and relived occasionally through rites (Mekeo) or in male initiations (Baruya).

Regular access to socially legitimate sexual relations and reciprocal access to the body of the other are the usual benefits of being married. To be sure, this reciprocal access does not necessarily exclude sexual relations with partners other than one's spouse. Furthermore, the fact that a man or a woman is entitled to have sexual relations with their spouse is not directly connected with the descent rule, which determines the social identity of the children that will result from these relations and their appropriation by a given kin category.

It is even because the parents' reciprocal sexual access is independent of the social form of the children's appropriation that it forms the basis of the Oedipus complex. And because it is independent of any given descent rule, this basis is universal and suggests that the Oedipus complex is itself universal. If this is true, Malinowski was wrong to criticize Freud for having defined the Oedipus complex in such a way that it fitted only the structures of the 'patriarchal' conjugal family typical of Judeo-Christian societies in the West.[12] He asked Freud to come up with a broader definition of the Oedipus complex so that it might apply equally to societies with a matrilineal descent rule, because in these societies it is often the mother's brother and not the father who exercises authority and repression on the child. But the Oedipus complex is not built around relations of authority but around the child's relations with the man who has sexual access to the mother.[13] Even among the matrilineal Nayar, where the husband disappears three days after the wedding without ever making another appearance in his wife's life, the children begotten by the mother's lovers live out the Oedipal relationship with the men who have access to their mother's gendered, sexual body. The only known case where the child does not encounter, in the early years of its life, a man who has regular sexual access to his mother is that of the Na, a minority group of China. But Cai Hua, the anthropologist who has studied this society and described it for us, says nothing about the construction of children's identity, all of whom, boys and girls, are under the strict obligation never to talk about sex in front of their mother or her brothers.[14]

In all events, and for reasons the reader has now perfectly understood, the analysis of the connections between the system of kinship relations in a given society and its representations of the person cannot content itself with the information garnered about the role played by male and female substances in

12   B. Malinowski, *Sex and Repression in Savage Society* (London, Routledge and Kegan), 1927, Chapter 1.

13   A. Green, 'Inceste et parricide en anthropologie et en psychanalyse', in P. Descola, J. Hammel and P. Lemonnier (eds.), *La Production du social* (Paris, Fayard, 1999), pp. 213–32.

14   C. Hua, *Une société sans père ni mari. Les Na de Chine* (Paris, Presses Universitaires de France, 1997).

making a foetus. A person is never simply the sum of the substances that make him or her. All the components of a person's being, as they are listed and articulated in the thinking of the members of this society, must be taken into account; in other words, not only the body substances, but also the breath, the life force, one or several souls, and so on. Indeed, it is usually via the non-corporal components of a person's being – their soul, their name, etc., that they present themselves as a specific, particular and indivisible being.

In short, the world over, the individual exists as a whole, both divisible, partible, in virtue of the substances and other components they share with others, and indivisible due to their acting from a place that is not that of others and, given this place, being responsible for their actions and the social and moral consequences they have for others or for the person doing the acting. In reality, the representations of the diverse components of a person, of their appearance and combination at different stages in the process of conception, are the vectors of several different kinds of social relationships, which are stamped into the child's sexed body and embed it in the overall social and cultural fabric of the society in which it has just been born.

The Baruya child, whose body is finished in its mother's womb by the Sun, who makes its nose, eyes, fingers and toes, is thereby given a place in a *socio-cosmic whole* that extends beyond its place in the system of kinship relations. The child is the product of a god who protects all Baruya and acts on the body of each to give them a human form. This god is a local tribal god. The surrounding tribes may have other gods, of whom the Sun is not necessarily the greatest or does not have a direct hand in making a child. Among the Khumbo, through the 'principle of consciousness or mind', which is added to the clan-soul embodied in a child, an individual is given a place in a religious universe that extends beyond the boundaries of their local community. They will learn to see themselves through the lens of the Buddhist reincarnation cycle and the path that leads to enlightenment. Alternatively, if the child owes its soul to the Christian god, it will experience itself through the concepts of a religion with universal claims, which seeks to lift all of humankind out of the sin that has stained it from the beginning. *In short, in all of these ethnotheories of the person and the process of procreation, the individual is enrolled in a social whole (tribe, ethnic group, religious community) and a cosmic whole that extend beyond the universe of kinship relations.*

These relationships feature in the ethnotheories at two levels: in the role played in conception by living humans, the child's 'parents', and in the role ascribed to the distant or close relatives, persons who are deceased but still alive and active. They are the ones who reincarnate themselves (Nzema, Trobriand), or instil in the foetus a life force which will become the soul (Melpa). The action of these deceased relatives is added to and combined with that of the living parents, who make the body of the foetus with their body substances and/or the foods they provide.

As we have seen, by endowing either sperm or mother's blood with the primary role in making the foetus' body, these representations legitimize the later appropriation of the child by a group of adults, the father's relatives or the mother's relatives, etc. Accentuation of the role of one substance or another corresponds roughly to the nature of the descent rule followed in the society. But the correspondence is not always as direct as it is in the case of the patrilineal Baruya or the matrilineal Trobrianders. The descent rule is sometimes combined with another principle, as with the matrilineal Maenge, where 'relatives by the penis', the descent ties traced through men, play an important political role and have a specific name. Another example: the importance attached to the blood transmitted by the mother in a patrilineal society like the Paici of New Guinea corresponds to the importance of the role of maternal kin – and particularly the maternal uncle – in Kanak societies.

All of which serves to underscore the fact that the notion of consanguinity as it is used in Western societies – to designate the set of both paternal and maternal kin – is not universally applicable. The notion supposes that a child is one flesh and one blood with its parents. How can this proposition be made to tally with the Khumbo view of parenthood, in which the child's bones come from the father and its flesh and blood from the mother? The concept of 'consanguinity' is a legacy of the society and culture of the Latin peoples of the ancient Roman world. To be sure, it can be used as a tool of analysis to distinguish the set of paternal and maternal relatives from the set of relatives by marriage. Provided one ignores all of the representations and theories historically (and unconsciously) conveyed by this notion. But the difficulties will resurface when it comes to dealing with affinity in certain kinship systems and it is discovered that the privileged affines are very close consanguines (the 'Arab' marriage with the father's brother's daughter) or fairly close cousins (cross cousins in the first, second, third degree, etc.).[15] How, in this case, can we distinguish and more particularly oppose consanguinity and affinity? Except to say that there are consanguines one can marry and others one cannot. But then the difference is no longer one between relations of consanguinity and other kinds, since the difference between potential and forbidden spouses cuts through consanguinity itself.

15   See Claude Meillassoux's excellent overview of the usual criticisms anthropologists make of their colleagues who use Western kin terms without sufficient critical distance in 'Parler parenté', L'Homme, no. 153 (2000), pp. 153–64.

THE IMAGINARY DIMENSIONS OF BODY SUBSTANCES

But let us go a step further. For the matrilineal Trobrianders, a man is the child's father but not its genitor, since his sperm does not make the foetus but only nourishes it once it is made. For the Mandak, who are also matrilineal, it is the father's sperm that makes the child, whose mother is not its genetrix. The mother is a nourishing vessel in which the child develops and is nourished. For the Canela, the husband's sperm does not suffice to make the foetus. The woman chooses several men as lovers so that, together with the husband, they all make the foetus. Here the husband is not considered to be the child's sole genitor.[16] For the Cashinahua, the pregnant woman multiplies her sexual relations with several men, but this time with the aim of nourishing the foetus conceived by her and her husband; when this child is born, as we have seen, the husband is publicly recognized as the only father in a ceremony organized for this purpose.[17]

These facts allow us to affirm, on the one hand, the imaginary character of the roles ascribed to body substances and the overdetermination of some – sperm, blood, breath, etc. – and, on the other hand, the importance attributed to certain foods – and, generally speaking, to the fact of nourishing as part of the process of creating a kin tie.

Let us take the case of sperm. First of all we see that, in many societies, this substance appears as a subcategory of a more encompassing term: water. Sperm is penis water, and female secretions are vagina water (cf. Telefolmin, Baruya). For other societies, sperm is a variety of blood, just as female secretions are another (Kako). We can therefore not project onto all cultures the representation of sperm as seed, a notion found in the Christian West but also in the Muslim world.[18] In some societies, sperm comes from bone marrow and makes the bones (Khumbo, Samo), in others, it comes from what one eats, in particular certain varieties of sugar cane forbidden to women (Baruya) or from pork fat (Melpa).

We also saw that sperm can change into mother's milk (Baruya), but that elsewhere it is incompatible with the same milk (Melpa, Samo of Upper Volta), that it is destroyed by menstrual blood (Baruya, Melpa), or that it mixes with menstrual blood to make a baby (Kako). In still other societies it is used secretly, together with menstrual blood, in the initiation rites held for boys (Telefolmin) or for boys and girls, brothers and sisters initiated together (Kasua).[19]

---

16   Crocker, 'Canela Other Fathers'.
17   Kensinger, 'The Philanderer's Dilemma'.
18   C. Delaney, *The Seed and the Soil: Gender and Cosmology in Turkish Village Society* (Berkeley, University of California Press, 1991).
19   Cf. F. Brunois, *Le Jardin du casoar. La forêt des Kasua. Savoir-être et savoir-faire écologiques* (Paris, Editions de la Maison des Sciences de l'Homme, 2008).

The nourishing role attributed to sperm (Trobriander, Khumbo, Baruya, etc.) or to the mother's blood (Mekeo, Mandak) raises the general issue of the role of nourishing and of the necessity of ingesting certain foods in making kin. The most spectacular example is that of the Kanak chief: in order to make the chief into an ancestor, he was served yams grown from very old clones, clones that had been grown and transported by the group's ancestors. In effect, food acts as a mediator between kinship by birth and kinship by co-residence and commensality. For one does not become a kinsman simply by holding a meal from time to time for passing guests. One must live together with the owners of a piece of land, have received the right to use it, and *this land must carry within itself something of the substance found in its occupants.*

An example of this circulation of substances between land and humans is the idea that, as it decomposes, the flesh of the deceased fertilizes the ground, adds 'fat' to the land and becomes part of the cultivated plants that people will eat. An illustration of this way of thinking is provided by the Baruya. Before the Europeans banned the practice, the Baruya used to expose their dead on platforms under which they planted shoots of taro and plants used in rituals.[20] As the corpse decomposed the body fluids would run onto the taros, which were then transplanted into the different gardens of the deceased's relatives so that they might make their crops grow big and plentiful. So human substances fertilize the ground, but reciprocally, substances from the earth enter human bodies and make them fertile. We also saw that, when she realizes she is pregnant, a Mekeo woman stops working and is force-fed with boiled plants because they are supposed to make blood, and blood nourishes the foetus.

The same is true in Tonga, where women were force-fed during their pregnancy and while nursing. In both of these societies, maternal blood, as we have said, is believed to play a highly important role in making the foetus. In other societies, the production of sperm requires men to eat a special diet – pig fat and certain varieties of sugar cane. The picture would not be complete if we forgot that all of the foods recommended for making sperm stand in opposition to those that are forbidden because they would spoil the sperm, dry up the blood, etc.

---

20   Taro has been grown in New Guinea since ancient times, or at any rate before the South American sweet potato was introduced in the sixteenth century by Portuguese and Spanish navigators. The effects of the introduction of the sweet potato on the economy and other aspects of the social life of the inhabitants of New Guinea were so great that one can justifiably speak of an 'Ipomean revolution'. Cf. J. Golson, 'The Ipomean Revolution Revisited: Society and Sweet Potato in the Upper Waghi Valley', in A. Strathern (ed.), *Inequality in New Guinea Highlands Societies* (Cambridge, Cambridge University Press, 1982), pp. 109–36. See also J. Golson and D. Gardner, 'Agriculture and Sociopolitical Organization in New Guinea Highlands Prehistory', *Annual Reviews in Anthropology*, 19 (1990), pp. 395–417; P. Wiessner and A. Tumu, *Historical Vines: Enga Networks of Exchange, Ritual, and Warfare in Papua New Guinea* (Washington DC, Smithsonian Institution Press, 1988), Chapter 4, pp. 101–18, on the introduction of the sweet potato.

One does not become a relative because one is occasionally invited to tea or regularly invited to share a meal. One becomes a relative through what one eats, and what one eats partakes in the process of making the human body and social identity. Without beliefs in the circulation of substances between nature and humans, commensality would not engender kinship. Behind these various ways of becoming a relative, of becoming kin, there lies the same logic: kinsmen are those who share all (or certain) of the components of their being, or share access to the land that produces the foods that will enter into the composition of the body of a human foetus. Absent an implicit or explicit theory according to which things are both persons and objects, without the idea that substances can circulate from things to persons and vice versa, kin ties would not exist in some societies. But once such a theory exists, this transformation can be thought and considered to be 'real'. This is the case in Tonga, among the Melpa, and so on. In this event, the rules prohibiting sexual relations, and even more strongly marriage, with those who share by birth the same elements automatically apply to food kin. The incest taboo also applies to these relatives.

Furthermore, all of these substances belong to sexed bodies, to male and female bodies, and all of the social meanings with which these substances or other components are loaded are *social attributes* of the sexes, which turn the sexes into *genders* whose roles and statuses differ even though they are often regarded as complementary. But gender complementarity does not prevent the existence of basic gender inequalities, which give rise to relations of domination and subordination between individuals depending on their sex.

We have seen this in the Baruya society. Not only does the man's sperm make the foetus, it also changes into the milk that swells the breasts of nursing women. Sperm also restores women's strength when they lose blood when menstruating and giving birth. Sperm makes the flesh and the bones, the flesh that will fatten the land and the bones that will be placed in trees or rocks to protect the clan's hunting territories and gardens. In short, sperm is not only pressed into the service of kinship relations and the continuity of kin groups, the lineages placed under male authority. *Sperm is also at the service of men's general domination over the rest of the society and of the governing of society by men.* But to be effective in serving this cause, the sperm must be that of young men who have never had sexual relations with a woman, young virgin men. It is this pure male substance that will circulate among the successive generations of men, who thereby give each other life, a man's life. The sexual and symbolic practices that raise men above women and legitimize their power over them thus take the form of a new conception, of a second birth, this time the birth of men without the help of women. Sperm is thereby overvalued, not merely because it legitimizes the appropriation of children by the father's clan, but because it legitimizes the political-ritual supremacy of men over women, their right to represent and to govern their society by themselves, alone. This is not the same thing as representing their clan and preserving its lands, functions and knowledge in order to transmit them to their descendants. In order to dominate, the bodies of the dominant must be disjoined from the dominated; and their substances, their essence, altered. The Baruya practice of ritualized homosexuality brings about this disjunction and this transmutation. And since substances do not exist in isolation, the overvaluation of sperm has its counterpart in the devaluation of menstrual blood. It is this blood that makes women a constant source of pollution, a threat to men's strength, and to the social and cosmic order. It is understandable that, if Baruya women are themselves convinced that they carry this threat in their bodies, they can not help feeling responsible for the disorders that might arise if they did not properly manage the products of their body that could detach themselves and come in contact with other bodies – men's bodies, children's bodies.

Here we measure the stakes involved in representations of the body, and singularly those of the sexed body, of the body designed to engage in (hetero- or homosexual) relations with others. The Telefolmin provide us with an exceptionally clear demonstration of such stakes. The women have a secret model of procreation: they claim that it is their blood alone that produces the bones, and more particularly the bones of the Great Men, which the men venerate and which they secretly use in the rites designed to prevent the expected destruction of the world – rites from which women, precisely, are excluded because their menstrual blood is a source of pollution.

In other strongly ranked societies, like Tonga, it is the sperm of male commoners that is devalued, stripped of the power to give life, to the benefit of the spermatic breath of the Tu'i Tonga, the man-god who fertilizes all the women in his kingdom, whose importance is not denied in the aristocratic theory of procreation. On the contrary, this theory amplifies the women's importance by attributing to them the power to make the entire body of the foetus that develops inside them and will become a human child by the intervention of the divine *mana* of the Tu'i Tonga – the keystone, together with his sister the Tu'i Tonga Fafine, of the kingdom's entire political-religious structure. This example provides a particularly clear illustration of how the theories of the way humans are made are not linked exclusively to a society's kinship system, but also to the forms of political-religious power that characterize the society and serve to reproduce the relationships and institutions through which these powers are exercised.

In all events, we are obliged to note that these imaginary representations of the body – its substances, its organs but also its breath, its soul or souls, their functions and their human and/or superhuman origins – give rise to social institutions and symbolic practices that materialize them and are essential structures of the society in which people are born, become aware of others and themselves and, as a consequence, act on both themselves and others.

These representations are, I repeat, *products of the imagination* and *objects of beliefs*. No one has ever 'seen' menstrual blood turn into the flesh or the bones of a foetus. No one has ever 'seen' sperm turn into milk. No one has ever 'seen' a life force carried by the blood or the sperm, or 'seen' an ancestor spirit or the Holy Spirit take possession of the developing body of an embryo. All of these representations belong to the universe of thought, to the realm of mind-prod-ucts (*l'idéel*), which is part of reality (*le réel*). No scientific experiment can disprove or prove these views. They are 'givens', as beliefs are givens, even if they are sometimes contested – for example by women who are not convinced that their milk is their husband's sperm, or by male commoners who are not convinced that they are mere insects that will not have a life after death and that they owe the birth of their children to the fecundation of a man-god.

As products of the imagination cut off from any 'experimental' basis that might prove or disprove them, these representations have an arbitrary character (like the words of a language). Why is the seat of thought the liver in one culture, the heart in another, elsewhere an invisible organ in the chest and yet elsewhere the brain? There is always a reason – also imaginary – for these choices, and the number of possible choices is not infinite. It does not take long to count the substances, organs, etc., in short the parts of the male and female anatomy and physiology, that can act as a vehicle for these discourses and provide the 'proof' of these interpretations. However, a more complete inventory than ours still needs to be made.

But above all, the body, with all of its visible and invisible components, is each time placed (according to a determined symbolic code) at the service of the produc-tion and reproduction of both kinship relations and the political-religious relations that encompass them and together with them make up the sites and forms of power that dominate a society at a given time. For the stakes involved in these imaginary representations are neither imaginary nor purely symbolic. It is with reference to these representations that, depending on whether one is a man or a woman, a younger or an older child, one inherits or does not inherit land, one bears or cannot bear arms, one has access or not to the most sacred places of worship.

Let us sum what we have covered so far. All of these representations, all of these singular interpretations of the process of human conception fulfil an essential social function: that of inserting a not-yet born child into three relationships which at birth are stamped into and buried in both the child's consciousness and its body. The child will take its place in a socio-cosmic order: it will be a child of Sila, the Inuit master of the universe, who gives children their soul and breath; it will be a child of the Sun for the Baruya. At the same time the child will take its place in a network of personal relationships with a number of individuals who are close or distant, of both sexes and of different generations, whom the child will come to know as being 'related' to it in various ways, and who therefore have various rights and duties with regard to the child. And the child will 'belong' by birth to one or several kin groups depending on the descent rule at work in the society. Lastly, at the same time, its sex, male or female, will mean that the child is placed in advance in relations of superiority (or even domination) or inferiority (or even subordination) with regard to those of the other sex.

The representations of the way (ordinary or extraordinary) human children are made and their appropriation thus express and attest to a cosmic, moral and social, and sexual order. It is these three dimensions of the order (or disorder) that prevail in a given society that are imprinted in a person's subjectivity at birth and will become conjoined with the person on the basis of the place he or she occupies by birth in this society.

HOW SEX BECOMES GENDER

We have observed, then, in all of these societies a *two-fold metamorphosis*. Social realities that have nothing to do with kinship or sexuality – such as (shared or private) ownership of the land, succession to political and/or religious offices, the existence of a dominant class or caste – make their way into kinship relations, install themselves and co-opt those relations into their service, into the service of their own reproduction. But at the same time, these realities metamorphose into aspects of kinship. For example, among the Yako of Africa, each person belongs simultaneously to the father's and the father's father's, and so on, patrilineage, and to the mother's and the mother's mother's, and so on, matrilineage. 'Realities' that make up this society circulate within the kin groups engendered by these two descent principles: land is transmitted by the men in their patriline, while religious functions go through the women in their matriline. Material means of existence (land) and essential – ritual, for example – social functions are transformed into *attributes of the relationship* a person entertains with relatives on the father's or on the mother's side.

But the transformation does not stop there, since the person who inherits land will be the son but not the daughter, and the person who inherits the religious function will be the oldest sister and not a younger sister (Kako). In short, all of the attributes of kinship relations are ultimately redistributed among individuals according to their sex and their age, and are transformed into *attributes of their person in accordance with their sex.*[21] Sex becomes gender.

---

21   Our analyses concur with the findings of Thomas Laqueur, *La Fabrique du sexe. Essai*

Through this two-fold metamorphosis, all kinds of social realities distinct from kinship find themselves attached to and (in part) reproduced by certain kinship relations before ultimately being vested in sexed bodies where they begin to *signify* the difference between the sexes, and give this difference a social meaning. We immediately see the incredible ideological work the human mind must do to enable the references to 'bone', 'blood', 'sperm', 'breath', and so on, to take on two functions complementary to the exercise of kinship: first, to legitimize the exclusion of certain categories of kin, close or distant, from access to land, titles, etc., in short those elements of social life that other relatives are going to inherit and that must be transmitted to them; and second, to establish the way the relatives that do inherit must use their inheritance and transmit it to following generations. Kinship thus finds itself compelled to attach certain rights and duties to relations of fatherhood, motherhood, siblingship, etc., and to exclude others, and to state the reasons for this in the language of kinship. That is why certain anthropologists, like Leach, have been able to claim that kinship is merely a language always used to talk about other things, about land ownership, for instance, as in Pul Elya. But Leach missed the essential point. The language of kinship is inevitable in so far as, from a person's birth, kinship relations are a source of rights and obligations that precede any contract this individual will later enter into during his or her lifetime. The great strength of kinship is that it embeds these rights and obligations in relationships between persons, between categories of persons and other categories of persons, in relationships which, for some, are intimate, nurturing, protecting and which provide the primary material and social support that greets the person at his or her birth.

From this standpoint, then, kinship is the site where the individual's appropriation of society and society's of the individual is prepared and begins. It is first of all within kinship relations that each sexed body begins, at birth, to operate as a ventriloquist's dummy for its society.

THE SEXED BODY: A VENTRILOQUIST'S DUMMY

All of our analyses point to one basic fact. *In all societies, sexuality is placed at the service of a number of realities – economic, political and religious – that have nothing to do with the sexes and sexual reproduction.*

We have seen that kinship relations are the privileged site where, from birth and directly, the first social control is exercised over the individual's sexuality, over the sexual drive that attracts them to persons of the opposite

sur le corps et le genre en Occident (Paris, Gallimard, 1992). As we show, we can no longer separate the analysis of kinship relations from that of gender relations. For an example of this two-pronged approach, see Jane Fishburne Collier and Sylvia Junko Yanagisako (eds.), *Gender and Kinship: Essays toward a Unified Analysis* (Stanford, Stanford University Press, 1987).

sex as well as that which draws them to persons of the same sex. This subordination of sexuality to realities that have nothing to do with the sexes is *not* the subordination of one sex to the other; it is the subordination of one domain of social life to the conditions of reproduction of other social relations. At stake is the place of this domain in the overall *structure* of the society, even before all of the personal relations of kinship between concrete individuals, in which persons stand face to face as father, mother, son, daughter, husband, wife, friend, enemy, master or slave.

This 'impersonal', as it were, and general subordination of sexuality is the starting point of a mechanism that stamps into each person's innermost subjectivity, into his or her body, the prevailing order (or orders) in society which must be respected if the society is to reproduce itself. The machinery works through representations of the body and the person, and of the role ascribed to each of the sexes and other agents in the process that ends with the birth of a child, with life. It is through these representations that the social and cosmic order is incised in the innermost person; furthermore, these same representations ensure not only the child's appropriation by those adults regarded as its parents and relatives but also the child's place in society as dictated by its sex.

Through these representations of the body, sexuality not only attests to the order prevailing in the society but also testifies that this order must continue to prevail. And it not only testifies but also testifies in favour of (and sometimes against) the order that reigns in society and the universe, since the universe itself is divided into male and female. For in all of the societies we have described, it is the person's sex that forms the identity of a body and the similarity or difference between individuals. Alongside flesh, blood and bones, which everyone possesses, there are some organs (penis, clitoris, vagina, breasts) and substances (sperm, menstrual blood, milk) that not everyone possesses. But where do the bones, flesh, breath and soul themselves come from? From the father? The mother? The ancestors? The gods? And which ancestors? The man's, the woman's? Which gods? And who invokes them?

In short, everywhere bodies and gender work like those ventriloquist's dummies that are hard to muzzle and which speak to an audience they cannot see words that they themselves do not utter. Like these dummies, sexuality of course cannot speak. Speaking goes on inside it. Someone speaks through it. But who speaks? And why there? For it is precisely to the extent that sexuality is forced, beforehand, into serving as a language and legitimizing realities other than itself that it becomes a source of fantasies and imaginary worlds. It is not sexuality that fantasizes about society, however, but society that fantasizes about sexuality. *It is not sexuality that alienates, but sexuality that is alienated.*

Here we touch on an essential point of social logics. These fantasized representations of the body are usually *ideas and images* shared for the most part by both sexes, which sum up and encode the social order and inscribe its norms in each and every body. It is this sharing of the same representations and their embodiment that, *beyond language*, seal a way of thinking and a given society into the body of each individual, thus making it a source of 'obvious truths' about the social and cosmic orders. From being alienated, sexuality goes on to become an instrument of alienation. Ultimately, when a Baruya woman sees the blood running down her thighs, she can no longer object to her fate; she knows she is guilty, she feels her guilt and, as a consequence, feels responsible for whatever happens to her. We now understand why sexuality is lived as something that can, at any time, challenge and subvert the order of society and the universe. And that is why it is hedged about with so many taboos.

These representations of the body are ideas, and these ideas are rooted somewhere beyond language, in both the conscious and unconscious mind. It is from there that they derive their meaning. But this meaning does not spring from vacuous thought or thought that has been reduced to its formal structures. It is the work of a mind turned toward social and cosmic realities, of a mind less concerned with expressing these realities than with organizing them, even producing them. But the body, too, surpasses what language can express. Ultimately, if everything buries itself in the body and if everything in it is masked or disguised, consent to the prevailing order and to the other culminates in silence. All a person has to do is live his or her body. He or she knows what can or cannot be done, what can be desired or what must be shunned.

In every society, representations of the body draw a sort of ring of social constraints around the individual, a mental ring that tightly encircles the person, a ring that is the very shape – paradoxically an impersonal and anonymous shape – of the individual's intimate inner subjectivity. It is in this anonymous form of personal intimacy imposed on the individual at birth and which already organizes its encounters with others that the child will begin to experience desire for the other. Whereas the child has already been appropriated by others, by its relatives, their social group, and so on, it is spontaneously going to want to appropriate them in turn. That is when the child will discover that it cannot appropriate everyone, that some – father, mother, sisters, brothers, etc. – are off limits to his desire. Sexuality as a 'desiring machine' is confronted with itself as a 'talking machine', a ventriloquist's dummy, which speaks on behalf of society. This is the source of the fantasized figures, which necessarily spring from our sexual nature. It is here that two opposing imaginary displacements and two symbolic productions occur. For society burrows in and hides here, disguised in the imaginary representations of the body. Desire, which has been repressed but has not disappeared for all that, buries itself in the body, beyond conscious awareness, only to resurface elsewhere, in 'respectable' forms and activities, betraying itself occasionally by a slip of the tongue and feeding as much on personal successes as on personal failures in society. In short, *sexuality conceals itself as much as it conceals, and it is this ambivalence that structures it.*

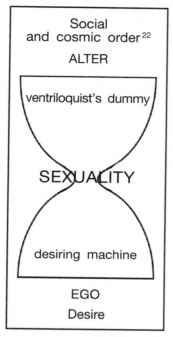

In the end, what the incest taboo stamps into the individual is not only that sexuality must submit to the reproduction of society. It is more basically that *it must be placed in the service of the production of society.* But for that, part of the spontaneous polytropism and (hetero- and homosexual) polyvalence of desire must be amputated. This is the insurmountable law that the many forms of incest taboo imprint into each individual. Partial amputation does not mean destruction of the individual, though, but rather promotion to the state of true human being, to humankind's generic being, which is not only to live in society but to produce society in order to live. It is from sexuality and its subordination that humans have in part drawn this energy and this capacity. From here, we should be able to say more about the nature of the unconscious.

---

22 See M. Godelier, 'Inceste, parenté, pouvoir', ibid., pp. 33–51.

CHAPTER TEN

Incest
(Sixth Component)
And a Few Other Misuses of Sex

In all societies, a certain number of uses of sex are formally prohibited because they are believed to endanger the reproduction of society – if not of the universe itself. Among those things that are forbidden are sexual relations with certain kin categories, with corpses, with animals; and the list is not exhaustive. Incest, necrophilia and zoophilia are variously disapproved and sanctioned, depending on the society and the time, necrophilia often being considered even worse than incest, and incest worse than zoophilia.

In all three cases, the criminal character of the act lies in the fact that persons or species that should be kept separate have united sexually. And the reasons advanced are the same throughout the world, based on the same logic. These species should be kept separate either because they are too different from each other (the case of humans and animals, or the living and the dead) or, on the contrary, they are too alike (the case of relatives sharing the same blood and/or sperm, or the same soul or name, or even the same food taken from the same land). In short, the proper uses of sex lie between these two extremes, between too different or too alike. Following the same principles, sexual relations, and even more so marriage, are also forbidden between persons from different ethnic groups, different religions (Christians and Muslims), from different castes (Brahmins and weavers) or from different classes (nobles and commoners).

But alongside these forbidden sexual unions and marriages, all societies have other prohibitions, this time on certain sexual practices, on acts that defile the person or persons who engage in them, whether or not they are married, whether or not they are related, or are from the same caste or of the same sex. Among these, I will cite sodomy (between men but also between a man and a woman), fellatio (between men but also between a man and a woman), cunnilingus (between women but also between a man and a woman), masturbation (solitary or collective), etc. The book of Leviticus lists an edifying inventory. Confessors' manuals formerly used by Catholic priests provide another, equally remarkable list.

Of course these various sexual practices are not condemned everywhere, and when they are, they do not have the same meaning or the same gravity. For Christians, for example, masturbation is a 'venial' sin which God easily forgives in exchange for penance and a few Our Fathers and Hail Mary's imposed by the priest, and a promise to do everything in one's power not to begin again. This is not the case for the Iqwaye of New Guinea.[1] For them, masturbation is an anti-human act that is as serious as incest, it is even incest taken to the extreme. In effect, masturbation is tantamount to having a sexual relation with oneself, to acting as though oneself were someone else. And to commit incest is to have sexual relations with a relative who shares the same identity as you, the same substance, the same breath, even the same soul, and so on. In a certain manner, it is copulating with oneself and consuming oneself. Masturbation, for its part, is a clear case of auto-sexuality. And the Iqwaye forbid boys to masturbate because their sperm does not belong to them. It belongs to the other initiates. The same goes for the Baruya.

But things are even more complicated in the case of the Iqwaye. They believe that humans were created by a cosmic being, Omalyce, a giant who filled the cosmos and held his penis in his mouth, ingesting himself and regenerating himself through this auto-fellatio. One day Omalyce decided to create some human beings in his own image. He made five men from the soil and insemi-nated them through the mouth with his sperm. But the fifth son had been made without a penis, and after having been inseminated by this father, became preg-nant. When the time came for the child to be born, his body, which had been closed up, split open and a vagina formed there where his brothers had a penis. For the Iqwaye, the woman's body is therefore a man's body on the inside, and her vagina is a slit made in a phallic body. Women can thus now make children with their bodies, but, unlike men, they cannot inseminate either men or women. And the Iqwaye regard the foetus in a woman's womb as a sort of penis. Men, on the other hand, can both inseminate men and re-engender them without the help of women through the male initiation rites. This means that male homosexuality, far from being condemned, is here a fundamental social act. When they orally inseminate the young boys who have just been separated from their mother, the oldest initiates, who have not yet had sexual relations with a woman, are repeating Omalyce's primordial act when he created men in his image and gave them life through the mouth, just as today the older initiates inseminate the young boys who tomorrow will in turn inseminate the new batch of younger boys. The life-bestowing male substance flows uni-direction-ally from generation to generation, since co-initiates are forbidden to have sexual relations with each other, and a younger initiate is forbidden to insemi-nate an older boy. This semen originally flowed from the body of Omalyce, the first cosmic man, and will disappear only when the Iqwaye disappear.

---

1   See J. Mimica, 'The Incest Passions: An Outline of the Logic of Iqwaye Social Organization', Part 1, *Oceania*, vol. 61 (1991), pp. 34–58 and Part 2, vol. 62, pp. 81–113.

In short, in this society, this form of male homosexuality – practised without the possibility of reciprocity[2] between young men having never had contact with a woman's vagina and its humours and the boys born from the womb of these women – is regarded as the best use a man can make of his sexual organ. It is a life-giving use, since it re-engenders men without the help of women, and it is a use that brings pleasure. Ritual homosexuality is here considered as indispensible for making a complete human being of the male sex. It stands in opposition to heterosexual relations. The ideal situation would be that homosexual relations sufficed to make a child and that it would no longer be necessary for a man to unite sexually with a woman. Unfortunately this is an inaccessible ideal, and so men must be content to create their own world, of which they are not a little proud because it is for them the proof of their superiority to women and of their right to represent and govern society. Around the age of twenty, the young man will be compelled to leave the men's house, marry and confront the dangers to which the women's world, and particularly their sexual organ, will subject his strength.[3]

I would like to emphasize that this world without women that the young man leaves in order to marry is, in fact, literally haunted by the forbidden presence of women. It is built with respect to and against women. And it is no accident if, in the men's house, the relations between inseminators and inseminated, between older and younger boys, are analogous at once to the hierarchical relations between elder and younger brother and to those between husband and wife.[4] The younger boy is subjected to all sorts of vexations by the older companion and all of the latter's co-initiates, compelled to perform all manner of jobs for him, much like a wife. The homosexual relations between men thus reproduce within this male space the hierarchical relations between the sexes and

---

2 Sperm-takers are not givers.

3 Among the Baruya, who belong to the same cultural and ethnic group as the Iqwaye, once married, men regularly have their wives drink their semen, initially during the first weeks of marriage (their sperm is said to fill their wife's breasts with the milk she will give their children), and then each time the woman menstruates or gives birth, in order to replenish her strength. For the Iqwaye, mother's milk is produced by the spinal cord, which makes women's milk and men's sperm. But the spinal cord is produced by the bones, and it is the man's sperm that makes the child's bones and skeleton. Once again, women's milk ultimately starts out as a male substance.

4 The disgust sexual relations with women arouse in Baruya men is so great that, after talking about the subject, they spit on the ground and purify their mouth by sucking on the fruit of a tree that grows in the forest, a flat brown disc that they carry with them all the time. In addition they use coded language women are not supposed to know about when speaking about such things. For instance, the word for penis (*lakala*) is replaced by the word *mwatdala*, which designates a variety of flat-tipped arrows used to kill birds without damaging their feathers. But this strong repugnance for talking about sex does not keep Baruya men from taking great pleasure in telling dirty stories. Cf. M. Godelier, 'Pouvoir et langage. Réflexions sur les paradigmes et les paradoxes de la "légitimité" des rapports de domination et d'oppression', *Communications*, no. 28 (1978), pp. 21–7.

between the generations, both between consanguineal kin and between husband and wife.

In other New Guinea societies, like the Kasua or certain groups in the Sepik, the initiation of boys entails their being sodomized by the married adults in charge of the rituals. For the idea of fellatio is repulsive to the Kasua, just as sodomy is to the Baruya and the Iqwaye. Thus male homosexuality is not everywhere the same.

But let us come back to the misuses of sex. There are others, of course, such as having homo- or heterosexual relations in a sacred place, on the altar of a god, on the tomb of an ancestor or a saint, in certain parts of the forest or the mountain that are the dwelling-places of usually benevolent spirits, and so on. Adultery and sexual relations outside of marriage with partners who are married or not, are frowned on and often sanctioned against. Finally, the most serious misuse is sexual relations imposed by violence on non-consenting persons, whether or not they are related, or of the same or opposite sex, in short: rape. Nor should we forget in this inventory certain positions of the body, certain gestures, words and of course looks, in sum, all of the signs that betray or serve forbidden desires.

In the end, we find ourselves confronted with a veritable sea of sexual taboos, of which incest is merely a specific case that, often, weighs more heavily than others on individuals and on society but which is inseparable from it, something we too often forget. Such a sea of prohibitions attests to the universal subordination, in varying degrees and forms to be sure, of sexuality (and therefore of bodies) to the reproduction of society. But we should not forget that the reproduction of social relations implies, in all periods and (almost) all societies, the reproduction of human relations with other actors, who are invisible but present and active: the dead, the spirits and the gods. It was not until the mid-nineteenth century that 'nature' began to be substituted for the gods and ancestors to found the sexual taboos, and that reasons of a scientific order (or more often appearance) began to be advanced to explain them. When it came to incest, the biological, genetic consequences that repeated – and even occasional – unions between close blood relatives would necessarily produce were advanced, but this explanation would not account for forbidding unions with relatives by marriage. Today we know that these negative consequences, if indeed they exist, are in no way the direct effect of consanguineous unions. Such unions merely reinforce and transmit already existing defects – but they do not create them.[5]

---

5   A. Langaney and R. Nadot, 'Génétique, parenté et prohibition de l'inceste', in A. Ducros and M. Panoff (eds.), *La Frontière des sexes* (Paris, Presses Universitaires de France, 1995), pp. 105–26; L. White, 'The Definition and Prohibition of Incest', *American Anthropologist*, no. 50 (1948), pp. 416–34.

These multitudinous sexual taboos are always accompanied by a profusion of forms of repression, from simple mockery or sarcasm to painful execution. And for the reasons we have just mentioned – namely: that relations between humans also go through their relations with the spirits and the gods – we understand that, to the punishments inflicted by humans in the name of God (the stoning to death of women convicted of adultery in Islamic law) or the gods, many societies add the fear of the punishment that the gods or ancestors might inflict, punishments that would be visited on the culprits – but also on their close relatives or even on their whole community. Drought or torrential rains will wipe out the crops, the women will become barren, the towns of Sodom and Gomorrah will be destroyed by fire from on High. The social order is not only a moral and a sexual order, it is also, through and through, as I have said, a cosmic order. And therefore the reasons invoked for forbidding and repressing these sexual practices are usually at the same time social, moral and religious (cosmic), in other words real and imaginary together and at the same time.

The imaginary we are talking about is not that of individual fantasies. It is a socially shared imaginary made up of collective representations that are the object of beliefs, crystallized in institutions and staged and enacted in symbolic practices understood by everyone. For in order to describe imaginary realities and show that they 'explain' and therefore legitimize the many prohibitions everyone encounters in daily life, for thousands of years humanity had no other recourse but to produce myths capable of providing the necessary and sufficient proof a culture needs to share the self-evident beliefs that have the force of truth and are embodied in symbolic practices, in rites that provide them with a tangible, concrete existence. It is this visible, concrete existence that will in turn indisputably attest to their 'truth'. We thus see that these imaginary 'explanations' are not merely an 'interpretation' of social reality, a 'mental' (*idéel*) reality that exists only in the mind and through the mind. They produce social reality at the same time as they explain it. It is for this reason that the analysis must both take them fully into account and account for them. But because these explanations refer to imaginary realities and are themselves imaginary, they are always somewhat arbitrary. And because they refer to entities – gods, goddesses, spirits, ancestors' words – which exist only as mental productions, prohibitions and sanctions are obvious and forceful only in so far as the mind that thinks them and the society that obeys them continue to find them meaningful.

Having taken these theoretical precautions, we will now tackle the question of incest, comparing several cultural universes, selected from a variety of societies on different continents, in an attempt to circumscribe the forms of sexual and matrimonial union that are forbidden between persons related by blood and by marriage, and of different or the same sex, for these unions are not everywhere necessarily considered to be 'incestuous'.

Another remark is called for here. Sexual taboos and prohibitions on marriage are two separate domains which overlap only where sexual taboos directly prohibit marriage. It is obvious that the prohibition on masturbation or on coupling with an animal do not necessarily or directly entail prohibiting marriage with a given person. But it is also obvious that, if heterosexual relations are forbidden between individuals because they are related or because they belong to different ethnic or religious communities, or to different castes or classes, the consequence, if not actually the raison d'être, of these prohibitions is to prevent these individuals from marrying each other.

Indeed, except for particular cases – for instance marriages of convenience in the West or fictitious marriages among the Nayar – why get married if sexual intercourse between the spouses is subsequently forbidden? For, as we saw in preceding chapters, whatever the kinship system and descent and marriage rules, whatever the roles ascribed to sperm, menstrual blood, the soul, etc., in making children, the overwhelming majority of societies think that marriage or its non-ritualized equivalent – living together, for example – implies that two persons of opposite sex, who are entitled to do so, unite sexually, and if children are born of their union, that they have specific duties and rights with respect to them. We will return below to the case of same-sex 'marriages', between women, as among the Nuer, or between men, as among the Azande. The cases of societies that practise fictitious marriages, like the Nyar, or that do not have marriage at all, like the Na, will also be examined.

I felt it necessary to begin the comparison of the definitions and cultural extensions of incest by an analysis of the Christian kinship system. For two millennia, Christianity shaped and dominated Western social representations and practices in the area of sexual relations and of authorized or forbidden, or even proscribed, marriages. Let us remember that, even if the various European civil codes of law did not adopt a certain number of marriage prohibitions defined by Christianity when they were created in the nineteenth century, Christianity nevertheless continued to provide the cultural backdrop for Western societies and to hover on the horizon of the codes even when they stood in opposition.

INCEST IN THE CONSTRUCTION OF CHRISTIAN KINSHIP IN THE WEST

It is impossible for us to understand the Christian representations of incest that spread to all Western societies beginning in the High Middle Ages and which still hover in the background of the 'secularized' conceptions of incest and marriage if we dissociate them from the Christian conception of marriage. This form was gradually worked out between the fourth and the twelfth centuries, when marriage was finally made a 'sacrament' and was added to those of baptism and communion. The process began in Byzantium, spread to Rome and ended, in addition to the transformation of marriage into a sacrament, in the progressive multiplication – up to the twelfth century as well – of the number of prohibitions on marriage, affecting not only blood relatives and relatives by marriage but also spiritual relatives through baptism – godparents. In the thirteenth century a movement began in the opposite direction, namely the progressive decrease in the number of prohibitions on marriage, a process that extended into the twentieth century.

The word 'incest' comes from the Latin *in-castus* and qualifies an act, a relationship or a person that has become 'impure' through a forbidden use of sex. This impurity defiles not only those persons who caused it, but also those close to them, their neighbours and friends, and even the places where the acts were committed. In Christian tradition, the defilement that attaches to persons owing to their acts is that of sin. What then are the sexual acts between opposite-sex relatives that are a sin and forbid their marrying?

In order to understand the link Christianity has established between sex, sin and marriage, we must go back to the passage in the Bible in the book of Genesis, which the Catholic Church used as a basis for the elaboration of these ideological constructions. In this passage, Adam comments on the birth of Eve, whom God has just created from a part of his body without Adam or God engendering her through a sexual act: 'This at last is bone from my bones, and flesh from my flesh! This is to be called woman, for this was taken from man. This is why a man leaves his father and mother and joins himself to his wife, and they become one body [or in some translations "one flesh"]' (Genesis 2: 23–4).

This is the dogma of *una caro*. When they join sexually, a man and a woman form a single body, which will also be that of their children. This dogma would determine the list and evolution of all of the incestuous sexual relations. But before continuing in this line, let us look at the nature of the tie the Christian religion establishes between sexuality and sin. The matter begins with Saint Paul, who, in his Letter to the Ephesians, alludes to this passage in Genesis to define the bond between husband and wife (Ephesians 5: 32). It will be quoted by all theologians.

Because Eve was engendered by God, Adam and Eve are the example of the perfect marriage, since they share the same body and the same spirit without uniting sexually. But when she urged Adam to eat of the fruit of the tree of knowledge, Eve broke this perfect union of body and spirit, causing them to be disjoined, thus giving rise to the opposition and the struggle between the soul and the body. Driven out of Paradise, Adam and Eve come together, sexually this time, and from their incestuous couplings the first ancestors of all humankind would be born.

The 'Fall', as it is known, thus made human sexuality into a source of lust, of sin, and at the same time brought death into the world. Humans in effect ceased to be immortal, as Adam and Eve had been before being driven out of the earthly paradise. Since that time, humans have transmitted this original sin, generation after generation, and no one can stop it happening, since it is propagated by the very act that enables humans to engender other humans, by sexual union.

From then on, to free oneself from sin and return to the path of salvation, every man and every woman was going to have to be re-engendered a second time, by God and the Church, and thus acquire new parents that were not defiled by a sexual relation like that which brought about their birth, parents joined to the child by pure spiritual ties: the godfather and the godmother. This second birth is brought about by the sacrament of baptism (followed, in the Catholic Church, by 'confirmation' when the child reaches the age of reason), and must be maintained throughout the person's life by the practice of confession, a sacrament which each time allows the soul to be reborn cleansed, as it were, of its sins.[6] The sacrament of baptism is performed by a rite during which, as Anita Guerreau-Jalabert describes it:

> The godfather, in the name of the community, presents to the priest a new member begotten carnally, so that, by means of ritual action, he may make the child a son of God and of the Church, that is, a fully fledged member of the Christian fellowship (Christianity, parish, and so on). Again in the name of the community, the godfather receives the newly engendered Christian from the baptismal fount. The priest thus plays a key role that is indispensable in the social birth of a child, and the community cannot reproduce itself without his mediation.[7]

Birth, marriage, death: the Church now presides over and dominates all of the major moments in a person's life, and thereby a share of the society's reproduction. Spiritual parenthood is moreover explicitly defined by the Church as being superior to real parenthood, because, for centuries in the West, there would be no social recognition of filiation between parents and children outside of baptism. Children born out of wedlock were bastards and often were not baptized. But baptism, confirmation and marriage are not enough to ensure Christians salvation. They must also regularly communicate with God through the sacrament of the Eucharist, founded on the sacrifice of a man-god who died

---

6   A. Guerreau-Jalabert, 'La désignation des relations et des groupes de parenté en latin médiéval', *Archivuum latinatis*, vol. 46–7, no. 46 (1988), p. 101.

7   A. Guerreau-Jalabert, 'Spiritus et caritas. Le baptême dans la société médiévale', in F. Héritier-Augé and E. Copet-Rougier (eds.), *La Parenté spirituelle* (Paris, Archives contemporaines, 1995), pp. 170–203.

on a cross[8] to save humanity from its sins and to whom he gives his body as food: 'This is my body, take it and eat', and 'Do this in remembrance of me'. At last, having taken all these sacraments, having lived in the love of God and neighbour (*caritas*), good Christians are promised a glorious resurrection at the end of time, when the soul and the body, separated by death, will be reunited and will go to sit at the right hand of God.[9]

This brief survey does not exhaust the special features of Christian marriage, which, in the space of a few centuries, led the newly converted Western societies to break radically with their traditions and their past, and increasingly to differentiate themselves from the surrounding societies of southern Europe and the Mediterranean Basin. In the majority of the ancient societies surrounding the Mediterranean – with a few exceptions such as ancient Rome – marriage with close, and even very close, relatives, such as the agnatic younger sister in Athens or the uterine younger sister in Sparta, was authorized; common-law marriage, divorce and the remarriage of widows and widowers were frequent; adoption (including that of adult men) was common practice. But beginning in the fourth and fifth centuries, Christianity gradually developed and imposed on all converts another form of marriage, which has become the Christian marriage.

This form was founded, in principle, on the consent of the spouses, both of whom must have been baptized either as adults or, from the fifth century, at birth. Marriage would little by little become a sacred bond uniting the spouses for life, which would result in the prohibition of both divorce and the remarriage of widows and widowers. Last of all, the Church would oblige everyone to choose his or her spouse among those persons situated beyond a very large number of degrees of kinship with respect to Ego, such that any remote trace of consanguinity would have disappeared. To this was added the prohibition of adoption in the event of a sterile union, a marriage without children. In the end, when marriage became a sacrament in the twelfth century it definitely ceased to be an act that joined first of all and directly the spouses and their families and occurred within the family; instead it became a vow taken by a man and a woman in the presence of God, outside the home, in a sacred place – one of the many churches or basilicas that had been erected throughout Christendom to celebrate its god.

But marriage is not only this spiritual union. It must be consummated, in other words must be followed by the carnal union of the spouses, by a *copula*

---

8   The crucified Christ, when he is represented naked, which is rare, is shown without a sexual organ. Cf. J.-C. Schmitt, 'Le corps en Chrétienté', in M. Godelier and M. Panoff (eds.), *Le Corps humain, supplicié, possédé, cannibalisé* (Paris, Editions du CNRS, 2009), pp. 339–53; pp. 347–8.

9   Cf. Schmitt, 'Le corps en Chrétienté', p. 346. Jean-Claude Schmitt is referring here to the work of C. W. Bynum, and in particular to *The Resurrection of the Body in Western Christianity, 200–1336* (New York, Columbia University Press, 1995).

carnalis. Without this carnal bond, Christian marriage does not fully exist and, as a consequence, can be annulled. In all events though, the children born of this sanctified carnal union must be baptized in turn, because *the parents' carnal union transmits to their children, without the man and the woman being able to do anything to prevent it, the stain of original sin.*

In short, Christian marriage presupposes a close connection between the body and sin, owing to the fact that the sexed body, because of its desires, emotions and lust, is the site and the instrument of sin. This was already definitively accepted by Christians from the time of Saint Augustine, at the start of the fifth century. But at the same time, Christian doctrine asserts that, if the flesh is docile to the spirit and the spirit to the word of God, the flesh can become, as Tertullian already asserted in the second century, 'the hinge of salvation'.[10]

This is a rough summary of the ideological field in which incest was rethought and redefined as Western Christianity developed over the millennia. Its redefinition was based, as we have seen, on a principle that the Bible traces back to Adam: when a man and a woman (married or not) come together sexually they form one flesh, a single body.

Once established, this principle would enable the extension to affines of a large number of the sexual and marriage taboos that formerly applied to Ego's close and distant consanguines. Because for a married man his wife becomes his flesh, and his flesh becomes one with his wife's, and because his wife's sister and his wife are also one flesh, his 'sister-in-law' becomes as his sister. The same goes for a woman, for whom her husband's brother becomes as her brother, her husband's father as her father, and so on. As a result, for a man, all of his affines' consanguines (AC) – wife's brother, sister, etc. – have become (equivalents of) his consanguines, as have his consanguines' affines (CA) – brother's wife, sister's husband, etc. The cultural postulate which holds that the sexual joining of a man and a women means that they form a single body results, in the Christian conception of sexuality, in turning all close affines into consanguines and subjecting them to the same sexual and marriage prohibitions as 'real' consanguines.

If we use AC to designate affines' consanguines and CA to designate consanguine's affines, we obtain AC = C and CA = C, or, if we use the sign $\approx$ to indicate equivalence between two kinds of relation: $AC \approx CA \approx C$.

In short, translated into abstract terms, the *una caro* principle defines and condemns as incestuous any sexual union, and marriage in particular, that brings together two beings who are identical or too similar to each other because they share the same flesh. And this shared identity (in the Christian vision of incest) has gradually been extended to relatives connected to Ego by ties of

---

10   See Schmitt, 'Le corps en Chrétienté', pp. 339–56.

consanguinity or affinity that over the centuries have become increasingly distant from Ego.

The starting point for the extension of the number of degrees of kinship that would prohibit individuals from uniting sexually, on pain of committing incest, is located in Byzantium. The Eastern Church, in effect, adopted Roman law, which, an exceptional event in the Mediterranean Basin, forbade marriage between consanguines to the seventh degree (by Roman calculation),[11] in other words up to and including first cousins (children of siblings); the same indications apply to affines. From the end of the seventh century, the Church adopted the method of calculating used by the Germanic populations, which calculated consanguinity by generation instead of by degrees. The passage from Roman calculation to the 'canonical' mode had the effect of doubling the number of degrees forbidden, since the 'canonical' seventh degree corresponded to the Roman fourteenth degree.

Peter Damien justified the number seven by the fact that 'it is also in six ages that the history of the world unfolded and that the life of humanity reached its fulfilment', and also by the fact that 'the power of nature itself enables brotherly love to be fully savored until the sixth degree of kinship and diffuses, as it were, an odor of natural community'.[12] Let us recall that it was only in the twelfth century that marriage ceased to be a 'profane' institution and became a sacrament. But in 1215, in view of the difficulties in getting married engendered by these prohibitions, which affected the noble or royal families[13] as well as the peasants and commoners in village and urban communities, the Lateran Council reduced the number of prohibited degrees from seven to four. This time another argument was advanced to justify the number of prohibited degrees, adducing that the body is made up of four elements and four humours, which means that incest extends to that degree. By the end of the twentieth century, the interdiction would apply only to cousins in the first degree. What happened in between? Might it be that the Word of God changed? Might it be that the Church doctors gradually came to understand better?

We are not competent to answer these questions, but without too much risk we can advance the hypothesis that these extensions and reductions of the field of application of marriage prohibitions for fear of incest have never drawn their reasons exclusively from the religious and symbolic universe in which these

---

11   See F. Héritier, *Two Sisters and Their Mother: The Anthropology of Incest* (New York, Zone Books, 2002), pp. 90–1; see also, by the same author, *L'Exercice de la parenté* (Paris, Gallimard/ Le Seuil, 1981), pp. 180–2.

12   Quoted by B. Vernier in 'Du nouveau sur l'inceste? Pour une théorie unitaire', *La Pensée*, no. 318 (1999), p. 78. See also Héritier, *Two Sisters and Their Mother*, p. 232.

13   Hugh Capet wrote to the pope complaining: 'We cannot find a spouse of equal rank, because of the affinity between us and the neighboring kings' (quoted by F. Héritier in *Two Sisters and Their Mother*, p. 97).

prohibitions were decreed but from that of necessity: Western societies had changed, and they needed to adapt to new social demands. Now, if it has been shown that the appearance of new social relations, and therefore new social demands, has led to the evolution and sometimes even disappearance of certain sexual and matrimonial taboos framed in religious terms, it is therefore in the social demands linked with prohibitions on sexual relations between relatives that the roots of these prohibitions must be sought – unless we think that the religious explanations advanced are sufficient in themselves and evolve automatically. We will return to this point.

But before we do, let us say a word about the third domain to which the Church extended the incest taboo, that of relatives by baptism, of relations between 'spiritual' kin. The Church would use the same principle of *una caro* to forbid sexual relations and marriage between a godfather and the mother of his godchild. And it is their union in God, their kinship of the soul through the sacrament of baptism that will forbid a godfather to marry his goddaughter.

As early as the sixth century, the Justinian Code (530) forbade marriage between a godfather and his goddaughter:

> A woman should, by all means, be prevented from marrying her godfather who received her in baptism whether she is his foster-child or not, as nothing else can be so productive of paternal affection and just prohibition of marriage as a tie of this kind, by means of which, through the mediation of God, the souls of the parties in question are united.[14]

And since the baptized child is one flesh with its parents, the godfather cannot have sexual relations with his godchild's mother. Vice versa, since the godfather's wife is one flesh with him, the godson cannot have sexual relations with her, and so on. Between the sixth and the twelfth centuries, in a manner similar and parallel to the extension of taboos on sexual relations and marriage between consanguines and between affines, prohibitions applying to spiritual kin also multiplied. In the twelfth century, this extension came to an end when it was suggested to prohibit marriage between the children of the godfather and the brothers and sisters of the godchild. The proposal was rejected because the spiritual kin tie between godfather and godchild concerned only the godchild received by his godfather into the Christian community. The godchild's siblings were in need of other 'godparents' to present them for baptism. The prohibition concerning the godchild could therefore not apply to his or her siblings.

---

14   Codex Justinianus V, 4, 20, quoted by Guerreau-Jalabert in *La Parenté spirituelle*, p. 184; see also Codex Justinianus: http://webu2.upmf-grenoble.fr/Haiti/Cours/Ak/Anglica/CJ5_Scott. htm#5.

I would like to stress an important point. If, from Carolingian times, the physical parents of a child could no longer be their child's spiritual parents on the pretext that they were the ones who in begetting the child had also transmitted the stain of original sin, it seems that there was never a prohibition on a sexual relationship between the child's godfather and its godmother. For, while each united spiritually, but separately, with the baptized child, their participation in the same rite of baptism did not create a spiritual tie *between them*.[15]

We have come full circle. Just as, through the carnal union between a man and a woman their affines become (the equivalent of) consanguines, so spiritual kin, through the spiritual union that binds them to their godchildren from the time of their baptism, become (the equivalents of) consanguineous relatives with whom sexual relations and marriage are henceforth forbidden. In short, step by step all these kin categories become in a certain way 'identical' (or nearly). All are reduced to equivalent forms of more or less close consanguineous relations. And since sexual union of same with same is forbidden, there is, from one end of this chain to the other, only one single principle at work. In the Christian vision of incest, therefore, there is only one kind of incest, incest between consanguineous kin, which extends to all categories of kin defined as equivalent to consanguines. In short, in Christian kinship, there is no room for incest of the 'second type', as defined by Françoise Héritier and to which we will return shortly.

In conclusion, let us recall that Christian kinship was implanted and diffused in the West in societies in which there were most often no (or no longer) kin groups based on unilineal descent principles (clans, lineages, etc.) and where undifferentiated, cognatic forms of kinship prevailed. In such systems, relatives on the father's side and those on the mother's side count almost equally for Ego and define his or her identity. Kinship relations were therefore increasingly centred on individuals born to monogamous families which the Christian prohibition on divorce compelled to endure until 'death us do part'. By multiplying the number of degrees of kinship constituting an impediment to sex and marriage, Christianity therefore obliged each person to seek their spouse at a great distance and forced families not to repeat their alliances for several generations. The prohibition on marrying one's wife's sister or one's husband's brother after the death of the husband or wife were in the same line.

This vast expanse of sexual taboos and marriage prohibitions stretching out around each Christian was thus engendered gradually, and it justified the combination of a *very special cultural interpretation* of the sex act as fusing into a single flesh, a single body, the man and the woman and a *religious* conception

---

15   See Guerreau-Jalabert, *La Parenté spirituelle*, p. 169, where she quotes Saint Thomas Aquinas: 'Since no spiritual relationship results between godfather and godmother, nothing prevents husband and wife from raising together someone from the sacred font' (*Summa theologica*, suppl. 9, LVI, a, 4).

of sexuality as being marked by *original sin*, and therefore as defiling and a source of defilement endangering humans' relationship with God and with each other. These ideas were already found in various Near Eastern mythologies and religions, and Christianity took them on while foregrounding the idea that the sexed body is defiled because it bears the mark of original sin from birth and because sex itself is a continual incitation to sin, to defile one's soul and turn away from God, the Creator, whose son died on the cross to redeem our sins.

In taking over and reworking these notions, Christianity also concluded that the only proper use of sex that was respectful of God and useful to humans is procreation, not pleasure. But carnal union in the service of procreation was permitted to only those men and women previously united by the sacrament of marriage. Finally the proper Christian use of sex came down to three simple, but hard-to-practise, rules: no sex before marriage, no sex outside of marriage, no sex after marriage for those who survived their spouse.[16]

And since the only legitimate use of sex was to make children within the family, the Church logically condemned sexual relations between an unmarried and unrelated man and woman (called fornication) and of course homosexuality, zoophilia, necrophilia – and generally speaking all practices designed purely for pleasure (masturbation, sodomy, cunnilingus, etc.).

Such is, roughly summarized, the ideological and cultural legacy Christianity left to Western societies and which has formed the context for modern thinking about incest and other breaches of the sexual code. But the development of Western societies since the Late Middle Ages has brought about all manner of changes – economic, political, scientific – which have deeply altered the nature and importance of kin ties and groups. Big kindreds – lineages, houses – have disappeared, leaving in their wake networks of kin more closely related to the individual and nuclear families. Following the French Revolution, civil marriage became the prevailing form in many European societies and was even often the only legally recognized form. People no longer need to get married, because cohabitation is recognized and the children of a cohabiting couple are also recognized. Divorce is allowed and widely practised. Church baptisms, marriages and funerals, in many European countries, have become a private affair. And yet it was not until the twentieth century that the civil codes of law began seriously to modify the list of marriage prohibitions.

---

16   One can understand why these many prohibitions that formed a close-knit web around individuals and families and whose infraction was heavily sanctioned by the Church (fasting, celibacy) might pose a problem for both aristocratic or royal families, who around the year 1000 were divided into 'lineages' and 'houses' concerned with extending but also reproducing their alliances, and for commoners concerned with marrying someone of their own rank in their local, rural or urban community. For more on these points, see J. Goody, *The Development of the Family and Marriage in Europe* (New York, Cambridge University Press, 1983) and *The European Family: An Historico-anthropological Essay* (Oxford/Malden MA, Blackwell Publishers, 2000).

Until then, the French and British codes of law, and those of many other countries, had implicitly or explicitly carried over a large portion of the prohibitions of marriage between consanguines in direct line or close collaterals and between (close) affines that had been established in previous centuries in the context of the Christian kinship system. It was not until 1907 in England that a man was allowed to remarry with the sister of his deceased wife, and only after a legal debate that had begun in 1842. In France, it was in 1914 that a man's marriage with his sister-in-law was authorized while his wife was living if he and his wife had divorced.[17] In short, something happened in the West that progressively eroded the Christian view of marriage and sexual relations.

For a portion of humankind living in Western societies, then, Christian symbolism has lost a large share of its meaning and its repressive force. Even if its dogmas and symbols still mobilize a large number of believers, some of them are living in a world that no longer has anything in common with the end of Antiquity or the Middle Ages.

The modern world, which Christianity has done little to shape and which it has proved incapable of bringing around to its ideas and rituals, as it did with feudal society, rose from the industrial and urban revolutions of the nineteenth century, which gave rise to Western capitalism. It was the capitalist social and economic system that created a partially 'disenchanted' world, to use Max Weber's expression, and which has, over the past two centuries and more, increasingly influenced the evolution of the family and kinship in the West. This impact alone is proof that the appearance of truth and the social effectiveness of symbols and dogmas are not only in the mind.

Whatever the fate of Christianity in Europe and in the parts of the world Christianized by Europe, one can not help but admire a theoretical construction that, by defining affinity and consanguinity as equivalent, managed bit by bit to reduce all forms of kinship to a single one and all forms of incest to a single type, that committed by closely related persons of the opposite sex: father–daughter, mother–son, brother–sister, etc. The focus on heterosexual relations was emphasized because only they were capable of engendering new lives, but homosexual relations were just as severely condemned between same-sex consanguines (and affines) as being against nature and divine law, which meant for sex to be used exclusively for the reproduction of the human race.[18]

---

17   A good summary of the recent evolution in French and English law on these points can be found in Héritier, *Two Sisters and Their Mother*, pp. 100–20.

18   As we know, Margaret Mead was probably the first to draw anthropologists' and sociologists' attention to the existence and importance of homosexual incest. In 1968, in her article 'Incest', published in the *International Encyclopaedia of the Social Sciences* (New York, Macmillan, 1968; vol. 7, pp. 115–22), she wrote: 'The prevailing emphasis on incest taboos as they are related to

Before leaving the Christian West to see how incest is conceived in other non-European and non-Christian societies, let us again pause and summarize what we have learned from a theoretical standpoint. By now the reader must be aware of the very particular character, culturally speaking, of Christian representations of human sexuality and marriage. By representations, I mean the ideas, concepts, judgements, images and symbols concerning sex and marriage, as well as the positive and/or negative values attached to the different types of sexual unions and acts.

The core of the Christian vision of kinship and the family lies in the combination of two ideas: the notion of *una caro* and the representation of sexuality as the vehicle of original sin.

When a man and a woman unite sexually, they are no longer two but one flesh, which will also be that of their children. One can well imagine the astonishment of a Baruya man at the thought that, when he makes love with his wife, he becomes her flesh and she his. He who thinks that his sperm alone makes children and nourishes the foetus and that, with the help of the Sun, who completes the foetus in the mother's womb, he is the main human producer the child. The idea of one flesh makes no sense to him and even contradicts his own representations and values. Or imagine the reaction of a woman in the Trobriand Islands if she were to learn that, when she unites sexually with a man, his blood becomes her blood, whereas the only blood that flows in the body of both men and women is women's blood, *dala*, which comes from the female ancestor who founded their matrilineage.

In this case, one understands the resistance and even repugnance felt by these men and women when missionaries – both Catholic and Protestant – opposed their conceptions of sex and marriage on the pretext that they were false, and instead tried to substitute their own doctrine of *una caro* and monogamous marriage.

For Christians, sex bears the mark of the original sin committed by the first couple, Adam and Eve, for all eternity. It is therefore the source not only of defilement, but also of sin. And parents unwittingly transmit this original sin to their children, even when they are begetting a new life.

---

the regulation of marriage has resulted in an almost total neglect of homosexual incest' (p. 115). Françoise Héritier, who cited this passage in the introduction to her book *Two Sisters and Their Mother*, unfortunately attributed them to Reo Fortune, who had published a short article entitled 'Incest' in a similarly titled but entirely different work, the *Encyclopaedia of Social Sciences* (New York, Macmillan, 1932, vol. 7, pp. 620–2); however this article made no mention of homosexual incest. This error was all the more surprising as Héritier, after having attributed Mead's phrase to Fortune, declared: 'Fortune's remark triggered my own inquiry into the possibility of incest of a different nature, between same-sex blood relatives who are not homosexual but who share the same sexual partner' (p. 12).

Imagine a Baruya's astonishment at the idea that, when his parents engendered him, they transmitted a sin that they themselves had not committed but which was committed by the first human couple on earth. For the Baruya, it was Kouroumbingac, the first woman, who invented everything – bows, arrows – and she alone who has the power to make children (without men). But Kouroumbingac used and misused her powers. She killed too much game with her weapons and sowed disorder in the universe. The men were compelled to steal her powers and confiscate the sacred flutes, which thereafter enabled them to give new birth to boys without the help of women. In this cultural universe, sex is a source of disorder because it defiles and pollutes beings, things and places. It is a threat to men's strength and power. It sows discord between and within clans. But in no case is sex a sin.

In a religion based on sin, one is guilty even before one is responsible. In the Baruya religion one is responsible before one is guilty. When they stole the women's sacred flutes and their powers, the Baruya's ancestors, the men from the Dreamtime, did what they needed to do to re-establish order in the society and the cosmos. At no moment does the Baruya's moral and religious conscience refer back to an original guilt – one that only penance and the grace of a god could redeem.

In 1956, more than thirty years before the original publication of Françoise Héritier's *Two Sisters and Their Mother*, which would at last raise the same questions, Jack Goody showed, in a remarkable article, the interest and the need to look beyond the West, to forget the artificial unity of the Christian representation of incest and seek to discover how this problem is formulated elsewhere. And scarcely seven years after Claude Lévi-Strauss published the original version of *The Elementary Structures of Kinship* (and Evans-Pritchard, *The Nuer*), Jack Goody had demonstrated that the thesis of the incest taboo as the condition for the exchange of women and the establishment of alliance relations could not account for all of the sexual taboos subsumed in the West under the word 'incest'.

Lévi-Strauss' theory of incest explains why a brother should not unite with his sister and even less marry her, for that would deprive him of the possibility of exchanging her for someone else's sister. But it by no means explains why, once a man is married, he cannot have sexual relations with his wife's sister. Before the marriage, both sisters were *equally* eligible, and therefore were outside the field of forbidden unions. Once one of the two sisters was married, however, the other became sexually off-limits for her brother-in-law and not eligible to marry him. This was something the theory of 'sister exchange' could not explain.

Had Jack Goody looked not at Africa but at Australia, dear to the heart of Lévi-Strauss, he would have found many examples of societies divided into marriage sections, and sometimes subsections, where all men in section A are potential spouses of women in section B, and in which custom has it that a man who has married a woman from B has the right to have sexual relations with his wife's real or classificatory sisters – because they are all classified as wives. In this cultural universe there is no fear of transferring the wife's vaginal humours to the body of a real or classificatory sister, no prohibition on bringing identical substances into contact and thus unleashing a social storm or a cosmic catastrophe.

Yet, despite its cultural singularity, the Christian conception of marriage and incest contains one apparently universal element. The term incest designates sexual unions that are prohibited between two persons (of the opposite but also the same sex) because they share a component that is essential to their being, whether tangible (sperm, breath, blood, bone, flesh, milk) or intangible (a soul, a name, etc.). And they share this component either because they received it from common ancestors – close or distant, real or classificatory (the case of incest between consanguines) – or because they acquired it through an alliance (incest between affines). The meeting and in some cases the potential combination of these identical components present in their body is an impediment to these individuals uniting sexually on pain of serious consequences for themselves, for their close relations and for their friends and neighbours, as well as for the overall order of society and the universe, and also on pain of sanctions inflicted by humans or by the ancestors, or by the spirits and the gods. But this does not tell us in advance what, in any given culture, the component is that, when shared by two individuals, would cause them to be committing incest if they were to unite sexually.

There are societies – as we shall see when we look beyond Christian or secular Western societies to peoples like the Na – where until now, for the majority of the population (with the exception of chiefly families connected to Chinese imperial power), marriage does not exist. And without marriage, there are no affinal relations and therefore no sexual taboos concerning affines. Sexual prohibitions in these cases concern only consanguines – or at least those linked to Ego through the female line, since, in this husband-less society, there is no father either. Incest therefore applies only to relations between brothers and sisters, as well as to sexual relations between consanguines belonging to different generations – mother–son, uncle–niece, aunt–nephew, mother–daughter, uncle–nephew, etc.

Other societies, as we shall also see, made still different choices. For instance, the ancient Egyptians, far from forbidding sexual unions between brothers and sisters, as the Na do, encouraged them, hence the large number of brother–sister marriages found in the archives of pharaonic Egypt, but also in Hellenized   Egypt,   since   the   Greeks   living   in   Egypt   had   also adopted brother–sister marriage. Not everything can be explained by the idea that Egyptians were imitating their pharaoh who, the product of a divine incest between Isis and Osiris, had to marry one of his own sisters. And they were not the only ones. The Inca also married his sister, as did certain Polynesian paramount chiefs. And in Africa among the Lovedu, the queen of the Rain kingdom was supposed to marry one of her brothers. To be sure these last examples concern exceptional human beings who belonged to the world of the gods or were closely related to them. But this was not the case with the Iranians who, until the eleventh century, used to marry their sisters in compliance with the precepts of the Mazdean religion.

Of course for those who do not share their beliefs, these kings and queens were human too, and crediting them with a higher, divine essence is a matter of the organization and functioning of their society. In order for these societies to function, then, the prohibitions on incestuous unions had to apply to the majority of ordinary humans but not to the minority of extraordinary humans. Prohibition *and* non-prohibition of incest thus operated as complementary principles necessary to these societies' functioning, and taken together they shed light on the rites and practices and the reproduction of these societies.

We now clearly see in what sense it is legitimate to speak of the universality of the incest taboo. It is a highly relative universality; and when it comes to formulating a theory, we have no right to set aside societies like the Na, the Nayar, the Egyptians, etc., as exceptions. There is perhaps one sexual union that is forbidden in all human societies: that between a mother and her son. But this remains to be verified.

FIRST TRIP OUTSIDE THE WEST: INCEST IN ASHANTI SOCIETY

The aim of Jack Goody's work was precisely to show the ethnocentricity of the concepts anthropologists used when talking about incest, the family, etc., and to point out the difficulties that were created when – as is the task of anthropology – one sought to compare different social and cultural logics at work in human societies.[19] Goody began by recalling that, for Europeans, the concept of incest applies indifferently to consanguineous and to affinal kin, because, when they marry, 'the spouses are assimilated into each others' natal groups and there is no distinction in this context of heterosexual offenses, between group members and group spouses'. Here we recognize the consequences of applying the *una caro* principle, which makes my wife's sister a sister (-in-law). But what

19   See Jack Goody's pioneering article, 'A Comparative Approach to Incest and Adultery', *British Journal of Sociology*, vol. 7 (1956), pp. 286–305.

about societies where there are kin groups (clans, lineages, etc.) stemming from the application of a unilineal descent rule, since such a rule simultaneously acts on internal family structure and creates gender-based differences of social status. Only the women transmit descent in a matrilineal system, and only the men in a patrilineal system.

As his first example, Goody chose the Ashanti, a matrilineal society of ancient Ghana, studied by Robert Rattray and Meyer Fortes.[20] If the Ashanti apply the matrilineal descent principle for the transmission of some components of the person's identity and for the sharing of some rights, they also give importance to descent traced through men, so that an Ashanti belongs to a matriclan through his or her mother and to a patriclan through his or her father, though the first carries greater weight than the second. The Ashanti classify (heterosexual) offences and crimes in two categories. In the first, crimes whose judgement demands intervention of the central authority, the chiefdom, and which are punished by death or banishment. These are called *oman akyiwadie*. In the other category they place all of the misdemeanours and offences judged and punished by the elders of the domestic group (*efiesem*). Here is the list of sexual crimes and misdemeanours as Goody reconstructed it.

TABLE OF SEXUAL CRIMES AND MISDEMEANOURS IN ASHANTI SOCIETY			
Terms used	*Nature of the crimes and misdemeanours*	*Judge*	*Punishment*
Mogyadie = 'to eat one's own blood'	Sexual intercourse with a woman from one's matriclan (*abusua*), with one's uterine sisters, with one's half-sisters by the same mother, or with one's mother	The chief and his representatives	Death
Atwebenefie (1) = to possess 'vaginas too close to home'	Sexual intercourse with members of the same patriclan (*ntoro*), among which relations between father and daughter	The chief and his representatives	Death or expulsion from the matriclan

---

20   R. Rattray, *Ashanti* (Oxford, Clarendon, 1923); *Religion and Art in Ashanti* (Oxford, Clarendon, 1927); and *Ashanti Laws and Constitution* (Oxford, Clarendon, 1929). M. Fortes, 'Parenté et mariage chez les Ashanti', in A. R. Radcliffe-Brown and D. Forde (eds.), *Systèmes familiaux et matrimoniaux en Afrique* (Paris, Presses Universitaires de France, 1953), pp. 330–72.

Baratwe	Sexual intercourse with a woman in a state of impurity or menstruating	The chief and his representatives	Death
Di obi yere = to eat a man's wife	Sexual intercourse with the chiefs wife, raping a married woman in the bush	The chief and his representatives	Death
Atwebenefie (2) = 'vaginas too close to home'	Sexual intercourse with a) wives of fellow matriclan members;	The elders of the domestic group	Special fee
	b) wives of fellow patriclan members	–	–
	c) wives of members of a military company in the vicinity	–	–
	d) wives of members of a local guild	–	–
	e) affines' consanguines, wife's mother, wife's sister, etc.	–	Payment from husband to wife
Di obi yere (2) = 'to eat another man's wife'	1) To make love in the bush with:	–	
	a) an unmarried woman		Ridicule
	b) with a married woman	–	Adultery fee
	c) with one's own wife	–	Ridicule + 1 goat
	2) Sexual intercourse between chief and a subject's wife	–	Special compensation
	3) Sexual intercourse between a master and a slave's wife	–	Compensation
Di obi yere (3)	Sexual intercourse with a married woman who does not fall into any of the above categories	–	Ordinary compensation for adultery

It is immediately obvious that here we are not in the cultural and social universe of the Hammurabi Code nor in that of the Bible or the Christian kinship system.

The Ashanti use different words for mother–son incest, which involves two people having the same blood, and for father–daughter incest, which involves two people from different matriclans but the same patriclan. The matrilineal descent rule thus profoundly separates intrafamily kinship relations that the West places in the same category of consanguineous kin. For a man, his daughter is the closest relative of all the women who do not belong to his matriclan, but she does not share the same blood. No *una caro* here. She is the 'closest vagina' of all the vaginas around him and who are close to him because they are the wives of his fellow matri- and patriclan members. If, to make things easy, we group these two categories of women (daughter and mother) into the Western category of consanguines (which they are not for the Ashanti), we can say that the taboos concern (maternal + paternal) consanguines (C), and these consanguines' affines (CA), but also the affines' consanguines (mother-in-law, sister-in-law) (AC). Missing are my affines' affines (AA), who would be consanguines in Australia or Amazonia. But African systems are neither section systems nor Dravidian systems, and are therefore not closed upon themselves.

Note that sexual relations with wives of fellow members of one's own matriclan or patriclan are judged by the authorities of the domestic group and not by the central power. They do not involve the society as a whole and are punished moderately. These taboos concern the brother's wife, the sister's husband, and so on. At the bottom of the list, a man's sexual relations with his wife's sister or mother (the paradigmatic case of Françoise Héritier's incest of the second type – i.e. an indirect sexual relationship between two persons of the same sex by the intermediary of a common partner of the opposite sex), far from being a 'primordial incest' for the Ashanti, are an 'incest' that does not involve one's own blood and are treated, according to Robert Rattray, much in the same way as Europeans would treat adultery.

It should also be noted that the Ashanti punish two kinds of sexual relations by death; these do not entail kinship relations but hierarchical ones: those between humans (sleeping with the chief's wife) and those involving the gods (raping a married woman in the bush and thus offending the Earth spirits, who can either grand good harvests or make the fields barren).

Crimes against the gods, crimes against the chief, crimes against the clan, crimes against one's allies, crimes against unrelated men whose wife one takes. In short, the Ashanti classification of misuses of sex is strictly embedded in their social relations, and the hierarchy of punishments that sanction infractions clearly reflects this. Incest, as we think of it here in the West after two thousand years of Christianity, does not exist for the Ashanti. They do recognize several types of sexual crimes, one of which is close to what we mean by incest: having sexual relations with 'blood' relatives, but this concerns only maternal kin and not relatives in the paternal line. Sexual relations between relatives from the same patriclan are also punished by death because something of each person's identity is also transmitted through the male line. But for the Ashanti there is no such thing as 'mixing' bloods, substances, etc. Different realities combine in each person, but they are transmitted separately, the ones in the *abusua* (matriclan) and the others in the *ntoro* (patriclan).

It must be stressed that sexual relations between a father and his daughter do not always result in death, but sometimes in the banishment of the guilty party – not from the patriclan that links the father and the daughter, but from the matriclan to which the father belongs but not the daughter. It is as though the crime the man committed with his daughter defiled all members of his matriclan, all those who share the same blood with him: his mother, his sisters, his maternal uncles, his brothers, his uterine nephews, and so on. In short, we are dealing with a type of incest that is different from mother–son or brother–sister incest; we are dealing with an incest of the second type. This crime is classified altogether logically in the category of the prohibitions on using 'vaginas that are close and even too close', because a man's daughter contains something of himself which positions her between the women of his father's matriclan and those of his own matriclan. It is because his daughter is not from his matriclan that intercourse with her is *atwebenefie*. And it is because she possesses something of himself, since she belongs to his patriclan, that the crime tops the list of *atwebenefie* crimes and is punishable either by death or (which shows the lesser degree of gravity with respect to incest within the matriclan) with expulsion from his own matriclan.

It is altogether curious to read in *Two Sisters and Their Mother*, that the father–daughter relation is an incest of the second type for the Ashanti because the 'maternal substance is fully present in the daughter' and that, therefore, by making love with the daughter and the mother, the father would bring the mother's substance in contact with itself, since the mother and the daughter share the same substances.[21] This is untrue from the ethnological standpoint, since the daughter contains something that the mother does not and which her father transmitted to her. And if we have properly understood the logic of the crimes of incest of the second type, the daughter and the mother would be the ones guilty of this incest, and it would be up to their matriclan to cleanse this stain. And yet it is the father's matriclan, the matriclan of the man, the husband, which banishes the culprit or calls upon the powers of the chief to put him to death.

---

21   Héritier, *Two Sisters and Their Mother*, pp. 142–3.

It should be noted that, in the example Françoise Héritier has chosen to demonstrate the existence of a secondary type of incest – sexual relations between a man and his wife's mother and/or sister – the Ashanti sanction this relationship with a light punishment: the man must give his wife a present to beg forgiveness. We are a long way from the primordial mother–daughter incest, the basis of all taboos, source of trembling, etc., as Françoise Héritier depicts it in the final pages of her book.

Jack Goody[22] then went on to compare the Ashanti with another matrilineal society, made famous by Malinowski: the Trobriand Islanders of Papua New Guinea. Unlike the Ashanti, the Trobrianders have only one unilineal principle and not two. There are therefore no patriclans, and the punishment for a man having had sexual relations with his daughter is very different. As we know, Malinowski believed that the bilateral family was the basic building block of all societies, and for him, incest occurred 'within the family' and was 'a breach of exogamy'.[23] As Goody observed, given this definition, the term *suvasova*, which the Trobrianders used to designate incest, should have covered a man's sexual relations with his mother or his sister within his birth family, and with his daughter in the family created by his marriage. But Malinowski was obliged to admit that the Trobriander term *suvasova*, which he had translated as 'incest', applied only to a man's sexual relations with his mother and his sister (this being the most heinous kind of incest) and not to relations with his daughter: 'It must be clearly understood that, although father to daughter incest is regarded as bad, it is not described by the word *suvasova* (clan exogamy or incest), nor does any disease follow upon it; and, as we know, the whole ideology underlying this taboo is different from that of *suvasova*.'[24]

Goody went on to note that the concept of *suvasova* was the exact counterpart of the Ashanti concept of *mogyadie*, but he said nothing about the fact that sexual relations between father and daughter would result only in reprobation and not in illness or some other plague sent by the ancestors and the gods, as in the case of a man's committing incest with a woman from his own matriclan. In fact, the punishments were different because in Trobriand society the father did not share any substance with his daughter, which was not the case in Ashanti society. For Trobrianders, a child's body is entirely made from its mother's blood (*dala*) and is brought to life by a spirit-child (*baloma*) that was a male or female ancestor from the woman's clan who had come to lead a new human life in the child's body. The father's role was merely to shape the foetus and to coagulate the mother's blood, which provided its substance.

Goody's text opened some significant perspectives. Comparing the

---

22   And not Robert Rattray, as Héritier wrote in *Two Sisters and Their Mother*, p. 161.

23   B. Malinowski, *The Sexual Life of the Savages* (London, Routledge, 1929), p. 339; quoted in Goody, 'A Comparative Approach to Incest and Adultery', p. 29.

24   Malinowski, *The Sexual Life of the Savages*, p. 447; quoted in ibid., p. 29.

matrilineal Ashanti and the patrilineal Tallensi, he brought out the difference between the mother's status in the two societies. In Ashanti society, the mother was her son's closest clanswoman in the generation above. For the Tallensi, the mother was regarded as the closest wife of Ego's closest clansmen of all the men in the generation above, in other words his father. It therefore follows that the status of the married woman and the mother was not the same in the two societies.[25] In Ashanti marriage, the woman's matriline transferred the right to her sexual services to her husband, but absolutely not the 'ownership' of her children. The husband was even obliged to supplement the 'marriage price' in order to guarantee exclusive sexual rights to his wife. For the Tallensi, the rights transferred at the time of marriage concerned both the wife's sexual services and her reproductive capacity. We see clearly why the gravity of the sexual offences is not the same when one involves sex but not descent and the other involves both.

Goody extended his comparison to the Nuer as well, using work done by Evans-Pritchard and Howell.[26] The Nuer descent rule was patrilineal, but relations with the mother and the maternal clan were very important in a person's life. The most heinous form of incest – declared unthinkable – was that of a son with his mother. Evans-Pritchard gave us two lists of sexual prohibitions he collected from the Nuer, one concerning marriage prohibitions and the other, sexual prohibitions having more or less to do with incest (called *rual* in the vernacular). The first list comes before the second, and Evans-Pritchard justified this order by reasons of theory (which placed him alongside Tylor, Fortune, Lévi-Strauss, etc.), namely: that marriage prohibitions, that is to say exogamy rules, explain the sexual taboos and not the other way around,[27] which seems erroneous to me. But in fact, by drawing up his lists of prohibitions on site, Evans-Pritchard must have seen that the fields covered by the two lists did not overlap and therefore could not be explained by rules of exogamy alone, by the obligation to marry out of one's clan.

In effect, the Nuer forbid marriage within the same clan (and therefore even more strongly within the same lineage). A man is also forbidden to take a wife in his mother's clan and thereby repeat his father's marriage. A man is forbidden to marry a woman with whom he shares a common ancestor, either on the paternal or the maternal side, traced through the men or the women (cognatic system) to the sixth generation; or relatives by adoption who have become members of his clan or that of his mother; or children of the man who paid his mother's brideprice (in cattle)

25   M. Fortes, *The Web of Kinship among the Tallensi* (Oxford, Oxford University Press, 1949), esp. Chapter 2, pp. 12–43.

26   E. E. Evans-Pritchard, 'Nuer Rules of Exogamy and Incest', in M. Fortes (ed.), *Social Structure: Studies Presented to A.R. Radcliffe-Brown* (London, Oxford University Press, 1949), p. 85, 101. P. P. Howell, *A Manual of Nuer Law* (London, Oxford University Press, 1954) and 'The Age-System and the Institution of "Nak" among the Nuer', *Sudan Notes and Records*, 1947.

27   Evans-Pritchard, 'Nuer Rules of Exogamy and Incest', pp. 85, 101.

What the Nuer say

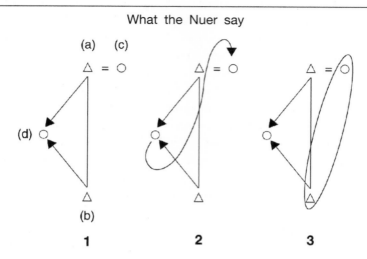

Mother–son incest occurs in 3 stages:
1. The father (a) and the son (b) have sexual relations with a woman (d), their shared mistress. Their sperms mix in this woman's vagina.
2. The father (a), after having made love with the woman (d) who has had sexual relations with his son (b), has sexual intercourse with his wife (c), the mother of his son.
3. He transports his son's sperm into his wife's vagina. Thereby the mother and the son have sexual relations with each other, but via the father; this happens even though neither the son nor the mother so wishes or knows. They have indirectly committed incest of the first kind.

Incest of the second type as invented by Françoise Héritier

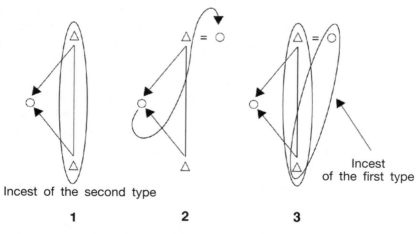

Incest of the second type

Incest of the first type

1. The father (a) and the son (b) (indirectly) commit an incest of the second type by mixing their substances in the vagina of their shared mistress (d).
2. The father transports his son's substance into his wife's womb.
3. In so doing, the father brings his wife and their son to commit an incest of the first kind, but not deliberately on their part.

and who became her children's 'pater' without being their 'genitor'. He is forbidden to marry the daughter of a man belonging to the same age-group as Ego's father, since the father calls her 'daughter', while her father calls Ego 'son'. The man and the woman are in this case classificatory 'brothers and sisters' and cannot marry. In short, the Nuer have a great number of marriage prohibitions (a little like the case of Christianity), whereas the number of sexual taboos inside the field of exogamy is much lower, and their gravity ranges, as Evans-Pritchard writes, from absolute condemnation to 'incestuous peccadillo or no incest at all'.[28] Taking the wife of one's father's half-brother is more serious than taking one's half-brother's wife, since the former belongs to a generation above Ego and so, in addition to being a sexual offence, it shows a lack of respect for an elder.

In principle a man is forbidden to have sexual relations with women from his own or his mother's clan, but relations with women from his mother's clan are regarded as worse than those with women from his father's clan. Fully incestuous relations (*rual*) are those with the mother (C), the mother's brother's wife (CA), the son's wife (CA) and the wives of brothers born of the same mother (CA). On the other hand, sexual relations with the wives of the father's brothers, of parallel patrilateral cousins and of agnatic half-brothers are regarded as 'peccadillos'. All of these men are 'bulls', members of the same lineage. They all have given some of their cattle to help with each others' brideprice payments and, as the Nuer say, 'the wife of one bull is the wife of all the bulls . . . she is our wife'. Siblings or half-siblings born of the same father can thus have sexual relations with each others' wives, while siblings born of the same mother cannot, just as they cannot have sexual relations with their mother's brother's wife or with the wives of relatives on the mother's side, because, as the Nuer say, any association between sex and the mother or with relatives on the mother's side, including the wives of maternal kin, must be forbidden (CA).

As a general rule, two men from the same clan 'are not supposed to make love with the same woman in the same time period', but they can at different times. Here again, 'bulls' are not subjected to this prohibition, whereas a father and a son or brothers born of the same mother are. Here we are approaching the shores of incest of the second type as described by Françoise Héritier. The Nuer give as an example of one of the most dangerous and heinous types of incest that of a father and a son having sexual relations with the same woman, their mistress, for, they say, 'the father then goes from the woman to the mother and thereby brings her into a sexual relationship with her son'.[29] Let us pause over this statement, which is of crucial importance.

---

28   E. E. Evans-Pritchard, *Kinship and Marriage among the Nuer* (Oxford, Oxford University Press, 1956), p. 45.

29   Evans-Pritchard, 'Nuer Rules of Exogamy and Incest', p. 92; *Kinship and Marriage among the Nuer*, p. 45.

Far from thinking that the father and the son, two same-sex consanguines, have committed secondary incest with each other through the intermediary of their shared mistress, the Nuer consider that they have brought the mother unwilling and perhaps even unwittingly to commit primary incest with her son. There has indeed been a transfer of substance – the son's sperm was transported by the father into the vagina of the mother. But nowhere do the Nuer mention the possibility of negative consequences for the father and the son because they have mingled their sperms in the same vagina. That is not where the crime lies for them. It lies in the transport and introduction of the son's sperm into his mother's vagina, *without mother and son having had intercourse*. It is clear that, for the Nuer, the primordial incest is that between a mother and her son, and not that between father and son, and even less homosexual incest between a mother and her daughter, between same-sex consanguines (which is mentioned nowhere).

Evans-Pritchard pointed out, too, that a man is forbidden to have sexual relations with two sisters because, according to the Nuer, two sisters are potential wives of men *belonging to different lineages*, to which they will give descendants. He takes the argument no further, but we know where he is heading, which has nothing to do with fear of secondary incest between a man and two sisters. In reality the argument is wholly in keeping with the principle followed by the Nuer when it comes to marriage. A man, as we have seen, cannot marry a woman from his mother's clan and thus reproduce his father's marriage. The general principle governing marriage is to diversify alliances and contract them with many different clans. Sisters, whether there are two or more, are therefore destined for different clans and meant to bring their clans the brideprice that will be paid by their husband's clan. The prohibition on a man making love with two sisters therefore has nothing to do with fear of incest of the second type between these two women via their lover's penis. This taboo guarantees each clan the capacity to diversify its alliances.

Evans-Pritchard also includes in his list the prohibition on a mother and her daughter having sexual relations with the same man, but does not give the reasons advanced by the Nuer. Howell indicates the opposite prohibition, that on two men, and especially two kinsmen (belonging to the same clan), having sexual relations during the same lapse of time with the same woman who is married to another man. The reason given by the Nuer, once again, has nothing to do with fear of incest of the second type. For the Nuer, to make love with another man's wife (what we call adultery) defiles both the man and the woman involved, and the defilement is even greater when two men from the same clan have the same woman who already belongs to another. This would explain why members of the same lineage may make love with the wives of their agnatic half-brothers, their patrilineal cross cousins, since all helped to pay the dowries needed for the ones' and the others' marriages. All of these men are 'bulls', and 'the wife of one bull is the wife of all the bulls', as we said. All of these women were married with the same cattle, and are the shared property, as it were, of all those who raised and gave these cattle for their brideprice.

Finally, we find no trace of the famous incest of the second type in Nuer society. Let us therefore look at how Françoise Héritier managed to introduce this notion in a cultural and social universe where it did not exist. Let us come back to her starting point: the prohibition on a man and his son making love with the same woman. What do the Nuer say about this and what reasons do they give for condemning and punishing this act? We give their reasons below in the form of diagrams.

The possibility of primary (heterosexual) incest between a mother and her son via a third party, in the event the father, is conceived and considered by the Nuer as incest (*rual*) and condemned as such. This is actually a remarkable case, for this kind of incest requires, in addition to the mother and the son, two other partners: the son's father and a woman who is unrelated to these three protagonists and is the mistress of both the father and the son. But in no case are the relations between father and son considered to be incestuous because they have the same mistress.

For Françoise Héritier, the sexual relations between these four persons give rise to and contain two different kinds of incest, one of which is recognized and conceals the other, of which the actors are completely unaware but which precedes the other in time. In effect, the father's and the son's relations with the same woman would bring them into an incestuous relationship of the second type, and it is then that the father, by transferring his son's sperm into the vagina of his wife, would lead the mother and the son to commit (indirectly) an incest of the first kind.

Of course the diagrams can be read this way at a purely formal level, but this formal possibility has no cultural or social meaning for the Nuer. Does an anthropologist have the right to completely disregard what people think and say about the way they are supposed to behave in their society? And can an anthropologist interpret these conscious representations and these explicit rules of conduct as a surface that covers and hides different rules which determine these individuals' conduct without their being aware? This is probably true in the case of the way people relate to their language, but it does not apply to the domain of the positive and negative norms or the explicit rules that govern the production and reproduction of kinship relations and are passed on from one generation to the next. Does an anthropologist have the right, on the pretext of explaining these norms, to introduce totally alien meanings into a culture and to claim that these meanings really exist in this culture but in forms of which those who experience and obey them are unaware? We do not think so.[30]

---

30 The same approach led Françoise Héritier to affirm – contrary to all of the Greek tragedies and their critics – that Oedipus' true crime was not having bedded his mother but having mixed his sperm with that of his father in his mother's vagina. However, when Oedipus, having vanquished the Sphinx, married Jocasta, he was unaware that she was his mother and that the man

But let us come back to the Nuer and Evans-Pritchard to see how Jack Goody was genuinely the first, in 1956, to show the limits of Claude Lévi-Strauss' proposed explanation of incest. Evans-Pritchard, as we have seen, wanted at all costs that rules of exogamy – that is, marriage prohibitions – sufficed to explain all prohibitions on sexual relations between related persons. To be sure, the argument could be valid for the prohibitions concerning consanguines, but what about affines? On this point, Evans-Pritchard expressed doubts about his own theory and recognized that it could seem inacceptable to some of his readers: 'It is true also that Nuer call *rual* relations with women already married to kinsmen, and because they are married to kinsmen, and that they cannot be counted as possible mates to whom any rule of exogamy could apply.'[31]

These lines were written in 1949, the year Lévi-Strauss' *The Elementary Structures of Kinship* appeared in French. And it was with reference to this doubt expressed by Evans-Pritchard that Goody, the first to our knowledge, pointed out the partial validity but also the limits of the interpretation of the incest taboo advanced by Lévi-Strauss a few years earlier. For Lévi-Strauss, in effect, the incest taboo can be explained basically by the obligation of human groups to respect exogamy and to exchange women among men. While declaring himself roughly in agreement with Tylor, Fortune and Lévi-Strauss on this explanation, Goody nevertheless pointed out that this reason by no means explained the sexual taboos on persons who had already married into this kin group and were therefore affines of consanguines (CA):

> For while the rule prohibiting marriage inside the group (exogamy) may be associated with the prohibition on intercourse within the group (intra-group prohibition), it cannot possibly be related, in any direct manner, to the prohibition on intercourse with the wives of the group, for these women must of necessity fall within the general category of permitted spouse. They cannot possibly be excluded by any marriage rule.[32]

Another explanation was therefore needed, and Goody suggested that it could be found in the need for these kin groups 'of necessity' to preserve their structure in the face of likely conflicts between their members over rights of sexual access to the women marrying into the group. This rule would apply to all clan members and not only to those belonging to the same family. The argument is convincing and should be explored, because it is not only cooperation, solidarity and

---

he had killed on the road to Cadmos was Laius, his father. In this line of reasoning, Oedipus would have unwittingly committed two kinds of incest: one of the first kind with his living mother, and one of the second type with his dead father. The thesis is startling, but has no basis in either the texts or tradition. (Cf. Héritier, *Two Sisters and Their Mother*, pp. 45–6.)

31   Evans-Pritchard, 'Nuer Rules of Exogamy and Incest', p. 99.
32   Goody, 'A Comparative Approach to Incest and Adultery', p. 302.

relations of authority that need to be preserved between members of a kin group (clan) in order for it to continue to exist; it is also the cooperation between this group and those with whom its members are allied by marriage. In the bulk of societies, kinship encompasses both descent and alliance, both consanguinity and affinity; and that is why kin groups need to control their members' sexual drives and forbid certain unions that might endanger their internal structure as well as relations with their allies – both consanguines' affines (CA) and affines' consanguines (AC).[33] To keep peace at home and not to create discord among one's affines – these are the two obligations incumbent on all members of a society if they wish their kin groups to be reproduced and their alliances to continue.

We now have a better grasp of the specific character of the notion of incest in the Western kinship system. Here the same term is used for forbidden sexual relations between consanguines who are close or removed to first the sixth and then to the fourth degree, but also those relations which are forbidden between affines' consanguines or consanguines' affines and, beyond them with spiritual kin, godparents through baptism. Among the Nuer, the term *rual* subsumes the taboos on sexual relations between consanguines to the sixth degree as well as other relations also concerning affines' consanguines and consanguines' affines, with the exception of some particularities ('bulls'' free access to each others' wives, etc.) which have nothing to do with Christian kinship and are certainly not based on the principle that two spouses unite to form a single flesh or body (*una caro*).

Yet even when the term 'incest' designates sexual prohibitions concerning different kin categories, these taboos address different social issues. For a medieval theologian, fornication with one's wife's sister was probably more serious than having sexual relations with the wife of a second cousin on the father's side. In many societies, these different sexual offences are designated by different terms, as Goody showed for the Tallensi or the Trobriand Islanders. Unfortunately, Goody never returned to these problems prior to publishing, in 1990, *The Oriental, the Ancient and the Primitive.*[34] Furthermore, in France it was not for another three decades that these issues were raised again, by Françoise Héritier, to whom the credit is indisputably owed, even though she does not always acknowledge her debt to Jack Goody. She writes:

---

33   In some societies characterized by Australian or Dravidian type kinship systems, affines of affines (AA) are necessarily Ego's consanguines, and the sexual taboos on consanguines automatically apply to the affines' affines. In most other societies, the sexual taboos do not apply to affines' affines. One interesting exception is that of the Bantu systems, where alliance entails a gift of cattle to the wife's family, who use it to pay the brideprice this woman's brother must pay in order to marry (*lobola*). A man is forbidden to have sexual relations with his wife's brother's wife, for she and her lineage were the ultimate destination of the cattle given to his wife's lineage. See C. Lévi-Strauss, *The Elementary Structures of Kinship*, translated by James Harle Bell, John Richard von Sturmer and Rodney Needham (Boston, Beacon Press, 1969), Chapter 28 passim.

34   J. Goody, *The Oriental, the Ancient, and the Primitive: Systems of Marriage and the Family in the Pre-industrial Societies of Eurasia* (Cambridge/New York, Cambridge University Press, 1990).

Lévi-Strauss' theory does not account for incest of the second type, and particularly for the prohibition on the sister of a man's wife . . . In effect, if the first sister married by a man is not his blood relative, which would have made her taboo, neither is her sibling. There is no reason to prohibit her in the perspective of the incest taboo on consanguines, unless one introduces explanations of an entirely different nature, for instance, a marriage strategy that would consist in contracting the greatest number of partners possible, and therefore not immediately repeating an already established matrimonial alliance.[35]

RETURNING TO THE WEST, IN SEARCH OF INCEST OF 'THE SECOND TYPE'

In 1994, then, Françoise Héritier, a disciple of Claude Lévi-Strauss, published a book that immediately attracted attention not only because it announced the discovery of a type of incest largely unknown to kinship specialists, but also because it showed the limits of the explanation of the incest taboo advanced by Lévi-Strauss.[36] The event caused quite a stir, less among anthropologists, though, than among psychoanalysts, and more in France than abroad.

Without contesting the arguments theologians 'always used to justify ecclesiastical prohibitions', Héritier asserted:

> Nevertheless, further inferences can be made. If the husband 'becomes' his wife's flesh and thus enters into a consanguineous relationship with her sister, it must also be true that, from an alternate point of view, the woman 'becomes' her husband's flesh; she is incorporated into him . . . But when she becomes her husband's flesh through marriage, he cannot touch her sister; therefore we may infer an identity of substances between the two sisters. The *una caro* argument must be understood in the full subtlety of its implications. Not only do the spouses become one, carnally as well as spiritually, but same-sex blood relations of the spouse also share the spouse's substantial identity.[37]

Nothing new up to that point. Two sisters are a single flesh because their parents became one flesh when they united sexually and gave them life. However, unlike the theologians, Héritier considers that this unity of flesh between parents and children makes same-sex consanguines more identical than opposite-sex consanguines: '*Una caro* implies the substantial identity of blood relations of the same sex, father and son, mother and daughter, two sisters, two brothers.'[38]

---

35   Héritier, *Two Sisters and Their Mother*, p. 20. This is precisely the argument advanced by Jack Goody, the Nuer, the Baruya, etc.
36   Ibid.
37   Ibid., pp. 84–5.
38   Ibid., p. 85.

It is not hard to measure how far this interpretation of *una caro* strays from that of classical theological exegesis, and even distorts it completely by adding an element that completely clouds the meaning. For theologians, when a man and a woman come together sexually, they become a single flesh, which is neither that of the man nor that of the woman. This flesh will become that of their children, who will become one with their parents. In short, if there is really a mixing of substances, the outcome of this mixture is the existence of one and the same substance shared equally by the husband, the wife and their children. This one and the same substance cannot therefore be 'more' identical between the father and the son or between a mother and her daughter, between same-sex or between opposite-sex consanguines – a father and his daughter or a mother and her son. This is, moreover, what Yves de Chartres affirms, whom Héritier quotes in support of her theory whereas he was saying just the opposite: '[It is] by the mingling of bodies, *commixtio carnis*, . . . that a couple become one flesh in the mingling of sperm.'[39] However, for Héritier, 'The Catholic Church, in its very first councils . . . used the argument of *una caro*: I am you, and being you, I cannot have sexual relations with your blood relative. But, as I see it, it is not because one *is* the other that they constitute one flesh, but because each is the bearer of the other's secretions.'[40] In short, for theologians, the spouses' substances have mixed and are no longer two but one; for Héritier, however, they *remain distinct*, and that is why each spouse can transport the other's humours to the body of all partners other than their spouse with whom they choose to have sexual relations.[41]

We find ourselves here in the presence of a theoretical *coup de force* which will turn everything upside down and produce a concatenation of theoretical propositions. The reversal resides in the affirmation that comes down to rejection of the *una caro* theory:

> The most fundamental identity seems to involve gender rather than biological or social relations of consanguinity. Because common substance and identity is greater between a father and son than between a father and daughter, certain societies may treat corporal union between a man and his son's wife . . . as more injurious than sexual relations between a father and daughter, for the father's substance comes into contact with the son's, and vice versa, through the common partner.[42]

39 Ibid., p. 98. Cited again by G. Duby, *Le Chevalier, la femme et le prêtre. Le mariage dans la France féodale* (Paris, Hachette, 1981), p. 187. For Yves de Chartres, as for Aristotle, the vaginal fluids are regarded as woman's 'sperm'.

40 Héritier, *Two Sisters and Their Mother*, p. 14. It is hard to think that by *commixtio carnis* a theologian means anything other than a mixture of substances. The notions of transporting and bringing into contact substances would have required different words in Latin.

41 Of course, whatever these relationships may be, since they occur out of wedlock, they are forbidden and sanctioned by the Church.

42 Héritier, *Two Sisters and Their Mother*, p. 13.

In short, once sameness of gender is posited as more basic than sameness of opposite-sex siblings, once the notion of *una caro* as the *mixture* of substances has been replaced, without theoretical justification, by that of *transporting and bringing into contact* humours, a new theory of incest emerges that no longer has much connection with the Western kinship system, which this theory nevertheless claims to explain.

The first conclusion Héritier has logically drawn from the shift in meaning she has just brought about is that, when a man has sexual relations with his sister-in-law while his wife is living, he is not committing one instance of incest, as theologians believed, but two. The first is the incest he commits in person with his sister-in-law, who has become his 'sister' by the principle of *una caro*. This is the incest that the Church condemns, as did the Civil Code for a long time. The second is the incest the two sisters commit *with each other* via the husband of one of them and which, paradoxically, *does not imply any direct sexual relationship* between the two women. When the man makes love with one and then the other, his penis *transports* the vaginal fluids (the 'sperm') of one into the vagina of the other and vice versa, thereby bringing them into contact.

Since the two women are sisters, and therefore come from the same flesh, and, by definition, from the same sex, from the same gender, the incest they commit via a third sexual organ would be more injurious than that which each could have deliberately committed with an opposite-sex relative – brother, father, son, cousin, etc. More injurious because the combination of sameness brought about by this act would be even greater. Likewise, if a woman were to make love with her husband's brother, she would be committing, and would cause the two brothers to commit, the same double incest. Her vagina would be the point of encounter of the sperms of her husband and his brother, who would thus have committed what Héritier calls an 'incest of the second type'.

Let it be clear that this incest between same-sex relatives (sister–sister, mother–daughter, brother–brother, father–son) is not a homosexual incest. It does not imply any direct sexual contact between the two persons, no touching, no practices such as fellatio, cunnilingus or sodomy, by which homosexual desires are usually satisfied. It does not even imply that the two persons linked by such an incest are both consenting partners, or even aware of what is happening. A woman can sleep with her husband's brother for years without the husband's knowledge. Likewise, a man can sleep with his sister-in-law without his wife's knowledge. And the pairing can be extended even further. A man can sleep with his wife, his sister-in-law and his mother-in-law – and in this case would link these three women by an incest of the second type. Of course, what Héritier only mentions in passing in order to minimize its importance is that these three women who share the same man and the same organ are more likely to become rivals than willing partners to the act. This is all the more likely because one of them is the man's publicly recognized wife and she sees her status, her rights, etc., flouted by members of her own family – her sister, her mother – unless, of course, she is agreeable.

Sexual activities are not without biological consequences either; but Héritier says nothing about this. These three women can be made pregnant by the same man, and if the children born of the legitimate wife will probably be recognized as legitimate, the children conceived with the sister-in-law and the mother-in-law – the first being perhaps married and the second perhaps a widow – will bear the consequences of their illegitimate birth – not to mention the social stigma that will surround their mothers for having borne them.

For the Church, the children of these unions were born in sin and could therefore not be baptized – with all of the consequences one can imagine. Such unions outside of marriage with consanguines or close or distant affines violated in many ways the taboos stemming from the principle which extended the application of primary incest to these relatives, namely: *una caro*. It is for this reason, and not in order to punish secondary incest, which had no doctrinal or theoretical existence, that the various Church councils regularly listed among the forbidden sexual unions that of a man with two sisters, with his mother-in-law, with his daughter-in-law etc., and symmetrically for a woman with her father-in-law, her son-in-law, etc.

In his penitential, Burkhardt of Worms writes that, if a man sleeps with his brother's wife without his knowledge, the first brother's marriage will be dissolved and the culprit sentenced to celibacy for life, while the innocent brother will be allowed to remarry, but only after having done penance, for he, too, has been defiled by the act of his brother and his wife.[43]

In sentencing the guilty party or parties to celibacy, in excluding them from the sacrament of marriage, the Church was actually forbidding them to reproduce both biologically and socially. Which meant that, for the Church, carnal union between two persons of the opposite sex was more important for people's relation with God and with each other than were sexual relations between two persons of the same sex. Homosexuality was condemned as being contrary to human nature and an obstacle to salvation. In short, *for the Church and for Christians, sexual difference was more important and otherwise important than sexual sameness.* The fullest identity that could exist between two persons of opposite sex or of the same sex was that engendered by the relations of consanguinity between them, a consanguinity that extended to and absorbed into itself

---

43   Cf. Vernier, 'Du nouveau sur l'inceste?', p. 67. Vernier quotes Burkhardt of Worms' penitentiary (c.1008–12) from the version reproduced in a book by Cyrille Vogel, *Le Pécheur et la pénitence au moyen-âge* (Paris, Editions du Cerf, 1969).

relatives by marriage and spiritual kin as well. The identity was not, as Héritier advanced, that which was founded on sameness of gender.

But let us return to an important point. The Christian kinship system represents sexual unions as the mixing of two fleshes, a mixture that begins with the mingling of sexual fluids. Of course, for there to be mixing, there must have first been contact between these fluids. Let us go further. The union of two unrelated persons of opposite sex is in no way incestuous. The mixing of their fluids comes about without producing incest. For there to be incest, the two persons must possess within themselves 'something' that makes them identical, either something they inherited from common ancestors or something they acquired by contracting alliances with persons with whom they are 'identified'. And the closer the ties (of consanguinity or affinity), the more the two persons are identical.

In short, in order for there to be incest, it is not the difference of fluids that matters, it is the fact that they bring into contact two persons who are socially and physically identical (who share the same 'blood', for instance). The sameness that matters is not in the sperm or in the vaginal fluids, it resides in the social identity of these who, in uniting, mix these fluids. And since the mixture makes them one flesh, two consanguines or two affines who unite are even more identical after their union than before. There is therefore an addition of sameness, and this addition is dangerous. It threatens the social order, and sometimes even the order of the cosmos if God (or the gods) wishes to punish the humans for misusing their sexual organs by sending catastrophes (drought, sickness, death of the cattle, etc.).

In short, in the case of classic heterosexual incest, we shall discover everything that Héritier sees as defining incest of the second type: transporting and placing in contact fluids and addition of sameness. But, and this is fundamental, the sameness that is placed in contact and added together is not that of two sexually identical fluids – a father's and a son's sperm, two sisters' or a mother's and her daughter's vaginal fluids. It is the fact that two persons are socially (and physically, i.e. in their 'flesh') identical, in spite of the difference of sex and fluids. And we understand the fundamental importance, from the standpoint of the social and historical evolution of humanity, of the condemnation of incestuous heterosexual unions and their position with respect to other forbidden sexual unions, among which homosexual relations. For not only do heterosexual unions procure pleasure and satisfy desire, they can also engender new human beings and introduce them into the process of reproducing society and social life. Other unions, between same-sex humans, between humans and animals or cadavers, cannot do this.

Héritier posits as a universal principle – despite all of the evidence to the contrary found in numerous societies – that sameness of gender is more fundamental than sameness of 'blood', that a father and a son are 'more identical' than a father and his daughter, that a daughter and her mother are 'more identical' than a son and his mother. We see that the modern problematic of 'gender' has become a key to her reading of present and past social and historical facts.[44]

But what right does an anthropologist have to advance this statement as a universal truth. The Trobriand Islanders, who live in the framework of a matrilineal kinship system, nevertheless affirm that *no substance* is shared between a father, his son and his daughter. The man's sperm does not enter into the substance of his children's bodies, which are entirely made from their mother's blood, even if their body is shaped by their father's penis and sperm as he continues to unite sexually with their mother while they are still a foetus in her womb.

Let us recall, too, the case of the Amazonian Cashinahua, where, as soon as a woman realizes she is pregnant, she takes a number of lovers in order, with their help, to build up enough sperm in her womb for her child to take shape. When the child is born, the mother publicly invites these men to take part in rituals that solemnly recognize them as co-authors of the child together with the husband. Generally speaking, as I have said, the woman chooses her lovers among the great hunters, who will be able to take care of her and her children in the event of her husband's death. And before the missionaries arrived and banned these customs, there were no feelings of jealousy and rivalry between the husband and the lovers his wife had chosen.[45]

These are two examples among many hundreds, and the Na, whom we shall soon observe, will provide us with another equally convincing instance. Héritier's postulate has no universal value then, and if this is the case, it is simply because the so-called relations of substance between parents and children vary widely and depend on the kinship system and cultural universe. And because, in addition, as we have shown, in no society is a child ever reducible to the 'substances' it has inherited from its parents. By placing the emphasis exclusively on the substances in question and the dangers of combining them, one ends up with a theory that makes the incest taboo the consequence of a branch of 'fluid mechanics' that arises in the human mind, which makes a game of posing and opposing formal categories of same and different. Paradoxically, this 'mechanical' theory, which is based on Lévi-Strauss' postulate of the primacy of the symbolic over the imaginary and the real, considers the representations members of a society have of the reasons for their sexual taboos and marriage prohibitions as superfluous, devoid of not only meaning but also reality and effectiveness. But let us read:

---

44   Héritier, *Two Sisters and Their Mother*, p. 13: 'The most fundamental identity seems to involve gender rather than biological or social relations of consanguinity.'

45   Cf. K. Kensinger, *How Real People Ought to Live: The Cashinahua of Eastern Peru* (Prospect Heights IL, Waveland Press, 1995), p. 402. Since Christian missionaries came to convert the Cashinahua these practices have been gradually been abandoned and they now are beginning to arouse jealousy among those who continue them.

One may question the explicative value of frequent notions of defilement, sin, purity, and impurity in anthropological or philosophical literature. These notions exist, of course . . . but they add a moral connotation to the primary notion of balance, danger, and rectification. Defilement may be grafted onto the notion of balance, but it cannot be substituted for it.[46]

But danger of what? Imbalance between what and what? The answer is equally significant:

'Religious and moral rationalizations in terms of misdeed, sin, or defilement are often superimposed where it is only a question of a mechanics of fluids with its underlying logic and objective, concrete, relative notions . . . that entail no value judgment in and of themselves.'[47] What is this anthropology, what is this social science that we have here? Religion and morality become mere rationalizations imposed 'after the fact' on a mechanics of sperm and blood that makes use of 'objective', 'concrete' notions entailing no 'value judgment'? But the whole of anthropology testifies against these affirmations, which reify cultural representations: they have nothing to do with 'objective knowledge' but are socially 'objective' representations for those who share them (and they all belong to the realm of ideologies). In short, we understand why Héritier allows herself to disregard the Nuer's interpretation of the prohibition on two men, a father and a son, having sexual relations with the same woman, or the Baoule's explanation when they justify forbidding a man to marry two sisters by saying that it is to keep them from becoming rivals. For Héritier, 'this justification is secondary; the essential lies elsewhere . . . The reason used to justify the prohibition of two sisters – they could not be sisters and rivals at the same time – is perhaps accurate on the psychological level of sexual fantasy, but it masks another, deeper one that supposes the meeting of "identical flesh" through a common partner.'[48] In this reading, the threats posed to institutions, to marriage, by certain sexual unions – with two sisters, for instance – would be merely 'sexual fantasies' which obsess the Baoule. Finally, for Héritier, the social content of the taboos and the explanations advanced to justify them come down to 'institutional and social trimmings: marriage is what matters. Yet sometimes . . . a detail makes meaning shift, allowing a glimpse of the primacy of the symbolic.'[49]

---

46   Héritier, *Two Sisters and Their Mother*, p. 216.
47   Ibid., p. 215.
48   Ibid., p. 157.
49   Ibid., p. 44. Here the symbolic is reduced to reified mental categories that completely transcend the social and historical context. In this Héritier follows Lévi-Strauss, who declared that 'symbols are more real than what they symbolize'. See C. Lévi-Strauss, 'Introduction à l'Œuvre de Mauss', in *Sociologie et anthropologie* (Paris, Presses Universitaires de France), p. xxxii; English translation: *Introduction to the Work of Marcel Mauss*, translated by Felicity Baker (London, Routledge and Kegan Paul, 1987). See also our comments in M. Godelier, *L'Enigme du don* (Paris,

We see where Lévi-Strauss' affirmation in 1950 of the 'primacy of the symbolic over the imaginary and the real' can lead. Not only is the meaning of the facts upended, but in addition a large portion of their social content disappears – or is reduced to its symbolic dimensions. We know that, just as representations cannot exist without symbols, neither can social relations exist without symbolic dimensions. But this by no means proves that social relations can be reduced to their symbolic dimensions or that symbols still have meaning (or the same meaning) when they are detached or disconnected from the social realities to which they have lent part of their form and their meaning.

In order to understand and measure the extremes to which Héritier's theses have led, let us follow her undertaking to its conclusion. First of all, she acknowledges that: 'One does not find a prohibition pertaining to a union with two sisters, or with a mother and her daughter, everywhere. In certain societies, these unions are, on the contrary, sought after.'[50] A remark she prefaces by saying '*I [will not] reduce it [the incest theme] to a universal uniformity*.'[51] Duly noted.

Yet, later in the book, this affirmation is absolutely contradicted. Convinced that she has discovered a kind of incest known since antiquity but masked by the Christian tradition and ignored by kinship specialists, including Claude Lévi-Strauss, Héritier undertakes the demonstration by rapidly passing in review a series of codes of law – Hittite, Assyrian, Biblical, Greek and Koranic – together with the body of common law found in a few societies in Africa and Madagascar. Everywhere she finds an explicit description of the incest of the second kind she has rediscovered. Here, for example, are three articles from the Code of Hammurabi quoted by Héritier in support of her thesis:

Fayard, 1996), pp. 39–44; English translation: *The Enigma of the Gift*, translated by Nora Scott (Chicago/Cambridge, University of Chicago Press/Polity Press, 1998).

50   Héritier, *Two Sisters and Their Mother*, p. 26.

51   Allow me to mention all of the Himalayan societies that practise adelphic polyandry (a woman is the wife of a group of brothers), or the Amazonian societies with non-adelphic polyandry (several men are co-husbands of the same woman). Héritier makes no mention of the famous chapter Lévi-Strauss devoted to 'The family' in Harry Shapiro's *Man, Culture and Society* (New York, Oxford University Press, 1966), pp. 261–95. In it he cited, alongside the polyandric societies of Tibet and Nepal, the example of the Toola, and that of the Tupi-Kawahib of central Brazil, where he had lived, and observed that, in this society, 'a chief may marry several women who may be sisters or even a mother and her daughter by former marriage . . . also the chief willingly lends his wives to his younger brothers, his court officers or to visitors. Here we have not only a combination of polygamy and polyandry but the mix-up is increased even more by the fact that the co-wives may be united by close consanguineous ties prior to their marrying the same man' (p. 265). Lévi-Strauss recalled, too, the ancient Russian custom known as *snokatchestvo*, which gave a father the right to have sexual congress with his son's young wife. Elsewhere, in some Southeast Asian societies, it is the sister's son who has privileged access to his mother's brother's wife (ibid., p. 278). Lévi-Strauss had therefore 'encountered' some of the relations that Héritier dubs 'incests of the second type', but he had not given them any particular theoretical status, at least not that of a concealed incest of the second type.

Article 191 states that 'a man may not have relations with several free women, as well as with their mother, in the same place'.

Article 191 – If a freeman cohabits with (several) free women, sisters and their mother, with this one in one country and that one in another country, there shall be no punishment. But if (it happens) in one and the same place knowing (of their relationship), it is a capital crime.

Article 194 – If a free man cohabits with (several) slave-girls, sisters and their mother, there shall be no punishment. If blood-relations sleep with (the same) free woman there shall be no punishment. If father and son sleep with (the same) slave-girl or harlot, there shall be no punishment.

Article 200 – If a man does evil with a horse or a mule, there shall be no punishment. He must not appeal to the King nor shall he become a case for the priest. If anyone sleeps with a foreign (woman), and (also) with her mother or (her sister) there will be no punishment.[52]

Clearly these articles in no way confirm Héritier's statements. Not only may two male relatives by blood, two close consanguines, sleep with the same woman without committing incest or incurring punishment. But above all, in each instance, the lawmaker has been at pains to specify the social status (free man or woman, female foreigner, prostitute, female slave . . .) of the partners because it is this status that determines whether or not they have committed a forbidden sexual act and deserve punishment – either by the priest or by the king. Nowhere is it said that two women – mother and daughter, or two sisters, or two sisters and their mother – are committing an incestuous or reprehensible act *with each other* because they have had sexual relations with the same man. Nowhere is there any mention of a possible encounter, via these successive and multiple couplings, between identical substances – the men's semen or the women's vaginal fluids. And yet, in the unions forbidden or authorized by the Code of Hammurabi, there is indeed a transfer and encounter of identical substances. As Bernard Vernier has stressed:

In all of these situations 'identical substances may be brought into contact' . . . But it is the woman's status that, alone, suffices to determine the meaning of the behavior and give rise to forbidding or allowing . . . consanguines to sleep with the same freewoman. And if the woman is a slave or a prostitute, even a father and his son can share her.[53]

<hr/>

52 Héritier, *Deux Sœurs et leur mère*, pp. 34–44; translation presented there taken from Vernier, 'Du nouveau sur l'inceste?', pp. 60–1.

53 B. Vernier, 'Théorie de l'inceste et construction d'objet. Françoise Héritier et les interdits de la Bible', *Social Anthropology*, vol. 4, no. 3 (1996), pp. 227–50; 'Théorie de l'inceste et construction d'objet. F. Héritier, la Grèce Antique et les Hittites', *Les Annales*, no. 1 (1996), pp. 173–200; 'Du nouveau sur l'inceste?', pp. 53–80.

Vernier shows us that in all of the cases cited by Héritier, from the Code of Hammurabi to the Bible, she has 'totally neglected in her interpretation' the social distinctions and oppositions present in the mind of those who drew up these codes. Through the erasure of these social relations and the stakes they entail, situations formally resembling incest (of the second type), between two close relatives via a third person of the opposite sex, will automatically appear to be nearly universal. In this event, the author felt authorized to skirt the objective fact that 'One does not find a prohibition pertaining to a union with two sisters, or with a mother and her daughter, everywhere', and to assert that: 'Incest of the second type is likely at the conceptual origin of the incest prohibition as we know it, that of the first type, and not the reverse.'[54] Or again, in an interview with the weekly *Le Nouvel Observateur* a few months after the publication of her book, Héritier further remarks: 'Today, pursuing my study of incest of the second type, which could be thought to be a sort of extension of the first kind, I have *turned around* my thinking and have come to see it as the *basis of all* of these taboos.'[55]

A paradoxical incest, this, which, *even though it is not found in any society*, is *conceptually* necessary for thinking the forms of incest taboo (and other improper uses of sex) that are to be found. What then are the facts that 'turned around' Héritier's thinking and provided her with arguments? We already know the answer. She claims to have discovered in the course of her research that the identity that arises between two blood relatives because they share the same sex (mother and daughter / father and son / brother and brother / sister and sister) is stronger, more identical, and therefore more basic or fundamental, than the identity shared by opposite-sex blood relatives (brother and sister / mother and son, etc.) because they are made from the same sperm or the same blood. In the end, incest between same-sex blood relatives is posited as the universal basis of all incests: 'Based on identity of gender within consanguinity, incest of the second type is the primordial incest' because 'the category of the identical as a primordial ideological category cannot be built on the similarity of crossed relatives [i.e. brother and sister] who, in filiation or collaterality, present a sexual difference.'[56]

However, if it were universally true that two consanguines of opposite sex will never be as identical as two consanguines of the same sex, and that the union of two same-sex consanguines will be more dangerous for the reproduction of the social and cosmic orders than the sexual union of two opposite-sex consanguines, it becomes impossible to understand why, in all societies, the primary target of the incest taboo is sexual relations between more or less close

54 Héritier, *Two Sisters and Their Mother*, p. 13.

55 F. Héritier, 'L'inceste du deuxième type', *Le Nouvel Observateur*, no. 1536 (April 1994), pp. 69–72.

56 Héritier, *Two Sisters and Their Mother*, p. 261.

relatives of the opposite sex because they are believed to share, in different degrees, the same components, the same substance, the same sperm, the same blood, the same name or the same soul inherited from common ancestors. At this stage, we need to recall that kinship is not only a matter of consanguinity, but also (with the exception of a few extreme cases, such as the Na of China) of affinity, and that unauthorized sexual relations between opposite-sex affines are *just as* dangerous – but for *other* reasons and with other consequences – for the reproduction of social groups and therefore the society.

Whether we consider consanguinity or affinity, the primary target of the lists of prohibitions on relations between kin are, as we have said, heterosexual relations and not direct homosexual relations between two relatives of the same sex or between indirect relations (between two same-sex relatives via a shared partner of the opposite sex). Furthermore, homosexual incest between a father and his son would not prevent the son from 'exchanging' his sister to obtain a wife. Alternatively, there is a likelihood that the son's homosexual relations with his father would disrupt the father's relations with his wife, the mother's with her son, etc. It is for this reason that Lévi-Strauss, concerned to prove kinship is based on alliance and that alliance always takes the form of the exchange of women between men, has not made the least allusion to the existence of homosexual incest between same-sex consanguines or affines. This silence is rightly the object of reproach on the part of Margaret Mead, in her brilliant article on incest, first delivered at a conference in 1961.[57]

Let us see where the thesis that incest of the second type is the basis of all incests has led Héritier. After having affirmed that incest between same-sex relatives and unrelated persons via a third person of the opposite sex is the primordial incest, she sorts through all the forms this kind of incest can take (between two brothers and a woman, between two sisters and a man, between a father, his son and a woman, between a mother, her daughter and the same man) and, with no scientific, cultural or historical justification of any kind, she posits that, of all forms of incest between same-sex relatives:

> the founding form is that of the mother/daughter relationship, for in addition to the identity of gender, there is the physical fact of the reproduction of the same form in the same mold. The mold and its product are identical. This also applies to the identity of two sisters. If the father/son and brother/brother identity involves the identity of gender induced by the force of the nourishing spermatic substance, it is inferior in the absolute sense to the perfect mother/daughter identity.[58]

57   M. Mead, 'Incest', *International Encyclopaedia of the Social Sciences* (New York, Macmillan, 1968), vol. 7, pp. 115–22.

58   Héritier, *Two Sisters and Their Mother*, p. 306. For the ancient Chinese, this statement would be meaningless. In the *Tang Yin Bi Shi*, a thirteenth-century jurisprudence manual, the

And she concludes that, of all forms of incest:

> In my eyes, the *fundamental* incest, so fundamental that it can only be expressed approximately, in texts as well as behavior, is *mother/daughter* incest. The same substance, the same form, the same sex, the same flesh, the same destiny, one issued from the other, ad infinitum, mothers and daughters live out this relationship in complicity or rejection, love or hate, always in tumult.[59]

There is no longer any question of discovering an incest masked in Western tradition. Through a succession of theoretical shifts, we have arrived at an entirely different theory, the idea that *direct* sexual relations between a mother and her daughter (therefore necessarily homosexual relations between these two women) are the primordial incest, the most injurious of all, so serious that practically no society speaks of it whereas all dare refer – often very indirectly – to the horror of mother–son incest.

Finally, the supreme contradiction for a kinship specialist who began her book by challenging and ridiculing all biological explanations of the origins of incest and declared, after Lévi-Strauss, that the only basis of the incest taboo could be sociological, we discover that the 'fundamental' form of incest, mother–daughter incest, is biological in nature: 'What is surprising is that nature in its most secret and most recently discovered mechanisms provides for this ideal discrimination of form and matter, mingled in the female sex: *all foetuses are female at first*, and half of them will become male as the result of a hormone' [italics added].[60] According to competent scientists, as soon as the egg is fertilized by a sperm, the sex of the foetus is immediately determined by its chromosomal make up. It is a girl (XX) or a boy (XY). Later a hormone will act to develop the traits of what the child will be – girl or boy – by switching off the features of the other sex that were also present in the foetus. In short, at the conclusion of a book purporting to be a rigorous scientific analysis of the sexual prohibitions in different societies at different times that have come down to us, or which ethnographers have collected in the field over the last two centuries, we find a pure fantasy, the dream of an ideal, non-incestuous, relationship between daughter and mother.

---

judge carefully reminded the reader that 'the tie that unites a father and his son is, of all forms of kinship, that which is the closest; these two beings are but a single form grown individually from the same seed ... The grandfather, the son and the grandson are, to be sure, three different generations, but they form a single body.' We thus understand that the most heinous crime for the ancient Chinese, as for the ancient Romans, was the killing of a father by his son, parricide. See *Tang Yin Bi Shi, Affaires résolues à l'ombre du poirier de Shi Po*, text established by R. Van Gulik (Paris, Albin Michel, 2000), p. 200.

59 Héritier, *Two Sisters and Their Mother*, p. 306–7.
60 Ibid., p. 306.

Whatever the case may be, if our global assessment of this book is very negative, we have never neglected its positive aspects. For this is the most systematic attempt in France since Lévi-Strauss to analyze the forms and foundations of the incest taboo. Positive, too, is the fact that it calls attention to forbidden sexual unions in many societies which have been masked in Christian tradition and/or ignored by (Western) kinship specialists. As we have shown, the unions Héritier calls incest of the second type are merely extreme cases of incest that she terms of 'the first type'. These are not homosexual unions nor do they ever bring related persons into *direct* sexual contact. Furthermore, the relationship between three (or four or five) persons is brought about by successive (sometimes simultaneous) heterosexual relations of each of the related persons with a third party of the opposite sex. We are therefore on the borderline of classic heterosexual incest. Whatever the case, it is clear that condemnation of these 'extreme unions' was not the primary concern of those responsible for the early legal codes.

Héritier must also be credited with having been the first in France, though thirty years after Jack Goody in England, to have opened the file on prohibited sexual unions and marriages with affines – affines' consanguines (AC), on the one hand, and consanguines' affines (CA), on the other. Missing are affines' affines, but the question arises only for societies with Dravidian and Australian kinship systems, and in this case the answer is simple: my affines' affines can only be my consanguines (AA = C). By opening this file, Héritier would, just as Goody was led to do in 1956, call into question the explanation of incest advanced by Lévi-Strauss in *The Elementary Structures of Kinship*, and would show its limits. Lévi-Strauss' explanation – namely, that kinship is basically a question of alliance and that men renounce their sisters in order to exchange them for other men's sisters – accounts only for prohibitions on incest between consanguines, and does nothing to explain the sexual taboos that, immediately following marriage, apply (in most systems, but not all, e.g. Australian kinship systems) to relatives by marriage (AC + CA). And why indeed should we continue to use the same term, 'incest', to designate prohibitions applying to both consanguines and affines? The Ashanti, the Trobrianders and many other peoples don't.

Another positive feature of the book is the fact of its having called the attention of anthropologists, psychoanalysts, theologians and philosophers to homosexual relations between relatives. The file is open. It needs to be revisited, for homosexual 'incest' between a father and son does not prevent the son from marrying a woman from another family or his sister from marrying a man from another family. Homosexual incest between consanguineous relatives by no means prevents the exchange of women (or men) between kin groups. On this point as well, Héritier was preceded by thirty years by Margaret Mead, in her remarkable article on incest (1968). We shall return to this point later.

Héritier also mentions other misuses of sex, which are likewise glossed over or completely neglected by kinship theory, such as necrophilia and zoophilia. And of course she is right to say that the justification of the prohibition in these cases is just the opposite of that advanced for incest between blood relatives or relatives by marriage, which join individuals who are too close, too identical, owing to birth or to marriage alliance. This time it is because the sexual relations join beings that are too dissimilar, the living and the dead, humans and animals, that they are prohibited.

Finally, and this is another quality, Héritier bases her thesis on numerous references to ancient or recent theological and legal documents, and shows their importance. Others had opened the way, which consists in looking beyond the ethnographic material: Jack Goody once again, but in France, Georges Duby, Pierre Legendre, and so on.[61] Anthropology cannot claim to solve the problems it poses alone. For that it needs to assimilate the wealth and diversity of the historical material built up by the other social sciences (history, law, sociology), just as these disciplines need the material and analyses provided by anthropologists in order to decentre their approach from our own times and societies.

SECOND TRIP OUTSIDE THE WEST: A JOURNEY TO THE NA OF CHINA —
A SOCIETY WITHOUT FATHERS OR HUSBANDS

With the Na, an ethnic minority which today lives in China, on the border of Yunnan and Sechuan provinces, we discover a society where there is no marriage and therefore no relatives by marriage, no affinity. (We must except the chiefly families that were in contact with and subjected to imperial power until the last century, today replaced by communist power.) Since there is no marriage, there is no 'father', not even a social father, and so relations with blood relatives are reduced to those between persons linked through women and therefore by a matrilineal descent principle. Two components of kinship usually present in societies with marriage or some other form of publicly recognized union (cohabitation, common-law marriage) are thus absent: relations of affinity (AC + CA) and relations of consanguinity through men. And of course there is no question of finding here any affines' affines (AA).

In reality, the Na are only an exception if one ignores the diversity of forms of kinship systems, although it is true that they are an extreme case of the

---

61   G. Duby, *Le Chevalier, la femme et le prêtre. Le mariage dans la France féodale* (Paris, Hachette, 1981); P. Legendre, *Le Dossier occidental de la parenté* (Paris, Fayard, 1988); *L'inestimable objet de transmission* (Paris, Fayard, 2004); *Filiation* (Paris, Fayard, 1996); *'Ils seront deux en une seule chair', scénographie du couple humain dans le texte occidental* (Paris, Editions de la Maison des Sciences de l'Homme, 2004) (Travaux du Laboratoire européen pour l'étude de la filiation, no. 3).

possible transformations of matrilineal kinship systems. And of course, we know other systems in which marriage exists but, instead of women being exchanged among men, men are exchanged among women, brothers by their sisters. And in place of *bridewealth*, there is *groomwealth*, which the women negotiate no less avidly than the men in patrilineal societies with dowries. This is the case of the Rhades of Vietnam or the Tetum of Timor.[62] With the Trobriand Islanders, then, we have a matrilineal society with real marriage and exchange of women; and with the Rhades, a matrilineal society with marriage and exchange of men.

Among the Nayar, on the other hand, another matrilineal society living on the Malabar Indian coast, marriage exists but it is purely fictitious.[63] The Nayar are a warrior caste of southern India. When girls reach menarche, a fictitious marriage is contracted with men who will subsequently disappear from their lives after two or three days, often without even having had sexual relations with their wife. Nevertheless, care is taken to ensure that the husband and wife are not close relatives, in order to avoid an 'incestuous' marriage. Then for the rest of their life, the women live with their brothers and are entitled to take as many lovers as they wish; the lover of the evening plants his lance in the ground in front of the house where he has joined his partner to indicate to the others that the place is already taken. Of course the brothers do what all men do and visit women at night, other men's sisters, other matrilines' women. The children born to these unions out of wedlock are raised by their mother and her brothers and sisters. Since this is a matrilineal system, the children do not belong to their mother's (fictitious) husband, who is never considered as a genitor. And so, marriage exists in this society, as do ties of affinity, but they are virtual, with no social impact. And of course, since the 'husband' is not the father of the children a woman brings into the world, consanguineous ties through men have literally no place in the society.

This is, it seems to us, one more step in the direction historically taken by the Na.

	Real marriage	Fictitious marriage	No marriage
Matrilineal societies	⟶	⟶	⟶
	Trobrianders, Rhades	Nayar	Na

62   A. de Hautecloque-Howe, *Les Rhades, une société de droit maternel* (Paris, Editions du CNRS, 1987); G. Francillon, 'Un profitable échange de frères chez les Tetum du Sud, Timor central', *L'Homme*, vol. 29, no. 1 (1989), pp. 26–43.

63   K. Gough, 'A Comparison of Incest Prohibitions and Rules of Exogamy in Three Matrilineal Groups of the Malabar Coast', *International Archives of Ethnography*, no. 46 (1952), pp. 81–105.

It seems to us that there are no more possible changes in the direction taken by the Na, for any further transformation would cause the disappearance of the last element of kinship, consanguinity through women, and a whole other human world would come into being.

If we are to believe the anthropologist Cai Hua, who devoted a fascinating and controversial book to this society,[64] the Na have no word in their language for 'father' or for 'husband', and basically the institution of marriage did not exist before it was imposed by the imperial dynasties of ancient China, and then only on the families of village or district headmen. Na society was thus made up of matrilines, each of which descended from a common female ancestor and was divided into households composed of groups of sisters and brothers living under one roof and raising the sisters' children together; to these were added members of the preceding generations – grandmothers, great-uncles, great-aunts, mothers, aunts, etc. Each household is under the authority of both a woman (often the eldest) and a man (her eldest brother). The first looks after internal household relations, the other is in charge of the group's relations with the outside. Inside the house any allusion to sexual matters is forbidden. Some relationships are regarded as unthinkable: sexual relations between an uncle and his nieces, between an aunt and her nephews, between a mother and her sons, and especially between brothers and sisters. Sexual exchanges must therefore occur between the men and women of the different households in order for these to reproduce themselves and continue to exist.

These exchanges take three forms: 'furtive' visits, visible visits and prolonged cohabitation; the first being the most prevalent and often coexisting with the others. The furtive visits take place at night: the man leaves his sisters to call on a woman who has previously agreed to the visit. The man and the woman are *açia*, each others' lovers, though each is free to carry on other *açia* relationships at the same time. It is thus possible for a man to have *açia* relations with two sisters, or for a woman to carry on such relations with two brothers for a given period of time. But the women never visit the men. When two partners decide to enter into a lasting relationship, they exchange belts, thereby signifying to those around them that they wish to establish a relationship that is clearly 'visible' to everyone. The woman speaks with the 'mother' of the house about it, and a ritual meal is organized that is not attended by the woman's male relatives living under the same roof. The lover presents himself accompanied by a go-between, and makes his request by offering the woman a few gifts. If his request is accepted, the man can call on the woman earlier in the evening and leave later the following morning. From then on, the man and the woman grant

---

64   Cai Hua, *Une société sans père ni mari. Les Na de Chine* (Paris, Presses Universitaires de France, 1997).

each other a sort of privilege when it comes to sexual matters, which not only they but others are supposed to respect. Nevertheless, this now-public relationship concerns them only, and not their respective matrilines; and it can be broken off whenever either of them so desires. This relationship does not create ties of affinity between the two 'families'.

With cohabitation, the nature of the relationship between the partners undergoes a change. 'No longer is it only nights that they spend together, but also days, during which they undertake activities in common: they work and produce together; they share the fruits of their efforts. In a word, they live together.'[65] Cohabitation is often determined by other factors than the partners' feelings and their desire for each other. A woman will move in with a man if there are no longer any women in his household – sister, mother, aunt. A man will move in with a woman for opposite reasons. Generally speaking – and this is very important – when a women comes into a family where only men are left, she becomes the 'head of the house'. On the contrary, a man who moves in with his partner is treated like a sort of 'servant' and can never become the head of house or perform rites or deal with outside business.[66] For the children of the women of the household, he is like a maternal uncle (ewu). In no case can he give preferential treatment to any children he has with his partner, for that would be violating the taboo forbidding any allusion to sex in the house. Here we glimpse the fragile nature of these matrilineal kin groups. It is the vicissitudes of births, sickness and accidents that will cause the households to lack women or to lack men. In this case the members of the household will have to fall back on either cohabitation or adoption in order to continue to perpetuate themselves.

Although cohabitation is usually motivated by these imbalances, it is also sometimes a response to the partners' desire to live together. Since their decision is subject to approval by the members of the man's and the woman's lineages, permission is often refused if there are no reasons other than their desire. But, when the two lineages agree, ties of what Hua calls 'friendship' (and not affinity) are contracted between the respective matrilineages and their members. However the adopted person (the man or the woman) does not cease to belong to his or her birth lineage. Alternatively, the children of a woman who has moved into another lineage acquire the goods and identity ('the bone') of this lineage. The relationship between the lineage that gives the woman and the lineage that takes her in becomes what Hua calls 'a relationship of eternal friendship', the receiving lineage being 'indebted' to the donor lineage. Since cohabitation is a publicly established relationship and meant to last as long as

65   Ibid., p. 200.
66   Ibid., p. 211.

the man and the woman live, even though it can be broken off, we are in the presence of a sort of *union libre*, as the French say (which is not a conjugal family since the couple becomes part of the workings of a matrilineage that it helps reproduce). In short, with the notion of the takers of a man or a woman being indebted to the givers, with these exchanges of goods and services that accompany the officialization of the union, we are not far from an affinity structure that generates 'friendship' behaviours reminiscent of the attitudes and feelings found elsewhere between affines and which are also fairly different from what one feels toward those with whom one has lived and grown up.

Summing up: with the Na we have a society whose kin groups and extended 'domestic' units reproduce themselves by what we can cautiously call the 'exchange' of men between groups of women related by common descent from a shared female ancestor. This exchange is not direct, with one exception, that which results in the cohabitation of two partners with one of their matrilineages. Otherwise, what are exchanged are male sexual partners. This exchange creates a generalized circulation of sperm between the lineages, each providing the others with the sperm needed for their reproduction. All of this is due to a strict taboo on sexual relations between members of the matrilineage which makes it impossible for households to perpetuate themselves in isolation, for example by means of unions between brothers and sisters, uncles and nieces, aunts and nephews.

We immediately see the theoretical interest of knowing how the Na represent sperm and the process of procreation. For the Na, sperm is 'penis water', a term that also designates urine.[67] Its function is like that of rain, without which 'grass will not grow from the ground'. Sperm therefore does not make the foetus, it only makes it grow. The foetus is already there in the woman's womb, waiting to start growing until it is watered by sperm, just as seeds planted in the ground come up after a rain. Foetuses thus exist prior to sexual intercourse; they were deposited in the woman's uterus before she was born by Abaodgu, the goddess who smiles on humans. It is also Abaodgu who nourishes the foetus in the woman's womb when she is pregnant.[68] It is therefore from the woman (and from Abaogdu) that the child gets its bones and its flesh, so that at birth the child automatically belongs to its mother's group, to a matrilineage. In the Na language, to designate a matrilineage, they in fact say 'people of the same bone'.[69]

---

67   Ibid., p. 96.
68   Ibid., p. 95.
69   Ibid., p. 97. We see that the Na have a conception of birth opposite to that of the Tibetan populations, like the patrilineal Khumbo, for whom the man's sperm makes the child's bones, while the mother contributes the blood and the flesh. That is why the Khumbo consider the circulation of women between patrilineal lineages to be like 'blood' circulating between all of the houses, which are regarded as the bones, stable, inalterable points. Among the Na the circulation of men between matrilineages is conceived as a circulation of sperm, which enables the

Every generation, then, sisters and brothers together live, eat and raise their descendants brought into the world by the sisters, boys or girls that have grown in the women's womb watered by the sperm of men belonging to other houses, to other 'bones'. For, as the Na say, however strong a woman may be, if she is not 'laid' by a man, she won't be able to make children.[70]

In this society, men are thus not considered to be their children's genitors – a fact we have already encountered in other matrilineal societies, like that of the Trobrianders – their sperm is only rain, which brings on the birth. They are catalysts. But they are not the child's 'father' either, in so far as they are not the mother's husband and have no particular responsibilities to her child when it is born. It is the woman's brother, the child's maternal uncle, who will bring up the child and look after it.

With the Na we therefore have a society in which kin groups reproduce by circulating among themselves male members of their society. This circulation is not an exchange, if we reserve the word for voluntary and deliberate gifts and counter-gifts between persons or groups. But it is an exchange if we consider that each matrilineage knows that its male members will bring the others the 'rain' that will enable them to have descendants and that it will receive in turn the same gift from the other groups. Here we find one of the basic conditions of the establishment of kinship relations: the exchange of sexed individuals between 'families'. But these exchanges have the particular characteristic – except in the case of the gift of a man or a woman between two lineages in order to ensure the continuation of one of the two – of being reduced to exchanges of substances and *not of individuals*, and of *not creating an alliance* between households or lineages which would subsequently structure their relations for one or several generations, making them true relatives by marriage, true affines.

These exchanges that enable each lineage to reproduce itself are imposed, as we have seen, by the ban on all sexual relations between members of the same household, between opposite-sex blood relatives. This prohibition is so strict that any allusion, any mention of sexual relations can lead to the guilty party's

---

reproduction of the 'bones', the women's households.

70   The Na say that, long ago, women were able to make babies by exposing their open vagina near a mountain top. There the wind (the mountain spirit) would enter them and they would become pregnant. But they add that today, if a woman tried to get pregnant without lying with a man, she would give birth to snakes or toads. They also maintain that, in the beginning, it was the men who made babies (without women) and carried them in the calf of their leg. But the children were too heavy when they tried to go up into the mountains for wood. The goddess Abaogdu therefore decided that children would be born from women's wombs. This idea of the incapacity of men, who were the first to bear children but were unable to continue, should be compared with the Baruya notion that it is the women who invented bows, arrows, etc., but used them incorrectly. And that is why the men were obliged to step in and take away their invention.

exclusion for several days or even longer. We have here, then, one of the basic conditions for the establishment of kinship relations: the incest taboo, which the Na do not designate by a specific word, but by an expression which means that those who engage in it are like 'animals'.[71] Those guilty of incest are condemned to hang themselves (a Han custom), to be thrown into a pit and burned (a Tibetan custom), or to be shut in a cave and left to starve (a specifically Na custom).

Sexual division of labour exists in Na society, as in all others, and the different chores are parcelled out among the brothers and sisters and among the generations. The land, the house, the domestic animals and all of the household goods belong to everyone. In the event of strife within a matrilineage, these goods are usually divided and shared between the two groups, which then go their separate ways. Sexual division of labour combined with shared ownership of the means of production, the means of subsistence and the means of exchange gives rise to social groups whose members are materially and economically interdependent and cooperate in their own material reproduction (which never comes down to the mere production and sharing of material means of subsistence). When the various forms of sexual division of labour are combined with the tasks of bearing and raising children, they form the basis of the different forms of 'family', even if these families, as in the case of the Na, do not entail sexual relations between their members. It is therefore not marriage that creates the 'family', but the twofold constraint obliging both sexes to cooperate in reproducing their material conditions of existence and in raising the children that certain members (the women) have conceived and borne by uniting with partners chosen outside the family.

If, coming back to an important observation made by Lévi-Strauss in 1956 in his article 'The family',[72] we see the sexual division of labour as the consequence of forbidding each of the genders to perform certain tasks reserved for the other, we must conclude that these two types of prohibition applying to both the sex and the labour – the taboo on incest between blood relations and the sexual division of labour, which is just as universal and no less varied in its forms – are two conditions necessary for the establishment of the more or less stable social groups we call 'families', within which persons of both sexes are united for a certain time in view of material survival and raising the children

---

71 The Baruya do not have a specific term for incestuous relations between consanguineous relatives either, but they do have an expression that means that the guilty parties behaved like *djilika*, dogs. The same idea is expressed by the Samo of Burkina-Faso.

72 Lévi-Strauss, 'The Family', p. 276: 'To return to the division of labor . . . when it is stated that one sex must perform certain tasks, this also means that the other sex is forbidden to do them'; and: 'If sexual considerations are not paramount for marriage purposes, economic necessities are found everywhere in the first place' (p. 274).

that they have engendered together or separately. With the help of the Na example, we now see more clearly that these two conditions *in no way* imply that the adults raising these children unite sexually in order to engender them, nor that those who engendered them are 'married'.[73] And the example of the Egyptians will show us that the taboo on incest between brothers and sisters can also fail to exist without bringing about the disappearance of the 'family'.

If marriage and – more rarely – sexual unions within the group are not universal conditions for establishing social units in which children are born and raised by adults who, in addition, cooperate in many ways to provide themselves with the material and social means of existence, we must conclude that the types of social units usually designated by the term 'family' (nuclear, extended, polyandrous, polygamous, and so forth) appear only when the sexual division of labour is directly associated with the birth and raising of children. In short, however people have represented the process of making children, and the role of each of the sexes in this process, wherever the sexual union of individuals occurs – inside or outside the family – until the twenty-first century, true 'families' existed only when there were children, engendered or adopted, that adults of both sexes worked together to raise.[74] The example of Nuer marriage between women does not contradict this proposition. In Nuer society, a childless widow can 'marry' another women for whom she has paid a brideprice in cattle, just like a man. She becomes the woman's 'husband' and chooses a male lover for her 'wife', who will give her children. The children will in turn belong to the patrilineage of the deceased husband. As we see, this marriage between two same-sex individuals does not imply homosexual relations, but it does imply the presence of a person of the opposite sex and heterosexual relations in order to produce the equivalent of a normal Nuer family. The Nuer example could therefore not be reasonably claimed to support the ideas of the proponents of Lesbian Kinship.

But we are not quite through with the Na, for three aspects of their social organization also open some general perspectives. The first is the existence of a twin authority at the head of the matrilineages, and the nature of the roles of the female and the male heads of a household. In this society where relations between women from different generations structure relations within lineages,

---

73   This analysis could provide a framework for comparing different forms of 'families', conjugal families, common-law marriage, cohabitation, reconstituted families, etc.

74   Sexual union may create couples, but not families. In many societies, a childless woman is not quite a wife, and she can be repudiated if she does not produce children, or can be relegated to a lower position in the family and in society. Note that, generally speaking, male domination means that it is the woman and not the man who is taxed with sterility. In some societies, it should be remembered, the husband and the wife hardly live together. In Ashanti culture, the husband returns to his sisters and brothers at night and goes to work with his wife at her home in the daytime.

the female head is in charge of making the daily offerings to the ancestors. She organizes the household chores and the fieldwork, manages the reserves and distributes meals. The male head's task is to represent his lineage in meetings with the other lineages in the village, and he is in charge of everything pertaining to relations with outsiders touching on land, cattle, helping neighbours, etc. All major decisions call for discussion by all members of the lineage. The division between inside and outside, even in Na society where women play such an important role and provide everyone, man or woman, with their life, their substance and their identity, has not disappeared. And as in (almost) every society known to us, the Na reserve those things having to do with 'the inside' for women. Among those things having to do with the outside, which, among the Na, are the basis of the men's power and in some contexts can raise them above their sisters and all other women, is recourse to violence in conflicts within the village or between villages or districts, trade with outsiders and Buddhism. Tibetan Buddhism, to which the Na converted a few centuries ago without forsaking worship of their ancestors and the mountain divinities, prompts all matrilineages to encourage one or several of their 'sons' in each generation to become a lama. There is an additional social division in Na society we have not yet mentioned, that between households which have land and those that do not (or not enough) and which work for those that lend them land. There, too, relations between 'houses' go through the men.

A second noteworthy fact is that, in this society, there is a tradition of helping other households and lineages when it comes time to sow and harvest crops, build a house, etc. This mutual aid rests on neighbourly relations between different matrilineages or on the help of distant blood relatives from the same matrilineage but living in separate households. In short, in this society, there is no need of brothers-in-law to lend a hand; neighbours and distant blood relatives fill the bill. And anyway, there are no 'real' brothers-in-law.[75]

Lastly, in this society which constantly stresses the obligation to treat all members of the household equitably, periodical conflicts erupt which divide the matrilineages and lead to splits. Most of these conflicts occur between two sisters who quarrel over authority in the household or between mothers who feel their children are treated unfairly, and so on. And, too, despite the fact that it is extremely easy for Na men and women to have sexual relations with

---

75   The Na are a far cry from the Arapesh, who told Margaret Mead: 'We don't sleep with our sisters. We give our sisters to other men, and other men give us their sisters . . . What, you would like to marry your sister! What is the matter with you anyway? Don't you want a brother-in-law? Don't you realize that if you marry another man's sister and another man marries your sister, you will have at least two brothers-in-law, while if you marry your own sister you will have none? Who will you hunt with, who will you garden with, who will you go to visit?' M. Mead, *Sex and Temperament in Three New-Guinea Societies* (New York, Morrow, 1935), p. 84, cited by Lévi-Strauss in *The Elementary Structures of Kinship*, p. 485.

members of other houses and to change partners frequently, sometimes a man will get it into his head to remain the lover of a woman who has decided to enter into a relationship of 'open visits' or 'official cohabitation' with another man. This obstinacy is called 'stealing the sex' of a woman, and it falls first of all to the woman to manage the situation, which often results in physical confrontations between the two men (in which the woman's brothers or uncles do not interfere). Despite the fact that children belong to their mother's lineage and no one cares about who their genitor is or that men do not pay any particular attention to the children whom they suspect may be the result of their attentions, the desire to enjoy a partner, even in a society that logically does not encourage jealousy, creates a problem when someone attempts to impose or perpetuate the relationship. Lastly, in this society, brothers sometimes clash with their sisters, and the rivalry can become ferocious when a brother imposes on his mothers and his sisters open cohabitation with a woman they do not approve of. In sum, while sex in this society does not have the capacity to create alliances between kin groups, alternatively, it can undermine them and make them fragile.

Our study of Na society allows us to draw a series of theoretical conclusions.

In this society which does not recognize marriage and makes of extended and public cohabitation between a man and a woman an exception rather than the rule, which does not recognize the existence of blood relatives on the father's side (since it does not care who a child's genitor is), and which gives importance to the blood relatives of a man or woman who unite sexually only when need be (to save a matrilineage that lacks women or men), in short, a society which recognizes only maternal consanguines (but not real affines), in this highly particular society, kinship is reduced to the relations and groups created by ties exclusively through women, which link individuals of both sexes and different generations and connect them to a common ancestress at least six generations above. Here incest of the so-called first type is completely forbidden and punished. But a man may unite with two sisters or a woman with two brothers, and no one finds this reprehensible.

Na kin groups are therefore obliged to look elsewhere for the means of reproducing themselves. They do this by exchanging among themselves men who, in the course of their discreet or visible visits, come seeking their own pleasure but also bring the other 'houses' the benefit of their sperm-rain. Instead of the women circulating between groups and between men, here we have men circulating among groups and among women. In place of gifts and counter-gifts of persons, we have gifts and counter-gifts of a substance, sperm, which helps the foetus already present in the woman's womb to become a child and to be born. The Na are therefore not an exception to the theory proclaimed by Tylor and Lévi-Strauss – but originally formulated by Saint Augustine and others well before them – that, by forbidding the union of brothers and sisters, societies are compelled to exchange. It is thus through exchange that each group that renounces incest is able to reproduce itself. One of the two theories advanced to explain the existence of the prohibition of incest of the first type is thus confirmed, even though it needs to be reformulated.[76] But the example of Egypt will show that it does not account for all of the societies in which marriage exists.

If the prohibition of heterosexual incest (of the so-called first type) compels the society to exchange, it does not seem necessarily and mechanically to oblige it to establish marriage alliances that are formally recognized between the kin groups that give each other the human means to reproduce themselves. In order for alliances to become established between groups, in addition to the exchange of sexual substances, the sexual unions between two (or several) individuals of the two sexes must:

1. be known publicly;
2. entail reciprocal obligations and different rights between the individuals involved;
3. entail for these different individuals obligations toward any children born of these unions;
4. concern not only the persons who unite but their kin groups (consan-guines), which through their union also enter into relationships of mutual obligations and obligations toward any children born of this union;
5. be remembered, up to a certain point, by the persons and the surround-ing society.

The example of the Na shows clearly that the exchange of substances is not enough to create alliances. This exchange must also be recognized as creating obligations between the persons and the groups giving and receiving these substances. And these obligations can arise only if what is given or received is seen and experienced as being an essential component of each person's identity. But what the Na women receive from the men, what their groups receive from other groups is not a 'substance' that mixes with their own, but a rain that sets in train what was *already theirs*, the foetus deposited in the woman's womb by a deity.[77] There is nothing in common between the furtive Na genitor and the Trobriander 'father', a man who shapes the foetus by repeated acts of coitus and

---

76 The two theories are that of Tylor and Lévi-Strauss in contrast to that of Malinowski, Seligman, etc.

77 For the Na, 'the woman's aim in having intercourse is to make babies, the man's is to have pleasure, "to have fun" and to perform a "charitable act"' (Hua, *Une société sans père ni mari*, p. 96).

nourishes it with his sperm without it contributing anything to making the bones and flesh of the child that in any event will belong to its mother's and mother's brothers' clan; a 'father' who, when the child is born will nourish it with the yams he has grown, will give it a name,[78] will help it enter the Kula ring, etc.

There is neither husband nor wife for the Na, but no mixing of substances either, no *una caro* that would turn affines into consanguines. This explains a major theoretical consequence: without affines, there can be no incest of the second type, in any of the three forms Héritier includes under this term: incest with affines of my consanguines, incest with consanguines of my affines, or indirect incest between same-sex consanguines via a third party of the opposite sex.[79] Yet, because the taboo on incest between consanguines via the female line exists (but, I stress, not the other sexual prohibitions which, in the Christian West, are covered by the term incest), two conclusions must be drawn. Incest between consanguines is distinct from the prohibitions concerning affines, which are not necessarily to be considered as incest taboos. Furthermore, as the example of the Na shows, where there is no taboo on unions of the second type (a man with two sisters, etc.), this type of union *cannot be the universal* basis for so-called incest of the first type.

But let us return one last time to incest in Na society, which, owing to the absence of 'husbands' and 'fathers' in the matrilineal consanguineous family, displays a highly specific aspect but still sheds a bright light on the other forms of incest that arise when marriage or other forms of socially recognized union exist. For sexual relations in Na society are forbidden not only between opposite-sex consanguines of the same generation, but also between opposite-sex consanguines of different generations. Not only may a woman not have sexual relations with her sons, but she cannot have intercourse with her sisters' sons, and an uncle cannot have sexual relations with his nieces, or a great-aunt with her great-nephew, and so on for all generations living together in the same place.

Incest within a Na 'family', as in practically all types of human family with the exception of the ancient Egyptians and a few other peoples, thus combines, as Brenda Seligman rightly observed, two taboos: 'One is the union of parent and child, the other is of siblings of opposite sex.'[80] From this she concluded that

---

78   Unlike the Trobrianders, whose children cannot help but look like their father, among the Na, the child can only look like its mother: 'If the sow's mouth turns up, the piglets' mouths turn up.'

79   Hua, *Une société sans père ni mari*, p. 212: he cites the example of a man living with two sisters at the same time, and of a man living with a woman and afterwards with her daughter.

80   B. Seligman, 'The Problem of Incest and Exogamy', *American Anthropologist*, vol. 52 (1950), p. 306.

the obligation to seek a marriage partner outside the family could explain the prohibition on sexual relations between brother and sister, but could not explain that on relations between parents and children, another limit to Lévi-Strauss' incest theory. She therefore suggested that incest has two functions: one directed outward, outside the family, which ensures the exchange of partners between families, thus paving the way for marriage alliances (Lévi-Strauss' theory), and the other directed inward, within the family, which ensures internal cohesion, founded both on cooperation between family members and on various kinds of relations of authority and responsibility between parents and children and between older and younger (Malinowski's theory). In the case of the Na, these two theories (which Lévi-Strauss tried to contrast and present as contradictory) are sustained, whereas this society does not have 'marriage alliances'.

Nevertheless, it must be noted that the 'outward' function of the incest taboo, the obligation to renounce sexual union with sames in order to enable exchanges or alliances with others, also works to prohibit incest between parents and children. Or to put it another way: when Na women renounce their brothers' sperm for that of other women's brothers, they must also renounce the sperm of their sons and their nephews, for, unless they allow their brothers to sleep with their daughters, in other words maternal uncles with their nieces, Na women know that their daughters will benefit from the sperm of the sons of other women.[81]

FINAL JOURNEY OUTSIDE THE WEST AND FAR FROM OUR OWN TIME: DISCOVERING ANCIENT EGYPTIAN AND IRANIAN 'ABOMINATIONS'

If we did not know about the Egyptian custom of brothers and sisters marrying, we would assert, wrongly, that it is universally recognized that men cannot marry their sister. [82]

---

81 For more information on the Na, see L. Barry, 'Le tiers exclu', *L'Homme*, no. 146 (1998), pp. 223–47; P. Bouchery, 'Interpréter l'exception. Une société qui questionne l'anthropologie de la parenté', *Archives européennes de sociologie*, vol. 40, no. 1 (1999), pp. 156–70; S. Chuan-kang, 'Tises and Its Anthropology Significance: Issues around the Visiting Sexual System among the Moso', *L'Homme*, nos. 154–5 (2000), pp. 697–712; C. Geertz, 'The Visit: Review of *A Society without Fathers or Husbands: The Na of China* by Cai Hua', *The New York Review of Books*, 18 October 2001. Nancy Levine and other Tibet specialists have also observed the disappearance of marriage in many zones practising polyandry subsequent to the land-ownership reforms imposed by the Chinese in 1959 (followed by more reforms in 1970 and 1980–1). Increasing numbers of men and women contracted informal unions that by no means implied their living together or sharing productive and domestic tasks or property. Cf. N. E. Levine, 'The Demise of Marriage in Purang Tibet: 1959–1990', in P. Kvaerne (ed.), *Tibetan Studies* (Oslo, Institute for Comparative Research in Human Culture, 1994), vol. 1, pp. 468–80.
82 Sextus Empiricus, Greek philosopher and physician, second century CE, *Outlines of Pyrrhonism*, 3, 324, quoted by K. Hopkins, 'Brother–Sister Marriage in Roman Egypt', *Comparative*

The Na provided us with the example of a society practising exchanges (of sperm) between matrilineages without these exchanges being the occasion to found alliances. Paying a visit to the ancient Egyptians, we discover a society where, over the centuries, it seemed normal for brothers and sisters to marry each other, and where such marriages were even strongly encouraged, not only within dynastic families but in the rest of the population. In this way a large number of marriages, in so far as they united two of the most closely related blood relations, were alliances without exchange, contrary to the Na, who practised exchanges without alliances. But, in marrying within their own families, the Egyptians did not create new alliances either.

Egypt was one of the Mediterranean societies that had not yet been exposed to the influence and pressures of either Christianity or Islam. In all of these societies around the Mediterranean Basin, and even in Rome,[83] marriages were contracted with close relatives, with first-degree cousins on the father's or the mother's side. An Athenian could marry his agnatic half-sister but not his uterine half-sister. A Spartan could marry both of these half-sisters. In Sparta, several brothers could marry the same woman and share her children among them (adelphic polygamy). But in Athens and Sparta a man could not marry a direct ascendant (mother, grandmother) or a direct descendant (daughter, granddaughter) or a real sister.[84] In Athens, again, when a man died leaving behind a daughter but no sons, this man's brother would marry his orphaned niece under the surveillance of the city's archontes, who saw to it that the 'houses' (oikoi) of Athenian citizens did not die out for lack of descendants and therefore authorized or imposed such epicleric marriages.[85]

In short, our visit to Egypt takes us into a world at the far pole from the Christian kinship system, which multiplied the degrees of relationship by blood

---

Studies in Society and History, vol. 22, no. 3 (1980), pp. 303–54. A shorter version of this article appeared in P. Bonte (ed.), Epouser au plus proche. Inceste, prohibition et stratégies matrimoniales autour de la Méditerranée (Paris, Editions de l'Ecole des Hautes Etudes en Sciences Sociales, 1994), pp. 79–95.

83   The case of Rome is more complex because, depending on the period, such close consanguineous or affinal unions were authorized or prohibited by law. But until the fifth-century CE, we find requests for dispensation to marry the sister's daughter or the father's brother's daughter, etc. See P. Moreau, 'Le mariage dans les degrés rapprochés: le dossier romain', in Bonte (ed.), Epouser au plus proche, pp. 59–78. See also Y. Thomas, 'Mariages endogamiques à Rome. Patrimoine, pouvoir et parenté depuis l'époque archaïque', Revue historique de droit français et étranger, 3 (1980), pp. 345–92; A. C. Bush and J. J. Mettugh, 'Patterns of Roman Marriage', Ethnology, vol. 14, no. 1 (1975), pp. 25–46; P. Corbett, The Roman Law of Marriage (Oxford, Oxford University Press, 1930); B. D. Shaw and R. P. Saller, 'Close-Kin Marriage in Roman Society', Man, vol. 19, no. 4 (1984), pp. 432–44.

84   Sally C. Humphreys, 'Le mariage entre parents dans l'Antiquité classique', in Bonte (ed.), Epouser au plus proche, pp. 31–58.

85   Ibid., p. 33. The order of succession for marrying an epikleros was very strict: FB, FZS, FFB, FFZS. No relative on the mother's side had the right.

or marriage that prohibited marriage and obliged people to marry far from home (in terms of genealogical distance). Yet the more we observe the ancient Mediterranean world, with the exception of Rome, the more the number of prohibitions on marrying close relatives diminishes. It is as though people and kin groups (families, *genos*, etc.) constantly practised twin strategies: marrying as close to home as possible and marrying far from home, thus combining the double advantage of reinforcing what one already has by not dividing it and adding to what one already has the advantages of new alliances. This twin policy is still practised today in Islamized societies governed by Koranic law. The preferred marriage in that case is with the father's brother's daughter, the patri-lateral parallel cousin, though the other cousins on both sides of the family are not forbidden.[86] And since a Muslim is allowed to take four wives, for his second or third marriage he can turn to groups further and further from home, and even to outsiders. In all events, in the nineteenth century, the existence in ancient or contemporary societies of forms of marriage with near kin that were unknown or forbidden in the West was the subject of a remarkable inventory by Alfred Henry Huth,[87] who based his study on earlier work by G. Wilkinson (1837) and W. Adam (1865). The Egyptians and the Iranians already had starring roles.[88] In France, the discussion on marriages with close kin would get under way only much later, so influential was Lévi-Strauss' thesis that kinship is basi-cally alliance and for there to be alliance, a brother and a sister must renounce sexual union and marriage with each other.[89]

---

86   P. Bonte, Introduction, in Bonte (ed.), *Epouser au plus proche*, p. 21.

87   A. H. Huth, *The Marriage of Near Kin* (London, 1875). See also W. Adam, 'Consanguinity and Marriage', *The Fortnightly Review*, nos. 12 and 13 (1865), pp. 80–90 and pp. 700–22; Sir G. Wilkinson, *Manners and Customs of the Ancient Egyptians* (London, 1841).

88   This led Westermarck to attack Huth in his *History of Human Marriage* (1891), since the Egyptian and Iranian data contradicted his thesis according to which the fact of a brother and sister being raised together extinguished all sexual desire between them. The argument was rekindled in the 1980s by A. P. Wolf (A. P. Wolf and C. S. Huang, *Marriage and Adoption in China, 1845–1945* [Stanford, Stanford University Press, 1980]) concerning Sim-pua marriage in China, in which a girl was adopted as a child in view of later becoming the son's wife, and was thus raised by her future parents-in-law as their own child. Earlier, M. Spiro had already attempted to show that children raised together in the same kibbutz later avoided marrying each other or found the idea repugnant. See M. E. Spiro, *Children of the Kibbutz* (Cambridge MA, Harvard University Press, 1958).

89   *Epouser au plus proche*, the work edited by Pierre Bonte, who claims to have been inspired by Lévi-Strauss' text, contributes much important documentation on societies of Antiquity; but it does not open up a serious discussion of the examples that challenge Lévi-Strauss' thesis of the universality of the brother–sister incest taboo (the atom of kinship) as the basis of exchange and kinship. Before the publication of this volume a few anthropologists in France, specialists on societies featuring 'Arab marriage', were uncomfortable with Lévi-Strauss' theses. But Lévi-Strauss himself took the first step and threw open the discussion in a new text, 'Du mariage dans un degré rapproché', *Le Regard éloigné* (Paris, Plon, 1982), pp. 127–40; English translation: 'On Marriage between Close Kin', *A View from Afar*, translated by J. Neugroschel and Phoebe Hoss (Chicago, University of Chicago Press, 1985), pp. 8–97. However, having rapidly mentioned

Let us therefore look at Egypt in this late stage of its history, after the Hellenistic period (332–31 BCE), an Egypt that would subsequently be absorbed by the Roman Empire and administered by a Roman governor (31 BCE–25 CE). Every fourteen years, the Roman administration took a census of the whole population by family so as to determine the tax base. Keith Hopkins' analysis of these censuses shows clearly that marriage between brothers and sisters was widespread throughout Egyptian society, including among the Greeks living in Egypt. In fact, the number of marriages between brothers and sisters and between half-siblings of the same father or the same mother is estimated at between 15 and 20 per cent. Since, beginning in the second century CE, those responding to the census were obliged to give the names of their ascendants – parents and grandparents – it is not hard to find brother–sister marriages repeated over two, or even three, successive generations.

It should be recalled that the status of women in Egypt at all periods – Pharaonic, Hellenistic and Roman – was exceptionally high compared to neighbouring societies. One hymn to Isis, who was still worshipped in the Roman period, proclaimed: 'You have made women equal in power to men.' Egyptian women could own goods, they were endowed upon marriage, they could sell or buy freely and enter into all sorts of legal acts.[90] They also had the right of life and death over their newborn children. When a brother and a sister married, a valid marriage contract was drawn up, and when they divorced, each recovered what was theirs (property they had managed separately during their life together). This was nothing new, since, a thousand years earlier, at the time of the New Pharaonic Empire, the Egyptian woman already enjoyed the same rights. A final point needs to be underscored: there is abundant documentation of the love and even passion that could exist between and unite a brother and sister in marriage. The love between a brother and sister was even the ideal of carnal love and passion, as attested by the wording of this love charm: 'Guide her to me . . . make my love bloom in her heart and hers in mine, as between brother and sister, I want to father her children.'[91]

In the end, brother–sister marriage appears as the ideal for Egyptians, and, as Keith Hopkins writes (with tongue in cheek?) that nothing suggests that a sister in marrying her brother, in Egypt, thought she was doing anything out of the ordinary.[92] With no play on words intended, in uniting, a brother and a

Athenian marriage with the agnatic half-sister, he quickly moved on, without mention of either the Egyptians or the Iranians.

90   An exceptional status even when compared with that of women in many twenty-first-century societies.

91   Hopkins, in Bonte (ed.), *Epouser au plus proche*, p. 86.

92   Ibid., p. 85. An Egyptian horoscope, which has come down to us in its Latin translation, states: 'A Favourable Horoscope: If a son is born when the Sun is in the terms of Mercury, he will be successful and have great power . . . He will be brave and tall and will acquire property and

sister were performing an altogether 'normal' act in their society, but at the same time they were making the ideal marriage, the very marriage that had always been practised by the pharaohs, who married their sisters in order to reproduce on earth the divine union that had brought forth their ancestors, the marriage of Isis and Osiris, both brother and sister and husband and wife. A sacred hymn from the fourth century BCE celebrates their union in the following terms:

> O Great Bull, lord of passion,
> Lie thou with thy sister Isis,
> Remove thou the pain which is in [her body],
> That she may embrace thee.[93]

Unlike their subjects, among whom polygyny, without being forbidden, was infrequent, the pharaohs could have several wives and concubines, but the 'great wife', the queen, was usually the Pharaoh's sister, or could also sometimes be a high-ranking foreigner. Marriages with close kin thus did not exclude marrying afar. The two completed each other. But the sister was chosen because, 'inheriting in the same degree and in equal proportions the flesh and blood of the Sun, [she] was the best qualified to share the bed and throne of her brother'.[94]

---

moreover will be married to his own sister and will have children by her' (cited in Hopkins, 'Brother–Sister Marriage in Roman Egypt', *Comparative Studies in Society and History*, vol. 22, no. 3 [1980], p. 303). We will see that brother–sister marriage, *xwêtôdas*, among the Iranians was also regarded as the ideal marriage.

93   Ibid., p. 344, citing Plutarch: 'Isis and Osiris were in love with each other even before they were born and had intercourse in the darkness of the womb.'

94   Goody, *The Oriental, the Ancient, and the Primitive*, Chapter 10, pp. 319–41, n. 4. Goody borrowed the quotation from G. Maspero, *Histoire ancienne des peuples de l'Orient classique*, I: *Les Empires* (Paris, 1968), p. 270. 'As queen she had her own followers, showed herself in public and played an important role in state ritual.' Goody cites a remarkable passage from Diodorus of Sicily (44 BCE), who had travelled extensively, written a history of all the (known) peoples of the world in forty volumes and considered that brother–sister marriage should be compared with the marriage of Isis and Osiris and with the very high status of women in Egyptian society: 'The Egyptians also made a law, they say, contrary to the general custom of mankind, permitting men to marry their sisters, this being due to the success attained by Isis in this respect; for she had married her brother Osiris, and upon his death, having taken a vow never to marry another man, she both avenged the murder of her husband and reigned all her days over the land with complete respect for the laws, and in a word, became the cause of more and greater blessings to all men than any other. It is for these reasons, in fact, that it was ordained that the queen should have greater power and honour than the king and that among private persons the wife should enjoy authority over her husband, the husbands agreeing in the marriage contract that they will be obedient in all things to their wives.' (D. de Sicile, *Bibliothèque historique* [Paris, Les Belles Lettres, 1993], I, 27, pp. 85–7, cited in Goody, *The Oriental, the Ancient and the Primitive*, p. 324.) Perhaps, being Greek, Diodorus attributed the Egyptian woman a higher status than she enjoyed in reality. (Cf. D. de Sicile, *Bibliothèque historique*, I, 27, p. 64.)

In short, the Egyptians were past masters at 'accumulating identity', and there was no threat of cosmic or social catastrophe attached to the union of siblings, regarded in the West as one of the worst kinds of incest. But other Eastern peoples are purported to have gone further still, and to have surpassed the closest degrees of marriage by allowing marriage not only between a brother and sister, but also between a father and his daughter, and lastly, the ultimate 'abomination', union of a son and mother. This was the crime of which Euripides accused the Persians, the Greeks' greatest enemies, whom they (the Greeks) regarded as barbarians but also feared.[95]

In 212 CE, the Emperor Caracalla made the Egyptians and the other peoples of the Roman Empire citizens of Rome. In order to become Roman citizens, the Egyptians were forbidden to practise their customs on pain of losing all they owned. 'Romans cannot marry their sisters or their aunts.' After Emperor Constantine's conversion to Christianity in 312, Roman law was reinforced by Christian dogma. Brother–sister marriages became inconceivable and were 'banished from popular memory'. Rome and Christianity had won. But a papyrus dating from the seventh century containing a Christian marriage contract recalls that the bride must be 'a virgin and neither the brother's sister, nor the sister's sister, nor the father's sister, nor the mother's sister'. The victory of the Christian West was short lived, though, since Egypt would soon be conquered by Islam.

In Iran, *xwêtôdas* marriages between close blood relatives, far from having disappeared under the influence of the Christian Churches, were restored and

---

95   See Euripides, *Andromache* (vv. 173–6): 'Foreigners, they're all alike. Father in bed with daughter, mother with son, sister and brother at it. Nearest and dearest kill each other. And no law to stop them!' It is interesting to recall that, when the people of Israel returned from exile in Babylon, they performed a series of purification rites because they had married foreigners and shared in the 'abominations' of these peoples: 'the leaders approached me to say, "The people of Israel, the priests and the Levites, have not broken with the natives of the countries who are steeped in abominations – Canaanites, Hittites, Perizzites, Jebusites, Ammonites, Moabites, Egyptians and Amorites – but have found wives among these foreign women for themselves and for their sons; the holy race has been mingling with the natives of the countries"' (Ezra, 9: 1–2; quoted in Goody, *The Oriental, the Ancient, and the Primitive*, pp. 341–2). Similarly, after their return from Egypt, when Moses forbade the Hebrews to continue doing like the Egyptians. In ancient Israel, marriage with the patrilateral parallel cousin, but also with cross cousins, sororal polygyny (Jacob's marriage) and levirate were practised. But, as in Egypt, marriage with only one wife was probably preferred. Let us recall that Moses himself was born from the union of a man and his father's sister. But Moses changed these customs so as to single out the tribes of Israel from the Egyptians but also from the neighbouring tribes in the land of Canaan. Before setting out the rules found in the book of Leviticus, the Lord had indeed said to Moses: 'Not like the deeds of the land of Egypt in which you dwelt shall you do, and not like the deeds of the land of Canaan into which I am about to bring you shall you do, and according to their statutes you shall not walk. My laws you shall do and My statutes you shall keep to walk by them. I am the Lord your God' (Leviticus 18: 3–4, translated by Robert Alter). These prohibitions required the Hebrews to give up some of the old Abrahamic customs.

consolidated at the end of the third century, when Mazdaism won out over Manicheanism. But from the seventh century and the end of the Sassanid Empire (224–650 CE), the Iranian 'abominations' would also disappear under the influence, this time, of Islam.[96] The oldest documents attesting to marriage between a brother and one or two sisters date to the Acheminide period (550–300 BCE), but there is no evidence to disprove that these practices existed before this time and were also found in strata of the population other than the royal dynasties, nobility and priests. In all events, these customs continued under the Parthians (200 BCE–224 CE) and until the end of the Sassanid Empire (650 CE).

As early as 1947, an anthropologist, J. C. Slotkin,[97] attracted the attention of his colleagues by publishing an article in the journal *American Anthropologist*, entitled 'On a possible lack of incest regulations in Old Iran'. Two years later, W. Goodenough[98] believed, wrongly, that he had refuted Slotkin's conclusions by affirming that the Parisis, descendants of Mazdeans who had fled to India in the tenth century, interpreted these unions as being not between brother and sister but between first cousins, and that, when the texts actually referred to unions between brother and sister, father and daughter, it was to strengthen the convictions of those peoples for whom these unions were repugnant.

Today the documentation has grown, the translations are more accurate and there is no longer any doubt that *xwêtôdas* unions were practised not only within the royal families but also in other segments of the population.[99]

Let us look first of all at the royal family and the nobility during the Acheminide Empire. Cambyse II, son of Cyrus, second king of the Acheminide dynasty, married two of his sisters. Artaxerxes II, son of Darius II, married two of his daughters. Finally, a very rare case, Quintus Curtius, satrap under Darius III, married his own mother, with whom he had two sons. After the fall of the Acheminide Empire, one of the Parthian kings in the first century BCE married two of his sisters. Later, the founder of the Sassanid dynasty, Ardachis, married his own sister. In addition to the royal families, the aristocratic families, too, practised brother–sister marriage. At the beginning of the seventh century, a noble relative of the Sassanid royal family and follower of Mazdeanism married his sister, then divorced her when he converted to Christianity.

Aside from these marriages with close relatives, other forms of marriage were practised with, it seems, a preference for marriage with the mother's

---

96   According to Al-Beidawi, soothsayers were forbidden to practise by Mahomet.
97   J. C. Slotkin, 'On a Possible Lack of Incest Regulations in Old Iran', *American Anthropologist*, N.S. vol. 49, no. 4 (1947), pp. 612–17.
98   W. Goodenough, 'Comments on the Question of Incestuous Marriages in Old Iran', *American Anthropologist*, vol. 51 (1949), pp. 326–88.
99   For more information on all these points, see C. Herrenschmidt, 'Le xwêtôdas ou "mariage incestueux" en Iran Ancien', in Bonte (ed.), *Epouser au plus proche*, pp. 113–25.

brother's daughter, the matrilateral cross cousin. Here we are back in a familiar world, that of cousin marriage, with the particularity that marriage with the mother's brother's daughter often went together with the fact that the wife-givers were not at the same time takers because they outranked the takers. Clarisse Herrenschmidt describes the dilemma confronting royal families: they had at once to affirm their incomparably superior status to that of the nobility and at the same time consent, out of self-interest, to an alliance.[100] On the other hand, the desire of aristocratic families to marry into the royal family, with nobles, to become the son-in law or brother-in-law of the king, is altogether understandable. This is attested by the fact that the nobles who had helped Darius I seize power after the assassination of Cambyse's brother, the legitimate heir to the throne, demanded that henceforth Darius marry women from their lineages.

But the problems of status and power strategies are not enough to explain the spread of *xwêtôdas* marriages to other parts of the population, among the Mazdean priests, known as *magi* (sg. *magus*), and the rest of the population, which shared these beliefs and rites. It was there, at the heart of these religious beliefs shared by all levels of society, that the reason for the spread of *xwêtôdas* marriages probably lies, and not only in the popular desire to imitate the practices of the upper classes.

Let us summarize, following Herrenschmidt, the main points of Mazdean cosmology and theology, which remained deeply rooted in Iran until the eleventh century CE, if not later, under the cloak of Islam. The most perfect *xwêtôdas* marriages are those 'between father and daughter, son and the one who bore him, and brother and sister'. *Xwêtôdas* is a word from the Sassanid era derived from the old Iranian *xwaêtvadatha*, which meant marriage (*vadatha*) within the *kwaêta* (family, lineage). Several *kwaêta* made a clan (probably patrilineal), and several clans, a tribe. Thus marriage among one's own people (*kwaê* = own) probably covered marriage with sisters but also with father's brothers' daughters – patrilateral parallel cousins. But owing to the fact that a man could marry his sister, he could perhaps also marry his mother's sisters' daughters.

---

100   Ibid. Herrenschmidt quotes this passage from an eleventh-century Persian novel, *Vîs ô Ramin*, by Gorgani, the theme of which can be traced back to Antiquity. The mother of Vîs tells her daughter: 'Your father is a king and your mother is a princess, in all the land I do not know of a husband worthy of you. Since you have no equal on earth, how am I to give you to someone who is not worthy of you? In all Iran there is no husband worthy of you except Prince Virou, who is your own brother.' The same dilemma existed on the other side of the world. The sister of the Tu'i Tonga, Tonga's paramount chief, who ranked higher than her brother, could not in theory marry any noble. The history of the Tu'i Tonga's dynasty reports one case of the Tu'i Tonga marrying his own sister. And on another occasion, the Tu'i Tonga's sister left to marry a paramount chief in the Fiji Islands, hundreds of miles from her home. Cf. F. Douaire-Marsaudon, 'Le bain mystérieux de la Tu'i Tonga Fafine. Germanité, inceste et mariage sacré en Polynésie', *Anthropos*, vol. 97 (2002): Part 1, pp. 147–62; Part 2, pp. 519–28.

Xwêtôdas are twice legitimized by Mazdean cosmogony and theology for the following reasons. First, they reproduce the acts of the deities that created the world. They guarantee that those who contract this type of marriage will enter paradise. They ward off or kill demons and reinforce the powers of Good in the universe. They are an obligation for followers of Mazdeanism. In effect, such marriages repeat the acts that founded the cosmos and humankind, which were the product of a triple union, between a father and daughter, a son and mother, and between the twins who were the primordial human couple. The first union took place between Ohrmazd, the chief deity and master of the Sky, and his daughter, Spandarmat, deity of the Earth. They begot a son, Gayomât, a giant who lay with his mother, Earth. From their union were born Mashya and Mashyani, the twins who in turn united in the desire to have a son. All humans therefore came from these three *xwêtôdas*. But in the beginning, there was no sexual difference between Mashya and Mashyani; it was only when they were fifteen that Ohrmazd breathed on them and made them different so that they might unite and mingle their seed. Now, female seed is cold, wet, red, etc., while male seed is hot, dry, white, etc. Bones are female; the brain and the spinal cord, male; and so on. If the proportions of water (female) and fire (male) are right, power goes to the brain, and knowledge springs from the union of intuitive intelligence (female) and acquired intelligence (male).

We see how highly the ancient Iranians valued *xwêtôdas* between brother and sister. In effect, it is the union of two beings with equally strong seed that produces beings 'remarkable for the balance of opposites' found in them. A son born of a *xwêtôdas* marriage realizes within himself the most exact proportion of female and male principles, he is a being armed to fight Evil and foster Good. For Mazdeans, innate intelligence is one and the same thing as the Mazdean religion, which is actually inborn in each human. And ultimately, Mazdeanism is identified with the 'consciousness' of all who believe in it.

The reader will have understood by now that, far from being forbidden in the eyes of commoners and practised only by an elite, brother–sister marriage was, for the ancient Iranians, the most valued, the most sacred form of union. It could be celebrated only by a priest, a magus, who had himself contracted a *xwêtôdas* marriage. And the reader will also understand the reasons for the references to *xwêtôdas* marriages in the major seasonal rites and sacrifices that each year reproduced the various moments of the world's creation from the union of the father of all the gods and humans, Ohrmazd, with his daughter and wife, Spandarmat, mother Earth.

We are here at the opposite pole from Christian kinship relations. Instead of prescribing the union of two persons of opposite sex in whom all traces of pre-existing ties of consanguinity or affinity have disappeared or never existed, the ancient Iranians prescribed marriage between the two closest blood relatives. In Christian kinship relations, by uniting sexually, a man and a woman who fulfil all of the Christian criteria for marriage nevertheless unwillingly and inevitably transmit the original sin committed by the original couple from whom all humans came, a couple that was not composed of twins but of a single being, Adam, a male being, whom God divided in two parts to make Eve, the first woman. On the contrary, the ancient Iranians made of the union of a brother and a sister the ideal of marriage, that by which humans prolonged and reproduced the divine creation of the universe and humanity, a marriage that, instead of condemning the couple to hell, was their best weapon for fighting demons and gaining access to paradise. The brother–sister *xwêtôdas* marriage was thus the ideal form of marriage for all humans. As for kings, who were closer to the gods, they could add unions that were even more rare and sacred, between a father and daughter or a mother and son, thus reactivating the first two stages in the creation of the world.

On the basis of these analyses we can make a few general theoretical remarks. Summing up, most ancient societies in the Mediterranean basin and the Near East combined two principles, two strategies for ensuring the continuity and development of their kin groups: marrying as close to home as possible or marrying into other more or less distant groups but which are of equal or, even better, higher rank. Marriages between a brother and an agnatic or uterine half-sister, or between an uncle and niece, were frequent, not to mention unions with more distant relatives, for instance father's brothers' daughters and cousins of all sorts. Of these societies, the Egyptians and the Iranians carried the practice of marriage with close relatives the farthest, allowing and even favouring marriages between brothers and sisters, and in Iran between brother and sister, father and daughter (very rare) and mother and son (still more rare). But even in these societies, marriages with distant relatives or with persons unrelated existed and probably made up the majority of unions. The first remark of theoretical import is that brother–sister marriages were not an obstacle to marriages with distant relatives or unrelated persons. Families simply kept some of their women (daughters) for themselves and used the others to contract alliances. But in that case, what becomes of Lévi-Strauss thesis?

Lévi-Strauss tells us that kinship is basically alliance, and that this implies exchanging women between the families contracting the alliance and carries as a universal condition the incest taboo bearing on unions between brothers and sisters in each family. But the Egyptians, for whom these unions were not forbidden but favoured, show us that it was possible to marry without exchange (marriage between a son and a daughter), and moreover that it was possible to exchange in the absence of the incest taboo on brother–sister marriages. In short, Lévi-Strauss' hypothesis is not universally confirmed. The truth of it is not absolute but relative, and its analytical effectiveness is thus limited. It is also clear that the opposite hypothesis set forth by Malinowski and Seligman – namely that father–daughter, mother–son and intergenerational unions, but also brother–sister unions, would destroy the universe of kinship and family from inside by setting daughter against mother (father–daughter union), son against father (mother–son union), son and daughter against father and mother (brother–sister union) – is not universally confirmed either.

In addition, we see that in the case of the Egyptians and the Iranians the fact of being brother and sister, of having been raised together, does not seem to have killed the sexual desire between siblings. The passionate love letters between brother and sister found in the Egyptian archives attest to that. The very fact of having been raised with the idea that they could one day marry, and that this union was constantly described and culturally and socially experienced as a great and good thing, far from killing desire, must on the contrary have nurtured and oriented it. *Xwêtôdas* marriages imbued those who practised them with more value than Egyptian marriages: they reactivated the work of the gods, fought evil and guaranteed a place in paradise, one of the best places even, all with the blessing of the priests and the protection of the king. What forces in this case could repress or castrate desire? In short, Freud seems the winner here, and Westermack the loser. But is it all that simple?

For Freud, in the nuclear family, the son spontaneously wants to take the father's place beside his mother; and the daughter, the mother's place beside her father. And the brother must renounce having his sister and the sister her brother so as to direct their desire toward strangers who strongly resemble the mother (for the son) and the father (for the daughter). In short, desire for the (forbidden) parents exists but it has to be repressed, denied if the family and relations of kinship are to exist and continue to exist. Can it be that, despite his talent for recognizing and exploring the role of sexuality in the individual psychic construction and in social relations, Freud remained a prisoner of the Judeo-Christian complex of the monogamous patriarchal family? Here and there in the world, humanity has explored possibilities and paths that have been forbidden or ignored elsewhere. And though Egyptians regularly practised brother–sister marriage for several millennia, it does not seem that they accumulated any more hereditary defects than the peoples held to the Christian prohibitions and horrified at the idea that a brother and a sister could not only have sexual relations but could also marry and found a family.[101]

---

101 The oldest information on Egyptian marriages goes back to the eleventh dynasty, 2000 BCE. Cf. J. Cerny, 'Consanguineous Marriages in Pharaonic Egypt', *Journal of Egyptian Archaeology*, vol. 40 (1954), pp. 23–9.

My last point. Many anthropologists or philosophers, when confronted with the close unions of the Egyptians, the Iranians but also the Incas and the Polynesian chiefs, ward off any discussion or reflection on these facts by affirming that they are the practices of humans who take themselves for gods or for descendants of gods and are therefore a minority who seek to mark their non-human origins and nature by committing incest. Yet we now know that these practices involved many other layers of the populations – Egyptian petty civil servants and even Greeks residing in the country, as well as many others.

Others recognize that religious beliefs may have inspired these practices but voice theoretical doubts inspired by a critical (and even 'Marxist') conception of the role of ideologies in the making of societies and history. As Keith Hopkins writes: 'We can hardly follow the creation myth literally and believe that the gods did it first and men simply imitated. And gods often reveal their divinity by doing what men cannot do, or even what they should not do.'[102] This is also the position of Jack Goody, who takes doubt about the explanatory value of the religious factor even further: 'In any case, if the gods are to be regarded as the imaginative creations of men, their deeds alone cannot provide a total explanation for human conduct, especially where some societies attempt to follow, others to reverse their ways of doing things.'[103] But this is a curious way of looking at religion, especially when it comes to the ancient Orient, where, all power over men sought its foundations and found its forms in religion. And how can a social reality be considered simply as a product of the imagination, in particular this religion that filled the land with temples and palaces which swallowed up a considerable portion of the labour and wealth of the society and legitimized princely power over priests and commoners?

There are, in effect, two ways for humans to position themselves with regard to the gods. Either they declare that there is a continuity among gods, kings and simple humans. This is the case with the Egyptians, who believed that the breath inhabiting all living creatures, and humans in the first place, was a parcel of the divine breath, of the Kâ of the pharaoh, a god living among men.[104] This was

102   Hopkins, 'Brother–Sister Marriage in Roman Egypt', p. 344.
103   Goody, *The Oriental, the Ancient, and the Primitive*, p. 332.
104   Cf. H. Frankfort, *Before Philosophy* (London, Pelican Books, 1949), pp. 11–38. For this reason, all humans were under a lifelong debt to the pharaoh, and this debt was inextinguishable, even at the cost of their existence, and justified the forced labour and tributes that the masses owed the gods, the priests and the pharaoh. See also A. R. Radcliffe-Brown, Preface, in M. Fortes and E. E. Evans-Pritchard (eds.), *African Political Systems* (Published for the International African Institute by the Oxford University Press, London, New York, 1950), p. xxi. 'In Africa it is often hardly possible to separate, even in thought, political office from ritual or religious office. Thus in some African societies it may be said that the king is the executive head, the legislator, the supreme judge, the commander-in-chief of the army, the chief priest or supreme ritual head, and even perhaps the principal capitalist of the whole community. But it is erroneous to think of him as combining in himself a number of separate and distinct offices. There is a single office, that of king,

even more clearly the case with the Iranians, since every person's conscience was considered to be the result of the presence within men and women of the true religion, Mazdeanism.

Other societies chose to look at things differently,[105] and to affirm that there was a discontinuity between the gods and men, that humans, for instance, had lost the immortality they originally shared with the gods, or with God, through the fault of Pandora (the Greeks)[106] or Eve (Christian tradition). For the Greeks, after humans had lost their immortality, they found themselves mid-way between animals and gods, and conscious that their fate was always in the end sealed by the gods. Unaware that Laius was his father and Jocasta his mother, Oedipus killed the first and married the second. And when he learned what he had done, conscious of the horror of his crimes but also of having been the unwitting instrument of the gods' curse on the Labdacides, he put out his eyes and went into exile, a wandering blind man led by his daughter. He knew he could not escape his fate, and that was his tragedy. But Oedipus was not a sinner in the eyes of God. He was guilty in the eyes of men, but, like him, they knew he was also, through his crimes, the tool of the gods.

This is by no means the vision of the universe and the place of humans within it that would be spawned and justified by the temptress Eve and her accomplice Adam. Their fault was a sin and a stain (*macula*) that would henceforth be borne by all humankind. Because of their sin, all of the descendants of Adam and Eve, the primordial couple, were condemned to 'seek redemption' from the original sin with which every man and every woman would henceforth be born, since it is by the act that transmits life, the union of the sexes, that the original defilement is also transmitted. Henceforth the fate of humanity would be to strive to ensure, each and everyone, their salvation, by being born a second time and, through baptism and the other sacraments, entering the Church. However nothing but the grace of God ensures that a sinner, even one who has repented, will be saved. It is through this vision of the relations between God and men that we can come to understand the many prohibitions Christianity has imposed on the relations between the sexes and on marriage. To marry as far from home as possible was to minimize the combining and mixing of

---

and its various duties and activities, and its rights, prerogatives, and privileges, make up a single unified whole.'

105   Cf. J.-P. Vernant, *L'Univers, les dieux, les hommes* (Paris, Le Seuil, 2006).

106   It is interesting to recall that the Indians and the Iranians, at the time of their common origin, shared the same myths. The union of two gods, brother and sister, Yima and Yimak, is found in India with the union of the first man and first mythic king, Yama, with his sister, Yami. But in Northern India, marriages with close kin were always banned, and monogamy preferred, while in South India, whose languages and kinship systems were Dravidian, marriage with close relatives – with the eldest sister's daughter or the mother's younger sister, was common practice. Good examples of the combination of identicals not being prohibited.

388 THE METAMORPHOSES OF KINSHIP

identical flesh marked by original sin and to multiply the benefits accruing from alliances with unrelated families and groups.

But for these points of Christian doctrine, we need only to do as others have done before us and listen to Saint Augustine (354–430 CE).[107] Augustine was born and grew up in Tunisia, where marriage between very close kin was commonly practised in town as in the countryside populated by nomadic tribes. The author of the *City of God* declared war on the incestuous customs of peoples who worshipped false gods and, fifteen centuries before Tylor[108] and Lévi-Strauss, boasted the advantages of exogamy and numerous alliances. And forestalling the objection that, according to the Bible itself, humankind was born from the incestuous union of Adam and Eve, two beings who literally were of one flesh, he explains that, since they were the only people on earth, our ancestors had no other choice:[109]

After the first sexual union between the man, created from dust, and his wife, created from the man's side, the human race needed, for its reproduction and increase, the conjunction of males and females, and the only human beings in existence were those who had been born from those two parents. Therefore, men took their sisters as wives. This was, of course, a completely decent procedure under the pressure of necessity; it became as completely reprehensible in later times, when it was forbidden by religion. For affection (*caritas*) was given its right importance so that men, for whom social harmony would be advantageous and honourable, should be bound together by ties of various relationships. The aim was that one man should not combine many relationships in his one self, but that those connections should be separated and spread among individuals, and that in this way they should help to bind social life more effectively by involving in their plurality a plurality of persons. 'Father' and 'father-in-law', for instance, are names denoting two different relationships. Thus affection stretches over a greater number when each person has one man for father and another for father-in-law. Adam was compelled to be, in his one self, both father and father-in-law to his sons and daughters, since brothers and sisters were joined in marriage. In the same way, his wife Eve was both mother-in-law and mother to her children of both sexes. If two women had been involved, one as mother and the other as mother-in-law, social sympathy would have been a binding force over a wider area. Finally, a sister also, because she became a wife as well, united in herself two relationships, whereas if

---

107 L. White, 'The Definition and Prohibition of Incest', *American Anthropologist*, no. 50 (1948), pp. 416–34; Vernier, 'Du nouveau sur l'inceste?', pp. 54–85.

108 E. B. Tylor, 'On a Method of Investigating the Development of Institutions; Applied to Laws of Marriage and Descents', *Journal of the Royal Anthropological Institute*, 18 (1889): 245–69.

109 Before Saint Augustine, Saint John Chrysostom, patriarch of Constantinople (347–407) had already developed similar theses.

these had been separated, and each had involved a different woman, one being a sister, and the other a wife, the number of people bound by intimate ties would have been increased. And so as soon as there came to be a supply of possible wives, who were not already their sisters, men had to choose their spouses from their number. Not only was there no necessity for unions between brother and sister; such unions henceforth were banned . . . With the growth and multiplication of the human race this rule is observed, we notice, even among the impious worshippers of many false gods, in that their corrupt laws may permit the marriage of brother and sister, but their actual practice is better than their laws, and they tend to abhor this licence. It was indeed generally allowed that brothers and sisters should marry in the earliest ages of the human race; but the practice is now so utterly repudiated that it might seem that it could never have been permitted . . . Nevertheless, an aversion was felt from an act which, though lawful, bordered on illegality, and union with a cousin was felt to be almost the same as union with a sister – for even among themselves cousins are called brothers and sisters because of their close relationship, and they are in fact the next thing to full brothers and sisters. The ancient fathers, for their part, were concerned that the ties of kinship itself should not be loosened as generation succeeded generation, should not diverge too far, so that they finally ceased to be ties at all. And so for them it was a matter of religion to restore the bond of kinship by means of the marriage tie before kinship became too remote – to call kinship back, as it were, as it disappeared into the distance. That is why, when the world was already full of people, they did not indeed like to marry half-sisters or full-sisters, but they certainly liked to marry wives from their own family. Yet no one doubts that the modern prohibition of marriage between cousins is an advance in civilized standards. And this not only because . . . the ties of kinship are thereby multiplied in that one person cannot stand in a double relationship, when this can be divided between two persons, and so the scope of kinship may be enlarged. There is another reason. There is in human conscience a certain mysterious and inherent sense of decency, which is natural and also admirable, which ensures that if kinship gives a woman a claim to honour and respect, she is shielded from the lust . . . which, as we know, brings blushes even to the chastity of marriage.[110]

Finally, after all these journeys through the different universes of kinship, what conjecture can we make concerning the origins and foundations of incest?

---

110 Saint Augustine, *City of God* (Harmondsworth, Penguin Books, 1972), Book 15, Chapter 16.

CHAPTER ELEVEN

Concerning the Origins and the Basis of the Incest Taboo

Freud and Lévi-Strauss

At the centre of the many misuses of sex rejected by every society as being bad and sanctioned by more or less serious punishments ranging from ridicule to death, we find the prohibition of incest. But incest is not necessarily the primal crime in the eyes of every society; in ancient Rome or China, for instance, this place was reserved for parricide. Certain sexual unions threaten to destroy more than kinship relations. They also endanger hierarchical relations between members of upper and lower castes, or between peoples of different 'races' – between black and white in Apartheid South Africa, or, until recently in the American South, where the Ku Klux Klan made the laws.[1]

In contrast to these misuses of sex, of course, there are all of the uses a society allows, recommends or even prescribes. These are not only heterosexual relations between people of the same rank, religion or those belonging to the category of kin who may or must one day marry. We have seen in the case of the Baruya that homosexual relations between initiates from different age groups are not only not forbidden but are imposed on the small boys when they leave the maternal world to live in the men's house. In short, in no society is sexual activity left entirely up to each person or each group. Sexuality is controlled directly or indirectly by society – not only subordinated to its reproduction but directly placed in its service, both when it is forbidden and when it is prescribed. What is it, then, about human sexuality that makes societies forbid certain uses and favour others, which it nevertheless seeks to channel? Attempting to answer this question implies proposing an explanation of the origins and foundations of the incest taboo, although this can be no more than conjecture.

Many authors – Morgan, Tylor, Westermarck, Durkheim, Freud, Lévi-Strauss, among others – have made an attempt to do this, with more or less fertile results. Before setting out our own views, let us look at two famous conjectures: those proposed by Sigmund Freud and by Claude Lévi-Strauss.

---

1   We know that, at the close of the Second World War, numbers of women in the German-occupied countries who had 'lain' with the 'occupiers' were brought before the court and sentenced, in France for example, to have their heads 'shaved' and sometimes to be paraded naked in front of the population of the liberated towns, who insulted and humiliated them.

FREUD'S CONJECTURE: THE FOUNDING ACT OF THE INCEST TABOO, RELIGION
AND SOCIETY WAS THE KILLING AND DEVOURING OF THE FATHER

The theme of the murder of the father as the originating act of the incest taboo
and the foundation of the human society that subsequently appeared is present
in all of Freud's major works, from *Totem and Taboo* to *Moses and Monotheism*,
by way of *Civilization and Its Discontents* and *The Future of an Illusion*. We will
not attempt an exegesis of these texts here but will simply examine how they
advance one of Freud's basic theories.

On numerous occasions, Freud depicts this murder as a real event that took
place at a remote time in the prehistory of mankind and was then repressed, in
other words both forgotten and conserved in the collective and individual unconscious. In other places, though, Freud presents an event that would throw a crucial
light on the foundations of human society as a purely imaginary happening.

What kind of life did Freud envision for the prehistoric ancestors of present-
day humans among whom this founding murder theoretically took place? He
begins by reviewing various earlier hypotheses advanced to explain the prohibition of incest. First of all, Westermarck, for whom there is 'an innate aversion to
sexual intercourse with those with whom one has been intimate in childhood'.[2]
Freud concurs with Frazer's objection to Westermarck, which Lévi-Strauss also
espoused thirty-five years later:

> It is not easy to see why any deep human instinct should need to be reinforced by law.
> There is no law commanding men to eat and drink or forbidding them to put their
> hands in the fire. Men eat and drink and keep their hands out of the fire instinctively
> for fear of natural not legal penalties, which would be entailed by violence done to
> these instincts . . . what nature itself prohibits and punishes, it would be superfluous
> for the law to prohibit and punish. Accordingly we may always safely assume . . . there-
> fore, from the legal prohibition of incest [not] that there is a natural aversion to incest,
> we ought rather to assume that there is a natural instinct in favour of it, and that if the
> law represses it, as it represses other natural instincts, it does so because civilized men
> have come to the conclusion that the satisfaction of these natural instincts is detri-
> mental to the general interests of society.[3]

Freud next sets aside another explanation, this time advanced by biologists or
authors claiming to have discovered a 'rational' explanation for the customs of

2   E. Westermarck, *The History of Human Marriage* (London, 1891); quoted in S. Freud,
Totem and Taboo, translated by James Strachey (London, Routledge and Kegan Paul, 1961), p. 122.
3   Freud, *Totem and Taboo*, p. 122; quoted in J. G. Frazer, *Totemism and Exogamy*
(London, Macmillan, 1910), vol. 4, p. 97.

'primitive peoples' according to which 'primitive peoples noticed at an early date the dangers with which their race was threatened by inbreeding and for that reason deliberately adopted the prohibition'. However, Freud replies,

> even to-day the detrimental results of in-breeding are not established with certainty and cannot easily be demonstrated in man. Moreover, everything that we know of contemporary savages makes it highly improbable that their most remote ancestors were already concerned with the question of preserving their later progeny from injury.[4]

Having eliminated psychological and biological explanations for the prohibition of incest, Freud finally mentions one 'more attempt at solving it [the origin of the incest taboo]', which is 'of a kind quite different from any that we have so far considered'. This attempt is based on the two hypotheses advanced by Charles Darwin in his famous text, *The Descent of Man*. Darwin begins by refuting the then common idea of generalized sexual promiscuity among mammals in the wild: one has but to look at the 'the jealousy of the oldest and strongest male' and the fact that many of them are 'armed with special weapons for battling with their rivals'. But what about our remote ancestors? Starting from the observation of the habits of the higher apes, Darwin advances two hypotheses that Freud copies word for word, the first being that 'the most probable view is that primeval man aboriginally lived in small communities, each with as many wives as he could support and obtain, whom he would have jealously guarded against all other men'. But Darwin also mentions another possibility: it may be that man was not a social animal, but 'may have lived with several wives by himself, like the Gorilla; . . . when the young male grows up, a contest takes place for mastery, and the strongest, by killing and driving out the others, establishes himself as the head of the community'.[5]

Freud resolutely lines up behind Darwin, but he takes a stance that is both surprising and significant. Instead of starting with the hypothesis Darwin considered to be the most probable, he immediately adopts the second hypothesis, without explaining why he deliberately rejects the first while acknowledging that the second describes the 'earliest state of society', which 'has never been an object of observation'.[6] In reality, one has only to compare the implications of the two hypotheses to see the reason for Freud's choice. According to the first hypothesis, our oldest ancestors already lived in a social group. In this society, all men possessed at least one woman, and sometimes several, whom they

---

4   Freud, *Totem and Taboo*, p. 123.
5   C. Darwin, *The Descent of Man* (London, 1871), vol. 2, pp. 362–363; quoted in ibid., p. 124.
6   Freud, *Totem and Taboo*, p. 140.

jealously kept from the others. But their rivalry rarely resulted in murder or exile. In the second hypothesis, our most remote ancestors were still living like animals. They did *not live in society* but in hordes dominated by a violent male who kept all the women for himself. The rivalry between males resulted in killing the leader of the group or driving him out.

To justify his choice, Freud cites the work of one of Darwin's followers, James J. Atkinson, who had spent his life in New Caledonia and published a book entitled *Primal Law*, in which he showed that Darwin's primal horde could 'easily be observed in herds of wild oxen and horses and regularly led to the killing of the father of the herd'.[7] Freud considered this to be 'a highly remarkable theory' and '[i]n its essential feature . . . in agreement with my own'.[8] However this was only one point, for Freud remarks that the theories of Darwin and Atkinson do not leave the least room for the origins of totemism. But Freud has need of totemism in order to develop his own theory, and we will see why. First, however, we need to understand the importance for Freud of the idea of 'killing the father of the herd'. It is this idea that will enable him to explain the shift from nature to culture and, completed by the notions of totemic belief and ritual sacrifice, to explain the appearance of religion, ethics and even art.

Why then, for Freud, did human society emerge with all of the components that make it what it is today? To understand his answer, we need to return to the objections he makes to Atkinson. In effect, Atkinson assumed that the killing of the Father must inevitably be followed by murderous conflict among the sons, and that this strife would have finished off the paternal horde without the intervention of a factor that had made them renounce all claim to their sisters and remain in the horde, and which was maternal love.[9] Freud rejects this explanation and, in an attempt to shed light on the shift from the state of nature to life in society, proposes a hypothesis which, he writes, 'may seem fantastic but which offers the advantage of establishing an unsuspected correlation between groups of phenomena that have hitherto been disconnected'.[10]

---

7   J. J. Atkinson, *Primal Law* (London, New York and Bombay, Longmans, Green, and Co., 1903); quoted in ibid., p. 141. This short treatise was included in a longer work entitled *Social Origins* (London, Longmans, Green, 1903), published by Andrew Lang, a highly respected anthropologist. At the time, a debate was raging between those who maintained that totemic beliefs (Durkheim) explained the existence of exogamy by prohibiting marriage within one's totem, with one's own blood, and those who, on the contrary, saw exogamy as the primordial rule which was subsequently sanctioned by religion. This was Lang's position. The jealous father imposes exogamy on his group and the rule becomes: 'You will not marry within your own group', and if the group is named after an animal totem from which it claims descent, another rule follows: 'You will not marry someone with the same totem.'

8   Freud, *Totem and Taboo*, p. 141.

9   In *Totem and Taboo*, Freud never mentions 'mothers'. He speaks only of the father's 'women'. Cf. N. Kress-Rosen, 'L'inceste aux origines de la psychanalyse', *Études freudiennes*, no. 35 (1994), pp. 61–82.

10   Freud, *Totem and Taboo*, p. 140.

One day, the brothers who had been driven out came together, killed and devoured their father and so made an end of the patriarchal horde. United, they had the courage to do and succeeded in doing what would have been impossible for them individually. Though the brothers had banded together in order to overcome their father, they were all one another's rivals in regard to the women. Each of them would have wished, like his father, to have all the women to himself. The new organization would have collapsed in a struggle of all against all, for none of them was of such overmastering strength as to be able to take on his father's part with success. Thus the brothers had no alternative, if they were to live together, but . . . to institute the law against incest, by which they all alike renounced the women whom they desired and who had been their chief motive for dispatching their father.[11]

In thus contracting with each other to renounce their claim on their sisters and their mothers, the brothers were also compelled to look elsewhere for their women, in other groups. Thus the prohibition of incest resulted in exogamy and at the same time made it both possible and necessary for men to exchange women. In short, the banning of incest brought forth within this new form of social organization kinship relations in their twin form of relations of descent and relations of alliance. For the prohibition of incest has two simultaneous consequences: it pushes to the fore and crystallizes in various forms the ties existing between individuals because they descend from common ancestors, and it obliges these same individuals to look outside their descent group for sexual partners. In short, it forces people to marry outside the group and to exchange women. We recognize here, thirty-five years before *The Elementary Structures of Kinship*, Lévi-Strauss' thesis linking the incest taboo to exogamy and the exchange of women.

But if the incest taboo sheds light on the emergence of human kinship relations, it cannot explain, as far as Freud is concerned, the appearance of other typically human institutions such as religion and moral codes. To do that, we need to turn once more to the founding event, the fact that the sons not only 'killed' their father, but 'devoured' him as well. For Freud – and his exegetes all too often forget this – dispenses with the father's murder in two pages but devotes many more to the cannibalistic meal that followed. What role and what importance did he ascribe to the devouring of the father's body? At this point, Freud calls on the concepts of totem and the totemic animal, as well as the concept of sacrifice, which he borrows from Robertson Smith, author of the famous *Lectures on the Religion of the Semites* (1889). For Freud, in killing and eating their father, the sons performed *the first religious sacrifice* in the history of humanity. In consuming their father's flesh, they once more accomplished

---

11   Ibid., p. 142.

their identification with him and at the same time reinforced their identity with each other – because they had shared the same crime and the same flesh. Yet, once he had been killed and devoured, the Father became even 'more powerful in death than he had ever been in life'.[12] For while they hated the father, who was such a formidable obstacle to their craving for power and their sexual desires, the sons also loved and admired him.[13] This love and this admiration would give rise to feelings of guilt and the desire to repent, two sentiments which, according to Freud, are found in the two prohibitions associated with the Oedipus complex: the ban on desiring one's mother and the ban on desiring the Father's death. Why is this called the Oedipus complex? Precisely because Oedipus killed his father and then married his mother.[14]

The murder of the father and the devouring of his flesh had thus sealed a pact between the brothers and reaffirmed their identification with each other and with their dead father. But the advantages accruing from this double crime, the fact of having appropriated and incorporated their father's powers, threatened to disappear over time, and therefore, in order to repeat the murder and devouring of the father, an animal was chosen as substitute, as the father's 'totem'. It was thereafter forbidden for all those who shared the same totem to kill and eat this animal except when, in order to reassert their shared identity and their solidarity, all shared the responsibility for the deed. With the invention of the totem as a substitute for the father and the periodical and symbolic re-enactment of his murder in the form of the sacrifice and consumption of the totem animal, according to Freud, the foundations of all religion were now present.

Thus, as humankind developed, the totemic ancestors were gradually deified, the father totem became a god, and the kings themselves became father figures. For Freud, the last manifestation of these successive metamorphoses was the appearance of Christianity, wherein the religion of the son replaced that of the father, and, he writes: 'As a sign of this substitution the ancient totem meal was revived in the form of communion, in which the company of brothers consumed the flesh and blood of the son – no longer the father – obtained sanctity thereby and identified themselves with him.'[15] For Freud, then, the murder of the father and the ensuing cannibalistic meal not only initiated the prohibition of incest, and thus engendered human kinship relations based on the exchange of women by men, but also laid the foundations for all religions. However, whereas the prohibition of incest is for all time, the murder and eating

---

12   Ibid., p. 236.
13   Ibid., p. 142.
14   Ibid., p. 155. Concerning Oedipus and his significance for the Greeks, see J.-P. Vernant, 'Œdipe', in Yves Bonnefoy (ed.), *Dictionnaire des mythologies* (Paris, Flammarion, 1981), pp. 190–2; and J.-P. Vernant and P. Vidal-Naquet, *Mythe et tragédie* (Paris, Maspero, 1972), pp. 75–132.
15   Freud, *Totem and Taboo*, p. 153.

of the father must be continually re-enacted symbolically in the form of sacrifices to the ancestors and the gods and performed by the religions: '*Society* was now based on complicity in the common crime; *religion* was based on the sense of guilt and the remorse attaching to it. While morality was based partly on the necessities of society and partly on the expiation which this sense of guilt demands.'[16]

Explaining all human religions by the primordial murder of a father, the memory of which lies buried and unknown in the unconscious of every individual while acting on the 'mass psyche', shows the extent to which Freud's explanation remains prisoner of Western Judeo-Christian religious representations; and it is this ethnocentrism that keeps us from adhering completely to his explanation.

In the end, we see that the two years devoted to writing *Totem and Taboo*, the voluminous reading that, via the work of Tylor, Durkheim, Darwin, Atkinson, Frazer and Lang, took Freud from the Australian deserts to the rites of the ancient Semites and the myths of the ancient Greeks, was undertaken solely for the purpose of consolidating and justifying results that he had arrived at long before using another method, that of analysis. And one of these results is the idea that sentiments between parents and children are characterized by a basic ambivalence composed of a mixture of love and unconscious hostility, and that from early infancy every person harbours two kinds of desires permanently held back in the unconscious: incestuous desires toward parents and relations of the opposite sex (but also of the same sex) and the desire to be rid of the persons who present an obstacle to the realization of these forbidden desires, and this desire takes the shape of the imaginary murder of the father. These forbidden desires, which were suppressed and repressed in the unconscious during the early years of life, never disappear. They merely change shape and attach themselves to new objects, which thereby become substitute objects. These desires make up what Freud called the 'Oedipus complex', which each person harbours and is obliged to 'resolve' at some point in order to live as a 'normal' adult. In short, what his ethnographic and historical readings had given Freud was the confirmation of discoveries he had already made concerning the mechanisms of the mind, the psychic apparatus present in each person, whatever their society and their time. It is therefore understandable that, in 1925, looking back on *Totem and Taboo*, he wrote:

> If I were to bring together all of that with my own observations of animal phobias
> [in little Hans], and Robertson Smith's theory on the totem meal, and Darwin's
> conjecture that all men originally lived in hordes, each of which was under the

---

16   Ibid., p. 145.

dominion of a strong, violent jealous male, I could construct from these components a hypothesis, or better yet, a vision.[17]

And on two occasions in 1911, although he had *not yet written* the chapter on the murder of the Father, Freud wrote to Carl Gustav Jung, whom he saw as a 'dangerous rival', saying that he too was engaged in writing a book on the origins of religion, entitled *Psychology of the Unconscious: A study of the transformations and symbolisms of the libido*:

'As soon as I read your essay, I saw that you knew what I had found . . . all this keeping of secrets can now cease, to my relief. You therefore already know that the Oedipus complex holds the root of all religious feelings.'[18]

In July of 1911, Freud had just begun his reading, and *Totem and Taboo* would not be finished until May 1913, two years later. Yet in late November 1911, he wrote to Sandor Ferenczi: 'The work on the Totem is a mess. I'm reading big books that are of no real interest because I already know what the conclusions will be. My instinct tells me.'[19]

Finally, if one wanted to sum up Freud's context and intention when writing *Totem and Taboo*, one could say this: Freud was a materialist and started from the fact he believed to have been definitively established by Darwin, whom he admired, that modern man, in both his 'primitive' and his 'civilized' states, is the outcome of a long evolution that separated him from the great apes to which he can be compared. Freud wanted to show that his discoveries on the organization of the human psyche, the notions of the unconscious and the conscious mind, the suppression and repression of forbidden desires, the ambivalence of sentiments, the Oedipus complex, and so forth, were a new contribution to the understanding of the known or still-unknown origins of religion, moral codes and society. In the scientific context of his time, dominated as it was by evolutionism in the natural and social sciences, he wanted to show that his discoveries were rooted in the biological and social evolution of humanity and that they shed new light on this evolution. Having written modestly at the start of Chapter 4 of his book that only a synthesis of the contribution made in the *all* fields of research would show the relative importance of psychoanalysis for understanding the genesis of religion,[20] he went on to assert in the final lines of *Totem and Taboo* that 'It does, however, follow from the nature of the new

---

17   S. Freud, in *Sigmund Freud présenté par lui-même* (Paris, Gallimard, 1984), p. 115.

18   S. Freud, Letter to Carl Jung, 20 July 1911. S. Freud, C. G. Jung, *Correspondance* (1910–1914), vol. II (Paris, Gallimard, 1975), p. 268; this letter was not included in the English-language edition of Freud and Jung's correspondence.

19   S. Freud, S., *Correspondance* (1908–1914), (Paris, Calmann-Lévy, 1992), p. 239; this letter was not included in the English-language edition of Freud and Jung's correspondence.

20   Freud, *Totem and Taboo*, p. 99.

contribution that it [psychoanalysis] could not play any other than *a central part* in such a synthesis, even though powerful emotional resistances might have to be overcome before its great importance was recognized.'[21]

The adjective 'emotional' is significant. Freud was persuaded of the newness and exceptional importance of his discoveries and did not even envisage the possibility that there could be any 'scientific' intellectual resistance to his theories, but only 'emotional' opposition. If, at the end of *Totem and Taboo*, Freud claims to be persuaded that, in the future, psychoanalysis will play the central part in the reconstruction of the evolution of human institutions and in the search for its foundations, it is because he believes he has already shown that all of these institutions – religion, moral codes, law, art, etc. – are merely 'substitutive formations'[22] of two events that happened a very long time ago within a 'horde' of men and women in their savage state, namely: the murder of a violent, overwhelming father by his sons and the subsequent devouring of his corpse. The two events had two distinct consequences. They gave rise to new social relations, relations of kinship in their two dimensions: descent (descendants of the same totem, the same blood) and alliance (groups with whom men exchanged the women they had given up), together with religion, law, moral codes, etc. Whatever the case may be, by founding the exchange of women on the prohibition of incest, Freud took his place in the theoretical movement initiated by Morgan and by Tylor, who in 1888 was the first to assert that kinship was founded on the alternative 'between either marrying out [or] being killed out'.[23] This explanation would be taken up in turn by Reo Fortune, Leslie White[24] and finally by Claude Lévi-Strauss.

It is clear that, in attempting to show that this double crime was the real origin of human institutions and, furthermore, provided the key to their evolution (such as it could be surmised on the basis of ethnographic or historical data), Freud could do nothing other than cobble together an imaginary history – which is not only a pseudo history but also an erroneous account. Yet when he asserted that any social order is at the same time a sexual order, and when he asserted that sexual desire divides humans more than it unites them, and when he showed that all social orders, all civilizations therefore required the control and repression of human sexuality, when he stressed the fact that human emotions are ambivalent, that love contains a measure of hatred

21 Ibid., p. 156.
22 Ibid., p. 140.
23 E. B. Tylor, 'On a Method of Investigating the Development of Institutions; Applied to Laws of Marriage and Descent', *Journal of the Royal Anthropological Institute of Great Britain and Ireland*, vol. 18 (1889), pp. 245–72.
24 Leslie A. White, 'The Definition and Prohibition of Incest', *American Anthropologist*, no. 50 (1948), pp. 416–34.

and hate a measure of love, and that the social order requires the repression of hatred – the desire to remove the obstacle to the satisfaction of desire, which culminates in wanting to kill – lastly, when he showed that what is repressed is not suppressed, does not disappear but continues to exist and manifest itself in other, socially acceptable forms, Freud advanced the scientific understanding of humankind by a big step.

But instead of being content to show that humans must sacrifice something of their sexuality in order for society to exist, he wanted to make his theoretical findings credible by connecting them with an imaginary event in the biological and social evolution of man. We now understand why *Totem and Taboo* was received with so little warmth by most anthropologists[25] and notably by one of the greatest, Alfred Kroeber,[26] who fired back a volley of criticisms. Lévi-Strauss would distance himself even further from Freud's work.

LÉVI-STRAUSS' CONJECTURES: SYMBOLIC THINKING IS THE FOUNDATION OF THE INCEST PROHIBITION AND OF THE EMERGENCE OF HUMANKIND

Claude Lévi-Strauss' attitude toward Freud's work evolved over his lifetime, going from lukewarm moderation in *The Elementary Structures of Kinship* (1949) to outright hostility, denying Freud's theories all scientific value in his late work such as *The Jealous Potter* (1985). In *The Elementary Structures*, he regards psychoanalysis as a 'social science' that is 'still wavering between the tradition of an historical sociology, looking . . . to the distant past for the reason for the present-day situation – and a more modern and scientifically more solid attitude, which expects a knowledge of its future and past from and analysis of the present'.[27] Or again: 'He ought to have seen that phenomena involving the most fundamental structure of the human mind could not have appeared once and for all. They are repeated in their entirety within each conscious-ness . . . Ontogenesis does not reproduce phylogenesis.'[28] The explanation given

---

25   With the exception of Malinowski, who proclaimed his admiration for Freud's book but made the objection that, among the Trobriand Islanders, there was no repressive father but that the function of repression was indeed present in the figure and the functions of the maternal uncle. For Malinowski, Freud's theory, however fertile it may have been, was too narrowly bound up with the Western world and thereby deprived itself of exploring other possible authority figures. Freud did not answer personally but left it to one of his disciples, Ernest Jones.

26   A. Kroeber, 'Totem and Taboo: An Ethnological Psychoanalysis', *American Anthropologist*, vol. 22 (1920), pp. 48–55; A. Kroeber, 'Totem and Taboo in Retrospect', *American Journal of Sociology*, vol. 45, no. 3 (1939), pp. 446–51. See also D. Freeman, '"Totem et Tabou": une nouvelle évaluation', in W. Muensterberger (ed.), *L'Anthropologie psychanalytique depuis 'Totem et Tabou'* (Paris, Payot, 1976), pp. 57–82. Freeman's article is a highly measured and well-informed assessment of Freud's ethnographic references.

27   C. Lévi-Strauss, *The Elementary Structures of Kinship*, translated by James Harle Bell, John Richard von Sturmer and Rodney Needham (Boston, Beacon Press, 1969), p. 492.

28   Ibid., p. 491.

by Freud in *Totem and Taboo*, is for Lévi-Strauss a highly dramatic myth. 'The desire for the mother or the sister, the murder of the father and the sons' repentance, undoubtedly do not correspond to any fact or group of facts occupying a given place in history. But perhaps they symbolically express an ancient and lasting dream.'[29] And 'The magic of this dream, its power to mould men's thoughts unbeknown to them, arises precisely from *the fact that the acts it evokes have never been committed, because culture has opposed them at all times and in all places.*'[30]

Yet from the outset, Lévi-Strauss traps Freud between his two interpretations of the murder of the Father. The first made of it an actual (pre-)historic event subsequently repressed into the collective unconscious of humanity but preserved and active down to our own era. This was the interpretation Freud preferred, and it corresponded to the scientific presuppositions of his time, which gave pride of place among the explanations of human institutions to the search for their origins and then the reconstruction of the stages of their later development. But, far from reconstructing the history of these institutions, this approach had merely produced a pseudo history, the result of 'a dialectic that is victorious every time'.

But Freud had also proposed another interpretation of the murder of the Father, which this time made it an imaginary historical fact but one whose dramatic telling would allow one to understand the inner conflict that all human beings of all eras must confront and overcome in order to construct their own identity: renounce the desire that attracts them to their close relatives of the opposite sex and repress the hostility toward the parent of the same sex which is experienced as an obstacle to the satisfaction of their desire. Later, once beyond this stage and the Oedipus complex being resolved, the grown-up child will turn, for the satisfaction of his now-conscious and explicit desires, to persons of the other sex who lie beyond the circle of close kin (or those persons regarded as such).

But Lévi-Strauss does not really discuss these analyses of Freud in *The Elementary Structures of Kinship*. He considers them to be the result of an ancient dream present in each of us, which is 'the permanent expression of a desire for disorder, or rather for a counter-order'.[31] But this means that these desires stemming from human sexuality and which spontaneously clash with the established sexual and social order are not a dream. They are well and truly present in each of us and throw light on both our past and our future. Because he had discovered these facts and explored their consequences for the

---

29   Ibid.
30   Ibid.
31   Ibid.

construction of human identity, Freud had produced a 'modern scientific work'[32] despite the mythic character of the story of the murder of the Father and his own inclination to consider it as a unique but real historical event that had influenced the subsequent evolution of humankind.[33]

In reality, what Lévi-Strauss basically objects to is the idea that sexual desire and its repression structure people's relationships with others and with themselves, and shape essential aspects of their identity. In 1962, in *Totemism*, he thus states: 'Actually, impulses and emotions explain nothing: they are always *results*, either of the power of the body or of the impotence of the mind. In both cases they are consequences, never causes. The latter can be sought only in the organism, which is the exclusive concern of biology.'[34] And in 1969, when Raymond Bellour writes that 'the divides he puts in place elude the fundamental dimension of the unconscious as producer of desire',[35] Lévi-Strauss replies:

But is that the fundamental dimension of the unconscious? I am by no means convinced . . . it seems to me that the usual interpretation that [Freud] gives [of dreams] as being the symbolic accomplishment of a desire remains particularly narrow: it is probably valid for some, and even there I doubt it is enough. For me, what is fundamental in the dream is the revelation of this crucial penchant of the mind, even when it is left to work automatically, to integrate heterogeneous material which, in the present case, consists of bits of experience, of images, of real organic sensations. This need, this demand for integration are more intellectual than emotional, and it would be confusing matters to put them under the heading of desire, a notion that, from the standpoint of my research, is not operative. It exists, of course, but covers obscure forces of which we cannot even say whether they are psychic or organic . . . What we call desire, drive, affect or whatever, is simply the confused and obscure way in which we feel the effects of complex

---

32 'Interpretation of our work, as it unveils the raw material that can be called sexual in broadest sense of the term, in a further development finds a variety of uses.' S. Freud, *Nouvelles Conférences d'introduction à la psychanalyse* [1933] (Paris, Gallimard, 1989), p. 37.

33 'The phantasized return to the mother's womb is beset by obstacles that cause anxiety; the incest barrier, where does that come from? Its representative is apparently the father, the reality, the authority, which does not allow incest. Why did they erect the barriers to incest? My explanation was a historical-social, phylogenetic one. I deduced the incest barrier from the prehistory of the human family and thus saw in the current father the real obstacle that erects barriers in the new individual too.' S. Freud, Letter to the International Psycho-Analytical Association, 15 February 1924, in E. Falzeder (ed.), *The Complete Correspondence of Sigmund Freud and Karl Abraham, 1907–1925* (London, Karnac, 2002), p. 482.

34 C. Lévi-Strauss, *Le Totémisme aujourd'hui* (Paris: Presses Universitaires de France, 1962), p. 103; English translation: *Totemism*, translated by Rodney Needham (Boston: Beacon Press, 1963), p. 71. The paradox is that here Lévi-Strauss's position is not as far from Freud's as he thinks since Freud locates the source of the libido in the body.

35 C. Lévi-Strauss, 'Entretien avec Raymond Bellour', in R. Bellour and C. Clément, *Claude Lévi-Strauss: Textes de et sur Lévi-Strauss* (Paris, Gallimard, 1977).

imbalances between [these] structural arrangements [of molecules and atoms] that lately emerged with life itself.[36]

Last of all, we see that Lévi-Strauss takes exception to Freud's notion of the unconscious as a psychic apparatus where desire is produced, repressed, displaced and overcome, in the name of the idea that, in his opinion, paradoxically united Marx and Freud in the same struggle:

> I retained from Freud much more than the idea of the unconscious: first of all the confirmation, as I had already learned from Marx, that the essential practical function of the unconscious is to lie to itself; then, and particularly, that behind the arbitrary and irrational aspect of certain constructions of the mind, it is possible to discover a meaning. These are intellectual and rational notions in which desire does not play a great role.[37]

The Freudian unconscious being eliminated, there remains the problem of the relationship between the human mind (and its fundamental structures, which operate beyond the scope of the conscious mind) and individual consciousness. For if the sole function of the conscious mind is to lie to itself, scientific analysis must distance itself from individuals' representations of themselves and of their relations with others and with their environment:

> What goes on in people's unconscious is very interesting, but only in so far as, by critical observation, we can gain access to the way things happen outside: not the subjective mixture but competing orders, of an organic, intellectual or social nature, of which the emotions merely reflect the conflicts or the difficulties of adjustment in the individual conscious.[38]

But why must people lie to themselves? Why do they not have the need or the means to know the truth? These are questions Marx raised when looking for the interests served by a refusal of lucidity that is not lucid about itself. Lévi-Strauss mentions Marx, but will not search in this direction.

Finally, all of Lévi-Strauss' allusions to Freud's work avoided from the outset a crucial fact over which he always passed in silence. Namely, the fact that, with the help of a myth, Freud had already drawn the conclusion Lévi-Strauss would himself turn into a hypothesis a half century later: that the

36   Ibid., pp. 206–8.
37   Ibid., pp. 201–2. In *Tristes Tropiques*, Lévi-Strauss confesses to having had two masters, Marx and Freud, and one mistress, geology. See C. Lévi-Strauss, *Tristes Tropiques* (Paris, Plon, 1955), p. 57–8.
38   Lévi-Strauss, 'Entretien avec R. Bellour'.

prohibition of incest obliges humans to renounce their close relatives and to look beyond this circle (exogamy) for the partners with whom they will unite sexually and socially. And since this prohibition applies not to one but to all human families, they can continue to exist only by exchanging among themselves those of their members whom the incest taboo tells them to renounce. Taming desire by the prohibition of incest in the early stages of the child's development would thus be a fact and a force that compels the adult to look beyond the circle of forbidden kin for the person with whom he or she will unite sexually and socially. But whether or not desire is repressed, it says nothing about the identity of the persons who are 'suitable' to satisfy it. And whether or not they are 'suitable' depends on two things: first of all, on the kinship system prevailing in the society where the person is born and has grown up (and which determines with whom one unites and how to do this in order for the union to be socially acceptable), and, second, on the political-social relations, hierarchical or not, that exist in a society and forbid or impose certain unions between the groups that make up this society. In explaining which person is chosen in a given society, Freud, Lévi-Strauss and Marx are therefore all right, each in his own way.[39]

ELEMENTARY STRUCTURES OF KINSHIP

The first thing we will attempt to do is present a summary of the essential elements of the way Lévi-Strauss saw the origins and foundations of the incest taboo when he wrote his major book on *The Elementary Structures of Kinship*, first published in France in 1949. We will then briefly enumerate the positive theoretical consequences he drew as he analyzed a number of kinship systems in view of identifying their 'structures', in other words their operating principles and the conditions of their reproduction. Last of all, we will review the limits of his approach and then close with a few remarks on the more recent developments of his thinking on kinship.

Indeed, from 1964 Lévi-Strauss turned to the study of Amerindian myths and seemed to have lost interest in kinship, leaving further development of the field to others and indicating the problems he thought should be tackled first. At the time, these were problems connected with the interpretation of the Crow and Omaha kinship systems, which he saw as typical examples of semi-complex systems and the obstacle anthropologists needed to overcome in order finally to address the analysis of the complex systems characteristic of modern (Western)

---

39   In a very interesting book, Alain Delrieux nevertheless claims that 'Freud's incest taboo is a purely internal institution that has nothing in common with a social reciprocity principle but which is a defense mechanism conceived in sexual terms'. See A. Delrieux, *Lévi-Strauss, lecteur de Freud* (Paris, Point Hors Ligne, 1993), p. 143.

societies.[40] Later he dealt with the problems of marriages with close kin and those raised by the notion of 'house'.[41] After that, aside from a few short interventions here and there,[42] little was added to his already immense work, but it is important to point out the changes, because they go back on certain points in the author's earlier positions and strongly – and even stubbornly – reaffirm others.

From the outset, it must be recalled that, for Lévi-Strauss, prohibition of incest is not only the precondition for establishing particular social relations between humans – kinship relations which can be divided into different systems – it is also and at the same time the moment when humanity emerges from its animal state, where culture suddenly develops and subordinates nature to its own ends. In this sense Lévi-Strauss' endeavour is both a global hypothesis about the reasons for the incest taboo and a 'conjecture' about its origins. It is similar to Freud's undertaking, but is based on real facts, which he believes go back to the appearance, sometime during the prehistory of humanity, of symbolic thought combined with articulated speech.

Lévi-Strauss, too, found himself obliged to imagine what might have been the lifestyle of our distant ancestors, as yet incapable of symbolic thought and communication with each other by means of articulated speech, and living therefore in a 'state of nature'.[43] Could the research being conducted at the time on the great apes help him to imagine early man's way of life? Yet the findings (prior to 1940) show, according to Lévi-Strauss, that 'The social life of monkeys does not lend itself to the formulation of any norm . . . in sexual life, as in other forms of activity'.[44] He believed that the absence of language in our early ancestors indicates that they were not yet living in society but were gathered together in 'biological families closed upon themselves' whose members were obliged to unite sexually with each other, living in a world dominated by blood ties.

40   C. Lévi-Strauss, 'The Future of Kinship Studies', Huxley Memorial Lecture, in *Proceedings of the Royal Anthropological Institute of Great Britain and Ireland*, vol. 1 (1965), pp. 13–22.

41   C. Lévi-Strauss, 'Du mariage dans un degré rapproché', in *Textes offerts à Louis Dumont*, reprinted as 'On Marriage between Close Kin', in *The View from Afar* (Chicago, University of Chicago Press, 1992), Chapter 6, pp. 88–97; 'La notion de Maison. Entretien avec Claude Lévi-Strauss', par Pierre Lamaison, *Terrain*, no. 3 (1987), pp. 34–9; C. Lévi-Strauss, 'Histoire et ethnologie', *Annales E.S.C.*, vol. 38, no. 6 (1983), pp. 1217–31; C. Lévi-Strauss, *Paroles données* (Paris, Plon, 1984), pp. 189–94; English translation: *Anthropology and Myth: Lectures, 1951–1982*, translated by Roy Willis (Oxford/New York, Blackwell, 1987).

42   C. Lévi-Strauss, 'La sexualité féminine et l'origine de la société', *Les Temps modernes*, no. 598 (March–April 1998), pp. 66–84, and 'Apologue des amibes', in *En substance, Textes pour Françoise Héritier* (Paris, Fayard, 2002), pp. 493–6.

43   Lévi-Strauss, *The Elementary Structures of Kinship*, p. 3: 'With his probable knowledge of language, his lithic industries and funeral rites, Neanderthal man cannot be regarded as living in a state of nature. His cultural level, however, places him in . . . marked contrast with his Neolithic successors. . . .'

44   Ibid., pp. 6–7, p. 37, and p. 31: 'it is certain that these great anthropoids practise no sexual discrimination whatever against their near relatives'.

Humanity thus began to emerge from its animal state and live in society when our first pre-human ancestors became aware that, in order to survive, families would have to become socially dependent on each other for their reproduction.

How did this awareness come about? For Lévi-Strauss, this is a problem we will never solve because humans have always lived in society since they emerged from animality. But, he adds:

> Indeed, it will never be sufficiently emphasized that, if social organization had a beginning, this could *only* have consisted in the incest prohibition since . . . the incest prohibition is, in fact, a kind of remodelling of the biological conditions of mating and procreation (which know *no rule,* as can be seen from observing animal life) compelling them to become perpetuated only in an artificial framework of taboos and obligations. It is there, and only there, that we find a passage from nature to culture, from animal to human life, and that we are in a position to understand the very essence of their articulation.

As Tylor has shown almost a century ago, the ultimate explanation is probably that mankind has understood very early that, in order to free itself from a wild struggle for existence, it was confronted with a very simple choice of 'either marrying out or being killed out'. The alternative was between biological families living in juxtaposition and endeavoring to remain closed, self-perpetuating units, over-ridden by their fears, hatreds and ignorances, and the systematic establishment, through the incest prohibition, of links of intermarriage between them, thus succeeding to build, out of the artificial bonds of affinity, a true human society, despite, and even in contradiction with, the isolating influence of consanguinity.[45]

This is a crucial text. In it we see Lévi-Strauss sharing the same vision as Freud of the human condition before the prohibition of incest. We remember that, far from adopting the position held by Darwin – for whom the most likely hypothesis, from the standpoint of natural history and the evolution of animal species, was that man's earliest ancestors were already a social species, living from the beginning in society and not in families isolated from one another under the authority of a solitary male – Freud had opted for the second hypothesis, describing in passing these families as 'primal hordes', terms not found in Darwin.[46]

---

45 Lévi-Strauss, 'The family', in H. Shapiro (ed.), *Man, Culture and Society* (London/ Oxford, Oxford University Press, 1956), p. 350.

46 S. Freud, *Civilization and Its Discontents*, Authorized translation by Joan Riviere (London, L. & Virginia Woolf at the Hogarth Press, 1930). 'In prehistoric times already, where man was close to the monkey, he had adopted the custom of founding families'; or again in S. Freud, *A*

The progress made in primate research since Freud and Lévi-Strauss confirms Darwin's theory. Humans are indeed a species of primates that, like their close primate relatives, chimpanzees and bonobos, lived in mixed male and female bands and descended from ancestors also familiar with this form of social organization. Being born and living in a band means that the band, by its existence and its organization, is the very condition for the existence and survival of its individual members. If man's remote ancestors became aware, in the course of their evolution, of the need to avoid and prohibit sexual relations and unions between members of the same family, the new rules they imposed on themselves could not have given 'birth' to society, because they were already living in society. What the imposition of these rules could produce was a fundamental *change* in their mode of social life, but not the *appearance* of society.

But Lévi-Strauss had a different vision. Humanity, in order to liberate itself from a savage struggle for life, from its hatreds and its fears arising from the isolation of consanguineous families, took upon itself the law that families would henceforth bind themselves to each other by creating alliances and that they would bind themselves to each other by exchanging the 'valuable par excellence', the 'supreme gift', the woman, women. And because the law was the same for all, this exchange could only take the form of reciprocal gifts between the groups, between the families contracting the alliance. At the same time, these exchanges would give rise to the properly human relations of kinship, which – in the immense majority of societies – combine ties of affinity and consanguinity, and would also produce society, 'true' society, society built on exchange and which could appear and continue to exist only because of the prohibition of incest. But for all of that to be possible, the symbolic function of thought had first to become fully developed and then place in its service the means of communication par excellence, articulated speech. Lévi-Strauss therefore looked to the evolution of mental structures to discover the preconditions for the formulation and the imposition of the incest taboo. What are these mental structures?, he asks, and replies:

> It seems there are three: the exigency of the Rule as a Rule; the notion of reciprocity regarded as the most immediate form of integrating the opposition between the self and others; and finally, the synthetic nature of the gift, i.e., that the agreed transfer of a valuable from one individual to another makes these individuals into partners and adds a new quality to the valuable transferred.[47]

Phylogenetic Fantasy: Overview of the Transference Neuroses, ed. by Ilse Grubrich-Simitis, and translated by Axel Hoffer and Peter T. Hoffer (Cambridge MA, Belknap Press/Harvard University Press, 1987): the 'individual hordes . . . were dominated by a strong and wise brutal man as father' (p. 16).

47 Lévi-Strauss, *The Elementary Structures of Kinship*, p. 84.

Rule, reciprocity and gift, and finally the reciprocal gift (of women) as the Rule. But why women? Why not men? And why does the Rule apply first of all to the field of sexual life?

> . . . sexual life is a beginning of social life in nature, for the sexual is man's only instinct requiring the stimulation of another person . . . That it should provide a transition, in itself natural, between nature and culture, would be inconceivable, but it does give one reason why the transition between the two orders of Nature and Culture can and must necessarily take place in the field of sexual life above any other. It is a rule which embraces that which in society is most foreign to it [the animal nature of man], but also a social rule which retains what in nature is most likely to go beyond it. The incest prohibition is at once on the threshold of culture, in culture, and in one sense . . . culture itself.[48]

For Lévi-Strauss '[t]he prime role of culture is to ensure the group's existence as a group, and consequently . . . to replace chance by organisation.'[49] The prohibition of incest asserts, in a field vital to the group's survival, that of the regulation or relations between the sexes, the 'pre-eminence of the social over the natural, the collective over the individual, organization over the arbitrary.'[50] And 'the first logical end of the incest prohibition is 'to freeze' women within the family, so that their distribution, or the competition for them, is within the group, and under group and not private control'.[51] But why women and not men? Once again, Lévi-Strauss looks to symbolic thought for the answer:

> The emergence of symbolic thought must have required that women, like words, should be things that were exchanged . . . indeed, this was the only means of overcoming the contradiction by which the same woman was seen under two incompatible aspects: on the one hand, as the object of personal desire, thus exciting sexual and proprietorial instincts; and on the other, as the subject of the desire of others, and seen as such, i.e., as the means of binding others through alliance with them. But woman could never become just a sign and nothing more, since even in a man's world she is still a person . . . In contrast to words, which have wholly become signs, woman has remained at once a sign and a value.[52]

---

48   Ibid., p. 12 (translation modified).
49   Ibid., p. 32. We are not far from Freud here: Let us recall Freud's superb definition of culture in *Civilization and Its Discontents*: 'The whole sum of the achievements and regulations which distinguish our lives from our animal ancestors' (p. 278).
50   Lévi-Strauss, *The Elementary Structures of Kinship*, p. 45.
51   Ibid.
52   Ibid., p. 496.

A vital text which, on the one hand, posits the domination of men over women as a universal, present at every period and in all societies and therefore, according to Lévi-Strauss' own criteria, as a *fact of nature* and which, on the other hand, sees this de facto state as an inevitable consequence, a require-ment of symbolic thought and therefore indissolubly attached to the fundamental structures of the human mind. Another argument, which does not overlap completely with the first, is that men's desire and their need to dominate women and to exchange them among themselves is justified by the fact that 'women [are] valuables par excellence both from the biological and the social points of view, without which life is impossible, or, at best, is reduced to the worst forms of abjection'.[53] Women are thus the valuable 'par excellence', the 'supreme gift among those that can only be obtained in the form of recip-rocal gifts'.[54] Valuables par excellence but also 'scarce' valuables, for, according to Lévi-Strauss, 'in man, these [polygamous] tendencies are natural and universal' and 'only limitations born of the environment and culture are responsible for their suppression'.[55]

Finally, according to a formula that has become famous, 'the prohibition of incest is less a rule prohibiting marriage with the mother, sister or daughter, than a rule obliging the mother, sister or daughter to be given to others'.[56] It is less a prohibition than a prescription. The acts that found kinship are strung out over three complementary moments. The *prohibition of incest* imposes exogamy and the giving of the women one has renounced to others. But this gift calls for a counter-gift, and these two acts constitute an exchange that seals an alliance: (Prohibition of incest → exogamy → exchange). 'But actually there is nothing in the exchange of women faintly resembling a reasoned solution to an economic problem . . . It is a primitive and indivisible act of awareness which sees the

---

53   Ibid., p. 481. Lévi-Strauss does not tell us anything about these forms of abjection (homosexuality, zoophilia). His affirmation thus presupposes that, in certain societies, men cannot be considered as the supreme valuable. Cf. China, where the wife is worthless unless she provides her husband with a son.

54   Ibid., p. 65.

55   Ibid., p. 37. For Lévi-Strauss, 'monogamy is not a positive institution, but merely incorporates the limit of polygamy in societies where, for highly varied reasons, economic and sexual competition reaches an acute form' (p. 37). He quotes from an article by G. S. Miller, 'The Primate Basis of Human Sexual Behavior', *Quarterly Review of Biology*, vol. 6, no. 4 (1931), p. 398, to assert that 'man shares the inherent tendency to tire of his sexual partner with the higher apes' (Lévi-Strauss, *Les Structures élémentaires de la parenté*, p. 20). One could conclude from this that, for Lévi-Strauss, the woman does not have a tendency to tire of her sexual partner and deeply desires to attach herself to one and only one man.

56   Lévi-Strauss, *The Elementary Structures of Kinship*, p. 481. Further on we will see that this formulation, which seems logical enough, and puts the daughter, sister and mother on the same footing, is not. We will understand that a father can exchange a daughter for a second wife or for a wife for his son. But it is hard to see a son exchanging his mother to procure a wife. The formulation sounds nice, but it is partially meaningless.

daughter or sister as a valuable which is offered, and vice versa the daughter and sister of someone else as a valuable which may be demanded.'[57]

Renouncing one's sister or daughter (here Lévi-Strauss has forgotten the mother) in order to give them in marriage to another man thus '*establishes a right to the daughter or sister of this other man*'.[58] Consequently, all exchange is exchange among men. '*Unlike exogamy, exchange may be neither explicit nor immediate, but the fact that I can obtain a wife is, in the final analysis, the consequence of the fact that a brother or father has given her up*'.[59] Certain systems even go on to specify on behalf of whom one renounces. This is the case with the Australian moiety, section and subsection systems, and also, but in another fashion, with the Dravidian systems. Exchange is thus 'the fundamental and common basis of all modalities of the institution of marriage'.[60]

What roles do men and women respectively play in these exchanges that are concretized by different types of marriage?

The total relationship of exchange which constitutes marriage is not established between a man and a woman . . . but between two groups of men, and the woman figures as only one of the objects in the exchange, not as one of the partners between whom the exchange takes place . . . This view must be kept in all strictness, even with regard to our own society, where marriage appears to be a contract between persons . . . this cycle of reciprocity is only a secondary mode of a wider cycle of reciprocity, which pledges the union of a man and a woman who is either someone's daughter or sister, by the union of the daughter or sister of that man or another man with the first man in question . . . The lack of reciprocity that seems to characterize these services . . . in most human societies is the mere counterpart of a universal fact, that the relationship of reciprocity which is the basis of marriage is not established between men and women, but between men by means of women, who are merely the occasion of this relationship.[61]

---

57   Ibid., pp. 139–40.
58   Ibid., p. 51.
59   Ibid., p. 62.
60   Ibid., p. 479.
61   Ibid., pp. 115–16. Lévi-Strauss, who knew that, in certain Southeast Asian tribes, it was as though women exchanged men among themselves, was already endeavouring to reaffirm the universal character of the exchange of women by men when he wrote: 'This would not be to say that in such societies it is the women who exchange the men, but rather that men exchange other men *by means of women*' (ibid., p. 115, n. 1). A verbal pirouette spirits away the facts and thus the problems. Since that time, research among the Rhades of Vietnam, the Tetum of Timor, and so on, have completely invalidated this interpretation, which Lévi-Strauss invented to save his thesis on the absolute universality of the exchange of women as the fundamental basis of all kinship relations and systems.

What characterizes human society, then, is the fundamental asymmetry of the rela-tionship between the sexes. And 'asymmetry' means the domination of one sex over the other, the control of one sex by the other. There is therefore no possibility of reciprocity between the sexes. It is as though the famous universal structure of the human mind, the notion of reciprocity as the most immediate way of integrating the opposition between ego and other, was present only in men's brains, and as though the Big Bang of symbolic thought had forgotten the brains of women. Let us be clear. We do not deny the very general phenomenon of the domination of men over women, but we recall, on the one hand, that its forms and severity vary enor-mously from one society to another[62] and, on the other hand, that, in our eyes, the deep-seated reasons for male domination should be sought elsewhere than in the invariant structures of symbolic thought. Moreover, in his article 'The family', Lévi-Strauss emphasized that the division of labour, which assigned war to men and child-raising to women, is as universal as the prohibition of incest. Is this opposition also grounded in symbolic thought, or is it merely justified and legitimized by it? In the event of the latter, it would have other reasons, which are social and material.

Whatever the case, the fundamental theoretical outcome of Lévi-Strauss' endeavour was to link together three social phenomena that previous generations of anthropologists had tried to explain in isolation: (1) the prohibition of incest, (2) exogamy, and (3) the exchange of women to seal matrimonial alliances.

Yet at a purely logical level, we know that exchange can take three forms. Either men exchange women among themselves. Or, as is the case in certain matrilineal and matrilocal societies, men are exchanged among women, broth-ers by their sisters. This is the case with the Rhades of Vietnam and the Nagovisi of Bougainville – instead of bridewealth, then we see the appearance of groomwealth. Or, thirdly, as is the case in most European and Euro-American societies as well as in a few cognatic societies in Madagascar[63] or Southeast Asia, two families unite with one giving a son and the other a daughter. In this case it is hard to say that one sex exchanges the other, whereas the prohibition of incest exists and applies, as in the two other cases, for both sexes. Each family makes half the effort in creating new alliances which will enable each to perpetuate itself through its descendants.

Of these three logical possibilities, of which he was perfectly aware, Lévi-Strauss retained only one, the only one that fits, he affirms, the historical data

---

62   Many feminists certainly must wish that women in our societies played the same social role as the Nagovisi women studied by Jill Nash in *Matriliny and Modernisation: The Nagovisi of South Bougainville* (Port Moresby and Canberra, The Australian National University, 1974). See also J. Nash, 'Women, Work and Change in Nagovisi', in D. O'Brien and S. W. Tiffani (eds.), *Rethinking Women's Roles: Perspectives from the Pacific* (Berkeley, University of California Press, 1990), pp. 94–119.

63   Cf. R. Astuti, *People of the Sea: Identity and Descent among the Vezo of Madagascar* (Cambridge, Cambridge University Press, 1995), Chapter 6, pp. 80–105.

and the ideologies of societies, all of which, he claimed, operated on the basis of the universal domination of men over women. And, of course, he explained himself:

> The female reader, who may be shocked to see womankind treated as a commodity submitted to transactions between male operators, can easily find comfort in the assurance that the rules of the game would remain unchanged should it be decided to consider the men as being exchanged by women's groups. As a matter of fact, some very few societies, of a highly developed matrilineal type, have to a limited extent attempted to express things that way. And both sexes can be comforted from a still different (but in that case slightly more complicated) formulation of the game, whereby it would be said that consanguineous groups consisting of both men and women are engaged in exchanging together bonds of relationships.[64]

To be sure, whether men take the place of women in the exchange or the converse, it does not alter the formal structure of the exchange relationship, but it does change the content of social life, for the destinies of men and women cannot be the same in the one case or the other. This is a strange blind spot for an anthropologist, but let us be clear here. We are not criticizing Lévi-Strauss for having regarded male domination as a universal phenomenon, or for having assumed that the situation must have been roughly the same in the case of our ancestors. And even less are we criticizing the idea that alliance very often rests on the exchange of women between groups represented by men. The Baruya have given us a clear example with their practice of *ginamaré*, or 'sister-exchange'. We are objecting to the idea that the social subordination of women is based on the unconscious structures of symbolic thought – in short, in the last analysis on the structures of the brain – and that male domination is the universal precondition for the appearance of kinship relations.

---

64   Lévi-Strauss, 'The Family', p. 356. It is understandable that *The Elementary Structures of Kinship* was, upon publication, the object of attacks by numerous feminists, with a few remarkable exceptions, like Simone de Beauvoir, who reviewed the book in 1949 after her own book, *The Second Sex*, had just appeared. Again in 1988, in *De près et de loin*, a series of interviews with Didier Eribon (*De près et de loin. Entretien avec Claude Lévi-Strauss* [Paris, Odile Jacob, 1988]; English translation: *Conversations with Claude Lévi-Strauss*, translated by Paula Wissing [Chicago/ London, University of Chicago Press, 1991]), Lévi-Strauss returns to these attacks: 'The feminists misunderstood or misread me, for I stress that there is no human society that does not see women both as valuables and as signs. The question is pointless: one could just as well say that women exchange men; one would have only to replace the + sign by the – sign and conversely; the structure of the system would in no way be altered. If I used the other formulation, it is because it corresponds to what human societies in their near totality think and say' (*De près et de loin*, p. 148). It is not because human beings are recognized as valuable by those who dominate them that this domination disappears. Slaves were 'valuable' to their Greek or Roman masters, but the social structure would have been very different if the slaves had taken the place of the masters, even if the society had formally still been a 'slave-owning' society. We see the blindness that results from the fetishization of social structures reduced to their forms or to their formal rules.

THE THEORETICAL SCOPE OF THE ELEMENTARY STRUCTURES

Lévi-Strauss' hypotheses, unlike those of Freud, immediately demonstrated their operational value, their analytical efficaciousness, when it came to explaining the logic behind the workings of a number of kinship systems.

We will explain. Having concluded, from the parable of the murder of the father, that men had chosen to give up incest within families and to exchange the women they had renounced with each other, Freud had nothing more to say about the diversity of kinship systems. According to a prevailing idea of his time, he briefly pointed out that kinship systems in which descent was calculated through women must have preceded patrilineal systems. But beyond these generalities based on the opinion of a few evolutionary anthropologists at the end of the nineteenth century, Freud never tackled the analysis of a particular system of kinship and finally contented himself with treating the European conjugal family dominated by the father.

Lévi-Strauss, on the contrary, in positing that kinship is fundamentally exchange, first of all, like Freud, linked together as moments of the same process the prohibition of incest, exogamy and the exchange of women. Later, however, he delved into the complexity of kinship systems and showed that, in those that made a division between ineligible parallel cousins and eligible cross cousins, marriage rests on an explicit rule of exchange of women, which exchange can be or cannot be repeated from one generation to the next and concerns persons who are in the genealogical position of cross kin with regard to each other or who are classified, with respect to each other, in categories that automatically make them potential spouses (cf. the Australian moiety, section or subsection systems).

Lévi-Strauss showed that, in other kinds of systems, marriage rests on negative rather than positive (prescriptive or preferential) rules. This is the case in the Crow and Omaha systems, in which a man cannot marry in the four lineages of his father, his mother, his father's mother and his mother's mother, and must marry beyond this circle. It therefore takes each clan or lineage several generations before they can repeat the same alliance, if not with the same clan, at least with the same lineage.[65] By contrast, in Western societies with cognatic kinship systems, where there are no clans or lineages but monogamous conjugal families, the rules organizing permissible marriages are exclusively negative and concern direct ascendants and descendants, close collaterals, members of the conjugal family and close relatives by marriage.

---

65   Lévi-Strauss nevertheless pointed out that not all Crow-type or Omaha-type kinship systems were organized into clans and lineages. Some were 'cognatic'.

These extensive analyses allowed Lévi-Strauss to classify all kinship systems into three broad groups. Systems with elementary structures are themselves divided into two subgroups, depending on whether the exchange of women is direct (givers are at the same time takers) or generalized (takers are not givers), which implies the existence of at least three groups among whom the women circulate in one direction and the matrimonial wealth in another. Then come the semi-complex systems and finally the complex systems, in which there is no positive rule for choosing a spouse.

These findings shed considerable light on the study of kinship systems. And Lévi-Strauss' analyses motivated hundreds of anthropologists over a span of at least two decades to make a closer examination, when doing fieldwork, of the kinship terminologies as well as the forms of marriage these systems allowed or proscribed. Among other positive aspects of Lévi-Strauss' work are the texts he devoted to the definition of the family, to analysis of its different forms, to the status of bachelor and orphan, and so on, in a large number of societies. He also showed that satisfaction of sexual desire had little to do in many societies with the reasons for marrying and establishing a new family. Alternatively, the fact that the sexual division of labour creates a material and social interdependence between the sexes seemed to him to be the major reason for the existence of what he preferred to call 'domestic families' rather than 'conjugal' families. But at the same time – and here we encounter one of the limits of his work – Lévi-Strauss minimized the fact that what matters in most societies when it comes to marriage is not only that two families derive many advantages from their alliance in terms of cooperation, solidarity, etc., but also that they will continue to exist through the descendants born of this alliance. For sexuality is not only desire, it is also reproduction. And it is no accident that this aspect of things was minimized by Lévi-Strauss, since, for him, the crucial aspect of kinship is not consanguinity but affinity, not descent but alliance.

THE LIMITS OF THE ELEMENTARY STRUCTURES

In this section, we address the question of the limits of a work whose impact no one will contest. As opposed to a certain tradition in anthropology and philosophy and to authors such as Meyer Fortes,[66] who saw in the ties of affinity a

---

66   M. Fortes, particularly in his article 'Primitive Kinship', *Scientific American*, no. 200 (1959), pp. 146–58. Meyer Fortes is also the author of an immense work. In particular, let us cite two books devoted to the Tallensi: *The Dynamics of Clanship among the Tallensi* (Oxford, Oxford University Press, 1945) and *The Web of Kinship Among the Tallensi* (Oxford, Oxford University Press, 1949); as well as his overview of kinship, *Kinship and the Social Order: The Legacy of L. H. Morgan* (Chicago, Aldine, 1969). Toward the end of his life, Fortes' views drew closer to those of Lévi-Strauss, but also to the theoreticians of altruism with *Rules and the Emergence of Society* (London, Royal Anthropological Institute, 1983).

'secondary' aspect of kinship, Lévi-Strauss gave pride of place in the workings of kinship systems to the principles governing alliance and marriage.

The function of a kinship system, he wrote in his 1965 Huxley Memorial Lecture, is 'to generate marriage possibilities or impossibilities'. It is the motor of a society's system of matrimonial exchange. In reality, the primacy given to alliance, to ties of affinity, is rooted in considerations that have to do more with philosophy than with science. For Lévi-Strauss, it was through exchange that mankind progressively distanced himself from nature and proclaimed the primacy of culture. In his eyes, the relations of descent and filiation always draw us toward nature, toward the universe of consanguinity. But this view is not unfounded. In Chapters 7 and 8, I showed that, in all societies, a man and a woman do not suffice to make a child, and that other agents, ones more power-ful than the men and women who unite sexually and than the groups that contract alliances, intervene to transform the foetus made by humans into a child that will take its place in the cosmos and in its society. We also saw that the notion of 'being of the same blood' as one's father or mother is quite specific. In other cultures one can be of the same bone as one's father and of the same blood as one's mother. In still others, one will be of the same 'breath' as one's father and one's body will contain no substance that comes from the mother. And so on.

In short, forms of descent are *just as cultural* as forms of alliance. They are entirely determined by culture. And in these cultural representations of descent are embedded considerable social stakes in terms of the appropriation of chil-dren, the transmission of status, lands, titles, etc., which are just as important (if not more so) as the social stakes connected with one or another form of alli-ance. And lastly, while the various forms of alliance and exchange (restricted, generalized, prescriptive, preferential, cyclical, acyclical) were closely exam-ined, the forms of descent, which are very few in number (unilineal, ambilineal, bilineal and undifferentiated) were not subjected to as thorough a theoretical analysis. It is as though it were a given that descent was traced either through men or through women or through both lines, or that wife takers should not in turn give wives to those from whom they had taken wives. Furthermore, the examples of the Na, the Nayar and so on show us that alliance can even disap-pear or be reduced to fictitious relations: what exists and is perpetuated in this case are groups of individuals of different sexes and ages brought together by a descent principle that excludes part of their ascendants ('fathers', for instance).

Another limit: when he made the exchange of women among men the only form of exchange actually practised historically, Lévi-Strauss had relegated the two other possible forms – namely, the exchange of men among women (rare but real) and the union of a man and a woman who give themselves to each other and, to a certain extent, make their families allies without them having 'exchanged' one for the other – to the imaginary domain of illusory satisfactions. In making the exchange of women the sole basis of kinship relations, Lévi-Strauss could only make women's subordination to men a universal, transhistorical phenomenon, which history could therefore not alter. History, however, and not only in the West as of late, has already shown the limits of this theory. For between really exchanging women, as the Baruya do, and marrying without being aware of having exchanged a brother or a sister for a husband or a wife, there lies a sociological gulf.[67]

It is not enough to say that, in this case as well, 'exchange' is present but implicit and invisible, on the pretext that, when a woman marries a man it is because her brother (or her father) 'gave her up', or that when a man marries a woman, it is because his sister 'gave him up'. For when marriage engages two people whose 'yes' carries equal weight from the standpoint of the official union, and whom the families cannot oppose if the man and woman are both adults and respect the degrees of kinship prohibited for marriage, the fundamental asymmetry between the sexes that is characteristic of human society, as Lévi-Strauss writes, has disappeared, at least in so far as the establishment of alliances between the persons, and through them their birth or adoptive families, are concerned. People contract bonds by giving themselves to each other, and their bond is composed precisely of this reciprocal gift, whether it is made publicly (marriage) or privately (free union).

In fact it was by allowing these forms of union (cohabitation, free union), by allowing divorce, by replacing paternal authority with parental authority shared equally by the father and the mother (which subsists even in the event of separation, divorce and remarriage), that most Western societies legally put an end to centuries of women's subordination to men, at least when it comes to choosing a partner, deciding whether to marry, and so on. This is so true that today one of the favourite topics of discussion in the West is the disappearance of fathers, male fragility and the sovereignty of mothers.[68]

---

67 '[N]o matter what form it takes, whether direct or indirect, general or special, immediate or deferred, explicit or implicit, closed or open, concrete or symbolic, it is exchange, always exchange, that emerges as the fundamental and common basis of all modalities of the institution of marriage' (Lévi-Strauss, *The Elementary Structures of Kinship*, pp. 478–9).

68 In 1947, Lévi-Strauss described the three characteristics of the modern European marriage as being: 'freedom to choose the spouse within the limit of the prohibited degrees; equality of the sexes in the matter of marriage vows; and finally, emancipation from relatives and the individualization of the contract' (ibid., p. 477). At the same time, he emphasized that it is 'a universal fact, that the relationship of reciprocity which is the basis of marriage is not established between men and women, but between men by means of women, who are merely the occasion of this relationship' (ibid., pp. 115–16). In a letter to Jean-Marie Benoist in 1947, he wrote: 'In our society, it is the woman who gives herself. The giver group actually fuses with the object of the gift' (Lévi-Strauss, *L'Identité* [Paris: Presses Universitaires de France, 1987], p. 104). Elsewhere he indicates that a logic of the emotions has replaced an economic logic and that, given the argument of longevity and the right to divorce, a new form of polygamy has come into being, this time as a succession of unions over a lifetime (Conversation with G. Kukukdjian, *Magazine littéraire* [November 1971], special issue on Lévi-Strauss).

To be sure, Lévi-Strauss' hypothesis has also shown its limits when dealing with 'non-Western' phenomena, such as the case of the Na, for whom exchange (of sperm) exists but does not create alliance, or the Egyptian and Iranian marriages, where a brother marries his sister and where there is 'alliance' without there having been 'exchange'. This is the case, too, with ancient Greece, where a brother could marry his half-sister (by the same father – Athens; or the same mother – Sparta), once again alliance without 'exchange'. But in these societies a brother will, of course, not marry all of his sisters, nor a sister all of her brothers. Family continuity therefore depends on the implementation of two principles: do not give but keep for yourself, and give to others, exchange. These close-kin marriages, which did indeed exist, pose a problem as much for Lévi-Strauss as for Freud. For Freud, how can a man or a woman construct their identity if, from childhood they know that they can unite sexually with their sister or their brother? And for Lévi-Strauss, how can one affirm that the prohibition of incest is meant less to forbid one uniting with one's sister than to oblige one to marry another's sister and give up one's own?

But let us return for a moment to Lévi-Strauss' famous statement: 'The prohibition of incest is less a rule prohibiting marriage with the mother, sister or daughter, than a rule obliging the mother, sister or daughter to be given to others.'[69] This general formulation, which puts mother, sister and daughter on the same footing, creates the illusion that the three possible exchanges are equivalent. But if it is thinkable for a father to exchange his daughter in order to get a second wife (with the possible consent of the girl's mother, his first wife), and if it is thinkable for a brother to exchange his sister to get a wife (with the consent of his father, who could also exchange her for a second wife, and with the possible consent of their mother), it is hard to visualize, as we have said, a son exchanging his mother in order to get a wife. We know of no such example. Lévi-Strauss' formulation created a sensation, but in the last example it is meaningless because it is no longer rooted in reality.

Nor should we forget other critical reactions, by Jack Goody, Françoise Héritier and Bernard Vernier, among others. Lévi-Strauss' formula turns the prohibition of incest into a means in the service of a single end: marriage beyond the circle of real or classificatory consanguines;[70] but it does not explain the fact that, in many societies, this prohibition extends to one's affines' consanguines (AC, my wife's sister), as well as to one's consanguines' affines (CA, my brother's wife), in other words to people who, *before* their marriage with Ego or with one of Ego's blood relatives, were not forbidden but, on the contrary,

---

69   Lévi-Strauss, *The Elementary Structures of Kinship*, p. 481.
70   In other words, genealogically close kin or who are made close kin by being classified in the same categories and designated by the same terms.

classified as potential spouses. By reducing the incest prohibition to the ban on marrying close consanguines or those who have been made close, Lévi-Strauss' formula accounts for only a portion of the facts covered by the incest taboo. That is a paradoxical aspect of a theory which constantly makes marriage and the creation of new alliances the primary driving force behind kinship, and which cannot manage to recognize that, once a marriage alliance and the ensuing bonds of affinity are established, if they are to endure they must also be protected from the various misuses of sex. To sleep with one wife's sister unbeknown to the wife and her family is to betray the relations of trust, transparency and cooperation established between the spouses and between their families at the time of their marriage. The same is true when someone, a man, married or not, sleeps with his brother's wife unbeknown to the brother and to the wife's family. That betrays the relations of trust and solidarity that 'should' exist between two brothers, but it also introduces discord into the wife's family and compromises the ties between the two families.[71]

In sum, kinship relations in most societies (at least in those that establish alliances through 'marriage') combine relations of consanguinity and affinity, and the misuses of sex threaten both relations *simultaneously* though in *different ways*. Furthermore, let us recall that relations of consanguinity and relations of affinity do not carry the same weight in all societies. Amazonian societies with Dravidian-type kinship systems often give more importance to ties of affinity than to ties of consanguinity, while the converse is often true in Africa. And more generally, the converse is often true when the alliance is not based on the direct exchange of women but on the exchange of wealth for a wife, which wealth can be recouped from one's affines if the woman wants to divorce or has not borne children.

IS EXCHANGE THE ULTIMATE BASIS OF SOCIETY?

A fundamental question remains to be answered: is human society based exclusively on exchange, as Lévi-Strauss would have it: exchange of women, exchange of wealth and exchange of words, three types of exchange which at the same time establish three domains of social life: kinship, economy, and language and culture? And we could add relations between humans and gods (religion), and relations between those governing and those governed (politics). All of these areas contain various forms of exchange, but these exchanges do not account for everything that goes on there – or even for the most important things that go on. For it has been forgotten – partly because of Mauss and the success of his essay on the gift[72] – that alongside things (and services) that are sold, alongside things

---

71   Concerning these two points, see the bibliography cited for B. Vernier.
72   M. Mauss, 'Essai sur le don. Forme et raison de l'échange dans les sociétés archaïques',

that are given, there are also things that must be neither sold nor given, but kept and transmitted.[73] Of course, among those things that are kept out of exchange and the circulation of gifts and commodities are 'sacred objects', gifts from the gods to humans to be kept and transmitted to their descendants. But there are also non-religious 'objects', like the 'Constitution' of a modern democratic state. Votes can be – and often are – bought, but a constitution cannot be bought. It is not a commodity. It is a set of standards that become a social reality only if all citizens exercise their rights and perform their duties, in other words if they put into practice the bit of (political) sovereignty that each possesses. For not everything is for sale, including in those societies whose economy is based entirely on the production and circulation of commodities, on markets which, today, are becoming more and more mere local fragments of the world capitalist system.

It could be shown that in all societies, including the most 'primitive' ones, where the share of things bartered or exchanged is much smaller than that of things circulating in the form of gifts and counter-gifts, social relations are organized around three principles. Some things are sold, and are detached by this act from the tie that connected them to their owner or their producer. These things are definitively alienated and in turn attach themselves to other individuals, to other groups, those that acquired them. Some things are given, and are both detached from their owner since this person has given them up, but remain attached to him or her, since they have been given and the giver remains present in the thing that has been given, thereby creating obligations to the giver. Lastly, some things are inalienable and non-alienated, such as the Baruya's *kwaimatnie*, the sacred objects and secret formulas that give the initiation masters the power to grow the strength and looks of the young boys who have been separated from their mother and the world of women in order to be made into warriors, husbands and fathers in charge of the future and the fate of their society. Thus, in order for some things to circulate, others must remain *stationary* and serve as anchor points for the basic components of the society's organization and thereby of the identity of the individual and group members. Because of their importance for the society, these components change only slowly over time, unless some pressure from outside causes them to disappear or alters their meaning.[74]

L'Année sociologique, nouvelle série, 1 (1925); reprinted in *Sociologie et anthropologie* (Paris: Presses Universitaires de France, 1950); English translation: *The Gift: The Form and Reason for Exchange in Archaic Societies*, translated by W. D. Halls, foreword by Mary Douglas (New York/London, W.W. Norton, 1990).

73   M. Godelier, *L'Enigme du don* (Paris, Fayard, 1996); English translation: *The Enigma of the Gift*, translated by Nora Scott (Chicago/Cambridge, University of Chicago Press/Polity Press, 1998).

74   When Japan was occupied by the American army at the end of the Second World War, the Emperor Hirohito was forced to write and pronounce in English the following text before General MacArthur, the new chief of the occupying forces, in which he disavowed his sacred nature and his function: 'The ties between Us and Our people have always stood upon mutual trust

It is this domain that Mauss failed to analyze in his essay, although he pointed it out, citing Boas:

> It would seem that among the Kwakiutl there were two kinds of copper objects: the more important ones that do not go out of the family and that can only be broken to be recast, and certain others that circulate intact, that are of less value, and that seem to serve as satellites for the first kind. The possession of this secondary kind of copper object doubtless corresponds among the Kwakiutl to that of the titles of nobility and second-order ranks with whom they travel, passing from chief to chief, from family to family, between the generations and the sexes. It appears that the great titles and the great copper objects at the very least remain unchanged [stationary] within the clans and tribes.[75]

In this passage, Mauss had thus mentioned in passing, following Boas, that the Kwakiutl had two categories of wealth: one alienable and used in potlatch, the competitive war carried on by the giving of gifts and counter-gifts between clans and their chiefs; and the other inalienable, intentionally kept out of the competition and stakes of the potlatch. But there was a problem Mauss did not see, for his object was neither the things that are not given, and not even those that are given in non-agonistic exchanges of equivalent gifts and counter-gifts. His fascination was with the agonistic gifts, the battles waged by dint of non-equivalent gifts and counter-gifts to win a title, a rank, a position of power. In Lévi-Strauss, the analysis of agonistic gifts and counter-gifts disappeared to the benefit of the analysis of equivalent gifts and counter-gifts, something barely addressed by Mauss but important for Levi-Strauss, who saw this as providing the formula for the exchange of women, which he believed to be the basis of kinship. Furthermore, it is clear that for Lévi-Strauss the category of things that are not sold or not given does not count, since society exists only through the exchanges it conducts.

Absent an analysis of agonistic exchanges as well as of inalienable goods, Lévi-Strauss' theories bypassed some of the most important aspects of the manufacture of political or religious power in human society. And just as he had dropped the analysis of kinship systems whenever, in order to determine possible alliances, they used criteria other than a rule drawn from the field of kinship – for example membership of the same caste, the same rank, the same religion – and no longer the categories of cross or other kinds of cousins,

---

and affection. They do not depend upon mere legends and myths. They are not predicated on the false conception that the Emperor is divine and that the Japanese people are superior to other races and fated to rule the world' (cited in Godelier, *The Enigma of the Gift*, p. 203). The Japanese divine monarchy thus was compelled to become a constitutional monarchy, a familiar step in the West.

75   Mauss, *The Gift*, p. 134, n. 245.

Lévi-Strauss also left aside the forms of gift-giving or bans on gift-giving that were nevertheless used in constructing certain forms of power, those arising outside the field of kinship but which subordinated it to their functioning and therefore to their reproduction.[76]

The Elementary Structures of Kinship was published more than a half century ago. There have been many changes since then in what we know about kinship and how we approach it. And Lévi-Strauss too changed over the years, amending when opportune his earlier theories. Taken together, these small adjustments and some clever side-stepping altered his first theoretical positions and placed him on a new theoretical trajectory which, on certain points, coincides with our own.

Let us return to the notion of 'unconscious structure of the mind', which resounded like a trumpet call in *The Elementary Structures*. Lévi-Strauss explained that the aim of analysis was to 'discover the underlying structure of each institution, of each custom'. But in 1965, in his lecture on 'The future of kinship studies' given in front of his British colleagues, Leach and Needham, the tone had already changed: 'I invoked rather hastily the unconscious processes of the human mind, as if the so-called primitive could not be granted the power to use his intellect otherwise than unknowingly.'[77] Or again: 'The capacity of the so-called primitives for theoretical thinking of a quite abstract nature deserves a great deal more respect than we usually give it.'[78] In short, these remarks raised in different ways the problem of the relationship between the unconscious mind with its symbolic thought and the conscious mind with its 'indigenous' theoretical constructions. But the author did not follow them up.

In the same text another important lead can be found, which opens onto the relationship between kinship, myth and prehistory. Lévi-Strauss had been analyzing Amerindian myths for several years when, in 1965, he was led to distinguish between two kinds and two layers of myths: those he called 'Palaeolithic' (whose themes were the acquisition of fire, access to cooking and the distinction between raw and cooked) and those he called 'Neolithic' (which dealt with the origin of agriculture, the increasing human population and the

---

76   Aside from a vague allusion to the Nambikwara chief's polygamy and to the 'feudal' structures engendered by or associated with generalized exchange of women and the hierarchy between wife-takers and wife-givers in Kachin society, and later a few references to the Japanese and European houses that combined marriage with close and distant kin and manipulated the calculation of descent through men and through women in order to survive or grow, there is no reflection to be found in Lévi-Strauss' work on power in its political or political-religious forms. It was necessary to wait until 1998 and an interview given to a somewhat confidential journal, *Mana*, for him to finally broach the subject, and then he merely said: 'It isn't a great discovery that not everything can be exchanged . . . of course not everything can be exchanged . . . but we've known that since Boas.'

77   Lévi-Strauss, 'The Future of Kinship Studies', p. 15.

78   Ibid., p. 16.

dispersal of human groups). Of course Lévi-Strauss denied that he 'load[ed] these terms [Palaeolithic and Neolithic] with historical content', and stopped his analysis there.[79] But whatever he may say, with these terms we are referred back to actual moments in the prehistory of human kind, since the domestication of fire took place at least 500,000 years ago and that of plants and animals began some 10,000 years ago in different places in both the Old and the New World.

These myths, then, describe the human conflicts arising from either the domestication of fire or that of plants and animals; and Lévi-Strauss himself was able to show that the underlying social structure of the two categories of myths was not the same. In the 'Palaeolithic' myths, the clashes break out around fire and the sharing of cooked meat with cross affines – the brother's wife or the husband's sister – whereas the conflicts in agricultural societies emphasize quarrels with parallel affines – the wife's sister or the husband's brother. The myths thus refer to a certain historical context and clearly attest to the existence of a conscious reflection on the part of prehistoric peoples about the problems they come up against in these different contexts.

In 1967, the first French re-edition of *The Elementary Structures* was published, with a new preface that attempted to update the author's thinking. One section of the text incorporates Lévi-Strauss' Huxley Memorial Lecture, which we have already analyzed, but the rest contains further theoretical shifts: 'the appearance of certain phenomena has made this line of demarcation [between nature and culture], if not less real, then certainly more tenuous and tortuous than was imagined twenty years ago'.[80]

Let us come back to 1949. For Lévi-Strauss, at this time, kinship relations presupposed the existence of the symbolic function of thought and articulated speech – to say language is to say exchange, and to say language and exchange

79   Ibid., p. 16. His stubborn refusal to see history as anything more than pure contingency (with the aim of leading us to the unconscious structures of the 'savage' mind) is so strong that it made him write, in *The Raw and the Cooked*, 'I therefore claim to show, not how men think in myths, but how myths operate in men's minds without their being aware of the fact. And . . . it would perhaps be better to go still further and, disregarding the thinking subject completely, proceed as if the thinking process were taking place in the myths, in their reflection upon themselves and their interrelation' (C. Lévi-Strauss, *Le Cru et le cuit, mythologiques* I [Paris: Plon, 1964], p. 20; English translation: *The Raw and the Cooked: Introduction to a science of mythology* 1, translated by John and Doreen Weightman [Harmondsworth, Penguin, 1986], p. 12). Just as the absolute Mind operated through the mind of Hegel, Amerindian myths would have operated through the mind of Lévi-Strauss. Is it not the case that to make the object the subject and the subject the object is an approach that cuts through, reverses and scrambles the relationship between humans, the products of their mind and their action? In 1998, Lévi-Strauss once more returned to his distinction between cold and hot societies inasmuch as it does not coincide with Sartre's between societies without a history and historical societies. (See C. Lévi-Strauss, 'Retours en arrière', *Les Temps modernes*, no. 598 [1998], pp. 66–77.)

80   Lévi-Strauss, *The Elementary Structures of Kinship*, p. xxix.

is to say society. But for Lévi-Strauss, language could only have come about all at once, and since, for him, symbolic thought, language and exchange are linked, the sudden appearance of society is something like the equivalent of a Big Bang that would have spawned, among others, kinship relations, since the incest prohibition and the exchange of women as signs and valuables are derivatives of symbolic thought:

> Whatever may have been the moment and the circumstances of its appearance in the ascent of animal life, language can only have arisen all at once. Things cannot have begun to signify gradually. In the wake of a transformation which is not the subject of study for the social sciences, but for biology and psychology, a shift occurred from a stage when nothing had a meaning to another stage when everything had meaning.[81]

In this text, we see Lévi-Strauss reject the idea of a gradual evolution of humankind (even if there may have been some 'qualitative leaps' or moments in which the processes speeded up) and affirm the primacy of the symbolic over the imaginary and the 'real'.[82] In 1967, Lévi-Strauss' vision thus has changed:

> [In 1949] my proposal was to trace the line of demarcation between the two orders [nature and culture] guided by the presence or absence of articulated speech . . . the appearance of certain phenomena has made this line of demarcation, if not less real, then certainly more tenuous and tortuous than was imagined twenty years ago. Among insects, fish, birds and mammals, complex processes of communication, which now and then bring true symbols into play, have been discovered. We also know that certain birds and mammals, notably chimpanzees in the wild state, can fashion and use tools. In that period which science has pushed further and further back and which saw the beginning of what is still conveniently called the lower palaeolithic, different species and even different genera of hominoids, fashioners of stone and bone, seem to have lived together on the same sites.[83]

And, he concluded: the upwelling of culture perhaps did not take the form of a Big Bang: 'Rather it takes the form of a synthetic duplication of mechanisms already in existence but which the animal kingdom shows only in disjointed

81   C. Lévi-Strauss, *Introduction to the Work of Marcel Mauss*, translated by Felicity Baker (London, Routledge and Kegan Paul, 1987), p. 59.

82   Ibid., p. 37: 'symbols are more real than what they symbolise . . .' Lacan, who would adopt some of Lévi-Strauss' ideas as early as 1950, went further, writing: 'The symbolic order is absolutely irreducible to what is commonly called human experience', and 'It cannot be deduced from any historical or psychological starting point' (Jacques Lacan, *Ecrits* [Paris, Le Seuil, 1960], p. 368).

83   Lévi-Strauss, *The Elementary Structures of Kinship*, p. xxix.

form and dispersed variously among its members – a duplication, moreover, permitted by the emergence of certain cerebral structures which themselves belong to nature.'[84] This was a new vision, but one that Lévi-Strauss would develop little, even though other findings would, it seems, bear it out.

After 1967, Lévi-Strauss felt obliged on three more occasions, to our knowledge, to take up his pen to comment very briefly on phenomena that seemed to cast doubt on his thesis of the purely social (and especially not biological) origins of incest and of kinship as the exchange of women among men. In 1988, responding to questions from Didier Eribon, he mentioned certain recent discoveries in ethology, which were said to have shown the existence of mechanisms 'for avoiding incest in the animal kingdom'. Lévi-Strauss acknowledged that 'observation of animals in the wild – great apes but other species as well – seems to establish that consanguineous unions are rare if not actually made impossible by certain regulatory mechanisms'. But this was immediately followed by a reservation: 'Specialists in this kind of study and, later, ethologists, hastily concluded that the incest taboo was rooted in Nature.'[85]

Here again the obsession with the idea that human society may have come out of natural evolution. This obsession was even stranger coming from a thinker who repeated time and again that 'man is part of life, the life of nature and the nature of the cosmos'.[86] At every opportunity, Lévi-Strauss would reassert his scepticism 'not about the phenomena observed but about their interpretation, all too often tinged with anthropomorphism. The fact that there is a general tendency to expel youngsters from the group when they reach puberty . . . can be explained in a variety of ways, among which competition for food seems the most likely.'[87]

In point of fact, Lévi-Strauss' hypothesis explaining the expulsion of young males or young females (depending on the species) by competition for food is probably the least likely. If the separation of generation occurs when youngsters reach puberty, it is because the competition that comes to the fore at that time is not over access to food but over access to sex, 'sex more than food'. And, as Lévi-Strauss himself said, sex is a 'drive' whose satisfaction, in its most usual forms, requires the presence and response of another (of the opposite or same

---

84   Ibid., p. xxx. In 1967, then, culture no longer arose 'all at once'. 'Consequently, to understand culture in its essence, we would have to trace it back to its source and run counter to its forward trend, to retie all the broken threads by seeking out their loose ends in other animal and even vegetable families' (ibid., p. xxix). In 1949, Lévi-Strauss had written: 'However we have been careful to eliminate all historical speculation, all research into origins, and all attempts to reconstruct a hpothetical order in which institutions succeed one another' (ibid., p. 142). The Preface to the first French edition of Les Structures had been written in New York in February of 1949.

85   Lévi-Strauss, Conversations with Claude Levi-Strauss, p. 111.

86   Lévi-Strauss, 'Retours en arrière', p. 70.

87   Lévi-Strauss, Conversations with Claude Levi-Strauss, p. 111.

sex). Sexuality is a relationship with oneself and with others, which is thoroughly both biological and social. And in humans, as in the other closely related social species, sexual drives can be satisfied only in *socially* regulated forms.

The problem here lies not with Lévi-Strauss but with the ethologists, who explain the dispersal of animals at puberty not as a biosocial mechanism designed to regulate and preserve bands as bands, or 'societies', but as a purely biological mechanisms designed to prevent the genetically harmful consequences of consanguineous sexual unions. But no decisive proof has yet been advanced in support of this claim. And yet it is this explanation, heavy with biological teleology, with the genetic finalism that it implies, which today holds pride of place in ethological discourse and is offered as the only valid explanation. There are other possible explanations, however, and Lévi-Strauss is right on this point. Nevertheless, it remains to be shown that the mechanisms that forestall intergenerational conflict at the time youngsters reach puberty are designed to regulate not the genetic structure of the animal populations but their social structure.

Last of all, the final series of phenomena invoked to explain the incest taboo, and Lévi-Strauss' most violently ironical riposte yet: the loss of oestrus in women and the features associated specifically with female sexuality purported to go with it and to act on male–female relations.[88]

In reality, two things were intertwined in the debate over the 'loss of oestrus' and gave rise to a theoretical confusion which Lévi-Strauss encountered in 1995, as we ourselves had a few years earlier.[89] First, the fact that men and women are able to make love at any time and in any season. Female sexuality is not governed by alternating periods of receptivity (heat) and non-receptivity. And second, the fact that, unlike other animals, human females do not signal their periods of oestrus (i.e. their periods of fertility) by changes in genital coloration and the emission of odours.[90] The expression 'loss of oestrus' is actually completely erroneous. There is no loss of oestrus in human females, only the disappearance of the physiological signs – if they ever existed – that acted as a signal to other members of the human species.

Without mentioning their names, Lévi-Strauss criticized a number of

---

88 Text published in 1995 in the journal *La Repubblica* (3 November 1995), entitled 'Quell'intenso profumo di donna'; and published in French in *Les Temps modernes*, no. 598 (1998), pp. 78–84, under the title 'La sexualité féminine et l'origine de la société'.

89 M. Godelier, 'Sexualité, parenté, pouvoir', *La Recherche*, no. 213 (September 1989), pp. 1140–55; and 'Meurtre du Père ou sacrifice de la sexualité? Conjectures sur les fondements du lien social', in M. Godelier and J. Hassoun (eds.), *Meurtre du Père, sacrifice de la sexualité. Approches anthropologiques et psychanalytiques* (Strasbourg: Arcanes, 1996), pp. 21–52. The developments below are an auto-critique of some of the hypotheses we advanced at the time but which have nothing to do with the theories of sociobiology.

90 Lévi-Strauss, 'La sexualité féminine et l'origine de la société', p. 80.

anthropologists and paleoanthropologists inspired by the theses of sociobiology.[91] He showed that, using the same facts, the theory-makers came up with very different theories which, for the most part, attempt to show that the 'loss' of oestrus had enabled women to turn their sexuality to their advantage by manipulating men:

> By concealing their time of ovulation, women would have compelled males in these primitive times when they were driven by the sole need to propagate their genes, to devote more time to them than would be required by the simple act of reproduction, thus guaranteeing themselves a durable production.[92]

In short, once again, Lévi-Strauss seized the pretext of the confusion and the theoretical weaknesses of what he calls 'robinsonnades génitales' (sexual exoticism) to omit from his analyses the area of sexuality, which is the prime object of the prohibitions of incest and other misuses of sex. And yet it is more probably in the fact that women make love and make babies than in the upwelling of symbolic thought that we should be looking for the reasons why it is usually women rather than men who are made to play the subordinate role in kinship relations.

In 1995, Lévi-Strauss brought other facts to light which pushed back by a few hundred thousand years the appearance of social phenomenon such as language and the use of tools, which humans are thought to share with other social animals:

> The origin of language does not lie in the anatomical structure of the speech organs. It is to be sought in the neurology of the brain. Now the neurological structure of the brain shows that language may have existed in the most remote times, well before the appearance of *Homo sapiens* some one hundred thousand years ago. Endocranial casts taken from the remains of the skulls of *Homo habilis* show that the left frontal lobe and what is known as Broca's area, which determines the production of language, were already formed over two million years ago . . . *Homo habilis* made tools that were rudimentary to be sure, but which corresponded to standardized forms. Alternatively, there can be no doubt about *Homo erectus*, our direct predecessor who, some five hundred thousand years ago, made stone tools whose symmetry required more than a dozen successive operations. All of these considerations place the appearance of conceptual thought, of articulated speech, in short of life in society, at such a remote time that one cannot, without exhibiting

---

91   Such as C. Knight, 'The Wives of the Sun and the Moon', *Journal of the Royal Anthropological Institute*, 3 (1997), pp. 133–53; or B. I. Strassmann, 'Sexual Selection, Paternal Care, and concealed ovulation in humans', *Ethology and Sociobiology*, no. 2 (1981), pp. 31–40.

92   Lévi-Strauss, 'La sexualité féminine et l'origine de la société'.

a degree of naiveté verging on inanity, conjure up hypotheses . . . These truly things that are truly interesting for understanding human evolution occurred in brains, not in wombs or larynxes.[93]

In short, *the Big Bang has vanished. Evolution has taken its place.* And evolution is supposed to dispel the mystery of the 'decisive leap from nature to culture' by which 'humankind cast off the animal state with the birth of human societies'. However, it is because humans, with their more highly developed brains, possessed the capacity to analyze the consequences of their acts for the reproduction of society, of their social existence, that they were able to prescribe laws, standards that placed sexual relations under the control of society, which regulated them. And if generalized sexual commerce, which is a constant possibility open to men and women, posed problems for the management not only of the relations between the sexes and between the generations within the families, but also that of the relations between the social units that made up the bands and societies – whose existence and continuation were a necessary condition of the material and social existence of both individuals and social units – who other than humans with their brains could think out these problems and deduce positive and/or negative rules, prescriptions and prohibitions? It is clearly not symbolic thought that invented all the problems with which it finds itself confronted.

AMOEBA, THE ULTIMATE BULWARK OF EXCHANGE THEORY

From the disappearance of the Big Bang to the dissolution of our origins in the flight of millions of years of human evolution, Lévi-Strauss nevertheless clung to the same explanation: 'Human society is based on exchange', but obviously at the cost of a succession of abandonments. In his final text, 'Apologue des amibes', he writes of Tylor's aphorism that early on men must have been reduced to the choice between 'marrying out or being killed out', that this was not a historical truth:

> It translates, in myth form, the retroactive vision of an imaginary past that biological families must create for themselves in order to understand that society forbids them to lead a separate life . . . if one were absolutely bent on speculating on how things really happened . . . a chimerical ambition . . . some hundreds of thousands if not even millions of years ago . . . one would have no need to postulate the logical or historical anteriority of biological families.[94]

---

93   Ibid., p. 79–80.
94   Lévi-Strauss, 'Apologue des amibes', p. 494.

428   THE METAMORPHOSES OF KINSHIP

Thus Tylor's formula, which Lévi-Strauss adopted on many occasions following the French edition of *The Elementary Structures of Kinship* or his text on 'The family', is now regarded, like the story of the ancient murder of the Father in *Totem and Taboo*, as a myth by which 'biological' families are supposed to explain to themselves the prohibition on leading a separate life. After the Big Bang of the appearance of symbolic thought, articulated speech and the exchange of women, the hoary hypothesis of the 'logical or historical' anteriority of isolated biological families, overwhelmed with fear and hatred, has also disappeared.

But in the name of what new facts does Lévi-Strauss renounce this postulate so crucial to his theory? In the name of amoeba. Tylor's mythical aphorism has been succeeded by the 'scientific' fable of the amoeba. We learn that unicellular beings, such as amoeba, alternate their living modes: a unicellular mode when food (bacteria) is present, and a social mode when food is lacking and they agglomerate into a multicellular body which moves toward sources of humidity and heat where food can be found. In short, Lévi-Strauss, quoting Durkheim, discovers that at this level, too, 'society is more than the sum of the individuals that compose it'. This piece of amoebic hypocrisy, which is just as bad as the neo-Darwinians' 'robinsonnades génitales', is not even an argument in support of the thesis dear to the author's heart according to which exchange gave rise to society, for amoeba live separately when there is plenty of food around. And when food is scarce, they clump together into a single body which ensures a number of complementary functions without any exchange taking place among the components. Amoeba turn into this single body because there is an inherent mechanism which, when they are starving, makes them secrete a substance, cyclic adenosine monophosphate, which attracts nearby amoeba and makes them converge and agglomerate. There is no exchange, no reciprocity involved.

But because this same substance is found in the cells of organisms as complex as mammals, Lévi-Strauss concludes that '*social life appears as the result of an attraction between individuals sufficient to make them seek each other out*',[95] and he calls this mutual attraction 'sociability'. But what do they seek each other out for? Lévi-Strauss goes on to posit, in the manner of a philosopher of human nature, that it is a question of cooperating rather than of dividing themselves up. In short, he suggests that society exists because each member is attracted by the others and needs them in order to live. Or conversely, society exists because we are spontaneously social beings and we need society in order to live. We are going in circles.

A constant in this stream of evolutions and partial abandonments of the initial theory is the thesis of the fundamental role of exchange in the institution

---

95   Ibid., p. 496.

of society and the introduction of the prohibition of incest. But this thesis is no longer the thundering affirmation that exchange exists because without it there is no society. We read: '*We would be mistaken therefore to deem that matrimonial exchange is like a contract.*'[96] This thesis already appeared in *The Elementary Structures of Kinship*, since a freely agreed marriage between a man and a woman merely 'has the appearance of a contract'. But why is it not a contract? Because it is not possible to marry if those who have rights over this person, the brother over his sister (and not the sister over her brother), have given her up: 'A single prohibited degree is enough for the mechanism of the exchange to be set off in the group, *outside of any awareness on the part of society*. Exchange is a property of social structure. Not everything in society is exchanged, but if there were no exchange, there would be no society.'[97] In this statement, Lévi-Strauss finally concedes that 'not everything in society is exchanged'. But he immediately minimizes the scope of this affirmation by hastening to add: 'But if there were no exchange, there would be no society.'

But if not everything is exchanged, the first question to ask is: What is not exchanged in societies? And why? And since the fact that not everything is exchanged is just as universal as the fact that 'many things – but not all – are exchanged' in societies, it becomes theoretically impossible and contradictory to write: 'but if there were no exchange, there would be no society'. The banality of the affirmation is surprising. The theoretical formulation that corresponds to reality is not that but the following: there would be no human society if exchange did not exist and if a certain number of things were not kept out of exchange in order to be kept out of the circulation of persons and goods and transmitted by their owners to the following generations.

But transmitting them to the generations that follow you means giving without the possibility of receiving in return.

The existence of society therefore is not based, as Lévi-Strauss affirmed in *The Elementary Structures*, on the implementation of a single mechanism – exchange – and of a single principle – reciprocal giving – but on a twofold mechanism and on two principles: the obligation to give and the obligation not to give what must be kept in order to transmit it. But transmitting means giving without the prospect of receiving in return, it means giving without the possibility of direct reciprocity (except for the descendants' 'gratitude' to their ascendants, the gratitude of the new generations to the old ones). And it is precisely the forms of non-reciprocal giving that Lévi-Strauss – deliberately or not – left to one side, condemned to inexistence, just as he had left to one side

---

96   Ibid., p. 494.
97   Ibid., p. 494, emphasis added.

the axis of descent and filiation in order to foreground and privilege the axis of alliance and affinity.

Whatever the case may be, a half century later, Claude Lévi-Strauss' work on the whole still stands, even though it may have been little by little altered and deformed – something that his disciples have not really wanted to see. Today it sits astride, and askew, on two theoretical axes: the axis of the Big Bang and exchange as the universal basis of society and kinship; and the axis of the thousands of years of evolution and interplay of the two opposing and complementary social principles of giving and not giving (keeping). After all, if the things we do not give are often those we consider to be the most sacred, those that benefit not only those who keep them but the whole society, then did not the ancient Iranian marriages between brother and sister, which were supposed to guarantee them the best places in the Mazdean paradise but also to contribute to increasing the share of Good in the world, make as much sense, in their violation of the incest taboo, as the marriages practised by the Arapesh of New Guinea, who forbid incest with their sister so as to enjoy the advantages of having a brother-in-law with whom to go hunting and clear the forest? Each act of forbidding or allowing produces social relations, makes society, a society where each person, according to their cultural choices, will have to live and to work for its reproduction.

Perhaps Lévi-Strauss remained too rooted in Western tradition, too little interested in religion to recognize that it has become possible, and no doubt necessary, to suggest another basis for the prohibition of incest, a conjecture free of the idea of a Big Bang that wrenched humankind from its animal state, a conjecture aware that the prohibition of incest in our culture has mixed a whole series of sexual taboos that other societies distinguish, that Freud made a decisive contribution, and above all, that human society is not based only on gift-giving and exchange, but also on the refusal to give, on the obligation to keep. It is to this new scenario that we will devote the next chapter.

CHAPTER TWELVE

Proposals for a Different Scenario

Any conjecture as to the nature and foundations of the incest prohibition is tantamount to an act of imagination. It means casting a particular light on certain known and relatively well-attested facts in the hope of bringing out ties, possible and plausible connections that might have a certain global explanatory power. Many regard this as a pointless or impossible exercise. Everyone knows that men and women the world over are born or incorporated into the kinship system that prevails in their society without being able to say why the system exists or since when. In sum, to make any conjecture as to the origins of something is to write the scenario of a play that has already been given, which is given and given again before our eyes without our really understanding the sequence of the scenes and the reasons behind it.

With Freud's conjecture, we had a purely imaginary event nevertheless regarded as genuinely prehistorical: the murder and the devouring of a father who exercised despotic control on the females of his horde. With the conjecture Lévi-Strauss presents in *The Elementary Structures*, we were referred to the upwelling of real facts, the appearance of conceptual and symbolic thought and of articulated speech. This event had already been dated to pre-Neanderthal times; but since conceptual and symbolic thought had subsequently not ceased to characterize human social being, the exchange of women, as a purported consequence of its appearance, had not ceased to characterize the human condition either and to serve as the basis of kinship relations and systems.

SIX CONSTRAINTS FOR A DIFFERENT SCENARIO

We too are going to propose a scenario. What criteria have we chosen for its construction? We posit that:

1. The analysis of the incest taboo should not be separated from the other prohibitions on uses of sex.

2. The prohibition of incest concerns forbidden sexual unions in the first place and only afterward forbidden matrimonial unions. If certain sexual unions are forbidden between two people of opposite sex then their marriage is forbidden all the more.

3. The sexual unions forbidden by the incest taboo concern as much heterosexual as homosexual relations. A priori the ban on two people of opposite sex having relations with each other should not stop them having relations with persons of the same sex (and vice versa). We will leave aside auto-sexuality, in other words masturbation, often forbidden in the name of forbidding individuals to satisfy themselves, to waste their substances, which are designed in principle for other purposes and can even belong to others.

4. The incest taboo is associated with prohibitions concerning relatives by marriage, either because the prohibitions on consanguines are 'extended' to affines, or because prohibitions of another kind apply to certain affines as a complement to the prohibitions concerning consanguines.

5. The incest taboo presupposes the development of conceptual thought and of various means of communication – protolanguage, articulated speech. However, these developments did not come to pass through a Big Bang but as processes occurring within human evolution over the long term. Such processes are for the most part unconscious, whereas prohibitions are conscious social facts expressed and assembled in codes of law or customs (the Hammurabi code, the abominations listed in the Biblical book of Leviticus, etc.). How then are we to discover the mechanisms that connect the two – conscious and unconscious – parts of the forms of human social existence?

6. There is no reason to suppose that primitive humanity lived in isolated biological families (Lévi-Strauss) or in hordes (Freud) before coming to live in society. There is no reason to suppose the logical and/or historical priority of the existence of consanguineous families living in a state of permanent sexual promiscuity when it comes to the development of the forms of society characteristic of our humanity's ancestors and their descendants.

SEXUALITY AND SOCIETY IN THE PRIMATES CLOSEST TO HUMANS

Let us begin with the last point. In what way does our present knowledge of the life of primates allow us to avoid Freud's and Lévi-Strauss' aporia, namely that the family must have come before society, a hypothesis Darwin already regarded as highly unlikely! We know that humans are one of the 152 species of primates still living on earth and that the two primate species closest to man, which share 98 per cent of their chromosomes with us, are the chimpanzees and the bonobos. It so happens that these two species live in multimale and multifemale bands that exploit the material resources of a territory, which the members of these bands strive to control and to defend against the intrusion of members of neighbouring bands. In chimpanzees as in bonobos, the males remain in their natal group, but at puberty the females disperse to neighbouring groups. In other primate species also living in multimale and multifemale bands, such as macaques, it is the young males that leave the natal band at puberty. In gibbons (a monogamous species) and gorillas (a harem species), the parents expel the young from the group at the onset of puberty: the fathers expel the young males and the mothers the young females.

In both chimpanzees and bonobos, each band in control of a territory forms a small society, and the existence of such bands is an indispensible condition for the existence and survival of their members. Society exists,[1] but, on the other hand, in these bands there are no 'families' that bring together in any durable and stable fashion a male and one or several females with their offspring. Most of the time the females live alone with their young, moving around the interior of the territory, while the adult and juvenile males 'patrol' the borders in search of food and on the lookout for possible predators or chimpanzees from other bands. Chimpanzees communicate with each other by means of a number of vocalizations each of which has a different meaning: some tell the band of the presence of a tree in fruit, others of the arrival of a predator, others that someone intends to attack another member of the band or intends to submit, etc. In addition to these vocalizations there are gestures, postures, behaviours (grooming, etc), which have meaning for all members of the band.

Chimpanzees make, transport and use tools, but they do not make tools for making other tools. They practise collective hunting and attack other species of monkeys or small antelopes. They anticipate the behaviour of their quarry and drive it toward several band members posted ahead. They kill and divide the body of their victims on the spot, and on this occasion the males frequently allow sexually receptive females to take from their hands and eat some of the victim's flesh and bones. Genuine wars between two bands have been observed in which the adults of one band, males but also females, enter the territory of another band and kill one or several of its members. At the finish of such clashes, the band with the most fatalities leaves the spot and gives up part of its territory.

The social organization of a band depends on the combination of two principles: competition and cooperation. Cooperation is manifested in defence of the territory, hunting and food sharing, though for the most part each individual finds

---

1   According to François Jacob, in *La Logique du vivant* (Paris, Gallimard, 1970), for certain species a society is the environment needed if a member of this species is to develop fully. Environment means resources, but also an organization, a set of relationships between individual members endowed with a logic of its own.

and eats its food alone (a hand-to-mouth economy). Competition exists between males, between females and between males and females, producing a hierarchy among the members of a band according to sex and age which lasts a few months or years but in all events is temporary. In this animal society, males dominate females, to be sure, but for this they need the help not only of other males but also of adult females to win and keep their rank. Among the social phenomena discovered in the past twenty years among chimpanzees and other primate species living in multimale and multifemale bands, some of the most important and the most significant are appeasement and reconciliation behaviours, and alliance strategies. The members of a primate group are at the same time rivals and allies in so far as they are at the same time competing for food and sexual partners but also need the help of others to achieve their goals. Individuals form coalitions to enable one of them to keep his rank in the face of a rival or, on the contrary, to enable this rival to win over the other's rank. Females play an important role in these coalitions. It is therefore crucial for a chimpanzee to know who are his friends and potential allies and who are his enemies or potential allies of his enemies.

But the other important discovery is that conflicts between members of a band have a limit. They are neither permanent nor so severe as to drive the loser out of the band. This is because the conflicts that end in the establishment of a domination-submission hierarchy between adversaries are immediately followed by gestures of reconciliation and appeasement, in other words by non-aggressive bodily contacts between the ex-adversaries. Among chimpanzees, the winner stretches out an upturned hand to the loser, who touches it; this gesture is systematically followed by kissing, hugging, petting, mutual grooming and sometimes sexual relations. Among bonobos, on the other hand, the gestures of reconciliation are strongly sexualized – homosexual: the males rub each other's penis, the females their vulva; and heterosexual: ventro-dorsal or ventro-ventral copulation (which exist only in bonobos and humans). It is as though, in making peace with each other, the individuals were acting in such a way that the band might *continue to exist as such*, and that the individuals involved in the conflict might continue to live side by side and benefit from its existence; in short, as if the preservation of a certain social cohesion entailing the coexistence of all members of the band was as necessary for its long-term continuation as the hierarchy produced and reproduced by their rivalry. And it is remarkable to learn that, among primates, reconciliation seems facilitated by the existence of relatively stable hierarchies.[2]

Reproduction in chimpanzees is a matter of sexual relations between adult males and females, and takes three forms. Most matings are 'opportunistic' and

---

2   See F. B. M. De Waal, 'La Réconciliation chez les primates', *La Recherche*, no. 210 (1989), p. 592, and F. De Waal and F. Lanting, *Bonobos, le bonheur d'être singe* (Paris, Fayard, 1999).

coincide with the periods when the females show external signs of oestrus – odours, colours, genital swelling. They are mounted several times by different males without any sign of active competition between them. The male's approach, intromission and ejaculation are rapid, taking only a few short minutes. In many cases the females do not respond to the males' advances and refuse intromission or disengage themselves. They thus exercise a choice of partners. Sometimes, though, a dominant male exhibits 'possessive' behaviour toward a female in oestrus. He stays by her side and prevents other males from approaching her by charging or intimidating them; this behaviour can last anywhere from a few hours to a few days.

Finally, a third form of tie between males and females has been observed, which has been called 'consortship'. A male and a female with young will separate from the band for a few hours, and even several days (the maximum observed was twenty-eight days). For this to happen, the female must consent. Furthermore she is the one who breaks off this preferential attachment by responding to the calls of other males and guiding them to her. It was her silence that kept the 'couple' separated from the others. The female role is therefore not a passive one. To be sure, dominant males have more access than the others to receptive females, but mating more frequently does not mean having more reproductive success than lower-ranking males.[3] Furthermore, it is now clear that the females willingly let lower-ranking males sneak a mating with them.

In chimpanzees and bonobos alike, the young take a long time to mature, and remain dependant and then attached to their mother until the age of three at least. They watch their mothers mate and generally interfere in the process. Female chimpanzees give birth every five or six years on average; female bonobos, every four or five years. Among bonobos, the females, all of whom come from neighbouring bands, enjoy high rank. Their (hetero- and homo-) sexual life is intense. They exercise more control than the males over access to food, which is abundant in their habitat. Bonds between females are very often friendly, except when their sons are concerned (the daughters leave the band at puberty and in the preceding months the mother and daughter become

---

3   To cite an example, B. Stern and G. Smith, from the California Primate Center, after having closely observed the matings that took place in 1980 in three groups of captive rhesus macaques – captivity reinforces competition – examined the genetic heritage of the young born of these matings the following year and found that the dominant males had not been any more successful at reproducing than the subordinate males. See B. R. Stern and D. G. Smith, 'Sexual Behaviour and Paternity in Three Captive Groups of Rhesus Monkeys (macaca *mulatta*)', *Animal Behaviour*, no. 32 (1984), p. 23. J. Maynard Smith, in *Evolution and the Theory of Games* (Cambridge, Cambridge University Press, 1988), showed that, while hierarchical relations between males, between females and between the two sexes are an element of the structure of an animal society, over the long term, if the dominant individuals were to have much greater reproductive success than the subordinate individuals, the reproduction of the very structure of their society would be endangered.

detached from each other), and their relationship with their mother has a bearing on the order of precedence among males, which show more hostility to each other than male chimpanzees do. Finally, a trait shared by chimpanzees and bonobos: males in these societies play with youngsters and often defend them; *but they do not raise them.* This is exclusively a female task.[4] Of course males do not recognize their biological paternity of a particular youngster born of a given female. And generally speaking, there is no sign that primates have understood that there is any connection between sex and procreation.

In the end, is there or is there not in primate societies one or several *biological* mechanisms that would prevent genetically close individuals from uniting sexually and that would protect their descendants, and thus their society, from the genetic disasters entailed in such matings? Is there any such thing as '*incest*' avoidance among primates? Primatologists have generally concentrated on the mother–son relationship, since there is no recognition among males of their blood ties with the young born in their band. They have found that, after a longer or shorter period of initial attachment to their young, females then undertake to force them to detach themselves. But they do not treat their sons and their daughters the same way, and are more aggressive with the sons than with the daughters.[5] The young male then gradually turns to other adult or juvenile females in the same band or in neighbouring bands. They also found that young males seem sexually more attracted by unfamiliar females than by familiar ones, and that the same is true for young females, who are more attracted to outside males. It would seem that familiarity inhibits sexual desire to a certain extent. This goes in the sense of Westermarck's thesis, generally taken up by the sociobiologists.

In point of fact, matings between mother and son exist and have been observed. Certain authors such as Ray H. Bixler have even specified the contexts in which they were observed. In the majority of cases, the mother was not in oestrus, and the mating appeared above all to be an appeasement behaviour toward a young male being chased by his fellow band members and in distress. Such matings were occasional and opportunistic, and never gave rise to a possessive relationship or to prolonged consortship.[6]

The theory has also been advanced that what would prevent a female and her mature son from mating is not nature's 'invisible hand' eliminating incest and its detrimental consequences but a social reason. What would stop and especially inhibit the young male would be the presence of older males that

---

4   See P. Mehlman, 'L'Evolution des soins paternels chez les primates et les hominidés', *Anthropologie et sociétés*, vol. 12, no. 3 (1988), pp. 131–49.

5   J-M. Vidal, 'Explications biologiques et anthropologiques de l'interdit de l'inceste', *Nouvelle revue d'ethnopsychiatrie*, no. 3 (1985), pp. 75–107. See in the same issue, B. Deputte, 'L'Evitement de l'inceste chez les primates non humains', pp. 41–72.

6   R. H. Bixler, 'Primate Mother–Son Incest', *Psychological Reports*, vol. 48 (1981), pp. 531–6.

outrank them. Here we would have socio-sexual mechanisms that result from the existence and the strength of hierarchical relations between individuals ordered by sex, age, physical capacities and social rank. We thus find ourselves faced with hypotheses that put the social before the biological, or that at least make a biological mechanism into a modality of social and species reproduction and not of the biological reproduction of the society. And lastly, certain authors, such as Jim Moore and Rauf Ali,[7] suggest a similar hypothesis as an explanation for the major phenomenon that serves as an argument for proponents of 'incest avoidance' in primates. For these authors, the moment when a new generation of primates reaches puberty and is about to enter into competition with the adult members of the band who outrank them (when it comes to access to females and food) *endangers the reproduction of the band as such*, whereas the dispersion of either the males or the females and their gradual individual incorporation into neighbouring bands are processes that do not threaten the reproduction of the bands when the arrival of unfamiliar males (or females) incites the females (or the males) to mate with them.

It is understandable that a great deal of caution is in order before asserting the existence of a 'biological' determinism of 'incest' avoidance in primates and humans. Yet this virtue is not typical of certain texts by primatologists or anthropologists, more concerned with showing, at the cost of verbal contortions, that the sociobiologists' hypotheses are borne out in all cases rather than discussing them. Instead of dispersion, they speak of 'exogamy', and instead of migration and incorporation into another band they speak of 'transfers' and 'exchanges'. A further step is taken when they go on to speak of 'patrilineages' among chimpanzees and 'matrilineages' among Japanese macaques. In the second instance, since it is the males that disperse at puberty and the females that spend their life in their natal band, we obviously find 'lines' containing an older female, her daughters and her daughters' offspring. But these lines are still not lineages, for in terms of human kin ties, a matrilineage is a group composed of men as well as women (brothers and sisters, sons and daughters, nephews and nieces, etc.) who share a common ascendance traced through the women, and reciprocal rights and duties. In macaques, however, males leave their band, brothers leave their sisters, sons leave their mother; and mothers' brothers – if they have not yet left the band when their sisters bear young – do not pay any particular attention to the fate of their 'nephews and nieces', except if they themselves remain attached to the group of females to whom the mother of these young belongs, in which case they exhibit solidarity. In short, we need to avoid projecting onto the primate societies closest to humans concepts such as incest, exogamy and exchange, which ipso facto

---

7   J. Moore and R. Ali, 'Are Dispersal and Inbreeding Avoidance Related?', *Animal Behaviour*, no. 32 (1984), p. 94.

endow their forms of social organization with the same operating principles as we encounter in human societies and anthropomorphize them.

Nevertheless, and I stress this, the lessons that can be drawn from the study of the primates closest to man have great theoretical importance for the issue that concerns us, namely: to advance a conjecture as to the origins and foundations of the incest prohibition in human societies:

1. Chimpanzees and bonobos naturally live in multimale and multifemale societies, like humans, and not in harems like gorillas or in monogamous families like gibbons. Chimpanzees and bonobos therefore live in 'society'; and although they do not have articulated speech or, it seems, do not have the capacity to think in general concepts, they understand signs and even symbols. They therefore have 'received' their form of social existence from natural evolution. This mode of living probably evolved since they became independent species, but it seems that these primates have never endeavoured or desired to change and replace the rules governing their social organizations. Analyses of the DNA of the three species tell us that the ancestors of man split away from the ancestors of chimpanzees and bonobos some six million years ago, and that chimpanzees separated from bonobos some four million years later. What can we conclude from this data?

    Human beings and their ancestors probably did not live in biological families, or in hordes or in harems like gorillas. The ancestor of the gorillas himself split off from the line containing humans, chimpanzees and bonobos one or two million years earlier. Freud's theory of the primal horde thus lies in ruins, as does that presented by Lévi-Strauss in *The Elementary Structures of Kinship*, according to which human society came about because of an upwelling of symbolic thought that resulted in the incest taboo, and the subordination and exchange of women.

2. If humans were *unable to endow themselves* with life in society, they *were able,* unlike the other primates, to *transform the ways* they lived in society, to invent new forms of society. This capacity they owe precisely to the development of their cognitive abilities, to the development of their brain, a 'strategic' development which apparently began long ago with the emergence of bipedalism as the normal means of locomotion, which in turn freed the hands.

    Now Broca's area, mentioned by Lévi-Strauss in his last works and which plays a major role in speech development, and the zone that controls the use of the hand lie next to each other, and we can trace their development from *Homo habilis*, over two million years back. We also know that this development increases in magnitude and speed with the appearance of *Homo erectus*, and of course with *Homo sapiens*, Neanderthal man and finally *Homo sapiens sapiens*, in other words, ourselves.

3. Chimpanzee and bonobo societies are characterized by separation between the sexes and gender subordination, females to males, which is strongly marked in chimpanzees and much less in bonobos. Within both of these societies we find distinct social units made up of females that have given birth and who raise their young separately. These social units stemming from procreation and raising the young do not mingle adults of both sexes. The males play with the youngsters and may even protect them. They also use them as a means of approaching the mother. But they do not raise them. In the absence of any awareness of the ties of paternity between males and their offspring produced by mating with a female when she is in oestrus, there are no social ties other than play or competition between the adult males and the children and adolescents that together compose the band. In all human societies, on the other hand, whether the 'families' are composed of brothers and sisters between whom all sexual relations are forbidden (e.g. the Nayar, the Na, the Rhades), or of men and women united or not by marriage but who have sexual relations, the units of procreation and child-raising imply the cooperation of both sexes in raising the children. And in primates close to man and in humans, it is many years before the youngsters leave adolescence and reach maturity. In chimpanzees this period is estimated to be eight to ten years, in humans, twelve to fourteen. That means that the coexistence of the mother with her children lasts a long time in primates and even longer in humans, but among the latter, the co-presence involves not only the mother but very often the man or men associated with the mother in caring for the offspring.

4. Sexuality in chimpanzees and bonobos displays three forms: heterosexual, homosexual and autosexual (masturbation). The importance of homosexual relations in these species is now acknowledged (as it is in other species, e.g. macaques), though biologists have as yet no satisfactory theoretical explanation for the role of homosexuality in natural selection. This would suggest that primate sexuality serves not only for reproduction, but also for pleasure. This would seem to be confirmed by Franz de Waal's observations on bonobos, on the existence of orgasm in female bonobos, on the frequency of their homosexual relations with other females. Furthermore, in these societies, sexual activity is precocious. Had Freud observed young chimpanzees or bonobos, he would have had little difficulty in discovering infantile sexual behaviour here as well. Youngsters

learn mating postures at a very early age, and sometimes the mother allows her son to rub against her and try to mount her. Adult and sub-adult females are continually pestered for sex by young males, and they themselves are interested in touching and smelling youngsters' genitals, not only those of their own young but the young of other females too.

Of course homosexual and autosexual relations go on all year round, whereas heterosexual relations are more frequent when the females are in season and exhibit external signs of oestrus. This is the time of the strongest male competition for access to females, but the females do not seem to submit automatically to the males' solicitations, even those of dominant males, and seem to possess a certain capacity to choose among them. A last very important social trait: when the young females reach puberty, they leave their natal band one by one and join neighbouring bands, where the fact of being 'outsiders' seems to make them more attractive to the local males. These two phenomena – precocious and intense infantile sexual activity, responded to by the males and females of the band including the mother (even though she may gradually distance her offspring when they reach a certain age), on the one hand, and, on the other, the dispersion of females when they reach puberty – are at the same time biological and social mechanisms. Because they are biological, in other words imposed by nature, the individuals experiencing them cannot be aware of their origin and even less of their meaning. But these mechanisms serve a social order that regulates relations between the generations and between the sexes. They operate at two key moments in the sexual life of the individuals, at the end of infancy for both sexes and at adolescence for young females (two key moments in the construction of individual identity for Freud), and are the result of forces that drive all individuals to leave, first, their mother and the 'family' in which they were raised, and then, in the case of females, the band in which they were born. They leave the brothers they played with and the fathers they do not know and who do not know them, and they will soon be replaced by young females from neighbouring bands, which will be much more 'attractive' than they were to their brothers and to the adult males of their natal band.

TWO OPPOSING FORCES ACT ON SEXUALITY IN CHIMPANZEES AND BONOBOS

Two interacting forces – one that repels and another that attracts: a push and a pull – act on individual sexuality and orient the relations these individuals will have with opposite- or same-sex members of their species. But there is no sign in either chimpanzees or bonobos of a 'primitive promiscuity' that would allow all members of the group to unite with all other members. The forces that push the individuals out of their 'family', out of the social unit in which they born and raised, and those that draw individuals to more distant members of their species are theoretically mechanisms that 'oblige' all individuals, male or female, to direct their 'sexual desires' toward those outside the small group in which they were born and raised, a group centred on the mother and where there was no 'father' or nurturing and protecting male associated with the mother. These potential sexual partners, which will, over an individual's lifetime, become his or her real partners, are first of all the members of his/her society, of his/her natal band that are the furthest removed in terms of kinship and child-raising, and then members of neighbouring bands – outside females, for the male members of a local band, outside males, for the females that join this band.

Two remarks are called for here. First, an individual's sexual partners will quickly, over his or her lifetime, and increasingly, be individuals that to not belong to the small circle of the birth family that raised him or her. Second, these forces that push the individual toward others or draw others to him or her are forces that 'oblige more than they forbid' sexual relations between closely related individuals, as is shown by the rare but existing mother–son unions. These 'oblige' the individual to turn to more distant members of his or her species without actually forbidding him or her to turn to close conspecifics. We are thus dealing here with facts that both invalidate the position taken by Lévi-Strauss in the first French edition of *The Elementary Structures of Kinship*, but at the same time confirm the twist he gave to his theory in the preface to the second French edition in order to take into account discoveries made in the meantime and which had shown the ability of great apes to make tools and to communicate with each other. The Lévi-Strauss of *The Elementary Structures* considered that there was a radical discontinuity between nature and culture resulting from the upwelling of conceptual, symbolic thought in human beings. Contrary to Freud and Malinowski, who, as he saw it, wrongly stressed the need to 'repress' sexuality as an explanation of the incest taboo, Lévi-Strauss maintained, in a striking formula that sparked countless, often highly critical comments:

> The prohibition of incest is less a rule prohibiting marriage with the mother, sister or daughter, than a rule obliging the mother, sister or daughter to be given to others . . . and it is clearly this aspect, too often unrecognized, which allows its nature to be understood . . . Thus it is that the reasons why marriage with the mother, daughter or sister can be prevented are sought in a quality intrinsic to these women. One is therefore drawn infallibly towards biological considerations, since it is only from a biological, certainly not a social, point of view that motherhood, sisterhood or daughterhood are properties of the individuals considered. However, from a social viewpoint, these terms cannot be regarded as defining isolated individuals, but relationships between these individuals and everyone else.[8]

---

8 C. Lévi-Strauss, *The Elementary Structures of Kinship*, translated by James Harle Bell, John Richard von Sturmer and Rodney Needham (Boston, Beacon Press, 1969), pp. 481–2.

For the Lévi-Strauss of *The Elementary Structures*, the prohibition of incest cannot have a biological basis because in nature nothing is forbidden, nothing is obligatory. 'Whatever the uncertainties regarding the sexual habits of the great apes ... it is certain that these great anthropoids practise no sexual discrimination whatever against their near relatives.'[9] Fifteen years later, on the basis not of new knowledge concerning the sexual life of monkeys but the fact that some kinds of monkeys make and use rudimentary tools and communicate with each other by means that sometimes make use of 'genuine symbols', he revised his previous positions and declared that the 'line of demarcation [between nature and culture] was if not less real, then certainly more tenuous and tortuous than was imagined twenty years ago'.[10] Without defining what he meant by 'tenuous' and 'tortuous', he pronounced himself ready to believe that:

> Ultimately we shall perhaps discover that the interrelationship between nature and culture does not favour culture to the extent of being hierarchically superimposed on nature and irreducible to it. Rather it takes the form of a synthetic duplication of mechanisms already in existence but which the animal kingdom shows only in disjointed form and dispersed variously among its members.[11]

Today we observe that new discoveries, this time about *sexual* behaviours, point to a 'synthetic takeover' by humanity of mechanisms that have already appeared in nature and can be found in a number of animal species, among which primates and humans. These mechanisms would thus be the backdrop and the raw material of what has become, in the human species and in the form of conscious prohibitions, the 'incest taboo'. These mechanisms, it should be remembered, are much more systems that 'oblige' individuals to direct their sexuality, during childhood and adolescence, toward members of their species that do not belong to the biological and social unit where they were born and raised, than systems that 'forbid' them to mate with their mother or their sisters (or with their brothers in the case of young females). Of course, since among primates there is no such thing as 'exchange' between individuals or groups, the prohibition of incest, when it applies in humans to affines and not to consanguines, *cannot* stem from mechanisms present in nature. It implies the existence of typically human kinship relations, which in the vast majority of societies are deployed along two axes: the axis of filiation and descent, and the axis of alliance.

Aside from this fundamental restriction, might we now have proof that the incest prohibition has its primary and remote basis in the biological and social

---

9   Ibid., p. 32; or again, on page 490: 'The natural state recognizes only indivision and appropriation, and their chance admixture.'

10   Ibid., p. xxix.

11   Ibid., p. xxx.

structures of certain animal species, in sum: in nature? To answer this question, we need to take a closer look at the nature of these mechanisms. It seems that their purpose is not to restrict consanguineous matings in view of preventing the deleterious genetic consequences that such matings might have for the survival of the species, but to regulate the sexual development of the individual members from infancy to the end of adolescence in such a manner that the satisfaction of their sexual desires does not endanger the reproduction of the society, in the event, the local band where they are born and grow up. For being born and living in society is the very condition of the survival and development of every individual of whichever sex. Another important fact, which we have merely touched on, points in the same direction. While until they reach puberty, young males and females practise their sexual behaviours with female and male adults, at the time of puberty two things happen. The young females, as we have said, leave their natal band one by one. As for the young males, their access to the receptive females is now *blocked* by the adult males. Sexual activity among the young animals also comes into competition with that of the adults. For months at a time, their sexual life is *inhibited* by these power relations, and it is only once the young males have made a place for themselves in the adult hierarchy of the band that they will have access to the receptive females. Their sexuality is thus subjected to the constraint placed on all members to take their place within a hierarchy, which, together with cooperation, are the two pillars of their social organization. These mechanisms found in the primates most closely related to man thus directly contribute to reproduction of the social form of existence characteristic of each species before indirectly contributing to the natural selection process that drives the evolution of all species.

Natural selection is probably the final cause of these mechanisms and of many others; but between the proximate cause – the constraints weighing on the reproduction of a species' social form of existence – and the final cause – the evolution of nature and the constraints of natural selection – there must exist a certain number of mediations and levels that we would like the primatologists, and more generally the biologists, to explain to us.

If today there is no longer any question of a Big Bang representing the passage from nature to culture and their articulation, and if the incest prohibition is (only partially) a sort of mutation of mechanisms already present and at work in nature, it must therefore be inferred that *the passage from nature to culture was a transformation from animality to humanity that was both continuous and discontinuous*, and that this continuity and this discontinuity can be found in the similarities and differences that exist between humans and the two primate species closest to us, chimpanzees and bonobos. We now know that the three primate species descend from lines that split off at different times from a common trunk, those lines that finally led to *Homo sapiens sapiens* having been the first to separate from the line of ancestors common to the chimpanzees and bonobos. The remaining two species then went on to split apart much later, some three or four million years ago, as I have said, which means that chimpanzees and bonobos stand at the same genetic distance from human beings. It is remarkable that, now we have realized that bonobos are a different species from chimpanzees, we observe that the two species exhibit strong differences in their social organization and that, out of fifty types of behaviours recorded, they share only half. We will outline these briefly before showing what distinguishes the human species from the other two taken together.

Chimpanzees and bonobos are thus primate species that live in society, in local bands made up of males and females of all ages, which exploit the resources of a space, a territory that they defend against the intrusion of other bands. Chimpanzees live in forests and grasslands, environments where resources are relatively dispersed. Bonobos live in dense forest where resources are abundant. Chimpanzees both make and use tools. Bonobos use tools more than they make them. Chimpanzees practise forms of collective hunting, make 'war' on neighbouring bands, wars in which adult females participate and which sometimes lead to the appropriation of a new territory. Nothing of the kind is found in bonobos. Male chimpanzees share food, even freshly captured and killed game, with females, and are particularly generous with those that are sexually receptive.

Generally speaking, chimpanzee social organization is male centred. Females are relatively hostile to each other. As with bonobos, female chimpanzees disperse at puberty, and the female adults present in a band come from outside. The oldest males in a band have thus known from infancy the young males that will grow up with them. *But there is no sign that the older males single out from among the youngsters those who are their 'sons'.* In chimpanzees, the males ostensibly dominate the females, and they have recourse to alliances to establish their rank and are dependent on their allies. This is reflected in the fact that they drive their rivals away from females they covet or protect, but allow their allies to approach and mate with them. Matings are always ventro-dorsal, *more canum*, that is, from behind.

Bonobo social organization, on the other hand, is female centred, and it is the males that show hostility to each other. When there is competition among adults for food, a high-ranking female can step in even in front of the alpha male. The alpha male's position is relatively clear, but the reciprocal position of the other males is much more uncertain. Males do not form alliances among themselves, and confrontations remain one on one.[12] Bonobos do not hunt collectively, and males do not usually share captured game with females. Females, on the

---

12   The females are the first to build their night nests, high up in the treetops. The adult males follow, lower down, and always fairly far apart.

contrary, frequently *share* food with each other, *whereas*, coming from different bands, *they are not related*, which shows that the existence of kin ties is not the necessary condition for food sharing. Female bonobos also share their food with their young and sometimes with a male. Mother–daughter ties loosen before puberty and then break off completely with the young females' departure for other bands. Mothers are strongly attached to their sons throughout life and defend them when need be. The older sons often stay with their mother when the band moves. Bonobos mature slowly and late, as do chimpanzees. Bonobos seem even more inclined than chimpanzees to seek peaceful outcomes to their conflicts, and they also practise gestures of 'reconciliation' and 'appeasement'. Of these gestures, the offer of sexual contact or relations of all forms – hetero- and homosexual – play a large role. Females have intense sexual relations with each other. Males also show homosexual behaviours, but to a lesser degree. When they mate with females, they do so *more canum*, like chimpanzees, but in 25 per cent of cases they mate face to face, like humans. The female chimpanzee cycle is thirty-five days, and for half of this time their genitals are tumescent. The female bonobo cycle is forty-nine days, and for three quarters of this time their sexual organs are tumescent. In each species, males and females multiply matings when the female's tumescence is at its peak. This gives observers the impression that bonobos are closer than chimpanzees to humans in so far as they are the only species that mates face to face and where the females seem receptive almost all year round (which is not in fact the case). Alternatively, chimpanzees have other behaviours – collective hunting, war, the sharing of game between males and receptive females, tool-making – that makes them seem closer to humans. In both species, the males play with the young and protect them; but they do not raise them and do not recognize their own offspring.

In chimpanzees as in bonobos, individual sexuality serves, as in humans, to produce social ties, and it is manifested by behaviours that show that individuals' sexuality is subordinated to the reproduction of their mode of social existence. But unlike humans, primates do not have the capacity to change, to modify the rules of their social life. They are capable of adapting to the material changes in their environment. And they can innovate, as in the famous example of the band of Japanese macaques in which one day one of the females washed the sandy sweet potatoes she had been given to eat; this innovation was not only imitated by the other adults in the band, it was also passed on to the following generations. Primates can thus act on nature by making and using tools, by selecting this or that resource as a food and by even changing the way they eat it; but they cannot act on their society so as to change its organization.

THAT WHICH IS UNIQUELY HUMAN

Human beings are not merely a species of primates that live in society. They are a species that produces society in order to live, in other words, that has the ability to modify its forms of social existence by changing the relations they entertain with each other and with their natural environment. And if humans have this capacity, it is because they are able to represent these relations to themselves, as abstractions, using concepts, images and symbols, and because they know how to act in a conscious and organized manner to introduce changes. To be sure, primates have an evolutionary history, but they have no social, economic, political or cultural history. Human history is made up of the sum of the many transformations humans have imposed on themselves and on their natural environment, and of the consequences of these changes on the fate of their societies. The rate at which these changes occur has varied considerably over time (over many millennia before the Neolithic era, and then over periods of less than a century in our time[13]). However, these multiple forms of social life that have differentiated human groups and each time moulded the social constraints on their sexuality are not comparable with the forms of social organization found in other primate groups, first among which are the chimpanzees and the bonobos, our nearest relatives.

It is therefore within the framework of human evolutionary history, which saw the appearance, disappearance and succession of multiple forms of social organization and existence, that we will pursue our attempt to imagine the conditions that might have led to humans' 'synthetic reworking' of the mechanisms present in nature and which today regulate individual sexual activity by subordinating it to the reproduction of forms of social existence.

One basic difference between humans and their ancestors, on the one hand, and our closest primate relatives, chimpanzees and bonobos, on the other, is that raising human children is no longer the task of women alone, and that the units charged with procreation and child-raising usually involve the co-presence of adult men and women. This co-presence by no means implies that these men and women are united by sexual ties, as husbands and wives are. We have seen that the procreation and child-raising units in certain matrilineal societies, the Nayar and Na for example, are composed of brothers and sisters between whom sexual congress is forbidden, as are forbidden sexual relations between mothers and children, and between aunts or uncles and their nephews or nieces. What is fundamental (and new) here is that adults of both sexes cooperate in the

---

13   Of course humanity has retained only a fragmentary memory, full of holes, of these changes and their succession. It is the task of archaeology, palaeontology, prehistory history and the other social sciences to reconstruct some of the steps – without ever being able to pretend to restore the whole picture.

establishment and maintenance of a social group where children are born and raised, in short, a family. Of course in most societies, the men and women of families cooperate not only in raising children but also in their procreation.

For what reasons have this co-presence and cooperation between the sexes come about and become generalized? Is it the outcome of the affective ties that arise between men and women owing to their sexual relations? Or on the contrary, is it, as Lévi-Strauss suggested in his article 'The family', the result of the sexual division of labour and the allocation according to gender of the many tasks – productive and others – whose necessity and complementarity have made daily cooperation between the sexes indispensible and encouraged them to build enduring material, social and affective ties, both for their own benefit and for that of the children the women bear, children who, even more than the adults, need this cooperation between adults of opposite sex in order to survive?

Let us examine first of all the features that are specific to human sexuality. It is well known that, of all the mammals, only humans can make love all year round.[14] Whereas female chimpanzees and bonobos alternate between periods when they are 'in heat' and those when they are not, human females are not subject to this alternation and can, like human males, have sexual relations any time. Heat in female chimpanzees and bonobos corresponds to their periods of ovulation and fertility, and this state is shown by bodily changes – tumescence of the perineum, emission of odours, etc. – which make them particularly attractive to males of their species. In human females, we do not see such mani-festations, which has led some biologists and primatologists to speak not only of 'loss of signs of oestrus' in humans, with respect to primates, which have purportedly kept them, but of women's deliberate 'concealment' of the signs of oestrus. This 'concealment' supposedly allowed them to negotiate more effec-tively with men the exchange of 'sex for food and care', the most desirable food being the game brought back to camp by the male hunters.

THE PURPORTED LOSS OF OESTRUS IN WOMEN

The idea that women managed to conceal their oestrus is senseless. Ovulation is always hidden in all mammals; it is a process independent of the individual will. But did the human species actually 'lose' the signs of oestrus that were purportedly present in human ancestors, as they are even today in chimpanzees and bonobos? Two theses are proposed. The first is based on the fact that, in certain primate species, like gorillas and orang-utans, the females' time of ovulation is not manifested, or only slightly, by external bodily signs, and

---

14   C. Lévi-Strauss, 'La Sexualité féminine et l'origine de la société', *Les Temps modernes*, no. 598 (1998), pp. 78–84; p. 79.

advances the hypothesis that perhaps genital tumescence and other signs did not exist in the final ancestors common to the lines of humans, chimpanzees and bonobos. If such signs did not exist in protohumans, their disappearance does not need explaining. However this thesis implies that the tumescence present in chimpanzees and bonobos appeared after the separation between their common ancestor and the line that led to humans.[15] It is this appearance, then, that needs explaining.

The second hypothesis proceeds in the opposite direction. Since the three species stem from a common ancestor – a primate that walked on all fours – these bodily signs of oestrus must have existed at the beginning of the evolution that led to humans, chimpanzees and bonobos. It would then have gradually disappeared with the development of the upright posture and bipedalism, which became the protohumans' permanent mode of locomotion. Upright posture and bipedalism must of necessity have led to important anatomical and physiological changes in our ancestors, which consisted in more than simply freeing the hands. The vulva was 'moved' from the back end of the body toward the front and became concealed between the thighs in human females. This would also have led to the disappearance of visual signs, now ineffective, and considerably diminished the role of odours. But, and this is the thesis advanced by two specialists in the morphological evolution of the human species, F. Szalay and R. Costello,[16] the ancestral signs of oestrus must have been replaced by a new system of signs which, this time, corresponded to the fact that female protohumans had become sexually receptive (and active) all year round.

These new signs must have satisfied the same function as the signs of oestrus present in primates, namely to make the human female sexually attractive – but continuously attractive, and therefore independently of the ovarian cycle. Continuously means from puberty and extending until menopause and beyond, independently of whether or not the women bears children over her lifetime. These specifically female signs are the breasts, which form at puberty and subsist independently of lactation, the size of the buttocks and the flare of the hips, and finally the skin texture, smoother and often almost entirely hairless, except in the pubic area and the under the arms.

All of these anatomic and physiological changes are spread widely over the erogenous and erotic zones of the female body and have become components of femininity.[17] And although body size and strength are not the only criteria used for measuring dimorphism in a species, we observe that the dimorphism between

---

15   De Waal and Lanting, *Bonobos, le bonheur d'être singe*, p. 191.

16   F. Szalay and R. Costello, 'Evolution of Permanent Oestrus Displays in Hominids', *Journal of Human Evolution*, no. 20 (1991), pp. 439–64.

17   The hormonal mechanism responsible for breast formation, independently of the ovulation cycle, is not perfectly known.

human male and female bodies is *greater* than that between male and female chimpanzees or bonobos. If we consider, too, that these aspects of the female body fulfil the same function as the signs of oestrus but are independent of ovulation, we are obliged to conclude that the evolution of the female body, far from 'concealing' or causing the disappearance of the signs of oestrus, which are a manifestation of the last stage of ovulation, and therefore a temporary sign, instead produced signs that form a sort of ongoing manifestation of sexual receptivity in female humans, signs equivalent to what would be *the manifestation of a permanent state of oestrus.*[18] And even if we now know that a female bonobo can have orgasms (even if among bonobos and chimpanzees coitus is over in less than a minute[19]), it is obvious that women can have orgasms much more often and all year round. Heterosexual relations between male and female protohumans thus were able to extend over the whole year, to become generalized.

The male body, too, acquired characteristics that are not present in primates. His body hair has also generally disappeared, but to a lesser extent than in women.[20] His penis is larger and longer in proportion to his body than that of other primates and it does not have the penile bone that is found in the males of these species. This seems to be connected to the fact that face-to-face copulation has become the position most widely used by human beings, without excluding the other modes found in primates. To be sure these changes in the male body happened without our human ancestors being aware of them or being able to act on them.

THE SPECIFIC CHARACTERISTICS OF HUMAN SEXUALITY

Over the course of evolution, human sexuality thus took on specific characteristics that set it apart from that of other primates. Since human sexuality was increasingly disconnected from the mechanisms of the biological reproduction of the species, it carried the distinction between sexuality-as-desire and sexuality-as-reproduction further than in all other species.[21] Desire and sexual pleasure exist in other primates, which alternate between autosexuality (masturbation), homosexual relations (rubbing penis against penis or vulva against vulva in bonobos, for instance) not linked with the female ovarian cycle, and heterosexual relations orchestrated by natural rhythms.

In point of fact, the disjunction in humans between the two sexualities – that of desire and that of reproduction – is carried even further because human sexuality reacts to internal representations, to internal stimuli of a social and cultural

---

18   Cf. ibid., pp. 44–5.
19   De Waal and Lanting, *Bonobos, le bonheur d'être singe*, p. 102.
20   Human beings are 'naked apes' as Desmond Morris puts it in the title of his well-known popularization, *The Naked Ape* (New York, McGraw-Hill, 1967).
21   M. Godelier, 'Sexualité, parenté et pouvoir', *La Recherche*, no. 213 (1989), pp. 1141–55.

nature, as much if not more than to external stimuli which are, in turn, always constructed and apprehended from a social and cultural standpoint. The effect of these internal representations is to make human sexuality capable of stimulating and fuelling itself.[22] It is also more responsive to meaning than to signs, and it responds more readily to the imaginary and the symbolic perhaps than to the signs deliberately or involuntarily emitted by the bodies of others.[23] In such conditions, it is understandable that human sexuality, having thus become 'cerebralized', permeates the whole body and is no longer confined to the genitalia. This separation of the genital and the sexual is inherent in human sexuality, which has carried it as far as it can go, since certain erotic states are induced by the mystical fusion of a believer with his or her god or goddess.

Human sexuality has thus carried primate sexual polymorphism even further, that is to say that sexual pleasure can be obtained through three types of relations – homosexual, heterosexual and autosexual – no one of which is exclusive of the others in biological terms, but of course not in cultural terms. Furthermore, human homo- and heterosexual relations can be carried on in a so-called 'masculine' or 'feminine' way – from a cultural standpoint – without consideration of the physiological sex of the individuals involved.

Human sexuality is more than cerebralized, generalized and polymorphous, though, it is also polytropic. When human infant sexuality awakens and begins to develop, children do not possess a biological mechanism that automatically forbids or compels them to direct their desire to a given person of a given sex. A child's sexual drives can spontaneously, that is to say unconsciously, direct themselves to the mother or the sister, in the case of a boy, or to the father or the brother, in the case of a girl. In short, in its spontaneous state, uncoupled from the biological process of reproduction of the species, *sexual desire* (sexuality-as-desire) *has no inherent social meaning*, except in that, in order to satisfy a homosexual or heterosexual desire, someone other than oneself must exist. But nothing determines in advance the identity of the others an individual will encounter in life. They will obviously be of the same or the opposite sex. But nothing can be assumed about the desire or absence of mutual desire or of the kinds of desire involved. It is also obvious that the first 'others' children encounter are those who ensure their survival on a day-to-day basis and raise them. There too it can be the woman who bore them or a nurse, etc. And still others will probably be present: brothers, sisters, half-brothers, etc., born before; but also grown men: husbands or brothers of the mother, companions, etc.

---

22   See J. D. Vincent, *Biologie des passions* (Paris, Odile Jacob, 2002).

23   But let us not forget that the triggering of sexual behaviours in primates and other animal species supposes that the individuals are capable of representing to themselves what characterizes members of their own species as male or female and the external signs that mark them as sexually receptive and attractive.

This is where the conceptions of Tylor, Freud, Lévi-Strauss and many others meet. For society and those who speak for it to children, and therefore those who raise them, will quickly make them understand that the 'others' are divided into two categories: those with respect to whom sexual desire is possible, proper and even to be encouraged; and those with respect to whom desire is forbidden, indecent, impure, proscribed, etc.

This being the case, in order to direct these sexual desires that manifest themselves spontaneously and are rooted in our unconscious, there will have to be a concerted and multiform direct and indirect effort to domesticate and socialize the child's sexuality, aimed at directing it toward suitable persons and taking suitable forms. It is during this period, which can last a longer or shorter time, that the prohibitions on masturbation, sleeping with one's brother, desiring one's father, and so on are stamped into the innermost conscience of the person. And forbidding also means threatening with punishment, ranging from disapproval to physical chastisement. It means associating certain desires with fear and encouraging their repression, their rejection from the conscious part of the mind, so that they slip into the shadows, without disappearing of course and without ceasing to act, welling up from time to time in forms and through acts that no longer allow them to be recognized socially.

Society has always preceded the individual, and the adults acting as (biological, social, symbolic, etc.) 'parents' precede the birth of their children and enable their survival in the society into which they are born. Every society rests on norms, values and prescriptions, but also on taboos and prohibitions, all of which taken together are what organizes society and establishes its 'order'. Every social order is thus at one and the same time a moral order and a sexual order, that is to say, a set of norms and standards that regulate relations between the sexes and are imposed on individuals, differently or not depending on their sex. Furthermore, nothing suggests that a society should have only one system of values and positive and negative norms, only one 'order'. There can be several orders, corresponding to different, and conflicting, social groups.

HOMOSEXUALITY, HETEROSEXUALITY AND AUTOSEXUALITY

Let us briefly recapitulate what we have learned from this quick look at the characteristics of human sexuality. Human sexuality takes three forms, also found in other animal societies, among which our closest primate relatives: autosexuality (pleasuring oneself), heterosexuality (the desire for others of the opposite sex), homosexuality (the desire for others of the same sex). All three forms are found in nature; they are natural. One of them is nevertheless associated through natural evolution with the reproduction of life, with the physical continuation of the species (and therefore of the society in which individuals are born and live): this is heterosexuality. The two other forms, without having been associated by natural evolution with the direct reproduction of life, are in themselves sources of pleasure, which is also, of course, the case with heterosexual relations.

Societies establish an order, a hierarchy among these three forms of sexuality and attach a list of positive and/or negative values to each. For instance, in the Baruya society, boys are forbidden to masturbate because their sperm is destined to initiate the other age groups and so 'belongs' to them, as it were. On the other hand, homosexuality among adolescent boys and young men is prescribed. But it is then forbidden when men marry. Male homosexuality is here seen as a necessary stage for men to become adults, warriors, fathers, clan leaders, and so on. The social stakes are clear. Male homosexuality legitimizes men's power over women and children, and gives them the right to represent their society and govern it. It legitimizes their repression of women and explicitly entertains their fear of them. But this phobia in no way results in the exclusion of sexual relations with women at another stage in life; it absolutely does not imply heterophobia. Moreover, male homosexuality in no way makes men effeminate, does not marginalize them further. On the contrary, it glorifies them, makes them fully masculine because they are nourished by the sperm of their elders; it also procures them pleasure by introducing them at a young age, collectively and individually, to the pleasures, desires and frustrations of sex.

In short, in each society, the three forms of sexuality are assigned distinct but interdependent meanings, and there is no universal reason that calls for everywhere assigning the same meaning and position to these forms. The Baruya example is a clear illustration, but there are many others. While the Baruya practise fellatio and ignore (or repress the desire for) sodomy, the Kasua of New Guinea practice sodomy but not fellatio. The Azande are today famous among certain European homosexuals because their young warriors used to marry, in a ceremony that imitated marriage with a woman, young boys whose parents consented and therefore paid a 'bride' price; they did not practise sodomy but 'intercrural' sex, that is, they took their pleasure between the boy's thighs. Later, when they married a woman, sometimes the boy's sister, the boy himself, now a man, would marry a boy often using the brideprice given by his former 'husband'. And the cycle of homosexuality, heterosexuality would begin all over, with the two forms of sexuality playing distinct but complementary roles in the life of a (male) individual.[24]

Sometimes, too, in certain societies, homosexual relations would temporarily serve as a substitute rather than as a complement for heterosexuality.

---

24 Female homosexuality existed but was apparently frowned on by men. Cf. E. E. Evans-Pritchard, 'Sexual Inversion among the Azandé', *American Anthropologist*, vol. 72 (1970), pp. 1428–34.

Here we are referring to little-known data that has been under-analyzed by Anglo-Saxon anthropologists, for reasons of Puritanism. For example, among Australian Aborigines, before the Europeans arrived, male homosexuality was relatively frequent, socially perfectly adopted, but was a private matter. Male homosexuality was never flaunted, it seems; and we do not know if homosexual relations between women occurred. It was forbidden to have homosexual relations with genealogical and classificatory brothers, but allowed between cross cousins, thus between two men who were each other's potential or real brothers-in-law. Australian Aboriginal men married women much younger than they. Men were often promised a wife even before she was born, and the actual marriage occurred only when the little girl became a woman, in other words when she began to get breasts. In the meantime, the two brothers-in-law were allowed to carry on homosexual relations.

This practice fulfilled two functions: one individual and the other social. It both satisfied the sexual needs of the brother-in-law/son-in-law until he could enjoy his wife, which could be several long years, but it also created ties between the two brothers-in-law and the two families. Among Australian Aborigines, the strongest ties, those involving the most solidarity, were, in the case of men, ties between brothers-in-law, followed by those between co-initiates; and in the case of women, the ties between sisters-in-law and then between co-initiates. It should be noted that homosexual relations were forbidden between real or classificatory brothers, just as heterosexual relations were forbidden with real or classificatory sisters. Exogamy thus applied to both forms of sexuality, and homosexual marriage and relations took place beyond the circle of siblings and parallel and even cross cousins. The same holds for the Baruya. The incest taboo applied thus in these societies simultaneously to homosexual and heterosexual relations and placed them at the service of the reproduction of the social order. This is something Lévi-Strauss, whose theory of incest is wholly focused on marriage and the exchange of women between men, failed to see.[25] Margaret Mead was the first, and one of the only ones, to mention homosexual incest.[26] Unfortunately few anthropologists heard her and thus failed to produce analyses accounting for all forms of sexuality, authorized or forbidden, in a society.[27]

But what then is the respective place of the two sexes and their sexualities in society? The fact that women are sexually attractive during a large portion

---

25 Cf. Lévi-Strauss, *The Elementary Structures of Kinship*, pp. 483–4.

26 M. Mead, 'Incest', in *International Encyclopaedia of the Social Sciences* (London, Macmillan, 1968), vol. 7, pp. 115–22.

27 Among them are a large number of specialists of New Guinea, a part of the world where male (and sometimes female) homosexual practices were widespread. We will cite for instance G. Herdt, B. Knauft, F. Brunois, etc. See F. Brunois, *Le Jardin du casoar. La forêt des Kasua. Savoir-être et savoir-faire écologiques* (Paris, Editions de la Maison des Sciences de l'Homme, 2008).

of their life, that they can make love (with men, but also women) the year round and night and day, does not make them different from men, who can also make love with women (or men) at any time. The difference has to do with the fact that only women make babies in their body, something that men cannot do however much they might wish to.[28] The question then becomes: did it become possible for women to attach men more closely to themselves, to interest them more in protecting them and helping raise the children they bore because they could exercise continual sexual attraction and make love at any time? *Is female sexuality the key factor that brought men into the procreation and child-raising units* that, ordinarily in man's closest primate relatives, are centred exclusively on the female, the mother of the young? Would not two of the forms of ties between males and females found in primates – the appropriation of the females in heat by dominant males, and the temporary consortship between a male and a female – be deeply changed by the fact of human female receptivity and proceptivity, i.e. the capacity to seduce and attach a man or men? Unless of course, on the contrary, the multiple, occasional 'opportunistic' (as primatologists say) matings were favoured by this permanent attractiveness and receptiveness and by females' (pro)active behaviours. Were men, who are naturally and universally 'polygamous', according to Lévi-Strauss, each chained to a single woman by the sexual pleasures she could 'dispense' to them all year round and throughout their life? But this would suppose that women are not naturally and universally polyandrous, and that if they did not give birth to children whose survival in the early years rested for the most part on their shoulders, they would not want to unite with other men, to change and multiply partners.

The experiential data proves the contrary. In all societies recorded in which divorce was allowed, woman sought divorce as often if not more often than men. A famous example is the Kikuyu society in Africa, where, both before and after the Europeans arrived, men and woman contracted up to six or seven successive marriages over their lifetime.[29] The families constantly reconfigured themselves with the departure or arrival of children from the previous marriages. The same thing is happening today in Europe and North America, where the number of divorces is on the rise and where the number of reconstituted families (heterosexual but now also homosexual) is growing. And we also see more

---

28   This is the underlying meaning of the male initiations practised by the Baruya, the Sambia and so on: to re-engender the boys without the help of women; to have them born anew from the belly of men alone. Cf. G. Herdt, *Rituals of Manhood: Male Initiation in Papua New Guinea* (Berkeley, University of California Press, 1982); G. Herdt (ed.), *Ritualized Homosexuality in Melanesia* (Berkeley, University of California Press, 1984).

29   J-C. Muller, *Parenté et mariage chez les Rukuba du Nigeria* (Paris/The Hague, Mouton, 1976) and *Du bon usage du sexe et du mariage* (Paris, L'Harmattan, 1982).

and more women raising their children on their own, because the market economy, and the various forms of state aid and protection for mothers and/or children, favour individual autonomy, unlike the gendered social division of labour and the control over individuals – especially women – characteristic of tribal societies and peasant communities.

To be sure, everyone knows that sexual desire can sometimes give rise to an enduring attachment between a man and a woman, but sex is not enough to explain why, in practically all societies, the sexual union of a man and a woman must be publically recognized if it is intended to last. Nor can individuals' sexual desire be the basis of the many forms of 'family' that humanity has produced over its history, since, in most cases, the two individuals have not been officially united by their own choice. In many societies – China and India for example – the bride and groom often did not know each other prior to their marriage. They had to adapt their lives and their sexual desires to each other after the fact. It is clear that the first goal of these unions decided and controlled by the families was not to enable the individuals involved to satisfy their sexual desires. The aim of their union was the birth of one or several children – a daughter in the Trobriand Islands, a son in China, India or ancient Rome, where only sons could offer the worship due to the spirits of the ancestors and beg them to bestow their blessings and protection on their descendants.

In short, a family is founded not on the union between the sexes but on the *birth and care of the children the women will bear over their lifetime.* The Nayar and the Na have given us the clearest demonstration of this, since, in these societies, the social groups within which the women bear their children and raise them with the help of a certain number of men, in sum, what we call 'families of procreation and child care', are social groups made up of brothers and sisters plus the children the sisters bear.[30] No sexual activity – hetero- or homosexual – is allowed among these persons. Brothers behave like 'fathers' toward their sisters' children. And yet they are not the ones who caused them to be born by their 'sperm-rain'. This was done by others, whose identity is of little importance and who never take care of these children, who in turn will not recognize them as their fathers and will not care who they are.

Yet, in the case of the Na (but also the Nayar, the Tetum, etc.), we cannot

---

30   It should be remembered that women can bear a child every year, but that in most societies they give birth only every two and half or three years – well beyond the period of post-partum amenorrhea – because they abstain from sexual relations with men before their child, which is usually breastfed, is weaned. This constraint applies equally to the men who have sexual access to the mother. Female bonobos give birth every four and a half years on average; and female chimpanzees, every six years. Furthermore, human children mature very late. They become materially – if not socially – relatively independent only around the age of fourteen. In chimpanzees the young mature relatively late as well, at between eight and ten years of age, but females mature faster than males, which is also the case in humans.

explain the attention and care the men give these children by the fact that they would be protecting the transmission of their genes – as the sociobiologists argue. Of course, while it is not the ties of 'fatherhood' that make a man take care of his sister's children, it is still a kin tie. In this matrilineal society, a man, his sister and her children share the fact that they descend in the female line from the same founding ancestor of the matriline. Furthermore, the absence of marriage between matrilines in Na society, which results in the absence of 'husbands' for the sisters and of 'fathers' for the children, shifts the responsibility for the functions ensured elsewhere by 'husbands' or 'fathers' to the brother–sister relationship and to that between the maternal uncle and his sister's children.

It must not be forgotten, though, that in the bulk of matrilineal societies, marriage does exist, children deal with their mother's husband all their life and, over their lifetime, men find themselves in the position not only of brother and maternal uncle, but also of husband, brother-in-law and 'father-in-law'. We have also seen that, in matrilineal societies, the role ascribed to the woman's husband in making children varies widely, from that of 'father' of the foetus, which he feeds but did not engender, to 'father' whose sperm made the child's body. And we would find even greater differences if we extended our comparison to societies whose descent systems are patrilineal, cognatic, and so on. If we do this, we find that *everywhere and at all periods, whatever the kinship system, the cultural definitions of fatherhood, motherhood, siblingship, etc., whatever the forms of political-religious power that structure the society as a whole and make kinship relations serve its reproduction, men find themselves involved (closely or more remotely, constantly or intermittently) in raising the children their woman relatives bear, and wield over them various forms of authority and control.* Generally speaking, men's involvement in child-raising increases once the children pass infancy, a time when women play the prime role. For, as children grow, their adult relatives find themselves in the position of sharing or transmitting things that belong to them as individuals or members of a group: knowledge, values, ranks, titles, functions, wealth, land . . .

COOPERATION BETWEEN MEN AND WOMEN IN CHILD-RAISING

In sum, what explains male investment in raising the children related to them by virtue of the fact that their mother is either a (real or classificatory) sister or one of their (real or classificatory) wives is not only the social and material division of labour between the sexes (which means that each sex depends on the other for its livelihood and that this dependence is even stronger in children than in adults); it is also the fact that the birth of children brings into play the continuity of social relations that have nothing to do with kinship. It is not only people's position in society that is in question, it is also the place of the group or groups to which they belong by birth or other ties. To have children or not, to be able to adopt children or not, to see them die before one has transmitted what, until then, ensured the material and social continuation of the group of which they became members: these are the reasons that, at all times and in all latitudes, have led men to associate, more or less closely, with female relatives in raising the children they bear without necessarily having to be the 'fathers' in order to care for them.[31] This is because, in all societies, social relations that have nothing to do with marrying and having children – for instance possession of a title or a function (master of initiation ceremonies), or shared ownership of agricultural lands and/or a hunting territory – can continue to exist only if they are passed on to new generations, only if kinship relations become the privileged vectors of these transmissions and a condition of their reproduction.

In the end, one can say that, if men associate with women to form families, it is not only, like male chimpanzees, in order to play with their children and win the mother's favours, but to raise and control their children and to transmit to them the material and immaterial means they possess so that the new generation may live and give life to the social group to which they belong by birth or adoption.

---

31   The case of matrifocal families, an institution typical of Afro-Caribbean groups or of the so-called Afro-American communities in some American cities, does not contradict this affirmation: on the contrary. The men's ideal is to get married and, depending on their means, to keep several mistresses, whom they visit more or less regularly and with whom they sometimes spend more time than they do with their wives. More rarely, their mistresses can also have several lovers. Of course children are born of these adulterous unions and often learn their father's identity from their mother. The father gives the mother material help to raise the child. The state aid to lone mothers of one or several children has only reinforced these practices. It must be remembered that these practices are rooted in a very particular history. The matrifocal Caribbean and Afro-American families date to the time when thousands of African men and women were wrenched from their natal societies and sold to work as slaves on the European plantations. Slaves were not allowed to marry and found families. They were permitted to have sexual relations, but the children born of these unions did not belong to them. They belonged to the master, who could take them away from their mother when they were grown and sell them as slaves in turn. Furthermore, the masters, who were white, Christian and 'civilized', had allowed themselves to make free use of the bodies of their slaves and to get them with child. The children born of these unions made up the stratum of those of mixed blood, ranked by the 'whiteness' of their skin. To unite with a White was often one of the goals sought by black women so as to 'lighten' the skin of their children and give them a better future in the social hierarchy dominated by 'békés'.

Today, in Western European societies and aside from the exceptional circumstances, such as war, that have multiplied the numbers of widows and orphans, women's entry into the economy together with state aid have enabled many women to have children and live alone, without getting married, or to raise their children alone if they divorced. But in other parts of the world, many societies do not allow women to divorce and oppose their living on their own. In the Baruya society divorce does not exist, and widows are 'inherited' together with their children, by one of their deceased husband's brothers or by a man from the same lineage. Cf. the thesis by S. Mulot, "'Je suis la mère, je suis le père!": l'énigme matrifocale. Relations familiales et rapports des sexes en Guadeloupe', Thesis, Ecole des Hautes Etudes en Sciences Sociales, 2 vol., and F. Gracchus, *Les Lieux de la mère dans les sociétés afro-américaines* (Paris, Editions caribéennes, 1986).

Because of the sexual division of labour and the presence in kinship relations of social concerns that do not originate in these relations but pass in part through them in order to reproduce themselves, *children are important to adults*. For it is by and through children that social groups continue to exist and the social relations characteristic of a society can in part reproduce themselves. But only in part. For the reproduction of an economic and/or political system generally characteristic of a society does not depend only on whether a given family or a given local social group ceases to exist or not: a global logic is always more than the sum of the movements of its parts.

To be sure, the fact that men, whatever the representations of their role in making babies, do not make them in their own bellies and do not give birth, makes children a stake in power relations and gender struggles. Children are one of the motivations, if not the most important, for men's desire to control women's bodies and sexuality and, through their bodies, to control (and even appropriate) the children they bear.

CONCERNING THE ASEXUAL CHARACTER OF HUMAN SEXUALITY

The generalized, cerebralized sexuality characteristic of humans can therefore not explain the historical development of the various forms of family (nuclear, conjugal, extended, polygamous, polyandrous, etc.) that associate, more or less durably and more or less closely, men and women in the task of raising children, nor does it explain the forms of authority we find there. For the human capacity to make love all year round and at any time of the day or night can just as well attach two beings in a durable relationship as cause them regularly to change partners (e.g. the Nayar, the Na), or to add new partners (a woman and several male partners, a man and several women, or in an institutional form such as harems, etc.). In *Totem and Taboo*, Freud stresses the fact that sexual desire and love are egotistical emotions that do more to divide people than to unite them.[32] Generalized, polymorphous, cerebralized human sexuality, which manifests itself in the various forms (homo, hetero, auto) of sexual desire has no social meaning in itself. Sexual desire isolates people more than it brings them together.

Sexuality-as-desire in combination with the possibility of generalized sexual commerce can even jeopardize the reproduction of social ties by becoming the source of strife and confrontations that threaten the reproduction of the political and religious kinship relations that uphold social structure. It seems to me that this threat sheds light on the operating logic at work in Na society.

---

32   S. Freud, *Totem and Taboo*, translated by James Strachey (London, Routledge and Kegan Paul, 1961), p. 142. Cf. Confucius (v. 551–479 BCE), in his *Analects*, book 15: 'It is all over! I have not seen one who loves virtue as he loves beauty [or "the flesh"].' Cf. also book 9, 17; text of the *Analects* available at http://classics.mit.edu.

Having chosen to allow men and women to enjoy generalized sexual commerce, every day and in accordance with each person's desire, the Na could not bring such sexual permissiveness to coexist with marriage which, when it exists in a society, sets limits on the desires and sexual activities of those who have become husband and wife. Extreme permissiveness in matters of sex seems to be incompatible with the workings of institutions such as marriage, but perhaps with those of other political, religious and economic institutions as well. It must be recalled here that the Na are permissive in the extreme when it comes to sex, but this permissiveness also has limits: it stops at the door of the 'house'. And this is fundamental from the theoretical standpoint. All sexual activity is forbidden between members of the household, who are all related by blood ties. The conclusion is clear: extreme permissiveness in sexual matters cannot extend to relations between adults of both sexes when they are related, live together and are associated in raising the children that the women of the group bear.

SEXUAL PERMISSIVENESS AND ITS CONSEQUENCES

In other words, the most extreme permissiveness in matters of sex, the case in which individuals are socially permitted to fulfil their every desire, must stop at the 'family' door, that is to say at the door of the groups which, in a society, are directly connected with child-raising, and in most cases with procreation. To cross these limits, would be, for those who make up these 'families' to commit what is known as incest.

Extreme sexual permissiveness concerns homosexual relations as much as it does heterosexual relations. In both cases sexual desire has the same effects: it isolates as much as it unites those who succumb to it, and it is a source of conflict, exclusion and rivalry. But of course there is a sizeable difference between the two: homosexual relations do not produce children. They come under what is called sexuality-as-desire and not sexuality-as-reproduction. If it were to become the only form of sexual activity practised, homosexuality would be a direct threat to society, and this reason has sometimes been advanced by those who condemn it. But as a form of sexuality, it is, I stress, just as 'natural' as heterosexuality – and it is practised by other animal species, chimpanzees and bonobos, for example, where it is part of the world of pleasure and play.[33]

But, as we have seen, there are two kinds of 'family': one brings together adults of both sexes and children related to each other by blood (Nayar, Na); the other brings together adults who live together because they are related by marriage whereas they belong to different birth groups. At the heart of this

---

33   See F. De Waal, 'Bonobo sex and society', *Scientific American*, March (1995), pp. 58–64; B. L. Deputte, 'Sexe et société chez les primates', *Sciences humaines*, no. 108 (2000), pp. 28–31.

second kind of family, the most frequently found, relations of alliance (between husband and wife) are articulated with relations of descent and filiation (between parents and children). In this case, by extending to the inner workings of these families, sexual permissiveness would jeopardize simultaneously the ties of affinity and those of consanguinity that are articulated within the unit that begets and raises children. It is for this reason that, in all societies where different kinds of alliance between kin groups legitimize the sexual union of individuals belonging to each of these groups and set out the rights each has over the children born of these unions, the prohibitions on sexual relations between members of the same 'family' apply simultaneously to the relations of descent and the relations of alliance that interconnect and form the family fabric. These prohibitions do not concern first of all relations between consanguines and then extend to affines. They concern both kinds of relations simultaneously, but in an order that starts from descent and works its way out to alliance, as it were, in so far as incest between parents and children would throw into question the alliance between the parents. The mother who unites with her son makes him a rival of her husband, the father who unites with his daughter makes her a rival of his wife. We also understand that a man who sleeps with his wife's sister unbeknown to his wife throws into question simultaneously the blood ties between his wife and her sister and the alliance ties that unite him with his wife and more broadly with his wife's kin. And if a man sleeps with his brother's wife unbeknown to the brother, he jeopardizes simultaneously the alliance ties that unite this woman with his brother and his own consanguineous ties with his brother.

In short, because marriage (or a more or less equivalent social form of alliance between kin groups) exists in most societies, sexual permissiveness affects simultaneously relations of descent and relations of alliance, and, among the latter, affects *in a different manner* relations with one's allies' consanguines (AC) and relations with one's consanguines' allies (CA). And if the descent principle is matrilineal, sexual relations between a father and his daughter will not have the same gravity as relations between a mother and her son or a brother and his sister.

TWO POSSIBLE CHOICES OF UNION

There remains to be examined the prohibition of sexual relations between a brother and his sister. This taboo is found in all societies where an exchange of persons (men or women) is the imperative condition for an alliance, and also in those societies where an exchange of sperm without exchange of partners does not result in an alliance. But it is not found in societies that have chosen not to exchange all of their children but to keep certain ones to unite with each other. This is the case with the ancient Egyptians and Mazdean Iranians. Here marriage between a brother and his sister, far from being a punishable abomination, was on the contrary glorified – and even considered to be the finest, the most noble of alliances, that which brings humans closer to the gods. In these societies, brother–sister marriage, far from being regarded as incest, was considered to be an almost divine union.

Humans have always been faced with two possible choices: (1) to marry with or without exchange and (2) to unite like the gods or differently from the gods. The Egyptian brother–sister marriage, as we saw, was a marriage without exchange, in the image of the gods (and of course the Pharaoh, son of Isis and Osiris). The same is true of the *xwêtôdas* marriages in ancient Iranian society, the three forms of which reproduced the three primal unions between the gods that had engendered the order of the world: the union of a father (the heavens) with his daughter (the earth), who bore a son, a giant who later united with his mother who bore twins, a boy and a girl, who themselves engendered a son, the first man. We can see why the Mazdeans glorified the union of a brother with his sister: it replicated the birth of the first man. And we also see why, in this society, the closer (or the more closely related) certain 'humans' believed themselves to be to the gods, the more they felt authorized (or compelled) to replicate the gods' unions. This is what Ataxerxes II did when he married two of his daughters. Such unions were not considered to be incestuous. They are only incestuous from the standpoint of another society.

One final point: there is no society where marriage takes place only between close kin. Many societies combine the two principles: marry within the group and with the closest relatives, and marry further away or with others than one's group. Muslim societies are a typical example.[34] Where unions between very close relatives are allowed, they are obviously not considered to be incestuous. But where brother–sister marriage was allowed, this by no means implied that before the marriage the son could sleep with his mother and the daughter with her father. Brother–sister marriage did not permit the father to possess his daughter before his son did or the mother to unite with her son before her daughter did.

---

34 The study of the way societies favouring strongly endogamous unions operate has finally begun. In 1976, Claude Lefébure had stressed 'the geographic area and the considerable historical weight of societies that practiced agnatic unions' and showed that *The Elementary Structures of Kinship* was a book that had chosen 'not to talk about it'. Recently, Laurent Barry brilliantly addressed this task and found more than fifty societies practising strong agnatic endogamy – in Africa and Madagascar – and well beyond the zones of strong Islamic influence. See C. Lefébure, 'Le Mariage des cousins parallèles patrilatéraux et l'endogamie de lignée agnatique: l'anthropologie de la parenté face à la question de l'endogamie', in *Production, pouvoir et parenté dans le monde méditerranéen de Sumer à nos jours* (Paris, EHESS/CNRS, 1976), pp. 195–207; L. Barry, 'Les Modes de composition de l'alliance. Le mariage arabe', *L'Homme*, no. 147 (1988), pp. 17–50, and 'L'Union endogame en Afrique et à Madagascar', *L'Homme*, nos. 154–5 (2000), pp. 67–100.

In the end, nowhere do we find a society where the individual is authorized to satisfy all of his or her sexual desires (and therefore all of his or her sexual fantasies). The most extreme forms of sexual permissiveness, of generalized sexual commerce between individuals, stop at the door of the social units within which men and women cooperate in raising children, whether or not they engendered them together. And when sexual unions within the family that are forbidden elsewhere are allowed in a given society, nowhere are these unions considered to be incestuous and condemned as such. In all places and at all times they have drawn humans closer to the gods and flow from a political and religious cosmosociology from which they derive their legitimacy, and which they help to reproduce.

INITIAL THEORETICAL CONCLUSIONS

Let us sum up some of the theoretical conclusions we believe we are entitled to draw from the foregoing analyses.

1. There is no society that allows individuals to satisfy all of their sexual desires (and fantasies). All societies set limits on the uses of sex.

2. There are two possibilities for ensuring the continuity of the groups that compose a society and whose survival depends on the birth of children that will prolong its physical and social existence: the groups can exchange sexual partners, usually women but sometimes men as well; or they can not exchange and instead reproduce within the group.

3. Exchange does not necessarily mean alliance. The exchange of substances is not an exchange of persons and does not give rise to a social alliance (as in the case of the Na).

4. Alliance does not necessarily mean exchange either, giving and receiving from others; it sometimes means keeping for oneself and contracting alliances within the family (ancient Egyptian and Iranian marriages).

5. Wherever exchange takes the form of exchanges of persons and gives rise to various forms of alliance, the procreation and child-raising units combine ties of affinity (between husbands and wives) and ties of filiation and descent (between parents and children), which are ties of consanguinity. When affines unite, they engender consanguines.

6. Wherever unions are based on the exchange of persons and are formalized by an 'official' alliance, the sexual permissiveness allowed the individuals stops at the door of the procreation and child-raising units. Sexual relations are forbidden between individuals of the opposite sex and different generations that make up these units; such relations are considered to be incestuous unless, on the contrary, they are regarded as unions that bring humans closer to the gods, as a way for humans to imitate the gods and be like them.

7. As a consequence, and logically, in societies that forbid sexual unions between close relatives, humans are not allowed to imitate the gods. The relations humans entertain with the gods are invoked here either to forbid or to allow relations between close blood relatives. Unions between humans always involve the whole of society and the cosmos.

8. There is no possible biological basis for the prohibition of sexual unions with affines' consanguines or consanguines' affines. Such prohibitions can be explained only by social reasons (which have no genetic impact on the humans species). These unions must therefore threaten social cooperation and the ties of solidarity created between two kin groups for them to be forbidden. But that also means that the development of partner exchanges giving rise to alliances is a specific feature of human kinship systems.

9. No society we know of operates solely on the basis of endogamous unions between very close blood relatives – brother/sister, father/daughter, mother/son. Even in the societies where such unions are allowed, there are also other unions that follow other principles – union with distant blood relatives or union with unrelated persons, foreigners or outsiders, and these unions can give rise to exchanges.

10. Even in societies where certain unions between close consanguines are not only allowed but sought (ancient Egypt, Iran and Greece – the case of marriage with an agnatic or uterine half-sister), other consanguineous unions are forbidden (between a mother and her son or a father and his daughter, for example). We must therefore conclude that no society operates without some form of what we call the incest prohibition.

11. The prohibition of unions between certain categories of consanguines is universal, but it does not follow that the prohibition of brother–sister

unions is universal and that the exchange of women or men between two kin groups is everywhere the basis of alliances (cf. ancient Egyptian or Greek marriages).

12. Reciprocal gifts of substances (sperm) between kin groups do not necessarily produce alliances between these groups.[35]

WHAT MAKES HUMANS DIFFERENT FROM THE OTHER PRIMATES?

Of all the inventions that gradually set humans apart from the other primates and restructured the gendered division of labour from top to bottom, there is one that was perhaps as important as the ability to make and use tools and weapons, and that was the domestication of fire.

The use of fire is (sporadically) attested 1.6 million years ago, but use does not imply domestication. Fire appears to have been completely domesticated some 500,000 years ago by *Homo Erectus,* and its use became widely diffused among our pre-human ancestors, including the Neanderthals and Cro-Magnons. Together with the gradual development of articulated speech and the diversification of tools and techniques, fire was a crucial factor that led men and women to cooperate durably in ways not found in the most closely related primate societies.[36]

Fire. We think of the old Greek myth of Prometheus, son of a Titan who stole the heavenly fire from Zeus and gave it to mankind. In those times, people lived with the gods without themselves being gods. One day Zeus told Prometheus to sacrifice an animal and to share it between the gods and men. Prometheus got a fine bull, killed it and cut it up. Of the pieces he made two shares. On one side, he put all of the white bones stripped of their meat and surrounded them with big pieces of appetizing white fat; on the other side, he gathered all the pieces of meat, and stuffed them into the slimy repellent belly of the animal. He

---

35   Just as a gay friend's gift of sperm to a lesbian does not make this man the child's father or uncle.

36   C. Perlès, 'L'Homme préhistorique et le feu', *La Recherche,* no. 60 (1975), pp. 829–39; S. R. James, 'Humanoid Use of Fire in the Lower and Middle Pleistocene', *Current Anthropology,* vol. 30 (1989), pp. 1–26; J. Goudsblom, *Fire and Civilization* (Penguin Books, 1992); A. Ronen, 'Domestic Fire as Evidence for Language', in T. Akazawa et al. (eds.), *Neanderthals and Modern Humans in Western Africa* (New York, Plenum Press, 1998), pp. 439–47; J. E. Frazer, *Myths of the Origins of Fire* (London, Macmillan, 1930); G. Bachelard, *La Psychanalyse du feu* (Paris, Gallimard, 1937); C. Lévi-Strauss, *Le Cru et le cuit* (Paris, Plon, 1964). The most recent work on this question is that by J. Collina-Gérard, *Le Feu avant les allumettes* (Paris, Editions de la Maison des Sciences de L'homme, 1988). See also R. A. Stein, 'La Légende du foyer dans le monde chinois', in J. Pouillon and P. Maranda (eds.), *Echanges et Communications. Mélanges offerts à Claude Lévi-Strauss* (Paris, Mouton, 1970), vol. 2, pp. 1281–305; S. J. Pyne, 'Keeper of the Flame: A Survey of Anthropogenetic Fire', in P. J. Crutzon and J. G. Goldammer (eds.), *Fire and the Environment* (New York, Wiley, 1993), pp. 245–66; R. Barkley, 'Fire as Paleolithic Tool and Weapon', *Proceedings of the Prehistoric Society,* no. 21 (1956), pp. 36–48.

presented the first package to the gods and the second to men. Zeus spotted the trick. And to punish Prometheus and the men who had helped him, he hid the fire and the wheat, thus depriving mankind of these things. Humans became like animals, thereafter forced to eat the raw flesh of animals and the leaves of wild plants. Once again Prometheus came to their aid. He travelled to heaven and there, unseen, stole a seed (*sperma*) of the divine fire, which he concealed in a stalk of fennel and returned to earth to give it to mankind. But this fire was only a seed. Like all seeds, it grew, matured and then died; whereas the heavenly fire fuelled itself and was immortal. To keep the fire alive, mankind had to tend it constantly, and had to bury the wheat seeds in the ground, let the sun 'cook' them and thus make them grow and ripen. In short, men had to work. Further-more, in these times, there were no women, only men.

Zeus was furious to have once more been tricked by Prometheus. He called a meeting of the gods and goddesses and had them mould the first woman, Pandora, the most beautiful and appealing of all creatures, made in the image of Aphrodite, Hera and Athena. And he sent her down to live with men, in the home of Epimetheus ('he who understands afterwards' – *epi*, while Prometheus 'understands beforehand' – *pro*). Epimetheus was dazzled and married Pandora the next day. He gave his house into her care, telling her never to raise the lid of a certain jar. Of course Pandora lost no time investigating and the next day, as soon as she had raised the lid, out of the jar rushed, invisible and silent, all of the ills that would henceforth beset mankind: cupidity, lies, sickness and death. As for Prometheus, Zeus punished him by chaining him to a column halfway up a mountainside, between heaven and earth. Each day Zeus's eagle comes and devours his liver, and each night it grows back.[37]

The beauty and richness of this myth, which is only one of hundreds of tales that societies have produced on this theme[38] and recorded in their mythologies, indicate the impact that must have been made on men's minds and on their subsequent evolution by the possession of fire. Its domestication was much more influential than the making and use of tools in bringing about the initial radical separation between protohumans and the rest of the animal kingdom, between the forerunners of humanity and animality. Furthermore, this initial separation preceded by several hundred thousand years the final transforma-tions of the protohuman languages into various sorts of articulated speech ultimately inherited by the ancestors of the Neanderthals and the Cro-Magnons, between 200,000 and 300,000 years before our era.

Animals eat their food raw and are afraid of fire. Fire is both a weapon and a tool. The possession of fire enabled humans to protect themselves from wild

---

37   J-P. Vernant, *L'Univers, les dieux, les hommes* (Paris, Le Seuil, 1999), pp. 67–8.
38   See Frazer, *Myths of the Origins of Fire*.

animals and from the cold. It enabled them to exploit the many resources – plants in particular – that are not edible if not cooked. It gave them access to new, cold, regions of the globe and, of course, allowed them to survive the last ice ages, which covered immense regions of the world with ice, and changed their fauna and flora. But above all, fire prompted man's ancestors to create places where food was cooked and shared out, 'base camps' separate from the spots where the game had been killed and cut up.

All of this had huge consequences for the organization of protohuman societies. Both before and after fire had been domesticated it had to be kept going, be fed and protected from the wind, the rain, etc. These operations demanded a certain organization on the part of society, a division of labour between the genders and the generations. Hence their cooperation for the good of the group that used fire for cooking, warmth and protection. And while they were learning to use fire as protection, humans had also to learn to protect themselves, to keep children away from fire.

These are important facts from the standpoint of the analysis of the circumstances that led to the appearance, in protohuman groups, of social units of procreation and child-raising where adult men and women worked together. Fire is indeed at the origin of cooking and of a new division of labour between men and women. It is also the origin of the place in the camp where people came together to warm themselves, to cook and to share food from the hearth. And the growing role of cooked food in the human diet reinforced the material dependence of children on the adults who fed them. *New material, social and emotional ties thus grew up between the sexes and between the generations* that found themselves brought together and bound to each other in the same places or in nearby places on a relatively continuous daily basis.

The domestication of fire also predated by hundreds of thousands of years the domestication of different plants and animals which, from ten or twelve thousand years before our era to the end of the Mesolithic, would again recast the economy and organization of societies, since people would now be able to produce a great portion of their means of existence for themselves. The gap between primates and man would grow even wider. Primates find their material means of survival in their natural environment. They do not produce them. The development of agriculture, of horticulture (in Oceania), of herding combined with agriculture (Europe, the Middle East) or of specialized nomadic herding (Central Asia, East Africa, etc.) would have three consequences.

The material and social interdependence of the sexes became increasingly complex. Certain new material forms of wealth – agricultural lands, herds, grazing territories, etc. – became fundamental issues for the functioning and reproduction of societies. Hence the even greater importance of controlling the sexuality of men and women and defining the rules that would legitimize the appropriation of the children born of the unions between the sexes. Children were henceforth regarded as a future labour force and the vector, depending on the child's gender and the descent principle at work in the society, of the transmission of the wealth, ranks, knowledge and so on of the group(s) into which it was born or had been adopted.

The third consequence of the development of agriculture, herding and the separation between towns and the countryside was the appearance, in numerous societies of the Old and New Worlds, in the East, the West and Africa alike, of new types of hierarchies between the groups specialized in various functions – sacrifices to the gods, war, various forms of production using complex technologies (metallurgists, potters, etc.). In short, priests and warriors, cut off from manual labourers and dependent on the other groups for their livelihood and the exercise of their functions, artists specialized in the service of the other castes or classes, made their appearance. To be sure, these new groups – priests, warriors, artisans – were composed of both men and women, and the hierarchy among these groups also gave a different status to the men and women who composed them.

To an even greater degree than in more egalitarian societies, children born in societies organized into hereditary chiefdoms, castes or classes became a strategic asset as much for the reproduction of the specific groups that composed the society as for the overall hierarchical structure that defined the places and functions to be preserved or to be occupied by each of these groups. *It is understandable that setting the social conditions of sexual unions and determining what group the children born of these unions belonged to were the two problems societies had to deal with.* The solutions to these problems came in the form of diverse kinship systems, which we listed earlier, and which combine rules defining who the children belong to (descent principle) and rules allowing and/or excluding certain unions. And we saw that these principles and rules are few in number, even though their combinations generate many varieties.

All of these social relations (sexual division of labour and material and social interdependence between men and women and between adults and children, on the one hand; and division of the society between ranked groups specialized in distinct and interdependent activities, on the other) are new; they never existed in any other primate species. And these new social relations are not rooted in the sexuality of individuals and are not directly linked to their desires. To be sure, the fact that it is usually men who become warriors and women who nurse babies is not unconnected with the position of each sex in the process of reproducing life and thus with sexuality as reproduction of life. But not with sexuality-as-desire.

It is in this uniquely human context – marked by the fact that not only can people not develop outside of society but they cannot survive without the cooperation of the two sexes bound together by their birth – that the problem of incest and the social 'misuses', the wrong uses, of sex arises. Without this twin presupposition – that humans live 'naturally' in society and that they have always evolved in societies *already* composed of families – the problem of the foundations of incest cannot be correctly posed. Instead of presupposing, as Freud and Lévi-Strauss did, that the ancestors of humans did not live in societies but in self-enclosed biological families in which generalized sexual promiscuity prevailed among the individual members and between the generations or which were under the sexual monopoly of a despotic male, we must, in accordance with the material unearthed by palaeontology and evolutionary morphology, posit that our ancestors lived in societies *already composed of families* and that the – very slow – emergence of new material and social relations between the sexes created new relations between the adults and children and between the groups in which these children were born and raised.

In itself, sexual desire as a drive is not of a social nature. Or, to be more accurate, sexual desire becomes a social trait because it can be satisfied only by the existence of others, of the same or opposite sex, who respond positively to it. But it is a-social in the sense that it can spontaneously direct itself towards individuals with whom, for various reasons (of religion, of social group, of kin ties) sexual union is socially forbidden. But sexual desire is not only a-social in that it is blind to social criteria, it is also a-social because it drives individuals to oppose each other as much as, if not more than, to cooperate. Finally, with a few notable exceptions that have been celebrated by poets or in song, sexual desire and passion never last for long, rarely a lifetime. They can never alone provide the social basis for prolonged cooperation between individuals belonging to the same or to different generations. Conversely, bearing and raising a child, whether born of a love union or not, can be a social and emotional reason for extended cooperation between adults. Desire and reproduction can thus lead completely distinct and separate lives. The Na are a spectacular example of this because in their society the disjunction is total and institutionalized. In the Trobriand Islands, sexual desire and commerce between young people are perfectly accepted and encouraged before marriage (except between brothers and sisters) but are forbidden after marriage.

HUMANS: THE ONLY ANIMAL CO-RESPONSIBLE WITH NATURE FOR ITS OWN EVOLUTION

By producing an increasing portion of their material and social conditions of existence, humans are the only animal species that has become co-responsible, with nature, for its own evolution.[39]

From this point on, evolution became history, and history was not the

---

39   See M. Godelier, *Meurtre du Père ou sacrifice de la sexualité. Approches anthropologiques et pyschanalytiques* (Paris, Arcanes, 1996), p. 30.

result merely of humans' capacity to act on their natural environment but also of their capacity to act on themselves, on their own nature. And among the actions humans undertook on themselves, in the forefront stands the control and management of their sexuality. In effect, humans are the only animal species that consciously and socially 'manages' its sexuality, that explicitly, in the form of oral and/or written laws, establishes prohibitions and limits on certain uses people can make of their sexual organs, in short, limits on sexual desires (and fantasies) of all forms, whether hetero- or homosexual.

The choice confronting humans has always been the same: either allow a man or a woman to unite with members of their natal group or oblige them to unite with individuals of the opposite sex from groups other than the one in which they were born. A third formula is possible, but it derives from the two others, since it combines the possibility of uniting within one's own group with that of uniting with individuals from other groups.

The two basic formulas correspond to two basic principles of social life, which are not restricted to the sphere of kinship. Social groups, like individuals, have the choice of keeping or giving away what they possess. These two principles – keeping and/or sharing – are principles of action and organization that apply to all areas of social life and serve as much (but in distinct ways) to establish the various social ties linking both individuals and groups.

Let us take the example of the division of labour between the sexes, which makes men and women materially, socially and emotionally dependent on each other. The obligation to share the products of their labours thus became included in the very functioning of these social relations, which are also material relations between the sexes and between the generations, between the adults of both sexes and the children. But obviously the obligation to share does not mean keeping nothing for oneself and one's dependants. There are, to be sure, examples of hunting societies in Australia where the hunter never eats the game he kills. He distributes it to the members of his band and waits to eat the meat another hunter shares out. That is an extreme case, where individuals deliberately place themselves in a relation of complete dependence on others and place others in the same relation with themselves. An even more extreme example is the Bushmen society, where hunters take with them an arrow belonging to a friend or a kinsman and choose precisely this arrow to kill their game. In this case, the game belongs to the owner of the arrow, which will enable him to share the game killed with his arrow with the whole camp.[40]

40 Cf. A. Testart, 'Essai sur les fondements de la division sexuelle du travail chez les chasseurs-cueilleurs (Paris, Ecole des Hautes Etudes en Sciences Sociales, coll. Cahiers de L'Homme, 1986), and 'Game Sharing Systems and Kinship Systems among Hunter-Gatherers', Man, vol. 22 (1987), pp. 287–304. Cf. also I. Glynn, 'Food Sharing and Human Evolution: African Evidence from the Plio-Pleistocene of East Africa', Journal of Anthropological Research, vol. 34 (1978), pp. 311–25.

But it is clear that, if the hunter gives away all or part of his game, it is in order to receive in turn, sooner or later, a portion of the game killed by the other hunters.[41] Nevertheless, there is one 'thing' that neither the male nor the female members of a hunting-gathering band can or are allowed to give away, and that is their territory. The band can share its use with a neighbouring band, but they cannot, on pain of disappearing as a band and being absorbed into other bands, yield the ultimate control of their land. Furthermore, gift-giving is not the only form of exchange, and the gift given in return, what is called a counter-gift, is not the only form of gift. Clan lands, the territories a society leaves to the generations yet to be born are gifts that these generations will never be able to 'return' and for which the only thing they will be able to give is their 'gratitude', and perhaps make them an object of veneration. Furthermore, the exchange of commodities, their sale and purchase, are in no way exchanges of gifts. In selling, the object sold is completely detached from its original owner and becomes attached to the buyer. No personal tie is created, no debt exists between seller and buyer. In the case of a gift, the object given is never completely detached from the person (or group) that has given it, and therefore giving creates a personal tie between giver and receiver – and obliges the receiver to give something in return. Giving creates ties and debts. Buying and paying for something creates no ties or debts.

Even in Western societies dominated by the production and sale of commodities, by the capitalistic obsession that 'everything is for sale', certain basic components of social life are not for sale. Take for example the sacred sites and objects associated with three great religions (Jerusalem, Mecca): these cannot be sold or given to the faithful of other religions, but must be kept and protected so as to be passed on to future generations. In short, reciprocal giving is not the ultimate basis of social life. Nor is the market the only basis of social life. Human society – whatever form it has historically taken – exists only because some 'things' (principles, values, goods, persons, etc.) circulate and are exchanged between individuals and groups, while *at the same time* other things do not circulate, are kept, either to be transmitted or simply to be used here and now. The life of societies, like that of the individuals that compose them, thus rests on two distinct but complementary and necessary obligations: the obligation to exchange and the obligation to keep and transmit.

THE FIVE FORMS OF SOCIALLY AUTHORIZED UNION

These two principles – exchanging/not exchanging – thus apply simultaneously to all spheres of social life. There is no reason to reduce them to a single

---

41   Male and female chimpanzees do not 'give' game, they 'let it be taken'. They give others the permission to help themselves, but this permission is not a right.

obligation: the obligation to exchange; or to reduce the obligation to exchange to the obligation to give; or finally to reduce giving to a single one of its varieties: reciprocal gifts, gifts followed by equivalent counter-gifts. There is no reason to posit reciprocal giving as the instrument of transition between animality and humanity, and to make 'sexual life, rather than anything else', as Lévi-Strauss says, the ground on which the passage between the two orders – from nature to culture – can and must of necessity occur. How does this distinction apply to the sphere of kinship?

The appropriation of children by given groups gained increasing strategic importance. And since it is women who bear the children after having united sexually with men, controlling and defining the rules governing the union of men and women (which also ultimately solved the problem of the appropriation by one or another adult group of the children born of these unions) became a constant social concern.[42] At the origin of the five forms of socially authorized unions we find the two main principles of social life.

The first possible formula is to *marry within one's group*, with one's closest relative – the closest being brother or sister, children of the same father and the same mother. This is the case of the brother–sister marriages in ancient Egypt and Iran; but also of the marriages between half-brother and half-sister of the same father or the same mother in ancient Greece; or in Rome the case of the paternal uncle and his niece in the event that the death of the girl's father leaves the family without boys. Brother–sister marriages are thus 'alliances' made within the group without an exchange of men or women with other groups. The group has preferred to unite within itself, to keep its members for itself rather than exchange them. Here we have kinship relations that are not based on the exchange of women or men but which nevertheless prohibit other possible forms of union between consanguineous relatives (father–daughter, mother–son).

The second and most frequent formula, from the standpoint of human history, consists in *uniting outside one's own group*, and, in order to do this, exchanging men and women with other groups. This union thus sets the seal on an alliance between groups. The children belong either to the man's group or to that of the woman, or to both. In order to be able to exchange women (or men) with other groups, each group forbids its members to unite with each other, and since an authorized union is an alliance, each group forbids its members unauthorized unions with the consanguines of these affines. Unions by exchange of men or women thus entail two kinds of sexual prohibition: between close, less close or distant consanguines; and between close, less close or even distant affines. It is this formula that Lévi-Strauss proclaimed to be universal.

The third formula is a *combination of the previous two*. One can marry very

42   Godelier, *Meurtre du Père ou sacrifice de la sexualité*, pp. 44–5.

close relatives, less close consanguineous relatives and/or strangers belonging to other kin groups. This is the case, for example, of marriage in Muslim countries. The preferred marriage is that with the father's brother's daughter, the closest parallel cousin in a patrilineal system, and next with the other types of cousins on the father's and the mother's side and then with more distant relatives and finally with strangers. When two brothers agree to the union between the one's son and the other's daughter, the alliance is contracted inside the same lineage but there is no exchange of women between the two lines. The honour of the lineages is threatened by bad conduct on the part of the women whether they are sisters or wives.

Let us return to an essential point. A group can at the same time keep some of its women for alliances within the group and give some of its women for alliances with other groups. But keeping means neither giving nor exchanging. It is impossible, unless we fiddle with the words, to pass off an exchange for something it isn't. Yet that is what Lévi-Strauss attempted to show in his conversations with Didier Eribon, speaking about the so-called 'Arab' marriage with the father's brother's daughter, and therefore from the same 'sperm' as Ego's father:

> The exchange, *if it does take place*, occurs within one lineage, between collaterals. However . . . this type of marriage represents a minority of cases . . . It is as if instead of exchanging their daughters the family exchanges *the right to keep* some of them, incurring the obligation to give up some of the others.[43]

We see that Lévi-Strauss, confronted with facts that challenge his theory of exchange as the universal basis of kinship, invents a formula that presents as an exchange something that is not: the exchange of the right to keep for the obligation to give. But nowhere is the right to keep negotiated in exchange for the obligation to give. The right to keep is distinct from and complementary to the right to give. It is not based on the obligation to give as subordinated to the obligation to exchange.

The fourth formula is very rare. It is the one we have encountered among the Na but also among the Nayar. The husband does not unite with his wife even for the time of a ceremony but disappears from her life immediately after the wedding. The woman then has every latitude to take lovers and bear children who will belong to her and to her brothers and sisters, who will help her raise them. A woman is forbidden to unite with men from other castes. In the Na case, sperm is exchanged between kin groups, matrilineages, but these exchanges

---

43   D. Eribon, *De près et de loin. Entretien avec Claude Lévi-Strauss* (Paris, Odile Jacob, 1988), p. 147; English translation: *Conversations with Claude Lévi-Strauss*, translated by Paula Wissing (Chicago, University of Chicago Press, 1991), p. 104, emphasis added.

do not give rise to alliances. All unions between a man and the women of the other matrilineages are allowed, even between a man and two sisters or between a man and a mother and daughter. The inverse is equally true for a woman, who can have two brothers as lovers at the same time. The Na therefore practise exchange without alliance, but sexual unions between consanguineous relatives through the female line – between brothers and sisters, mother and son, uncles and nieces, aunts and nephews – are strictly forbidden.

Finally we must mention one last formula, in which one marries outside one's group without exchange. This is the case of marriage with a woman who has been captured or abducted by force. These women are taken without anything being given in return. There are, however, matrilineal societies, like the Makhuwa of Mozambique, where, when a lineage does not have enough women to exchange, the men go out in search of captives, whom they ritually make into fictitious 'sisters', and then exchange with men of other matrilineages.[44]

Generally speaking, male domination weighs more heavily on women when the marriage formula is based on the exchange of women by men, and when it is the husband – and not the woman's brothers and sisters – who appropriate the children she bears. But the roots of male domination also plunge into the sphere of the political and religious functions and relations that enable the society to exist as a whole and which use for their own purposes the kinship relations which, as such, are enough to make society into a whole.

IT IS FORBIDDEN SEXUAL UNIONS THAT GIVE THE INCEST TABOO ITS FORM AND CONTENT

We now come to the fact that all of these formulas for the union of the sexes and the appropriation of children are hedged about with prohibitions bearing on other possible unions, on the pretext that these would be incompatible with the realization of authorized unions or would destroy them once they were contracted. To be sure, we do not reduce the field of forbidden sexual unions to the narrower field of forbidden marriages. The prohibition of homosexual relations between relatives is not directly connected with marriage, although it can be (see the case of brothers-in-law in Australia). However here we will privilege unions that are forbidden because they are incompatible with maintaining formulas of alliance or descent.

For example, the union of a father and his daughter, or of a mother and her son in ancient Egypt, prevented the son from subsequently marrying the daughter – in other words prevented the brother from marrying the sister – whereas the union of a brother and a sister was not forbidden and did not constitute

---

44 Cf. C. Geffray, *Ni père, ni mère, le cas Makhuwa* (Paris, Le Seuil, 1990).

incest. The incest prohibition existed, therefore, but between blood relatives in *successive* generations, for such unions would prevent alliances between blood relatives of the same generation. The number and gravity of the prohibitions varies, depending at once on the nature of the descent principles and on the nature of the alliances – within the group (endogamous marriages) or between two or several groups (exogamous marriages) in which the takers could also be givers (Baruya) or the takers could not be givers (Kachin).

Sexual permissiveness stops, in all societies, either there where the alliance formula would be jeopardized or there where the relations of cooperation and authority between consanguines would be at risk of collapsing and, in merging with each other, of disappearing (Na). But this time we are no longer talking about sexuality-as-reproduction but about sexuality-as-desire which, as we have seen, is fundamentally a-social. Sexuality-as-desire has never been the basis of lasting cooperation between individuals, whether within their birth group or between the individual and the groups with whom he or she is allied. And it is not only hetero-sexual desire that unites and divides. This is just as true in another way of homosexual desire between a father and his son, a mother and her daughter, but also between two sisters or two brothers. It is because, as we have said, sexual desire in itself is a-social that no society can allow everything to be allowed.

And this process of self-domestication is never finished, whereas the domestication of plants and animals seems to have reached its limits.[45] Sex and the sexed body, determined by its genital organs, by its substances, by all of the anatomical and physiological differences that distinguish one sex from the other, was compelled not only to submit to the social (and cosmic) order prevailing in each society, but to constantly testify *to*, but also *for* or even *against*, this order. This is perfectly illustrated by all of the representations of the respec-tive roles men and women play in making babies. Everywhere, the spontaneous nature of desire has had to be sacrificed in order to produce a social order that is always and at the same time an order between the sexes and a sexual order. Everywhere the a-social character of sexuality had to be eliminated, the poly-morphism of desire sacrificed, generalized sexual permissiveness forbidden in order for society to organize and reproduce itself.

Sexuality was forced to take on forms that were mandatory for all members of society in accordance with their respective places in the social order, and even for kings and queens when it came to the cosmic order. These social forms forced the desires of individuals to bend and converge in such a way that society might subsist through and over and beyond the meeting of these desires. We can thus understand why, of all the ages of the human life, it is first childhood and then adolescence that are the most strongly marked by the domestication

---

45 For all these points, see Godelier, *Meurtre du Père ou sacrifice de la sexualité*, pp. 21–52.

of sexuality. For it is in and on the bodies of children, and in their innermost selves – which are composed in the first place by ties with their closest family members and with the members of the social groups to which they belong – that this bending of sexuality is brought about, this imposition of orientations and of the social meanings that will make – but not always – these desires 'appropriate', that is to say, both appropriate in themselves (heterosexual rather than homosexual, for instance) and directed toward the appropriate persons (not the mother or the father, etc., not toward persons of another religion, another class, another race, a 'bad' family in the village, and so on).

But if sexual desire can be suppressed, it can never disappear. It can merely be repressed, pushed below the level of what the conscious mind and society are willing or able to see, somewhere in the shadows where it will lie in wait until it can reappear in other forms. Yet sacrificing the a-social character of sexuality is not simply an amputation. It is also a kind of creation. It is acting on oneself in order not only to live in society but to produce society in order to live; this is a feature unique to humankind and which will always separate humans, increasingly with every passing day, from our distant cousins, the primates.

The ancestors of humankind, faced with a mode of existence they did not chose – living in society, which they inherited from nature – over the course of evolution that has been going on for many thousands of years, completely reworked the conditions in which they lived at the outset. It is thus that they gradually became the only 'naturally social' species to co-manage its evolution, to be co-responsible, along with nature, for its fate. A unique phenomenon: humans are the only natural species that has become more and more implicated in the production of itself, pursuing its evolution in another world that it produces itself, that of culture and history, through the many forms of social life and the cultural worlds it has invented. And that is a universal phenomenon.

Over the course of this evolution, the new social relations that arose between the sexes and between the groups that make up societies, the new forms of dependence, of cooperation and hierarchy, would reshape the original forms of social organization – living in multimale and multifemale bands where the care and raising of children fell primarily to the women and where conflict concentrated on access to sex and means of subsistence. There was no wealth, no secrets in these societies, but perhaps territories and skills to transmit. Since that time, new social relations not found in nature – kinship relations – have emerged; nowhere can they be confused with the family, that social unit associated with the birth and raising of children, but nowhere are they completely detached from it either.

These new relationships gave rise to original social groups that did not exist in nature either, and which brought together men and women of several generations, bound, affiliated by a shared descent principle to clans, lineages, households, demes and kindreds, which inserted themselves between the individual and the family in which he or she was born and/or raised, and society. And these new relations and social groups, which were broader than the family, each time restructured existing family forms according to their own logic. That is why there are no 'matrilineages' or 'clans' in primate societies. For in order for such social groups to exist, the members of these groups must learn after birth to recognize not only their mother but also their father, their mother's brother or their father's sister, not to mention their grandparents, classified as fathers and mothers, etc.

But even when it was vested with various political, economic and religious social stakes, the family, or something close to it, has remained the place where individuals are initially socialized and where are stamped on their bodies and into their sexuality the standards and forms that will make this sexuality socially 'appropriate'. It is through this twofold movement of the development of kinship relations (which are not to be confused with the direct ties a child may have with those who raise him or her) and the fact that these relations have always been vested with other social relations, that a twin metamorphosis can be found at work in all societies. Social relations have become 'matters of kinship', and since kin ties are ties between men and women, these social relations that have become an aspect of kinship mark the difference between the sexes. Boys rather than girls, the eldest son rather than the youngest (or the contrary), inherit land, girls inherit the jewels, the oldest girl inherits her mother's house, and do on.[46]

When these metamorphoses are complete, the sexes become 'genders', masculine and feminine. It is then that sexually typed bodies – because some have a penis and others a vagina, some secrete sperm, others milk – which are now bodies of a particular 'gender', begin to function as ventriloquists' dummies, constantly holding forth a discourse on the prevailing order in their society – an order between the sexes, a sexual order, but also a political order; in sum the order, in all its forms, that brings together the different components of society, all of the activities engaged in by these individuals and groups, into a whole which must be reproduced. That is why human sexuality, which is basically a-social, would thus interfere even more frequently than the sexuality of primates in the development of new forms of social life.

At first humanity could only undergo this condition and shape it, but not explain it. Humanity could explain it as a gift from the gods, since women gave birth to children, or as a curse, since sexual desire divided and opposed men as much or more than it united them – unless precisely, it was domesticated and made to serve society and the reproduction of life. Likewise humanity justified the multiple taboos, prohibitions and punishments it unleashed against one or another form of sexual union between individuals of the opposite or same sex. The explanation was

---

46   M. Godelier, 'Inceste, parenté, pouvoir', *Psychanalyse*, no. 36 (1990), pp. 33–51.

everywhere the same: this is what the gods or the ancestors want. Nowhere have humans been able or willing to recognize themselves as having been the source of the proscriptions and prescriptions they imposed on themselves. It was the Sun who gave Kanaamakwe, the Baruya's ancestor, the rules of their society and established the position that men and women were to occupy in it. It was Yahweh who gave Moses the Tables of the Law and promised to help him lead the Jewish people back to the land of Israel. Everywhere customs and their human sanctions are cloaked in the authority of the gods, the spirits, divine ancestors. Nowhere for thousands of years has humanity been able to recognize itself in its works.

We know of no better proof of everything we have advanced than the customs of Bali dealing with the treatment of twins at birth. If opposite-sex twins are born in a noble family, they are greeted with joy and honoured. They are considered already to be united as husband and wife in their mother's womb and they are raised to marry each other like gods when they come of age. By contrast, if opposite-sex twins are born to commoners, the parents and their children will be banished from the village for a time, their house torn down, and the whole village will have to undergo a ritual cleansing. In this case, the birth of twins, their union in their mother's womb, are considered as an act of incest, and both parents and children will have to be punished for it.[47] It therefore comes as no surprise that, in these Southeast Asian societies, nobles marry their closest relatives, their first cousins, and that close marriages are forbidden and looked upon in horror by commoners, even though, as Clifford Geertz pointed out, here incest is less a sin than a social fault, an act that is forbidden them by their status.[48]

Can there be any more eloquent proof that humanity, which invented its own rules of conduct, its own hierarchies, cannot at the same time produce them and ascribe them to itself? They are attributed to the gods or to nature. Why not to humanity itself? The examples of the societies of Bali teach us that we cannot or will never be able to understand sexual prohibitions and incest taboos by viewing them, as so many anthropologists have done, as purely a problem of kinship.

47   J. Belo, 'A Study of Customs Pertaining to Twins in Bali' (1935), in J. Belo (ed.), *Traditional Balinese Culture* (New York, Columbia Press, 1970), pp. 3–56. See also J. Boon, *The Anthropological Romance of Bali* (Cambridge, Cambridge University Press, 1977), p. 133; S. Errington, 'Incestuous Twins and the House Societies of Insular Southeast Asia', *Cultural Anthropology*, vol. 2, no. 4 (1987), pp. 403–44.
48   C. Geertz, cited by Errington, 'Incestuous Twins', p. 403.

CHAPTER THIRTEEN

Of the Past, We Cannot Make a Clean State
Assessing the Theories

We are coming to the end of this long and sometimes difficult journey. We have, it seems to me, taken stock of and analyzed sufficient facts (and highly diverse ones at that) to be able to answer the questions we asked ourselves at the outset.

THAT WHICH IN KINSHIP HAS NOTHING TO DO WITH KINSHIP

What was at stake was to understand the nature and importance of kinship relations at two levels, which intersect and fuse in life but must be carefully distinguished when it comes to their analysis: that of the role of kinship relations in personal life, in the construction of social and sexual identity, in affective and emotional intimacy; and that of their role in the workings of the different types of society that have arisen in the course of history (and often disappeared after having reproduced themselves for a longer or shorter period of time over a tiny or huge portion of the earth).

The connection between these two levels, the individual and the societal, is easy to identify and simple to understand. It is part and parcel of the very nature of human kinship. What are we talking about when we talk about kinship and the diverse ties it creates between individuals? What we are talking about, as we have abundantly shown, are, first, the socially authorized or forbidden unions between individuals of the two sexes – sexual unions, and all the more, matrimonial unions – and second, the social appropriation of the children born of these unions. The child is at the heart of kinship, at the heart of the stakes involved. That does not mean that kinship is only filiation and descent, though. For if one sex has to unite with the other in order for children to be born, who should this other be? Can the two people be already related (and to what degree), strangers (and to what extent)? And then, who will the children born of these authorized unions belong to: To the woman and her group? To the man and his group? To both, and in what proportions? And for what reasons will adults of both sexes appropriate the children, equally or unequally, either because they engendered them or because they are relatives of those who engendered them? Finally, what ties will the children born successively of these unions have with each other? What status will they derive from their sex and their birth order? What will be the fate of forbidden sexual and matrimonial unions, and of the children born of them (will they be regarded as bastards, for example?)? But also, what will be the fate of orphaned or abandoned children who have no one to take them and to substitute for their deceased or defective parents?

It is clear, then, that kinship relations, which are ties between persons of different sexes and ages, play an important, if not decisive, role in people's lives in so far as in all known societies, nearly all of the children born are recognized by adult relatives. These children survive and are raised, at least in the early years of their life, in groups of related adults. And everywhere, these groups have a known, if not recognized, social status (cohabitation, common-law union, monogamous family, single-parent family, polygynous or polyandrous family, line, lineage, clan, deme, house, etc.). These relations and these ties, which from its birth bind a child to other people who have rights and duties with respect to it and constitute its first form of integration in society, will continue to influence the child as it grows and becomes first an adolescent then an adult, and comes to occupy other positions in the kinship network and the society.

This person will marry or remain unmarried. He or she will have children, which may be all boys or all girls. He or she will also become the uncle or the aunt of the children that are born to his or her brothers or sisters if they, too, have children. In short, through their choices and through the choices of their relatives, individuals pass in the course of their lifetime from one kin position to others, occupying simultaneously with regard to other relatives several positions at once. He is at the same time (or successively) the son of, the father of, the uncle of, the brother of; she is the daughter of, the mother of, and so on.

Observing the destinies reserved for each individual by the fact of being born male or female, or being born first or last in a group of related adults who thereby have rights and duties in regard to this person, which they may or not exercise, takes us immediately to the other side of kinship relations, to another aspect of their workings, which determines the place and importance of kinship relations in the functioning and reproduction of a given society. This other aspect entails all of the social functions that have nothing to do with kinship per se and which attach themselves to individuals owing to their position (father, son, oldest or youngest brother, oldest daughter, etc.) in the kinship network. The reason for this is clear if not simple. It has to do with the fact that in all societies, social relations that are not directly connected with the actual functions of kinship come to reside in a given kinship relation and make all kinship relations serve their own functioning and reproduction while being broader than the sphere of kinship by their very nature. This is easy to see when the social relations that penetrate the sphere of kinship and subordinate it to their own workings are caste or class relations that run through the whole society and divide its members, whatever their age and sex, into social groups occupying a specific place in the social hierarchy owing to the functions they ensure – Brahmins or Kshatriya, peasants or untouchables, etc.

These social relations involve forms of power, ownership and wealth as well as their distribution among the groups that make up the society; the unequal or equal access of individuals, depending on their sex, their age and the group they belong to, to the worship and rites owed to the ancestors, spirits or deities; etc. Some of which do not belong to any one clan and are worshipped by everyone.

These social relations take over kinship relations, enter them and attach themselves to one of the two axes that, in the overwhelming majority of societies, constitute the supports of kinship relations – relations of descent and filiation, on the one hand, and alliance ties, on the other. Countless examples, of the greatest variety, attest to this! Even recently, in certain rural areas of Europe, when a boy child was born, if he was the first born and not a younger son, he alone would inherit the family land and its ancestors, and would work the land in order to transmit it to his own oldest son (if he had one). But this privilege and this responsibility also required him to give his younger brothers and sisters their inheritance, in the form of either money or other chattels. In other parts of the world, this privilege went to the last-born child, with the obligation to take care of his or her aged parents until their death.

Such examples are legion, and show the ties that exist between a social status and the place an individual occupies, owing to sex or birth order, in the network of kinship relations and in the group these create. Evidence of this can still be seen in the Indian caste system, a global social system that emerged over two thousand years ago in the north of the country and which over the centuries spread to the southern tip of the subcontinent and to Sri Lanka. Moreover, the caste system is far from having disappeared in spite of its official abolition after the country's independence.

In this system, one is born a Brahmin or a Kshatriya; one does not become one. But the son is a Brahmin by birth only if his father married a woman of the same caste; if not, the father's function and the social status attaching to it are not transmitted. This function, as we know, consists in performing the rites and sacrifices demanded by the gods and the *sri*, the 'fathers', in view of preserving the order of the society and the universe. Given the obligation to marry in one's caste, kinship contributes directly to reproducing the Brahmin caste, as it does the other castes, since caste endogamy is a general principle. But it takes more than kinship to reproduce each caste and subcaste (*jati*) in its place within the hierarchy of the four major *varna*: priests (Brahmans), warriors (Kshatriyas), farmers and craftsmen (Vais'hya) and the rest of the low-status population (Shudras, out-castes, untouchables).[1]

---

1   This is only a very rough image of a complex system that arose in Vedic times but became rigidified through a ban on inter-caste marriages only in the tenth and eleventh centuries CE, perhaps in the wake of Muslim supremacy in the north and west of the country.

Owing to this division of functions and the assignment of religious, political and economic activities to different castes and subcastes, everyone depended on everyone else to reproduce their material and/or social conditions of existence. Before the English colonized India, various complex systems, such as the *jajmani* system, regulated material exchanges between castes for the services they provided each other and set the contributions imposed on the lower castes that would enable the Brahmins and Kshatriyas to live in accordance with their rank and status by performing their religious and political-military functions. Of course the social division between groups specialized in mutually exclusive functions and tasks cannot be seen as a social division of labour in so far as it is based on a ranking of all these functions and tasks according to their degree of purity or impurity. It therefore had nothing to do with the desire to increase the productivity of labour by dividing it up.

The system appeared in the north and the west of the Indian subcontinent with the arrival of Indo-European peoples in the Vedic period (c. 1200 BCE) (but that is controversial). It was formalized at the time of the composition of the great lyric epics, the *Mahabharata* and the *Ramayana* (between the second and the seventh centuries CE), and spread from the north to southern India in the period between the tenth and the twelfth centuries CE. The caste system gradually subordinated all of the local groups to its order and restructured them, with the exception of a certain number that resisted and have preserved their tribal organization even today. The other groups, the majority, thus found their place in the caste hierarchy. This system became the global scaffolding of Indian societies, whereas, until the time of the British conquest, the Indian subcontinent had been divided into more than a hundred larger or smaller kingdoms that ruled over populations speaking a great variety of Indo-European languages in the north, Dravidian languages in the South, Sino-Tibetan languages in the North-East as well as Austro-Asian languages.[2] All of these kingdoms and local societies were organized according to the same system which at once united and separated all casts and all local groups, and which calmly survived the disappearance of all of the local dynasties and even entire kingdoms. However, and this is the key point in our demonstration, the kinship systems found in India today fall into two big groups: Indo-European-type systems from the north to the centre and Dravidian systems from the centre to the southern tip of the continent.[3] It was therefore the *same* global system that

---

2   The 1971 linguistic survey counted 1,652 languages for India alone, not including Bangladesh.

3   The Indo-European systems have distinct vocabularies for consanguines and affines, and do not prescribe marriage with a cross cousin, unlike the Dravidian systems. Cf. T. Trautmann, *Dravidian Kinship* (Cambridge/New York, Cambridge University Press, 1981), pp. 91–237 and Chapter 4, 'The Dharmasastra and the Indo-Aryan kinship system', pp. 293–301.

took over two *different* sets of kinship systems and subordinated them to its own reproduction by attaching the same political-religious content to different logics of kinship. If we look at other parts of the world where Dravidian-type systems are found, at Amazonia for example or perhaps very ancient China, it is even more evident that the same types of kinship relations can be invested with different social contents depending on the political-religious and economic systems that co-opt them for their re-production.

From this we must conclude that the social relations that invest kinship and each time give it different 'social' contents have nothing to do, as far as their origins and raisons d'être are concerned, with kinship itself.

But not all social relations subordinate kinship relations to their own repro-duction. The ones that do cut across the whole society, concern all specific social groups, in so far as they situate them with respect to each other within a global architecture that assigns each group a place that connects all groups to each other. These are therefore social relations that have the capacity to create *a general state of interdependence* between all of the groups and individuals that compose the society and to make the society into a *whole* which can and must reproduce itself as such. This is something kinship *per se*, that is, the relations of descent and alliance between the people and kin groups in a society, is precisely incapable of doing.

NOWHERE ARE KINSHIP RELATIONS, AND EVEN LESS 'THE FAMILY', THE FOUNDATION OF SOCIETY

Kinship relations everywhere divide as much as they unite individuals and groups. They do not have the capacity in and of themselves to create a general state of dependence between all individuals and all groups. History is full of violent ruptures, deliberate separations between lineages that had declared themselves 'brothers', even boasted the same ancestor and claimed to found their solidarity on this reason alone. But it is precisely the 'social' content of kin relations that sets lineages against each other in land disputes or ambitions for a different place in the tribal hierarchy.

Of course there are also many occasions for conflict over women, over the honour of the clan or the husband, over livestock, etc. And this is why kinship relations are not merely, as Meyer Fortes would have it, a matter of feelings inspired by the purest of altruisms, with flawless solidarity, in short, what he called 'Amity'.[4] Kinship is also the site where love changes to hate, amity to 'enmity', concord to discord, because the love and solidarity owed one's kin have

---

4   On the notion of 'Amity', see M. Fortes, *Kinship and the Social Order* (London, Routledge and Kegan Paul, 1969), pp. 110, 123, 132, 239, 251.

been eaten away, shattered by conflicts of interest that had nothing to do with kinship: the sharing of land, parents' unfairness to one or another of their children, plotting between sisters, etc. Perhaps the feelings of love or hate are more violent between persons who are not strangers but are personally connected, who share, really or mentally, components of the same identity, of the same being (the same blood, the same name, the same ancestors, the same cults). However these clashes between relatives, these family novels and these clan stories may arise, *nowhere does kinship alone allow the creation of material and social dependence among all of the individuals and groups that make up a society. Kinship cannot make them into a whole, or close the society upon itself. And in societies without classes and castes, the economy cannot do this either.*

In all cases, what makes a society, what holds all of the groups together and makes them dependent on each other, for imaginary as well as for other, less intangible reasons, are the relations that cut across the whole society, and these relations are of a political-religious nature. But they are never sufficient to establish the outlines, the boundaries of a society. In all societies more is needed: these political-religious relations must be exercised over a territory, must define the sovereignty and the privileged ties a certain number of social groups, kin groups, castes or other, have over and with a territory, its inhabitants and its resources. This is as true of classless or casteless societies as it is of societies with castes or classes. But when these exist, when social groups do not produce their own material conditions of existence and depend on other groups (usually of lower status) to be able to perform the functions on which they have the monopoly, then the material content of the relation of general interdependence between the groups is not only the various forms of appropriation of a territory and its resources, it also takes the form of a direct material tie between the higher castes and classes, who control the land and the other productive resources, and the lower castes or classes, who are subordinated to them at the political and religious levels. This direct material tie can take many shapes: payment of a rent in labour or in kind, offering of first fruits of the land and sea to the heads of the *kainga*, and then part of these offerings by the heads of the *kainga* to the Tu'i Tonga, who in turn would take the best products to offer to the Tu'i Tonga Fafine. But this direct material tie between all castes, orders or classes never exists without being legitimized by political-religious relations that reserve the monopoly of the exercise of power, the performance of rites and the wielding of repressive violence for certain social and kin groups.

All of these analyses show that it is not longer possible to assert, as so many anthropologists did for over a century, that so-called 'primitive societies', that is, societies without castes or classes and without a state, were 'kin based'. There has never been any such thing as 'kin-based' societies, except in the anthropology and sociology textbooks. But to affirm this is not to claim, as Leach did, that kinship is merely a language or a veil, or worse, an invention on the part of anthropologists and therefore of the West.

THE IMPORTANCE OF ANCESTOR WORSHIP AND FILIAL DUTY IN CHINA: A COUNTER-EXAMPLE?

Reading the *Book of Filial Piety*, attributed to Confucius,[5] or his *Analects*, as well as the many commentaries his disciples added to the thoughts of master Kong, it seems indisputable that filial piety was, as Marcel Granet said: 'from the most ancient times the basis of domestic morality and even of civil morality . . . the duties one owes to the state are seen only as an extension of the duties one owes to one's family. The loyal subject flows from the pious subject.'[6] But Granet, and many other sinologists after him, actually showed that, as soon as historical data are actually taken into consideration, 'one sees that, far from flowing from a simple codification of natural emotions, civil morality is by no means a projection of domestic morality: on the contrary, it is the law of the feudal city that instead permeates domestic life.'[7]

Worship of the ancestors was first a privilege of princes and their vassals before gradually spreading down to the other strata of the population. Only those clans or lineages one of whose members had become a servant of the state or of princes (before the disappearance of the old, so-called feudal nobility upon the creation of the first empire, in 221 BCE) systematically venerated their ancestors and garnished their altars with the tablets of their illustrious forebears. Nevertheless, the rites connected with ancestor worship and performed by the eldest son of the last descendant of a clan's oldest lineage spread well beyond the descendants of the state civil-service lineages. Thus the expansion of ancestor worship and the obligations attached to the position of eldest son or older brother with respect to one's younger brothers was not the result of the influence of kinship in China but that of the subordination of kinship relations and groups to the functioning of the state. But let us hear what master Confucius says:

> The disciple Zeng said, 'Immense indeed is the greatness of filial piety!'
>
> The Master replied, 'Yes, filial piety is the constant (method) of Heaven, the righteousness of Earth, and the practical duty of Man.' . . . 'The ancient kings, seeing how their teachings could transform the people, set before them therefore

---

5   The book was probably written sometime between the time of Mencius (350 BCE) and the Han dynasty (200 BCE).

6   M. Granet, *La Civilisation chinoise* (Paris, La Renaissance du Livre, 1929), p. 366; English translation: *Chinese Civilization*, translated by Kathleen E. Innes and Mabel R. Brailsford (New York, Meridian books, 1958), p. 310.

7   Granet, *La Civilisation chinoise*, p. 367; translated here from the French edition.

an example of the most extended love, and none of the people neglected their parents ... They led them on by the rules of propriety and by music, and the people were harmonious and benignant. They showed them what they loved and what they disliked, and the people understood their prohibitions.'[8]

The six kin relationships Confucius regarded as important were those between father and son, between older and younger brother, and between husband and wife and, vice versa, between son and father, younger and older brother, wife and husband. The relationship between father and daughter, brother and sister, mother and daughter or sister and sister are never mentioned, which sheds light on the following statement: 'The Master said, "For teaching the people to be affectionate and loving, there is nothing better than filial piety. For teaching them (the observance of) propriety and submissiveness, there is nothing better than fraternal duty." '[9] It is said in *The Book of Filial Piety*:

> The happy and courteous sovereign
> Is the parent of the people.[10]

Thus, far from providing the basis of Chinese society, kinship relations were made to serve the state through the extension to all levels of society of the sacrificial rites offered by the Emperor or his vassals to the heavens and to the spirits of their ancestors. Hence the idea commonly found in ancient China that 'it was the meticulous execution of the royal rites [performed mainly in the ancestral temple] that determined the successful running of the state, the fertility of the fields, peace and the happiness of the people.'[11] 'When those who are in high stations perform well all their duties to their relations, the people are aroused to virtue.'[12]

According to this thinking, society ultimately depends on the rigorous performance of the rites by the sovereign and the civil servants, followed by the fathers and their eldest sons, and so on down to the head of the humblest cottage.

That is why we are justified in asserting that, in China too, neither kinship relations nor the family were the basis of society. They only appeared to be because they had been subordinated to the state's functioning, which had seen in the son's respect for the father, in the children's respect for their parents, the virtue that prepared the people to be loyal to their superiors and to the 'One

---

8   *The Book of Filial Piety*, Book 8.
9   Ibid., Book 12.
10   Ibid., Book 13.
11   A. Cheng, 'Introduction aux Entretiens de Confucius', in *Entretiens de Confucius*, translated by A. Cheng (Paris, Le Seuil, 1981), p. 24. Cf. *The Analects*, book 1, § 9.
12   *The Analects*, book 8.

Man',[13] placed at the centre of the state and the society. Let us recall that the education of the prince royal, the future Wang, began in his mother's womb while he was still a foetus. In the seventh month of her pregnancy, the queen mother retired to her apartments, and for weeks, the great intendant and the great tutor ensured that music was played for the future prince and that the food provided for the mother was, like the music, 'in every way according to the rites'.[14] Once again it is the political-ritual practices that crosscut the society and gather into a whole all groups – kin, clans, lineages, families – and all classes – nobles, scholars, peasants, craftsmen, etc. – that compose the society. But the functioning of these political and religious relations is closed to the people. Their performance is the role of the One Man according to the 'Path of Virtue and Justice'.

We will now look at another and much more formidable counter-example.

THE CASE OF THE AUSTRALIAN ABORIGINAL PEOPLES: AN EXCEPTION?

It has been argued that the proof that Australian societies are kin based is the great number of them that are divided into four or eight groups known as sections or subsections, each of which incorporates various categories of kin without being centred on a specific individual. The functioning of these societies, it is claimed, thus rests wholly on the relations between these sociocentric kin groups.

Let us take the case of the Kariera, a tribe living on the west coast of the Australian continent regarded as exemplary of a section society. This society is divided into two matrilineal moieties (A and B) and two patrilineal moieties (1 and 2), and each moiety is further divided into two sections. Each section combines a matrilineal principle of belonging with a patrilineal principle, which produces four sections as follows: A1, A2/B1, B2; they are named Banaka, Marimera, Bunung, Palyeri.

Relations between the sections are determined by both an alliance rule and a descent rule between parents and children. From the standpoint of alliance, A1 marries B2, B2 marries A1; and A2 marries B1; while B1 marries A2. Spouses are thus exchanged between A1 and B2, and between A2 and B1. From the standpoint of descent, when a man from A1 marries a woman from B2, their children belong to another section altogether, in the present case to B1 (a section that belongs to the same matrilineal moiety as their mother and at the same time to the same patrilineal moiety as their father, since the two patrilineal moieties are composed of A1 + B1 and A2 + B2). According to the same principle, when a man

---

13   *The Analects*, book 20. The One Man because he is the sole tie between heaven and earth, as indicated by the Chinese character 'emperor', Wang. Because of this, the One Man is also divine.

14   See J. Lévi, *Les Fonctionnaires divins. Politique, despotisme et mystique en Chine ancienne* (Paris, Le Seuil, 1989), p. 152.

from B2 marries a woman from A1, their children belong to section A2 (the same matrilineal moiety as their mother and the same patrilineal moiety as their father). And so on . . . We thus see that children never belong to their parents' sections and that the union of two sections allowed to intermarry produces the members of the two other sections, which in turn produce those that produced them in the first place. Here we have complementarity and a cycle.

This system is shown in the following formal diagram. The arrows indicate the mother–children relationship; and the lines, the alliances between sections.

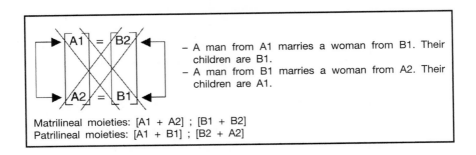

– A man from A1 marries a woman from B1. Their children are B1.
– A man from B1 marries a woman from A2. Their children are A1.

Matrilineal moieties: [A1 + A2] ; [B1 + B2]
Patrilineal moieties: [A1 + B1] ; [B2 + A2]

If we substitute Kareira section names for the abstract symbols, the letters and numbers we have used to show the formal structure of the system, we have:

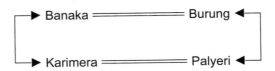

Using these rules, we observe that each section includes, with respect to Ego, a certain number of kin categories linked to Ego by distinct relationships and genealogical paths. Let us take the example of a woman from B1 who marries a man from A2.

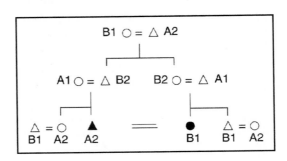

A2 marries B1, who is his father's sister's daughter, his patrilateral cross cousin, and B1 marries her mother's brother's son, her matrilateral cross cousin. The Kariera marriage rule is therefore to marry one's first-degree female cross cousin. Men in the Aranda society, whose system has eight subsections, marry their second-degree cousin. Among the Ngaatjatjarra and the other societies with so-called Aluridja kinship systems, which do not have sections, the rule is to marry a female cousin of the second degree and beyond, in sum, to marry as far away genealogically and geographically as possible.

We see in the preceding diagram that every individual, even though they do not belong to their parents' sections, nevertheless belong to their mother's and their father's moieties. B2 belongs to moiety B through his mother and to moiety 2 through his father. From this double belonging each individual receives the different components of his or her being, of his or her physical and social identity. The mother, as Elkin showed, transmits the child's blood and flesh; the father transmit's the child's membership in a local group that exploits the resources of a territory but at the same time has specific rights and responsibilities regarding a number of sacred sites. These sites are the dwelling places of the spirit-children who, sometimes, enter a woman's womb and mingle with her blood to make the foetus that will become a child. These sacred sites were created by the Dreamtime Beings that, in the course of their fabled travels throughout Australia, left behind them here a lake, there a strange rock formation and elsewhere an ochre-coloured chain of mountains, etc.

From this short summary we can see why certain anthropologists, among whom Claude Lévi-Strauss, expressed their admiration for the 'crystalline beauty' of these both complex and simple social systems, complex in the multiplication of the tasks ensured by kinship relations and simple in their construction principles. For Lévi-Strauss their beauty stemmed from the fact that all social relationships could be expressed in two languages, which, for him, seemed to be perfectly equivalent: that of genealogical relations and that of categories (i.e. sections, which in Fison and Morgan's time were called 'marriage classes').

However, new fieldwork going back some thirty years, and conducted separately by linguists and anthropologists, has yielded findings that converge but deeply modify the vision the bulk of anthropologists[15] had of the nature of sections in the 1950s, at the time Lévi-Strauss wrote his *Elementary Structures of Kinship*.

---

15   With the exception of Radcliffe-Brown, who published an important series of articles in *Oceania* in 1930–31 on 'The social organization of Australian tribes', *Oceania*, vol. 1, nos. 1–4 (1930–31), pp. 34–63, 206–46, 322–41 and 426–56. Forty years later, M. Megitt, in a much-remarked article, challenged the idea that sections were essentially kin categories. See M. Meggitt, 'Understanding Australian Aboriginal Society: Kinship Systems or Cultural Categories', in P. Reining (ed.), *Kinship Studies in the Morgan Centennial Year* (Washington, Anthropological Society of Washington, 1972), pp. 64–87.

In effect, sections do not really form the basis of the Aboriginal marriage rules. For instance, in the section where Ego will find his potential wives, there are other categories of women who are not cross cousins, not even classificatory ones, and therefore are not potential wives. In the Kariera system, these are: Ego's father's mother (FM) or Ego's wife's mother's mother (WMM) (see preceding diagram where A2 marries B1, and the section of B2 contains his wife's mother's mother [B1] and his father's mother [B1]). Upon closer inspection, then, the two languages – that of sections and that of genealogical ties – are not 'equivalent', contrary to what Lévi-Strauss believed.

Today it is clear that sections and subsections are primarily ceremonial and totemic groups composed of different genealogical and/or classificatory kin categories, and which ensure three main functions. The first is the organization of the male and female initiation rituals, since a man and women cannot marry if they have not been initiated. The person who initiates the man and spills his blood[16] is usually a 'mother's brother', a classificatory maternal uncle, who, in exchange for the spilled blood, will promise him a wife. The second function is the organization of the complex rites for the multiplication of the plant and animal species found in the band's territory,[17] and the rites by which men bleed themselves into a 'hole' dug in the ground thereby encouraging spirit-children to come and take up residence in their wife's womb. The third function is that of a common reference system, a *lingua franca*, enabling individuals from different friend or enemy tribes to position themselves with respect to each other. This last function has gained even greater importance since the arrival of the Europeans, with the multiplication of encounters and the intermingling of Aboriginal groups that previously had not met but which are now thrown together on the reservations created by the Europeans.

Recent research has uncovered two major facts. First, the fact that the dozens of local and regional groups scattered over the 600,000 km² of the Great Western Desert, did not have sections and nevertheless often performed the rites for the multiplication of the plant and animal species and the male and female initiations. Furthermore, the same groups, whose kinship systems Elkin

---

16   Depending on the group, initiating young men entailed circumcision of the penis and, in some societies, for instance those in the Great Desert, circumcision and subincision.

17   The linguist C. G. von Brandenstein's research on the meaning of section and subsection names clearly shows that one of the functions of sections is to perform the rites that ensure the reproduction of the universe and to ascribe qualities to human beings that bring them into harmony with their environment. For instance, Brandenstein showed that the Pannaga and Purungu sections are associated with 'cold blood', and the Karimarra and Paltjarri sections, with 'warm blood'. Reptiles are therefore an integral part of the Pannaga and Purungu sections, whose members can communicate with and act on them. The sun and fire are 'Harimarra', and so on. See C. G. von Brandenstein, 'The meaning of section and sub-section names', *Oceania*, vol. 41, no. 1 (1970), pp. 39–49, and *Names and Substance of the Australian Subsection System* (Chicago, University of Chicago Press, 1982).

had dubbed 'Aluridjha' and which he, and later Lévi-Strauss, declared to be 'aberrant', turned out to be in no way aberrant but instead driven by the logic of the Dravidian systems whose presence in Australia had never before been imagined.[18] While these systems prescribed marriage with a real or classifica-tory female cross cousin, like the Australian section and subsection systems, they were also egocentric and favoured marriage with classificatory and/or at least third degree cousins. They had, although to a lesser degree, the same asso-ciative properties as the section systems – i.e. the equations (CC = C; AC = A; CA = A; AA = C) – but differed from these systems when it came to the classi-fication of certain cross-kin categories.

The kinship systems of Western Desert groups divide society in two gener-ational moieties, one of which contains Ego, Ego's grandparents and Ego's grandchildren ($G^0 + G^{+2} + G^{-2}$) and the other Ego's parents and children ($G^{+1} + G^{-1}$). The two moieties are named, among the Ngaatjatjarra, and oppose and complete each other like the 'shadow side' and the 'sun side'. The division into two moieties served to divide the roles to be performed in the initiation and multiplication rites between people of different generations and sexes.

Now here is where things get interesting. It has been proven that it was only at the start of the twentieth century that the section and subsection systems entered the Western Desert groups, first among the Pintupi around 1930, and then among the Ngaatjatjarra around 1940. Initially the Pintupi tried to adapt a four-section system to their kinship system and then, after a short period in which they toyed with six sections, they finally opted for a system with eight sections. The Ngaatjatjarra, on the other hand, adopted and adapted a four-section system, then abandoned it for managing alliances but kept it for the purpose of communicating with the other Aboriginal groups they encountered, for example, in the stations opened by the Government, which contained a school, a small hospital, etc., or in the mission centres.

These findings once again posed the problem of the origin and nature of sections and subsections, and it is on this point that linguists came up with some surprising answers. In effect, it appeared, following the work of McCo-nvell and his team,[19] that sections made their appearance on the southwestern coast of Australia sometime during the first millennium CE and from there diffused first northward and then westward, along with the language of the

---

18   See Laurent Dousset's work, already cited.

19   P. McConvell, 'The Origin of Subsections in Northern Australia', *Oceania*, vol. 56, no. 1 (1985), pp. 1–33; P. Sutton, *Native Titles and the Descent of Rights* (Canberra, Publication Commonwealth of Australia, 1998); J. Keen, 'Seven Aboriginal Marriage Systems and Their Correlates', *Anthropological Forum*, vol. 12, no. 2 (2002), pp. 145–58; J. Avery, 'Jura Conjugalia Reconsidered. Kinship Classification and Ceremonial Roles', *Anthropological Forum*, vol. 12, no. 2 (2002), pp. 221–32.

Western Desert groups, Wati and its dialects. According to these linguists, subsections appeared several hundred years later southwest of Darwin and then diffused in all directions until they reached the Aranda and their neighbours. These diffusions are believed to have taken the traditional trade routes that followed the coastline and penetrated the interior of the continent.[20]

At this point, we would like to advance the following hypotheses. If the original Australian kinship systems did not have sections, they must have looked like the systems found in societies that did not yet have sections a century ago. The basic type of kinship system in Australia, before the invention of sections, was probably Dravidian. These Dravidian systems also included in their structures a dualist principle that made it possible to associate diverse kin categories in the opposing distinct but complementary ceremonial groups that celebrated the rites which, for the Aborigines, ensured the reproduction of the cosmos and founded men's right to represent and govern their society.

In this case, why sections? It seems that the fact of dividing society in two, four or eight decentred groups – that is to say, not connected with an Ego or a reference generation – was a response to the need to simplify to the maximum the distribution of all the members of a local society in different places and moments of the ritual cycles by uncoupling them from their real place in the genealogical network. The recourse to sections would thus be a remarkable sociological invention that allowed increasingly populous groups to place given individuals in given kin categories that were both real (linked by genealogical ties) and classificatory (since in Dravidian systems father and father's brother [F = FB] are given as identical, merged, as are mother and mother's sister [M = MZ], which is the mark of all merging collateral systems).

To put things simply, the invention of sections would not have been used to resolve problems of kinship. This could be done by the Dravidian systems. But they served to organize rituals, that is, political-religious relations that concerned all members of the society, whatever their sex or age, but not all in the same way, depending on whether a person was a man or a woman, had or did not have the right and responsibility to initiate the younger generations, etc. For rites concern the whole society as soon as they involve the reproduction of the cosmos and of society.

In order to mobilize the entire population and to assign each person a place in the (highly complicated) rites, the Aboriginal peoples of Australia set out to find a simple means of calculation, based on kinship but broader. The simplest and most complete formula of which we know is that in which the associativity of the relationship between consanguinity and affinity, descent and alliance, is

---

20   P. McConvell, L. Dousset and F. Powell, 'Introduction', *Anthropological Forum*, vol. 12, no. 2 (2002), pp. 137–44.

automatic and total. And indeed, associativity exists in Dravidian systems – with respect to Ego, everyone is either a consanguine or a real or potential affine; but it is not total. To be total, and also automatic and easy to calculate, it had to no longer be based on Ego being a reference. That was accomplished by the invention of sections. But the consequence was that the children of a couple could no longer belong to their parents' sections, although their belonging to a third section depended on the nature of these two sections (e.g. A1 x B2 → B1).

The new constraints affected the deep structures of the Dravidian systems, which were thus compelled, over a long period of time, to adapt to the way the sections worked and gave rise to the Kariera- and Aranda-type kinship systems which, until Lévi-Strauss, had been regarded as typical of Australian systems and the basis of the social organization of almost all of the continent's peoples. In reality this is not so. And Australian societies are no more kin based than societies elsewhere. Only political-religious relations can bind into a whole the kin groups that compose a society which must reproduce itself. The division into sections and subsections is one such relation. But why did this system, which is so effective in organizing the rites and power found in a society, spread from one society to the next, hundreds of kilometres from the coastal society where they originated, to the point where the same words for a given section are found in completely different languages? There seem to be two reasons.

The first reason is that the representations of the beings that existed in primordial times, in the Dreamtime, and which gave the universe the aspect and order it has today, are a mental and cultural world that seems to be shared by the hundreds of tribes that populate the continent and date from well before the appearance of sections and subsections. Each of these tribes thus found itself responsible for performing the rites that reproduced what the original beings had left behind when they crossed its territory. In Australia, it is as though each tribe, each local group, had the responsibility for part of the Dream World and was duty bound to reproduce it not only for itself but for all of the other groups that, in turn, ritually reproduce for themselves and for all others the portion of the myths and primordial itineraries that concern them.

The second reason for the diffusion of sections has to do with the fact that each local group had ritually to ensure the reproduction of the plant and animal species found in its territory and which where the group's totems. This was done not only for the benefit of that group but for that of the neighbouring groups (friends or enemies) which did not have the same totem species. The species-multiplication rituals thus made up a vast system of imaginary cooperation between all of the local groups and all of the tribes, whose livelihood was based on hunting, gathering and fishing, a system that extended beyond their borders and was rooted in the mental world shared by all Australian Aboriginal peoples:

the belief in the Dreaming, in the primordial world as it was when the world began.[21]

But to say that in Australia political-religious relations mean that local groups exist for the duration of the rites as 'totalities' is tantamount to saying that these rites legitimize the power relations in these societies. For these hunter-gather or seafisher/collector societies were (and are still) characterized by strongly asymmetrical relations between the genders and between the generations working on behalf of men and the elders.

The domination of men over women, and of adults over young people who had to be initiated, operated at two levels: in the framework of the production of the material conditions of existence and in that of the ritual reproduction of the cosmos and society.[22] As we saw, and this point was already noted by Durkheim,[23] a man's blood is actually female blood transmitted by his mother. During the rituals designed to 'set free' the nature spirits that fertilize the plant and animal totem species but also the spirit-children that will enter women's bodies, men bleed themselves, either by opening a vein in their arm or by opening the circumcision scars and, when they exist, the subincision scars on their penis. This blood is allowed to flow into a hole dug in the ground and which is the inverse of the woman's vagina, a hole from which the spirit-children will issue and then enter into the women's bodies. No woman must be present at these times, on pain of death.[24]

While the mother transmits her blood to both her sons and daughters, only the sons are given the power by this blood to reproduce the species and set free the spirits that will fecundate their own wife and make her a mother.[25] To quote Laurent Dousset: 'the men thus suppress the women's power of auto-procreation given them by the simple penetration of a spirit'.[26] As we see,

21   The anthropological publications on this topic are numerous. The indispensable ones are: R. M. and C. H. Berndt, *The World of the First Australians: Aboriginal Traditional Life, Past and Present* (London, Angus and Robertson, 1992 [1964]) and B. Glowczewski, *Du rêve à la loi chez les Aborigènes. Mythes, rites et organisation sociale en Australie* (Paris, Presses Universitaires de France, 1991).

22   On all these points we have followed Laurent Dousset's remarkable analyses. See esp. his article, 'Production et reproduction en Australie. Pour un tableau de l'unité des tribus aborigènes', *Social Anthropology*, vol. 4, no. 3 (1996), pp. 281–98.

23   E. Durkheim, *Les Formes élémentaires de la vie religieuse* (Paris, Presses Universitaires de France, 1960 [1912]) quoted by Dousset, 'Production et reproduction en Australie', p. 290.

24   As Webb and Elkin showed, the Murngin did not have such rites for the reproduction of the species. For more information on this point, see Dousset, 'Production et reproduction en Australie', p. 292. For the Murngin, blood is not transmitted by the women and therefore the ritual system changes completely.

25   On the role of sperm in child conception as seen by Aboriginal peoples, see R. Tonkinson, 'Semen Versus Spirit-Child in a Western Desert Culture', in L. R. Hiatt (ed.), *Australian Aboriginal Concepts* (New Jersey, Humanities Press, 1978), pp. 81–91.

26   Dousset, 'Production et reproduction en Australie', p. 291.

Aboriginal men (with the exception of the Murngin), even though they believe that women alone transmit a life-giving substance, blood, have appropriated this substance for themselves and introduced it into the process of reproducing life, claiming to contribute more than the women to making babies, since it is due to their capacity to ritually sacrifice and manipulate their own blood that spirit-children come out of the ground, leave their hole, and enter women's bodies. Furthermore, because they are responsible for the ritual reproduction of the plant and animal species that are now their group's totem species, the reproduction of the universe and their own society now lies wholly in their hands.

The same thinking intervenes at the economic level, owing to the social and ritual importance given to game and therefore to hunting, from which women are banned. Even though in Australia, as in many hunter-gatherer societies, women provide the daily fare through their gathering and their collecting and capture of small animals, game is the most valued food, both when it comes to group consumption and to exchanges between the sexes and between groups. Whereas the products the woman gathers are eaten by her entire family, the game is not eaten by the hunter himself; it is meant for the whole group. It should be kept in mind that, before being accepted as a son-in-law, a man sometimes used to have to follow his future wife's group for three years, regularly providing them with hunted game while avoiding contact with his future mother-in-law and his future wife. In sum, game, and therefore hunting, had greater social value than gathering and collecting (in which the men also participated).

But of course these unequal relations between the sexes and between the generations were presented as 'exchanges', and that is what ensured the passive, and sometimes active, consent of those who were subjected to them.[27] We have a hard time imagining the effort of imagination and ideological elaboration humankind must have furnished to justify the power of the One Man, the Chinese Wang, who had the monopoly on the veneration of Heaven and on that of the ancestors, of the Brahmins who were the only ones allowed to spill the blood of the victims sacrificed to the gods and the ancestors, and finally of the men of Australia, who bled themselves so that spirit-children might impregnate their wives.

---

27   M. Godelier, *L'Idéel et le matériel* (Paris, Fayard, 1984), p. 21; English translation: *The Mental and the Material: Thought, Economy and Society*, translated by Martin Thom (London/New York, Verso, 1986), p. 10.

CONCERNING THE TWIN METAMORPHOSIS THAT OCCURS IN ALL SOCIETIES

We thus see the social contents, the highly diverse political-religious relations that kinship relations everywhere can and especially must support. Which explains the general theoretical proposition already advanced. Everywhere and at every period, we see a twin metamorphosis. Social relations that have nothing to do with kinship make their way into kinship relations and subordinate them to their own reproduction. *Social content becomes the stuff of kinship.* And everything that falls under kinship is transformed into relations between the sexes in the first place and then between parents and children.[28] And finally everything having to do with kinship is imprinted into sexed bodies from birth and becomes an attribute of a person's sex. *Through this twin metamorphosis, sexual differences become 'gender' differences*, become masculine and feminine, categories that characterize not only men and women but the Sun and the Moon, and the myriad beings that populate the universe.

THE BASIS OF MALE DOMINATION

Assigning women, but also men, distinct tasks, undervaluing women's tasks and overvaluing men's, giving women a minor role in or excluding them from the rites supposed to reproduce the cosmos and life itself,[29] excluding them, in sum, from access to the most important spiritual powers, are all processes applied in every area of social life and which engender and continually increase the distance and the social inequality between men and women.

Using these facts, which were gathered in casteless and classless societies far beyond Western Europe, we can extend the comparison to contemporary Western societies. If one gives any credit to our demonstration – namely, that nowhere in the world are kinship relations the basis of society, that only political-religious relations have the capacity to bind human groups into a whole that forms a society and that in societies divided into castes or classes, economic relations join with the political relations to bind the groups into a whole – it then appears that one of the essential conditions for establishing equal status between women and men is to allow women access to the political functions

---

28   That is what makes certain anthropologists say that, in analyzing the social content of kinship relations, they go 'beyond kinship'. See e.g. Rosemary A. Joyce and Susan D. Gillespie (eds.), *Beyond Kinship: Social and Material Reproduction in House Societies* (Philadelphia, University of Pennsylvania Press, 2000).

29   However, we should not forget that Aboriginal women in Australia perform secret rites from which men are banned. On this point see A. Hamilton, *Timeless Transformations: Women, Men and History in the Western Australian Desert* (Sydney, University of Sydney Press, 1979) and Glowczewski, *Du rêve à la loi chez les Aborigènes.*

and the religious responsibilities that exist in the society. However it is a rare religion in the West that gives women an if not equal then at least important role in the celebration of its rites.[30]

When it comes to producing and raising children, it is well known that, traditionally, these two activities were not only reserved for women (a given for pregnancy and childbirth) but were also all the more highly valorized since doing so made it possible to justify their exclusion from political, economic and religious responsibilities – hence the famous German saying 'Kinder, Küche, Kirche'. Feminists rightly rebelled against this overvaluing of the family and parenthood as an exclusively feminine area. But we should not forget, for all that, that it is in women's bodies and not in men's that babies are made, and it is women who take all the risks in bearing children, and that it is also women who usually care for the newborn baby and provide the bulk of ongoing infant care. That does not exclude (nor do I seek to minimize) the fact that today a minority of men play an increasing role in child-raising, and that the difference between male and female tasks is tending to fade in that area too.[31]

In short, giving birth to a child and raising it through infancy should be much more highly valued than they are in Western societies, and particularly for reasons diametrically opposed to those that have been used by all the conservative tendencies, on the right or the left, to justify excluding women from the sphere of economics or politics. Likewise, men's decision to withdraw for a time from their professional activities to raise their infant should also be valorized.[32]

KINSHIP SYSTEMS EVOLVE

Here I will simply indicate what the specialists are beginning to see in the evolution of kinship systems in a few parts of the world. This evolution can sometimes, when the sources exist, be reconstructed for several periods – Antiquity, the Middle Ages and the modern and contemporary periods. But before we begin, a few points should be recalled so that the reader may be aware of the limits of such an undertaking.

First of all, we know that a kinship system is not simply the terminology people use to talk about kin ties and to guide their actions. And we know that terminologies evolve very slowly over time. Nevertheless, certain old terms

30 The ordination of women is a very recent phenomenon in certain Protestant Churches and a highly minority practice. It has nonetheless created an upheaval in the Anglican Church. Roman and Orthodox Catholics reject the idea, as does Islam, which does not have a true clergy.

31 Nevertheless we must not forget that men's and women's bodies, and their physical gestures and attitudes, are different and do not provide infants with the same things.

32 Cf. M. Godelier, 'Anthropologie et recherches féministes. Perspectives et rétrospectives', in J. Laufer, C. Marry and M. Maruani (eds.), Le Travail du genre (Paris, La Découverte, 2003), pp. 23–34.

disappear and new ones appear, produced in the society itself or borrowed from neighbouring languages and societies. We also know that certain changes within a kinship terminology can go well beyond these disappearances and borrowings, and call into question the very structure of the system, that is to say, the principles that organize the definition and distribution of the terms designating the kin ties. Such structural changes then lead to the replacement of one type of terminology by another. These are the changes that matter most and which can be detected when a society's history is observed over the long term.

That is precisely where a considerable number of problems crop up, many of which are nowhere near being resolved. For a kinship terminology does not tell us anything about the political, religious or economic relations prevailing in a given society, and therefore nothing about the social content of and the stakes involved in the kin ties in this society. And since we know that kin terminologies do not change of their own accord and do not evolve without a reason, we must at all costs discover the forces and interests that have brought the members of a society to alter the rules that organized their marriage alliances and even the principles that organized descent reckoning, inheritance and transmission.

It is only when the evolution of social relations that have nothing intrinsically to do with kinship lead people, lead the groups that compose a society, to change their ways of regulating alliances and descent that kinship relations begin to take on a different content and that, after a certain lapse of time, a rearrangement of the terms for the kin ties and positions becomes necessary. This happens first of all through the loss of old terms or a change in their meaning, and then through an overall change in the architecture of the terminology. Among the most powerful forces capable of acting in this sense is of course religion. We saw this in the case of Christianity, which intervened abruptly and continuously to forbid marriages with close kin, remarriage of widows, adoption of children, which deprived families and kin groups of the capacity to celebrate the marriages of their members themselves, and so on. Likewise in Islam with the prime importance of marriage with the father's brother's daughter (or for a woman, with the father's brother's son).

Another important fact. A kinship system transforms into another kinship system, and not into anything else. It never gives rise to caste or class relations. Furthermore, the evolution of a kinship system can have only two outcomes. Either the new system is merely a variant of the old one, or it becomes a variant of another type of system. For example, a society where kinship is organized according to a Dravidian-type system, which entails marriage with a cousin, can be led to forbid marriage with a first-degree cross cousin and make it mandatory to marry a second-degree cross cousin, which means renewing the same alliances but at a greater distance in time (or space). In this case, the prohibition on marrying a first-degree cross cousin will be reflected by the fact that cross cousins are treated like parallel cousins who, in a Dravidian (or Iroquois) system are treated like siblings. The categories of brother and sister will therefore be extended to include parallel and cross cousins of the first degree, and because all of these individuals will therefore be regarded as brothers and sisters, marriage between them will be forbidden: it will therefore be necessary to look further abroad for a spouse. From the standpoint of kin terminology, this situation is expressed by the equation (Sb = // = X) (siblings = parallel cousins = cross cousins). This is the case in G^{o}, while the distinction between parallel and cross kin will continue to exist in G^{+1} and G^{-1}.

From another standpoint, as we saw in the example of the Australian systems, the invention of sections and their diffusion transformed a certain number of originally Dravidian-type kinship systems into another type, one with sections and subsections, characterized by much greater associativity. This property was both the condition and the consequence of the division of the whole population into kin classes constituted without reference to a particular Ego. Another case of a shift from one system to another can be found in Ancient Europe, when the Latin system, which was of the Sudanese type, yielded to one of the Eskimo type, which today still characterizes a large portion of European kinship systems. In this case, too, the transformation affected the very structure of the system as well.

The old Latin system was what is called a *bifurcate collateral* system, in other words each kin position was designated by its own term.

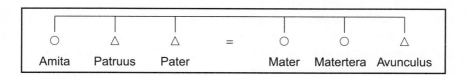

| Amita | Patruus | Pater | = | Mater | Matertera | Avunculus |

It evolved through the simultaneous disappearance of the terms *patruus* and *matertera*, which created a bifurcation between father and father's brother and between mother and mother's sister. *Avunculus* took over the spot left empty by *patruus* (which gave the French *oncle* and the English *uncle*), and *amita* took over the spot left by *matertera* (which gave *aunt* in English and *tante* in French).

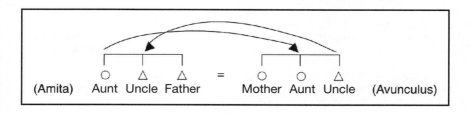

| (Amita) | Aunt | Uncle | Father | = | Mother | Aunt | Uncle | (Avunculus) |

Whereas in a Sudanese-type system there are different terms for father's brother and mother's brother, this difference disappears in an Eskimo system. Here it is necessary to specify 'my paternal uncle' or 'my uncle on my mother's side', and so on. But the disappearance of *matertera* and *patruus* automatically led to a change in the terms that designated their children with respect to Ego. Brothers by a same father were called *fratres*; the children of the father's brother (patrilateral parallel cousins) were called *fratres patrueles*; the children of the paternal aunt were called *amitini*, while those of the mother's sister were *consobrini*, like those of the mother's brother. The disappearance of *patruus* and *matertera* thus led to the disappearance of *fratres patrueles* and *amitini*, and to their replacement by *consobrini*, which gave the French and English term 'cousin'.[33]

THE WORLD OF KINSHIP SYSTEMS IS NOT ROUND

Another remarkable fact was discovered. The world of kinship systems is not round like that of Lévi-Strauss' Amerindian myths. The essential point is not so much that kinship terminologies and systems evolve, even very slowly, but that the transformations are *irreversible* and do not move in only one direction. From a perspective of several thousands of years in some cases, centuries in others, several lines of evolution now appear clearly.

Today certain specialists such as M. Y. Kryukov tend to think that the ancient Chinese kinship system was Dravidian. Between the third and the fifth century of our era, the Dravidian features of the system disappeared, and it evolved toward a Sudanese-type system (similar to the ancient Latin system), which it remains, even if certain recent developments are taking it toward an Eskimo-type system. Another very important and little analyzed fact is that the ancient Chinese system, which was Dravidian[34] and therefore egocentric,[35]

---

33   This transformation caused numerous problems for linguists, for *consobrini* originally designated the children of two sisters. Emile Benveniste gave the explanation in his article 'Termes de parenté dans les langues indo-européennes', *L'Homme*, no. 34 (1965), pp. 5–16, and of course in the chapters devoted to kinship in his *Vocabulaire des institutions indo-européennes* (Paris, Minuit, 1969), 2 vols.; see vol. 1, Chapters 3, 4, 5. See also F. Wordick, 'A Generative-Extensionist Analysis of the Proto-Indo-European Kinship System with a Phonological and Semantic Reconstruction of the Terms', Doctoral Dissertation, University of Michigan, Ann Arbor, University Microfilms, 1970, and more recently S. Kullanda, 'Indo-European Kinship Terms Revisited', *Current Anthropology*, vol. 43, no. 1 (2002), pp. 89–111. On the French kinship system, see P. Maranda, *French Kinship. Structure and History* (The Hague, Mouton, 1994).

34   Even in the most ancient sources, like the oracular inscriptions carved on bones, which date from the fourteenth to the eleventh century BCE, kin terms abound; this is explained by the nature of the texts, which are connected with everyday ceremonial life. Cf. M. V. Kryukov, 'The synchro-diachronic method and the multidirectionality of kinship transformations', in M. Godelier, T. R. Trautmann and F. E. Tjon Sie Fat (eds.), *Transformations of Kinship* (Washington/London, Smithsonian Institution Press, 1998), pp. 297–8.

35   Marcel Granet had pointed out that, at the end of the first millennium BCE, Chinese

existed side by side with a sociocentric division of society into four categories similar to the Australian sections and probably connected, like these, with ritual divisions in the society. The four classes were called Bo (A), Shu (B), Zhong (C) and Ji (D). They regulated marriage alliances according to a principle of symmetric exchange: A married D, D married A, B married C, C married B. And the children born from these unions belonged to a different category from their parents according to a patrilineal and not a matrilineal criterion as in Australia. In Australia it is the mother's blood that is transmitted to her children, in China it is the father's breath.

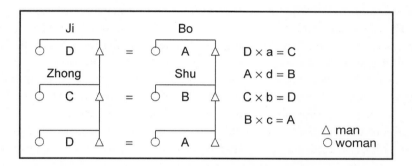

The evolution was thus the outcome of two transformations: of the differentiation of kin into direct and collateral lines, on the one hand, and of the split between consanguines and affines, on the other. These transformations resulted in the formation of a terminology we class under the heading of 'bifurcate collateral' systems. Mikhail Kryukov suggests that, in the West, the system that preceded the Latin system, also of the bifurcate collateral type, could have been, as was the case in China, a Dravidian-type system in so far as the terms *patruus* and *matertera* are clearly derived from *pater* and *mater* and may have arisen from the need to distinguish between father and father's brother and mother and mother's sister, which had previously been merged under the same terms *pater* (F = FB) and *mater* (M = MZ), a feature of Dravidian (or Iroquois) systems. This is in fact what happened in China, where originally the same term, *fu* was used for father and father's brothers.[36] Likewise, in ancient China, the term *gu* was used for father's

---

kinship terminology suggested the existence of a cross-cousin marriage rule. The term *sheng* designates at the same time FZS, MBS, cross cousins on the fathers and the mother's side, as well as WB and ZH, which implies sister exchange and cross-cousin marriage. See M. Granet, 'Catégories matrimoniales et relations de proximité dans la Chine ancienne', *Annales sociologiques* (1939), series B, fasc. 1–3.

36 Kryukov, 'The Synchro-diachronic Method and the Multidirectionality of Kinship Transformations', p. 299. Unfortunately there is no historical document or testimony to validate or invalidate Kryukov's suggestion that the Latin terminology may have been the outcome of the transformation of a Dravidian-type terminology (bifurcate merging) into a Sudanese type (bifurcate

sister (FZ), mother's brother's wife (MBW), wife's mother (WM) and husband's wife (HM). The equation (FZ = MBW = WM = HM) was the consequence of the exchange of spouses in G+1 and in G0. In the fifth century BCE, however, the wife's mother, the mother-in-law, was no longer called *gu*, but *po*.[37]

Kryukov also reconstructed the evolution of several kinship systems found in Tibeto-Burman groups living in Yunnan province. Using Chinese documents going back several centuries, nineteenth-century dictionaries and his own field-work, he showed that the terminologies used in the societies in the Yi ethnic group (formerly called Lolo) had evolved in two different directions after these groups separated at the end of the Bronze age, as attested by archaeological finds in Yunnan, around Deli in the west and around Kumming in the east. In the west, the Dravidian terminology, which corresponded to a symmetrical system that prescribed marriage with cross cousins and therefore had no specific vocabulary for affines, turned into an Iroquois type. In the east, the transformation of the Nasupo's terminology took another direction. Their symmetric-prescriptive kinship system yielded to an asymmetric-prescriptive system very similar to the so-called Jinpaw terminology used in the Burmese Kachin groups described by Leach, but without the Omaha-type skewing found in the Kachin system. The reason for this transformation is clear. Whereas in a Dravidian system, givers are also takers, in the Kachin society, givers are not takers. We are therefore in the presence of a system of generalized exchange, which implies the existence of at least three clans or kin groups, A, B, C. B gives women to C and receives women from A, A gives to B and receives from C, C gives to A and receives from B.

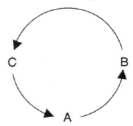

collateral). See the recent discussion in *Current Anthropology*, vol. 43, no. 1 (2002), pp. 89–111, of S. Kullanda's article, 'Indo-European Kinship Terms Revisited', which merely repeats well-known facts, for instance that a kin term like *pater* designates both a status and a form of authority, hence the term *patres conscripti*, used to designate senators. But everyone knows that it is impossible to derive direct knowledge of the nature of the institutions that organize a society from the kinship terminology used there. Debates on the proto-Indo-European kinship system have been ongoing since the publication of Berthold Delbrück's book, *Die Indogermanischer Verwandtshaftsnamen* (1889) and then the speculative article by A. M. Hocart, 'The Indo-European Kinship System', *Ceylon Journal of Science*, no. 1 (1928), pp. 79–204. See Benveniste, *Vocabulaire des institutions indo-européennes* and P. Friedrich, 'Proto Indo-European Kinship', *Ethnology*, vol. 5, no. 1 (1966), pp. 1–36.

37   M. V. Kryukov, *Sistema rodstva kitaitsev* [The Chinese kinship system] (Moskow, Nauka, 1972), pp. 177, 205.

In other ethnic groups, such as the Mong-Khmer-speaking groups in South Vietnam, we find matrilineal societies using terminologies that were originally Dravidian but whose kinship systems are asymmetric and prescribe marriage with the mother's brother's daughter and this time feature Crow-type skewing, that is, equations which cancel differences of generation for certain kin positions.[38] There are thus several possible transformations of Dravidian kinship systems, which are summarized in the following table:

Dravidian → Sudanese (China)
Dravidian → Iroquois (Lolo)
Dravidian → asymmetric Dravidian (Jinpaw) → Crow (Mnong-Gar)
Sudanese → Eskimo (Europe)
And if we suppose that the Latin system stemmed from the transformation of a Dravidian system, we would have had in Europe: Dravidian → Sudanese → Eskimo.

Turning now to the Polynesian societies, which, as we know, come from Austronesian-speaking populations that left South China and the island of Taiwan sometime between 2500 and 1500 BCE, we can suggest that the so-called Hawaiian-type terminologies are transformations of kinship systems that were also originally Dravidian. This hypothesis is based on four facts: first of all the existence, in the societies of western Polynesia – an area where the so-called 'Polynesian' societies formed – of terms that distinguish cross cousins (*ilamutu/ sakafotu*) from parallel cousins, who are merged with siblings. Next, the fact that the terms for father (*tamai*) and mother (*fae*) designate both the father and the father's brothers, and the mother and the mother's sisters. But these two features alone do not tell us whether these terminologies derive from Dravidian or from Iroquois terminologies, since they are found in both types of systems. But two other features could allow us to decide. For *tamai* means 'father', but also 'father-in-law', the wife's father. Affines are therefore treated like consanguines. Last, in Polynesia, my affines' affines are in principle consanguines, which is typical of Dravidian (and Australian) systems. This, then, is probably another example of a transformation of a Dravidian system, this time into a Hawaiian system.

Turning to North America, we observe the juxtaposition of Dravidian, Iroquois, Crow and Omaha systems. But their evolutionary sequences all seem to have followed that of the transformation of Dravidian systems into Iroquois

38   M. V. Kryukov, personal communication based on G. Condominas' work among the Mnong-Gar of Vietnam. See G. Condominas, 'The Mnong-Gar of Central Vietnam', in G. P. Murdock (ed.), *Social Structure in Southern Asia* (Viking Fund Publications, Anthropology, Wenner-Gren Fondation for Anthropological Research, 1960), no. 29, pp. 15–23.

systems, and then, for some of the latter, into Crow or Omaha systems. In North America, only one group, the Eyak, is known for having a Dravidian B-type terminology[39] (i.e. close to the Australian Kariera systems) with exogamous moieties. In South America, the Amazon is strongly dominated by Dravidian systems, but among the Jivaro groups one finds societies that suggest transformations of Dravidian into Iroquois and of Iroquois into generational Iroquois (of the Ngawbe type), in other words, which forbid repeating the same alliances for at least four generations. But one also finds Dravidian systems among the Panoan groups that are combined with a division of the society into ritual and ceremonial sections.

Continuing our overview: We have seen that India is divided into two major sets of kinship terminologies and systems: Indo-European in the north and Dravidian in the south; that New Guinea features a mosaic of terminologies of the Iroquois, Yafar, Kuma, Hawaiian and Eskimo types; that Africa has many varieties of systems of the Sudanese, Eskimo, Crow and Omaha types; and so on.

In reality a systematic, region-by-region inventory of kinship terminologies and systems exists only for a few regions of the world, those for which we have archives, testimony or published fieldwork. A huge amount of research remains to be done, which may yield the most unexpected – and always fascinating – results. The new data piling up every day forces us, at any rate, constantly to relativize, rethink, complete and complexify conclusions or generalizations that are already a part of anthropological tradition. For instance, Jean-François Guermonprez, a specialist in Eastern Indonesian kinship systems, was led to challenge Needham's earlier hypotheses, which had been considered unshakable. Guermonprez advanced the idea that the asymmetric prescriptive systems (so widespread in Indonesia and Southeast Asia) had been superposed on earlier cognatic systems, because these kinship systems were associated with a type of political power that tended to diffuse and impose itself in this region. Until then the reverse had been thought to have happened, and that the cognatic systems found in the area had grown out of earlier asymmetric systems.

To sum up: kinship terminologies form systems. These terminologies evolve, and when a terminology evolves, it gives rise to another terminology, which in turn forms a system. The evolution of the different types of terminology inventoried to date took several directions, which constitute series of irreversible transformations because there is no going back. Thus, in the end, given the extent

---

39   We are indebted to Thomas Trautmann for having identified this type of Dravidian terminology and kinship system, whose structure is very close to that of the Kariera-type four-section systems found in Australia. In Dravidian B terminologies, the distinction between cross and parallel kin reappears in G+2 and G-2, and cross kin are affines. Trautmann mentions another case of Dravidian B in Amazonia, this time among the Western Panare, Carib groups living on the middle Orenoco.

of our present knowledge, we can advance the hypothesis that the Dravidian type seems to be the starting point of several lines of evolution even as it continues to exist side by side with the systems derived from it (drifts). We have here a major sociological and historical fact that is a scientific finding of prime importance, even though it raises as many questions as it opens new perspectives.

WHY THESE TRANSFORMATIONS?

We know neither in what circumstances nor for what reasons Dravidian kinship terminologies and systems turn into 'Sudanese' systems, as was the case, for example, in ancient China and perhaps in the pre-Roman Latin society. We posit that the Australian kinship systems were originally Dravidiniate and that a large number turned into section and subsection systems in response to the need to divide all members of a society into kin groups that were not necessarily connected by genealogical ties but each of which was responsible for certain tasks, for distinct but complementary functions in the collective rites meant to ensure the reproduction of the cosmos and the society. Perhaps an analogous reason, the organization of collective rites, explains the presence of sections in ancient China and among the Amazonian Pano, of sociocentric divisions existing side-by-side with Dravidian-type kinship systems, but without replacing them, as they did in Australia.

Alf Hornborg's work[40] allows us perhaps to glimpse the reasons for the transformation of certain Dravidian systems into Iroquois systems, the most frequent type of transformations occurring in Dravidian systems we know of. As long as 'sister' exchange is the marriage rule, the terminologies distinguish between cross and parallel kin. This is the case with all of the terminologies classed as bifurcate merging, among which the Dravidian and Iroquois. But if marriage with a cross relative is no longer the rule, but merely a possibility, in other words if there is no longer an obligation to renew the exchange of women between the same groups, then the cross–parallel distinction is limited to Go, and a distinct vocabulary differentiating real affines appears. This is now an Iroquois system. And if it is forbidden to repeat alliances for a certain number of generations, this gives rise to Kuma, Ngawbe, Yafar, etc., systems. The reason is clear. The groups in question choose to marry with their most distant relative, in genealogical and even perhaps in geographic terms.

To what sociological and historical conditions does this decision correspond? We do not have a clear answer yet, although we now understand the advantages kin groups can derive from opening up and multiplying their alliances. The reasons are the same – prohibition on repeating alliances for several generations – but in

---

40   A. Hornborg, 'Social Redundancy in Amazonian Social Structure', in Godelier, Trautmann and Tjon Sie Fat (eds.), *Transformations of Kinship*, pp. 168–86.

addition this time to the prohibition of direct 'sister' exchange, which would have given rise to the so-called Crow-Omaha systems usually found in societies close to those with Dravidian or Iroquois systems. Furthermore, Crow-Omaha systems forbid, depending on the case, two or three of the four groups above Ego – those of his father, his mother, his father's mother and his mother's mother – and they often forbid marriage in all four.[41] We also see that Crow-Omaha systems are on the same trajectory as the Yafar, Ngawbe, etc., systems, but they differ in that they clearly define the lineages in which one can take a spouse and they forbid marriage by direct 'sister' exchange between two men, two lineages.[42]

But this leaves unilluminated one feature encountered in the Crow-Omaha kinship systems, which is the fact that this terminology raises a series of kin positions one or several generations above Ego and, symmetrically, lowers a certain number of positions on the other side. The terminology becomes skewed around Ego. This is what is called the skewing principle, i.e. the 'skewing' of Crow-Omaha terminologies. In the end, the generation difference is cancelled, being caught between several kin positions that are all, whatever their role and position, given as identical or equivalent. The mother's brother's son (the matrilateral cross cousin) becomes an uncle for Ego; the father's sister's son (the patrilateral cross cousin) becomes a nephew for Ego. One is raised with respect to Ego, the other is lowered.

We do not yet know whether this 'skewing' of the Crow and Omaha terminologies is a specific feature, consubstantial with the internal structure of these kinship systems, or whether it is independent of these marriage prohibitions and is a superstructure that can appear and grow on different kinship systems.[43] David Kronenfeld showed that the Fanti of Africa, which have a Hawaiian terminology and groups that operate, in some circumstances, according to a matrilineal descent principle, use the same terminology but modified according to a 'Crow' skewing rule. Their circumstances are of a political or ritual nature and are the source of roles and statuses that are locked into the same kin position from one generation to the next, which makes them equivalent and skews the nearby kin terms. Kronenfeld[44] reiterates the hypothesis about the skewing

---

41   For the Crow-Omaha systems, see F. Lounsbury, 'A Formal Analysis of Crow-Omaha Type Kinship Terminologies', in W. Goodenough (ed.), *Explorations in Cultural Anthropology: Essays in Honour of George Peter Murdock* (New York, McGraw-Hill, 1964), pp. 351–94, and F. Héritier, *L'Exercice de la parenté* (Paris, Gallimard/Le Seuil, 1981).

42   We are indebted to Françoise Héritier for having shown that the exchange of women lies at the heart of Crow-Omaha systems, but that, instead of giving a woman back to the wife-giving lineage, you give a woman to another lineage in the wife's clan. See Héritier, *L'Exercice de la parenté*, pp. 112–24.

43   One proof would be the presence of 'Omaha features' in the ancient Latin system, which was of the Sudanese type.

44   David B. Kronenfeld, 'Fanti Kinship: The Structure of Terminology and Behavior', *American Anthropologist*, no. 75 (1973), pp. 1577–95, and 'A Formal Analysis of Fanti Kinship Terminology (Ghana)', *Anthropos*, no. 75 (1980), pp. 586–608.

principle already tentatively advanced by Lounsbury in 1971, that: 'The equivalence rules express laws of succession.'[45] Nevertheless, this hypothesis requires confirmation in the other cases of terminologies with Crow or Omaha features, as, for example, the Kachin (or the Mnong-Gar).

Let us therefore return to the different transformations we have seen and which are far from being representative of the hundreds of other examples I could have cited. In all events the particular place of Dravidian kinship terminologies and systems is striking. These terminologies are capable of step-by-step transformations into four other terminology types: Australian, Iroquois, Sudanese and Hawaiian. Alternatively, in no case do they transform directly into Eskimo or even Crow-Omaha terminologies. To arrive at these, an intermediary step is needed, perhaps a prescriptive asymmetric system (of the Kachin, Nasupo, etc. variety), but more surely of the Iroquois type. As for the Eskimo-type terminologies, in a few known cases they clearly derive from a Sudanese type (in Western Europe for example). With what types of kin groups are these various types of terminologies associated?

Dravidian, Sudanese and Iroquois terminologies are compatible with the existence of kin groups organized according to a unilineal or duolineal principle (clans, lineages, the Latin *gens*, etc.). This is also the case with the Australian terminologies. But where there are 'clans' in Australia, they come into play only in the performance of rituals and not in the day-to-day management of kinship. Hawaiian terminologies are compatible with cognatic descent principles and kin groups living together on the same land, like the Tongan *kainga*, which are cognatic groups closed by a principle of co-residence and not of descent. This organization produces what has sometimes been termed *demes*[46] or what Firth, speaking of the Tikopia, called '*ramages*' rather than lineages.

Eskimo terminologies are associated with societies without a lineal descent principle, and which therefore do not have clans and lineages but kindreds. This terminology type is found among the Iban of Borneo, the Garia of New Guinea and in Western Europe (with the exception of societies of Slavic origin, like Russia and Poland, for instance), and of course in Euro-America. These facts exclude directly and mechanically associating, as Morgan and the evolutionists had done in the nineteenth century, the existence of such and such a terminology, of such and such a kinship system, with a given stage in the development of

45   Lounsbury, 'The Formal Analysis of Crow-Omaha Type Kinship Terminologies', p. 383: 'Laws of succession: linear succession, uniform for the two sexes, in the skewing rules, and lateral succession in the merging rules.'

46   The term is associated with Cleisthenes' reformation of the Athenian constitution; it was used by Howitt and Fison in 1855, then forgotten until reintroduced by Murdock in 1949. Howard A. W. Fison, 'On the Deme and the Horde', *Journal of the Royal Anthropological Institute*, no. 14 (1885), p. 142; G. P. Murdock, *Social Structure* (New York, The Free Press/ London, Collier-Macmillan, 1949), pp. 63, 64, 158–64.

civilization or, more modestly, with a given mode of production. In Europe, the Eskimo kinship terminology and bilateral, cognatic kin ties have existed since the end of the Roman Empire and since then have existed side by side with two of the main forms of social organization found successively in the West from the Early Middle Ages to our day: feudalism and the capitalist system, associated from the early nineteenth century in certain Western European countries with various forms of constitutional and democratic political regimes.

Below is a summary of the different lines of evolution we believe to have resulted from the diverse transformations of Dravidian-type kinship systems:

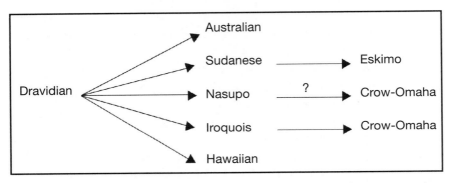

If we superpose on this diagram of the lines of known transformations Robert Lowie's classification in four groups according to the presence or absence of collaterality and bifurcation in the terminology's structure[47] we obtain the following table:

---

47 Presented for the first time in a short but famous text published in *American Anthropologist*, April–June 1928, p. 267: 'The merging of uncles and aunts with parents constitutes a *generation* terminology. If the males or females of the first generation ascending are dichotomized on the principles explained [FB = F; MZ = M; MB; FZ], the terminology may be called *birfucate merging*, bifurcate because paternal and maternal kin are distinguished, merging in so far as there is a partial merging with the parents. Where this merging fails to obtain so that each collateral relative is distinguishable, the nomenclature becomes *bifurcate collateral*.

If collaterals are confounded with each other but remain separate from the direct line of descent, such emphasis on the latter merits the term *lineal*.

In 1932, in *Zeitschrift fur Ethnologie* ('Verwandschaftsbezeichnungen und Verwandtenheirat', *Zeitschrift fur Ethnologie*, no. 64 [1932], pp. 41–72), Kirchhoff presented an equivalent classification. But it was F. G. Lounsbury who, in 1964, completed the definition of (merging and collateral) bifurcate systems by introducing the concept of crossness (cf. Lounsbury, 'A Formal Account of Crow-Omaha Type Kinship Terminologies', p. 387). In 1949, G. P. Murdock had named the four types of terminology distinguished by Lowie using ethnonyms: Hawaiian (generational), Iroquois (bifurcate merging), Sudanese (bifurcate collateral) and Eskimo (lineal). If we use the signs + and – to indicate the presence (+) or absence (-) of collaterality and bifurcation, we obtain -- Hawaiian, -+ Iroquois, ++ Sudanese and +- Eskimo.

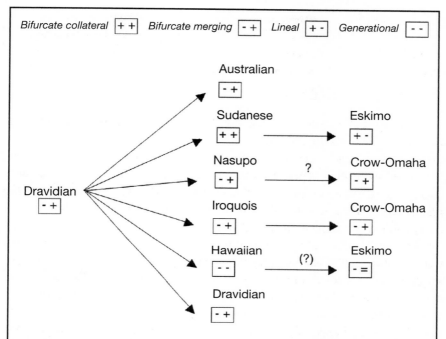

Transformations of the Dravidian kinship systems and terminologies and the directions taken by these transformations; modified version, after Kryukov ('The synchro-diachronic method and the multidirectionality of kinship transformations', pp. 311–12).

We agree for the most part with Kryukov's reconstruction of the evolution of kinship terminologies and systems. However, we have a few reservations about the hypothesis of Hawaiian systems having turned into 'Eskimo' systems – because we do not know of any thoroughly convincing example – and about that of the Nasupo systems having become Crow-Omaha systems.[48] To complete the picture, we need to add two other criteria to the two advanced by Lowie, bifurcation and collaterality: whether or not the terminology in question uses different vocabularies to distinguish consanguines and affines, and whether or not it distinguishes generational levels (presence or absence of skewing). If we include the criterion of the presence or absence of a specific terminology for affines, we obtain this other classification:

---

48   The Nasupo system is asymmetric prescriptive; a Crow or Omaha system is one that defines alliance by a certain number of prohibitions bearing on certain lineages: two in the case of the Cherokee, three for the Hopi, four for the Samo. The two logics are different. To get from one to the other requires a rupture. Cf. C. Lévi-Strauss, 'The Future of Kinship Studies', Huxley Memorial Lecture, in *Proceedings of the Royal Anthropological Institute of Great Britain and Ireland*, vol. 1 (1965), pp. 13–22; p. 19. N. J. Allen nevertheless attempted to reconstruct the transformation of a Dravidian system, that of the Sherpa, into an Omaha system. See N. J. Allen, 'Sherpa Kinship Terminology in Diachronic Perspective', *Man*, vol. 11 (1976), pp. 569–87.

ABSENCE	PRESENCE
Dravidian	Iroquois
Australian	Crow-Omaha
Nasupo	Sudanese
Hawaiian	Eskimo

Distribution of the kinship terminologies according to whether or not they have specific terms for affines[49]

If we accept the hypothesis that kinship systems analogous to the Dravidian type may have been the starting point for several series of structural transformations, as yet largely unexplained but which gave rise to other kinship systems associated with other types of terminologies without the possibility of going back, then we can revisit the important findings reported by Lévi-Strauss in *The Elementary Structures of Kinship* (1949) and in 'The future of kinship studies' (1965), and even complete them with a new meaning.

For putting Dravidian systems at the outset of these diverse lines of evolution is tantamount to resting everything on one of the 'elementary structures' of kinship that occupied much of Lévi-Strauss' major work. The book was constructed around the hypothesis that the existence of a distinction between cross and parallel cousins was proof that kinship is basically 'exchange' (for Lévi-Strauss, exchange of women by men, as we know), with cross cousins being potential spouses for Ego, and parallel cousins – assimilated to sisters – being for this reason prohibited. Lévi-Strauss called those systems where there was not only a distinction between parallel and cross kin but also the presence of a positive alliance rule prescribing marriage with the patri-, matri- or bilateral cross cousin, 'elementary structures of kinship'. We will not go back over these points, which we have already discussed, but let us recall that the kinship systems that have such structures are: the Dravidian systems and the Australian systems – with the exception of the Murngin (Yolngu) and the Nasupo-Jinpaw (Burma, China, etc.), which are generalized-exchange systems. In the first, 'wife-givers' are at the same time 'wife-takers'. In the second, givers cannot be takers. In this case there must be at least three groups for people to be able to marry (A gives its women to B and receives women from C, and so on).

But we saw that certain Dravidian systems in Australia have acquired sections or subsections, thus falling into either the formula of restricted exchange (Kariera and Aranda systems) or that of generalized exchange (Murngin). And we saw, with the example of the Lolo (or Li) and the Nasupo of China, that prescriptive symmetric Dravidian systems (which therefore come under the heading of elementary structures with restricted exchange) had

---

49   This classification in two groups is quite rough, since it omits the fact that many Dravidian terminologies have a few specific terms for distinguishing real and classificatory affines and, on the other hand, certain Iroquois terminologies have terms corresponding to Dravidian equations, since the same word designates the mother's brother and the wife's father (MB = WF).

turned into asymmetric prescriptive systems with generalized exchange (Nasupo, Kachin, etc.).

We gave examples of the transformation of Dravidian systems into Iroquois systems. Iroquois systems distinguish between cross and parallel cousins, but this distinction is not accompanied by a marriage rule requiring Ego to marry a cross cousin. Ego can marry someone who is not related, hence the presence of a specific vocabulary for affines. In fact, generally speaking, in Iroquois systems, if direct 'wife' exchange remains the rule, it is forbidden, unlike in the case of 'elementary' structures, to repeat these exchanges for several generations (Iroquois systems of the Baruya, Yafar, Ngawbe, etc., type).

But if we add to this negative rule (the ban on repeating the same alliance for three or four generations) the prohibition this time on exchanging a 'sister' directly with the lineage that has given you a wife, we obtain the Crow-Omaha-type systems, those Lévi-Strauss chose to call 'semi-complex'. Finally, if we separate all of the collateral lines of the two direct lines descending from the father and the mother, and we designate the collaterals on both sides by the same terms, while multiplying the marriage prohibitions that forbid repeating the same alliances for several generations, we produce, as was the case in Europe, the transformation of a Sudanese (Latin) system into an Eskimo system. Christian kinship reckoning is an extreme example of those systems that forbid marriage, for a certain number of generations, with all those connected to Ego by diverse degrees of consanguinity or affinity, and who therefore belong to Ego's kindred. Descent reckoning is undifferentiated (with a patrilineal bias, nevertheless) and no distinction is made between cousins on the father's side and those on the mother's side. But Eskimo-type systems are found not only in Europe or among the Inuit of Canada but also among the Iban of Borneo.

These are what Lévi-Strauss called 'complex' systems, because the reasons for the preferred or prescribed marriage depend on other considerations than kinship and on other criteria (marrying someone of the same religion, from the same ethnic group, of the same class or rank, etc.) and therefore because of social relations that have nothing to do with kinship.[50] We thus see that all of the systems distinguished by Lévi-Strauss find their place and meaning in the pattern of structural transformations we have reconstructed and offered as a hypothesis. These structural transformations lay out what is commonly called a network of evolutionary lines, which strike out in different directions and are irreversible. Why do we speak of evolution? Precisely because these transformations start from the same type of system and never come back to their point of departure.[51]

---

50 C. Lévi-Strauss, Preface to the second edition of *The Elementary Structures*, p. xxxiii.

51 It is interesting to recall Jean-Claude Muller's suggestion that Lévi-Strauss' distinctions between elementary, semi-complex and complex structures be understood as phases in an evolutionary pattern. Cf. J-C. Muller, 'Structures semi-complexes et structures complexes de

Lévi-Strauss had thus distinguished a certain number of systems, and this was a remarkable achievement. But he never actually attempted to connect them up using rules of transformation. It is true that he wrote *The Elementary Structures* at a time when anthropologists still felt the need to set themselves apart from any 'evolutionary' approach *à la* Morgan, that is to say, a unilineal approach to evolution that had long depicted the different social and kinship systems as so many stages in human progress, from savagery (Hawaiian systems) to civilization (Eskimo systems) via barbarism (Iroquois systems). Of course we have gone beyond Morgan. Today we can serenely show that a system evolves and turns into another without going on to claim that the second shows 'progress' with respect to the first. Thus all of the systems identified by Lévi-Strauss today find their logical place in a multilineal pattern of irreversible structural transformations. We do not see, for example, how today's French kinship system could tomorrow change into a Dravidian system prescribing marriage with a cross cousin, daughter of the mother's brother and potential father-in-law.

But when they take up their place in such a pattern, the systems Lévi-Strauss distinguished as being elementary, semi-complex or complex must be renamed, for these terms give rise to theoretical confusion and do not correspond to the realities they designate. From the standpoint of their structure, the systems Lévi-Strauss termed 'elementary' are structurally complex. And it is the so-called 'complex' systems – such as the European or American cognatic systems with an Eskimo terminology – that are structurally simple. This does not contradict Lévi-Strauss' analysis, which finds that the choice of a spouse is relatively simple when the person already belongs to a kin category. But for this choice to be simple, there has to be a pre-existing system that is 'structurally' complex. Example: the Australian section systems where Ego already knows in what section his or her potential spouses are to be found. It should be noted however that this in no way enables Ego to guess with exactitude which of these people will become his or her real spouse. In prescriptive systems, there is also room for contingency, for randomness, if indeed this term can be applied to the choices made by individuals living in small societies where everyone, or nearly, knows everyone else and must combine several criteria in order to choose a spouse.

At the opposite end of the spectrum, in our societies where no kin category is prescribed for marriage and where a certain number of categories are forbidden for reasons of incest, people nevertheless never marry 'purely at random'.[52] Not just anyone will do as a companion, and the number of possible choices is not unlimited – even though it is infinitely greater than the number of choices open

---

l'alliance matrimoniale: quelques réflexions sur un ouvrage de Françoise Héritier', *Anthropologie et sociétés*, vol. 6, no. 3 (1982), pp. 155–72.

52   Lévi-Strauss, Preface to the second edition of *The Elementary Structures*.

to someone living in Dravidian, Australian, Iroquois or Crow-Omaha-type societies. Lévi-Strauss' analyses and conclusions on this point are entirely founded.

To sum up, we can say that, if the starting point of the different structural transformations in kinship relations lies in the Dravidian systems, these transformations
concerned the distinction between cross and parallel kin, which in certain systems
was reduced only to Ego's generation (Iroquois) or disappeared altogether (Eskimo).
But they concerned a second component as well, which explains the reduction of
the impact of the parallel/cross distinction, the disappearance of prescriptive
marriage rules, and, a third component, the disappearance of direct spouse
exchange, which was replaced by various forms of bride/groom price.

Lastly, these transformations may also have affected a fourth component of
kinship relations, perfectly disjoined from the first two: descent reckoning. But we
know almost nothing about this point. No one has yet explained why the descent
rule in some societies is patrilineal, in others matrilineal and in others undifferentiated. In Europe, societies are thought to have gone from the ancient Latin system,
which was strongly patrilineal, to a cognatic system with merely a patrilineal bias.
Some authors suggest that elsewhere, in Central Asia, large-scale animal husbandry
had placed male tasks in the foreground and ensured that men controlled the
society to the extent that all social relations entailed gifts or exchanges of livestock.
This practice would have encouraged them to adopt a patrilineal descent mode.
The hypothesis is plausible. But the problem is to go over each region, paying close
attention to the details of the activities, the ecosystems, the pre-colonial historical
contexts and so on. The domain is still unexplored.[53] Other development sequences
have been suggested in the past, based either on ideological and epistemological a
priori (Morgan) or on logical and epistemological a priori (Kirchhoff, Lowie,
Murdock). Here are the outlines for the record.

Morgan started with the epistemological postulate of the evolutionary theory of his
time, namely: that evolution always proceeds from the simple to the complex. Since
the simplest terminology is the one Lowie called 'generational' and Murdock
dubbed 'Hawaiian', for Morgan this must have been the starting point of kinship
systems.[54] To his mind, this terminology bore the stigmata of the era when humankind lived in a stage of 'savagery' and practised 'group marriage', which had partially
put a stop to the sexual promiscuity of the primitive animal horde. Morgan thus

---

53 See Jack Goody's essay, *Production and Reproduction* (Cambridge, Cambridge
University Press, 1976) and Alexander Spoehr's now-classic monograph, *Changing Kinship Systems:
A Study in the acculturation of the Creeks, Cherokee, and Choctaw* (Chicago, Field Museum of
Natural History, Chicago, 1947), Anthropological Series, vol. 33, no. 4, pp. 155–235. As early as 1947,
Spoehr showed how, after having been dispossessed of their territories by land-hungry settlers, the
Indian societies, and especially the Oklahoma Creeks, had been devastated by the discovery and
exploitation of oil.

54 Morgan used the term Malayan.

came to see the Polynesian societies as the remnants and evidence of the most ancient stage of human evolution. Later, according to Morgan again, other human groups graduated to the stage of 'barbarism', of clans, of *gentes*, to which corresponded the Iroquois-type terminologies[55] (which do not yet distinguish the father from his brothers and the mother from her sisters). Last of all, a few societies in Europe and Euro-America went on to the stage of 'civilization', to which corresponds the modern European terminology (which Morgan called 'Aryan', and which was later renamed Eskimo). This terminology showed that, finally the real, biological roles of the father and the mother had been understood, and that the human family had at last reached its ultimate, rational form, based on monogamy. This view saw terminologies as having become purely descriptive, starting from Ego and the monogamic nuclear family and constructing all kinship relations from those genealogical ties linking Ego with his father, grandfather, great-grandfather, and so on. Such was the epistemological (monolineal evolutionism) and ideological (Eurocentrism) background of Morgan's attempt, in *Ancient Society*, to reconstruct human evolution. But we should not forget that Morgan had first literally founded a scientific discipline that did not exist before him and that he was motivated by the desire to answer a major question: How to show the cultural unity of all of the American Indians and their Asiatic origin? In an attempt to reply, he had sent out hundreds of questionnaires, which were filled out by people working at the four corners of the earth; he carried out numerous structural analyses, and ultimately was able to lay the foundations of a veritable Mendelian table of kinship terminologies.

Other patterns of evolution have been proposed. Paul Kirchhoff's,[56] for example, was based on another epistemological principle, namely: that human thought advanced by stages, from concrete and specific realities to general abstractions. This is why, according to Kirchhoff, the evolution of kinship started from 'bifurcate collateral' systems, where all kin positions were designated by specific terms (he gave the Chinese system as an example), and ended with the generational-type systems, in which all terms were merged and took on a definitively abstract character (the Hawaiian system). Like Morgan's, this hypothesis was not based on the slightest historical evidence, but instead on the idea that human thought took several tens of millennia to go from concrete to abstract thinking, a hypothesis that is not only contradicted by the sources but

---

55   Morgan called these 'Ganowinian' or 'Eurasian'. Concerning all these points, see Thomas Trautmann, *Lewis Henry Morgan and the Invention of Kinship* (Berkeley, University of California Press, 1987), esp. pp. 260–2. Morgan's schema forms Part Three of his *Ancient Society or Researches on the Lines of Human Progress from Savagery through Barbarism to Civilization* (Tucson, University of Arizona Press, 1985 [1887]), entitled 'Growth of the Idea of the Family', pp. 205–534.

56   P. Kirchhoff, 'The Principles of Clanship in Human Society', *Davidson Journal of Anthropology*, vol. 1, no.1 (1954), pp. 1–10.

is absurd. As Lévi-Strauss showed, mythical thinking, which is as old as kinship systems, is based on a mixture of abstract and concrete thought.

More recently, other diagrams of evolution have appeared. One of these, which we will adopt with a few modifications, is that of Kryukov, based on historical evidence, on fieldwork and on structural analyses. The other is that of Nick Allen, published in an article in the same book, entitled 'The prehistory of Dravidian-type terminologies'.[57] Allen imagines as the starting point of all kinship systems, a 'tetradic' system with two generation levels – parents/children – each level being reduced to two brother–sister pairs who marry each other. At level one, the two brothers exchange their sisters, or vice versa. At level two, the children of the two couples marry according to the cross-cousin formula (MB = FZH = SpF). Allen then endows this reduced model with two properties, declaring it to be at the same time egocentric and sociocentric, in other words, that groups A and B in generation I have children that make up two groups, C and D, in generation II, who in turn unite with each other and engender groups A and B and so on. There are two types of time, then: lineal (generation I engenders the members of generation II) and cyclical (I engenders II which engenders I, and so on.). The combination of the two times can be illustrated by a double helix model, each helix representing one generational moiety:

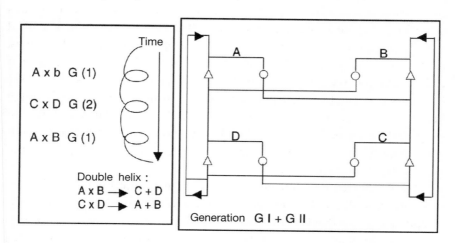

---

57   N. Allen, 'The Prehistory of Dravidian-Type Terminologies', in Godelier et al., *Transformations of Kinship*, pp. 314–31. The text refers to two other attempts by the same author to construct a schema of the evolution of kinship terminologies: 'Tetradic Theory: An Approach to Kinship', *JASO*, vol. 17, no. 2 (1986), pp. 87–109, and 'The Evolution of Kinship Terminologies', *Lingua*, no. 77 (1989), pp. 173–85. In one of his latest articles, Allen investigates this time the origins of human society: N. Allen, 'Effervescence and the Origins of Human Society', in N. J. Allen, W. S. F. Pickering and W. Watts Miller (eds.), *On Durkheim's Elementary Forms of Religious Life* (London, Routledge, 1988), pp. 149–61. In a completely different vein, let us mention the work of Gertrude Dole, and in particular 'Developmental Sequences of Kinship Patterns', in Priscilla Reining (ed.), *Kinship Studies in the Morgan Centennial Year* (Washington DC, Anthropological Society of Washington, 1972), pp. 134–46.

516 THE METAMORPHOSES OF KINSHIP

Allen goes on to suppose that all members of the society are really or virtually related to each other, and he constructs their relations using three series of equations. The first posits identity between alternate generations and distinguishes them from the adjacent generations. Ego is identified with his grandfather and his grandson (FF=SS). The second prescribes a cross-cousin marriage rule (MBD = W): the wife will be the mother's brother's daughter. Affines are therefore cognates. The third and last type of equations, this time classificatory, posits the equivalence of siblings: father = father's brother (F = FB), son = brother's son (S = BS), mother = mother's sister (M = MZ), and so on.

Based on this hypothetical starting point, which looks very much like an Australian four-section system, Allen posits that human evolution gave rise to all known kin types through a *series of ruptures* that caused the *disappearance* of these three types of equations one after another. The first to go, he writes, were the equations that conflated alternate generations, followed by the equations prescribing various marriage formulas and making certain cognates potential affines, the last rupture being that of the classificatory equations (F = FB, M = MZ, S = BS, and so on). In the end, according to Allen, when the evolution finds its way to certain parts of the world, it will lead to terminologies without any equation, that is to say, to systems that distinguish paternals from maternals, and lineal kin from collaterals, and collaterals among each other. In short, one would end up with so-called 'Sudanese' systems, classified as collateral bifurcate systems (the ancient Latin, Chinese or Polish systems, etc.). In this theory, evolution thus began with the Australian systems and ended with the Sudanese systems via Dravidian or Iroquois systems. The lineal systems would have been marginal, ignoring as they do bifurcation between collateral maternals and paternals. At this point, Allen is obliged to suppose the existence of 'counter-tetradic' equations that spring up independently of each other, do not develop or have a cumulative effect, and are of secondary importance.[58]

These views are intellectually very exciting, to be sure, but for me they are not quite receivable. It does not seem realistic to take as the starting point of the evolution a system that is both egocentric and sociocentric. Recent discoveries show, in effect, that this was not the case for the Australian systems on which Allen modelled his hypothesis. And this is because the sociocentric character of the Australian systems seems to be linked not to the desire to regulate alliances but to that to divide the whole society into groups responsible for distinct and complementary ritual functions, which have nothing to do with kinship but instead concern the reproduction of the universe and the power relations between men and women.

---

58   Allen, 'The Evolution of Kinship Terminologies', pp. 182–3.

In addition, this hypothesis is obliged to call on the existence of counter-tetradic equations to explain the existence of lineal systems (Eskimo), generational systems (Hawaiian) and bifurcate merging systems (Crow-Omaha).[59] That makes a lot of exceptions, and the argument for the existence of counter-tetradic equations looks like an ad hoc explanation. Furthermore, history has shown us that a so-called zero-equation system, the ancient Latin system, evolved into a lineal system, whereas it should have been the end point. In short, imagining that history proceeds by a well-ordered series of disappearances of three kinds of originally combined rules (equations) is an abstract view that leaves aside the fact that transformations not only proceed by multiplying the distinctions between kin positions but also work the other way, conflating into a single term, for instance, *avunculus*, both mother's and father's brother, or calling all of Ego's cousins *consobrinus*, thus extending the meaning of a term to three other types of cousins that were previously designated by distinct terms.

Of course, kinship terminologies and systems have not finished evolving. Today and before our eyes, the Polish[60] and Chinese terminologies, which have an overall 'Sudanese'-type structure, are increasingly (and more and more rapidly) heading toward an Eskimo-type terminology, perhaps because of the growing importance of the nuclear family in these societies at the cost of more extended family forms. In addition, as Thomas Trautmann reminds us, history provides us with numerous examples of Brahmin communities in South India that are believed to have come from North India, and to have abandoned their Indo-European kinship systems (lacking distinct terms for cross cousins and a cross-cousin marriage rule) and adopted a Dravidian system. In fact, isn't this what happens in many parts of the world, where populations who have converted to Christianity are encouraged to adopt the Western kinship system, centred on the monogamous family, and to marry genealogically distant partners, a system that the Protestant and Catholic missionaries brought with them together with its Eskimo terminology, and which they regard as both 'rational' and 'Christian'.

In all events, kinship systems change profoundly over centuries, whereas kinship terminologies, like languages, evolve much more slowly, since the same terms 'father', 'uncle', etc., take on new meanings while others are abandoned, as in French *parâtre*, *marâtre*, which have been replaced by *beau-père* and *belle-mère*,

---

59   Ibid., pp. 178–9.

60   R. Parkin, 'The Contemporary Evolution of Polish Kinship Terminology', *Sociologus*, vol. 45, no. 2 (1995), pp. 140–52. Concerning the evolution of the Russian system from bifurcate collateral to lineal, comparable to the evolution of contemporary terminologies in Polish and Chinese, see E. Gessat-Anstett, 'Les terminologies russes de parenté', *L'Homme*, nos. 154–5 (2000), pp. 613–34.

thus leading to the conflation of kin positions that were distinguished in old French, while English continues to distinguish father-in-law and stepfather.[61] Hypotheses such as those made by Murdock, that in changing residence modes (from virilocal to uxorilocal, for instance) people would be brought to change descent principles (from patrilineal to matrilineal, for example), or those made by Bourdieu, explaining the appearance of a kinship system and its terminology (for example the Arab system) as the consequence of the aggregation of the strategies of groups pursuing their own interests, have never been proven.[62]

Kinship systems change. And to my mind, the forces that drive the changes originate much more in the political-religious relations that fashion society into a whole than in economic relations. A spectacular proof is provided by the evolution of kinship in the West since the end of the Roman Empire. The role of religion, of Christianity and the Church, in this evolution was fundamental. As Jack Goody showed in a pioneering work,[63] the Church successively banned polygamy, cohabitation, divorce, remarriage of widows, adoption, marriage with close kin and the marriage of priests. It made marriage, which had initially been an alliance between two families and as such was their business, a 'sacrament' celebrated in the Church, by the priest, before God. It imposed baptism, without which a child had no social existence and was sentenced to purgatory if it died in infancy, or to hell if it died later. But Christianity also imposed marriage by mutual consent, and affirmed the equality of men and women in the eyes of God, without however ever allowing women, the source of original sin, to accede to the highest ranks of the ecclesiastical hierarchy.

But Christianity was not merely a religion, a system of beliefs and rites directed at God, the Virgin Mary or the saints. The Church and Christianity also became the agents that legitimized the feudal powers, the right of kings and

---

61   T. Trautmann, 'Kinship as Language', in P. Descola, J. Hammel and P. Lemonnier (eds.), *La Production du social* (Paris, Fayard, 1999), pp. 433–44.

62   Murdock, *Social Structure*, pp. 201–18; P. Bourdieu, 'Les stratégies matrimoniales dans le système de reproduction', *Annales*, nos. 4–5 (1972), pp. 1105–27.

63   J. Goody, *The Development of the Family and Marriage in Europe* (Cambridge/New York, Cambridge University Press, 1983). It is worth recalling here the tribute paid by the great medieval historian, Georges Duby, in his preface to the French translation of Goody's work: 'As the good historian that he is, Jack Goody takes care to pin down the high points of this evolution in time. After the initial period of the 4th century, he rightly stresses the time of the so-called Gregorian reform spanning the 11th and 12th centuries, where the power of the organized Roman Church reached its peak. It was at this time that the prescriptions concerning sexuality and the family came into full force, that the prohibition of incest was immoderately extended to the seventh degree of canonical kinship . . . that the model of marriage, whose collapse has recently accelerated before our very eyes, reached its ultimate form . . . Jack Goody gives professional historians a superb lesson in rigour: applying to the materials they are in the habit of handling a far sharper conceptual tool, he shows the proponents of an historical approach to anthropology how to break out of the routines of the traditional critical method.' See J. Goody, *L'Évolution de la famille et du marriage en Europe* (Paris, Armand Colin, 1985), p. 7.

nobles to rule over society and to govern it. In effect, ever since the Emperor Constantine's conversion, the new religion has been conjoined with political power and the state. And if the prohibitions on marriages between close kin created many a problem for the aristocracy (to which the bishops who pronounced these prohibitions in different councils often belonged), it should not be forgotten that the bishops were also feudal lords in their own right.

In contrast, the changes Islam brought to kinship relations in the societies and communities that converted to its principles were less sweeping. To be sure, the traditional Bedouin form of marriage with the father's brother's daughter was regarded as the ideal, but marriages with close relatives, which were frequent since Antiquity on both sides of the Mediterranean, were not forbidden by the new religion. Polygamy was maintained but restricted to four wives, and repudiation and divorce continued to exist. Only adoption was forbidden by the Prophet, although subsequently various practices and institutions made it possible to get around this prohibition when it was expedient.

This brief overview shows the full importance and interest of encouraging the social sciences to coordinate their efforts in order to reconstruct and understand a past that *reaches down to our day*, all of these practices and representations involving millions of people and which are part of their ways of thinking and acting, of their identity, and which are not about to disappear. Jack Goody, Thomas Trautmann, M. Kryukov and a few other anthropologists and historians (too few) have been working in this direction for two decades.[64] Theirs is the kind of research that needs to be followed up and extended even further with the collaboration and competence of those who, in all societies, Western and non-Western, possess the memory and knowledge of their history, are familiar with its complexity and are in a better position than others to measure what has disappeared or appeared, or has been reproduced in other forms over the last decades of the twentieth century.

---

64   Cf. Andrzej Plakans' all too 'rapid' *Kinship in the Past: Anthropology of European family life (1500–1900)* (Oxford, Basil Blackwell, 1994). Also worth noting are the two volumes of *L'Histoire de la famille*, edited by A. Burguière, C. Klapish- Zuber, M. Segalen and F. Zonnabend (Paris, Armand Colin, 1986), as well as J. Delumeau and D. Roche (eds.), *L'Histoire des pères et de la paternité* (Paris, Larousse, 1990), a work combining approaches from several disciplines, and notably psychoanalysis.

Conclusion:
What Future for What Kin Ties?

The world's population in 2010 was estimated at over six billion eight hundred million, and counting. Some one billion four hundred million live in China and annexed Tibet. Over a billion live in India, two hundred million in Indonesia, four hundred million in Europe, three hundred and eight million in the United States, etc.

Seen from another angle, the world contains nearly two billion Christians, more than a billion Muslims, three hundred million of whom live in Arab countries, close to one billion Hindus and between five and six hundred million Buddhists. These great religions are themselves divided and subdivided into movements and denominations, often opposed to each other, and impose different religious practices and social behaviours on their followers. Three – Christianity, Buddhism and Islam – are driven by the desire to convert all humanity to their beliefs. Hinduism lays no claim to conversions and is, moreover, hard to export: this would require transporting the entire caste organization along with its gods.

These facts are worth bearing in mind, since all religions, whether or not they claim universality, have a very direct impact on the relationships between men and women, both in the area of sexuality and the unions allowed or forbidden between the sexes but also on relations between parents and children, between living or deceased ascendants and descendants. It must also be remembered that, to the impact of religion, which is capable of unifying the family practices of members of societies whose culture, history and importance in the world are very different, must be added the impact of power and wealth, which invest the kinship relations found in a society with specific social stakes that are the source of solidarity but also of diverging interests, conflicts and ruptures.

If one confronts these facts and figures with the theories developed in the present work, one will conclude that it is highly unlikely that today's kinship and family practices are moving everywhere in the same direction. Nevertheless, some prevailing trends can be outlined.

THE IMPACT OF THE WEST

Beginning at the start of the nineteenth century, an economic system born in the West, capitalism, began spreading to all societies on the face of the earth, either by including them directly or by subjecting them from a distance (China, for example). In association with capitalism, various forms of democratic and constitutional political regimes developed, at least in Western Europe and America, where this system arose and developed, replacing – sometimes through violent transitions – the feudal and monarchical regimes of what is known as the Ancien Régime. Without being as widely exported as capitalism, whose worldwide spread was borne up by both financial (investments) and impersonal (firms, national and multinational companies) competitive relations of power, democracy is hailed by the West as a fundamental value and used, when in the interests of a given state or coalition of states, as both a measure of the backwardness of other countries and civilizations compared with the West and as a model to be proposed to or imposed on non-Western countries.

The task of bringing 'true' religion, Christianity, to the other peoples of the world was one of the missions shouldered by the Westerners who discovered and conquered America, Oceania and Africa. Even today Oceania, Africa, South America and the Far East remain missionary countries. But the idea of democracy underpinned by the charter of human rights has replaced Christianity.

It can therefore be reasonably supposed that the growing global hegemony of the capitalist system and the appearance of democratic political regimes in the Western countries of its birth had an impact on the reproduction of kinship relations in the societies subjected to their domination or their influence.[1]

The research perspectives are enormous. Development of this area requires associating practically all of the social sciences: history past and present, economics, sociology, anthropology, demographics, linguistics. Anthropology cannot go it alone. Nevertheless, anthropologists do have two advantages. They strive to analyze all aspects of a local society and often go back to their site over a period of ten or twenty years, thus witnessing minor or major changes and resistances. They also have access to data built up over more than a century on the different types or varieties of kinship systems found in the world. Unfortunately, very few anthropologists have worked or are working in urban environments. Yet 75 per cent of sub-Saharan Africa's people live in towns today. Urban ethnic strife, unemployment, poverty, political and/or tribal clientelism all create a new context for those who, in order to survive in the city, need to call on village or ethnic solidarities or, on the contrary, try to escape the obligations to share with those of their village, clan etc., who daily turn up in town. Here sociology is called for.

But anthropologists and sociologists, demographers or geographers will still not be equal to the task. Historians and linguists are also needed, as well as

---

1   See J. Friedman (ed.), *World System History: The Social Science of Long-Term Change* (London, Routledge, 2000).

all of those, first among which the indigenous populations, who possess the memory of the past and their traditions.

Based on present knowledge, what can be said about the important changes underway in the major regions of the world?

BACK TO OCEANIA

Let us shift to the other side of the world, to Oceania, and more particularly to New Guinea, with which we are better acquainted. We will take the case of the Telefolmin, about whom we have data going back to 1940, nearly twenty years before the Europeans arrived and established a patrol post, at the end of the 1950s and in the 1960s. We owe many rich and precise observations to several anthropologists, among whom Ruth and Barry Craig[2] in the 1960s, and Dan Jorgensen[3] starting in the 1980s.

In the mid twentieth century, the Telefolmin lived in highly endogamous villages perched on the mountainside at the headwaters of the Sepik river. Their kinship system was cognatic and therefore without lineages or clans. Marriage was carried out by direct 'sister' exchange, but it was forbidden to repeat the same alliance for at least two generations. The alliance principle was the exchange of a person for a person and was based on the idea that all women were equivalent. 'Sister' exchange was always accompanied by reciprocal gifts of goods between the kindreds involved: the bridegroom's family gave the young woman's people shells obtained through trade with southern tribes; the bride's family in turn gave a certain amount of pork. This gift of meat was meant to forestall any later demands on the woman's children. The meat was consumed and the shells stored away for future marriages and funerals.

When the Australian government took over administration of the tribes and established a patrol post, things began to change in the area of kinship, and especially marriage. The government began by punishing all acts of violence committed on a woman when her family forced her to marry a man she did not want. Then the government refused to grant 'sister' exchange the status of 'customary law'. The first Western intervention was thus political and adminis-trative. The second was economic. A few years later, Western multinationals began digging huge open-pit mines (for gold and other precious metals) at Ok

---

2   R. Craig, 'Marriage among the Telefolmin', in R. M. Glasse and M. Meggitt (eds.), *Pigs, Pearl-shells and Women* (Englewood Cliffs, Prentice Hall, 1969), pp. 186–7.

3   D. Jorgensen, 'Money and Marriage in Telefolmin', in R. A. Marksbury (ed.), *The Business of Marriage: Transformations in Oceanic Matrimony* (Pittsburgh, University of Pittsburgh Press, 1995), pp. 57–82, and 'Big Men, Great Men and Women: Alternative Logics of Gender Difference', in M. Godelier and M. Strathern (eds.), *Big Men and Great Men: Personifications of Power in Melanesia* (Cambridge, Cambridge University Press, 1991), pp. 256–71.

Tedi, a few days' walk from the Telefolmin. Young men were hired en masse by the mines, received relatively high salaries for New Guinea, and experienced life on housing projects with supermarkets.

Little by little, sister exchange disappeared and the exchange of goods that accompanied marriage turned into a 'brideprice', a payment made by the groom's family to that of the bride. The return payments disappeared. After an intermediary stage, where the young men still converted their money into shells or traditional goods, all of the prestations were made in money, and the brideprice soared. From 150 kina around 1970, it rose to 6,000 kina in 1983 and finally to between 10 and 12,000 kina today, which is one or several years of salary for a mine worker. Marriage has become a purely 'family' affair. This is something entirely new in so far as marriages now no longer connect families as they used to do with the practice of sister exchange. The brideprice ceiling is no longer set by the number of pigs or shells available to the families but by the amount of 'cash' they can get together. This means there are no set limits. We are witnessing the 'monetarization' of social relations. Today among the Telefolmin, as in many other societies, wealth circulates in the form of money, and this is procured by producing and selling commodities or labour. In this way a mechanism came into being that made the reproduction of non-economic, non-commercial social relations – marriage alliances for instance – dependent on individuals' participation in the market economy. And thus non-economic social relations were monetarized.

The sphere of the production and circulation of commodities, which in New Guinea is always linked to the financial and commercial capitalism of foreign countries – Australia, the United States, Japan, Great Britain, but also France – is constantly expanding, not only under the impact of the extension of markets but also because of the monetarization of non-economic and non-market relations. At the same time, another factor, which also arose in the West, has slowed this evolution. American fundamentalist Protestant Churches have appeared among the Telefolmin, and have made a large number of converts, primarily women. The slogans of these Churches are *Behainin Jisis* (Follow Jesus) and *Makin bisnis* (Do business). They frown on the considerable expense involved in marriage and especially the inflation of brideprices.[4] They now discourage marriage with brideprice and impose Christian marriage between a man and a woman who have chosen each other freely and have united before

---

4   In 1989, the Catholic Bishops of Papua New Guinea held a conference to address the problem of brideprice and inflation of dowries. See *Braid Praise* (Umben Publication, Melanesian Institute, 1989), vol. 5, no. 3. We also recommend reading Colin Filer, 'What Is This Thing Called Bride Price?', *Mankind*, vol. 15 (1985), pp. 163–83; R. Wagner, 'A Theology of Bride Price', in E. Mantovani (ed.), *Marriage in Melanesia: An Anthropological Perspective* (Goroka, The Melanesian Institute, 1992, 'Point Series', no. 11), pp. 153–72.

God to form a couple which, following the birth of its children, will form a Western-style nuclear family.

The old Western model of the monogamous Christian family without the right to divorce has all but disappeared in the West, but it is taking root at the other side of the world due to a combination of several factors: the appearance of a post-colonial state whose laws are modelled on those of Western states; the development of an industrial and commercial economy entirely independent of local populations (but which integrates them by means of the market); small local societies ill equipped to resist the combined pressures of the representatives of the state and of the Christian churches of all denominations that have come to stamp out the various forms of idolatry and satanic practices, etc. The weapons of conversion are no longer the direct violence and auto-da-fés perpetrated by the Spanish and the Portuguese between the sixteenth and eighteenth centuries in that part of the Americas conquered and divided up between two European Catholic countries. Conversions are now obtained through the material support given the populations by missionaries, who build schools, bush hospitals and air strips, and who perform the tasks that the 'independent' states artificially created at the end of the colonial period do not, either because they do not have the means or because they use their resources for other purposes (enrichment of the so-called 'evolved' elites, etc.).

If we now turn to Polynesia, and to Tonga and Samoa in particular, two societies where the old hierarchies of local kinship and co-residence groups, the *kainga*, still exist and reproduce themselves under the mantel of a European-style parliamentary regime; alliances continue to be contracted according to the old principles; and marriages occasion huge 'displays' of wealth followed by reciprocal gifts and counter-gifts of old or modern mats, but also of many industrial goods made in the USA or Europe (cars, home appliances, electronics, etc.). Of course, all of these populations are Christian, and usually Protestant. They have their national Churches, and their bishops and pastors hold an important rank in the society, but alongside the heads of the principal *kainga*. Here, too, the new Christian family is monogamous, but owing to the persistence of the old hierarchies, there is less freedom to choose one's spouse than in New Guinea.

CHINA

In China, the communist regime had outlawed the selling of children, eliminating the dowry to be paid to the bride's family, the keeping of concubines, etc. Following Mao's death and the new era inaugurated by Deng, many things have changed, and some of the changes give the impression of a return to the past. The major change was the 'One family, one child' policy. Confronted with a population explosion and slower economic growth, China adopted a radical demographic policy several decades ago. In theory, families are allowed no more than one child, with the exception of non-Han ethnic minorities, who are allowed three, together with an economic and social package designed to bring them up to the Chinese 'level of civilization'. This has created numerous problems for millions of families who continued to venerate their ancestors and therefore absolutely to need a son to perform the rites. Hence, of course, the multiplication of female infanticides. In addition, certain women who had their first child in a people's clinic were, unbeknown to them, permanently sterilized. Nevertheless, many families decided not to declare the birth of a girl, and these children remain without a social identity. Today in China there is a growing interregional traffic of women. Women are being bought and sold. One of the reasons for this is that hundreds of thousands of women have left the countryside because they no longer wanted to live there, and the men who stayed behind are looking for wives to have a family. Dowries have reappeared in two forms: the brideprice the future husband brings to the woman's family and the woman herself, and the dowry provided the bride by her family. This second form is very important for a woman, because it signals to everyone that she was not purchased.[5]

Not so long ago, a man's duty to put together the money for a brideprice was expressed by the formula of the so-called 'sixteen feet': the man needed to have the means to buy the bed (four feet), the table (four feet), chairs, etc. By the end of the 1990s the sum needed already amounted to several thousands of yuan, in other words the equivalent of more than a year's earnings. Today the amounts required are even greater: the sum has grown with the booming development of capitalism and China's growing integration in the world market. But this integration has equally contributed to revitalizing a far-from-dead past, which has given rise to new practices. We must bear in mind that in 2003, 42 per cent of European and American foreign investments were made in China. The global trend in favour of the monetarization of non-market social relations – with the creation of new social inequalities based on private ownership of wealth and profits from capital – is growing relentlessly and impacts on relations between men and women and between the populations of the soaring cities and those of the countryside which is gradually being emptied of many of its young people.

---

5   Of course these facts do not appear in the official Chinese publications such as *New Trends in Chinese Marriage and the Family* (Beijing, China International Book Trading Company, 1987). Nevertheless, the book gives a clear picture of the new marriage laws, the right to divorce, parents' responsibility toward their children after divorce, etc. For a very subtle analysis of the consequences of these laws see the excellent book by J-L. Domenach and H. Chang-Ming, *Le Mariage en Chine* (Paris, Presses de la Fondation Nationale des Sciences Politiques, 1987).

INDIA

We have already discussed the case of India at length.[6] Traditionally marriages in India can be contracted only between persons from the same caste; the marriage is arranged by the bride's parents, who look for a husband for their daughter and preferably a man of higher rank. The bride is supposed to be a virgin, and to the gift of a virgin is added a considerable dowry, which, contrary to the practice in China, is given to the parents of the groom (gold, jewellery, cloth, etc.). Here too, the marriage of a son or a daughter is the occasion for the families to display their wealth and their rank.

Although after independence, when India was adopting Western-style political institutions, the practice of providing a dowry was abolished by law, in 1961,[7] and while other measures were taken to allow low-caste people access to schools and universities, the practice did not change substantially, even though the dowry was increasingly paid in rupees and no longer in gold or jewellery. And if the promised dowry is not paid, or is paid only in part, the woman is often subjected to reprisals, to ill treatment that can even cause death. Nevertheless, as many Bollywood films attest, the ideal marriage for millions of young people is the form the Vedic texts call *Gandharva*, in which a woman chooses the man she wants, the one she loves, on condition of giving up her inheritance, her dowry. These two trends – individualization of marriage on the one hand, and submission to caste norms on the other – have been at odds in Indian society for decades, and the recent rise of anti-Muslim and in part anti-Western Hindu fundamentalism tends to reinforce the conservative tendencies within the field of kinship and the family, sexuality and gender relations.

THE MUSLIM WORLD

A few words on Muslim countries. Here, as well, two opposite trends weigh on the development of kinship and family relations.

In some countries, such as Turkey after Atatürk's accession to power in 1919 or Tunisia after the Second World War, and later Iraq after the Ba'ath party's seizure of power, polygamy was abolished by law, and women were no longer forced to veil themselves. Divorce is authorized by the Koran, but remained much harder to obtain for women than for men. In other Muslim countries

---

6   See Chapter 4.
7   Bear in mind that the custom of obliging widows to sacrifice themselves on their husband's funeral pyre (*sati*) was abolished in Delhi in 1809 by Metcalfe, and in the rest of India by Bentik in 1829. The practice nevertheless continued in 'orthodox' Hindu communities until the twentieth century.

polygamy continued to be practised but paradoxically by two opposite layers of society: the rich at the top and the poor at the bottom. As in India, people's desire for more freedom to choose their spouse has grown apace and today finds expression in movies and songs. The monogamous family has thus spread to almost all layers of society. But kinship, in these countries, is often linked to the existence of lineages, clans and tribes, which have not disappeared with the globalization of the economy and Western political hegemony. And often these clans, lineages and tribes act at once as a bulwark against the effects of globalization but also as effective instruments to achieve a place in the economic and political power relations that grew up during the colonial period and after independence. In the final years of the twentieth century, after the so-called third-world countries won independence, resistance to Western hegemony and its cultural influence, accused of corrupting minds and leading the masses astray into ungodly practices, grew; and movements strove to bring back old customs, to force women to again don the veil or the burqa, to ban women from school or the medical professions, etc. This was and still is the case in Afghanistan and Pakistan, in particular. Their relationship with the West had the effect of prompting the desire to return to Islam as it was in the beginning, a more imaginary than real Islam, somewhat as in Europe when certain Christian denominations claimed to go back to the true Gospel, to the Christianity of the first centuries.

SUB-SAHARAN AFRICA

In the Islamized countries of Africa, kinship relations have been remodelled on Koranic principles while retaining many aspects of the local kinship systems characteristic of the traditional ethnic or tribal groups. In other first colonized and now independent African countries (Rwanda is exemplary), different Christian Churches have converted large portions of the populations to Catholicism or one of the Protestant denominations. Conversion led to the disappearance of the direct exchange of women in those places where it existed (among the Tiv of Nigeria), of polygamy, and to the spread of the monogamic family, the partial replacement of old marriage and funeral ceremonies by church marriages, baptisms and funerals,[8] but also to the inflation of dowries. In all events, a two-pronged movement is at work in kinship relations; either they act as a bulwark against the economic and social changes induced by economic globalization and direct or indirect Western hegemony,

---

8   P. Bohannan, 'The Impact of Money on an African Subsistence Economy', *Journal of Economic History*, vol. 19, no.4 (1959), pp. 491–503. C. Murray, 'High Bridewealth, Migrant Labour and the Position of Women in Lesotho', *Journal of African Law*, vol. 26, no. 1 (1977), pp. 79–96.

or they act as a springboard to a place in the new society emerging from these changes. But there is another trend, too, which goes in the opposite direction: the growing individualization of people's choices, which refuses the duties of sharing, hospitality and mutual aid traditionally imposed by kin ties, whether these be of consanguinity or alliance, or by the fact of belonging to the same village, the same tribe or the same ethnic group. Yet everywhere one observes the inflation of dowries; everywhere one sees people who have 'succeeded' in the administration or in trade lodging dozens of relatives and friends who have arrived from their home village for a visit and who stay on and on. 'Individualism', in these circumstances, cannot claim or hope to accompany individual success all the way.

EUROPE AND EURO-AMERICA

We will limit ourselves to information on France,[9] some of which has already been presented in this volume. Some of this information is, in fact, tied to changes that appeared in other Western European countries, both Catholic and Protestant, and in North America.[10] The mutations affected both the axis of descent and that of alliance.

Concerning descent, which in cognatic kinship systems includes filiation, the major effect in France was the abolition in 1970 of the notion of 'paternal authority' and its replacement by 'parental authority' shared equally by a child's father and mother, and which continues to exist even if the father and mother divorce and remarry. It was also in 1970 that contraceptives went on sale without a prescription, which enabled women to disconnect sexuality and reproduction, and to bear children when and with whom they pleased.

In 1975 divorce by mutual consent was brought in, and in the same year abortion was legalized under certain conditions. Various laws also accelerated

---

9 For Europe: R. Ganghofer (ed.), *Le Droit de la famille en Europe. Son évolution depuis l'Antiquité jusqu'à nos jours* (Strasbourg, Presses Universitaires de Strasbourg, 1992) and V. Feschet, 'La transmission du nom de famille en Europe occidentale. Fin XXᵉ–début du XXIᵉ siècle', *L'Homme*, no. 169 (2004), pp. 61–88. The author shows that recent development accentuates the tendency gradually to do away with 'all discrimination between the man and the woman' in the choice of who transmits the name to the children, to no longer give the parents the last word in this area, and to bolster filiation with respect to alliance, which goes in the direction of the profound changes in Western societies over the last century: greater gender equality, stronger value attached to the child and childhood, almost complete freedom in choice of a spouse. For Euro-America: R. Rapp, 'Family and Class in Contemporary America', in B. Thore and M. Yalom (eds.), *Rethinking the Family: Some Feminist Questions* (Boston, Northeastern University Press, 1992), pp. 49–70. Read in the same work: J. Collier, M. Rosaldo and S. Yanagisako, 'Is there a family? New anthropological views', pp. 31–48.

10 Let us remember the now-classic book by Michael Young and Peter Willmott, first published in 1957 and revised in 1962 before being reissued nearly twenty times: *Family and Kinship in East London* (London, Routledge and Kegan Paul, 1957; Pelican Books, 1962).

the 'liberalization of mores' and classic representations. The notion of conjugal became dissociated from the notion of parental, and the couple was no longer synonymous with the family (which comes into existence only with the birth of a child). In addition, a growing proportion of couples no longer get married, or else marry later (often after several years of shared life and the birth of one or more children). The average age of marriage is thirty for a man and twenty-seven for a woman. The age at which a woman has her first child, which was twenty-six on average in 1980, was twenty-nine in the year 2000. Thirty per cent of couples are not married, and forty per cent of children born every year in France are born out of wedlock. Eighty-two per cent of these children are recognized by their father either immediately or within a year of their birth. (Bear in mind that unmarried couples in France have the right to the same family benefits as married couples.)

In France, then, *marriage is no longer the act that founds the couple*, which also means that the old Christian prohibition of 'no sex before marriage, no sex outside of marriage' no longer holds – even for Christians. Young people are initiated into sex at an ever-earlier age. Another change: the growing number of divorces and separations. One marriage in three ends in divorce or separation. Hence the multiplication of reconstituted and one-parent families, with, in most cases, a woman heading the single-parent family. This has been made materially possible by the massive entry of women into the labour market after the Second World War. As women begin earning a salary they acquire a decisive economic weight in the family, since their financial contribution becomes indispensible as needs expand. But in times of economic downturn or crisis, women are the first to be affected, and life becomes more difficult for single-parent families. In 2003 more than a million children in France were living in poverty,[11] and these were often children of divorced or single parents.

If not everyone gets married in France, we are not looking at the end of marriage either.[12] More simply, we no longer expect marriage to create life-long ties.

How do these facts sum up? What trends do they express? First of all that the union of the sexes and the decision to give it an official, even enduring, status have become more and more an individual, private affair, a relation to the other in which emotions outweigh social pressure (whether from the family or the social environment) and outweigh the material interests people have to consider in making their life choice. That was already true in the nineteenth century for the working classes, who had few valuables to transmit. And it was often among the working classes that unmarried couples with children were to be found.

---

11   The population of France in 2003 was 59.8 million.
12   Cf. F. Battagliola, *La Fin du mariage?* (Paris, Syros/Alternatives, 1988).

WHAT HAS CHANGED IN THE WEST

Three things, basically, have changed in the West when it comes to kinship. People's relationship with sexuality, gender roles in society (and therefore gender relations), and the place of children.

The discovery of sexuality occurs in early adolescence, and people are sexually active before living as a couple (as well as outside the couple when the couple exists). In the couple and even in the family, the trend is toward more gender equality, toward a less dissymmetrical distribution of day-to-day responsibilities. This equality and sharing are more easily achieved or imposed when the woman works, thus contributing her share to the material upkeep of the family. Outside the private sphere, in the firm or the world of politics, gender inequality has certainly decreased, but to date only slightly. The responsibilities accessible to men and to women are not the same, the pay for equal work is not equal, and in times of crisis, women are, after immigrants, the first to be let go when the company downsizes, or, as they say in France, 'takes off the fat'.

Continuing an already centuries-long trend, the child occupies a growing place in Western society and in the eyes of the law. Society has reacted in a fundamental way to the fact that, since divorce became lawful and relatively easy when requested by mutual consent, families are decomposed and recomposed in accordance with choices made by adults. Thus the changing relations between parents and children are now governed by law so as to better protect the child. This is reflected in the substitution of parental authority (which belongs to the father and the mother and to them alone) for paternal authority (formerly reserved for the man, who had total authority in the family and over the children). Today, whatever their life choices, the parents have the moral and legal obligation to fulfil their parental responsibilities to their children until they reach adulthood in four areas essential to their development and set out by law: health, education, security, and an often-neglected area, morality.[13] The parents' authority is thus both an individual moral responsibility but also a 'function of public order',[14] a social obligation incumbent on every citizen.

13 Articles 371–372 of the *Code civil*.
14 Article 376 of the *Code civil*. The law on parental authority (passed 4 June 1970) was reformed twice, once in 1987 and again in 1993, so that all children would be treated equally, whatever their parents' legal status, and in view of ensuring the continuity of parental authority in the event of the couple's breakup. Cf. I. Théry (ed.), *Couple, filiation et parenté aujourd'hui, le droit face aux mutations de la famille et de la vie privée* (Paris, Odile Jacob/la Documentation française, 1998), pp. 189–207.

RECONSTITUTED FAMILIES

The family has thus been compelled to evolve in order to cope with the problems facing parents and children and stemming from the multiplication of divorces and the logically ensuing reconstituted or single-parent families.

The problem was first that facing the adults associated in the raising of children born of other unions than their own and who arrived with the new companion. It was also the problem posed to the children born of these various unions when they shuttled between homes. Many children today fear that their parents will divorce and that they will be abandoned by one or the other, or cut off from one or the other. Many children suffer from the fact that their parents are divorced and that they find themselves with one parent in a new family where they are obliged to find new bearings, having lost the old ones. But it is also a problem for the adults, who will live for years with children who are not their own and for whom they must take day-to-day responsibility even though they did not know them and have no legal authority over them, which authority continues to belong 'to the child's mother and father and to them alone'.

In reality, for adults and children alike, brought together by a third party and finding themselves obliged to live together on a daily basis, the reconstituted family becomes a world where, to the classic Western family ties, which combine biological and social kin ties – a father and his children by the same mother, a mother and her children by the same father, brothers and sisters by the same father and mother – are added 'quasi-kinship relations' with the mother's or the father's new companion and his or her children from a former couple. These are 'step-relatives' – step-father, step-mother, step-children, step-sister, and so on. They are the father's or the mother's new 'affines' but have no paternal or maternal blood ties with the children of the former couple. The tie established between these adults and their partner's children is thus a purely social kin tie, but society expects them to behave toward children who are not their own like 'real' parents. And this situation implies that the children in turn behave toward these adults who care for them on a daily basis as though they were their 'real' children, as it were.

A new form of parenthood is thus growing up and developing in Western societies, in which the union of persons of opposite sex depends entirely on their individual decision, in which the family no longer automatically coincides with the couple, and where parents' authority over their children does not disappear – and is in no way diminished – when the parents separate. This new parenthood in reconstituted families obviously has nothing to do with the adoption of children by adults who are not their biological parents.[15] It is a parenthood based on a principle familiar to anthropologists and which is almost universal: the parents are not only or even necessarily those who made the children by uniting sexually. They are also, and sometimes primarily, the adults who feed them, bring them up and ensure their future.

The parenthood exercised by quasi-kin is developing in France on this basis, with one restriction, that it has no foundation in law. In effect, it has turned out to be very difficult to find a legal status for the 'quasi-parent', considering the heterogeneity of the situations that give rise to reconstituted families and the diversity of the possible ties between children and step-parents, which vary with the children's age, the longevity of the reconstituted family, and so on. The lawmaker's role has been merely to define the relations between step-parents and step-children by multiplying the legal protections surrounding the child. Still, the new social parents are increasingly driven to reproduce the ideal model of the traditional family and to adopt its obligations and prohibitions. One striking example is the moral and social obligation incumbent on a 'step-parent' to abstain from sexual relations with the children of his or her new companion even though they are biologically unrelated. These forbidden sexual relations are assimilated to interfamily incest and condemned by public opinion. The prohibition has no basis in law, especially in France, where incest is not enshrined in law, but the law can nevertheless intervene if there is proof of violence, rape or abuse of authority by the adult on a minor.[16] Developments in the legislation on marriage, divorce, decomposition and recomposition of families should impose legal action sooner or later, for which France could take inspiration from the Children Act passed by Great Britain in 1989, which gives the 'step-father' the power to discharge those acts relative to the child's supervision and education.

Thus new forms of kinship and family relations are taking shape before our eyes, which are actually only new forms of the social character of kinship, that is to say, parental social behaviours disjoined from the biological ties that bind children to a man and a woman who are their genitors. For centuries the West – with its cognatic kinship system that links a child equally to its parents

---

15   Simple adoption of the partner's child is authorized by law. It does not affect filiation and requires the consent of the adopted child if he or she is over thirteen years of age. The consent of the partner is sufficient if the other parent has lost his or her rights or is deceased. Full adoption of the partner's child, long favoured by lawmakers, is now forbidden except in special cases so as not to sever the child's genealogical and family ties with his or her grandparents. See Théry, *Couple, filiation et parenté aujourd'hui*, pp. 212–23, and A. Fine (ed.), *Adoptions: ethnologie des parentés choisies* (Paris, Editions de la Maison des Sciences de l'Homme, 1998).

16   Articles 222/8, 222/24, 222/28 of the *Code pénal*. The question of the social parent's status arises also and more importantly for homosexual families, posing the whole question of co-parenthood.

and grandparents by biological ties of consanguinity or social ties of affinity, with its absence of kin groups, lineages and clans connecting a large number of individuals by real or classificatory kin ties, and finally with its extreme social mobility that results in distinct social destinies for the members of a same family (brothers and sisters) or for related individuals (cousins, nephews, nieces) – has privileged biological and genealogical ties between individuals in defining family relations and justifying the duties and rights incumbent on its members. Social kinship, independent of biological ties, has therefore occupied only a minor place over the centuries, adoption, for example, having been forbidden by the Catholic Church before being reinstated in the nineteenth century in a certain number of countries. That is why the present obsession with the genetic basis of parenthood will have to disappear if we are to integrate and regulate the new forms of parenthood and family. For these, we stress, are neither bliss nor a nightmare. They are simply the offspring of our societies – and our times.

In reality people do at the same time what their society allows them to do and what it compels them to do. Contemporary Western society, after its various revolutions, has been built on the principle of the equality of everyone before the law, whatever their sex, race or religion, on condition, however, of being a citizen of the state that makes and applies the law. Equality before the law signifies the abstract sharing of popular sovereignty, that is to say equal rights in the political sphere and (in theory) in the areas of education, health, culture and security. But Western societies are also built on the idea of unequal access to the ownership and use of productive capital and therefore to the sharing of profits and wealth, as well as on commercial and individual competition.

It is in this global framework that the notion of kinship has evolved and will continue to do so. We readily speak of 'individualism' as a source of disrespect for values, for the past and for the rejection of solidarity, but we forget that our society constantly encourages people to make their own choices and to look after their own interests. This same kind of society, by authorizing divorce by mutual consent, has given individuals the legal and social possibility of separating after having lived and produced children together. And this separation no longer needs to be justified by the misconduct of one of the partners – unfaithfulness, domestic violence, drunkenness, child abuse, etc. The law now allows people to cite the real evolution of the couple's relationship and their mutual feelings to justify separation. The consequences are easy to understand: the couple no longer coincides with the family, the conjugal domain is dissociated from the parental sphere, and parenthood therefore increasingly takes on a social content independent of biological or genetic ties.

In another fashion, by providing those who make children with state aid regardless of their marital status, Western societies, or at least those of 'Old

Europe', have opened new possibilities for choice in matters of sexual union. Indeed, the law has moved with the times, and tends to dissociate filiation from the form of union chosen by the adults, and from their durable or temporary, or even ephemeral character when the union is sought not in order to form a couple but to satisfy someone's desire for a child. For the massive arrival of women in the labour market and their education today enables those who so desire and who have a steady job to satisfy their desire to have a child, to found a family without forming a couple, since the salary and family allowance, in other words the material assistance provided by society via the state, ensures up to a certain point the material security of the one-parent family thus created.

THE FAMILY AND THE NEW ASSISTED-REPRODUCTION TECHNOLOGIES

Another feature of the recent development of Western societies are the new technological and biomedical discoveries in the area of reproduction; these have given new hope to couples who want children but cannot have them. There are several situations, which have sparked numerous debates on motherhood, fatherhood, in short on what makes someone the parent of a child. The new reproductive technologies[17] for example allow a woman who cannot have children to get pregnant by her husband if she receives an ovocyte from another woman, which has been fertilized by her husband's sperm. The child she bears will therefore have no genetic tie with her and her ascendants, but will be genetically linked to her husband and his ascendants as well as to the woman who donated the egg. Here we see that the classic process of motherhood, whereby a woman's body undergoes fertilization, pregnancy and birth, can be broken down into separate moments accomplished in two separate bodies: that of the woman who gives one of her eggs and that of the wife, who receives the egg fertilized by her husband and goes through all of the stages and emotions of pregnancy and birth and then cares for the newborn infant.

In short, we see the partial dissociation of parenthood from sexual relations. The husband's sperm fertilizes another woman who is not his wife without his having had sexual relations with the woman. The wife is pregnant by her husband without having had sexual relations for this. But she becomes a mother, and that is what the couple desired. To be sure, if the woman knows anything about biology, she knows that she does not transmit her and her ancestors' genes to the child. But she is the mother of the child, for she felt it growing

---

17 R. Rapp, 'Moral Pioneers. Women, Men and Fetuses on a Frontier of Reproductive Technology', in M. Di Leonardo (ed.), *Gender at the Crossroads of Knowledge: Feminist Anthropology in the Postmodern Era* (Berkeley, University of California Press, 1991), pp. 383–95. And especially R. Rapp, *Testing Women, Testing the Fetus: The Social Impact of Amniocentesis in America* (New York, Routledge, 2000).

inside her, she gave birth to the child with all the pain and risks that involves, and she brings it up. She may therefore be less of a 'biological mother' than women who are pregnant by their partner, but she made more of a 'biological' contribution than an adoptive mother to the birth of her child.[18] And like other mothers, she will continue to be a mother because she will bring up the child.

The kin tie between this woman and the child is finally in part biological and in part social (she recognized it as hers, brings it up, gives it a name, etc.). Later, with the passage of time, she may even forget that this child is not completely hers and project onto it her own family story, the real or imaginary memory of her own ancestors.

The situation is not the same for a couple where it is the man who is sterile and accepts, in order to satisfy his and/or his partner's desire for a child, that she be inseminated with the sperm of an anonymous donor. This man will have none of the emotions or bodily sensations connected with the child before its birth, unlike his partner when she becomes pregnant. And he will have a problem to overcome, in so far as, in our societies, virility has often been associated with the capacity to father children. In accepting that another than he inseminates his partner, a man will have to accept his masculinity deprived of the attribute of virility. But as in the previous case, he will feel like a father when he recognizes this child as socially his and begins to bring it up, to protect it and to love it. His fatherhood will be only (but fully) social.

Let us now turn to the two figures which, in these two examples, remained in the wings: the sperm donor and the egg donor. What kin ties do they have with the child they helped to make? A purely biological one, which means that they disappear as persons endowed with a past, a personality, ancestors, etc. This purely biological tie does not confer kinship. Even in matrilineal societies, where it is not thought that the husband's sperm engenders the child, this man is expected to conduct himself with respect to the child differently from those who are not married to the child's mother. It is this *social* behaviour, characterized by responsibility, protection, affection, material assistance, that designate a man as the child's 'father', even if later the child will leave the house to live with his maternal uncle, who will hand on to him his titles and his goods, and who exerts over the child, from birth, another form of authority than that exercised by the father. To be sure, in our society, the anonymous sperm and egg donors justifiably think they have contributed to giving a child life but also the joy of parenthood to other adults. But if there is nothing that subsequently links them with the child, if nothing else but this gift ties them to the child and the child to

---

18   M. Strathern, *Reproducing the Future: Anthropology, Kinship and the New Reproductive Technologies* (New York, Routledge, 1992), Chapter 9. See also A. Clarke and E. Parson (eds.), *Culture, Kinship and Genes* (London, Macmillan, 1997).

them, the initial gift of a biological component of the child's body will not be enough to make them parents, the child's parents.[19]

This is, as we know, a hotly debated subject: should the woman who has had a baby conceived by embryo transfer tell her child that she is not 'fully' its mother? Should the man who accepted that his partner be inseminated by sperm from an anonymous donor tell his child that he is not its biological father? Should children be told the 'genetic truth' about themselves? And should a further step be taken and should the identity of the anonymous donor(s) be revealed at the time the child is told that its father is not its (biological) father or that his mother is not completely its (biological) mother?

We do not have a definitive answer to these questions, but we do have doubts about the importance and the interest for the child of making such a revelation.[20] For what is most important is for the child to construct its identity, its personality with respect to the adults who brought it up, protected it and loved it, who acted like parents should act in a given society and who helped the child find a place in this society. A drop of sperm is not a man. An ovocyte is not a woman. A man and a woman are concrete, unique individuals, persons who have a life story and ancestors, individuals who interact with others: this cannot be given, cannot be transmitted when a man or a woman give or sell a bit of themselves, of their genetic substance. A man who donates or sells[21] his sperm is not a father. He would be a father only if he subsequently claimed the child born of his sperm as his own and took responsibility for and care of it. But the moral contract between a donor of sperm and the couple who receive it is that the donor will not claim the child, will have no rights to it. This is even truer of the man who sells his sperm. His contract prohibits any claim to the child born of his seed.

ARE SURROGATE MOTHERS REAL MOTHERS?

This is precisely the rule in certain Western countries, where a woman can legally place her body at the service of a couple wanting a child and become this child's surrogate mother. Let us recall what these terms mean. Modern technologies now make it possible to separate the conception of a child from its gestation. This made it possible for couples who wanted a child, but where the woman could not carry through a normal pregnancy, to choose this means in

---

19   See J. Edwards, S. Franklin, E. Hirsch, F. Price and M. Strathern, *Technologies of Procreation: Kinship in the Age of Assisted Conception* (Manchester, Manchester University Press, 1992), and especially Chapter 4 by Sarah Franklin, 'The Parliamentary Debates on the Human Fertilization and Embryology Act', pp. 96–131.

20   See the discussion in G. Delaisi and P. Verdier (eds.), *Enfant de personne* (Paris, Odile Jacob, 1994).

21   As is the case in Denmark, a major exporter of sperm on the world market.

preference to adoption. In the case of adoption, the child is an outsider who becomes a relative. Alternatively, when a couple uses a surrogate mother, the child is 'genetically' theirs, because an egg from the wife is fertilized by her husband or partner and, after a hormonal preparation, is implanted in the surrogate mother's womb. When the child is born, it will be socially (and genetically) entirely theirs. In the meantime it will develop in the body of another woman, who will bear the problems of pregnancy and the risks of birth and then hand over the child to its father and mother.

This is a new situation. Whereas in the previous example the man's wife or partner received another woman's egg fertilized by her husband's or partner's sperm and then went through two of the three phases of normal maternity, namely: pregnancy and birth, but not the first, conception, and then delivered a child that was not genetically linked to her, in the case of surrogacy, the child has no genetic link with the woman who carries and delivers it, since they do not share any genes.

Let us take a closer look at this new form of motherhood. It is growing in certain American states and, for example, has given rise to the creation of agencies[22] advertising the services of candidates for surrogacy, substitute mothers, and which deal professionally with the supply and demand resulting in a commercial transaction (with a few particularities[23]). The agencies deliberately keep the fee for surrogate motherhood low[24] so as to avoid assimilating the transaction to the purchase of a body by a couple wanting a child, an act entailing the prostitution not of sex but of motherhood.[25]

What motivates a woman to offer herself as a surrogate mother and to confront the considerable risks of biological complications entailed in the transfer and implantation of fertilized ovocytes? If the surveys carried out by H. Ragone are to be believed, these women cite three motives by decreasing order of importance. The first is helping couples unable to have children. The gift of life is the gift par excellence, the perfect altruistic act. The second is to earn money while staying home. The third concerns only some women, who say they 'love being pregnant'.

What is the relationship between the surrogate mother and the mother of the

---

22   There are several American sites on the Internet run by agencies of this kind, on which candidates for 'surrogacy' communicate with each other and congratulate each other when, having signed a contract with a couple, one of them becomes pregnant – and then when she delivers the child she was carrying.

23   See Hal. B. Levine, 'Gestational Surrogacy: Nature and Culture in Kinship', *Ethnology*, vol. 42, no. 3 (2003), pp. 173–86.

24   Limited to 40,000 dollars. Cf. H. Ragone, *Surrogate Motherhood: Conception in the Heart* (New York, Boulder Publishing House, 1994).

25   H. Ragone, 'Chasing the Blood Tie: Surrogate Mothers, Adoptive Mothers and Fathers', *American Ethnologist*, vol. 23 (1996), pp. 352–65.

child? These relations, it should not be forgotten, are based on a contract. The child's parents must be assured that no claim, no right on the child will be demanded by the surrogate mother after the birth. The woman who lends her body and feels the child growing inside her, who delivers it successfully, must prepare herself psychologically for the fact that the child is not hers and never will be. 'When the baby has its first cry, our job is over.' Of course while this woman is 'doing her job', the parents are anxious to see that nothing happens to her, that she does not lack anything. Friendship can even develop between the couple and the surrogate mother, though always mingled with reciprocal interests.

We recognize in this transformation of motherhood all of the features of Western civilization: a contract monetarizing a relationship between persons for services rendered, with an emphasis on the 'gift of life' which transforms a relationship of reciprocal interests into an act of altruism imbued with all of the moral, and even religious, virtues – for Christianity is always lurking in the wings of ethics in the West, and particularly in the United States.

Another face of this transformation of motherhood has as yet been little explored, but should be one day. That is the relationship between the surrogate mother's own children and herself when she is pregnant with a child that is not their brother or sister, and their own relationship with this child when it is born and their mother breastfeeds it and cares for it. A few surveys show that these children often have difficulty understanding that the child delivered by their mother is not their brother or their sister. In one case, the children of a surrogate mother who had given birth to twins asked her if they could not keep one, buy it from the woman who was coming to take them. In a few cases, the children express the fear that they, too, might one day be given to another woman like the baby their mother carried and delivered.

What conclusions can be drawn from these different cases? In the case of surrogate mothers, things are clear. These women are not mothers. They do not want to be nor should they be. And if they were to try to keep the baby they delivered, they would be guilty of breach of contract and kidnapping. She does not become the child's mother, even though she probably felt all of the emotions and feelings a mother traditionally feels when she is pregnant and when she delivers. The loan of her body and the gift of the attentions and precautions she lavishes on the child she carries can be compared with the gift of blood or an organ. Giving blood to someone does not make this person a blood relative. But a personal tie is created by the gift, which, like all gifts, makes the recipient indebted; the couple who receives the baby incurs a debt. In the latter case, the debt is twofold. Socially it is defined by the terms of the contract between the parties to the transaction, and this social debt is cancelled when the agreed responsibilities have been fulfilled and the child has been handed over to its parents. But what a legal act can never establish is the amount of the *moral* debt the parents feel with respect to the woman who enabled them to have a child. Likewise, nothing can measure the moral satisfaction felt by the surrogate mother at the fact of having helped a couple to have a child.[26]

Here we are halfway through the latest transformations to the family and kinship in Euro-American societies. All share the fact of enabling heterosexual couples to satisfy their desire for a child with the help of the possibilities delivered by the new reproductive technologies. All end in the same result: a heterosexual couple that was unable to have children has a child they will now raise with all the more love and care as it was long and painfully desired. Nothing new here. What is new is that the child has mobilized a third party in order to be born: the sperm donor who stands in for the infertile husband, or the egg donor who stands in for the barren wife, or finally the surrogate mother who enables a fertile woman who regularly miscarries to have a child she has conceived with her partner or husband. What is new is that it takes *three bodies instead of two to make a baby* and that the third person who has helped the other two become parents is not herself or himself recognized as a parent of this child, nor should he or she be or desire to be. Here the gift of genetic material, sperm or egg, in sum the gift of gametes, is not enough to make a donor a parent.

In the case of reconstituted families the inverse was true.[27] When he marries a divorced woman with children from a first marriage, a divorced man with children from a previous union acts as a social parent, but without having a legal status because he has no biological tie with his partner's children. The same is true for the woman with regard to her new partner's children, even though she may treat them like her own. Here social kinship and parenthood make their appearance. They are developing, but have no legal status, because they have no biological basis. In the cases analyzed earlier, there is a biological tie between sperm or egg donors and the child, but that does not make them parents, because they do not have the legal right to claim parenthood and they do not act like parents, and therefore will not exercise any form of social parenthood with regard to the child.

REPRODUCTIVE CLONING

There remain three other changes in kinship to analyze that are at work in certain Western European and North American (USA, Canada) societies. The first has not yet been done and is unanimously banned: human reproductive

---

26   See M. Tort, *Le Désir froid: procréation artificielle et crise des repères symboliques* (Paris, La Découverte, 1992).

27   Cf. A. Martial, *S'apparenter, ethnologie des liens de familles recomposées* (Paris, Maison des Sciences de l'Homme, 2003).

cloning, the reproduction of oneself by oneself, the gateway to immortality.[28] The second is the appearance of transsexual kin ties, when a man who had children in one phase of his life can no longer tolerate being in a male body because he feels he is a woman and wants to live and be recognized as a woman. Or, vice versa, a woman who feels she is a man and wants to live and be recognized as a man. After a long course of hormones and surgery (phalloplasty, for instance), the person takes on the bodily appearance that seems to correspond to his or her inner identity. It was in 1953 that Professor Christian Hamburger and his team transformed Georges Jorgensen into Christine Jorgensen, an event that made the headlines and which has been repeated many times since.[29]

In the case of reproductive cloning, the avowed motivation is eventually to give birth to oneself in a world where sexuality has disappeared. Given that the lure of profit or the ambition to be the first will drive certain researchers and laboratories to pursue their research in secret and illegally, it is crucial to make clear that reproductive cloning is the very epitome of the antisocial act. Born as ordinary mortals, persons who aspire to have themselves cloned are basically seeking to avoid dying. Perhaps they imagine that everything they were in life, their experience of others and of the world, will be passed on to a double of themselves who will begin life equipped with all this experience, with this life story that they have not lived. The present state of science obviously does not extend such possibilities, but that is not what should motivate the prohibition of reproductive cloning. Other reasons, of a philosophical and ethical nature, condemn reproductive cloning as an antisocial act whereas the same reasons do not oppose, quite the contrary, therapeutic cloning, which will in the future help save thousands of human lives.

TRANSSEXUAL FAMILIES

The second case, that of transsexual families, is a marginal social phenomenon today and will remain so.[30] No one has yet discovered the genetic and/or social causes behind the intense desire felt by certain individuals to be rid of the body

---

28 Did the three births announced by the Raelians actually take place?

29 C. Hamburger, B. M. Stürup and E. Dahl-Iversen, 'Transvestism, Hormonal, Psychiatric and Surgical Treatment', *Journal of the American Medical Association*, no. 152 (1953), pp. 391–96. For more on these questions, see Colette Chiland, *Le Transsexualisme* (Paris, Presses Universitaires de France, 2003). We would like to thank the author for having provided us with her paper to the 11th International Congress of the European Society For Child And Adolescent Psychiatry (Hamburg, ESCAP, September 1999).

30 Transexuality is known if not accepted in many societies, and it happens that some institutionalize the phenomenon. This is the case among the African Nuba, in Polynesia, in Oman and among the Mohave Indians. See e.g. the article by Unni Wikan on the transsexuals (*xanith*) of Oman, and the many reactions it prompted when it was published: Unni Wikan, 'Man Becomes Woman: Transexualism in Oman as a Key to Gender Roles', *Man*, vol. 12 (1977), pp. 304–19.

they have, to erase their original sex because it does not coincide with what they feel they are inside – to erase the sex one was born with in order to take on and live the gender one is. If it is possible to ease such suffering, why oppose it? Providing the person is aware that this suffering may return, and even more intensely! How many men who have become 'women' and changed their name discover that they can never have children because they would need a uterine or ovarian graft? They were no doubt told, but can one hear what one does not want to hear?

MARRIAGE AND HOMOSEXUAL FAMILIES

The third and final change in kinship and the family is neither virtual nor marginal but very real and has become of major importance. Since it made its entrance on the stage of history it has not ceased to expand: this is the multiplication, in the West, of homosexual families formed by the adoption of children or by insemination with donor sperm, anonymous or not.[31] In France today the problem is posed in the form of demands on the part of certain homosexual groups to 'go beyond the PACS'[32] and obtain legal recognition of their right to found families.[33]

PACS stands for the French 'Pacte Civil de Solidarité', or Civil Solidarity Pact. It was voted into law in France on 15 November 1999. The PACS is a 'contract established between two adults, of opposite or same sex, to organize their life together'. The immediate outcome of the law was to establish legal recognition of homosexual couples desirous of being bound by a contract.[34] But the PACS does not give the parties the right to adopt a child.[35] Nor does it allow a same-sex couple access to medically assisted procreation. In sum, the PACS is

31   Cf. K. Weston, *Families We Choose* (New York, Columbia University Press, 1991); E. Dubreuil, *Des parents de même sexe* (Paris, Odile Jacob, 1998).

32   Cf. D. Borillo and E. Fassin (eds.), *Au-delà du PACS. L'expertise familiale à l'épreuve de l'homosexualité* (Paris, Presses Universitaires de France, 1999).

33   The rate of homosexuality in France is estimated at 1 per cent. But several studies show that 4.1 per cent of men declare having had at least one homosexual relation in their lives, as compared to 2.6 per cent of women. Cf. N. Bajos and A. Spiraa, *Les Comportements sexuels en France* (Paris, La Documentation française, 1993).

34   Cf. M. Gross, *L'Homoparentalité* (Paris, Presses Universitaires de France, 2003), pp. 50–1. This is an indispensable work that summarizes and clearly analyzes the problems posed by the appearance and multiplication of gay and lesbian families. All of the criticisms of homoparenthood are taken into account and the author responds with both subtlety and rigour. We would like to thank Martine Gross, now honorary president of the Association des Parents et Futurs Parents Gays et Lesbiens (APGL), for our fruitful exchanges and for the American, English and Dutch documentation she so generously placed at our disposal.

35   Direct ascendants and descendants, collaterals to the third degree included, and direct affines cannot get PACSed. See V. Feschet, 'Nouveaux Pères et 'dernières épouses'. Les formes de la parenté en France à travers le droit et la famille (1999–2003)', *Terrain*, no. 42 (2004), pp. 33–52.

a step forward for many living together and sharing their worldly goods, among whom are numbers of homosexuals, but it is fundamentally different from marriage and remains completely dissociated from the family.

This new institution was on the whole well received by French society and, of course, by homosexuals. And this reception attests to a deep evolution in attitudes toward homosexuality. By 'getting PACSed', homosexual couples were finally able to come out of the closet where they had been hiding in order to escape homophobic aggressions and repressions. But since the PACS does not allow homosexuals who so desire to found a family, a certain number are asking that the law go even further and that family law and the concept of parental authority be overhauled. This goal was the subject of debate in the homosexual community and in the APGL (Association de Parents et Futurs Parents Gays et Lesbiens) even before the PACS was voted in. Those taking part in the debates included a number of jurists, sociologists, anthropologists and psychoanalysts concerned to listen to and understand these struggles for the legalization of new forms of parenthood and kinship and to measure the consequences both for society and for the theoretical development of their disciplines.[36]

How would Freud and Lacan have reacted if they had been told that sexual difference is on the verge of deserting the family? How could a child raised by same-sex parents overcome his or her Oedipus in the absence of a mother or a father with whom to identify? What will become of the taboo on incest within the family, so useful in turning the child's sexual desire in the 'right' direction, in other words toward persons of the opposite sex? And might not the disappearance of incestuous heterosexual desires leave the way free for homosexual desires? But what do we really know about incestuous homosexual desires and their consequences for the construction of the personality when, with the exception of a few anthropologists, historians and psychoanalysts,[37] homosexuality has been the object of very little serious and long-term research in the West?

And what will become of the theories of Lévi-Strauss and his disciples, for whom kinship is based on the exchange of women by and for men? It had already been discovered that women could exchange men, their brothers, among

---

36   See the transcription of the discussions organized by the APGL between 1997 and 1989 in *Débathèmes* (published by the APGL, Paris). After two No votes in the Assemblée Nationale in 1998, the PACS was passed in the Fall of 1999. It was almost a 'non-event', Irène Théry wrote in an article that sparked some polemics: 'Pacs, sexualité et différence des sexes', *Esprit*, October (1999), pp. 139–81.

37   S. Freud, 'The Psychogenesis of a Case of Homosexuality in a Woman' (1920), 'Some Neurotic Mechanisms in Jealousy, Paranoia and Homosexuality', in J. Strachey (ed.), *The Standard Edition of the Complete Psychological Works of Sigmund Freud: Beyond the Pleasure Principle, Group Psychology and Other Works*, vol. 18 (1920–1922) (London, Hogarth Press, 1953–74). See also F. Pasche, 'Note sur la structure et l'étiologie de l'homosexualité masculine', *Revue française de psychanalyse*, no. 4 (1965), pp. 344–55; J. McDougall, 'Introduction à un colloque sur l'homosexualité féminine', *Revue française de psychanalyse*, no. 4 (1965), pp. 356–66.

themselves. And now we have men proposing to create kin ties by exchanging men among themselves. And what will happen if women start doing the same thing and exchanging women among themselves? How will the child construct its identity with two fathers and no mother, or with two mothers and no father? And where will the child come from, since same-sex relations are sterile?

With the demand for legal recognition, homosexual parenthood appeared to many as a subversive, and even terrorist, practice which threatened the very basis of society and the social sciences. A few psychoanalysts and philosophers believed it their duty to call on the state to put a stop to this madness and 'to safeguard the bearings of reason, that is to ensure the equality of the two sexes in reproduction, to protect the images of the man and the woman and to make them into founding images of the father and the mother by the intermediary of the law'.[38] Others, without going that far, brandished the texts in which Freud analyzed the connections between homosexuality and narcissism, taxing homosexuals desirous of founding a family with 'treating themselves to children' to satisfy their basic and asocial narcissism. But other voices were heard among psychoanalysts,[39] anthropologists, sociologists, etc., advocating stepping back and substituting analysis of the facts and listening for anathemas or dogmatic hypotheses.

WHAT SHOULD WE THINK ABOUT HOMOSEXUAL PARENTHOOD?

The PACS (or its equivalent) exists in France, Belgium, Spain (but not in all provinces) and Switzerland (but not in all cantons). A more open formula is available to same-sex partners in Denmark, Finland, Germany, Iceland, Norway, Sweden and the Netherlands. In the Netherlands, same-sex civil marriage is allowed. The second parent can adopt his or her partner's children in Denmark, Iceland and the Netherlands. The joint adoption of a child by two same-sex adults is authorized in the Netherlands, Sweden and the United Kingdom. In the Netherlands, parental authority is automatically shared in the case of a homosexual couple when one partner has given birth to a child by anonymous sperm donation.[40] In the Netherlands, Belgium, England, Wales, Spain and Portugal, no law forbids unmarried women or lesbian couples using artificial insemination with donated sperm to have a child.[41]

---

38   P. Legendre, 'Entretien avec Antoine Spire', *Le Monde*, 23 October 2001, and *Télérama*, 30 December 1998, cited in Gross, *L'Homoparentalité*, pp. 95–7.

39   M. Tort, 'Homophobies psychanalytiques', *Le Monde*, 14 October 1998; C. Eliacheff, 'Malaise dans la psychanalyse', *Esprit*, nos. 3–4 (2001).

40   Gross, *L'Homoparentalité*, pp. 53, 55, 62. See also N. Boursier, 'L'Europe est divisée sur la question de l'homoparentalité', *Le Monde*, 28 June 2002.

41   In the Netherlands a person is legally authorized to know the identity of his or her genitor if the genitor agrees and if the child has reached a certain age and demands to know the name of the sperm donor.

Lastly, in the European Union being a 'mother for someone else' (surrogacy) is authorized in Denmark, Belgium, the Netherlands, Finland, the United Kingdom and Greece.

In the United States it is possible for a same-sex couple to adopt, but only in certain states such as Vermont and New Jersey. In the Canadian province of Ontario, same-sex marriage is allowed, hence the flood of gay and lesbian couples going to get married in Canada. In the United States, on the other hand, the Supreme Court ruled in 1996 that marriage was between individuals of opposite sex. Nevertheless, in 2004, the mayor of San Francisco and some mayors in New Jersey ignored this prohibition and authorized the celebration of homosexual marriages. Finally, one last important point, some Catholic priests in France, the United States and a few other countries agree to baptize the children born to a homosexual couple but refuse to marry the same couple. Here marriage remains a sacrament that unites, in the eyes of God and with the priest's blessing, two persons of opposite sex who, once united, become one flesh.

These facts show that the Western societies where the question of recognition of homosexual families has come up (which is not the case in Poland, Bulgaria, Romania, etc.) do not all respond in the same way. What is forbidden in one country is authorized in another. Alongside a country like France, where there are many prohibitions when it comes to adoption and artificial insemination, not to mention Italy where there is no equivalent of the PACS, other countries have tackled the problem of the appearance of homosexual families and have provided them with legal conditions of existence, while others still have paved the way for these conditions one day to come about. This imbroglio of diverging responses enables women who so wish, and who have the means, to travel to Brussels for insemination, while Danish sperm banks, on the other hand are experiencing a growth in their exports. What conclusions can be drawn from these facts?

The first is clear. No law can now stop the trend. Homosexual parenthood exists and can only spread with the multiplication of lawful or unlawful gay and lesbian families. And since the trend cannot be stopped, it needs to be recognized and socially accompanied so that it may acquire legal structures and limits acceptable to both the homosexual community and society at large. To accompany a trend entails an ongoing dialogue with those who are asking that attention be paid and answers given to their problems. This dialogue should involve representatives from a wide swathe of society: politicians, scientists, religious figures, social workers, physicians, paediatricians, and so on. But these debates must be nourished by a real knowledge of the facts, in all their complexity and diversity. For that to happen, sufficiently broad studies must be available that are not limited to surveys but carefully reconstruct the life paths of homosexual couples, taking into consideration the circumstances of their past that have led to the present state. But what is basically at issue?

It is the matter of children born and raised in these homosexual families.

Ultimately what should retain our attention is not the problem of homosexuality but that of homoparenthood.

We have seen that homosexuality is a form of sexuality found in nature, that it is 'natural', as it were, since it is abundantly practised by bonobos, chimpanzees and other species of primates. Homosexuality, as it is found in animal societies, is prompted by desire and pleasure. It is not limited to periods of reproductive sexuality, to heterosexual sex practised primarily when the females are receptive. For a long time, primatologists left to one side, or ignored, this aspect of primate sexuality, perhaps projecting onto these primates the homophobic prejudices present in our societies, embarrassed, above all, in terms of theory, by this sexuality with no reproductive purpose. If all animal behaviour can be explained by the (unconscious) desire to maximize individual reproductive success, to ensure their genes a successful future, how is this sexuality disconnected from reproduction to be interpreted? What makes a female bonobo choose another female to have sex with?

If homosexuality is 'natural' for primates, then the human species is also endowed with a two-sided sexuality, one side heterosexual and the other homosexual; and every human being is therefore potentially bisexual at birth. And in some cases he or she may remain bisexual, but in the vast majority of cases, the family and social context in which people grow up will lead them unconsciously and consciously to repress one of these possibilities and to cultivate the other. We know the result. In all societies, the overwhelming majority of people become heterosexual because heterosexuality is the only reproductive sexuality, and that to have children, whether or not they are desired, is a necessity if the groups that make up a society want it to last. We therefore understand that homosexuality exists in all societies, but that its meaning and status vary considerably from one society to another and from one period to another. These practices range from homosexuality as a condition for initiation to knowledge and access to powers forbidden to other members of the society, the homosexuality-as-erotic-pleasure practised by men in ancient Athens and Rome, to homosexuality considered as a mental illness and sexual pathology (for European or North American medicine and psychiatry until the middle of the twentieth century), and therefore belonging to the field of medicine, to homosexuality regarded as an unnatural practice (Christianity) or an extreme form of impurity (Islam) and therefore condemned and repressed. In certain Muslim countries, homosexuals can even be stoned to death.[42] But in the Judeo-Christian

---

42   There are at least eighty countries in the world where homosexuality is illegal and, in a dozen of these – among which Afghanistan, Iran, Saudi Arabia – it is punishable by death. See the important *Dictionnaire de l'homophobie*, edited by L-G. Tin (Paris, Presses Universitaires de France, 2003). The word '*gai*' is a French term that goes back to the Middle Ages. It was borrowed by English and then reintroduced into French with a 'Y' – *gay*.

West, the condemnation goes even further back in time – to the Bible and the Book of Leviticus.[43]

Let us take a further look at homosexuality regarded as an initiation.[44] By chance, we lived and conducted fieldwork for over seven years in a society where all boys between the ages of nine or ten, when they are torn away from their mothers and the world of women, and twenty or twenty-two, when they leave the men's house to live with a young women they have not personally chosen as a wife, develop in a world of male homosexuality in which they play two successive roles, that of sperm receivers (between the ages of nine/ten and fourteen/fifteen) and that of sperm givers (between the ages of fifteen and twenty/twenty-two). Male homosexuality in this society is not an individual matter, not the consequence of a personal bent. It is a social practise imposed on all boys[45] with the purpose of 're-engendering' them in a purely masculine world, of ridding them of all the female impurities transmitted by their mothers, of 'hypermasculinizing' them in view of their future responsibilities as warriors and husbands. Homosexuality is here an attribute of the men's 'virility' and a political as much as a sexual and erotic practice. It is important to know that the young initiates living in the men's house are treated 'like women' by those who give them their sperm. They do chores and odd jobs for the older boys. And they become 'men' when, after puberty, they become givers of sperm in turn, and active where they had once been 'passive'. Homosexual practices may well exist among young Baruya women as well, but we know nearly nothing about them.

It is also interesting to keep in mind that, in ancient Greece, male homosexual practices were probably initially an aspect of military training and the integration of the young men into the body of citizens. Female homosexuality, illustrated by the poetry of Sappho, was probably associated with the education provided in what were effectively 'initiation schools'[46] for girls preparing to marry citizens. In the classical period, homosexuality was part of a religious type of initiation. It was widely practised in Athens and Rome, where it took

---

43   'The man who lies with a man in the same way as with a woman: they have done a hateful thing together; they must die, their blood shall be on their own heads' (Leviticus 20: 13). 'You know perfectly well that people who do wrong will not inherit the kingdom of God: people of immoral lives, idolaters, adulterers, catamites, sodomites, thieves, usurers, drunkards, slanderers and swindlers will never inherit the kingdom of God' (I Corinthians 6: 9–10). 'It would not be fair to draw from this the conclusion that sexual inversion in woman is rare, for if this anomaly is really a manifestation of functional degeneration, then degenerative influences will prevail alike in the female as well as in the male' (Richard von Krafft-Ebing. *Psychopathia sexualis*, 1886).

44   In China, male homosexuality is regarded as one of the paths of the Dao, i.e. the Way. It is also interesting that the word *tronjeu*, which during the Communist period designated a 'comrade', also meant someone with homosexual tendencies. This is still the case today.

45   On pain of death for boys who refuse to swallow the sperm.

46   See S. Bernard, *L'Homosexualité initiatique dans l'Europe ancienne* (Paris, Payot, 1986), Chapter 1, and the work of reference, J. Boswell, *Les Unions du même sexe dans l'Europe antique et médiévale* (Paris, Fayard, 1996 [1994]).

different forms. Generally speaking, homosexuality and heterosexuality were not mutually exclusive. It was not considered deviant or antisocial behaviour for a man to love another man. In Rome, on the other hand, female homosexuality was not allowed, whereas in Greece it disappeared after the seventh or sixth century.[47]

In these cases, male homosexuality fell under the triple sign of desire, pleasure but also love and passion. Yet a dichotomy existed, which is reminiscent of that found in the Baruya culture, between passive and active homosexual activity. In Greece as in Rome, a man who accepted a passive role in a homosexual relationship was considered to have dishonoured himself and was disqualified as a citizen. Whereas among the Baruya, men go successively from a passive sexuality to an active one, becoming full-fledged men in the process,[48] in classical Athens, the passive role marked a man or a boy negatively and classed them among women, servants or slaves.

Whatever may be the case of the past history of homosexuality,[49] what is new in our era is the appearance in Western societies of homoparental families demanding recognition as 'families' in their own right, defined by law following a change in family law – or even in the constitution of the state in question. Homosexuality, which is a biologically sterile form of sexuality, has pretentions to being a life-giving reproductive form. To the desire for a same-sex other is added the desire for a child. And what if to desire is added love, and to love for a same-sex other is added the love of children that have been, if not engendered – which is possible only for a lesbian – at least adopted?

Herein lies the new element: in the desire for a child and in the will to fulfil it. This desire and this will are not restricted to homosexual couples. More and more single women are adopting children and creating single-parent families

---

47   See the important book by Eva Cantarella, *Selon la nature, l'usage et la loi. La Bisexualité dans le monde antique* (Paris, La Découverte, 1991). See also the article by D. Cohen, 'Law, Society and Homosexuality in Classical Athens', *Past and Present*, no. 117 (1987), pp. 3–21, as well as K. J. Dover, *Greek Homosexuality* (Cambridge MA, Harvard University Press, 1978) and M. Foucault, *Histoire de la sexualité*, vol. 1: *L'Usage des plaisirs* (Paris, Gallimard, 1984).

48   Hence the importance of the studies devoted to homosexuality in Melanesia, which have brought to light new findings and deeply changed our approach to the problems. We are indebted to Gilbert Herdt, who followed us several years later among the Baruya's neighbours, the Sambia, for a series of studies that have become indispensable reading: G. Herdt, *Guardians of the Flutes: Idioms of Masculinity* (New York, McGraw-Hill Company, 1981); G. Herdt (ed.), *Rituals of Manhood: Male Initiation in Papua New Guinea* (Berkeley, University of California Press, 1982); G. Herdt (ed.), *Ritualized Homosexuality in Melanesia* (Berkeley, University of California Press, 1984). Cf. also B. Knauft, 'Homosexuality in Melanesia', *The Journal of Psychoanalytic Anthropology*, vol. 10, no. 2 (1987), pp. 155–91.

49   Past but also recent. See F. Tamagne, 'Histoire comparée de l'homosexualité en Allemagne, en Angleterre et en France dans l'entre-deux-guerres', *Actes de la recherche en sciences sociales*, no. 125 (1998), pp. 44–62; E. Fassin, 'Homosexualité et mariage aux Etats-Unis', *Actes de la recherche en sciences sociales*, no. 125 (1998), pp. 63–73.

where these children live without their father. The children of these homosexual or single-parent families come from Romania, Haiti or Colombia, and one day their adoptive parent(s) will have to talk to them about their origins, without ever being able to tell them about their ancestors.

Homoparenthood thus has nothing in common with the examples mentioned by certain promoters, who cite without understanding them the Nuer marriages between women,[50] or the Azandé marriage between a warrior and an adolescent boy. In the first case the female husband and the female wife do not have sexual relations, and the female wife must take a lover to give children to her female husband or, if the latter is a childless widow, to the lineage of the widow's deceased husband. As for the Azandé, as soon as the warrior can marry he does, and he gives his former lover the necessary cattle and means to take an adolescent spouse in turn. The man often marries his former lover's sister, as we have said, and all of these marriages are contracted with the lover's parents and his sister's consent, and with the approbation of society.

But what happens in Western societies? First let us recall that the majority of gays and lesbians do not want to get married and have and/or raise children. For them, being homosexual, affirming the fact and living openly is a dearly won freedom. For these people, being homosexual is first of all belonging to a minority not like the others, in which artists rub shoulders with scientists, etc.[51]

But of course people who recognize themselves as homosexuals and choose to live their sexuality are found not only in the middle classes and the more well to do or in the most educated levels of society or in the best educated societies of Europe or North America. It is hard to assess the actual number of homosexual persons, however, for national censuses usually avoid asking people about their sexuality.[52] Nevertheless we know that in the Netherlands some 20,000 children are raised in families where at least one of the parents is gay or lesbian. In the United States, in 2002, the number of children being raised by gay or lesbian parents was estimated at three million. A majority of these were born before one of the parents identified him- or herself as being homosexual and began living with a same-sex partner together with the children born during his or her first, heterosexual life. In this case, the children will have begun to construct their identity in a family where there was a difference between the sexes, therefore a 'normal' family, before living in a family where this difference has disappeared. And if they continue to visit the parent their

---

50   This is also the case among the Nandi. See R. Smith Oboler, 'Is the female husband a man? Woman/woman marriage among the Nandi of Kenya', *Ethnology*, vol. 19, no. 1 (1980), pp. 69–88.

51   See D. Eribon, *Dictionnaire des cultures gays et lesbiennes* (Paris, Larousse, 2003) and *Réflexions sur la question gay* (Paris, Fayard, 1999).

52   In the United States, 2003 was the first time the Census Bureau recorded the number of same-sex couples. See Gross, *L'Homoparentalité*, pp. 14–16.

father or mother left in order to live his or her homosexuality, these children will find themselves immersed in a world where hetero- and homosexuality exist side by side – and they will find their bearings.

A certain number of questions arise here. What happens when a child is raised by parents who, from the outset, have chosen to be exclusively homosexual, just as the majority of people are exclusively heterosexual? Or in other words, what is the process of subjectivation, internalization, a child goes through when it is born and raised in a homosexual family?[53] Will all of these children be homosexual or more often homosexual when they reach adulthood than children born and raised in heterosexual families? How will a boy raised by two women construct his masculinity, or a girl raised by two men her femininity?

We do not have enough distance or sufficiently rigorous studies to reach a clear conclusion. Some American studies commissioned by gay and lesbian associations have concluded that children's sexual orientation is the same whether they are raised in homosexual or in heterosexual families. But these studies were accused of being partial and biased, of seeking to convince the American government to legalize homosexual marriages and the families that would result. Other studies conducted in Great Britain showed that there was an undeniable, though not large, difference in the sexual orientation of the children in favour of homosexual relations.[54] On the other hand, no disorder affecting identity or intelligence, no lack of ability to act as a responsible being was found in the children raised in these families. On 4 February 2002, the American Academy of Pediatrics released a statement recommending that the children raised by a same-sex couple be adopted by the second parent. The consequence, ipso facto, would be to create homosexual families, whereas they are not yet recognized by law, since homosexual marriage is widely prohibited in the United States.[55]

This is where we stand for the moment. It is clear that, for a given individual, society is not limited to the family, and that children born and/or raised in a homosexual family will discover sexual difference via their uncles, aunts, grandparents, school mates, etc. They may even find themselves surrounded by

---

53   See D. Julien and E. Chartrand, 'La Psychologie familiale des gays et des lesbiennes: perspectives de la tradition scientifique nord-américaine', *Sociologie et sociétés*, vol. 29 (1999), pp. 71–81.

54   See the very important studies by the team led by Susan Golombok, professor at London's City University, 'Children in Lesbian and Single-Parent Households: Psycho-sexual and Psychiatric Appraisal', *Journal of Child Psychology and Psychiatry*, vol. 24, no. 4 (1983), pp. 551–72; S. Golombok, F. Tasker and C. Murray, 'Children Raised in Fatherless Families from Infancy: Family Relationships and Socio-emotional Development of Children of Lesbian and Heterosexual Mothers', *Journal of Child Psychology and Psychiatry*, vol. 38, no. 7 (1997), pp. 783–91; J. Stacey and T. J. Biblartz, 'How Does the Sexual Orientation of Parents Matter?', *American Sociological Review*, vol. 66 (April 2001), pp. 159–83. These are a selection of texts from a list of dozens.

55   Gross, *L'Homoparentalité*, p. 81.

more people acting as parents of both sexes than a child in a single-parent family. We know too – and for an anthropologist this is obvious – that the paternal and maternal functions can be ensured by persons with no genetic or other link with the child and that the paternal functions are not necessarily attached to a person of the male sex nor the maternal functions to a person of the female sex. It is certain, too, that the liberation of sexuality we have been witnessing for a half-century in the West as well as in other parts of the world and the affirmation of an attitude of tolerance (and even complete recognition) toward homosexuality are going increasingly to lessen the risks of a European or North American child undergoing public homophobic attacks (at school or elsewhere) on the homosexual couple raising the child and aimed at him or her as the son or daughter of these parents. Homosexual parenthood is already no longer the gateway to hell or the psychiatric hospital.

Two problems remain. What if homosexuality were to give way to hetero-phobia? What if the roles were reversed? What if certain homosexuals started preaching 'rejection or fear of heterosexuality . . . that might be expressed by negative and even discriminatory attitudes toward people of heterosexual orientation'?[56] One can imagine the consequences of this 'backlash of hate', even though it might be understandable coming from people who had suffered for decades from social, physical and symbolic violence because of their sexuality.[57] Social consequences in the first place: people's latent homophobia might be awakened, with psychological consequences for the children of homosexual parents, who would feel like they were living in a different world than other children of their age.

This is where things sometimes become hard to analyze, very awkward to assess. When lesbians stress that they want sperm but not a man, there is the risk of forgetting that the sperm is emitted by a man who has a life story, ascend-ants, dreams, in short, there is the risk of sperm becoming dehumanized,[58] of it becoming a pure 'genetic substance' which, unfortunately for some, cannot yet be synthesized and produced in a laboratory. And when we read in one Ameri-can study that two women had themselves been inseminated on the same day with the sperm of the same anonymous donor so that their children would be

56   Comments by Erik Rémes, cited in J-L. Jeannelle, Article 'Hétérophobie', in *Dictionnaire de l'homophobie*, pp. 205–7. See S. Jackson, *Heterosexuality in Question* (London, Sage, 1999).

57   It should not be forgotten that it was only in 1982 that homosexuality was legalized in France. Until then it had been a crime. Earlier, in 1974, the American Psychiatric Association (55,000 members) had taken homosexuality off its list of mental diseases (DSM 3 (Diagnostics and Statistical Manual of Mental Diseases)). See D. Welzer-Lang, P. Dutey and M. Dorais (eds.), *La Peur de l'autre en soi. Du sexisme à l'homophobie* (Montreal, Editions Québec, 1994).

58   C. Hayden, 'Gender, Genetics and Generations: Reformulating Biology in Lesbian Kinship', *Cultural Anthropology*, vol. 10, no. 1 (1995), pp. 41–63.

genetically related, and so that they would both have not one but two mothers,[59] a sort of 'supermother' in two persons, one might well find these actions and representations worrying. There is legitimate concern that once again these children could become the victims or the supports of the fantasies of adults desirous above all of satisfying their 'desire for a child', whatever the price to be paid by the child. But we also know that adult fantasies and narcissistic desires for a child are not restricted to homosexuals.

In short, there is an urgent need to gain a better knowledge of the facts, to locate the problems, to open debates and to identify the decisions to be taken at the political, juridical and societal levels in order to give people new rights, but rights that are accompanied by commitments and responsibilities which would be covered by the law, as is the case when heterosexual parents fail in their duties and endanger the mental balance and the personality of their children.

Our journey through kinship is drawing to a close. Humans began inventing kinship relations well before the ancestors of our direct ancestors, the Cro-Magnon people, appeared on earth. If we give any credit to the theory that one does not bury one's enemies, one kills them and leaves their body where it lies or even eats it, then the discovery of ancient burials attests to at least two things: first, the existence of ties of kinship or friendship between those who were buried and those who buried them, and, second, the existence of beliefs that death is not the end of life, that something of the deceased person lives on after death.

The oldest burial known to this day in Europe dates back 300,000 years, and was discovered in a cave in the Sierra de Atapuerca, near Burgos in Spain.[60] Thirty-two individuals of all ages were buried there, and near one of the skeletons had been placed a magnificent biface made from red quartz and meant, it would seem, to accompany the deceased. All of the individuals were identified as belonging to the *Homo heidelbergensis* species, which preceded the appearance of the Neanderthals and the Cro-Magnon people. This discovery would confirm our hypothesis that the appearance of kinship relations preceded that of articulated speech, and that the ability to imagine an invisible world beyond and to symbolize it existed before this appearance as well.

Here we can see the beginnings of an archaeology of kinship, which holds yet another surprise. Archaeologists have discovered other, later burials, both

---

59   H. Lewin, *Lesbian Mothers: Accounts of Gender in American Culture* (Ithaca, Cornell University Press, 1993).

60   See Pascal Picq, *Au commencement était l'homme* (Paris, Odile Jacob, 2003), pp. 154–60. The author highlights the evolutionary importance of *Homo ergaster*, whose arrival some 1.8 million years ago signalled the decline of the other hominids. It seems that it was this species that left Africa (ibid., pp. 101–24), and in his wake appeared *Homo erectus*.

on Neanderthal habitation sites and on those inhabited by Cro-Magnon people. This would mean that kinship relations, beliefs in the beyond and the symbolic rites enacting them appeared twice in two species which evolved side-by-side for thousands of years, one of which disappeared for reasons unknown some 30,000 years ago, giving way to the only surviving human species, our own.[61]

The reader will have understood that, being a specific component of the humanity of mankind for some tens of thousands of years, kinship is not about to disappear, and kinship relations have not seen their last metamorphosis. Both real and imaginary, abstract, sometimes even purely symbolic but always brimming with concrete interests, rooted in each of us from infancy, accepted or rejected when we reach adulthood, imposed by others or chosen in the teeth of everyone, kinship relations and all of the representations (images, positive and/ or negative values) that go with them would be threatened with fossilization and, ultimately, disappearance, only if that which is the distinctive feature of human-kind were to disappear or be destroyed, that which definitively separated humans from the other primates, their natural cousins, namely: the fact that *humans not only live in society, but can and must produce society in order to live.*

POSTSCRIPT

This book, which was written between 1996 and 2004, takes a position in favour of legalization that recognizes homosexual unions and the use of surrogate mothers by those unable to bear children, therefore acknowledging the rights of same-sex families. At the time of writing, there were very few French anthro-pologists who were interested in the contemporary metamorphoses of kinship, thanks to the misguided belief that as far as this was concerned there was noth-ing new under the sun and these aforementioned phenomena were marginal if not aberrant. Since 2004, I have continued to keep abreast of the work of Anglo-phone colleagues with regard to these questions, and I have noted how their analyses have really helped us advance our understanding of the transformations of societies and reinforced our responsibilities towards those living within them.

Andros, Greece, October 2011

---

61   Ibid., pp. 156–7. See also J. Riel-Salvatore and G. Clark, 'Grave Markers, Middle and Early Upper Palaeolithic Burials and the Use of Chronotypology in Contemporary Paleolithic Research', *Current Anthropology*, vol. 42, no. 4 (2001), pp. 449–79, and the earlier work by F. May, *Les Sépultures préhistoriques. Etude critique* (Paris, CNRS, 1986).

Glossary

A

ADOPTION
The legal act that establishes jural relations between the individual adopted and the person or persons who adopt him or her analogous to those conferred by descent.

– *full adoption*: the adopted person severs ties with the birth-family group.

– *simple adoption*: the adopted person preserves ties with his or her original family group to which he or she adds the new ties with the adopting group.

AFFILIATION
Belonging by birth or by choice to a given social group.

AFFINES
Persons who become relatives following a matrimonial alliance or marriage. A distinction is made between real affines and classificatory affines; between real affines (brother-in-law, sister-in-law, etc.) and virtual affines (all of one's cross cousins, for instance) and potential affines (non-relatives whom one can marry). Affines are therefore people with whom one is 'allied' by marriage. Co-affines are persons having common affines.

AFFINES OF AFFINES
These are the affines of your affines, for example your wife's sister's husband or your wife's brother's wife, as opposed to consanguines of affines, which are your husband's brother or your wife's sister, for example.

AFFINITY
Kinship ties created by a matrimonial alliance, usually in the form of a marriage.

AGAMY
Absence of any marriage rule, whether inside or outside of one's social group.

AGE (AGE GROUP)
Persons of a same generation and usually of the same sex who recognize themselves as a particular group to which society ascribes a certain number of rights and duties. In many societies, age groups are formally recognized and subjected to a system of progressive initiations, which change by stages the individual's

social status over his or her lifetime. This status varies with the person's sex, age, membership of a given clan, caste, etc.

AGNATES
Individuals related to a person through the male line, as opposed to 'uterine kin'.

ALLIANCE (BY MARRIAGE)
A socially recognized bond between two persons, usually of opposite sex, and through them of the two kin groups to which they belong. Social recognition of the bond does not necessarily imply a marriage.

ALTER
Someone who has one or several kinship ties with Ego.

AMITY
A term used by Meyer Fortes to characterize the rules guiding the reciprocal relations between related individuals: rules of solidarity, generosity, etc. According to Fortes, these rules constitute the ethical dimension of kinship. The opposite of *amity* is *enmity*.

ANCESTOR
A man or a woman who is supposed to be at the origin of a descent group. In this case we speak of the 'apical' ancestor, i.e. who is at the top (*apex*) of the descent group's genealogical tree. Sometimes this ancestor has given his or her name to the group of descendants and has thus become the 'eponymous' ancestor.

ANISOGAMY
Marriage between two persons of different social status.

ASCENDANTS
All those from whom Ego is descended and who are divided into several generations before Ego (parents: G+1; grandparents: G+2; great-grandparents: G+3, etc.).

AVOIDANCE
Behaviour of those who shun physical contact, sexual relations, verbal exchanges or other face-to-face interaction with a certain number of persons linked to them by certain social, kin or other relations. These behaviours are associated, for example, with the taboo on sexual relations between mother and son, father and daughter, brother and sister, or with the prohibition on any physical contact

between members of different castes. These behaviours can also be observed in some primates.

AVUNCULATE

Codified relations between a man and his sister's son. These relations are characterized in different ways, by respect or familiarity, and are associated with various forms of transmission of property, statuses, knowledge and functions from uncle to nephew.

B

BIFURCATION/CROSSNESS

In some kinship terminologies, Ego's relatives are designated by a different term depending on whether they are related through the male or the female line. This principle is at the origin of the distinction between parallel cousins (e.g. father's brother's son) and cross cousins (father's sister's son).

BILATERAL

A term that describes someone related to Ego on both the father's and the mother's side. For example, Ego's mother's brother's daughter is a bilateral cross cousin if Ego's mother's brother married Ego's father's sister.

BRIDEWEALTH

Valuables, material goods and sometimes rights in a piece of land that are transferred from one family or kin group to another on the occasion of the marriage of one of their members. The term *brideprice* is also used, but is objected to by those who consider that the word 'price' introduces market logic into relations that have nothing to do with the market.

C

CAPTURE (MARRIAGE BY)

Marriage in which the bride is abducted by the man who wishes to marry her.

CATEGORY (KIN)

Kin term that designates a certain number of persons related to Ego by the same ties (real or classificatory), or by different kin ties which are regarded as equivalent. For example: in English the term 'cousin' is used for both father's brother's children and mother's brother's children, and for father's sister's children and mother's sister's children, etc.

CHIEFDOM

A society (usually a tribe) in which power is concentrated in the hands of a small number of kin groups, sometimes only one, which have exclusive access to those functions that appear to the members of the society as ensuring the reproduction of the cosmic and social orders. When these functions and the powers associated with them are inherited within certain clans or local groups, these groups form a sort of tribal aristocracy.

CIRCULATION

Transfers and movements of persons, goods, services, statuses and functions within a group or between groups. There are several kinds of circulation: the circulation of goods and services in a market (commercial circulation), which is different from the circulation of goods and services in the form of gifts and counter-gifts (non-commercial circulation), but also the circulation of persons (men, women or children) exchanged between social groups contracting a marriage alliance.

CLAN

Group of individuals who consider themselves to be descended, in the male or the female line, from a common male or female ancestor. In this case we speak of a patriclan or a matriclan. The ancestor can be purely imaginary or not even human. A clan is usually, but not necessarily, exogamous.

CLASS (MARRIAGE) ALSO KNOWN AS 'MARRIAGE SECTION'

An exogamous kin group that is obliged to marry into another specific exogamous group. The children of these marriages automatically belong to a third marriage class, which differs according to whether descent is reckoned through the men or through the women. For example, men in class A must marry women in class B. Their children will belong to class C and will marry members of class D. The children of the CD marriages will once again belong to class A, their paternal grandfather's section. The cycle then starts over again.

CLASSIFICATORY KIN

Kin terms that place in the same category persons related to Ego by genealogical ties but also individuals not genealogically related but who are considered to stand in an identical or equivalent relationship with Ego.

COGNATES

Those persons related to Ego through both the male and the female lines.

COLLATERALS

Kin or lines of kin not in a direct line of descent from an individual, as opposed to relations between ascendants and descendants in direct line. Siblings are first-degree collaterals.

COMPLEX KINSHIP STRUCTURE

A term used by Lévi-Strauss to designate kinship systems lacking a positive (prescriptive or preferential) marriage rule but which have a certain number of negative rules.

CONCEPTION (THEORIES ABOUT)

Theories that describe the different roles humans (father and mother), ancestors, spirits and gods play in making babies.

CONSANGUINES

Ego's relatives on both father's and mother's side. The notion of consanguinity comes from Latin, referring to all those with whom Ego shares the same 'blood' (Latin, *sanguis*). The anthropological notion is no longer connected with this particular theory of the creation of kin ties through the transmission of blood.

COUSINS

Children of siblings:

     – cross cousins: children of opposite-sex siblings (a brother and a sister).
     – parallel cousins: children of same-sex siblings (two brothers or two sisters).
     – matrilateral cousins: cousins related to Ego through Ego's mother.
     – patrilateral cousins: cousins related to Ego through Ego's father.

COUVADE

The practice in some societies where, at the birth of a child, the father takes to his bed and participates virtually in the birth as well as in the rites the two parents must observe in the first weeks after the birth.

CULTURE

The principles and rules for thinking and acting to which positive or negative values are attached and which are shared (up to a certain point) by the individuals and groups that make up the society, who turn them into acts and works in order to reproduce themselves individually and socially.

CYCLE (MATRIMONIAL)

The succession of marriage alliances that comes full circle after a certain number of generations (e.g. marriage with a third-degree cross cousin).

D

DEGREES OF KINSHIP
The level of relationship with Ego. A first cousin is said to be closer to Ego than a second cousin. The way of calculating these distances varies with the type of system adopted. In the common system children of siblings are first cousins, and their children are second cousins, etc. This system is different from that defined by Canon law and used by the Catholic Church, which had borrowed Germanic customs. In this system, brothers and sisters are kin of the first degree, and children of siblings are kin of the second degree. It is also different from the ancient Roman system, which calculated degrees of kinship by counting the number of genealogical links between two individuals, going through their common ancestor. In this system, Ego's father's brother's son (a first cousin in the common system) is a fourth-degree relative, since the link runs through Ego's father (1) then through Ego's father's father and Alter's father's father (2), and drops back down to Alter's father (3), ending at Alter (4).

DEME
A division of land in ancient Greece. Anthropologists sometimes use the term to designate cognatic descent groups whose membership is defined by descent links traced through both the male and the female lines. The term is the counterpart of 'clan', which designates descent groups created by unilineal descent reckoning.

DESCENT RULE/PRINCIPLE
The criterion defining a person's belonging, at birth, to a group of individuals claiming to descend from one or several common ancestors. These criteria are few in number:
- The descent system can be unilineal, and in this case descent is traced exclusively through the male line (patrilineal descent rule), or exclusively through the female line (matrilineal descent rule).
- The descent system can be defined by two calculations at once, one traced through the male line, the other through the female line. In this case, the person belongs to both descent groups, from which he receives different 'things', for example land from the mother's side and political-religious functions from the father's side. This way of reckoning is said to be ambi- or duolineal.
- Descent can be reckoned differently for men and women. In this event, two cases are possible. Girls belong to the father's group and boys to the mother's (cross bilineal descent), or, on the contrary, girls belong to their mother's group and boys to their father's (parallel bilineal descent).

    – Children can belong to both their father's and their mother's group, and, in this case, descent reckoning is indifferent, unlike the sexes. This is the case of cognatic systems, also called undifferentiated systems.
A descent group (lineage, clan) often exists and acts as a corporate group.

DESCRIPTIVE

An adjective applied to kinship terminologies that designate genealogical links by terms which add together equivalent relationships, for example: 'father', 'grandfather', 'great-grandfather', etc. The English term 'cousin', on the other hand, is not descriptive but classificatory, because it does not indicate whether the individual is a paternal or maternal cousin.

DEVOLUTION

Hereditary transmission of material or immaterial assets. Devolution differs with the sex of the heirs and their degree of kinship with the deceased. Devolution is divergent when transmission follows different rules for a son and a daughter, etc.

DOWER

A widow's rights in a share of her deceased husband's goods.

DOWRY

Goods given at the time of a marriage either by the groom's family to that of the bride, or by the bride's family to the bride herself, or by the groom's family to the groom himself. In the last two cases the dowry is an advance of sorts on the inheritance.

DYSHARMONIOUS

The term used by Lévi-Straus to designate kinship systems in which residence does not coincide with the descent rule, for example when the descent system is matrilineal and residence is virilocal. Harmonious systems are those where residence and descent rule coincide, for instance, the descent system is matrilineal and the couple's residence after the marriage is uxorilocal (i.e. the husband leaves his own group and goes to live with that of his wife).

E

EGO

The male or female reference who is the point of departure or arrival of kin ties.

ELDEST/ELDER
- A firstborn or an individual born before certain brothers and sisters.
- A person who is older than another. The opposite of firstborn is last-born. In many societies, the firstborn enjoys different and greater rights than brothers and sisters born later (*see 'Primogeniture'*). In certain societies, the firstborn, whether male or female, has absolute priority over younger male and female siblings.

ENDOGAMY/EXOGAMY
- Endogamy rules that an individual must marry within his or her own kin group, caste, class, religion, ethnic group, etc.
- Exogamy rules that an individual must marry outside his or her own kin group, caste, etc.

EPICLERE
The rule in ancient Greek law that, after her father's death, a girl without a brother had to marry her father's brother or one of his closest male relatives.

EQUATION (KINSHIP)
Way of representing the fact that the same individual can occupy several positions in a kinship system. For example, the equation (MB = FZH = WF) means that the mother's brother is at the same time Ego's father's sister's husband and Ego's wife's father, in other words his father-in-law, which implies an exchange of women between Ego's father and Ego's mother's brother.

ETHNIC GROUP
The set of local groups (tribes, village and/or urban communities, etc.) that recognize a remote common origin, speak the same or closely related languages (because they derive from a common protolanguage), follow to a certain extent the same rules for organizing social life, and share values that are similar or which diverge within or from a common core of values. Example: the Pashtuns, who live astride Afghanistan and Pakistan.

EXTENSION
There is extension when the same kin term applies to a close kinsman and to relatives that are more or less genealogically remote. Some theoreticians explain this by saying that the application of this term has been 'extended' to other genealogical positions regarded as identical or equivalent. Others, like Hocart and Leach, consider, on the contrary, that the category takes priority, in other words, affirmation of the equivalence of all or several kin positions of which those closest to Ego are merely a special case and not the point of departure. For

them, the notion of extension is inadequate. The positions of Ego's close kin (e.g. father) appear in this case as a 'reduction' of the category 'fathers' to a single individual, the mother's husband.

F

FAMILY
All persons related by blood ties (consanguinity) and, with regard to spouses, by marriage (affinity). Several family types are commonly distinguished. There is the conjugal or nuclear family, made up of a man, a woman and their children. And there is the extended, joint or undivided family, which includes several related families comprising different generations. There is also the family 'of orientation', the one in which the individual was born and/or raised and the family 'of procreation', the one founded by an individual through marriage or another form of union. Families in which a man has several wives are called polygynous; those where a woman has several husbands, polyandrous. Single-parent families are made up of a parent (usually a woman) and his or her children. Reconstituted families are created when individuals remarry after a divorce or after the death of their former spouse.

FILIATION
The ties between an individual and both his or her father and his or her mother, without regard to a descent rule. Example: in a patrilineal descent system, a person is the descendant of his or her father alone, but is the son or daughter of his or her father *and* his or her mother.

FISSION
The event in which lineages split off from their clan of origin to found a new clan.

FOSTERAGE
Temporary care of a child by an adult to whom the parents have entrusted him or her for education and training (*see also* 'Adoption').

G

GENDER
Term increasingly used to describe all social differences, functions, statuses, symbols, positive and/or negative values attaching to a person because of his or her sex. These differences are often presented as opposing complementary and hierarchical terms. Gender relations are thus presented as unequal and

indicative of forms of domination or even exploitation of one sex (usually women) by the other (usually men).

GENEALOGY

The description or hypothetical reconstruction of kin ties between a person and his or her ascendants, descendants, collaterals and their descendants. Genealogies are usually preserved in people's memories, but their 'depth' varies according to these individuals or to the interest a society has for this memory. In societies with writing, genealogies are written down, at least in certain families or social classes. In the West it has become customary to represent these genealogies as a tree, a cross or some other graphic design. Genealogies can be very important in establishing claims to land, material assets, statuses and functions. They are therefore often the object of interested and interesting manipulations and are in part fictional.

GENERATION

All those persons situated at the same distance of lineal descent from a common ancestor and therefore at the same genealogical level. In kinship terminologies, Ego's generation is designated as G^0; Ego's parents, G^{+1}; Ego's grandparents, G^{+2}; Ego's children, G^{-1}; Ego's grandchildren, G^{-2}, etc.

Two generations that follow each other without interruption are called 'consecutive' generations.

Two generations separated by a third are known as 'alternate' generations.

GENITOR/GENETRIX

Man (or woman) having physically contributed to making a child. In some societies, the genitor is not the social 'father' if he has not helped, for example, with payment of the brideprice to his wife's family and if another man has done so in his stead. The children the genitor has helped bring into the world belong to the other man, who becomes the socially recognized 'father'.

GENS

A term designating in ancient Rome the group of families descending from a common ancestor in the male line and governed by the *patria potestas*, the legal authority held by the *pater familias*, or 'father of the family'. The *gens* is the equivalent of the Greek word *genos* and refers to the idea of engendering or birth.

GINAMARE

Baruya term designating 'sister' exchange between two men, which is actually the exchange of women between two lineages.

GIVERS OR TAKERS

The 'givers' are those groups that give one of their members, a man or a woman, in marriage to another group. This yields two possible cases. The takers are also givers, and in this case the exchange is reciprocal. The takers are not givers and, in this case, there is no exchange of persons but gifts of goods (dowry, bridewealth) in exchange for a person (a man or a woman). As far as the status of givers and takers goes, there are three possibilities. The givers are superior to the takers, the takers are superior to the givers, or takers and givers are on an equal footing.

H

HARMONIOUS

A term used by Lévi-Strauss to designate a system where residence pattern and descent rule coincide, for example when residence is virilocal and the descent rule patrilineal.

HOMOGAMY

Marriage between a man and a woman of same social status.

HOMOPARENTHOOD

Parental relations between children and same-sex adults. Parenthood is established through the 'adoption' of children by a male couple or by recourse to a surrogate mother; by adoption or by the artificial (or natural) insemination of one of the two women living as a couple; and finally, for men and for women, by co-parenting.

HOUSE

A group of individuals related by ties of blood or marriage and functioning as a corporate group in possession of a domain including material assets (land) and immaterial assets (titles, insignia, myths, etc.), and bearing a name passed from one generation to the next independently of the individuals who occupy and utilize the domain.

HOUSE SOCIETIES

Societies whose kinship system and social organization are built on the existence of houses often hierarchically articulated within a system of titles, ranks and functions.

HYPERGAMY

Marriage between a woman of lower social status and a man of higher social status (as opposed to hypogamy, where the woman marries a man below her status).

I

INCEST
Homo- and/or heterosexual sexual relations prohibited between consanguineous kin or between affines considered to be too close or too similar. The taboos on heterosexual relations therefore also imply prohibitions on marriage between opposite-sex relatives.

ISOGAMY, SEE 'HOMOGAMY'

J

JOKING RELATIONSHIPS
In certain societies, relations between two individuals of the same or opposite sex, related by a given kin tie (e.g. cross cousins) are characterized by great familiarity, sometimes even obscenity, which are not authorized in other relationships. Joking and public or private provocations are regarded as a game or as part of the normal course of these kinship relations.

K

KIN
All persons related to Ego by blood (consanguinity), marriage (alliance) or adoption.

KINDRED
Kin group centred on an individual, Ego. The group includes the consanguineous kin on both father's and mother's sides and their affines. Brothers and sisters of the same father and mother share the same kindred. This is not the case for half-brothers and half-sisters. Kindreds are typical of undifferentiated cognatic systems but actually exist in all kinship systems whatever their descent rule.

KINSHIP
Those biological and/or social ties arising from the union of persons (most often of the opposite sex) and which determine the belonging and social identity of the children born to or adopted by this couple. These ties are of two kinds: ties of consanguinity, i.e. ties with the father and father's kin, and with the mother and mother's kin (ascendants and collaterals), and ties of affinity, created by marriage or other forms of union between opposite-sex or same-sex partners.

KINSHIP (FICTITIOUS)

Social kin ties created by reciprocal choices and according to certain conventions between two unrelated persons or between an individual and a kin group that recognizes the person as one of them without going through a formal adoption.

KINSHIP TERMINOLOGY

The set of terms used in a society to refer to kinship relations between two or several persons, or to address an individual who has a kin tie with Ego. A distinction is therefore made between reference terms (e.g. so-and-so is someone else's mother's brother) and address terms (e.g. 'Dad', 'Mom', etc.). All kinship terminologies are variations on a small number of types that anthropologists, since Morgan, have identified: Hawaiian, Eskimo, Australian, Dravidian, Iroquois, Sudanese, Kachin (asymmetrical prescriptive), to which must now be added Ngabwe, Yafar . . . The Crow-Omaha terminologies have not yet been definitively established as a separate type.

KWAIMATNIE

A Baruya sacred object used by the masters of the initiations to grow (*nimatnie*) boys and men (*kwala*).

L

LEVIRATE

Obligation for a widow to marry her deceased husband's brother.

LINE

A lineage segment, sometimes also a chain of individuals connected by a succession of descendants of the same sex.

LINEAGE

A group descended through the male or the female line from one of the sons or daughters of a clan founder or one of their known descendants. A lineage often takes the form of a local group whose members hold material and immaterial assets in common, help each other and show solidarity with each other. A lineage is an exogamous unit, which is often at the same time a religious unit practising ancestor worship. A lineage acts as a corporate group with respect to other lineages. Anthropologists differentiate between matrilineages and patrilineages according to the descent rule operating in the society. They also differentiate between eldest and youngest lineages according to the position of their founding ancestors among descendants of the clan founder or founders.

M

MARRIAGE
A socially recognized bond between two individuals of opposite or same sex (cf. marriage between women in Africa). The bond is often established following a series of negotiations between the partners' families, lineages or houses, which set the marriage compensation and other related prestations. It determines to whom the children born of this couple or adopted by them belong. It also implies distinct rights and duties incumbent on the individuals united by marriage: in the areas of sexual relations, household chores, residence, the name carried by the spouses and by their children, inheritance in the event of death, etc. Marriage often involves specific rites and ceremonies.

MARRIAGE (ARAB)
Union between two patrilateral parallel cousins, e.g. between the son and the daughter of two brothers belonging to the same agnatic lineage.

MATRIFOCAL
A family or domestic group is matrifocal when it is centred on a woman and her children. In this case the father(s) of these children are intermittently present in the life of the group and occupy a secondary place. The children's mother is not necessarily the wife of one of the children's fathers.

MATRIMONIAL COMPENSATION, SEE 'BRIDEWEALTH'

MERGING
The inclusion under the same term of several distinct genealogical positions in the same generation. Example: father and father's brother in Baruya = *noumwe* (*see also* 'Skewing').

MILK BROTHERS OR SISTERS
Bonds created between two or several persons by having been suckled by the same woman. These bonds concern not only the woman who nursed them but often a certain number of her kin as well (e.g. children, husband, brothers).

MOIETY
Many societies are divided into two groups, or moieties, which have distinct, opposing but complementary functions. Moieties are often but not always exogamous groups between which women (sometimes men) circulate. Women from moiety A marry men from moiety B, and women from moiety B marry men from moiety A. The children belong to one moiety or the other in

accordance with the descent rule followed by the society. Moieties provide the framework and the raison d'être of reciprocal exchanges of goods and services, each moiety playing a particular role in the rites intended to ensure the reproduction of the cosmic and social orders. There are also what are known as 'generational' moieties, which put Ego, Ego's grandparents and Ego's grandchildren (G0, G+2 and G-2) into one moiety and Ego's parents and Ego's children (G+1 and G-1) into the other. Generational moieties are usually not exogamous.

MONOGAMY
Marriage rule that prohibits having more than one spouse at a time.

N

NOMENCLATURE (KINSHIP)
Terminology used by a kinship system; it is expressed using a particular vocabulary of terms.

P

PARENTHOOD
Those roles that should or can be ensured by the adults who are related to a child by blood (consanguinity) or marriage (alliance). These functions impose a certain number of duties and obligations on the adults and give them certain rights. Parenthood includes the bonds and forms of 'fatherhood', 'motherhood'.

PARENTS
Ego's father and mother (*see also 'Kin'*).

POLYGAMY
The publicly recognized marriages an individual has the right to contract with several other persons simultaneously. Polygamy is termed polyandry when the person is a woman married to several men. It is termed polyandry when a man is married to several women. Polyandry is adelphic when a woman is married to several brothers. Polygyny is sororal when a man is married to several sisters.

PRIMOGENITURE
The tradition of inheritance by the first-born in some societies (*see also 'Eldest', 'Ultimogeniture'*).

R

RAMAGE
A cognatic descent group. Segment of a deme (*see* '*Deme*').

RESIDENCE
The rule that determines where a couple will live after their marriage.
Residence is termed:
- neolocal: if the couple does not live in the same place as the man's or the woman's parents;
- virilocal: if the couple lives with the husband's kin group;
- uxorilocal: if the couple lives with the wife's kin group;
- patrilocal: if the couple lives with to the husband's father;
- avunculocal: if the couple lives with the husband's maternal uncle;
- bilocal: if the couple lives for a time with the husband's parents and for another time next to the wife's parents;
- duolocal: if the spouses live separately;
- natolocal: if the husband and wife continue to live in their own separate family households.

S

SIBLINGS
The group composed of an individual's (real or classificatory) brothers and sisters.

SKEWING
The merging under a single term of several genealogical positions in distinct generations. These positions can be either skewed upward or skewed downward. In the first case, an adult man will call a little boy 'great-uncle', for example. These forms of skewing are found in so-called Crow-Omaha systems, which Lévi-Strauss defined as 'semi-complex' structures. But they are also found in other systems: Australian, Hawaiian, Sudanese. No satisfactory explanation for skewing has yet been advanced.

SORORATE
The right or obligation for a widower to marry one of his wife's sisters (*see* '*Levirate*').

SPIRITUAL KINSHIP
A fictitious kin tie created by the religious bonds that are established for instance in Christianity between the child (or newly converted adult) and the persons who agreed to be his or her godfather and godmother.

T

TRIBE

Set of kin groups that have joined together to exploit and defend a particular territory, which they share according to a variety of rules. These groups are at the same time associated in various ways in view of reproducing themselves together, materially, socially and symbolically. Membership in a tribe is often marked by the existence of a 'big name', an overarching name shared by all the clans or other individual groups that compose it, for example the Baruya. This big name is added to each of the clan names or names of other particular groups. The Andavakia are a clan of the Baruya tribe.

U

ULTIMOGENITURE

The tradition in some societies of inheritance by the last-born (*see 'Primogeniture'*).

UNDIFFERENTIATED, SEE 'COGNATES' AND 'DESCENT RULE'

UTERINE KIN

Individuals related exclusively through the female line, as opposed to agnates.

STANDARD ABBREVIATIONS FOR RELATIONS

F	father
M	mother
B	brother
Z	sister
H	husband
W	wife
S	son
D	daughter
P	parent
Sb	sibling
C	child
c	cousin
e	elder
y	younger
X	cross

Bibliography

Adam, W., 'Consanguinity and Marriage', *The Fortnightly Review*, nos. 12 and 13 (1865), pp. 80–90 and pp. 700–22.

Allen, N., 'Hinduism, Structuralism and Dumézil', *Journal of Indo-European Studies Monograph*, no. 33 (2000), pp. 241–60.

Allen, N., 'Marriage by Capture', *Journal of the Royal Anthropological Institute*, vol. 6, no. 1 (2000), p. 135.

Allen, N., 'Tetradic Theory: An Approach to Kinship', *JASO*, vol. 17, no. 2 (1986), pp. 87–109.

Allen, N., 'The Evolution of Kinship Terminologies', *Lingua*, no. 77 (1989), pp. 173–85.

Allen, N., 'The Prehistory of Dravidian-Type Terminologies', in M. Godelier, T. R. Trautmann and F. E. Tjon Sie Fat (eds.), *Transformations of Kinship*. Washington/London, Smithsonian Institution Press, 1998, pp. 314–31.

Allen, N. J., 'Effervescence and the Origins of Human Society', in N. J. Allen, W. S. F. Pickering and W. Watts Miller (eds.), *On Durkheim's Elementary Forms of Religious Life*. London, Routledge, 1988, pp. 149–61.

Allen, N. J., 'Sherpa Kinship Terminology in Diachronic Perspective', *Man*, vol. 11 (1976), pp. 569–87.

Assoun, P. L., 'Fonctions freudiennes du père', in *Le Père. Métaphore paternelle et fonctions du père: l'interdit, la filiation, la transmission*. Paris, Denoël, 1989, pp. 25–51.

Astuti, R., 'Food for Pregnancy: Procreation, Marriage and Images of Gender among the Vezo of Western Madagascar', *Social Anthropology*, vol. 1, no. 3 (1993), pp. 227–90.

Astuti, R., *People of the Sea: Identity and Descent among the Vezo of Madagascar*. Cambridge, Cambridge University Press, 1995.

Atkinson, J. J., *Primal Law*. London/New York/Bombay, Longmans, Green, and Co., 1903.

Augustine, *City of God*. Harmondsworth, Penguin Classics, 1972.

Avery, J., 'Jura Conjugalia Reconsidered: Kinship Classification and Ceremonial Roles', *Anthropological Forum*, vol. 12, no. 2 (2002), pp. 221–32.

Bachelard, G., *La Psychanalyse du feu*. Paris, Gallimard, 1937.

Bachofen, J. J., *Das Mutterrecht, un ouvrage qui a influencé à la fois Morgan et Marx*. Stuttgart, 1861.

Bajos, N. and A. Spiraa, *Les Comportements sexuels en France*. Paris, La Documentation Française, 1993.

Barkley, R., 'Fire as Paleolithic Tool and Weapon', in *Proceedings of the Prehistoric Society*, no. 21 (1956), pp. 36–48.

Barnard, A. and A. Good, *Research Practices in the Study of Kinship*. London, Academic Press, 1984.

Barnes, R., 'Marriage by Capture', *Journal of the Royal Anthropological Institute*, no. 5 (1999), pp. 57–73.

Barnes, R., *Two Crows Denies It: A History of Controversy in Omaha Sociology*. Lincoln/London, University of Nebraska Press, 1984.

Barraud, C., *Tanebar-Evav, une société de maisons tournées vers le large*. Cambridge/Paris, Cambridge University Press/Maison des Sciences de l'Homme, 1979.

Barry, L., 'Les Modes de composition de l'alliance. Le mariage arabe', *L'Homme*, no. 147 (1988), pp. 17–50.

Barry, L., 'Le tiers exclu', *L'Homme*, no. 146 (1998), pp. 223–47.

Barry, L., 'L'Union endogame en Afrique et à Madagascar', *L'Homme*, nos. 154–5 (2000), pp. 67–100.

Barth, F., *Political Leadership among Swath Pathans*. New York/London, The Athlone Press, 1959.

Barth, F. (ed.), *Ethnic Groups and Boundaries: The Social Organization of Culture Difference*. Boston, Little, Brown and Company, 1969 (London School of Economics Monographs on Social Anthropology, no. 19).

Battagliola, F., *La Fin du mariage?* Paris, Syros/Alternatives, 1988.

Beattie, J. H. M., 'Kinship and Social Anthropology', *Man*, vol. 64, no. 130 (1964), pp. 1–23.

Belo, J., 'A Study of Customs Pertaining to Twins in Bali' (1935), in J. Belo (ed.), *Traditional Balinese Culture*. New York, Columbia Press, 1970, pp. 3–56.

Bensa, A. and A. Goromido, 'Contraintes par corps: ordre politique et violences dans les sociétés kanak d'autrefois', in M. Godelier and M. Panoff (eds.), *Le Corps humain. Supplicié, possédé, cannibalisé*. Amsterdam, Editions des Archives Contemporaines, 1998, pp. 169–97.

Benveniste, E., 'Termes de parenté dans les langues indo-européennes', *L'Homme*, no. 34 (1965), pp. 5–16.

Benveniste, E., *Vocabulaire des institutions indo-européennes*. Paris, Minuit, 1969, 2 vols.

Bernard, S., *L'Homosexualité initiatique dans l'Europe ancienne*. Paris, Payot, 1986.

Berndt, R. M. and C. H., *The World of the First Australians: Aboriginal Traditional Life, Past and Present*. London, Angus and Robertson, 1992 (1964).

Biersack, A. (ed.), *Papuan Borderlands: Huli, Duna and Ipili Perspectives on the New Guinea Highlands*. Ann Arbor, University of Michigan Press, 1995.

Bixler, R. H., 'Primate Mother–Son Incest', *Psychological Reports*, vol. 48 (1981), pp. 531–536.

Bloch, M. (ed.), *Marxist Analyses and Social Anthropology*. London, Malaby Press, 1975.

Boas, F., 'The Social Organization of the Kwakiutl', *American Anthropologist*, vol. 22 (1920), pp. 111–26.

Bogoras, W., *The Chukchee. Jesup North Pacific Expedition*, vol. 7, parts 1–3. New York, G. E. Stechert, 1904–9 (Memoirs of the American Museum of Natural History, vol. 11).

Bohannan, P., 'Marriage in a Changing Society', *Man*, no. 14 (1953), pp. 11–14.

Bohannan, P., 'The Impact of Money on an African Subsistence Economy', *Journal of Economic History*, vol. 19, no. 4 (1959), pp. 491–503.

Bohannan, P., *The Tiv of Central Nigeria*. London, International African Institute, 1953.

Bonnemère, P., 'Considérations relatives aux représentations des substances corporelles en Nouvelle-Guinée', *L'Homme*, vol. 114 (April–June 1990), pp. 101–20.

Bonnemère, P., 'L'Anthropologie du genre en Nouvelle-Guinée. Entre analyse sociologique, psychanalyse et psychologie du développement', *L'Homme*, vol. 161 (January–March 2002), pp. 205–24.

Bonnemère, P., *Le Pandanus rouge. Corps, différence des sexes et parenté chez les Ankave*. Paris, Editions du CNRS/Editions de la Maison des Sciences de l'Homme, 1996.

Bonnemère, P., 'Maternal Nurturing Substance and Paternal Spirit: The Making of a Southern Anga Society', *Oceania*, vol. 64, no. 2 (1993), pp. 159–86.

Bonnet, D., 'Le retour de l'ancêtre', *Journal des africanistes*, vol. 51, nos. 1–2 (1981), pp. 149–82.

Bonte, P. (ed.), *Epouser au plus proche. Inceste, prohibition et stratégies matrimoniales autour de la Méditerranée*. Paris, Editions de l'Ecole des Hautes Etudes en Sciences Sociales, 1994.

Boon, J., *The Anthropological Romance of Bali*. Cambridge, Cambridge University Press, 1977.

Borillo, D. and E. Fassin (eds.), *Au-delà du PACS. L'Expertise familiale à l'épreuve de l'homosexualité*. Paris, Presses Universitaires de France, 1999.

Boswell, J., *Les Unions du même sexe dans l'Europe antique et médiévale*. Paris, Fayard, 1996 (1994).

Bouchery, P., 'Interpréter l'exception. Une société qui questionne l'anthropologie de la parenté', *Archives européennes de sociologie*, vol. 40, no. 1 (1999), pp. 156–70.

Bouquet, M., *Reclaiming English Kinship: Portuguese Refractions on British Kinship Theory*. Manchester, Manchester University Press, 1993.

Bourdieu, P., 'Les stratégies matrimoniales dans le système de reproduction', *Annales*, nos. 4–5 (1972), pp. 1105–27.

Boursier, N., 'L'Europe est divisée sur la question de l'homoparentalité', *Le Monde*, 28 June 2002.

Brady, I. (ed.), *Transactions in Kinship, Adoption and Fosterage*. Honolulu, The University of Hawaii Press, 1976 (ASAO monograph. no. 4).

Brandenstein, C. G. von, *Names and Substance of the Australian Subsection System*. Chicago, University of Chicago Press, 1982.

Brandenstein, C. G. von, 'The Meaning of Section and Sub-section Names', *Oceania*, vol. 41, no. 1 (1970), pp. 39–49.

Brunois, F., *Le Jardin du casoar. La forêt des Kasua. Savoir-être et savoir-faire écologiques*. Paris, Editions de la Maison des Sciences de l'Homme, 2008.

Burguière, A., C. Klapish- Zuber, M. Segalen and F. Zonnabend (eds.), *L'Histoire de la famille*. Paris, Armand Colin, 1986.

Busby, C., 'On Marriage and Marriagibility: Gender and Dravidian Kinship', *Journal of the Royal Anthropological Institute*, no. 3 (1997), pp. 21–42.

Bush, A. C. and J. J. Mettugh, 'Patterns of Roman Marriage', *Ethnology*, vol. 14, no. 1 (1975), pp. 25–46.

Bynum, C. W., *The Resurrection of the Body in Western Christianity, 200–1336*. New York, Columbia University Press, 1995.

Cantarella, E., *Selon la nature, l'usage et la loi. La Bisexualité dans le monde antique*. Paris, La Découverte, 1991.

Care, R., *Lewis Henry Morgan, American Scholar*. Chicago, University of Chicago Press, 1960.

Caroll, V. (ed.), *Adoption in Eastern Oceania*. Honolulu, The University of Hawaii Press, 1970 (ASAO monograph no. 1).

Carsten, J., 'The Substance of Kinship and the Heat of the Earth: Feeding, Personhood and Relatedness among Malayo in Palau Lankaudi', *American Ethnologist*, no. 22 (1995), pp. 223–41.

Castelain-Meunier, C., *La Place des hommes et les métamorphoses de la famille*. Paris, Presses Universitaires de France, 2002.

Catholic Bishops of Papua New Guinea, *Braid Praise*. Umben Publication, Melanesian Institute, 1989, vol. 5, no. 3.

Cerny, J., 'Consanguineous Marriages in Pharaonic Egypt', *Journal of Egyptian Archaeology*, vol. 40 (1954), pp. 23–9.

Chiland, C., *Le Transsexualisme*. Paris, Presses Universitaires de France, 2003.

Chuan-kang, S., 'Tises and Its Anthropology Significance: Issues around the Visiting Sexual System among the Moso', *L'Homme*, nos. 154–5 (2000), pp. 697–712.

Chun, A. J., 'Conceptions of Kinship and Kingship in Classical Chou China', *Toung Pao*, vol. 76, nos. 1–3 (1990), pp. 16–48.

Clark, J., 'Pearl-shell Symbolism in Highlands Papua New Guinea with Particular References to the Wiru of Southern Highlands Province', *Oceania*, vol. 61, no. 4 (1991), pp. 309–39.

Clarke, A. and E. Parson (eds.), *Culture, Kinship and Genes*. London, Macmillan, 1997.

Clastres, P., *Chronique des Indiens Guayaki*. Paris, Plon, 1972.

Clifford, J. and G. E. Marcus, *Writing Culture: The Poetics and the Politics of Ethnography*. Berkeley, University of California Press, 1986.

Cohen, D., 'Law, Society and Homosexuality in Classical Athens', *Past and Present*, no. 117 (1987), pp. 3–21.

Collier, J. F. and S. J. Yanagisako (eds.), *Gender and Kinship: Essays toward a Unified Analysis*. Stanford, Stanford University Press, 1987.

Collier, J. F., M. Rosaldo and S. Yanagisako, 'Is There a Family? New Anthropological Views', in B. Thore and M. Yalom (eds.), *Rethinking the Family: Some Feminist Questions*. Boston, Northeastern University Press, 1992, pp. 31–48.

Collina-Gérard, J., *Le Feu avant les allumettes*. Paris, Editions de la Maison des Sciences de l'Homme, 1988.

Comaroff, J. L. (ed.), *The Meaning of Marriage Payments*. London, Academic Press, 1980.

Commaille, J. and F. de Singly (eds.), *La Question familiale en Europe*. Paris, L'Harmattan, 1997.

Condominas, G., 'The Mnong-Gar of Central Vietnam', in G. P. Murdock (ed.), *Social Structure in Southern Asia*. Viking Fund Publications, Anthropology, Wenner-Gren Fondation for Anthropological Research, 1960, no. 29, pp. 15–23.

Confucius, *Entretiens de Confucius*, translated by Anne Cheng. Paris, Le Seuil, 1981; English version: Confucius, *The Analects*, available at http://classics.mit.edu/Confucius/analects.mb.txt

Confucius, *The Book of Filial Piety*, available at www.chinapage.com/confucius/xiaojing-be.html

Copet-Rougier, E., 'Tu ne traverseras pas le sang. Corps, parenté et pouvoirs chez les Kako du Cameroun', in M. Godelier and M. Panoff (eds.), *Le Corps humain. Supplicié, possédé, cannibalisé*. Amsterdam, Editions des Archives Contemporaines, 1998, pp. 87–108.

Copet-Rougier, E. and F. Héritier-Augé, 'Commentaire sur commentaire: réponse à E. Viveiros de Castro', *L'Homme*, vol. 33, no. 1 (1993), pp. 139–48.

Coquery-Vidrovitch, C., 'The Political Economy of the African Peasantry and Modes of Production', in P. W. Outkind and I. Wallerstein (eds.), *The Political Economy of Contemporary Africa*. London, Sage, 1976, pp. 40–6.

Corbett, P., *The Roman Law of Marriage*. Oxford, Oxford University Press, 1930.

Corbier, M. (ed.), *Adoption et fosterage*. Paris, De Boccard, 1997.

Craig, B. and D. Hyndman (eds.), *Children of Afek: Tradition and Change among the Mountain-Ok of Central New Guinea*. Sydney, Oceania Monograph, 1990.

Craig, R., 'Marriage among the Telefolmin', in R. M. Glasse and M. Meggitt (eds.), *Pigs, Pearl-shells and Women*. Englewood Cliffs, Prentice Hall, 1969.

Crocker, W., 'Canela Other Fathers: Multiple Paternity, Its Changing Practices', Paper presented at the 49th international meeting of Americanists, Quito, 1997.

Crocker, W. and J. Crocker, *The Canela: Bonding through Kinship, Ritual and Sex*. New York, Harcourt Brace, 1994.

Damon, F., *From Muyuw to the Trobriands: Transformations along the Northern Side of the Kula Ring*. Tucson, University of Arizona Press, 1990.

Darwin, C., *The Descent of Man*. London, 1871.

De Waal, F. and F. Lanting, *Bonobos, le bonheur d'être singe*. Paris, Fayard, 1999.

Delaisi, G. and P. Verdier (eds.), *Enfant de personne*. Paris, Odile Jacob, 1994.

Delaney, C., *The Seed and the Soil: Gender and Cosmogony in a Turkish Village Society*. Berkeley, University of California Press, 1991.

Delbrück, B., *Die Indogermanischer Verwandtshaftsnamen*. 1889.

Delrieux, A., *Lévi-Strauss, lecteur de Freud*. Paris, Point Hors Ligne, 1993.

Delumeau, J. and D. Roche (eds.), *L'Histoire des pères et de la paternité*. Paris, Larousse, 1990.

Deputte, B. L., 'L'Evitement de l'inceste chez les primates non humains', *Nouvelle revue d'ethnopsychiatrie*, no. 3 (1985), pp. 41–72.

Deputte, B. L., 'Sexe et société chez les primates', *Sciences humaines*, no. 108 (2000), pp. 28–31.

Derlon, B., 'Corps, cosmos et société en Nouvelle-Irlande', in M. Godelier and M. Panoff (eds.), *La Production du corps*. Paris, Editions des Archives Contemporaines, 1998, pp. 163–86.

Desveaux, E., 'Parenté, rituel, organisation sociale. Le cas des Sioux', *Journal de la Société des américanistes*, no. 80 (1997), pp. 111–40.

Desveaux, E. and M. Selz, 'Dravidian Nomenclature as an Expression of Ego Centered Dualism', in M. Godelier, T. R. Trautmann and F. E. Tjon Sie Fat (eds.), *Transformations of Kinship*. Washington/London, Smithsonian Institution Press, 1998, pp. 150–67.

De Waal, F., 'Bonobo Sex and Society', *Scientific American* (March 1995), pp. 58–64.

De Waal, F., 'La Réconciliation chez les primates', *La Recherche*, no. 210 (1989), pp. 588–97.

Diemberger, H., 'Blood, Sperm, Soul and the Mountain', in T. Del Valle (ed.), *Gendered Anthropology*. London, Routledge, 1993, pp. 88–127.

Diemberger, H., 'Montagnes sacrées, os des ancêtres, sang maternel: le corps humain dans une communauté tibétaine du Népal', in M. Godelier and M.

Panoff (eds.), *La Production du corps*, Paris, Editions des Archives Contemporaines, 1998, pp. 269–80.

Diodore de Sicile. Paris, Les Belles Lettres, 1993 (Bibliothèque historique).

Dole, G., 'Developmental sequences of kinship patterns', in Priscilla Reining (ed.), *Kinship Studies in the Morgan Centennial Year*. Washington DC, Anthropological Society of Washington, 1972, pp. 134–46.

Domenach J-L. and H. Chang-Ming, *Le Mariage en Chine*. Paris, Presses de la Fondation Nationale Des Sciences Politiques, 1987.

Dores, M., *La Femme village*. Paris, L'Harmattan, 1981.

Douaire-Marsaudon, F., 'Je te mange, moi non plus', in M. Godelier and J. Hassoun (eds.), *Meurtre du père, sacrifice de la sexualité. Approches anthropologiques et psychanalytiques*. Paris, Arcanes, 1995, pp. 21–52.

Douaire-Marsaudon, F., 'Le bain mystérieux de la Tu'i Tonga Fafine. Germanité, inceste et mariage sacré en Polynésie', *Anthropos*, vol. 97 (2002), Part 1, pp. 147–62; Part 2, pp. 519–28.

Douaire-Marsaudon, F., 'Le Meurtre cannibale ou la production d'un homme-dieu. Théories des substances et construction hiérarchique en Polynésie', in M. Godelier and M. Panoff, *Le Corps humain. Supplicié, possédé, cannibalisé*. Paris, Editions des Archives Contemporaines, 1998, pp. 137–67.

Dousset, L., 'Accounting for Context and Substance: the Australian Western Desert Kinship Systems', *Anthropological Forum*, vol. 12, no. 2 (2002), pp. 193–204.

Dousset, L., 'Diffusion of Sections in the Australian Western Desert: Reconstructing Social Networks', *Assimilating Identities: Social Networks and the Diffusion of Sections*. Sydney, Oceania Publications, 2005 (Monograph 57).

Dousset, L., 'L'alliance de mariage et la promesse d'épouses chez les Ngaatjatjarra du désert de l'Ouest américain', *Journal de la Société des océanistes*, vol. 108 (1999), pp. 3–17.

Dousset, L., 'On the Misinterpretation of the Aluridja Kinship System Type (Australian Western Desert)', *Social Anthropology*, vol. 12, no. 1 (2003), pp. 43–61.

Dousset, L., 'Production et reproduction en Australie. Pour un tableau de l'unité des tribus aborigènes', *Social Anthropology*, vol. 4, no. 3 (1996), pp. 281–98.

Dover, K., *Greek Homosexuality*. Cambridge MA, Harvard University Press, 1978.

Dubreuil, E., *Des parents de même sexe*. Paris, Odile Jacob, 1998.

Duby, G., *Le Chevalier, la femme et le prêtre. Le mariage dans la France féodale*. Paris, Hachette, 1981.

Dumézil, G., *Mariages indo-européens*. Paris, Payot, 1979.

Dumont, J-C., 'L'Imperium du pater familias', in J. Andreau and H. Bruhns (eds.), *Parenté et stratégies familiales dans l'Antiquité romaine*. Rome, Ecole française de Rome, 1990, pp. 475–95.

Dumont, L., *Affinity as a Value: Marriage Alliances in South India with Comparative Essays on Australia*. Chicago, University of Chicago Press, 1983.

Dumont, L., *Dravidien et Kariera. L'alliance de mariage dans l'Inde du Sud et en Australie*. Paris, Mouton, 1971.

Dumont, L., *Homo hierarchicus. Essai sur le système des castes et ses implications*. Paris, Gallimard, 1966; English translation: *Homo Hierarchichus: The Caste System and its Implications*. Complete revised English edition, translated by Mark Sansbury, Louis Dumont and Basia Gulati. Chicago, University of Chicago Press, 1970.

Dumont, L., *Une sous-caste de l'Inde du Sud. Organisation sociale et religieuse des Pramalai Kallar*. Paris/La Haye, Mouton, 1957; English translation: *A South Indian Subcaste: Social Organization and Religion of the Pramalai Kallar*, translated by M. Moffatt, L. and A. Morton; revised by the author and A. Stern; edited with an introduction by Michael Moffatt. Delhi/New York, Oxford University Press, 1986.

Dupré, G. and P. P. Rey, 'Reflexions on the Pertinence of a Theory of the History of Exchange', *Economy and Society*, vol. 2, no. 2 (1973), pp. 131–63.

Durkheim, E., *Les Formes élémentaires de la vie religieuse*. Paris, Presses Universitaires de France, 1960 (1912).

Edwards, J., S. Franklin, E. Hirsch, F. Price and M. Strathern, *Technologies of Procreation: Kinship in the Age of Assisted Conception*. Manchester, Manchester University Press, 1992.

Eliacheff, C., 'Malaise dans la psychanalyse', *Esprit*, nos. 3–4 (2001).

Elkin, A. P., 'Kinship in South Australia', *Oceania*, vol. 8, no. 4 (1938–40), pp. 423–4.

Eribon, D., *De près et de loin. Entretien avec Claude Lévi-Strauss*. Paris, Odile Jacob, 1988; English translation: *Conversations with Claude Lévi-Strauss*, translated by Paula Wissing. Chicago/London, University of Chicago Press, 1991.

Eribon, D., *Dictionnaire des cultures gays et lesbiennes*. Paris, Larousse, 2003.

Eribon, D., *Réflexions sur la question gay*. Paris, Fayard, 1999.

Errington, S., 'Incestous twins and the house societies of insular Southeast Asia', *Cultural Anthropology*, vol. 2, no. 4 (1987), pp. 403–44.

Evans-Pritchard, E. E., 'Heredity and Gestation as the Azande See Them', *Social Anthropology and Other Essays*. New York, Free Press, 1962, pp. 243–56 (originally published in 1932 in *Man*).

Evans-Pritchard, E. E., *Kinship and Marriage among the Nuer*. Oxford University Press, 1956.

Evans-Pritchard, E. E., *Nuer Religion*. Oxford, Clarendon Press, 1956.

Evans-Pritchard, E. E., 'Nuer Rules of Exogamy and Incest', in M. Fortes (ed.),

Social Structure: Studies presented to A. R. Radcliffe-Brown. London, Oxford University Press, 1949.

Evans-Pritchard, E. E., 'Sexual Inversion among the Azandé', *American Anthropologist*, vol. 72 (1970), pp. 1428–34.

Evans-Pritchard, E. E., *The Nuer*. London, Oxford University Press, 1940.

Fajans, J., *They Make Themselves: Work and Play among the Baining of Papua New Guinea*. Chicago/London, University of Chicago Press, 1997.

Fassin, E., 'Homosexualité et mariage aux Etats-Unis', *Actes de la recherche en sciences sociales*, no. 125 (1998), pp. 63–73.

Feinberg, R., 'Kindred and Alliance in Anuta Island', *The Journal of the Polynesian Society*, vol. 88, no. 3 (1979), pp. 327–48.

Feschet, V., 'La transmission du nom de famille en Europe occidentale. Fin XXᵉ–début du XXIᵉ siècle', *L'Homme*, no. 169 (2004), pp. 61–88.

Feschet, V., 'Nouveaux Pères et 'dernières épouses'. Les formes de la parenté en France à travers le droit et la famille (1999–2003)', *Terrain*, no. 42 (2004), pp. 33–52.

Fezas, J., 'La dot en Inde: des textes classiques aux problèmes contemporains', *Annales de Clermont*, vol. 32 (1996), pp. 183–202.

Filer, C., 'What Is This Thing Called Brideprice?', *Mankind*, vol. 15 (1985), pp. 163–83.

Fine, A., 'Adoption et parrainage dans l'Europe ancienne', in M. Corbier (ed.), *Adoption et fosterage*. Paris, De Boccard, 1999, pp. 349–54.

Fine, A., 'La Parenté spirituelle: lieu et modèle de la bonne distance', in F. Héritier-Augé and E. Copet-Rougier (eds.), *La Parenté spirituelle*. Paris, Editions des Archives Contemporaines, 1995, pp. 51–82 (coll. Ordres sociaux).

Fine, A. (ed.), *Adoptions: ethnologie des parentés choisies*. Paris, Editions de la Maison des Sciences de l'Homme, 1998.

Firth, R., 'A Note on Descent Groups in Polynesia', *Man*, vol. 57 (1957), pp. 4–8.

Fishburne Collier, J. and Sylvia Junko Yanagisako (eds.), *Gender and Kinship: Essays toward a Unified Analysis*. Stanford, Stanford University Press, 1987.

Fison, H. A. W., 'On the Deme and the Horde', *Journal of the Royal Anthropological Institute*, no. 14 (1885).

Forde, D., 'Double Descent among the Yako', in A. R. Radcliffe-Brown and D. Forde (eds.), *African Systems of Kinship and Marriage*. London, Oxford University Press, 1950, chap. 7.

Fortes, M., 'Descent, Filiation and Affinity: A Rejoinder to Dr Leach', *Man*, vol. 59, no. 309 (1959), pp. 193–7 and vol. 59, no. 331, pp. 206–12.

Fortes, M., 'Kinship and Marriage among the Ashanti', in A. R. Radcliffe-Brown and D. Forde (eds.), *African Systems of Kinship and Marriage* (London, Oxford University Press, 1950), chap. 6.

Fortes, M., 'Kinship and Social Order: The Legacy of L. H. Morgan', *Current Anthropology*, vol. 13, no. 2 (April 1972), pp. 285–96.

Fortes, M., *Kinship and the Social Order: The Legacy of L. H. Morgan*. London, Routledge and Kegan Paul, 1969.

Fortes, M., 'Primitive Kinship', *Scientific American*, no. 200 (1959), pp. 146–58.

Fortes, M., *Rules and the Emergence of Society*. London, Royal Anthropological Institute, 1983.

Fortes, M., *The Dynamics of Clanship among the Tallensi*. Oxford, Oxford University Press, 1945.

Fortes, M. 'The "Submerged Descent Line" in Ashanti', in I. Shapera (ed.), *Studies in Kinship and Marriage*. London, Royal Anthropology Institute of Great Britain, 1963.

Fortes, M., *The Web of Kinship among the Tallensi*. Oxford, Oxford University Press, 1949.

Fortune, R., 'Incest', *Encyclopaedia of Social Sciences*. New York, MacMillan, vol. 7, pp. 620–2.

Fortune, R., *Sorcerers of Dubu*. London, Routledge, 1932.

Foucault, M., *Histoire de la sexualité*, vol. 1: *L'Usage des plaisirs*. Paris, Gallimard, 1984.

Fox, R., *Kinship and Marriage*. London, Penguin Books, 1967.

Fox, R., *Reproduction and Succession: Studies in Anthropology, Law and Society*. New Brunswick NJ, Transactions Publisher, 1993.

Francillon, G., 'Un profitable échange de frères chez les Tetum du Sud, Timor central', *L'Homme*, vol. 29, no. 1 (1989), pp. 26–43.

Frankfort, H., *Before Philosophy*. London, Pelikan Books, 1949.

Franklin, S., 'The Parliamentary Debates on the Human Fertilization and Embryology Act', in J. Edwards, S. Franklin, E. Hirsch, F. Price and M. Strathern, *Technologies of Procreation: Kinship in the Age of Assisted Conception*. Manchester, Manchester University Press, 1992, pp. 96–131.

Frazer, J. E., *Myths of the Origins of Fire*. London, Macmillan, 1930.

Frazer, J. G., *Totemism and Exogamy*. London, Macmillan, 1910.

Freeman, D., 'On the Concept of Kindred', *Journal of the Royal Anthropological Institute*, vol. 91 (1961), pp. 192–220.

Freeman, D., 'The Family of Iban of Borneo', in J. Goody (ed.), *The Development Cycle in Domestic Groups*. Cambridge, Cambridge University Press, 1968.

Freeman, D., '"Totem et Tabou": une nouvelle évaluation', in W. Muensterberger (ed.), *L'Anthropologie psychanalytique depuis 'Totem et Tabou'*. Paris, Payot, 1976, pp. 57–82.

Freud, S., *A Phylogenetic Fantasy: Overview of the Transference Neuroses*, ed. by Ilse Grubrich-Simitis, translated by Axel Hoffer and Peter T. Hoffer. Cambridge MA, Belknap Press/Harvard University Press, 1987.

Freud, S., *Civilization and Its Discontents*, Authorized translation by Joan Riviere. London, L. and Virginia Woolf at the Hogarth Press, 1930.

Freud, S., *Nouvelles Conférences d'introduction à la psychanalyse* (1933). Paris, Gallimard, 1989.

Freud, S., *Sigmund Freud présenté par lui-même*. Paris, Gallimard, 1984.

Freud, S., 'The Psychogenesis of a Case of Homosexuality in a Woman' (1920), 'Some Neurotic Mechanisms in Jealousy, Paranoia and Homosexuality', in J. Strachey (ed.), *The Standard Edition of the Complete Psychological Works of Sigmund Freud: Beyond the Pleasure Principle, Group Psychology and Other Works*. Vol. 18 (1920–22). London, Hogarth Press, 1953–74.

Freud, S., *Totem and Taboo*, translated by James Strachey. London, Routledge and Kegan Paul, 1961.

Friedman, J., (ed.), *World System History. The Social Science of Long-Term Change*. London, Routledge, 2000.

Friedrich, P., 'Proto Indo-European Kinship', *Ethnology*, vol. 5, no. 1 (1966), pp. 1–36.

Ganghofer, R. (ed.), *Le Droit de la famille en Europe. Son évolution depuis l'Antiquité jusqu'à nos jours*. Strasbourg, Presses Universitaires de Strasbourg, 1992.

Geertz, C., 'The Visit. Review of *A Society without Fathers or Husbands: The Na of China* by Cai Hua', *New York Review of Books*, 18 October 2001.

Geffray, C., *Ni père ni mere. Critique de la parenté, le cas Makhuwa*. Paris, Le Seuil, 1990.

Gell, A., *Metamorphosis of the Cassowaries: Umeda Society, Language and Ritual*. London, Athlone, 1975.

Gessat-Anstett, E., 'Les terminologies russes de parenté', *L'Homme*, nos. 154–5 (2000), pp. 613–34.

Ghasarian, C., *Honneur, chance et destin. La Culture indienne à la Réunion*. Paris, L'Harmattan, 1991.

Girard, F., *Manuel élémentaire de droit romain*. Paris, Librairie Rousseau, 1918.

Glowczewski, B., *Du rêve à la loi chez les Aborigènes. Mythes, rites et organisation sociale en Australie*. Paris, Presses Universitaires de France, 1991.

Glynn, I., 'Food Sharing and Human Evolution: African Evidence from the Plio-Pleistocene of East Africa', *Journal of Anthropological Research*, vol. 34 (1978), pp. 311–25.

Godelier, M., 'Anthropologie et recherches féministes. Perspectives et rétrospectives', in J. Laufer, C. Marry and M. Maruani (eds.), *Le Travail du genre*. Paris, La Découverte, 2003, pp. 23–34.

Godelier, M., 'Ethnie, tribu, nation chez les Baruya de Nouvelle-Guinea', *Journal de la Société des océanistes*, vol. 41, no. 81 (1985), pp. 159–68.

Godelier, M., *Horizons, Trajets Marxistes en Anthropologie*. Paris, Maspero, 1973; English translation: *Perspectives in Marxist Anthropology*, translated by R. Brain. Cambridge, Cambridge University Press, 1977.

Godelier, M., 'Inceste, parenté, pouvoir', *Psychanalyse*, no. 36 (1990), pp. 33–51.

Godelier, M., 'Introspection, rétrospections, projections: un entretien avec Hosham Dawood', *Gradhiva*, no. 25 (1999), pp. 1–25; English translation: 'Insights into an Itinerary. An Interview with Maurice Godelier', by Hosham Dawod; translated by N. Scott, *Folk*, vol. 41 (1999), pp. 5–44.

Godelier, M., *L'Enigme du don*. Paris, Fayard, 1996; English translation: *The Enigma of the Gift*, translated by N. Scott. Chicago, University of Chicago Press; Cambridge, Polity Press, 1998.

Godelier, M., *L'Idéel et le matériel, pensée, économie, sociétés*. Paris, Fayard, 1984; English translation: *The Mental and the Material: Thought, Economy and Society*, translated by Martin Thom. London/New York, Verso, 1986.

Godelier, M., 'L'Occident est-il le modèle universel de l'humanité? Les Baruya de Nouvelle-Guinée entre transformation et décomposition', *Revue internationale des sciences sociales*, no. 128 (1991), pp. 411–23.

Godelier, M., 'La Monnaie de sel des Baruya de Nouvelle-Guinée', *L'Homme*, vol. 11, no. 2 (1969), pp. 5–37.

Godelier, M., *La Production des grands hommes. Pouvoir et domination masculine chez les Baruya de Nouvelle-Guinée*. Paris, Fayard, 1982; English translation: *The Making of Great Men: Male Domination and Power among the New Guinea Baruya*, translated by R. Swyer. Cambridge, Cambridge University Press, 1986.

Godelier, M., 'Le Concept de tribu. Crise d'un concept ou crise des fondements empiriques de l'anthropologie?', *Diogène*, no. 81 (1973), pp. 3–28.

Godelier, M., 'Les Baruya de Nouvelle-Guinée, un exemple récent de subordination économique, politique et culturelle d'une société "primitive à l'Occident"', in M. Godelier (ed.), *Transitions et subordinations au capitalisme*. Paris, Editions de la Maison des Sciences de l'Homme, 1999, pp. 379–99.

Godelier, M., 'Meurtre du Père ou sacrifice de la sexualité? Conjectures sur les fondements du lien social', in M. Godelier and J. Hassoun (eds.), *Meurtre du Père, sacrifice de la sexualité. Approches anthropologiques et psychanalytiques*. Strasbourg, Arcanes, 1996, pp. 21–52.

Godelier, M., *Meurtre du Père, sacrifice de la sexualité. Approches anthropologiques et pyschanalytiques*. Paris, Arcanes, 1996.

Godelier, M., 'Objet et méthodes de l'anthropologie économique', *L'Homme*, vol. 5, no. 2 (1965), pp. 32–91.

Godelier, M., 'Outils de pierre, outils d'acier chez les Baruya de Nouvelle-Guinée', *L'Homme*, vol. 13, no. 3 (1973), pp. 187–220.

Godelier, M., 'Pouvoir et langage. Réflexions sur les paradigmes et les paradoxes de la 'légitimité' des rapports de domination et d'oppression', *Communications*, no. 28 (1978), pp. 21–7.

Godelier, M., 'Quelles cultures pour quels primates: définition faible ou définition forte de la culture?', in A. Ducros, J. Ducros and P. Joulain (eds.), *La Culture est-elle naturelle?* Paris, Errance, 1998, pp. 217–23.

Godelier, M., *Rationalité et irrationalité en économie*. Paris, Maspero, 1966.

Godelier, M., Review of Bernard Vernier's book *Frère et sœur. La genèse sociale des sentiments* in *L'Homme*, vol. 130 (1993), pp. 191–5.

Godelier, M., 'Sexualité, parenté, pouvoir', *La Recherche*, no. 213 (1989), pp. 1141–55.

Godelier, M. and M. Panoff (eds.), *La Production du corps*. Amsterdam, Editions des Archives Contemporaines, 1998.

Godelier, M. and M. Panoff (eds.), *Le Corps humain. Supplicié, possédé, cannibalisé*. Amsterdam, Archives Contemporaines, 1998.

Godelier, M., T. R. Trautmann and F. E. Tjon Sie Fat (eds.), *Transformations of Kinship*. Washington/London, Smithsonian Institution Press, 1998.

Golombok, S., A. Spencer and M. Rutter, 'Children in Lesbian and Single-Parent Households: Psycho-sexual and Psychiatric Appraisal', *Journal of Child Psychology and Psychiatry*, vol. 24, no. 4 (1983), pp. 551–72

Golombok, S., F. Tasker and C. Murray, 'Children Raised in Fatherless Families from Infancy: Family Relationships and Socio-emotional Development of Children of Lesbian and Heterosexual Mothers', *Journal of Child Psychology and Psychiatry*, vol. 38, no. 7 (1997), pp. 783–91.

Golson, J., 'The Ipomean Revolution Revisited: Society and Sweet Potato in the Upper Waghi Valley', in A. Strathern (ed.), *Inequality in New Guinea Highlands Societies*. Cambridge, Cambridge University Press, 1982, pp. 109–36.

Golson, J. and D. Gardner, 'Agriculture and Sociopolitical Organization in New Guinea Highlands Prehistory', *Annual Review of Anthropology*, vol. 19 (1990), pp. 395–417.

Good, A., 'Prescription, Preference and Practice: Marriage Patterns among the Kondaiyankottai Maravar of South India', *Man*, vol. 16, no. 1 (1981), pp. 108–29.

Good, A., *The Female Bridegroom: A Comparative Study of the Life Crisis Rituals in India and Sri Lanka*. Oxford, Clarendon Press, 1991.

Goodenough, W., 'Comments on the Question of Incestuous Marriages in Old Iran', *American Anthropologist*, vol. 51 (1949), pp. 326–88.

Goodenough, W., *Description and Comparison in Cultural Anthropology*. Chicago, Aldine, 1970.

Goodenough, W., 'Residence Rules', *Southwestern Journal of Anthropology*, vol. 12, no. 1 (1956), pp. 22–37.

Goody, E., *Parenthood and Social Reproduction. Fostering and Occupational Roles in West Africa*. Cambridge, Cambridge University Press, 1982.

Goody, J., 'A Comparative Approach to Incest and Adultery', *British Journal of Sociology*, vol. 7 (1956), pp. 286–305.

Goody, J., 'Inheritance, Property and Marriage in Africa and Eurasia', *Sociology*, vol. 3 (1969), pp. 55–76.

Goody, J., 'Marriage Prestations, Inheritage and Descent in Preindustrial Societies', *Journal of Comparative Family Studies*, vol. 1 (1970), pp. 37–54.

Goody, J., *Production and Reproduction*. Cambridge/New York, Cambridge University Press, 1976.

Goody, J., *The Development of the Family and Marriage in Europe*. Cambridge/New York, Cambridge University Press, 1983.

Goody, J., *The European Family: An Historico-anthropological Essay*. Oxford/Malden MA, Blackwell Publishers, 2000.

Goody, J., *The Oriental, the Ancient, and the Primitive: Systems of Marriage and the Family in the Pre-industrial Societies of Eurasia*. Cambridge/New York, Cambridge University Press, 1990.

Goody, J. and S. J. Tambiah, *Bridewealth and Dowry*. Cambridge, Cambridge University Press, 1973.

Goudsblom, J., *Fire and Civilization*. Harmondsworth, Penguin Books, 1992.

Gough, K., 'A comparison of incest prohibitions and rules of exogamy in three matrilineal groups of the Malabar Coast', *International Archives of Ethnography*, no. 46 (1952), pp. 81–105.

Gracchus, F., *Les Lieux de la mère dans les sociétés afro-américaines*. Paris, Editions Caribéennes, 1986.

Granet, M., 'Catégories matrimoniales et relations de proximité dans la Chine ancienne', *Annales sociologiques* (1939), series B, fasc. 1–3.

Granet, M., *Catégories matrimoniales et relations de proximité dans la Chine ancienne*. Paris, Félix Alcan, 1939.

Granet, M., *La Civilisation chinoise*. Paris, La Renaissance du Livre, 1929; English translation: *Chinese Civilization*, translated by Kathleen E. Innes and Mabel R. Brailsford. New York, Meridian books (1958).

Green, A., 'Inceste et parricide en anthropologie et en psychanalyse', in P. Descola, J. Hammel and P. Lemonnier (eds.), *La Production du social*. Paris, Fayard, 1999, pp. 213–32.

Gregory, C., *Gifts and Commodities*. London/New York, Academic Press, 1982.

Gross, M., *L'Homoparentalité*. Paris, Presses Universitaires de France, 2003.

Grottanelli, V. L., 'Pre-existence and Survival in Nzema Beliefs', *Man*, vol. 61 (1961), pp. 1–5.

Guerreau-Jalabert, A., 'La désignation des relations et des groupes de parenté en latin médiéval', *Archivuum latinatis*, vols. 46–7, no. 46 (1988).

Guerreau-Jalabert, A., 'La parenté dans l'Europe médiévale et moderne: à propos d'une synthèse récente', *L'Homme*, vol. 29, no. 110 (1989), pp. 63–93.

Guerreau-Jalabert, A., 'Spiritus et caritas. Le baptême dans la société médiévale', in F. Héritier-Augé and E. Copet-Rougier (eds.), *La Parenté spirituelle*. Paris/ Amsterdam, Editions des Archives Contemporaines, 1995, pp. 133–203.

Guerreau-Jalabert, A., 'Sur les structures de parenté dans l'Europe médiévale', *Annales*, no. 6 (1981), pp. 1028–49.

Hamburger, C., B. M. Stürup and E. Dahl-Iversen, 'Transvestism, Hormonal, Psychiatric and Surgical Treatment', *Journal of the American Medical Association*, no. 152 (1953), pp. 391–6.

Hamilton, A., *Timeless Transformations: Women, Men and History in the Western Australian Desert*. Sydney, University of Sydney Press, 1979.

Hautecloque-Howe, A. de, *Les Rhades: une société de droit maternel*. Paris, Editions du CNRS, 1987.

Hayden, C., 'Gender, Genetics and Generations: Reformulating Biology in Lesbian Kinship', *Cultural Anthropology*, vol. 10, no. 1 (1995), pp. 41–63.

Herdt, G., *Guardians of the Flutes: Idioms of Masculinity*. New York, McGraw-Hill Company, 1981.

Herdt, G. (ed.), *Ritualized Homosexuality in Melanesia*. Berkeley, University of California Press, 1984.

Herdt, G. (ed.), *Rituals of Manhood: Male Initiation on Papua New Guinea*. Berkeley, University of California Press, 1982.

Héritier, F., *L'Exercice de la parenté*. Paris, Gallimard/Le Seuil, 1981.

Héritier, F., 'L'inceste du deuxième type', *Le Nouvel Observateur*, no. 1536 (April 1994), pp. 69–72.

Héritier, F., *Les Deux Sœurs et leur mère. Anthropologie de l'inceste*. Paris, Odile Jacob, 1994; English translation: *Two Sisters and Their Mother: The Anthropology of Incest*, translated by J. Herman. New York, Zone Books, 2002.

Héritier-Augé, F. and E. Copet-Rougier (eds.), *La Parenté spirituelle*. Amsterdam, Editions des Archives Contemporaines, 1995.

Herrenschmidt, C., 'Le xwêtôdas ou "mariage incestueux" en Iran Ancien', in P. Bonte (ed.), *Epouser au plus proche. Inceste, prohibition et stratégies matrimoniales autour de la Méditerranée*. Paris, Editions de l'Ecole des Hautes Etudes en Sciences Sociales, 1994, pp. 113–25.

Hewlett, B. S., *Intimate Fathers: The Nature and Context of Aka Pygmy Paternal Infant Care*. Ann Arbor, University of Michigan Press, 1992.

Hiatt, L., *Kinship and Conflict: A Study of an Aboriginal Community in Northern Arnhem Land*. Canberra, Australian National University, 1965.

Hiatt, L., 'Towards a Natural History of Fatherhood', *The Australian Journal of Anthropology*, vol. 1, nos. 2–3 (1990), pp. 110–30.

Hindness, B. and P. Hirst, *Pre-capitalist Modes of Production*. London, Routledge and Kegan, 1975, pp. 45–78.

Hocart, A. M., 'Kinship Systems', *Anthropos*, vol. 32 (1937), pp. 545–51.

Hocart, A. M., 'The Indo-European Kinship System', *Ceylon Journal of Science*, no. 1 (1928), pp. 79–204.

Holy, L., *Anthropological Perspectives on Kinship*. London, Pluto Press, 1996.

Hopkins, K., 'Brother–Sister Marriage in Roman Egypt', *Comparative Studies in Society and History*, no. 22 (1980), pp. 303–54.

Hornborg, A., 'Social Redundancy in Amazonian Social Structure', in M. Godelier, R. Trautmann and F. E. Tjon Sie Fat (eds.), *Transformations of Kinship*. Washington/London, Smithsonian Institution Press, 1998, pp. 168–86.

Houzel, D., *Les Enjeux de la parentalité*. Paris, Erès, 1999.

Howell, P. P., *A Manual of Nuer Law*. London, Oxford University Press, 1954.

Howell, P. P., 'The Age-System and the Institution of "Nak" among the Nuer', *Sudan Notes and Records* (1947).

Hua, C., *Une société sans père ni mari. Les Na de Chine*. Paris, Presses Universitaires de France, 1997.

Hughes, O., 'From Brideprice to Dowry in Mediterranean Europe', *Journal of Family History*, vol. 3 (1978), pp. 262–96.

Hecht, J., 'The Culture of Gender in Pukapuka: Male, Female and the Mayakitanga Sacred Maid', *The Journal of the Polynesian Society*, vol. 86, no. 2 (1977), pp. 183–206.

Huth, A. H., *The Marriage of Near Kin*. London, 1875.

Ives, J. W., *A Theory of Northern Athapaskan Prehistory*. Boulder CO, Westview Press, 1990.

Ives, J. W., 'Development Processes in the Pre-contact History of Athapaskan, Algonkian and Numic kin systems', in M. Godelier, T. R. Trautmann and F. E. Tjon Sie Fat (eds.), *Transformations of Kinship* (Washington/London, Smithsonian Institution Press, 1998, pp. 94–139.

Jackson, S., *Heterosexuality in Question*. London, Sage, 1999.

Jacob, F., *La Logique du vivant*. Paris, Gallimard, 1970.

James, S. R., 'Humanoid Use of Fire in the Lower and Middle Pleistocene', *Current Anthropology*, vol. 30 (1989), pp. 1–26.

Jeannelle, J-L., Article 'Hétérophobie', in *Dictionnaire de l'homophobie*. Paris, Presses Universitaires de France, 2003, pp. 205–7.

Jeudy-Ballini, M., 'Naître par le sang, renaître par la nourriture', in A. Fine (ed.), *Adoptions. Ethnologie des parentés choisies*. Paris, Editions de la Maison des Sciences de l'Homme, 1998, pp. 19–44.

Jolas, T., M-C. Pingaud, Y. Verdier and F. Zonnabend, *Une campagne voisine*. Paris, Editions de la Maison des Sciences de l'Homme, 1990.

Jorgensen, D., 'Big Men, Great Men and Women: Alternative Logics of Gender Difference', in M. Godelier and M. Strathern (eds.), *Big Men and Great Men: Personifications of Power in Melanesia*. Cambridge, Cambridge University Press, 1991, pp. 256–71.

Jorgensen, D., 'Mirroring Nature? Men's and Women's Models of Conception in Telefolmin', *Mankind*, vol. 14, no. 1 (August 1988), pp. 57–65.

Jorgensen, D., 'Money and Marriage in Telefolmin', in R. A. Marksbury (ed.), *The Business of Marriage: Transformations in Oceanic matrimony*. Pittsburgh, University of Pennsylvania Press, 1995, pp. 57–82.

Joyce, R. A. and S. D. Gillepsie (eds.), *Beyond Kinship: Social and Material Reproduction in House Societies*. Philadelphia, University of Pennsylvania Press, 2000.

Juillerat, B., *Les Enfants du sang. Société, reproduction et imaginaire en Nouvelle-Guinée*. Paris, Editions de la Maison des Sciences de l'Homme, 1986; English translation: *Children of the Blood: Society, Reproduction and Cosmology in New Guinea*, translated by Nora Scott. Oxford/New York, Berg, 1996.

Juillerat, B., 'Terminologie de parenté yafar. Etude formelle d'un système dakota-iroquois', *L'Homme*, vol. 17, no. 4, pp. 5–34.

Julien, D. and E. Chartrand, 'La Psychologie familiale des gays et des lesbiennes: perspectives de la tradition scientifique nord-américaine', *Sociologie et sociétés*, vol. 29 (1999), pp. 71–81.

Karsten, R., *La Civilisation de l'Empire inca*. Paris, Presses Universitaires de France, 1986.

Keen, J., 'Seven Aboriginal Marriage Systems and Their Correlates', *Anthropological Forum*, vol. 12, no. 2 (2002), pp. 145–58.

Keesing, R., *Kin Groups and Social Structure* New York, Holt, Rinehart and Winston, 1975.

Kensinger, K., 'Hierarchy Versus Equality in Cashinahua Gender Relations', paper presented at the Wenner-Gren symposium 'Amazonia and Melanesia: Gender and Anthropological Comparison', Mijas (Spain) 1996.

Kensinger, K., *How Real People Ought to Live: The Cashinahua of Eastern Peru*. Prospect Heights IL, Waveland Press, 1995.

Kensinger, K., 'The Philanderer's Dilemma', Paper presented at the 49th international meeting of Americanists, Quito, 1997.

Kirchhoff, P., 'The Principles of Clanship in Human Society', *Davidson Journal of Anthropology*, vol. 1, no.1 (1954), pp. 1–10.

Kirchhoff, P. 'Verwandschaftsbezeichnungen und Verwandtenheirat', *Zeitschrift fur Ethnologie*, no. 64 (1932), pp. 41–72.

Knauft, B., 'Homosexuality in Melanesia', *The Journal of Psychoanalytic Anthropology*, vol. 10, no. 2 (1987), pp. 155–91.

Knight, C., 'The Wives of the Sun and the Moon', *Journal of the Royal Anthropological Institute*, 3 (1997), pp. 133–53.

Krafft-Ebing, R. von, *Psychopathia sexualis*. 1886.

Kress-Rosen, N., 'L'Inceste aux origines de la psychanalyse', *Etudes freudiennes*, no. 35 (1994), pp. 61–82.

Krige, E. J. and J. D., *The Realm of the Rain Queen*. London, Oxford University Press, 1943.

Kroeber, A., 'Classificatory Systems of Relationship', *Journal of the Royal Anthropological Institute*, no. 39 (1909), pp. 77–84.

Kroeber, A., 'Totem and Taboo, an Ethnological Psychoanalysis', *American Anthropologist*, vol. 22 (1920), pp. 48–55.

Kroeber, A., 'Totem and Taboo in Retrospect', *American Journal of Sociology*, vol. 45, no. 3 (1939), pp. 446–51.

Kronenfeld, D. B., 'A Formal Analysis of Fanti Kinship terminology (Ghana)', *Anthropos*, no. 75 (1980), pp. 586–608.

Kronenfeld, D. B., 'Fanti Kinship: The Structure of Terminology and Behavior', *American Anthropologist*, no. 75 (1973), pp. 1577–95.

Kryukov, M. V., *Sistema rodstva kitaitsev* (The Chinese kinship system). Moskow, Nauka, 1972.

Kryukov, M. V., 'The Synchro-diachronic Method and the Mutidirectionality of Kinship Transformations', in M. Godelier, T. R. Trautmann and F. E. Tjon Sie Fat (eds.), *Transformations of Kinship*. Washington/London, Smithsonian Institution Press, 1998, pp. 297–313.

Kullanda, S., 'Indo-European Kinship Terms Revisited', *Current Anthropology*, vol. 43, no. 1 (2002), pp. 89–111.

La Pensée, no. 327 (July/September 2001), Special issue, 'Quelle place pour le père?' (articles by Françoise Hurstel, Anne Thevenot, Marie-Thérèse Meulders-Klein, Patrick de Neuter)

Lacan, J., *Ecrits*. Paris: Le Seuil, 1960.

Lallemand, S., 'Adoption, fosterage et alliance', *Anthropologie et sociétés*, vol. 12, no. 2 (1988), pp. 25–40.

Lallemand, S., 'Génitrices et éducatrices mossi', *L'Homme*, vol. 16, no. 1 (1976), pp. 109–24.

Lallemand, S., *La Circulation des enfants en société traditionnelle: prêt, don, échange*. Paris, L'Harmattan, 1993.

Lang, A., *Social Origins*. London, Longmans, Green, and Co., 1903.

Langaney, A. and R. Nadot, 'Génétique, parenté et prohibition de l'inceste', in A. Ducros and M. Panoff (eds.), *La Frontière des sexes*. Paris, Presses Universitaires de France, 1995, pp. 105–26.

Laqueur, T., *La Fabrique du sexe. Essai sur le corps et le genre en Occident*. Paris, Gallimard, 1992.

Lawrence, P., *The Garia*. Melbourne, Melbourne University Press, 1984.

Le Gall, D. and Y. Bettachar (eds.), *La Pluriparentalité*. Paris, Presses Universitaires de France, 2001.

Leach, E., 'Aspects of Bridewealth and Marriage Stability among the Kachin and Lakher', *Man*, vol. 57 (1957), pp. 50–5.

Leach, E., 'Descent, Filiation and Affinity', *Man*, vol. 60 (1960), pp. 9–10.

Leach, E., 'Proceedings of the Royal Anthropological Institute', 1966; reprinted in *Genesis as Myth and Other Essays* (London, Cape Editions, 1969).

Leach, E., *Pul Elya, a Village in Ceylon: A Study of Land Tenure and Kinship*. Cambridge, Cambridge University Press, 1961.

Leach, E., *Rethinking Anthropology*. London, University of London/The Athlone Press, 1961.

Leach, E. Review of D. Schneider and K. Gough (eds.), *Matrilineal Kinship*, *American Journal of Sociology*, vol. 67, no. 6 (1962), pp. 705–7.

Leach, E., 'The Atom of Kinship, Filiation and Descent: Error of Translation or Confusion of Ideas?', *L'Homme*, vol. 17, nos. 2–3 (1977), pp. 127–9.

Lederman, R., *What Gifts Engender: Social Relations and Politics in Mendi*. New York, Cambridge University Press, 1986.

Lefébure, C., 'Le Mariage des cousins parallèles patrilatéraux et l'endogamie de lignée agnatique: l'anthropologie de la parenté face à la question de l'endogamie', in *Production, pouvoir et parenté dans le monde méditerranéen de Sumer à nos jours*. Paris, Ecole des Hautes Etudes en Sciences Sociales/CNRS, 1976, pp. 195–207.

Legendre, P., 'Entretien avec Antoine Spire', *Le Monde*, 23 October 2001.

Legendre, P., *Filiation*. Paris, Fayard, 1996.

Legendre, P., *'Ils seront deux en une seule chair', scénographie du couple humain dans le texte occidental*, Paris, Editions de la Maison des Sciences de l'Homme, 2004 (Travaux du Laboratoire européen pour l'étude de la filiation, no. 3).

Legendre, P., *Le Dossier occidental de la parenté*. Paris, Fayard, 1988.

Legendre, P., *L'Inestimable Objet de transmission*. Paris, Fayard, 2004.

Lehman, F. K., 'On Chin and Kachin Marriage Regulation', *Man*, vol. 5 (1970), pp. 118–25.

Lemonnier, P., 'Maladies, cannibalisme et sorcellerie chez les Anga de Papouasie-Nouvelle-Guinée', in M. Godelier and M. Panoff (eds.), *Le Corps humain. Supplicié, possédé, cannibalisé*. Amsterdam, Editions des Archives Contemporaines, 1998, pp. 7–28.

Lemonnier, P. 'Mipela wan bilas. Identité et variabilité socioculturelle chez les Anga de Nouvelle-Guinée', in S. T. Tcherkézoff and F. Marsaudon (eds.), *Le*

Pacific sud aujourd'hui: identités et transformations culturelles. Paris, Editions du CNRS, 1998, pp. 196–227; English translation: *The Changing South Pacific: Identities and transformations.* Canberra: Pandanus Books, Australian National University, 2005.

Lévi, J., *Les Fonctionnaires divins. Politique, despotisme et mystique en Chine ancienne.* Paris, Le Seuil, 1989.

Levine, H. B., 'Gestational Surrogacy: Nature and Culture in Kinship', *Ethnology*, vol. 42, no. 3 (2003), pp. 173–86.

Levine, N. E., 'The Demise of Marriage in Purang Tibet: 1959–1990', in P. Kvaerne (ed.), *Tibetan Studies.* Oslo, Institute for Comparative Research in Human Culture, 1994, vol. 1, pp. 468–80.

Levine, N. E., *The Dynamics of Polyandry, Kinship, Domesticity and Population of the Tibetan Border.* Chicago, University of Chicago Press, 1988.

Levine, N. E., 'The Theory of Rü Kinship, Descent and Status in a Tibetan Society', in C. von Fürer-Haimendorf (ed.), *Asian Highland Societies in Anthropological Perspective.* New Delhi, Stirling, 1981, pp. 52–78.

Lévi-Strauss, C., 'Apologue des amibes', in *En substance, Textes pour Françoise Héritier.* Paris, Fayard, 2002, pp. 493–6.

Lévi-Strauss, C., Conversation with G. Kukukdjian, *Magazine littéraire*, November (1971), special issue on Lévi-Strauss.

Lévi-Strauss, C., 'Du mariage dans un degré rapproché', in *Le Regard éloigné.* Paris, Plon, 1982, pp. 127–40; English translation: 'On Marriage Between Close Kin', in *A View from Afar*, translated by J. Neugroschel and Phoebe Hoss. Chicago, University of Chicago Press, 1985, pp. 8–97.

Lévi-Strauss, C., 'Entretien avec Raymond Bellour', in R. Bellour and C. Clément, *Claude Lévi-Strauss: Textes de et sur Lévi-Strauss.* Paris, Gallimard, 1977.

Lévi-Strauss, C., 'Histoire et ethnologie', *Annales*, vol. 38, no. 6 (1983), pp. 1217–31.

Lévi-Strauss, C., 'Introduction à l'Œuvre de Mauss', in *Sociologie et anthropologie.* Paris, Presses Universitaires de France, 1950, pp: i–lii; English translation: *Introduction to the Work of Marcel Mauss*, translated by Felicity Baker. London, Routledge and Kegan Paul, 1987.

Lévi-Strauss, C., 'La notion de maison: entretien avec Claude Lévi-Strauss', par Pierre Lamaison, *Terrain*, no. 9 (October 1989), pp. 34–9.

Lévi-Strauss, C. *La Pensée sauvage.* Paris, Plon, 1962; English translation: *The Savage Mind*, (no translator mentioned). Chicago, University of Chicago Press, 1969.

Lévi-Strauss, C., 'La Sexualité féminine et l'origine de la société', *Les Temps modernes*, no. 598 (1998), pp. 78–84.

Lévi-Strauss, C., *La Voie des masques.* Paris, Plon, 1979; English translation: *The Way of the Masks*, translated by Sylvia Modelski. Seattle, University of Washington Press, 1982.

Lévi-Strauss, C., *Le Cru et le cuit, mythologiques* I. Paris, Plon, 1964; English translation: *The Raw and the Cooked: Introduction to a Science of Mythology*: 1, translated by John and Doreen Weightman. Harmondsworth, Penguin, 1986.

Lévi-Strauss, C., *Le Totémisme aujourd'hui*. Paris: Presses Universitaires de France, 1962; English translation: *Totemism*, translated by Rodney Needham. Boston: Beacon Press, 1963.

Lévi-Strauss, C. *Les Structures élémentaires de la parenté*, Paris, Presses Universitaires de France, 1949; English translation: *The Elementary Structures of Kinship*, translated by James Harle Bell, John Richard von Sturmer and Rodney Needham. Boston, Beacon Press, 1969.

Lévi-Strauss, C., *Paroles données*. Paris, Plon, 1984; English translation: *Anthropology and Myth: Lectures, 1951–1982*, translated by Roy Willis. Oxford/New York, Blackwell, 1987.

Lévi-Strauss, C., 'Réflexions sur l'atome de parenté', *L'Homme*, vol. 13, no. 3 (1973), pp. 5–30.

Lévi-Strauss, C. 'Réponse à Edmund Leach', *L'Homme*, vol. 18, no. 2–3 (1977), pp. 131–3.

Lévi-Strauss, C. 'Retours en arrière', *Les Temps modernes*, no. 598 (1998).

Lévi-Strauss, C., 'The Family', in H. Shapiro (ed.), *Man, Culture and Society*. London/Oxford, Oxford University Press, 1956, pp. 261–95.

Lévi-Strauss, C., 'The Future of Kinship Studies', Huxley Memorial Lecture, in *Proceedings of the Royal Anthropological Institute of Great Britain and Ireland*, vol. 1 (1965), pp. 13–22.

Lévi-Strauss, C., *Tristes tropiques*, Paris, Plon, 1955; English translation: *Tristes Tropiques*, translated by John and Doreen Weightman. Penguin books, 1973.

Lewin, H., *Lesbian Mothers: Accounts of Gender in American Culture*. Ithaca, Cornell University Press, 1993.

Lewis, E. D., *People of the Source: The Social and Ceremonial Order of Tana Wai Brama of Flores*, Dordrecht, Foris, 1988.

Liu Pi-chen, 'Les Mtiu, femmes chamanes: genre, parenté, chamanisme et pouvoir des femmes chez les Kavalan de Taiwan (1895–2000)', Doctoral dissertation, Ecole des Hautes Etudes en Sciences Sociales, Paris, 2004.

Lloyd, R. G., *A Baruya–Tok Pisin–English Dictionary*. Canberra, The Australian University, 1992 (Pacific Linguistics).

Lloyd, R. G., 'Baruya Kith and Kin', in D. Shaw (ed.), *Kinship Studies in Papua New Guinea*. Ukarumpa, Summer Institute of Linguistics, 1974, pp. 97–114.

Lloyd, R. G., 'The Angan Language Family', in K. Franklin (ed.), *The Linguistic Situation in the Gulf District and Adjacent Areas. Papua New Guinea*. Canberra, The Australian University, 1973, pp. 31–110.

Lounsbury, F. G., 'A Formal Account of Crow-Omaha Type Kinship Terminologies', in W. H. Goodenough (ed.), *Explorations in Cultural Anthropology: Essays in Honor of George Peter Murdock*. New York, McGraw-Hill, 1964, pp. 351–94.

Lowie, R., 'A Note on Relationship Terminologies', *American Anthropologist*, no. 30 (1928), pp. 263–7.

McCarthy, J. K., *Patrol into Yesterday. My New Guinea years*. Melbourne, F. W. Cheshire, 1963.

McConvell, P., 'The Origin of Subsections in Northern Australia', *Oceania*, vol. 56, no. 1 (1985), pp. 1–33.

McConvell, P., L. Dousset and F. Powell, 'Introduction', *Anthropological Forum*, vol. 12, no. 2 (2002), pp. 137–44.

McDougal, C. *The Social Structure of the Hill Juang*. Ann Arbor, University Microfilms, 1963.

McDougall, J., 'Introduction à un colloque sur l'homosexualité féminine', *Revue française de psychanalyse*, no. 4 (1961), pp. 356–66.

Maine, Sir H. *Ancient Law*. London, Murray, 1861.

Malinowski, B., *Argonauts of the Western Pacific*. London, Routledge, Kegan, 1922.

Malinowski, B. *Coral Gardens and Their Magic: Soil Tilling and Agricultural Rites in the Trobriand Islands*. New York, American Book Company, 1935, 2 vols.

Malinowski, B., 'Parenthood: The Basis of Social Structure', in V. F. Calverton and S. D. Schmalhausen (eds.), *The New Generation: The Intimate Problems of Modern Parents and Children*. New York, The Macaulay Comp., 1930, pp. 113–68.

Malinowski, B., *Sex and Repression in Savage Society*. London, Routledge and Kegan Paul, 1927.

Malinowski, B., *The Father in Primitive Psychology*. New York, Norton and Company, 1927.

Malinowski, B., *The Sexual Life of Savages in North-Western Melanesia: An Ethnographic Account of Courtship, Marriage, and Family Life among the Natives of the Trobriand Islands, British New Guinea*, with a preface by Havelock Ellis. London, G. Routledge and Sons, 1929.

Maranda, P., *French Kinship; Structure and History*. The Hague, Mouton, 1994.

Marcus, G. E., *Ethnography through Thick and Thin*. Princeton University Press, 1998.

Marcus, G. E. and M. J. Fisher, *Anthropology as Cultural Critique: An Experimental Moment in the Human Sciences*. Chicago, University of Chicago Press, 1986.

Marshall, L., 'The !Kung Bushmen of the Kalahari Desert', in J. L. Gibbs (ed.), *Peoples of Africa*. New York, Holt, Rinehart and Winston, 1965, pp. 241–78.

Martial, A., *S'apparenter, ethnologie des liens de familles recomposées*. Paris, Editions de la Maison des Sciences de l'Homme, 2003.

Maspero, G., *Histoire ancienne des peuples de l'Orient classique*, I: *Les Empires*. Paris, Hachette, 1886. (ed. cited 1968)

Massard, J., 'Engendrer ou adopter: deux visions concurrentes de la parenté chez les Malais péninsulaires', *Anthropologie et sociétés*, vol. 12, no. 2 (1988), pp. 41–62.

Mauss, M., 'Essai sur le don. Forme et raison de l'échange dans les sociétés archaïques', *L'Année sociologique*, n.s. 1 (1925), pp. 30–186 (re-printed in M. Mauss, *Sociologie et anthropologie*. Paris, Presses Universitaires de France, 1950, pp. 143–279); English translation: *The Gift: The Form and Reason for Exchange in Archaic Societies*, translated by W. D. Halls, foreword by Mary Douglas. New York/London, W.W. Norton, 1990.

May, F., *Les Sépultures préhistoriques. Etude critique*. Paris, Editions du CNRS, 1986.

Maynard Smith, J., *Evolution and the Theory of Games*. Cambridge, Cambridge University Press, 1988.

Mead, M., 'Incest', in *International Encyclopaedia of the Social Sciences*. London/New York, Macmillan, 1968, vol. 7, pp. 115–22.

Mead, M., *Sex and Temperament in Three New-Guinea Societies*. New York, Morrow, 1935.

Meggitt, M., *Desert People: A Study of the Walbiri Aborigines of Central Australia*. Chicago, University of Chicago Press, 1975.

Meggitt, M., 'Understanding Australian Aboriginal Society: Kinship Systems or Cultural Categories', in P. Reining (ed.), *Kinship Studies in the Morgan Centennial Year*. Washington DC, Anthropological Society of Washington, 1972, pp. 64–87.

Mehlman, P, 'L'Evolution des soins paternels chez les primates et les hominidés', *Anthropologie et sociétés*, vol. 12, no. 3 (1988), pp. 131–49.

Meillassoux, C., *Anthropologie économique des Gouro de Côte-d'Ivoire*. Paris/The Hague, Mouton, 1964.

Meillassoux, C., 'Essai d'interprétation du phénomène économique dans les sociétés traditionnelles d'autosubsistance', *Cahiers d'études africaines*, no. 4 (1960), pp. 38–67.

Meillassoux, C., *Femmes, greniers et capitaux*. Paris, Maspero, 1969.

Meillassoux, C., 'From Reproduction to Production', *Economy and Society*, vol. 1, no. 1 (1972), pp. 93–105.

Meillassoux, C., 'Parler parenté', *L'Homme*, no. 153 (2000), pp. 153–64.

Menget, P., 'Note sur l'adoption chez les Txicao du Brésil central', *Anthropologie et sociétés*, vol. 12, no. 2 (1988), pp. 63–72.

Miller, G. S., 'The Primate Basis of Human Sexual Behavior', *Quarterly Review of Biology*, vol. 6, no. 4 (1931).

Mimica, J., *Intimations of Infinity*. Oxford, Berg, 1988.

Mimica, J., 'The Incest Passions: An Outline of the Logic of Iqwaye Social Organization', Part 1, *Oceania*, vol. 61 (1991), pp. 34–58; Part 2, vol. 62 (1991), pp. 81–113.

Mimica, J., 'The Incest Passions: An Outline of the Logic of Ye Social Organization', Parts I–II, *Oceania*, vol. 62, no. 2 (1991), pp. 34–58.

Monberg, T., 'Fathers Were Not Genitors', *Man*, vol. 10, no. 1 (1975), pp. 34–40.

Montague, S. 'Trobriand Gender Identity', *Mankind*, vol. 14 (1993), pp. 33–45.

Moore, J. and R. Ali, 'Are Dispersal and Inbreeding Avoidance Related?', *Animal Behaviour*, no. 32 (1984), pp. 94–112.

Moreau, P., 'Le mariage dans les degrés rapprochés: le dossier romain', in P. Bonte (ed.), *Epouser au plus proche. Inceste, prohibition et stratégies matrimoniales autour de la Méditerranée*. Paris, Editions de l'Ecole des Hautes Etudes en Sciences Sociales, 1994, pp. 59–78.

Morgan, L. H., *Ancient Society or Research in the Lines of Human Progress from Savagery through Barbarism to Civilization*. Tucson, University of Arizona Press, 1985 (1887).

Morgan, L. H., *Systems of Consanguinity and Affinity of the Human Family*. Washington DC, Smithsonian Institution, 1871.

Morris, D., *The Naked Ape*. New York, McGraw Hill, 1967.

Mosko, M., 'Conception, De-conception and Social Structure in Bush Mekeo Culture', *Mankind*, vol. 14 (1983), pp. 24–32.

Mosko, M., 'Motherless Sons: "Divine Kings" and "Partible Persons" in Melanesia and Polynesia', *Man*, vol. 27 (1992), pp. 697–717.

Mosko, M., 'Peace, War, Sex and Sorcery: Non-linear Analogical Transformation in the Early Escalation of North Mekeo Sorcery and Chiefly Practice', in M. Mosko and F. Damon (eds.), *On the Order of Chaos: Social Anthropology and Science of Chaos*. New York, Berghahn, 2005.

Mosko, M., *Quadripartite Structures, Categories, Relations, and Homologies in Bush Mekeo Culture*. Cambridge, Cambridge University Press, 1985.

Mosko, M., 'Rethinking Trobriand Chieftainship', *Journal of the Royal Anthropological Institute*, vol. 1, no. 4 (1995), pp. 763–85.

Muller, J-C., *Du bon usage du sexe et du mariage*. Paris, L'Harmattan, 1982.

Muller, J-C., *Parenté et mariage chez les Rukuba du Nigeria*. Paris/The Hague, Mouton, 1976.

Muller, J-C., 'Structures semi-complexes et structures complexes de l'alliance matrimoniale: quelques réflexions sur un ouvrage de Françoise Héritier', *Anthropologie et sociétés*, vol. 6, no. 3 (1982), pp. 155–72.

Mulot, S., '"Je suis la mère, je suis le père!": l'énigme matrifocale. Relations familiales et rapports des sexes en Guadeloupe', Thesis, Ecole des Hautes Etudes en Sciences Sociales, 2 vol.

Munn, N., *The Fame of Gawa: A Symbolic Study of Value Transformation in a Massim Society*. Cambridge, Cambridge University Press, 1986.

Murdock, G. P., 'Correlations of Matrilineal and Patrilineal Institutions', *Studies in the Science of Society*. New Haven, Yale University Press, 1937, pp. 445–70.

Murdock, G. P., *Social Structure*. New York, The Free Press; London, Collier-Macmillan, 1949.

Murray, C., 'High Bridewealth, Migrant Labour and the Position of Women in Lesotho', *Journal of African Law*, vol. 26, no. 1 (1977), pp. 79–96.

Myers, F., *Pintupi Country, Pintupi Self: Sentiment, Place and Politics among Western Aborigines*. Washington DC/London/Canberra, Smithsonian Institution Press, 1986.

Nakane, C., *Garos and Khasis: A Comparative Study in Matrilineal Systems*. Paris, Ecole Pratique des Hautes Etudes; The Hague, Mouton and Co., 1967 (Cahiers de L'Homme, New Series V).

Nash, J., 'A Note on Groomprice', *American Anthropologist*, no. 80 (1978), pp. 106–8.

Nash, J., *Matriliny and Modernisation: The Nagovisi of South Bougainvill*. Port Moresby/Canberra, The Australian National University, 1974.

Nash, J., 'Women and Power in Nagovisi Society', *Journal de la Société des océanistes*, vol. 60, no. 34 (1978), pp. 119–26.

Nash, J., 'Women, Work and Change in Nagovisi', in D. O'Brien and S. W. Tiffani (eds.), *Rethinking Women's Roles: Perspectives from the Pacific*. Berkeley/San Francisco, University of California Press, 1990, pp. 94–119.

Needham, R. 'A structural analysis of Purum society', *American Anthropology*, vol. 60, no. 1 (1958), pp. 75–101.

Needham, R., *Structure and Sentiment: A Test Case in Social Anthropology*. Chicago, University of Chicago Press, 1962.

Needham, R., 'Remarks on the Analysis of Kinship and Marriage', in R. Needham (ed.), *Rethinking Kinship and Marriage*. London, Tavistock Publications, 1971, pp. 14–16.

Needham, R. (ed.), *Rethinking Kinship and Marriage*. London, Tavistock Publications, 1971.

Obeyesekere, G., *The Cult of the Goddess Pattini*. Chicago, University of Chicago Press, 1984.

Ottino, P., *Rangiroa, parenté étendue, résidence et terres dans un atoll polynésien*. Paris, Cujas, 1972.

Panoff, M., 'Patrifiliation as Ideology and Practice in a Matrilineal Society', *Ethnology*, vol. 15, no. 2 (1976), pp. 175–88.

Panoff, M., 'The Notion of Double Self among the Maenge', *The Journal of the Polynesian Society*, vol. 77, no. 3 (1968), pp. 275–95.

Parkin, R., 'The Contemporary Evolution of Polish Kinship Terminology', *Sociologus*, vol. 45, no. 2 (1995), pp. 140–52.

Parkin, R., *The Munda of Central India: An Account of Their Social Organization*. Delhi, Oxford University Press, 1992.

Pasche, F., 'Note sur la structure et l'étiologie de l'homosexualité masculine', *Revue française de psychanalyse*, no. 4 (1965), pp. 344–55.

Peletz, M. G., 'Neither Reasonable nor Responsible: Contrasting Representations of Masculinity in a Malay Society', *Cultural Anthropology*, vol. 9, no. 2 (1994), pp. 135–78.

Perlès, C., 'L'Homme préhistorique et le feu', *La Recherche*, no. 60 (1975), pp. 829–39.

Phillpots, B. S., *Kindred and Clan in the Middle Ages and After*. Cambridge, Cambridge University Press, 1974 (1913).

Picq, P., *Au commencement était l'homme*. Paris, Odile Jacob, 2003.

Plakans, A., *Kinship in the Past: Anthropology of European Family Life (1500–1900)*. Oxford, Basil Blackwell, 1994.

Pyne, S. J., 'Keeper of the Flame: A Survey of Anthropogenetic Fire', in P. J. Crutzon and J. G. Goldammer (eds.), *Fire and the Environment*. New York, Wiley, 1993, pp. 245–66.

Radcliffe-Brown, A. R., Preface, in Meyer Fortes and E. E. Evans-Pritchard (eds.), *African Political Systems*. Published for the International African Institute by the Oxford University Press, London, New York, 1950.

Radcliffe-Brown, A. R., 'The Social Organization of Australian Tribes', *Oceania*, vol. 1, nos. 1–4 (1930–1), pp. 34–63, 206–46, 322–41 and 426–56.

Radcliffe-Brown, A. R. and D. Forde, *African Systems of Kinship and Marriage*. London, Oxford University Press, 1950.

Ragone, H., 'Chasing the Blood Tie: Surrogate Mothers, Adoptive Mothers and Fathers', *American Ethnologist*, vol. 23 (1996), pp. 352–65.

Ragone, H., *Surrogate Motherhood: Conception in the Heart*. New York, Boulder Publishing House, 1994.

Raheja, G., *The Poison in the Gift: Ritual, Prestation and the Dominant Caste in a North Indian Village*. Chicago, University of Chicago Press, 1988.

Rapp, R., 'Family and Class in Contemporary America', in B. Thore and M. Yalom (eds.), *Rethinking the Family: Some Feminist Questions*. Boston, Northeastern University Press, 1992, pp. 49–70.

Rapp, R., 'Moral Pioneers: Women, Men and Fetuses on a Frontier of Reproductive Technology', in M. Di Leonardo (ed.), *Gender at the Crossroads of Knowledge: Feminist Anthropology in the Postmodern Era*. Berkeley, University of California Press, 1991, pp. 383–95.

Rapp, R., *Testing Women, Testing the Fetus: The Social Impact of Amniocentesis in America*. New York, Routledge, 2000.

Rattray, R., *Ashanti*. Oxford, Clarendon, 1923.

Rattray, R., *Ashanti Laws and Constitution*. Oxford, Clarendon, 1929.

Rattray, R., *Religion and Art in Ashanti*. Oxford, Clarendon, 1927.

Razafintsalama, A., *Les Tsimahafotsy d'Ambohimanga*. Paris, Selaf, 1984.

Reiter, R. (ed.), *Toward an Anthropology of Women*. New York, Monthly Review Press, 1975.

Riel-Salvatore, J. and G. Clark, 'Grave Markers, Middle and Early Upper Paleolithic Burials and the Use of Chronotypology in Contemporary Paleolithic Research', *Current Anthropology*, vol. 42, no. 4 (2001), pp. 449–79.

Ring, V. T. (ed.), *Essays on Borneo Societies*. Oxford, Hull, 1978.

Rogers, G., 'The Father's Sister Futa-Helu is Black: A Consideration of Female Rank and Power in Tonga', *The Journal of the Polynesian Society*, vol. 86 (1977), pp. 157–82.

Rohatynskyj, M., *The Larger Context of Omie Sex Affiliation*. New York, Morrow, 1990.

Ronen, A., 'Domestic Fire as Evidence for Language', in T. Akazawa et al. (eds.), *Neanderthals and Modern Humans in Western Africa*. New York, Plenum Press, 1998, pp. 439–47.

Rousseau, J., *The Social Organization of the Baluy Rayan*. Cambridge, Cambridge University Press, 1973.

Rubellin-Devichi, J. (ed.), *Des concubinages dans le monde*. Paris, Editions du CNRS, 1990.

Rubin, G., 'The Traffic in Women: Notes on the "Political Economy" of Sex', in R. Reiter (ed.), *Toward an Anthropology of Women*. New York, Monthly Review, 1975, pp. 157–210.

Sagant, P., 'Mariage "par enlèvement" chez les Limbu (Népal)', *Cahiers internationaux de sociologie*, no. 48 (1970), pp. 71–98.

Sahlins, M., *Islands of History*. Chicago, University of Chicago Press, 1985.

Saladin d'Anglure, B., 'Du fœtus au shamane, la construction d'un troisième sexe inuit', *Etudes/Inuit/Studies*, vol. 10, no. 102 (1986), pp. 25–113.

Saladin d'Anglure, B., 'L'Election parentale chez les Inuit: fiction empirique ou réalité virtuelle?', in A. Fine (ed.), *Adoptions. Ethnologie des parentés choisies*. Paris, Editions de la Maison des Sciences de l'Homme, 1998, pp. 121–49.

Saladin d'Anglure, B., 'Le "troisième sexe"', *La Recherche*, no. 245 (1992), pp. 836–44.

Saladin d'Anglure, B., 'Nom et parenté chez les Eskimaux Tarramint du Nouveau-Québec (Canada)', in J. Pouillon and P. Maranda (eds.), *Echanges et communications. Mélanges offerts à Claude Lévi-Strauss*. The Hague, Mouton, 1970, pp. 1013–38.

Saladin d'Anglure, B., '"Petit-Ventre", l'enfant géant du cosmos inuit. Ethnographie de l'enfant dans l'Arctique central inuit', *L'Homme*, vol. 20, no. 1 (1980), pp. 7–46.

Saladin d'Anglure, B., 'Violences et enfantements inuit, ou les nœuds de la vie dans le fil du temps', *Anthropologie et sociétés*, vol. 4, no. 2 (1980), pp. 65–99 (special issue devoted to 'L'Usage social des enfants').

Salomon, C., *Savoirs et pouvoirs thérapeutiques kanaks*. Paris, Presses Universitaires de France, 2000.

Sangre, W. H. and N. E. Levine (eds.), *Journal of Comparative Family Studies*, vol. 11, no. 3 (1980) (special issue on polyandry).

Scheffler, H. W., *Australian Kin Classification*. Cambridge, Cambridge University Press, 1978.

Scheffler, H. W., and F. G. Lounsbury, *A Study in Structural Semantics: The Siriono Kinship System*. Englewood Cliffs NJ, Prentice Hall, 1971.

Schmitt, J.-C., 'Le corps en Chrétienté', in M. Godelier and M. Panoff (eds.), *Le Corps humain. Supplicié, possédé, cannibalisé*. Paris, Editions du CNRS, 2009, pp. 339–53.

Schneider, D. M., *A Critique of the Study of Kinship*. Ann Arbor, University of Michigan Press, 1984.

Schneider, D. M., *American Kinship: A Cultural Account*. Englewood Cliffs NJ, Prentice Hall, 1968.

Schneider, D. M., 'Introduction', in D. M. Schneider and K. Gough (eds.), *Matrilineal Kinship*. Berkeley, University of California Press, 1961.

Schneider, D. M., 'The Meaning of Incest', *The Journal of the Polynesian Society*, vol. 85, no. 3 (1976), pp. 149–69.

Schneider, D. M. and K. Gough (eds.), *Matrilineal Kinship*. Berkeley, University of California Press, 1961.

Schneider, D. M. and R. T. Smith, *Class Differences and Sex Roles in American Kinship and Family Structure*. Englewood Cliffs NJ, Prentice Hall, 1973.

Segalen, M., 'Parenté et alliance dans les sociétés paysannes', *Ethnologie française*, vol. 11, no. 4 (1891), pp. 307–29.

Seligman, B., 'The Problem of Incest and Exogamy', *American Anthropologist*, vol. 52 (1950), pp. 306–7.

Shaw, B. D. and R. P. Saller, 'Close-Kin Marriage in Roman Society', *Man*, vol. 19, no. 4 (1984), pp. 432–44.

Sinclair, J. P., *Behind the Ranges: Patrolling in New Guinea*. Melbourne, Melbourne University Press, 1966.

Slotkin, J. C., 'On a Possible Lack of Incest Regulations in Old Iran', *American Anthropologist*, N.S. vol. 49, no. 4 (1947), pp. 612–17.

Smith, M., *Evolution and the Theory of Games*. Cambridge, Cambridge University Press, 1988.

Smith Oboler, R., 'Is the Female Husband a Man? Woman/woman Marriage among the Nandi of Kenya', *Ethnology*, vol. 19, no. 1 (1980), pp. 69–88.

Sousberghe, L. de, 'Cousins croisés et descendants: les systèmes du Rwanda et du Burundi comparés à ceux du bas Congo', *Africa*, vol. 35, no. 4 (1965), pp. 396–421.

Spiro, M. E., *Children of the Kibbutz*. Cambridge MA, Harvard University Press, 1958.

Spoehr, A., *Changing Kinship Systems: A Study in the Acculturation of the Creeks, Cherokee, and Choctaw*. Chicago, Field Museum of Natural History, 1947 (Anthropological Series vol. 33, no. 4).

Stacey, J. and T. J. Biblartz, 'How Does the Sexual Orientation of Parents Matter?', *American Sociological Review*, vol. 66 (April 2001), pp. 159–83.

Stein, R. A., 'La légende du foyer dans le monde chinois', in J. Pouillon and P. Maranda (eds.), *Echanges et communications: Mélanges offerts à Claude Lévi-Strauss*. Paris, Mouton, 1970, vol. 2, pp. 1281–1305.

Stern, B. R., and D. G. Smith, 'Sexual Behaviour and Paternity in Three Captive Groups of Rhesus Monkeys (*Macaca Mulatta*)', *Animal Behaviour*, no. 32 (1984), pp. 23–32.

Steward, J. H., *Basin-Plateau Sociopolitical Groups*, Washington DC, US government Printing Office, 1938 (Bureau of American Ethnology Bulletin no. 120).

Strassmann, B. I., 'Sexual Selection, Paternal Care, and Concealed Ovulation in Humans', *Ethology and Sociobiology*, no. 2 (1981), pp. 31–40.

Strathern, A., 'Keeping the Body in Mind', *Social Anthropology*, vol. 2, no. 1 (1994), pp. 43–53.

Strathern, A., 'The Central and the Contingent: Bridewealth among the Melpa and the Wiru', in J. L. Comaroff (ed.), *The Meaning of Marriage Payments*. London, Academic Press, 1980, pp. 49–66.

Strathern, A., 'The Female and Male Spirit Cults in Mount Hagen', *Man*, vol. 5, no. 4 (1970), pp. 571–85.

Strathern, A., *The Rope of Moka: Big Men and Ceremonial Exchange in Mount Hagen, New Guinea*. London, Cambridge University Press, 1971.

Strathern, A. and M. Strathern, 'Marriage among the Melpa', in R. Glasse and M. Meggitt (eds.), *Pigs, Pearl-shells and Women*. Englewood Cliffs NJ, Prentice Hall, 1969.

Strathern, M., *Reproducing the Future: Essays on Anthropology, Kinship and the New Reproduction Technologies*. Manchester University Press, 1992.

Strathern, M., 'Subject or Object? Women and the Circulation of Valuables in Highlands New Guinea', in R. Hirschon (ed.), *Women and Property, Women as Property*. London, Croom Helm, 1984.

Strathern, M., *The Gender of the Gift*. Berkeley, University of California Press, 1988.

Strathern, M., *Women in Between: Female Roles in a Male World. Mount Hagen, New Guinea*. London, Seminar Press, 1979.

Sutton, P., *Native Titles and the Descent of Rights*. Canberra, Publication Commonwealth of Australia, 1998).

Szalay, F. and R. Costello, 'Evolution of Permanent Oestrus Displays in Hominids', *Journal of Human Evolution*, no. 20 (1991), pp. 439–64.

Tamagne, F., 'Histoire comparée de l'homosexualité en Allemagne, en Angleterre et en France dans l'entre-deux-guerres', *Actes de la recherche en sciences sociales*, no. 125 (1998), pp. 44–62.

Tambiah, S. J., 'The Structure of Kinship and Its Relationships to Land Possession and Residence in Pata Dumbara, Central Ceylon', *Journal of the Royal Anthropological Institute*, vol. 88, no. 1 (1958), pp. 21–44.

Tang Yin Bi Shi, Affaires résolues à l'ombre du poirier de Shi Po, text established by R. Van Gulik. Paris, Albin Michel, 2000.

Taylor, A. C., 'Jivaro Kinship: A Dravidian Transformation Group', in M. Godelier, T. R. Trautmann and F. Tjon Sie Fat (eds.), *Transformations of Kinship*, Washington DC, Smithsonian Institution Press, 1998, pp. 187–213.

Taylor, A. C., 'Remembering to Forget. Mourning, Memory and Identity among the Jivaro', *Man*, vol. 28 (1993), pp. 653–78.

Terray, E., *Le Marxisme devant les sociétés primitives*. Paris, Maspero, 1969.

Testart, A., *Essai sur les fondements de la division sexuelle du travail chez les chasseurs-cueilleurs*. Paris, Ecole des Hautes Etudes en Sciences Sociales (coll. Cahiers de L'Homme), 1986.

Testart, A., 'Game Sharing Systems and Kinship Systems among Hunter-Gatherers', *Man*, vol. 22 (1987), pp. 287–304.

Testart, A., 'Manières de prendre femme en Australie', *L'Homme*, vol. 36, no. 139 (1996), pp. 7–57.

Théry, I., *Le Démariage: justice et vie privée*. Paris, Odile Jacob, 1999.

Théry, I., 'Pacs, sexualité et différence des sexes', *Esprit*, October (1999), pp. 139–81.

Théry, I. (ed.), *Couple, filiation et parenté aujourd'hui, le droit face aux mutations de la famille et de la vie privée*. Paris, O. Jacob/la Documentation française, 1998.

Thomas, Y., 'A propos du parricide. L'interdit politique et l'institution du sujet', *L'Inactuel*, no. 4 (1996), pp. 167–87.

Thomas, Y., 'A Rome, pères citoyens et cité des pères (IIe siècle av. J-C.–IIe siècle ap. J-C.)', in A. Burguière, C. Klapish-Zuber, M. Segalen and F. Zonnabend (eds.), *Histoire de la famille*. Paris, A. Colin, 1986, vol. 1, pp. 193–229.

Thomas, Y., 'Le "ventre", corps maternel, droit paternel', *Le Genre humain*, vol. 14 (1986), pp. 211–36.

Thomas, Y., 'Les Artifices de la vérité', *L'Inactuel*, no. 6 (1996), pp. 81–96.

Thomas, Y., 'Mariages endogamiques à Rome. Patrimoine, pouvoir et parenté depuis l'époque archaïque', *Revue historique de droit français et étranger*, vol. 3 (1980), pp. 345–92.

Thomas, Y., 'Parricidium', *Mélanges de l'Ecole française de Rome*, vol. 93 (1981), pp. 643–715.

Thomas, Y., 'Remarques sur la juridiction domestique à Rome', in J. Andreau and H. Bruhns (eds.), *Parenté et stratégies familiales dans l'Antiquité romaine*. Rome, Ecole française de Rome, 1990, pp. 449–74.

Tibetan Book of the Dead, translated by F. Fremantle and C. Trungpa Berkeley, Shambala, 1975.

Tin, L-G. (ed.), *Dictionnaire de l'homophobie*. Paris, Presses Universitaires de France, 2003.

Tjon Sie Fat, F., 'On the Formal Analysis of "Dravidian", "Iroquois" and "Generational" Varieties as Nearly Associative Combinations', in M. Godelier, T. R. Trautmann and F. Tjon Sie Fat (eds.), *Transformations of Kinship*, Washington DC, Smithsonian Institution Press, 1998, pp. 59–93.

Tonkinson, R., 'Semen Versus Spirit-Child in a Western Desert culture', in L. R. Hiatt (ed.), *Australian Aboriginal Concepts*. New Jersey, Humanities Press, 1978, pp. 81–91.

Tort, M., 'Homophobies psychanalytiques', *Le Monde*, 14 October 1998.

Tort, M., *Le Désir froid: procréation artificielle et crise des repères symboliques*. Paris, La Découverte, 1992.

Trautmann, T., *Dravidian Kinship*. Cambridge/New York, Cambridge University Press, 1981.

Trautmann, T., 'Dravidian Kinship as a Cultural and as a Structural Type', Paper presented at the symposium 'Kinship in Asia: Typology and Transformation', Moscow, 1992.

Trautmann, T., 'India and the Study of Kinship Terminologies', *L'Homme*, no. 154–5 (2000), pp. 559–72.

Trautmann, T., 'Kinship as Language', in P. Descola, J. Hammel and P. Lemonnier (eds.), *La Production du social*. Paris, Fayard, 1999, pp. 433–44.

Trautmann, T., *Lewis Henry Morgan and the Invention of Kinship*. Berkeley, University of California Press, 1987.

Trautmann, T., 'The Whole History of Kinship Terminology in Three Chapters: Before Morgan, Morgan and After Morgan', *Anthropological Theory*, vol. 1, no. 2 (2001), pp. 268–87.

Tylor, E. B., 'On a Method of Investigating the Development of Institutions; Applied to Laws of Marriage and Descent', *Journal of the Royal Anthropological Institute of Great Britain and Ireland*, vol. 18 (1989), pp. 245–72.

Van Wouden, F. A. E., *Sociale Structuurtypen in de groote Oost*. Leiden, J. Ginsberg, 1935; English translation by Rodney Needham: *Types of Social Structure in Eastern Indonesia*. The Hague, Nijhoff, 1968.

Vernant, J-P., *L'Univers, les dieux, les hommes. Récits grecs des origines*. Paris, Le Seuil, 2006.

Vernant, J-P., 'Œdipe', in Yves Bonnefoy (ed.), *Dictionnaire des mythologies*. Paris, Flammarion, 1981, pp. 190–2.

Vernant, J-P. and P. Vidal-Naquet, *Mythe et tragédie*. Paris, Maspero, 1972, pp. 75–132.

Vernier, B., 'Du nouveau sur l'inceste? Pour une théorie unitaire', *La Pensée*, no. 318 (1999), pp. 53–80.

Vernier, B., *Frère et sœur. La Genèse sociale des sentiments*. Paris, Editions de l'Ecole des Hautes Etudes en Sciences Sociales, 1991.

Vernier, B., *Le Visage et le nom: contribution à l'étude des systèmes de parenté*. Paris, Presses Universitaires de France, 1999.

Vernier, B., 'Théorie de l'inceste et construction d'objet. F. Héritier, la Grèce Antique et les Hittites', *Annales*, no. 1 (1996), pp. 173–200.

Vernier, B., 'Théorie de l'inceste et construction d'objet. Françoise Héritier et les interdits de la Bible', *Social Anthropology*, vol. 4, no. 3 (1996), pp. 227–50.

Vidal, J-M., 'Explications biologiques et anthropologiques de l'interdit de l'inceste', *Nouvelle revue d'ethnopsychiatrie*, no. 3 (1985), pp. 75–107.

Vincent, J. D., *Biologie des passions*. Paris, Odile Jacob, 2002.

Viveiros de Castro, E., 'Dravidian and Related Kinship Systems', in M. Godelier, T. R. Trautmann and F. Tjon Sie Fat (eds.), *Transformations of Kinship*, Washington DC, Smithsonian Institution Press, 1998, pp. 332–85.

Viveiros de Castro, E., 'Structures, régimes, stratégies', *L'Homme*, vol. 33, no. 1 (1993), pp. 117–33.

Viveiros de Castro, E., 'Une mauvaise querelle', *L'Homme*, vol. 34, no. 129, (1994), pp. 181–91.

Vogel, C., *Le Pécheur et la pénitence au moyen-âge*. Paris, Editions du Cerf, 1969.

Vogel, C., *Les "Quatres Mères" d'Ambohibaho*. Paris, Selaf, 1982.

Wagner, R., 'A Theology of Bride Price', in E. Mantovani (ed.), *Marriage in Melanesia: An Anthropological Perspective*. Goroka, The Melanesian Institute, 1992, pp. 153–72 ('Point Series', no. 11).

Wagner, R., *Asiwinarong: Ethos, Image and Social Power among the Usen Barok of New Ireland*. Harvard, Princeton University Press, 1986.

Wagner, R., *The Curse of Souw: Principles of Daribi Clan Definition and Alliance*. Chicago, University of Chicago Press, 1967.

Weber, M., *The Theory of Economic and Social Organization*. New York, Free Press, 1947.

Weiner, A., 'The Reproductive Model in Trobriand society', *Mankind*, vol. 11 (1978), pp. 175–86.

Weiner, A., *The Trobriand Islanders of Papua New Guinea*. New York, Holt, Rinehart and Winston, 1988.

Weiner, A., 'Trobriand Kinship from Another View. The Reproductive Power of Women and Men', *Man*, vol. 14, no. 2 (1979), pp. 328–48.

Weiner, A., *Women of Value, Men of Renown*. Austin, University of Texas Press, 1976.

Welzer-Lang, D., P. Dutey and M. Dorais (eds.), *La Peur de l'autre en soi. Du sexisme à l'homophobie*. Montreal, Editions Québec, 1994.

Westermarck, E., *The History of Human Marriage*. London, 1891.

Weston, K., *Families We Choose*. New York, Columbia University Press, 1991.

White, L., 'The Definition and Prohibition of Incest', *American Anthropologist*, no. 50 (1948), pp. 416–34.

Wiessner, P. and A. Tumu, *Historical Vines: Enga Networks of Exchange, Ritual, and Warfare in Papua New Guinea*. Washington DC, Smithsonian Institution Press, 1988.

Wikan, U., 'Man Becomes Woman: Transexualism in Oman as a Key to Gender Roles', *Man*, vol. 12 (1977), pp. 304–19.

Wilkinson, G., *Manners and Customs of the Ancient Egyptians*. London, 1841.

Williams, P. E., *Drama of Orokolo*. Oxford, Clarendon Press, 1940.

Wittgenstein, L., *The Blue and Brown Books*. Oxford, Blackwell, 1958.

Wolf, A. P. and C. S. Huang, *Marriage and Adoption in China, 1845–1945*. Stanford, Stanford University Press, 1980.

'Women of China', New Trends in Chinese Marriage and the Family. Beijing, China International Book Trading Company, 1987.

Wordick, F., 'A Generative-Extensionist Analysis of the Proto-Indo-European Kinship System with a Phonological and Semantic Reconstruction of the Terms', Doctoral Dissertation, University of Michigan, Ann Arbor, University Microfilms, 1970.

Young, M., *Ngawbe: Tradition and Change among the Western Guaymi of Panama*. Urbana, University of Illinois Press, 1971.

Young, M. and P. Willmott, *Family and Kinship in East London*. London, Routledge and Kegan Paul 1957; Harmondsworth, Pelican Books, 1962.

Zimmermann, F., *Enquête sur la parenté*. Paris, Presses Universitaires de France, 1993.

Index of General Terms

Abaodgu: 367

abduction (marriage by): 56–58, 136, 140–42, 169, 473, 557

abjection: 409

abusua: 115, 258, 338, 341

Adam: 279, 304, 325–26, 328, 334, 384, 387, 388

address term: 76, 183, 567, 167

adolescence: 241, 439, 440, 442, 443, 452, 474–75, 531, 549

adoption: 108–12, 155, 177, 519, 533, 534, 537–38, 544–45, 555, 565

adultery: 43, 60, 322, 323, 339, 346

affection: 48, 61, 221, 222, 241, 250, 259, 263, 264, 330, 388, 536

affiliation: 91, 96, 267–68, 288, 555

affinity: 3, 51, 68, 78, 115, 123, 147, 179, 183, 192, 202, 207–17, 307, 329, 333, 349, 354, 360, 363, 364, 366, 367, 383

affine: 3, 33, 47, 50, 51, 52, 54, 58, 76, 99, 108, 134, 144, 147, 156, 158, 163, 184, 185n4, 191–92, 194, 196n16, 202–17, 328–33, 336, 339, 349, 374, 396, 307, 532, 566; affine of affines, 51, 207, 212, 215, 340, 349n33, 362, 363, 491, 503, 555; affine of consanguines, 3, 207, 212, 215, 328, 340, 345, 348–49, 362, 363, 417, 460, 491

age group: 60, 61, 345, 391, 452, 555–56

agnates: 87, 149, 167, 556, 571

agriculture: 84, 281, 421, 466–67

Ahoʼeitu: 290–91

Akaisa: 297–98

alliance: asymmetric prescriptive, 170–72, 174, 197, 207, 211, 411, 416,

494, 502–504, 507, 509n48, 511, 567; axis of, 23, 430, 442, 529; symmetric prescriptive, 172, 196, 197, 207, 502, 510; theories about, 170–71

Alter: 207, 209, 213, 560

amity: 85n9, 119, 483, 556

amoeba: 428

Ancien Régime: 3–4, 522

androcentrism: 116

anima: 62, 301, 303

anisogamy: 143, 556

antiquity: 4, 109, 279–80, 333, 357, 497, 519

aoulatta: 30–31, 42

Apartheid: 391

APGL (Association de Parents et Futurs Parents Gays et Lesbiens): 543

Aphrodite: 465

'Arab' marriage: 307, 377n89, 472

Ardachis: 381

aristocracy: feudal, 92, 94–95, 97, 279n54, 381–82, 519; tribal, 92, 94, 113, 269, 277–78, 290, 311, 558

Artaxerxes II: 381, 461

artificial insemination: 2, 103, 177, 536, 537, 542, 544, 545, 551, 565

ascendance: 89, 437

associativity: 207, 212, 491–93, 499

authority: of husband, 4; parental, 5–7, 416, 529, 531, 543, 544; paternal, 4–7, 141, 416, 529, 531

autochthon: 41, 289

auto-da-fé: 525

autosexuality: 439–40, 449, 450, 451

avoidance (sexual): 424, 436–37, 556–57

Index of Personal Names

Index of Societies

MAPS

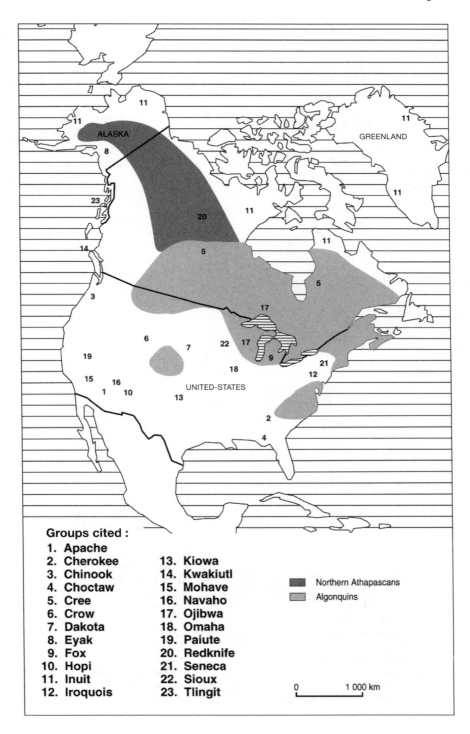

Groups cited :
1. Apache
2. Cherokee
3. Chinook
4. Choctaw
5. Cree
6. Crow
7. Dakota
8. Eyak
9. Fox
10. Hopi
11. Inuit
12. Iroquois

13. Kiowa
14. Kwakiutl
15. Mohave
16. Navaho
17. Ojibwa
18. Omaha
19. Paiute
20. Redknife
21. Seneca
22. Sioux
23. Tlingit

Northern Athapascans
Algonquins

0   1 000 km

Groups cited:
1. Ashuar (Jivaro)
2. Aguaruna (Jivaro)
3. Apinaye (Ge)
4. Arawete (Tupian)
5. Bororo
6. Canela
7. Cashinahua (Panoan)
8. Guahibo
9. Guarani (Tupian)
10. Guayaki (Atche)
11. Kadiweu (Guaykuru)
12. Kagwahiv (Tupian)
13. Kaiowa-Guarani (Tupian)
14. Kandoshi, Shapra (Candoa)
15. Kayapo (Ge)
16. Matis (Panoan)
17. Ngawbe (Chibchan)
18. Panare (Carib)
19. Shipibo-Conibo (Panoan)
20. Shuar (Jivaro)
21. Siriono (Tupian)
22. Trio (Carib)
23. Tupinamba (Carib)
24. Txicao (Carib)
25. Yanomani

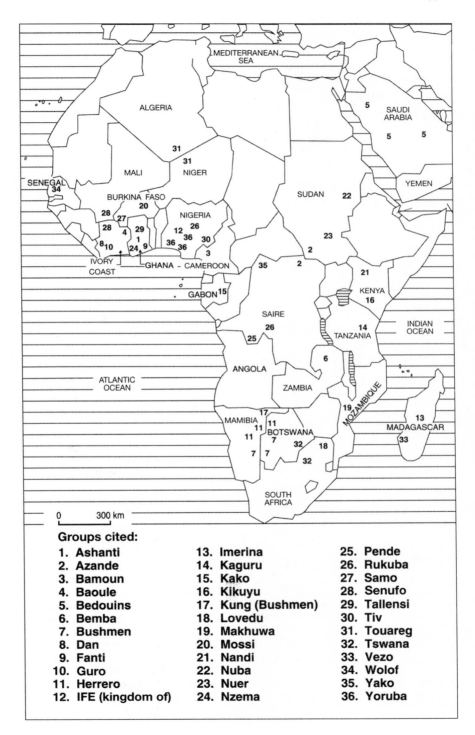

Groups cited:

1. Ashanti	13. Imerina	25. Pende
2. Azande	14. Kaguru	26. Rukuba
3. Bamoun	15. Kako	27. Samo
4. Baoule	16. Kikuyu	28. Senufo
5. Bedouins	17. Kung (Bushmen)	29. Tallensi
6. Bemba	18. Lovedu	30. Tiv
7. Bushmen	19. Makhuwa	31. Touareg
8. Dan	20. Mossi	32. Tswana
9. Fanti	21. Nandi	33. Vezo
10. Guro	22. Nuba	34. Wolof
11. Herrero	23. Nuer	35. Yako
12. IFE (kingdom of)	24. Nzema	36. Yoruba

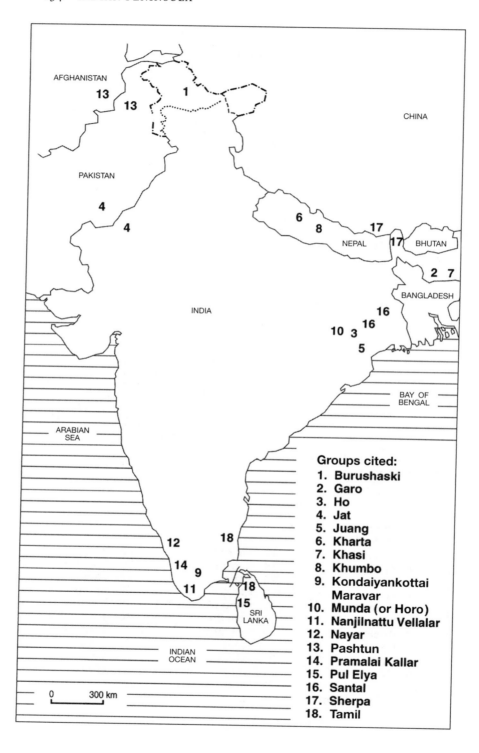

Groups cited:
1. Burushaski
2. Garo
3. Ho
4. Jat
5. Juang
6. Kharta
7. Khasi
8. Khumbo
9. Kondaiyankottai Maravar
10. Munda (or Horo)
11. Nanjilnattu Vellalar
12. Nayar
13. Pashtun
14. Pramalai Kallar
15. Pul Elya
16. Santal
17. Sherpa
18. Tamil

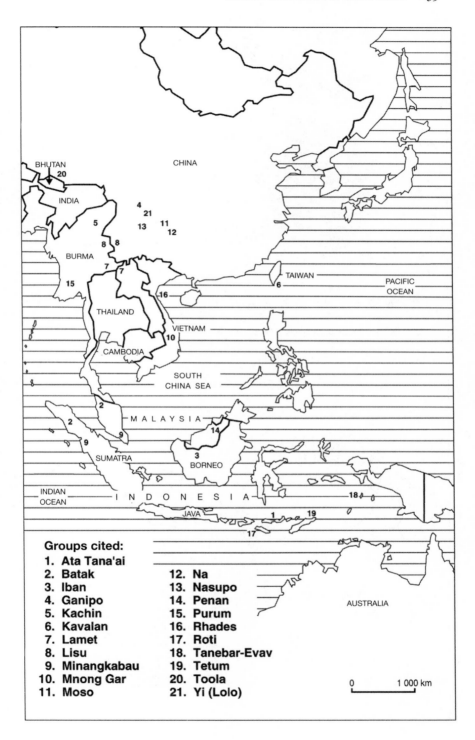

BHUTAN
20
CHINA
INDIA
4
21
5
13
11
12
8   8
BURMA
7
7
15
TAIWAN
6
PACIFIC
OCEAN
16
THAILAND
VIETNAM
10
CAMBODIA
SOUTH
CHINA SEA
2
M A L A Y S I A
2
14
9
9
3
SUMATRA
BORNEO
INDIAN
OCEAN
I N D O N E S I A
18
JAVA
1
19
17
AUSTRALIA

Groups cited:
1. Ata Tana'ai
2. Batak
3. Iban
4. Ganipo
5. Kachin
6. Kavalan
7. Lamet
8. Lisu
9. Minangkabau
10. Mnong Gar
11. Moso

12. Na
13. Nasupo
14. Penan
15. Purum
16. Rhades
17. Roti
18. Tanebar-Evav
19. Tetum
20. Toola
21. Yi (Lolo)

0   1 000 km

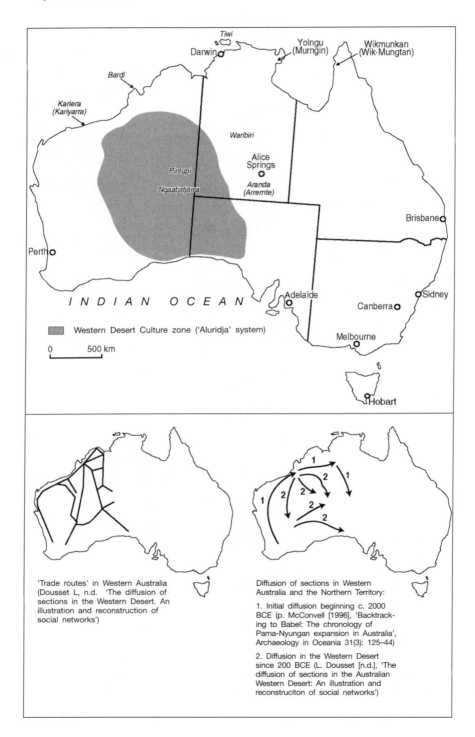

Western Desert Culture zone ('Aluridja' system)

0   500 km

'Trade routes' in Western Australia (Dousset L, n.d. 'The diffusion of sections in the Western Desert. An illustration and reconstruction of social networks')

Diffusion of sections in Western Australia and the Northern Territory:

1. Initial diffusion beginning c. 2000 BCE (p. McConvell [1996], 'Backtracking to Babel: The chronology of Pama-Nyungan expansion in Australia', Archaeology in Oceania 31(3): 125–44)

2. Diffusion in the Western Desert since 200 BCE (L. Dousset [n.d.], 'The diffusion of sections in the Australian Western Desert: An illustration and reconstruciton of social networks')

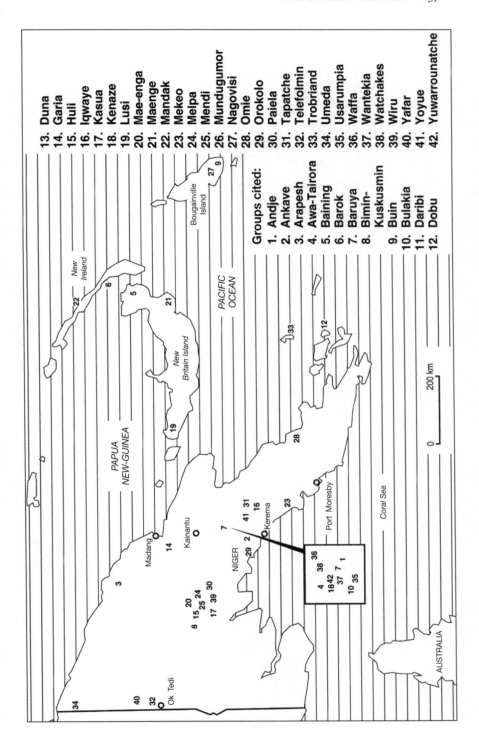

13. Duna
14. Garia
15. Huli
16. Iqwaye
17. Kasua
18. Kenaze
19. Lusi
20. Mae-enga
21. Maenge
22. Mandak
23. Mekeo
24. Melpa
25. Mendi
26. Mundugumor
27. Nagovisi
28. Omie
29. Orokolo
30. Paiela
31. Tapatche
32. Telefolmin
33. Trobriand
34. Umeda
35. Usarumpia
36. Waffa
37. Wantekia
38. Watchakes
39. Wiru
40. Yafar
41. Yoyue
42. Yuwarrounatche

Groups cited:

1. Andje
2. Ankave
3. Arapesh
4. Awa-Tairora
5. Baining
6. Barok
7. Baruya
8. Bimin-Kuskusmin
9. Buin
10. Bulakia
11. Daribi
12. Dobu

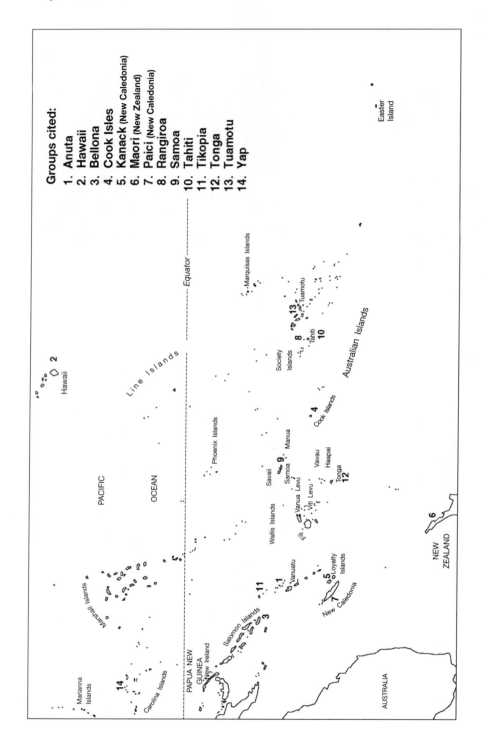

Groups cited:

1. Anuta
2. Hawaii
3. Bellona
4. Cook Isles
5. Kanack (New Caledonia)
6. Maori (New Zealand)
7. Paici (New Caledonia)
8. Rangiroa
9. Samoa
10. Tahiti
11. Tikopia
12. Tonga
13. Tuamotu
14. Yap